PIMLICO

ONE WEEK

THE CITY OF LONDON

I

A WORLD OF ITS OWN 1815-1890

David Kynaston was born at Aldershot in 1951
and educated at Wellington College, New College, Oxford, and the London School of Economics. He has been a professional historian for
twenty years. Since 1979 his principal interest
has been the City of London, interrupted by
three excursions into cricket history. His publications include *King Labour: The British Working
Class 1850-1914*, the historical surveys *The Secretary of State* and *The Chancellor of the Exchequer*,
and major histories of the *Financial Times* and of
the leading stockbrokers Cazenove & Co.

THE CITY OF LONDON

Volume I
A World of Its Own 1815-1890

DAVID KYNASTON

PIMLICO

PIMLICO

An imprint of Random House
20 Vauxhall Bridge Road, London SW1V 2SA

Random House Australia (Pty) Ltd
20 Alfred Street, Milsons Point, Sydney
New South Wales 2061, Australia

Random House New Zealand Ltd
18 Poland Road, Glenfield
Auckland 10, New Zealand

Random House South Africa (Pty) Ltd
PO Box 337, Bergvlei, South Africa

Random House UK Ltd Reg. No. 954009

First published by Chatto & Windus 1994
Pimlico edition 1995

5 7 9 10 8 6

Printed and bound in Great Britain by
Bookcraft, Bath

ISBN 0-7126-6200-6

This book is dedicated to Laurie and George

In 1711 the essayist Richard Steele introduced the members of the Spectator Club. One was Sir Andrew Freeport, 'a Merchant of great Eminence in the City of London', a man 'acquainted with Commerce in all its Parts' who, as a favourite jest, 'calls the Sea the British Common'. Over the next two centuries Freeport and successive generations of merchants, bankers and others built the City of London into the pivot of the world's entire commercial system, as sterling reigned supreme and Britain exported capital to all quarters of the industrialising globe. *A World of its Own* tells that story. It is also a collective biography of the people behind it, the clerks at the high sloping desks as well as their superiors who made such enviable fortunes. Ultimately, this book confronts Steele's proposition that 'a General Trader of good Sense, is pleasanter Company than a general Scholar', Sir Andrew 'having a natural unaffected Eloquence, the Perspecuity of his Discourse gives the same Pleasure that Wit would in another man'. By their own words and deeds these practical men are to be judged.

Contents

PART ONE

Prologue

At the corner of Wood Street, when daylight appears,
Hangs a Thrush that sings loud, it has sung for three years:
Poor Susan has passed by the spot, and has heard
In the silence of morning the song of the Bird.

'Tis a note of enchantment; what ails her? She sees
A mountain ascending, a vision of trees;
Bright volumes of vapour through Lothbury glide,
And a river flows on through the vale of Cheapside.

WILLIAM WORDSWORTH, *The Reverie of Poor Susan* (1800)

CHAPTER ONE

Outsiders

Picture the prosperous underwriter at home:

> We dined at 6 oClock. The dinner consisted of two Courses. viz: a Fine Turbot at the top, A Sirloin of Beef at the bottom & vermicelli Soup in the middle, with small dishes making a figure of dishes. The remove roast ducks at the top & a very fine roast Poulet at the bottom, macaroni, tartlets &c &c. afterwards Parmesan & other Cheese & Caviare with toast. – Champaigne & Madeira were served round during dinner . . . I observed that Mr. Angerstein drank very little wine *after dinner*. – While the Conversation went on He for some time slept, – after He awoke He eat an orange with Sugar. – He appears to consider His Health but looks very full and well.

The appreciative guest was the diarist Joseph Farington, his host John Julius Angerstein, in his late sixties in 1804 but still the best-known man at Lloyd's. 'When his name appeared on a policy, it was a sufficient recommendation for the rest to follow where he led without further examination.' From uncertain beginnings, Angerstein's life had charted an exemplary course. He was born in St Petersburg in 1735, nominally into a well-known Hanoverian family recently settled there, though it is at least possible that he was the natural son of the Empress Anna of Russia and the merchant Andrew Poulett Thomson. Either way, Angerstein was in Thomson's counting house in the City of London by the age of fifteen; he was soon making his way as a marine insurance broker and underwriter; and in 1774 he had a handsome country villa built for him in Blackheath. There, at Woodlands, he was not only a munificent and particular host but also such an acute collector of pictures that after his death in 1823 the collection formed the nucleus for the National Gallery. Yet always, requiring even less sentiment of judgement, there was Lloyd's, and in 1810 we hear the authentic, dispassionate voice of Angerstein giving evidence to a parliamentary committee. The question was nervous enough: 'Do not you believe, in point of fact, that there are a great many Underwriters in the

Coffee-house in Lloyd's, though not among those with whom you deal, who have very little capital?' His reply was unanswerable: 'I suppose this may be the fact, but I cannot say; I go into the Coffee-house to do my business with those I have business to do with . . .'[1]

William Hancock also found the streets of London paved with the right stuff. The son of a Berkshire innkeeper, he entered in 1773 the service of Smith, Payne & Smiths, a leading bank in Lombard Street, and speedily rose to be confidential clerk. From 1780 he became a compulsive defalcator, robbing his trusting employers of enormous sums of money, until just before Christmas 1798, expecting at last to be uncovered at the annual balancing of books, he wrote them an almost boastfully wretched letter of confession:

> I shudder when I behold the enormity of my guilt but it would be a mockery of too detestable a nature to affect remorse while I have continued almost to the present moment to follow up a principle of such dishonourable conduct . . . I anticipate the inevitable necessity of self murder which guilt will force me to because altho' I have been base enough to turn your confidence to the most dishonourable purposes I cannot endure to meet you when you know me guilty, much less can I stand the infamy of a public stigma . . . Before this reaches you, the hand which dictates these lines will be lifeless and happy would it have been for those connected with me that I had many years since died.

But Hancock's crimes were not discovered, the letter was not sent, and over the next eight years there took place an annual ritual of more defalcations, the remorseful missive composed and the losses not noticed. By 1805 he was expressing a wish to retire, which prompted a letter between partners: 'Mr Hancock's abilities, fidelity, long services & zeal are so great that in my opinion it will be very injudicious to suffer him to quit us. He hinted that he knew the Banking business was not so productive as formerly & that since our attention had been turned to the *expences* he had not presumed nor should he ever again give any orders which might incur expence.' At last, in January 1807, Hancock's nerve cracked. One Tuesday, instead of going to work, he travelled to Brighton, from where he sent the senior partner the key to his desk and an accompanying letter: 'When you open the desk, summon all your fortitude and self-command to prevent those who may be near to you suspecting the infernal confessions which the papers in the packet will place before you. It is beyond all of the worst systems of private treachery ever known. When this reaches your hand, mine will be lifeless.' So it was, and it transpired from Hancock's

3

meticulously kept red leather pocket book that since 1780 his defalcations had amounted to £87,800, worth at least £4m in present-day values. No one knew what had become of the money or why he had done it.[2]

Hancock's death caused few ripples in the wider world, but perhaps the Goldsmid brothers, being of broad sympathies, nodded mutely. Benjamin and Abraham Goldsmid were the youngest sons of a Dutch merchant who had settled in London shortly before their birth in the 1750s; and after going into business together in 1776 they achieved an astonishing ascent, so that by the beginning of the nineteenth century they were the dominant figures in the City. Their firm did all sorts of business – bill broking, money dealing, loan contracting, dealing in the funds, merchanting, virtually the lot – and to each they brought dexterity, resource and attention to detail. Their fame grew, so did their fortune, and inevitably they acquired country houses. Abraham's was Morden Hall, while Benjamin built his own resplendent mansion at Roehampton, fervently described by a contemporary biographer: 'Every thing is here on a scale of magnificence and beauty equal to any Nobleman's country seat. Drawing, Music and Dancing Rooms furnished with the highest taste and latest fashions . . . Ice houses, hot houses, the whole forming an accommodation fit for the reception of a Prince.' Both men were also prominent philanthropists, Benjamin being the founder of the Royal Naval Asylum, and both were friendly with the royal family. Yet the end came with remarkable suddenness. Benjamin had become fat, gout-ridden and melancholic; and in 1808 he hanged himself, by the silk cord that he normally used for levering himself out of bed. It was a huge blow to Abraham, the gentler, less socially ambitious of the two. He seemed to recover, but in 1810 a loan for which he had contracted began to go badly wrong, an over-driven ox knocked him down in Lombard Street, and by the last Thursday in September he was in a strangely savage mood on the Royal Exchange, talking of revenge against his enemies in the money market. That evening at Morden Hall he played a distracted hand of cards and early the next morning he shot himself, in the part of his grounds called the Wilderness, given over to a rookery. News of his death caused intense consternation in the City, to the outrage of William Cobbett, who issued a characteristic blast in his *Weekly Political Register*:

> All this for the death of a Jew merchant! The *king* and the *heir apparent* to be informed of it by a royal Messenger! And, is it really true, that this man's having shot himself made the citizens of London forget almost

every thing else? Is it really true, that such an event put business nearly at a stand? Is it really true, that it produced an effect equal to *peace* or *war* suddenly made? And is it true; is there truth in the shameful fact, that a Jew Merchant's shooting himself produced *alarm* and *dismay* in the capital of England, which is also called, and not very improperly, perhaps, the emporium of the world?

There may have been truth in these dreadful impeachments, but for Abraham and his brother, both interred in the Jews burial ground at Mile End, it hardly mattered.[3]

Altogether more robust was the next great Jewish financier. The brewer Sir Thomas Buxton encountered him – a short, heavy figure with protruding lips and bulbous eyes – at a dinner party in 1834, and fragments of a life story spilled out:

> There was not room enough for all of us in Frankfurt. I dealt in English goods. One great trader came there who had the market to himself. He was quite the great man, and did us a favour if he sold us goods. Somehow I offended him, and he refused to show me his patterns. This was on Tuesday. I said to my father, 'I will go to England'. I could speak nothing but German. On the Thursday I started. The nearer I got to England, the cheaper goods were. As soon as I got to Manchester, I laid out all my money, things were so cheap, and I made good profit . . .
>
> When I was settled in London, the East India Company had £800,000 worth of gold to sell. I went to the sale, and bought it all. I knew the Duke of Wellington must have it. I had bought a great many of his bills at a discount. The Government sent for me, and said they must have it. When they had got it, they did not know how to get it to Portugal. I undertook all that, and I sent it through France; and that was the best business I ever did.

The monologue was only briefly interrupted when someone at the dinner table expressed the hope that his children were not too fond of money and business:

> I wish them to give mind, and soul, and heart, and body, and everything to business; that is the way to be happy. It requires a great deal of boldness, and a great deal of caution, to make a great fortune; and when you have got it, it requires ten times as much wit to keep it. If I were to listen to all the projects proposed to me, I should ruin myself very soon.

The speaker was Nathan Mayer Rothschild, a nonpareil figure in the City's entire history, and for once the recollections late in life of a successful self-made man bear some relation to historical fact.

Rothschild was born in 1777 the third son of a Frankfurt merchant, was based in Manchester from 1799 and prospered as a textile merchant, and in 1808 opened a permanent office in the City, at first in Great St Helen's Street but moving to New Court in St Swithin's Lane shortly after. During the latter stages of the Napoleonic Wars he made his fortune through the audacious conduct of crucial bullion operations on behalf of the British Government, in the course of which he was much helped by large credits from his four brothers who were based in various financial centres on the Continent. That was the prime source of his initial great wealth; it was not (contrary to legend) a major killing on the stock market from being on the inside track over the battle of Waterloo. The Rothschild of these decisive years was quite as masterful and single-minded as the relatively benign latter-day version, though not without a neurotic and self-aggrandising streak. Usually on the receiving end were his brothers, one of whom, Salomon, showed some letters to an Amsterdam associate who in turn wrote to Nathan in June 1814: 'I have to confess sincerely, dear Mr Rothschild, that I was embarrassed for your own brother, when I found these big insults in your letters. Really, you call your brothers nothing but asses and stupid boys.' He went on: 'Now God gave you the good fortune to carry out large-scale transactions, such as, I think, no Jew has ever done. So you should be happy about it together with your brothers.' Six months later and Nathan, unabashed, was writing to brother Carl in Frankfurt:

> I have taken the firm resolution to put the Frankfurt House on a new basis . . . I would rather give up business in Frankfurt than to have you cry for money all the time . . . Speaking quite frankly your letters sometimes drive me crazy. They are written in such a crude way. You use some horrible expressions . . . I am risking wife and children and am content with a fifth, quite apart from the fact that I drive myself crazy . . .

He need not have worried, for 1815 was to be the year in which he netted about a million in connection with the payment of the British army and its allies. 'I do not read books, I do not play cards, I do not go to the theatre, my only pleasure is my business', Nathan informed his brothers at the start of 1816, before adding astutely of the place he had made home: 'As long as we have a good business and are rich everybody will flatter us'.[4]

City houses rose, City houses fell, and in October 1812 an anxious clerk wrote to his mother in Scotland:

The situation of this house is truly disastrous . . . You can have no idea of the Extravagance of both nay all the partners. They are men of the most generous, easy disposition imaginable – but all their friends are disgusted with their ridiculous stile which has resembled that of Princes more than Merchants. These things must have an end – a variety of unfortunate, ill contrived, ill advised, Speculations carried off in the last two years £50,000, a great property say £140,000 lies in Jamaica unsaleable. Mr Murphy's Brother a great scoundrel in Spanish America owes us £300,000 which he disputes & will not pay a halfpenny of. These things added to the Expenditure of the partners which may amount yearly to £25,000 have brought the house to its present state of humiliation wherein it cannot obtain credit for a £100 – after being thought the richest house in London. All are afraid of us – all have envied us – so all now laugh at us hate us & wait with impatience to see our ultimate fall . . . Yet so sanguine are the partners about their affairs that tho' we are struggling from day to day – they conceive themselves perfectly safe & think because they have large property in various hands that it must all be recovered & their distresses relieved & such is their infatuation that whilst at this moment one lives in a Gothic Castle on the Banks of the Thames & at Grosvenor Square the other is contesting the Worcester Election tho' absent in Spain.

The castle-dweller was Colonel Murphy, the parliamentary candidate Sir William Duff Gordon, the house Gordon, Murphy & Co. And the much-harassed clerk was John James Ruskin, who as a young man in Edinburgh had hoped to study law but had been overruled by his grocer father and compelled in 1801 to begin a commercial career in London. 'I cannot but say I have turned from my profession for moments repeatedly with disgust', he wrote in his apocalyptic letter home, adding that 'had I my life to lead over again, nothing should make me a Merchant'. For years he had been working fearsomely long hours, which were compounded by Sir William's habit of coming from the House of Commons to the City in the evening; and in August 1813, with the firm still staggering on, he took his first holiday in almost a decade. He later recalled it: 'I left by Coach for Edinburgh after being in Counting House till Midnight – totally exhausted & was seized with Typhus fever at Ferry bridge'. On Ruskin's eventual return to the City he left the firm and set up with two others a successful sherry-importing business.[5] In 1819 his wife gave birth to the Victorian prophet whose most abiding dictum would be that 'there is no wealth but life'.

Angerstein, Hancock, the Goldsmids, Rothschild, Ruskin senior – all outsiders who experienced intensely contrasting fortunes. Over the next two centuries the City would flourish inasmuch as it was susceptible to outside influences and the rise of new men, congeal inasmuch as it allowed itself to be dominated by dynastic conservatism. Clubs, like families, are capable of renewing themselves; but they still remain clubs. Such was to be the City's inner history until the late twentieth century.

CHAPTER TWO

The Whole Earth Emporium

Once upon a time the City was London, and by Tudor times at the latest it had established itself as a leading international trading centre. Thomas Gresham's successful establishment of the Royal Exchange in 1570 consolidated the fact. By the end of the seventeenth century London towered over the rest of the country in almost all types of trade (its population of half a million was meekly followed by Norwich with 30,000). In the eighteenth century came the great surge in British commerce, which took three main forms: a growing domestic demand for American and Asian consumer goods (above all sugar, tea, tobacco and coffee) and North European raw materials (such as forest products like timber); a growing European market for re-exports of American and Asian consumables; and a growing protected market for British manufacturers in the American colonies and Africa.[1] The City of London was to the fore in servicing all three markets. This prosperity could not have been achieved without a growing naval dominance that brought Britain spectacular colonial gains in Canada, the West Indies and India, more than offsetting the subsequent loss of America, which anyway still left intact much of Britain's growing transatlantic commerce. It was this imperial thrust that gave a particular trading primacy in the City to so-called 'colonial goods', which included not only food and drink, but also cotton, dyestuffs and printed textiles.[2] 'London is become, especially of late, the trading metropolis of Europe, and, indeed, of the whole world', asserted the banker-cum-economist Henry Thornton in 1802. And soon afterwards *The Picture of London* said much the same thing in best guide-book purple: 'London is the centre of the trade of the whole world, and more ships sail from it in a year than from all other places in the world united. It has fifty times more trade than ancient Carthage, than Venice in its glory; than all the Hans Towns, or Amsterdam could ever boast.'[3]

The historic heart of this mercantile community remained the Royal Exchange, rebuilt after the Great Fire of 1666 and the single great meeting-place for the City's merchants and the several hundred specialist brokers who acted as intermediaries between them. Defoe in the 1720s called it 'the greatest and finest of the kind in the world', while a few years later a revised edition of Stow's *Survey of London* explained how 'for the more easy expediting of their work the merchants dealing in the same Commodities have by custom fixed on these different Parts of the Exchange to meet one another, called Walks' – walks that included the Norway Walk, Virginia Walk, Jamaica Walk, Spanish Walk and Jews Walk. These walks, with their specialist implications, prefigured the ultimate decline of the Royal Exchange as a commercial assembly, but it was not a rapid process. During the eighteenth century, despite the emergence of the odd specialist exchange such as the Corn Exchange in Mark Lane in 1749 and the Coal Exchange in Thames Street in 1770, the celebrated heyday of the coffee house served to complement rather than rival the Royal Exchange in the daily rhythm of City life. Most of the main coffee houses were centres for trade with particular areas of the world, though Garraway's of Change Alley, for instance, was renowned for the length of its hours and the variety of its sales of commodities. Thus the Jamaica was largely frequented by those involved in the West Indies trade, the Jerusalem by those concerned with the East, the Virginia and Baltic (forerunner of the Baltic Exchange) by those whose merchandise came from either the American colonies or Baltic seaboard, and so on. What did these coffee houses provide? Partly working premises when offices were still rare, a place where merchants and others could do a certain amount of business as well as their paperwork either side of a session on 'Change; partly sustenance; but above all the very latest information, as 'the coffeemen vied with each other in maintaining the supply of a wide variety of domestic and foreign newspapers, news-sheets, journals, and bulletins, customs-entry forms, auction notices, price-current lists, &c, in addition to making known their particular brand of punch and other beverages'.[4]

And the merchants themselves? 'There is no place in the town which I so much love to frequent as the Royal Exchange', wrote Addison in *The Spectator*. 'It gives me secret satisfaction as an Englishman to see so rich an assembly of countrymen and foreigners making this metropolis a kind of emporium for the whole earth. Sometimes I am jostled by a body of Armenians, sometimes I am lost in a crowd of Jews or Dutchmen, sometimes Danes, Swedes or Frenchmen . . .'[5] It was of course no new thing for foreign merchants to settle in London in order to sell the goods of their home region and to buy return cargoes, but from the late seventeenth century there were successive waves of immigration. Huguenots, Dutch Jews and Germans handled much of the trade to and from northern Europe, while Portuguese Jews traded to and from the Iberian Peninsular, the Mediterranean and even beyond.[6] Of the 810 merchants who kissed the hand of George III on his accession in 1760, at least 250 were (on the basis of their surnames) of palpably alien origin. It was typical that during this third quarter of the century the first members of the Cazenove family to make an impact in the City, the merchanting cousins John Henry and James, were grandchildren of a French Huguenot who had left France for Geneva in the wake of the Revocation of the Edict of Nantes. Or take Levi Barent Cohen: he was a Dutch merchant who settled in England in about 1770 and in due course became a great City patriarch, with Nathan Rothschild as a son-in-law.[7]

However, Addison gazed upon 'countrymen' as well as 'foreigners', and the City remained a strong pull to more homegrown mercantile talent. Matthew Wood was born about 1768 the son of a Devon serge manufacturer, worked for eight years for druggist firms in Exeter, and at the ripe age of twenty-two was head-hunted by Crawley & Adcock of Bishopsgate Street. Further moves followed, until in 1797 he went into prosperous partnership as a hop merchant just off Cripplegate. Also from Exeter (though his wool-merchant father had come from Bremen) was young Francis Baring, who after a suitably arithmetical education at Mr Fuller's Academy in Lothbury opened a merchant house at Queen Street, Cheapside in 1763. Forty years on and Farington was noting in his diary: 'Sir Francis Baring's House is now unquestionably the first Mercantile House in the City. He is a General Merchant. The Partners are respected. Other Houses, comparatively, only come in for gleanings.' It was a remarkable achievement and on his death in 1810 he was described by Lord Erskine as 'unquestionably the first merchant in Europe', being 'first in knowledge and talents, and first in character and opulence'.[8]

A strong international connection was virtually a prerequisite of successful merchanting, typified in the case of Barings in the late eighteenth century by its close links with the powerful Amsterdam house of Hope and Co and its increasing ability to provide credit to leading merchants in North America. 'London is the principal centre of the American Commerce, London houses acting almost solely as bankers for the America trade, receiving the proceeds of consignments', wrote Alexander Baring in 1808. Also operating in that field, between 1782 and 1802, was the firm of Bird, Savage & Bird. It exported manufactured goods to South Carolina and in effect provided the finance for such semi-tropical products as rice and indigo to be shipped to London. Credit was the crux, especially since many merchants, at home and abroad, began business with little or no capital. Systems of credit could be complicated things, but the basic mechanism on which they increasingly revolved was the sterling bill of exchange, a negotiable instrument through which a seller was able to receive payment for goods as soon as he had sent them on their way. Towards the end of the century a few of the leading London merchants, above all Barings, were taking on a 'finance' function and becoming what would eventually be termed merchant banks – or, more narrowly, accepting houses – to service the international trading community. It was a profitable business, done on a commission basis; but since it involved guaranteeing bills of exchange that would eventually be sold in the London bill market centred on the Royal Exchange, it was one that demanded the nicest possible judgement of clients, of trades, and of countries.

So the substantial eighteenth-century City merchant was rarely a merchant pure and simple – he might easily do any number of other things, including dealing in bullion or negotiating foreign drafts and remittances. William Braund (1695–1774) was not untypical: his main business was the wholesale export of woollens to Portugal, but he took advantage of the Seven Years' War to win a small fortune in the Portuguese bullion trade; and quite apart from being a Manager of the Sun Fire Office and a Director of the East India Company, respectively representing merchanting and shipping interests, he became increasingly prominent in marine insurance.[9] Merchants like Braund *defined* the eighteenth-century City and would help to give it for long after a character that was as much 'commercial' as specifically 'financial'.

No merchant could be without insurance. Back in 1691 Edward Lloyd had moved his coffee house from near the river to Lombard Street in order to be as close as possible to the General Post Office, prime source of shipping intelligence, and over the next half-century Lloyd's Coffee House specialised increasingly in marine insurance, with *Lloyd's List* beginning publication in 1734. In 1769 a new, more morally upright Lloyd's Coffee House split from and superseded the old one, moving in 1774 into new premises on the first floor of the Royal Exchange, with Angerstein negotiating the agreement. Three aspects of the Lloyd's of the late eighteenth century stand out: that many of the underwriters were little more than speculators of slender means; that it was the brokers who during the eighteenth century largely held the market together and had to make correct assessments of risk on behalf of merchants; and that the small family firm was the norm, such as the insurance broking firm started by John Robinson in Birchin Lane in about 1800 that was the precursor of Hogg Robinson. Did it work? Angerstein certainly thought so, telling the 1810 inquiry into marine insurance that at Lloyd's 'every Insurance almost can be done with fair connections, and at a considerable advance of Premium'. Not everyone came out of the experience with a prized picture collection and roseate memories – 'the labour, the agitation of mind, the perpetual vexation, is not to be described', stated the experienced broker Thomas Reed, adding that 'I would rather begin the world again and pursue any other line' – but that was another matter. Some of the merchant witnesses complained that underwriters were too prone to take to the spas during the autumn and thus avoid winter risks, but the underwriter James Forsyth, an autumn regular, laconically remarked that 'it has not been in my own experience such a bad business at that time of the year, because I exact a high Premium'. Overall the select committee gave Lloyd's a clean enough bill of health, and the following year saw significant internal reorganisation, building on the introduction of a modicum of quality control in 1800 after which subscribers to the coffee house had to be elected.[10]

Another central pillar of the City now taking shape was the Bank of England, established in 1694 by opportunistic merchants in order to fund the war against France. Over the next century there were few pauses for peace, the national debt grew inexorably, and the Bank of England not only managed that debt but became a government bank, looking after the accounts of most of the departments of state. Moreover, backed by its considerable bullion reserves, it issued a large volume of notes, becoming the dominant influence in the London money market. In the course of the eighteenth century it came to seem indispensable: in 1745, as the looming presence of the Young Pretender threatened a potentially fatal run on the Bank, a powerful group of merchants met at Garraway's and agreed to accept its notes as payment; in the financial crisis of 1763 the Bank for the first time acted as lender of last resort; and in 1781 the prime minister Lord North famously referred to it as 'from long habit and usage of many years . . . a part of the constitution'. Yet what is now forgotten is that in the eighteenth century the Bank of England was essentially a profit-making bank run by merchants on behalf of the mercantile rather than banking community, that 'rival' bankers were not allowed to be Bank directors, and that it saw itself fulfilling a private at least as much as a public function. There was certainly no continuous sense in which it was a central bank

regulating a national financial system: indeed, it was still often called
the 'Bank of London', a reflection in part of its aloofness from the
emerging network of country banks and the fact that the use of its notes
was more or less confined to London and the south-east. Yet what the
Bank did exercise was a considerable degree of influence within the
City, especially through its provision of short-term finance by means of
discounting commercial bills. This increased rapidly from the 1760s
and the main beneficiaries were City merchants and traders. 'Before the
[French] Revolution our Bank was the centre upon which all credit and
circulation depended, and it was at that time in the power of the Bank
to affect the credit of individuals in a very great degree by refusing their
paper', recalled Sir Francis Baring in the early 1800s.[11] It was a first
step on the road to becoming village policeman, immigration officer
and magistrate rolled into one.

There were plenty of other London banks – some fifty by the 1770s,
nearly seventy by the end of the century – and at any one time at least
half of these were City-based. Some firms, such as Barnett, Hoare &
Co or Willis, Percival & Co, both of Lombard Street, had been bankers
in the City since the reign of Charles II. Others, like Smith, Payne &
Smiths or Hanbury, Taylor, Lloyd & Bowman (the modern Lloyds) or
Jones, Loyd & Co, essentially represented well-established provincial
banking families (from Nottingham, Birmingham and Manchester respectively) who during the second half of the eighteenth century set up
London offices and often moved their main interests there. What is
most striking is the mercantile background of many of the private
banks that were coming into existence. The firm of Barclay, Tritton,
Bevan & Co (the modern Barclays) derived partly from large-scale linen
merchants trading in Cheapside; the three original partners of Vere,
Glyn & Hallifax (the later Glyn Mills) were respectively the sons of a
Paternoster Row mercer, a Hatton Garden drysalter and a Yorkshire
clockmaker; or as Henry Thornton of Down, Thornton & Free put it,
'we are all City people and connected with merchants and nothing but
merchants on every side'. It is a key point, for whereas West End banks
lent on mortgage and had many landed families as clients, City banks
purchased bills of exchange and, broadly speaking, serviced the world
of trade. The banks, for the most part tightly clustered in Lombard
Street, were fundamentally deposit banks, and the note-issuing function gradually died out; many of them, especially the newer ones, not
only facilitated mercantile credit by acquiring (as an investment) the
bills of merchants, but also enjoyed a lucrative, expanding business by
acting as London correspondent to banks in the country. This agency

role included the clearance of payments with other banks through the London Bankers' Clearing House, established in 1773. But more important from the point of view of the larger economy, they functioned as a more or less benign conduit: rural banks would deposit in London the surplus savings of rural areas; banks in undercapitalised industrial areas, where the paramount need was for circulating capital rather than fixed capital, would secure short-term credit from their London agents. Altogether it was a virtuous circle that played a larger part in the financing of the Industrial Revolution than has often been recognised.[12]

The private bankers themselves comprised a distinctive breed of men who in time would come to represent the very bloom of the City. Henry Thornton for one had no doubts of the standards to uphold:

> I consider myself to possess as a Banker the character in a great measure of a trustee to our customers, & as not entitled to commit their property to hazard to any serious extent . . . I, as elder partner, & as one who possesses, I trust not ostentatiously, principles of this sort which connect themselves indeed with still higher principles am counted on as a guarantee that all is safe.

Thornton – Treasurer of the Bible Society, the Church Missionary Society and the Religious Tract Society as well as a prominent writer on banking and currency questions – may not have been entirely typical, and indeed he found that his partners 'lent no very willing Ear to the religious observations' that he 'sometimes endeavoured to press upon them'; yet in his high seriousness he was far from unique among private bankers. Take John Henton Tritton, who came to Barclays in 1782 after the traumatic experience of his uncle's firm failing through defalcations. Robert Barclay II described him in his prime:

> He was the most deliberate and exact man I ever knew . . . He followed up the details of every part of our concern with minute particularity which kept all the clerks up to the mark, silently overlooking their work and making all his observations in a low tone of voice, so that the same quiet habit of transacting the business prevailed throughout the House. Extreme caution, inflexible integrity and firmness were his characteristics as a man of business, and to these he added punctuality and self-command. He was scrupulously exact in not revealing the secrets of others, and especially careful of being dragged into ill-precedents by the influence of names.

In short, in a haunting phrase, 'he lived in the entire subjection of his natural temperament and passion'. Nevertheless, one is perhaps nearer the human mainstream with James Martin II of Martin, Stone & Foote (the modern Martins Bank). He could be lofty enough – for example, reading Priestley's history of the Christian Church to his family at the breakfast table – but he was also immensely fat, enjoyed going to the theatre and playing cards, and had the homely habit of recording in his diary the weather at noon. 'Incorruptible integrity compensated for the mediocrity of his talents' was how Wraxall described his parliamentary contribution as Member for Tewkesbury between 1776 and 1807.[13] Contemporaries would not have expected otherwise, for despite the odd glittering exception it was bottom, not brilliance, that made a private banker.

One pillar remains. 'The Stock Exchange is a poor substitute for the Holy Grail', thought Schumpeter, and no doubt he had a point. The stock market's effective origins lay in the war finance of the 1690s, and during the next century and beyond it dealt primarily in British government securities ('the Funds'). Home to this market during most of the eighteenth century were the coffee houses of Change Alley, most famously Jonathan's and Garraway's. In a sense the modern organisation of the market began in 1734 when, over a decade after the stock manipulation that culminated in the South Sea Bubble, legislation introduced by Sir John Barnard, himself a merchant, sought severely to reduce the range of stockbroking business. In particular, it attempted to outlaw the highly profitable but speculative end of the business known as 'time bargains' – by which traders in effect gambled on future prices without actually buying or selling stock. Confronted by this hostile legislation, the brokers and jobbers of the day simply ignored it and developed their own self-regulating mechanism, in which the sanctity of the bargain was paramount. 'My word is my bond' became no idle boast. Economic logic was also on the market's side: holdings in the funds were not just investments to merchants but the means by which they effected many of the loans between themselves; and for the property-owning nation at large, there was, following the introduction of Consols (British government stock) in 1751, nothing quite like 'the sweet simplicity of the three per cents'. It is clear from modern econometric historians that the capital market of the age was highly efficient and surprisingly well integrated with those of Paris and Amsterdam.

In 1773, with space increasingly at a premium despite the emergence of the Rotunda of the Bank of England as an alternative place for dealing in the Funds, the stockbrokers abandoned their coffee houses and found a home at the corner of Threadneedle Street and Sweetings Alley. The building had the words 'The Stock Exchange' inscribed above the door and an entrance fee was levied of sixpence a day. Payment of this tanner allowed a member of the public to pass through a waist-high bar, but his problems were not over: 'If he entered within the bar, either to watch his broker, or for essay, he was sure to be hustled, find lighted squibs put into his pocket, or his hat and wig canted out before him, until it was ascertained that he came for other purposes than espionage'.[14]

Until late in the eighteenth century there was little distinction between brokers (dealing on behalf of the public) and jobbers (making a market in securities in order to service brokers), and even then there were many who continued to perform both functions. Similarly mixed were the social origins of those who operated in the stock market: back in the 1690s a list of brokers included such names as Henry Contigno, Stephen Mahieu, Benjamin Nunes and Elias Paz. There was undoubtedly a strong Jewish element, and between the 1730s and 1750s there was no one more dominant at Jonathan's Coffee House than Samson Gideon. He made a fortune for himself, offered crucial advice to government over a series of war loans and other financial operations, and possessed a superbly sardonic touch: when during the crisis of 1745–6 the private banker Thomas Snow requested the repayment of a substantial loan, Gideon sent the money by return in bank notes wrapped round a bottle of hartshorn.[15]

What, though, was the stock market actually like? Although motivated by hostility, in 1761 Thomas Mortimer provided the closest description of the 'daily tumult' at Jonathan's, here shortly after noon:

Tickets – Tickets – South-Sea Stock for the opening – Navy-Bills – Bank Stock for the rescounters – Long Annuities – (*here the waiter calls*) Chance – Chance – Chance – *Mr. Chance is not here, Sir, he is over at his Office* – Here Tickets for August – Omnium gatherum for September – Scrip for the third payment – 3 per Cent. consolidated, gentlemen – Here Mr. Full (*whispers a friend, but is overheard*) they are all BULLS by G—d, but I'll be d—d if they have any of my Stock, I'll go to Bath, and not come near them till the rescounters – Here Bank Circulation, who buys Bank Circulation – Tickets for the drawing gentlemen – Well, what have you to do in Tickets for the drawing, Mr. Mulberry. – I am a seller of five hundred, Sir – and I am a buyer, Sir, but pray at what price? – Why, as you are a friend, Mr. Point-royal, I shall give you the turn, you shall have them at 14. The turn, Mr. Mulberry, why do you think I do not know what I am about? they are all sellers at 13 – Well then, you shall have them at 13s. – I will take them at 12, and no otherwise – Well, you, shall have them, put 'em down (for the drawing mind) but, d—n it, Tom, where did you get that paste wig? – Why, you son of a b—h, it is as good as your mop . . .[16]

Joining the lottery at about this time was Abraham Ricardo, a stockbroker in Amsterdam before moving to London. His son was David Ricardo, the leading economist who also doubled as an immensely successful jobber and loan contractor; and when in 1814 he was asked by a fellow-economist which members of the market would be able to give advice on the thorny subject of circulation, his reply was objective:

> The Stock Exchange is chiefly attended by persons who are unremittingly attentive to their business, and are well acquainted with its details; but there are very few in number who have much knowledge of political economy, and consequently they pay little attention to finance, as a subject of science. They consider more, the immediate effect of passing events, rather than their distant consequences.[17]

Short-termism has a long history.

By the time Ricardo wrote, he and his fellow-members had for over a decade been occupying their own purpose-built home in Capel Court, the first stone of which was laid in May 1801. Unlike its predecessor the new Stock Exchange was a fully closed market, for 'instead of a breastwork barricado, as in the old house, they ran up high folding double doors, to prevent further interview from the out-door stockholder, than with the porter at the porch, distinguished by a gold laced hat to call out by name any member wanted by his principal . . .' Members had to be elected (though the entrance qualifications were not formidable), these members in turn elected their own committee, and at last a modicum of respectability beckoned. That there was some ground to make up is shown in a plaintive letter from one member of the Smith banking family to another (Robert Smith, recently created Lord Carrington) in April 1802, reflecting dashed hopes of entering the business:

> The interest which your Lordship has taken in my welfare – the repeated marks of kindness which you have shown me – and the desire which I believe you have of seeing me respectably established in life, make me feel anxious to communicate to you the proposition which your Brothers have this morning made to me, of placing me in business with some Stock-broker, whose name they have not mentioned . . . This last unexpected affair has occasioned in me a considerable degree of morti-

fication and disappointment . . . I am apprehensive that my friends would probably consider the Stock Exchange as a sort of transportation – a punishment for misconduct. The business of a Stockbroker is so little congenial to my feelings, that, setting aside all other considerations, and looking to it only as a means to independence, I do not believe that I should succeed . . .

Banking would long have a social cachet denied to stockbroking, and a clue lies in the despairing tone of the Stock Exchange's first set of rules and regulations, drawn up in 1812: 'The Committee earnestly recommend, to the several members, that *order and decorum* which is so essentially necessary to be observed in all places of business, and that they forbear on their own parts, and discourage as much as possible in others, those rude and trifling practices which have too long disgraced the Stock Exchange in the estimation of the public, which would not be tolerated in any other place; and which, it is seriously apprehended, may have been injurious to the best interests of the House'.[18] Injurious yes, but to be tired of making butter slides or throwing paper balls was to be tired of Capel Court.

There was, of course, much else to the eighteenth-century City. For one thing there was the emergence by the 1770s, with the Goldsmid brothers to the fore, of specialist bill broking, further refining the process of mercantile credit; for another there were the bullion brokers headed by Mocatta & Goldsmid (Asher Goldsmid, an older brother) who conducted the business of London's increasingly important precious-metals market. Or take the specialist foreign exchange dealers: on Tuesdays and Fridays, between noon and three o'clock, they serviced with acute, competitive attention the merchants of the Royal Exchange, matching the needs of importers for remittances with the supply of bills from exporters. Bills were negotiated at the keenest rates and those rates were published immediately after the close of business in *The Course of the Exchange*. But there were many other types of dealing trades in the City, not least the drapers, mercers and silkmen who operated in London's extremely large textile and clothing market; while as for the City's many shops, a popular song called 'Country Commissions to my Cousin in Town' had the lively refrain, 'a skein of white worsted from Flint's', referring to the well-known haberdasher near the Monument. There was also the traditional manufacturing sector: although there took place a general emigration during the century to the regions, where labour costs were lower, not only did London continue to provide much of the finance but significant manufacturing trades remained, such as coopering on the banks of the Thames. Perhaps an epitome of the variegated eighteenth-century City were the parents of Thomas Gray, born in 1716 in a house in Cornhill: his father was a money scrivener on 'Change, his mother with her two sisters kept a milliner's shop in the City; and between them they prospered sufficiently to send the young elegist to Eton.[19]

*

Outsiders were little enough impressed. 'Now Men seem vastly rich upon the sudden, set up for Greatness presently, and live profusely, and, in a little time, sink unaccountably, and carry their Acquaintance with them, to the Bottom', preached Bishop Fleetwood of Ely in a sermon in the City in 1718. The following year Defoe anatomised the denizens of Exchange Alley in the shrillest possible tones and in 1720 the trauma of the South Sea Bubble confirmed any critic's worst suspicions. By the 1730s there had emerged a clear 'country' critique of the City, depicting it as inherently unstable, parasitic and even treacherous. Bolingbroke declared that stockjobbing was to trade as faction was to liberty, while Joseph Danvers, MP for Bramber, inveighed in the Commons against 'the Plumb Men of the City of London' who through manipulation of the Funds were 'enabled to deck their Wives in Velvet and rich Brocades, while poor Country Gentlemen are hardly able to afford their Wives a Gown of Lindsey Woolsey'. So it went on, with Dr Johnson defining in his dictionary the stockjobber as 'a low wretch who gets money by buying and selling shares in the funds', the 'cit' as 'a pert low alderman or pragmatical trader', and remarking to Boswell in 1778 that the wives of City tradesmen were 'the worst creatures upon the earth, grossly ignorant, and thinking viciousness fashionable.'[20]

Apart from the larger question of what did or did not constitute a healthy society and economy, there were two particularly sharp strands to the critique. One, as implied by the great cham, was almost a matter of taste, so that successive generations of social satirists and caricaturists made savage butts of City people, pointing up their corpulence, their mundane recreations, their general lack of elegance. The culminating example was Peter Pindar's depiction of the prominent, grossly overweight self-made merchant-cum-banker Sir William Curtis ('Sir William Porpoise'), with his 'nose as red as rose in June'. The other strand was even less benign and came out implicitly in 1785 when the Marquis of Lansdowne urged Francis Baring to stand for the House of Commons: 'It's the highest Injustice to consider every Merchant as a

Jew, as if he were incapable of looking forward to anything but a Fraudulent Contract or a Line of Stockjobbing – the consequence of which is that their talents are left to prey upon the Publick instead of serving it . . .'[21] Anti-Semitism was a crude perspective on the City that had plenty of mileage left in it.

Whatever the emotional force of the critique from the country, the fact was that during the eighteenth century the landed came at least to some extent to accept that there existed an interdependence between themselves and the monied in the City. By the end of the century it was hardly possible for a latter-day Bolingbroke to declare that 'the landed men are the true owners of our political vessel, the moneyed men but passengers in it'. There was starting to crystallise that compact between the aristocracy and the commercial middle class: gentlemen were becoming capitalists, capitalists were becoming gentlemanly, and henceforth the twain would meet. Both sides seemed to have few qualms. 'It is gone into the city to look for a fortune', Dr Johnson flatly explained to a young nobleman in 1770 about where the gallantry and military spirit of the old English nobility had vanished; while from the point of view of the monied interest, there were several prominent examples of City men obtaining Parliamentary seats, acquiring country estates and marrying their offspring into the aristocracy or gentry. This particularly applied to merchants – who on the whole made the real fortunes – and indeed as a pattern of social mobility became virtually a caricature in its own right. What, though, was the nature of the interdependence that shaped this compact? Essentially it lay in the City's crucial, highly profitable role in managing the national debt, thereby enabling the ruling landed class simultaneously to enhance national power through protracted warfare, consolidate the Hanoverian settlement and keep taxation not only low but also thoroughly regressive. The economic case was compelling for bringing the moneyed men on board.[22]

Nevertheless, it was in many ways a chequered, fractured sort of *rapprochement*. Even its strictly economic basis was somewhat patchy: thus research into who held stock in the East India Company has shown no significant scale of investment on the part of the landed interest; instead, it was fairly tightly held within the City. But it was at the social level that the key ambiguities lay, as exemplified by the painful ascent of Samson Gideon. From the late 1740s he was on the way up, acquiring a grant of arms, a country house in Kent and a collection of pictures; but in 1758 he was refused when he asked for a baronetcy in return for his considerable services to successive ministries, being mollified only when his fourteen-year-old son instead was created a

baronet the following year. Almost forty years later the transformation
of the banker Robert Smith into the peer Lord Carrington prompted a
widespread jingle:

> Billy Pitt made him a peer,
> And took the pen from behind his ear.

When in 1801 Sir Francis Baring's son, Alexander, became a member
of a fashionable West End political dining club, the King of Clubs,
Sydney Smith observed that it was only 'upon the express promise that
he lends £50 to any member of the Club when applied to'. And in *Sense
and Sensibility* (1811), Lady Middleton regretted that her mother, the
sturdy Mrs Jennings, had never dropped 'a few old city friends'. Nor
was integration entirely whole-hearted, let alone complete, on the
City's part. Bankers tended to go into Parliament strictly in order to
benefit the business; the average mildly prosperous merchant was at
least as likely to acquire a cosy riverside villa within striking distance
of the City as any sort of country estate proper; and during much of
the eighteenth century the influence of the lesser merchants and tradesmen put the City into a state of quasi-permanent opposition to the
government of the day. The City had its own culture, its own tradi-
tions, and altogether a pride that rendered it not entirely susceptible to
aristocratic buy-outs. In 1803 Farington noted shrewdly of his orange-
eating host: 'Mr Angerstein might have been at the head of popularity
in the City, but has chosen to associate chiefly at the west end of the
town'.[23]

Who then did run the City? In one sense it is a meaningless question
to ask – granted the inherently discrete, fragmented nature of the place
– but it is clear that at any one time there existed a group of immensely
wealthy merchants and financiers who had their fingers in most of the
important pies. Overlapping directorships were rife, as is apparent
from an examination of the directors of the Royal Exchange Assurance
during the eighteenth century: twelve were at some time directors of
the Bank of England, six of the East India Company and six of the
South Sea Company. Most of the REA's directors were merchants
(though with a significant minority of bankers), and there was a strong
tendency towards dynasticism, especially on the part of those Huguenot merchant families who were on the REA's Court. Samuel Bosanquet, son of a Huguenot refugee from France who had come to London
and built up a highly prosperous Levant trade, married in 1733 into
the family of a leading Levant merchant who had helped to found the

REA; and he subsequently enjoyed a seat on the Court for twenty years. His eldest son, Samuel II, not only in time became Governor of the Bank of England but in the 1780s went into banking partnership (Forster, Lubbock, Bosanquet & Co) with Edward Forster, Governor of the REA from 1785 to 1812; while as for Samuel Bosanquet's second son, William, he was a successful merchant, deputy-governor of the Levant Company and for many years a member of the REA's Court. But if the Bosanquets readily enough found their way into the charmed circle, not everyone was so fortunate. Particularly this applied to those of the City's Jews who, unlike Gideon or later the Goldsmids, were not manifestly the dominant financiers, through ability and force of personality, of their generation; and here one cannot ignore the anti-Semitic policy of the leadership of the Bank of England for most of the eighteenth century.[24] The Bank, with its power of refusing paper, for a long time made life very difficult for those merchants and others whose faces, in the timeless phrase, did not fit.

Yet approaching the end of that century the City was on the verge of momentous change. The catalyst was the state of almost continuous European warfare between 1792 and 1815 which severely blunted the activities of Britain's main trading rivals and greatly increased the proportion of world trade conducted by merchants based in Britain. Amsterdam declined as the leading international financial centre and was replaced by the City of London. There took place during these years a wholesale flight of capital to London; the French occupation of Amsterdam in 1795 was a final nail in the coffin for that city's financial future; and the transformation of Hope and Co from a powerful independent house into a virtual subsidiary of Barings was eloquent testimony to the profound shift of fortunes. It was also in this period that for the first time foreign stock was marketed in London in significant quantity, though the grudging response to the Austrian loans of the 1790s revealed a certain innate prejudice on the subject. Nevertheless, taken together with the marketing of American securities pioneered in London first by Bird, Savage & Bird and then by Barings, the beginnings were at hand of what would become the City's historic role as exporter of capital.[25]

The City, moreover, similarly grew in *national* importance on the back of warfare. Three symbolic moments stand out: in 1793 a monumental commercial crisis was only avoided through Pitt, Angerstein and the directors of the Bank of England coming up with a timely issue of Exchequer Bills; three years later Pitt's ennoblement of Smith was a tacit recognition of the importance of financial advice, though Disraeli was right in spirit only when he famously claimed that the state's wartime dependence on the City had meant that Pitt 'caught them in the alleys of Lombard Street and clutched them from the counting houses of Cornhill', thus creating 'a plebian aristocracy'; thirdly, in 1797, the beginning of Restriction (by which the drain on the Bank's gold reserves made it necessary to stop paying out gold in exchange for the Bank's notes) not only caused Gillray to draw his immortal, nick-name-coining cartoon of 'Political Ravishment, or The Old Lady of Threadneedle-Street in danger!', but it also raised to near the top of the politico-economic agenda for the next half-century the whole question of the Bank's public responsibilities. In Bagehot's later words: 'It was said to be the "manager" of the paper currency, and on that account many expected much good from it; others said it did great harm; others again that it could do neither good nor harm. But for the whole period there was an incessant and fierce discussion.'[26]

Wars were also fought, and during them Lloyd's found favour with the Admiralty thanks to the coffee house's unique news-gathering service; towards the end it was Rothschild who came up trumps in the task of keeping Wellington's army and its allies in the field. But above all what paid for the war was a series of government loans, amounting to a total borrowing of some £475m and creating a wider, even more permanent market in government securities. For the leading men of the City the potential rewards were enormous but the risks were great, and in practice a handful of loan contractors dominated the scene. The way was led by Walter Boyd, a resilient Scot who had served his mercantile apprenticeship in the Austrian Netherlands and Paris before coming to London in 1793; and during the intensely fluctuating years that followed he believed that he could ride the forces of rising interest rates, the drain of gold and restricted credit, but in the end they unseated him. Then it was the turn of the Goldsmids and, with increasing prominence, Barings, who in 1813 made a tidy £77,000 from two loans. Two years later, following Napoleon's return from Elba, Barings together with Smith, Payne & Smiths were responsible for a £30m issue in 3 per cent bonds, and at a critical juncture the house successfully placed large blocks of the loan with its correspondents in Amsterdam, Basle, Frankfurt, Hamburg, St Petersburg and Vienna – a harbinger of how over the ensuing decades it would often be in the strength of a firm's international connection that much of its City stature would depend.

No one ever denied that loan contracting could be a rough, tough business. Abraham Goldsmid discovered this (if he had not already) when from 1809 he fell foul of the Stock Exchange's jobbers, who accused him of undercutting the very profitable continuation facilities they offered to holders of stock. The jobbers were led by Ricardo, who in brilliantly destructive fashion wore his economist's hat to put forward views on monetary policy designed to undermine Goldsmid's ability to support the market and his jobber's hat to depress prices and thus imperil the success of the 1810 loan for which Goldsmid contracted. The rest followed ineluctably: the over-driven ox in Lombard Street, Ricardo's own triumphs as a loan contractor, and soon his acquisition of the handsome, almost royal estate of Gatcombe Park in Gloucestershire.[27]

These were also the years when the City's specialist ability to service the needs of trade increased significantly and thereby set a pattern for the rest of the nineteenth century. Its role on behalf of Britain's rapidly booming textile trade was a prime example: from the 1790s there developed in and around the Wood Street area off Cheapside (home of poor Susan's plane tree) what was in effect a textile quarter. It usually provided the wholesale warehousing arm, together with a retail outlet, for exporting manufacturers in the provinces, such as the Belper-based hosiery firm Ward, Brettle & Ward, which from about 1809 shared warehouse premises in Wood Street with the lace manufacturers W. Welbury & Co.[28] Finance, however, was even more than before the crux for trade, especially with the wartime growth of the consignment system; and here the City's emerging merchant banks (or accepting houses) held the key, not only enabling foreign producers to draw bills on London as soon as they had shipped their goods, but also, having provided those credit facilities, ensuring the safe warehousing of the goods, often in secure bonded warehouses on the banks of the Thames.

Credit was also at the heart of the increasingly sophisticated money market, where bill broking, building on the pioneering example of the Goldsmids, was starting to become an occupation in its own right. During the 1800s these brokers became increasingly effective in their role of sending bills for 'discount' (i.e. to be purchased) from bankers in industrial areas to bankers elsewhere looking for safe investments. The leading firm of bill brokers, following the demise of the Goldsmids, was Richardson, Overend & Co, of whom the four partners from 1807 were all Quakers, including Samuel Gurney from Norfolk. Another, smaller Quaker firm was started by William Alexander in 1810. He came from Rochester, where his father had been a schoolmaster, and worked for two City banks before starting his own bill-broking establishment in Lombard Street. For a time he quietly prospered, but in

1812 two City houses (one bank, one merchant) to whom he had lent money failed; and he was compelled to relinquish the services of his extremely able clerk John Allcard, who went to Richardson, Overend & Co. It was a great blow for Alexander, though in the end it was his firm that lasted the course rather than that of his more ambitious Quaker rivals.[29]

Trade may have been booming, but a merchant operating during the French wars was a poor insurance prospect. 'A medical gentleman, of great practice in the City, assured me, that it was very usual for him to have several merchants, of great respectability, under his care, previous to the arrival of the Hamburg mails, after a prevalence of contrary winds, and that soon after the winds had shifted to a favourable point they blew away their disorders', noted one visitor to London. The Continental blockade and embargo, extreme fluctuations in commodity prices, the temptation to speculate or stock-pile in order to exploit sudden gluts or scarcities – all these things meant a high wastage rate amongst the City's merchants. Following on from the large-scale casualties caused by the American War of Independence, the City's mercantile landscape of 1815 looked very different from what it had been thirty or forty years earlier. The over-supply crisis of 1810 alone saw the failure in March of five merchants dealing in Baltic hemp, followed in July by the West India brokers Thomas Coles & Sons and their Lombard Street bankers Brickwood and Co.[30]

Nature, however, performed its usual act of abhorrence, and during these wartime years there arrived a host of new entrants in the City. They included (in chronological order between 1800 and 1809): Johann Friedrich and Johann Heinrich Schröder, sons of a wealthy Hamburg merchant who from their arrival in London concentrated, as both principals and agents, on commodity trade to Europe; Emanuel Henry Brandt, son of a Hamburg insurance broker, soon prospering through growing trade with Russia; Antony Gibbs, originally from the West Country but who had spent much of his mercantile life in Spain before coming to London to export textiles there and to South America; Nathan Rothschild, from Frankfurt via Manchester; and Frederick Huth, from Hanover via Corunna, specialising in exports to the west coast of South America. There were others, but the pattern is clear enough of a 'push' in the form of continental Europe becoming an untenable base for business and a 'pull' in the form of a critical mass of support facilities existing in London to maximise the trading or trade-financing potential of distinct areas of local knowledge. Often this knowledge was supplemented by extensive, far-flung family connections, and it is no coincidence that several of these new entrants were or would become genuinely international networks.

Equally crucial, however, to this creation of a more 'open' City was the weakening power of the Bank of England as, in effect, social and business arbiter. Sir Francis Baring in the 1800s described the Bank's traditional exercise of its power to refuse paper, and went on in a passage of fundamental importance: 'The Bank is still the pivot for circulation but no longer for credit and discount. In the distress of 1793, they committed a fatal error by deciding that all merchants and traders were entitled to their proportion of accommodation as the Bank was a public body and ought not to discriminate between individuals . . .' It may have been a fatal error from Baring's point of view, but the direct result was a City more open to merit, much of it Semitic, and judicious risk-taking.[31] There was no clearer sign of the changing times than the failure of the East India Company in 1813 to retain its monopoly of the India trade. With the chips down, and the maintenance of traditional Anglo-Indian mercantilism at stake, the merchants of the City failed to hang together, revealing a split not only between merchants of different trading interests but also between the older merchants and the new men. It was symptomatic when in 1812 one merchant wrote to the vice-president of the Board of Trade referring almost hysterically to German and other alien newcomers who 'make their harvest now by perjury and fraud, thereby staining the character of England'.[32] The ill-mannered game would go on, but this time the new men held the winning cards.

CHAPTER THREE

Vanity Fair

What was the City of 1815 actually like? Thackeray's wonderful panorama gives a point of entry – the stockbroker Sedley who falls in those febrile months before Waterloo, the overproud tallow merchant Osborne, and as an underlying motif Becky Sharp's envy of all those with holdings in the Funds – but a still better one lies in the Post Office Directory for that year. To take a page at random and pluck out the City addresses is to get a broader flavour of the place than even a great novelist can provide, albeit a touch less readable:

Thomas Nightingale, warehouseman, 26 Bucklersbury
N. A. Nilsen & Co, merchants, New Court, Crutched-friars
B. Nind, solicitor, 32 Throgmorton-street
J. Nind, paper-hanging manufactury, 10 Beech-street, Barbican
T. Nisbett, stock-broker, 11 Warnford-court, Throgmorton-street
Nissen, Williams & Nissen, merchants, Swan-street, Minories
James Nix, glover, 32 Bishopsgate-Street-within
John & Richard Nixon, merchants, 5 Basinghall-street
J. Nixon, corn-factor, 33 Great Tower-hill
M. Nixon, grocer, 28 Red-lion-street, Spitalfields
R. Nixon, merchant, 24 Change-alley, Cornhill
J. Noakes, clock-maker, 24 Bishopsgate-within
Noble and Hunt, merchants, 5 Laurence Pountney-hill
Noble, Sampson and Co, wine and hop merchants, 40 St Mary-hill
John Noble, merchant, 15 Tokenhouse-yard
R. Noble, Breeches-maker in general, 118 Leadenhall-street
S. Nock & Co, mattress-manufacturer, 15 Birchin-lane
Christian Nockles, merchant, 3 Nag's-head-court, Gracechurch-street
Henry Nodin & Co, Customhouse and general commission agents, 56
    Great Tower-street
John Nodin & Co, commercial & general agents, & shop & insurance-
    brokers, 2 Beer-lane, Tower-street
John Noel, merchant, 6 Three-king-court, Lombard-street
J. Nonnen, merchant, 2 Pope's-head-alley, Cornhill
Robt. Norcutt, linen-draper & hosier, 28 Chiswell-street
John Wm. Norie & Co, at the Naval Academy, 157 Leadenhall-street

Prologue

George Norman, merchant, 23 Earl-street, Blackfriars
John Norman, general Ship broker & agent, 1 Water-lane, Tower-street,
    and Little Thames Street, St Catherine's[1]

So predominantly commercial, so little explicitly financial: that is one's
dominant impression from this snapshot, together with the sheer range
of often muscular occupations being pursued.

An awestruck spectator was Richard Rush who, soon after arriving
in London in December 1817 to take up the post of U.S. minister, set
out exploring:

> Went through Temple Bar into the *city*, in contradistinction to the west
> end of London, always called *town*. Passed along Fleet street, Ludgate-
> hill, St Paul's, Cheapside, the Poultry, Cornhill, and other streets in the
> direction of the Tower. Saw, by a hasty, exterior glance, the Bank, Royal
> Exchange, Lord Mayor's house, Guildhall, India house, the Excise build-
> ings. If I looked with any feeling of wonder on the throngs at the
> west-end, more cause is there for it here. The shops stand, side by side,
> for entire miles. The accumulation of things, is amazing; it would seem
> impossible that there can be purchasers for them all, until you consider
> what multitudes there are to buy; then, you are disposed to ask how the
> buyers can all be supplied. In the middle of the streets, coal wagons and
> others as large, carts, trucks, vehicles of every sort, loaded in every way,
> are passing. They are in two close lines, like great tides, going reverse
> ways, and reaching farther than the eye can see. The horses come so near
> to the foot pavement which is crowded with people, that their hoofs, and
> the great wheels of the wagons, are only a few inches from the people. In
> this manner the whole procession is in movement with its complicated
> noise; it confounds the senses to be among it all; you would anticipate
> constant accidents – yet they seldom happen. The fear of the law pre-
> serves order; moreover the universal sense of danger if order were viol-
> ated, prevents its violation. I am assured that these streets present the
> same appearance every day in the year, except Sundays, when solitude
> reigns in them.[2]

The modern cliché of the pin-striped banker with rolled-up umbrella
seems remote enough.

Socially mixed, populous by night as well as by day, and still retaining
its medieval street pattern, though now studded with the glories of
Wren's churches, the Georgian City was a place of much fascination.
Another foreigner, visiting it in 1815, found that it 'consists of little,
narrow, crooked streets, forming a labyrinth, out of which it is not easy
to extricate yourself when you have once entered it'. Moreover, already
cramped to begin with, the City by the early nineteenth century was

coming under severe pressure on space as the volume of its business increased; and the result, in an era before the purpose-built office block, was often multiple occupancy and the conversion of domestic property into a rabbit-warren of tiny offices. Nevertheless, despite this trend and the fact that many did commute daily to the square mile (ranging from clerks on foot who lived nearby to the prosperous merchant William Manning who each morning drove eight miles in a coach and four from his Totteridge residence), there was still about the City in the pre-railway age a distinctly traditional and residential character. 'A capital Family-House, very desirably situate for a merchant, between the Royal Exchange and Custom-house . . .' was how one property advertisement began in January 1815, while not long afterwards another extolled the attractions of 'a substantial and desirable Brick-built Dwelling House, and Counting-house, in excellent repair, eligibly situate No. 9 Cooper's-row, Crutched friars, containing six bed chambers, drawing and dining room, breakfast parlour, counting house, excellent entrance, convenient domestic offices, paved yard, arched vault, coal, beer, and wine cellars'. When Barings moved to 8 Bishopsgate in 1805–6, the firm took possession of a substantial house with an archway and open courtyard at the front, stables at the side and a garden at the back; and when in 1808 Jones, Loyd & Co rebuilt its premises, there was still a separate entrance to the upper floors housing a partner, his family and servants. Somehow it was fitting that if one future cardinal had a merchant father commuting to and from Totteridge, another (Newman) was the son of a banker and first saw the no doubt opaque light of day at the family home in Old Broad Street.[3]

In 1815 the residential population of the City was some 122,000 (about a tenth of the population of London as a whole) and about 8,500 firms were operating there. The overwhelming majority of these firms were small, specialised and family-owned. Glyns, for example, was one of the larger banks, but still had only thirty-six staff in 1815; while Antony Gibbs the same year employed only five men in its London office in addition to the three partners. The major exception was the Bank of England, where between 1792 and 1813 the number of clerks increased from 300 to 900. To cross the threshold of one of these firms was usually to enter an austere world. Take Prescotts in Threadneedle Street: massive oak doors opened into a dimly lit banking hall, as elsewhere known as 'the Shop', where clerks dealt with customers over an ancient oak counter and with quill pens and snuff boxes at hand to meet all needs; while beyond was the oak-panelled partners' parlour, directly above the strong room in the basement. The

City clerk was *sui generis* and Charles Lamb provides the classic description:

> His dress is plain without singularity; with no other ornament than the quill which is the badge of his function, stuck under the dexter ear, and this rather for convenience of having it at hand, when he hath been called away from his desk, and expecteth to resume his seat there shortly, than from any delight which he taketh in foppery or ostentation. The colour of his clothes is generally noted to be black rather than brown, brown rather than blue or green. His whole deportment is staid, modest and civil. His motto is Regularity.

William Jerdan would not have disagreed. Brought up in the Scottish borders, he sailed in 1801 from Berwick upon Tweed to Wapping and soon entered the West Indian merchant house of Samuel Turner. There, in City Chambers, he 'found a perfect sample of the quiet, contented and sedulous London clerk: a Mr Drew, dressed in a brown Quakerish garb, and ever most punctually attentive to his day-books and ledgers, his dinner-hour and all his other duties'.[4]

City hours could vary enormously: if Lamb in East India House liked to joke that 'it is true that I come late, but I always leave early', probably more typical was the experience of the young George Crow, writing to his parents in Yorkshire in 1812 that at Todd & Co's textile warehouse in Fore Street 'we open shop before seven in the morning and never shut up before nine in the evening and sometimes twelve o'clock, and we have to sleep in the shop . . . I never get out except on Sunday.' City rewards likewise varied. At Prescotts a clerk's salary averaged about £100 a year, which was handsome enough in national clerical terms, yet in relation to partners it is a figure put in some perspective by a piece of non-evangelical gossip from Mrs Henry Thornton to Hannah More in 1814: 'Did you hear that old Mr Down is dead? He has left £150,000 after educating fourteen children and marrying six daughters – so you see banking is a good trade even in these bad times.' But whatever the rewards, whatever the prevailing black-coated dourness, there was sometimes laughter to be heard in the counting houses of the City. The young Jerdan was a duffer of a clerk and only lasted a year, but the senior partner's son, who sat near him, had the sense not to worry at all: 'If I disliked the movements of reptile turtles which I had not seen before, it was rare fun; and if I spoilt a cask of madeira by ignorantly breaking several dozen of whole eggs into it to fine it, the laugh against me appeared to make amends for the loss, or deterioration of the wine'.[5]

31

One can exaggerate the homeliness, for there was in the City's set-piece buildings a certain trend towards monumentalism. The new Stock Exchange in Capel Court was something of an exception, rather tucked away and with the only feature of note being the perhaps ironic one of a bust of Mercury on the keystone of the main entrance; but near it from 1808 in Bartholomew Lane was the Auction Mart, put up by surveyors and auctioneers for the purpose of property sales and ecstatically described by one paper as the first building 'which perfectly corresponds with our national character, that of simple grandeur, combining the simplicity of the Grecian with the massy grandeur of the Roman'. Soon afterwards, in 1811, the City's commodity traders, dealing mainly in colonial produce, erected by subscription the London Commercial Sale Rooms, aiming thereby to rival the coffee houses by providing a complete market for the sale of sugar, cotton, coffee, tobacco, indigo and other imported goods. The new building was in Mincing Lane and the front part comprised 'a magnificent coffee-room' on the ground floor and two public salerooms above, the back part counting houses on the lower floors and five showrooms above.[6]

But the heart of the City remained that well-known, semi-circular triad of Mansion House, Royal Exchange and Bank of England. 'If it stood on elevated ground, with a fine area round it, proportioned to its magnitude, it would not be found deficient in magnificence', was how *The Picture of London* in 1815 damned with faint praise the cribbed and confined Mansion House built by George Dance in the 1730s. The same guide was more enthusiastic about the Royal Exchange: 'It has two principal fronts, one in Cornhill, and the other in Threadneedle-street . . . Each of the two fronts has a piazza, which gives a stately air to the building . . . In the centre of each front is a lofty gate, leading to a noble area, in which the merchants assemble.' But for an Irish legal student, writing home in 1807, the Royal Exchange was 'a great and heavy fabric' whose exterior 'is sadly disfigured by a number of little shops that adhere to it, like barnacles upon the bottom of a noble ship', and overall 'is infinitely inferior to our Royal Exchange in Dublin'. Most contemporary eyes, though, were on the Bank of England, in 1815 approaching the end of its thorough, masterly rebuilding by John Soane. 'This immense pile of building is more extensive in its range of offices, and more eminent for its architectural ornament, and interior arrangement, than any single public office in the metropolis', asserted *Leigh's New Picture of London* soon afterwards. A later generation can only think with bitter-sweet admiration of the Bank Stock Office, the Lothbury Court, the Consols Transfer Office, the Rotunda and, most evocative of all, the Five Pound Note Office adjoining the Governor's Court.[7]

Soane's workmen were still busy when in about 1808 Robert Hawker, a clergyman from Plymouth staying in town with a merchant friend, agreed to accompany his host to the Royal Exchange:

> On our arrival, my mind was wonderfully arrested with all I saw and heard. The place, though spacious, was full of persons; and earnestness was strongly pictured upon every countenance ... One general feature marked every character, whether buyer or seller: – I mean, the unwearied perseverance, uniformly distinguishing all, to accomplish the object of their distinct pursuits. Here were no vacant countenances. Nothing like the shew of indifferency. Every one appeared alive, zealous, and indefatigable.

As Hawker continued to gaze at the 'busy multitude' before him, he realised after a while that there were 'many faces carrying with them the aspect of disappointment'; and then something prompted further reflection:

> I remarked a great number of advertisements hung in frames, or pasted on boards, on the walls of the Royal Exchange: many of them containing a sorrowful want; but, whether from their being considered as commonplace things; or, whether from the imperious demands which every man's own separate concern made upon him, – it appeared that their tales of woe were not much regarded. Alas! I said, here is but little time for Charity of any description, to put in her claim. The whirlpool runs round too rapidly, and drags into the vortex too powerfully, to allow attention, much less relief to such as are not within the tide.

Refusing to be dismayed, however, the moral scrutineer concluded his observations in a fine passage not without its lasting verities:

> But what of that? Those that are out, and want places; and those that are in, and want none, by and by will all be upon a level. The most successful in the whole circle ... what is the final upshot of his gains? He only dies somewhat richer than his neighbour; that's all; and his son, or heir, will take care to let the world know it. The enquiry at the Exchange, when his death is announced from every mouth, is, What did he die worth? Like a carcase at the shambles, the question only turns upon one point, Doth he turn out well? And it is for such ends as these, one generation after another is for ever projecting schemes of gain, pursuing the phantom to the very close of life, and dying in the very moment of grasping a bubble?[8]

CHAPTER FOUR

Icons in the Making

Napoleon was beaten and during the first decade of peace the framework was created for the City's international dominance – a dominance that would last for the rest of the nineteenth century and beyond. The return to gold in 1819 enabled sterling to reassert its claim to be the indispensable currency of international finance and commerce; and during the first half of the 1820s there began a seemingly irresistible drive towards free trade, opening up the world's markets to ever more penetrative British commerce. Mercantilism was dead, 'rational capitalism' flourished as never before, and the City was superbly placed to exploit these developments. Yet *at the time* the attitude of the City was at best sceptical, more often downright hostile. What follows[1] is a story with a moral.

It begins with the fact that the immediate post-war years were ones of appalling distress in large parts of Britain, agricultural as well as industrial. Chancellor of the Exchequer was the hopeless Vansittart, who in a state of almost abject dependence on the City – above all the Bank of England and Nathan Rothschild – staggered through each financial year with an improvised mixture of loans and advances. Without the resource of an income tax, which City interests among others had repudiated, 'Van' by 1818 could muster a revenue for the year of only £56m, of which £54m was spent on servicing the national debt and providing for the sinking fund. Enough was enough. In March that year William Huskisson, not yet in the Cabinet but an influential Tory figure, in effect spoke for a rising generation of commercially minded middle-class radicals-cum-economic-liberals when he put the following proposition to the Prime Minister, Lord Liverpool:

> In time of War the wants of Government are so urgent and so great in their amount that the Treasury is at the mercy of the money market; but in the third year of peace, it would be hard for the Public and discreditable for the Minister to submit as of necessity whether to the terms or the

arrangement which the Speculators are now attempting to prescribe as most conducive to their sordid Views.

Huskisson's rhetoric reflected a popular feeling that City speculators had been benefiting from the national distress, as earlier in the paper money era, following the suspension in 1797 of bank notes being issued with the backing of bullion, they had benefited from wartime; and an accompanying detailed plan, involving the issue of exchequer bills and thus a smaller loan, sought to achieve the government's 'political ease and independence of the money market'.[2]

The plan was adopted with only partial success, and the ministry's thoughts soon turned to cash payments and the question of gold. The City took fright, associating resumption of bullion with monetary tightness, liquidity problems and an inevitable diminution of trade. Typical was the appeal of a Fenchurch Street man, George Bartley, to Liverpool in May 1818: while not denying that under the system of paper money the Bank of England's profits 'have been immense and ought without ceremony to be reduced to their proper level', he stressed that 'the resort to Cash payments would cut up by the Roots the principal part of our Commerce'.[3] Yet for Huskisson, the key figure in all this, his motives were by no means anti-City. Quite the reverse, as he explained to Liverpool later that summer about the fruitful implications of a return to gold:

> I have no doubt that with the extent of our commercial dealings and operations of Exchange, which make this Country the Emporium not only of Europe but of America North & South, the Bank of England would make London the chief Bullion Market of the World ... The facility it would give to Trade in affording them the means of promptly rectifying the Exchange with any particular Country, and probably in the particular Coin of that very Country to which it might be desirable to remit Bullion, could not fail to form one of those inducements which would make London the *settling House* of the Money transactions of the World.

Indeed, the Old Lady of Threadneedle Street, though she might never regain her unsullied virtue, would have a pivotal role to play under a gold standard so properly regulated from the outset that there could be no possibility of mismanagement let alone greed:

> The Bank would be the great Steam Engine of the State to keep the Channel of the Circulation always pressing full, and the power of

converting its Notes at any time into Gold Bullion at 78s per ounce the
Regulator and Index of the Engine, by which the extent of its operations
and the sufficiency of the supply would be determined & ascertained.[4]

The City itself, temperamentally averse to the big idea, could never
have enunciated such powerful, visionary stuff: it preferred to take
things as they were and, again for preference, leave them like that.

'It is very difficult to say when the Bank could with propriety resume
its cash payments, it must always be judged of by experience', the
Governor of the Bank of England, George Dorrien, told the Commons
secret committee on the question early in 1819. Nathan Rothschild,
unconstrained by office, was crispness itself:

> In what line of business are you? – Mostly in the foreign banking line.
> Have the goodness to state to the Committee in detail, what you
> conceive would be the consequence of an obligation imposed upon the
> Bank to resume cash payments at the expiration of a year from the
> present time? – I do not think it can be done without very great distress
> to this country; it would do a great deal of mischief; we may not actually
> know ourselves what mischief it may cause.
> Have the goodness to explain the nature of the mischief, and in what
> way it would be produced? – Money will be so very scarce, every article
> in this country will fall to such an enormous extent, that many persons
> will be ruined.

Whereas under paper currency, the only system he had known since
coming to England, 'every thing has gone smooth'. Generally the City
representatives before both the Lords and Commons committees took
a fairly similar line. They accepted that at some distant, usually unspe-
cified point in the future it was inevitable that cash payments be
resumed, but their main thrust was that a precipitate return to gold
would be disastrous. 'Fixing a period, and not adhering to it, always
creates a great deal of dissatisfaction and disappointment in the public
mind', insisted the veteran Bank director Jeremiah Harman. He emphasised that such was the state of the foreign exchanges that 'what
further time may be necessary must depend on circumstances not
under our control', though adding helpfully that 'we always look on
the bright side of things'.[5] The committees, however, were largely
unimpressed with the City's evidence and recommended a decision to
return to gold within four years. There matters rested a few weeks until
the denouement in May.

It was an exciting, charged sequence of events. An anti-resumption
meeting took place on the 18th, at the City of London Tavern in

Bishopsgate Street, in a 'considerably crowded' room. It was meant to be for merchants and other City folk but soon found itself being hijacked by such dubious types as New Lanark's Robert Owen, already well known for his doctrine of co-operation. Owen declared that 'if the resumption of cash payments were attempted, it would no longer be possible to give even the present low rate of wages to labourers' – hardly the consideration uppermost in mercantile minds. Many of those present seem to have fled to the safety of their counting houses, but from an extremely disorderly meeting there did emerge for Parliament's perusal a petition against resumption, as likely to lead to a 'highly injurious contraction of the circulating medium of the country', signed by some four or five hundred merchants. Two days later the directors of the Bank made their own formal representation to government, in the course of which they tried to have it both ways. They eschewed responsibility, through an admission that 'it is certainly not a part of the regular duty of the Bank, under its original institution, to enter into the general views of policy, by which this great empire is to be governed, in all its commercial and pecuniary transactions'; but declared the committees' proposals were 'fraught with very great uncertainty and risk'. The next day the Lords debated, including the prime minister:

> No body of men, he believed, was ever entrusted with so much power as the Bank of England, or had less abused the power entrusted to them: but would Parliament consent to commit to their hands what they certainly would refuse to the sovereign on the throne, controlled by Parliament itself – the power of making money, without any other check or influence to direct them, than their own notions of profit and interest?

But the crux was the Commons, where on the 24th Robert Peel reiterated Liverpool's point – the fear that indefinite suspension would give permanent and potentially mischief-making discretion to the Bank over matters of circulation. A pained Manning on the Bank's behalf warned that 'if the House withdrew its confidence from the Bank at a moment like the present, they could not be answerable for the consequences'. Immediately following Manning was Ricardo, who had long despised the 'company of merchants' as he dubbed the Bank, and had recently become an MP. He made a vigorous speech, combining an authoritative analysis of how resumption should proceed with some high-class knockabout, not least over the Bank's complaint that government had failed to repay its advances:

But how came they to make those advances to government, if not assured of repayment at a certain time? The Bank had not been forced to make those advances, but the directors had such an extraordinary disposition to act as ministers [a laugh, and hear, hear!]. It would, however, be better if those directors would rather attend to their own interests, and those of their constituents.

At the end the wealthy ex-jobber 'sat down amidst loud and general cheering from all sides of the House', and the debate was effectively over.[6] A unanimous vote followed on the 25th. Over the next few days the City surrendered to a blue funk, as Consols fell sharply, but legislation in June confirmed that by 1823 at the latest the country would be returning in full to the disciplines of gold.

The argument behind this victory had at least as much a moral as an economic dimension: somehow it was assumed that bringing the paper money era to an end would cleanse the body politic of unpatriotic speculators and generally repair the social fabric, damaged by war and its aftermath. 'For a permanent and peace system, the only wise course either in policy or for impression is a system of simplicity and truth' was how Huskisson himself put it to Liverpool in February 1819.[7] That autumn, soon after the Peterloo massacre had led to a heightening of social tension, Rothschild (via Vansittart) put pressure on the prime minister to reverse the policy, but Liverpool in his reply to the Chancellor would have none of it:

> If we are quiet things will come right. I know from a person who has seen Baring within these few days, that he is of opinion that there will be a great reaction as to our funds, and that the French funds cannot rise much beyond their present price.
> The point, however, upon which I feel most anxiety is the idea suggested by Rothschild, of a continuance of the Bank restriction. I am satisfied that no measure could be more fatal, and that the very notion of its being a matter for consideration would do harm . . .
> Let us therefore determine to stand upon our present system, and let no one entertain a doubt that this is our determination. I am persuaded the Bank, for their own interest, when they see we are firm, will not make any improper reduction of their circulation . . .[8]

So it was: the government duly stood firm, supported by an eclectic range of public opinion whatever the misgivings in the world of commerce; and in 1821, after almost a quarter of a century, the restriction period at last ended. Within a few years the return to gold was starting to assume an almost absurdly symbolic quality that it would not readily lose.

Free trade was the other icon in the making. It began, according to the textbooks, with the famous petition by almost 200 of the merchants of London presented to Parliament in May 1820 – a petition that included the classical assertion 'that the maxim of buying in the cheapest market and selling in the dearest, which regulates every merchant in his individual dealings, is strictly applicable as the best rule for the trade of the whole nation'. The author was Thomas Tooke, keen student of political economy and leading Russia merchant. Almost forty years later, with the momentous battle for free trade safely won, he recalled with some amusement how he had persuaded his fellow-merchants to sign the pioneering petition:

> From my experience among the merchants of London, I was quite convinced that they understood little, and cared less, about the doctrines and principles of Political Economy . . . and that from their general unwillingness to sign petitions, as to matters in which their individual interests or political feelings were not very obviously and immediately concerned, it was highly improbable that such a number of signatures of persons of commercial eminence could be obtained as would be requisite . . .

In consequence Tooke sought the help of Samuel Thornton, prominent merchant, long-standing Bank of England director, Governor of the Russia Company, and intimate of Vansittart. He listened with apparent sympathy to Tooke's arguments about how much the objects of the petition would benefit the Russia trade, but declined to sign it. Tooke then tried other Bank directors, but only three would sign. At that point, however, Thornton *did* agree to sign, whereupon Tooke presented the position with Thornton's signature on it and found that 'more than half of the Court of Directors immediately signed it'. Explaining subsequently this rather abrupt U-turn by the City's opinion formers, Tooke's laconic comment was that 'the signature of Mr Thornton was a guarantee against anything in the Petition being considered as inconsistent with Tory principles', that in other words there did not 'lurk a leaven of the democratic principle of political reform'.[9]

The petition was presented on 8 May by Alexander Baring. Barely a week later a numerous body of shipowners and others met at the inevitable City of London Tavern to draw up a counter-petition. This time the meeting was 'highly respectable', and among the speakers was Alexander Baring, who was in an invidious position and quickly found himself being forced on to the back foot:

First, he should observe, that the [original] petition was not of his drawing up. He had never seen it until it was put into his hands to be presented. Undoubtedly it was very ably drawn up. It laid down some principles upon which it was said our trade should be regulated; but he would admit, that many of those were too general in their nature, and therefore it was natural that they should be looked upon with a jealous eye. They were rather of too sweeping a character, and might, perhaps, apply better to a new country than to one which had a long experience of previous regulations.

Or as Ricardo coolly referred to Baring a few weeks later, that eminent merchant was 'the professed but I think lukewarm friend of free trade'.[10]

Only a relatively small part of the City was pushing for free trade in 1820 and almost without exception those doing so were heavily motivated by their own particular sectional interests. One notable group were the north European merchants keen to put an end to the preferential treatment given to Canadian timber. Tooke himself made, at least in retrospect, no bones about it: 'The simple truth is, that the Government were, at that time, far more sincere and resolute Free Traders than the Merchants of London'. There lay the core of the matter, for during the first half of the 1820s it was the ministry's economic liberals (Huskisson to the fore) who pushed through a sustained programme of free trade and related measures – rarely to City enthusiasm and sometimes, as in the case of lowering the duties on imported silk, to outright opposition. The assiduous diarist Mrs Arbuthnot recorded a conversation in April 1825 with Herries, financial secretary to the Treasury and staunch supporter of the old ways:

> He told me that Mr Huskisson's indecent presumption and haste in altering the trading laws was creating great alarm and dissatisfaction among the merchants of the City ... Rothschild had told him that the consequence of admitting foreign goods (which had not been met by corresponding liberality on the other side of the water) was, that all the gold was going out of the country. He had himself sent two millions within the last few weeks; the funds fell rapidly, and *no advantage* is gained by any human being.

Rothschild's great rival did not disagree:

> He would beg leave to suggest, that the political economists should refrain from abusing the practical man, and treating him as the greatest fool in existence, because he proved, by facts, that, though the result should, according to theory, be as they stated, it was not always so.

So spoke Alexander Baring not long afterwards.[11] If free trade was on the way to becoming the omnipotent commercial religion of the nineteenth century, few of the square mile's practical men were yet among its worshippers.

CHAPTER FIVE

Parcels of Stock-jobbers

On 2 December 1815 the merchant Antony Gibbs wrote a letter to his
son that mixed paternal commendation with the sharpest possible
advice:

> I am very glad that you succeeded in drawing what you did on Cadiz
> tho' the exchange was so low as 35, and shall be glad for you to succeed
> in drawing the same sum at ye same exchange on Tuesday . . . I think it
> likely at ye same time that you may find it for your purpose not to lead
> the brokers to suppose in ye morning of Tuesday that you shall want to
> draw, but keep that information for your arrival early on Change. They
> themselves are the people who fix the rate at which to print ye exchange,
> and they are much governed in this by ye advice they receive in ye
> morning from Houses that wish to draw or take, and you might not be
> likely to draw less on account of your not telling them what you mean to
> draw before they go on Change . . .[1]

Three days later Antony had a stroke and by the 10th he was dead –
the founder of a commercial dynasty, a businessman to the last.

He was perhaps fortunate to miss four years of fairly unrelieved
depression in the City, characterised by restricted trade, restricted
money and countless failures. John Newman's bank failed in 1816,
resulting in the future cardinal's father becoming manager of a brewery
in Alton; in the same year the stockbroker Jeremiah Lear, whose
twentieth child was the four-year-old Edward, was forced to vacate his
handsome house in Holloway. But the worst of these post-war years
was 1819. 'A much greater scarcity of money than has been felt for a
long time prevails', wrote Barclay, Tritton & Bevan that February to a
correspondent in Liverpool, while according to the leading bill broker
Samuel Gurney a few days later, 'We have had a very stormy time in
the City, many failures to the right and to the left'. At the end of
February a timber broker tried to explain what had been going on:

> During the whole of these two months the Commercial world has been
> kept in a continued alarm by the repeated heavy Failures which have

occurred followed by a languor & heaviness in every Branch of Business & in almost all Trades.

All sorts of Produce in abundance, but no buyers . . .

Various causes assigned & perhaps have all combined to produce this Crisis. The French Loan, the limitations of Discount at the Bank & among the Country Bankers, & the agitation of the Bank Restriction in Parliament – all occurring at a time when every Mercantile Establishment had been laying themselves out to the full stretch of their Capital . . .

Things were no better by the autumn. 'Prices dreadfully low' on 21 August, 'great failures at the Stock Exchange' on 28 August, 'business still dull' on 15 October. And at the end:

Thus closes a trying Year in the Commercial World, having been full of successive Shocks on Confidence – with falling Markets in every Branch of Trade – & from Month to Month going from bad to worse – we have to thank God for having hitherto escaped without any Losses of Consequence.

The grateful diarist was Charles Churchill, in his mid-thirties and a partner in the recently established firm of Churchill & Sim. He thus completed his first year's journal, and well might inscribe at the start of the following volume: 'If in the hurry of Business and cares of the World, I forget thee, do not thou Oh God forget me'.[2]

The most notable exception to post-war City gloom was in the area of foreign loans. Barings led the way and raised its name to new heights in 1817 by successfully bringing out three issues for the indemnity-laden French Government that raised a total of 315m francs (over £12m). Tributes from back as well as front of the hand followed this massively lucrative operation. The Duke of Wellington: 'The fact is, that Baring having the French finances in his hands, and French loans being in fashion in England, has to a certain degree the command of the money market of the world . . .' The Duc de Richelieu: 'There are six great powers in Europe: England, France, Prussia, Austria, Russia and Baring Brothers . . .' James Rothschild: 'The Baring lot is and was well versed in the way of using influence, as we are.' In 1818 another French loan was less successful, but Barings had made its point.[3] That same year Nathan Rothschild began the fight back, issuing a £5m loan for the Prussian Government. The loan had been negotiated in the first place by a City-based merchant from Prussia called Barandon, but he lacked sufficient credit to bring it to the market and sold out to the opportunistic Rothschild for some £30,000. It proved a great success and, for the first time with a foreign loan, dividends were to be payable in London and in sterling.[4] The era of the foreign security as an attractive, readily marketable counter was under way.

It has to be said that the greater part of the money for the French indemnity loans was raised in France itself, and analysis of the Prussian loan shows that Rothschild distributed about two-thirds of it to his continental connections. In general at this time, and indeed for a very long time thereafter, London had little more than an agency role, giving its imprimatur to the loans being sought by foreign governments and using its manifold international connections to ensure the widest possible distribution.[5] To contemporaries, however, it did not seem quite like that. 'It exposes in its true light the base and wretched avidity of the Monied Interest, which, at the prospect of gain, is ready to forget all the claims of patriotism', declared the *Commercial Chronicle* in January 1817 about what Barings was doing, and other papers agreed. In the context of severe domestic trade depression, the notion of so much capital going abroad was, hardly surprisingly, repugnant. It was a sentiment shared by some in the City:

> What are the inducements to individuals in this country, to divert their capital from the purposes to which it is now applied, in order to invest it in foreign funded securities? – Gain . . .
> Which do you consider the prevailing object of gain in speculation, the increasing amount of stock, or the positive amount in the advance of interest? – There is, at this moment in London, almost as much jobbing in the French funds, as in our own, among that class of persons, I presume it is for the selling again; but there is another class whose incomes are limited, and who have been taught to know that by selling out their English stock, and investing in the French funds, they will get a larger income; I am very apprehensive indeed, that that has increased, and is increasing.

Thus growled Jeremiah Harman to a resumption committee in 1819, conceding that foreign securities provided a higher yield than that available from 'the Funds' but clearly unhappy about the implications. Rothschild by contrast was wholly matter of fact: 'There is no doubt that the English people invest a part of their money in foreign securities on account of getting a better interest, besides its being a growing passion at the present time; we lay out fifty to sixty thousand pounds a week in the foreign funds for different English houses'. And when it came to the distinction between investment and speculation – that most agonising of nineteenth-century distinctions – Rothschild's reply was robustness itself: 'You may divide it in half, half speculative people and half for permanent investment, but in case a real rise takes place, which has been the case, they will all go out . . .'⁶

It was interesting fodder for debate, but for most people in the City day-to-day commercial life was plodding, painstaking and repetitive. George Henry Gibbs (Antony's son) kept a small notebook between 1819 and 1821, in the course of which he composed an *aide-mémoire* on 'My Department in Business':

> *Letters.* Read the letters rec^d and written & extract from them any thing worth notice.
>
> *Orders.* Give out all the orders received and see that they are properly executed & copied into the Inland & For Order B^k. Look frequently into Mr Wainwright's Shipping Book – see what goods can be shipt & make enquiries of the Ship Brokers about Ships, Freights &c. When goods are ordered mark them in the form order Book thus √. When the packing instructions are completely given, add a stroke to the mark, thus ⅄.
>
> *Revise the Price Current every Saturday.*
>
> *Lloyds.* After sending the foreign letters go to Lloyds and extract from the Books & the Boards anything new. See Willis, and collect any news from him or others. On Post days go again to Lloyds before Change & get the latest information. Generally go every day to Lloyds at about 3. See Lloyds List in the Reading room published twice a week, and the Cadiz Lists received.
>
> *Change.* Go to Change generally every day at 4. On Post days when any Bills to draw or take at $\frac{1}{4}$ past 3, & stay *patiently* till $\frac{1}{2}$ past 4. See Brokers of all sorts, and make enquiries about Prices of Produce, Stock, in the market &c &c. Pay particular attention to Wool.
>
> *Insurances.* Attend to the execution of all Insurance orders, the recovery of Averages &c & in short everything connected with Insurance Business.
>
> *Sales.* Superintend the Sale of all Produce. Make out Account Sales.
>
> *Correspondence.* Carry on the whole of the inland correspondence & part of the foreign. Be as particular as possible in giving every informa-tion wch may be interesting to each correspondent, especially with regard to their orders, keeping them well informed of the state of forwardness in wch they are, the prices at wch we have contracted for them &c &c. The letters sh^d be written as soon as possible in order that they may be copied in the Books from the originals, and that there may be no hurry in sending them to the Post. Keep a memorandum Book with each Correspondent's name in a separate page under wch may be enter'd any thing that occurs to be said to each. Refer always to this Book before writing any letter. Also read the last letter written unless we have rec^d an answer to it, and recapitulate the important parts of it.

Relevant detail was what counted in mercantile correspondence, and in June 1821 the London house of Antony Gibbs wrote to a corres-pondent in Lima, where it was seeking to set up a branch:

We have almost resolved on an expedition from hence & Gibraltar to your consignment. We ship about £40,000 from hence, and send the Vessel to Gib. to complete her Cargo, as many things could be shipt there well suited to your Market, which could not be got here, and besides there are many English Goods lying there, which would do very well . . . It will of course be very important that you should keep us well advised of the state of your Market for European Articles, and we wish to direct your attention very particularly to all those little trifling Articles, which are worth but little here, but in which immense Profits are made with you, such as Dutch & French Toys, Gum Ben, Naples Soap, Quicksilver, Flasks, Glasses, &c &c . . .

Unconsidered trifles were, in short, the very stuff of a merchant's business.[7]

By that autumn there were signs that the trade depression was over. Some, like Charles Churchill, operating at the coalface, were hard to convince, especially after the relaxation of the timber duties had encouraged a host of unwelcome new entrants to the Royal Exchange:

31 *August*. Business fair, but not without Interruptions from the small fry of Brokers starting up at every Corner, buzzing about without being able either to gather Honey or to Sting.

8 *September*. Keep our Stand in the Market tolerably well.

22 *September*. Business moderate, but maintain ourselves pretty well against all opposers.

29 *September*. Continue our usual routine with indifferent Success.

13 *October*. Business a little better, heal our quarrel with Mr Warburton [Henry Warburton, the prominent timber merchant], sell the Laurence & Mary's Cargo . . . Turn off Hogan in a huff.

27 *October*. Sell the Neva's Riga Timber to Copland, & begin the Onega deals with Montgomery at £18. Otherwise but indifferent success.

22 *November*. Stocks continue high (Consols 78) & something more like Confidence than has been felt for some time.

29 *December*. In business nothing going on, but still keep about, getting wet every day to very little purpose.[8]

All diarists like a good grumble – this timber broker, for over a quarter of a century, was no exception.

*

Generally though, as Churchill himself admitted, confidence was starting to pick up in the City by the early 1820s, inevitably accompanied by widespread speculation, in which the Stock Exchange was to the fore. Late in 1821 a squall took place over the contentious question of option dealings, also known as puts and calls, where a speculator would pay an agreed sum for the right to buy or to sell a stock at a certain price on a given date in the future. The founding Committee of 1802 had unanimously condemned such dealings as injurious, but the first rule book in 1812 had failed to distinguish them with sufficient clarity from the more acceptable (though still technically illegal) time bargains for the settlement. The row began with the Committee considering two rival requisitions from members. One demanded the outright abolition of puts and calls, 'which are now so frequent as to constitute the greater part of the business done in the House and which operate materially against the interests of those who do not comply with this practice'. The other took positive pride in 'the immense jobbing which is now consequent upon Options' and declared that 'viewing the community of the Stock Exchange with those feelings of consideration due to persons of honor, Independence and property we cannot but consider that any further restraint upon the bargains in question would more resemble the severity of School discipline than those wise and liberal Regulations proper for the Stock Exchange'. The Committee, conscious of the extremely dubious legal standing of such dealings, sided with the first petition and ruled that henceforth members would only be re-elected each March if they promised not to engage in them. Reaction was immediate, as members queued to express their outrage in person. The minutes record of Jacob Ricardo: 'That after transacting business honorably for so many years he shall be deprived of his free agency is very disagreeable'; of John Higgins: 'He protests against the interference of the Committee in every circumstance between man and man'; William Wright: 'Nobody can deny that the Business of the Stock Exchange is at all times greatly encreased by optional Bargains'; and John Easthope: 'It is as much out of the cognizance of the Committee as a bet, or a game at Whist'.

The turning point came on Christmas Eve, when some appeared who had signed the original requisition. Among them was James Capel, who stressed his individual support for the Committee's actions but then conceded that 'in the present temper of the House it would be better to try a mild measure first'. But it was John Hensley who gave the game away: 'Finding so many persons adverse to the regulation proposed, and that it was possible many might leave the House, he repented of having signed, as he was sorry to see dissension likely to take place'. That was indeed the danger, for the option dealers had already subscribed a considerable sum of money with a view to founding a rival

stock exchange; and at this point the Committee backed down.⁹ This
pattern of surrender would frequently recur over the next century; after
all, what is the point of a club unless it exclusively serves the interests
of its members?

In 1822 came the year of the foreign loan. Nathan Rothschild
established his dominance in this market by floating sizeable loans for
Prussia, Russia (traditional Barings country) and the Neapolitan Government, and above all there was widespread enthusiasm for making
loans to the newly liberated countries of Latin America. Emissaries
from Columbia, Chile and Peru all came to London, all were greeted
warmly by merchants-turned-contractors who knew a handsome
margin when they saw one, and all were ruthlessly exploited.¹⁰ The
Peruvian loan was underwritten at 75 by Thomas Kinder junior of
Basinghall Street, but marketed at a price way above. Such was the
popular capacity for self-delusion, and the appetite for higher rates of
return than those provided by British government stock, that it even
proved possible to issue bonds for an imaginary country, apparently
somewhere in Central America, called Poyais. Yet the contractors did
not have it all their own way, as Kinder himself found one Saturday
morning in October when, at the Royal Exchange, shares in the
Peruvian loan were for the first time offered publicly for sale. A crowd
of brokers and others gathered, demanding to know the issue price:

> The confusion and pressure was so great, that nothing for some time
> could be distinctly heard; and the impression was, that the agents were
> playing on the eagerness of their customers, and did not in fact declare
> any price at which they thought it proper to sell. Meantime different
> prices were audibly vociferated from various parts of the assemblage; but
> not, as it appears, reaching the point desired by the agent, he remained
> silent, and did not close with any of the offers. At length 88 was named,
> and was followed by a burst of indignation from the crowd, and the
> words 'Shame, shame!' 'Gross extortion!' resounded on all sides. Even at
> that price, however, such is the mania that at present exists for speculat-
> ing in foreign securities – bidders were to be found; and many of those
> who were able to bear the extreme pressure, and to approach sufficiently
> near to the contractor, entered into engagements for taking the Scrip in
> sums varying in amount from 5,000 to 10,000 each. Thus encouraged,
> the contractor in a few minutes advanced his price to 89, a notice which
> was attended with the same indignant exclamation as before, but he still
> found adventurers hardy enough to close with his proposals. In con-
> sequence, however, of the confusion, not many of those who were eager
> to buy could be supplied, and of numerous and loud applications made
> to the contractor, few were heard; or, if heard they were honoured with

no answer ... Meantime the crowd, having received a large accession from the Stock Exchange, increased round the contractor and his agents; and the confusion rose to such a height, that the possibility of transacting business was out of the question. All were excessively indignant at the supposed backwardness of the contractor to take the offers made him; and pressing round him in still greater numbers, he and his agents were forced by the multitude surrounding them from the Dutch walk, where the confusion began, to the opposite corner of the Exchange, where the Swedish merchants assemble. Here the brokers became so highly exasperated, being still unable to come to terms with the agents, that they forced the whole party off the Exchange, out at the North gate, opposite to Bartholomew-lane. They succeeded, however, after a desperate struggle, in re-entering the Exchange; and having at length, with some further effort, effected a lodgment on one of the seats of the Exchange, they became once more visible, if not audible, to the brokers, who surrounded them. They were then tumultuously called on to name a price, and one of the agents at last named 90 as the minimum of the contractor. We could not ascertain if any persons closed at that price, but with the auditors generally it operated as a *quietus*, and they answered the proposal by liberally bestowing the epithets of 'shameful extortion'. Soon afterwards the contractor quitted the Exchange, and the hubbub for the most part terminated.[11]

The Royal Exchange witnessed plenty of other disturbances during these hectic months. Brokers and jobbers, unable to use the Stock Exchange itself because dealings there were confined to British government stock, had already complained in vain to the Stock Exchange Committee about 'the want of an open and fair Market for Foreign Securities'. The day before the Peruvian fracas the *Morning Chronicle*'s City correspondent pointedly congratulated 'the Gentlemen from the Stock Exchange' on having 'behaved themselves this day in a peaceable manner on the Royal Exchange'; a week later the same writer was complaining that 'the Royal Exchange has been numerously attended by pickpockets, and many Gentlemen have had their books cut out of their pockets'. Towards the end of October the following handbill, addressed to dealers in foreign stocks, was posted at the entrance of the Royal Exchange:

Gentlemen – You have selected for the theatre of your operations one of the most frequented parts of the Exchange, particularly on foreign post days, of those whose habitual places you have usurped; you removing a few yards further to the north-east corner, a quarter always very thinly attended, will be considered as an act of courtesy for which the Merchants who frequent the French and Italian Walks will feel much obliged.[12]

The Stock Exchange eventually acquired a new room for dealing in foreign securities, which opened for business at the start of 1823. Connecting physically with the main house but separately organised and managed, it constituted a cumbersome, just about workable arrangement.

Rampant speculation also led to institutional change in the equally volatile world of Baltic produce. Here the central protagonist was Richard Thornton,[13] a merchant who had originally made his fortune through a series of daring wartime feats between 1810 and 1812, involving a mixture of patriotic importation of hemp on behalf of the Royal Navy and less than patriotic use of inside information about Napoleon's retreat from Moscow.

Thornton was a prominent figure at the Baltic Coffee House and was in a position, through his connections with Russian exporters, to make another killing in the autumn of 1822. The article in question was tallow, which was vital to everyday life and at this time came almost entirely from St Petersburg, in supplies sufficiently uncertain to make it a favourite object of speculation. What seems to have taken place was a well-worked corner, buying up all available tallow, arousing enormous hostility on the Royal Exchange as well as in the Baltic itself. 'The parties engaged in this extraordinary mercantile operation are powerful in the needful, and their spirits are fully equal to the occasion', reported the *Morning Chronicle* in late October about speculative demand raising the price of tallow. By 8 November the nerves of those engaged in tallow dealing on the Baltic Walk were probably starting to fray, as the price rose sharply: 'It is pleasing on the Royal Exchange to contemplate the good will and temper with which the transactions in this most important article of consumption are conducted'. Exactly a week later someone, presumably Thornton, jumped ship, though at least one correspondent did not share the hostility felt by those left on board:

> A Gentleman, celebrated for his speculative genius, and who has followed the opinions of those by whom for some time now the market has been regulated, is reputed this day, in the phraseology of the Stock Exchange, to have changed his account, and to have sold no less than 4,000 casks of tallow to those who have regularly thwarted the operations of the great Bulls in this article. The seller of this quantity is supposed to have made a good thing of the transaction, and as it is rumoured that he first offered it to those with whom he has till now acted, there is nothing unfair in his disposing of his share in the speculation . . .[14]

The outcome of this speculative episode was the formation the following spring of the Baltic Committee, with Thomas Tooke a prime mover.

More or less following the precedent of Lloyd's in the 1770s, the Committee imposed a maximum of 300 subscribing firms to the Baltic Coffee House's subscribers' room, a crucial repository of newspapers and commercial intelligence. A closed market, less speculation, greater respectability: these were the aims of Tooke and friends, and to an extent they succeeded, especially as the Baltic Exchange (as it would eventually become known) developed increasingly as the market for chartering ships as well as dealing in tallow, timber and grain.[15]

But one man dominated the City of the early 1820s. 'You have beaten your antagonists so frequently that I am surprised there are any so hardy to be found in the Stock Exchange to oppose you in any considerable operation', Moses Montefiore applauded his brother-in-law Nathan Rothschild. Nathan's brother Carl, writing to another brother, was even more eloquent: 'We owe everything, really everything to him'. No one, extended family or otherwise, ever denied that Nathan Rothschild was a consummate operator; on the Stock Exchange, scene of some of his greatest coups, he invariably employed several brokers at any one time in order to ensure that the precise positions he had taken remained a matter of secrecy. The sense of his omnipotence is writ large in a pathetic letter (original punctuation) from Francis Millard, packer, of Size Lane, Bucklersbury:

> May the Almighty preserve you & your family (for the sake of mine) I entreat do not take your business from me I am wretched I cannot sleep if you will once more try me; I will examine every price myself I will not trust to servants with regard to charges you shall not have cause to complain, it is my great misfortune your *present broker* is not my friend, he prefers others. In the hope you will give peace to my mind . . .

Inevitably some hated him in their hearts. In the spring of 1818 when Liverpool was considering Huskisson's plan to reduce government dependence on the City, he received two letters in quick succession from an anonymous member of the Stock Exchange:

> Let me inform you, the Capitalists of the Money Market . . . have set their faces against your Plan because it serves not their purpose or puts Money in their Pockets. The Jew interest alias Mr Rothschild are disappointed and straining every nerve to defeat your objects . . .
>
> If a Man asks Mr Rothschild, what is his opinion of the Funds, he answers they must be better & at the very same time he acts contrary himself & sells to knock them down. It is a deplorable Circumstance that in so great a Country as this, Your Lordship & Colleagues should be the Sport [&] the caprice of a Jew Party, it is truly lamentable.

Rothschild was conscious enough of such anti-Semitism directed against him, but being a businessman first and foremost he showed himself perfectly willing over the years to enter into syndicates with leading Gentile houses.[16]

At least twice a week he was to be seen in the Royal Exchange, conducting his extensive foreign exchange operations:

> He never hesitated in fixing the rate, either as a drawer or a taker, on any part of the world, and his memory was so retentive, that, notwithstanding the immense transactions into which he entered on every foreign post day and that he never took a note of them, he could dictate the whole on his return home with perfect exactness to his clerks. His liberality of dealing was another conspicuous feature of these operations, and many merchants whose bills were objected to elsewhere found ready assistance from him, and his judgement was proved by the very small amount of loss which he incurred in consequence of such liberality.

If foreign bills were one speciality, so were bullion transactions; for as Rothschild truly told the resumption committee, 'I am no merchant in goods'. This systematic specialisation, which also included government stocks, was a way of maximising the potential of his high-level connections, which by 1815 were even better at home than they were abroad. His brother James wrote to him on one occasion from Paris, about not wanting to do anything in French Rentes without asking Nathan's opinion: 'One of the reasons is, that in respect of the English stocks, you always knew through H— what is going on, while here one remains always in the dark'. The reference was undoubtedly to Herries, the Tory minister. This specialisation paid off, for by the 1820s the capital of the London house alone was well over a million pounds, way ahead of all rivals, even Barings.[17]

Underwriting this ascendancy was the man himself, shrewdness and determination personified, day-in, day-out. Visiting Nathan at New Court in the summer of 1818 was the young diplomat Woodbine Parish, seeking to arrange banking facilities for the British party at the forthcoming Congress of Aix-la-Chapelle. After discussing the matter, Nathan handed Parish a letter of credit for £10,000:

> He then wrote a few lines to his brother, which he handed to me open to read, and then burst out laughing at my face on finding it was written in Hebrew!
> Business over he rang the bell and ordered coffee, which was brought in by a servant in gorgeous livery, upon a splendid silver salver, with all its

appurtenances of the same, strikingly contrasting with his own appearance, 'en déshabille' in an old dressing-gown, with his black silk breeches loose and unbuttoned at the knee, his ordinary costume in the Counting House, as I was told, but cutting a very different figure to his appearance on Change, as I have seen him with all eyes upon him.

What struck me very much was his correct information as to the details of our party and his knowledge of the persons likely to compose it, some of whose names I believe had not even transpired at the Foreign Office . . .[18]

A couple of letters give something further of the crisp flavour of Nathan in action. On 21 October 1817 he wrote to the Lords of the Treasury: 'Having about 150,000 oz of foreign bar Silver to ship to Hamburg, and there being no Court of Aldermen sitting at this time, nor will there be before 12 or 14 days, and the winter may set in, in a few days, I therefore humbly pray your Lordships order to pass the entry at the custom house without the certificate signed by the Court of Aldermen'. Or six years later, addressing the governor and deputy governor of the Bank of England: 'Gentlemen – An opportunity offering itself in which I could employ from One to Three Millions of Spanish Dollars, I beg leave to state the terms upon which I should be willing to receive from you the whole or any part of that quantity . . .' After briskly stating his terms, he ended with a characteristic sting in the tail: 'In the event of your compliance with these propositions, I must request that this affair may not be conducted through the agency of your Broker, who being himself a Merchant & Loan Contractor, it is desirable should not be apprised of the Arrangement'.

Although Nathan Rothschild would never lose his native toughness, by 1825 he not only possessed a country residence in Stamford Hill but had also moved into an elegant town house in Piccadilly, thus no longer living above the counting house in New Court. Many years later a relative recalled going to Stamford Hill at about this time to visit Nathan's sons during their school holidays: 'The two boys were surrounded by their father with every luxury. They had a miniature carriage with four white goats to drive about the grounds.'[19] An Anglicised dynasty was in the making.

What of 'Christian Baring', who according to Byron in 1818 held 'the balance of the world' alongside 'Jew Rothschild'? The following year one of the Bishopsgate partners, Swinton Holland, told the resumption committee that his firm was 'very extensively engaged, I may say, in correspondence with all commercial parts of the world, or nearly so', and it was a justified boast. Yet in fact, after the glory years under Sir Francis, Barings was entering a period of relative decline. The problem lay partly with Holland himself, whose over-rigid control lost the firm its unrivalled ascendancy in Anglo-American trade. But the head of the house, Alexander, had a more harmful influence. Intellectually able but ultimately a vain dilettante, and far too distracted by matters of state and estate ever to concentrate on the more mundane aspects of business, he went a fair way towards undoing the work of his father. Such were the attractions of rolling acres and country houses that in the early 1820s the firm's capital dipped to about £¼m, more or less putting it out of contention in terms of contracting the major foreign loans. There is no doubt some truth in the argument that the partners of Jewish firms encountered, because of their continuing legal disabilities, far fewer distractions than their Gentile counterparts, but the heart of the matter surely lies in character. Nevertheless, one should neither exaggerate the decline nor underestimate those increasingly traditional Baring qualities of caution and sobriety. As the house wrote in June 1824 to an American correspondent, in the context of turning down a proposed operation in Philadelphian bank shares:

> In other times it might have suited us . . . to have entered into your views, but at the moment, being engaged in large financial operations in France, we do not feel disposed to divest ourselves of our own Capital, by placing it at a distance from us. Indeed, our object always is to have our Capital within reach that we may command it as necessary.[20]

Admirable sentiments, and indispensable for long-term survival.

Meanwhile, there were plenty of international houses – embryo merchant banks – starting to come through as significant City presences. Some were new, like Ralli Brothers, being Greek merchants forced abroad by Turkish persecution and reaching London in 1818. Others were longer established, but most derived from the migration to London towards the end of the Napoleonic Wars. Frühling & Göschen, for instance, was the 1814 combination of a wealthy merchant from Bremen and the young son of a prominent Leipzig publisher. Some years later Barings described them in action:

> Their Business has been conducted with uniform steadiness. It consists almost entirely in the exporting of Colonial Produce on Commission to Germany: and of E. I. Cotton they are becoming the largest Shippers. They have considerable Connexions at Bremen . . . They are both single men. Mr Frühling is generally on the Continent whilst Mr Göschen who

is a clever active intelligent man, resides here. From their success in Business and their economical Habits, there can be no doubt but that they must have saved money . . .[21]

Also from Germany was John Henry (formerly Johann Heinrich) Schröder, who at the end of 1817 resigned his partnership with his elder brother and started his own merchanting firm, J. Henry Schröder & Co. It financed international trade, did a wide range of import-export business with St Petersburg and shipped large quantities of refined sugar to Hamburg, where Schröder himself concurrently ran another firm (J. H. Schröder & Co) and lived for most of the year, leaving the London end in charge of a German confidential clerk. Also much involved with Russian business was Emanuel Henry Brandt, in effect acting as London agent for his brother's Archangel firm, and in 1822 he was able to move premises from Bateson's Coffee House in Cornhill to 34 Lombard Street. Another City firm originating from Germany was Frederick Huth & Co; that same year, 1822, a French merchant temporarily based in its offices pondered with wry admiration:

In this country it is necessary to have plenty of occupation, and plenty of reasonableness, to get on at all. There is very little sociability, and, as in Holland, commercial interests are the dominant feature. You must not expect much friendliness from a John Bull who does not see his way to get something out of you. On the other hand, for learning commerce, London is without exception the best school. You are here in the centre of universal business, and you can know here what goods come from each country, and what goods they want in return.[22]

The attentive recipient of this letter was Daniel Meinertzhagen; a few years later, when his family house in Bremen met with disaster, he too came to the City.

A more indigenous, equally vigorous group were the textile merchants and warehousemen clustered to the east of St Paul's. William Cook was the son of a Norfolk sheep farmer, who set off for London in 1805 with five sovereigns in his pocket. By 1807 he was in partnership with a Clerkenwell linen draper, by 1814 he took the lease of a shop and warehouse at Fish Street Hill, in the shadow of Wren's Monument, and by 1818 he was 'William Cook, Manchester & Scotch Warehouseman of Cheapside'. John Bradbury and Jeremiah Greatorex were Midlanders who in 1815 resigned their jobs as travellers for two Manchester warehouses and came to London. By 1820 they were established as Bradbury, Greatorex & Teale – originally in King Street off Cheapside but soon in Aldermanbury – and were doing a wholesale trade in Manchester-made cotton piece goods (sheets, towels and so on), as well as textile goods produced in Scotland and France. Particularly thriving in these years was Ward, Brettle & Ward of Wood Street (north of Cheapside), so much so that by the 1820s George Brettle was well ensconced at Raleigh Lodge, a substantial residence on Brixton Hill, complete with fifteen acres of land. There was no sector of British trade growing faster than textiles. City merchants, through their considerable working capital, enjoyed a control of credit and marketing denied to the disintegrated textile manufacturers of the north; this aspect of the square mile, linked closely to British industry, was more important than has tended to be recognised. The kingpin was undeniably James Morrison. He was the son of a Hampshire innkeeper, started at the Fore Street wholesale and retail haberdashery business of Todd & Co in 1809, and within five years was not only a partner but also the son-in-law of Todd. Under his direct influence turnover rose phenomenally: £65,000 in 1813, £650,000 in 1817, over £1½ m in 1822, by which time Morrison was sole managing partner. (In 1818 he is said to have cleverly anticipated the death of Queen Charlotte and bought up most of the available crêpe.) His business methods over a longer period are well described by his friend Sir John Bowring:

> Morrison told me that he owed all his prosperity to the discovery that the great art of mercantile traffic was to find sellers rather than buyers; that if you bought cheap, and satisfied yourself with only a fair profit, buyers – the best sort of buyers, those who have money to buy – would come of themselves. He said he found houses engaged with a most expensive machinery, sending travellers about in all directions to seek orders and to effect sales, while he employed travellers to buy instead of to sell: and if they bought well, there was no fear of his effecting advantageous sales. So, uniting this theory with another, that small profits and quick returns are more profitable in the long run than long credits with great gains, he established one of the largest and most lucrative concerns that has ever existed in London . . .

No wonder that Morrison himself wrote to a junior partner in the 1820s: 'None can approach us in the science of business, independent of success and profit. There is an intellectual pleasure in this.'[23]

The selling of crêpe to fashionable London impinged but little on the Stock Exchange, though according to one thoroughly jaundiced critic not through any lack of aspiration to *bon ton*.

Mark the process; the town of Brighton, in Sussex, 50 miles from the Wen, is on the seaside, and is thought by the stock-jobbers to afford a *salubrious air*. It is so situated that a coach, which leaves it not very early in the morning, reaches London by noon . . . Great parcels of stock-jobbers stay at Brighton with the women and children. They skip backward and forward on the coaches, and actually carry on stock-jobbing, in 'Change Alley, though they reside at Brighton.

Thus Cobbett in *Rural Rides* in 1823. That was perhaps true during the summer, but for the rest of the year this was not the reality. In 1823 itself the great majority of those whose surname began with 'A' lived either in the City or, more commonly, pretty nearby in such places as Islington, Vauxhall, Walworth and Kentish Town – respectable enough, but hardly the height of fashion.

By this time several of what would become the main stockbroking firms were taking shape. The future James Capel & Co was called Marjoribanks, Capel & Co. James Capel had come from Worcestershire to the City early in the century to enter the office of John Capel, a stockbroking cousin who was also one of the Stock Exchange's original managers. He soon teamed up with two other brokers, whose most important connection was with Thomas Coutts; James Capel himself became a partner in 1813, and other partners, including Coutts connections like David Marjoribanks, followed. Connection was indeed everything: John Helbert Israel (he later dropped the 'Israel') and John Wagg were uncle and nephew; by the 1830s both were related by marriage to the Rothschilds. Both operated profitably as brokers to New Court, and eventually the two became partners. In 1823, John Menet took into partnership his brother-in-law Philip Cazenove, who through his father's merchant business enjoyed a useful connection with Rothschild, and thus founded the modern Cazenove & Co. The future R. Raphael & Sons was a firm with a difference. Raphael Raphael was a Dutch Jew who as a young man had left Amsterdam to come to London as a merchant. He made a considerable fortune during the war, and from the 1820s with great deftness reshaped his business into a specialised mixture of stockbroking, foreign banking and bullion broking – creating for himself and his firm an exception to the rule that Stock Exchange members should not pursue outside business activities.[24]

These nascent figures and firms all had to rub along with the humour of Capel Court. The foreign loan boom of 1822 caused a few new japes, like the plausible creation of entirely fictitious bonds called

Chinese Turnpikes, a favourite ploy on novice brokers ever after. Sometimes Stock Exchange humour was linked to Stock Exchange obstinacy, as the City report for 5 November 1824 explained:

> The Bank was shut today, and so was the Royal Exchange until twelve o'clock; but the British and Foreign Stock Exchanges were both open; the opening of the two Stock Exchanges, however, gave great offence to a large majority of the members, who claimed the right of a holyday upon the ground of immemorial custom; and these gentry appeared to be determined that no business should be transacted, for, from the opening to the close of the houses, one incessant discharge of fireworks, of all sorts and descriptions, was kept up, accompanied by loud and repeated cries of 'Holyday! Holyday!' &c; and, to enliven the scene, an effigy of Guy Faux was introduced, and conveyed through the Foreign Market, amidst loud uproar and laughter.

The particular grouse on this occasion was that the first payment of the Neapolitan loan (contractor, N. M. Rothschild) was due that day. 'And it was observed', the report went on, 'that if a contractor of a loan, for his own private convenience, chose to fix a day which is well known as being a holyday, such contractor should take the consequences of his own act . . .'[25]

Expansion was in the air in the specialised craft of bill broking, a slightly less boisterous area of the City. 'Has the business of your house, as bill brokers, increased since the year 1810?' the resumption committee asked its principal exponent, Samuel Gurney of Richardson, Overend & Co; he simply answered, 'Yes, very much'. Four years later his firm's annual turnover was up to a colossal £20m. Crucial to this prosperity was the continuance of cheap money after 1815, which meant that London banks were no longer able to make their customary turn of one per cent on the balances that their country correspondents lodged with them. Instead, much of this short-term money passed to the bill brokers, who employed it not only to buy and sell bills on a differential rates basis, but also to make their own short-term loans with it, whether to major capitalists like Rothschild, or to members of the Stock Exchange needing to carry over stock from one account to another, or to commission merchants temporarily requiring funds in order to meet acceptances. It was an attractive business on the face of it, and by 1822 there were some twenty-five bill-broking firms operating in the City, though in practice many failed to last the course.[26] One that did, by the skin of its teeth, was the firm immortalised by Jos Sedley's boast in *Vanity Fair* that 'Alexander will cash my bill down on the counter, Sir'. When its founder, William Alexander, died in 1819, the business of Alexanders was in a poor way.[27] His widow Ann was determined to keep it going until their son, George William Alexander, came of age in 1823, and this she succeeded in doing. The boy had been working in the firm since he was thirteen, showed a business-like cast of mind from the start, and on attaining his majority was made a partner. Appropriately, the style of the firm now became Ann & G. W. Alexander – one of the very few instances ever of a woman being the senior partner in a firm doing business in that male bastion, the City.

The hermetic world of private banking yielded another piquant family story. The origins of Prescotts Bank lay in two eighteenth-century City merchants, George Prescott and Andreas Grote (originally from Bremen), who started a banking business in 1766. In due course a new generation, in the persons of William Willoughby Prescott and George Grote, continued the firm. Grote was a hunting and shooting man, owned large farms in Kent and Oxfordshire, and, though married to an Evangelical, was a thoroughgoing secular Tory. In 1810 his eldest son, also called George, entered the bank as a clerk at the age of fifteen. Almost from the start George junior's letters to friends complain of the wearisome burdens imposed on him by his father, above all dreadful evenings of drunken stupidity at Threadneedle Street with his father's City friends. The adolescent took refuge in classical studies, learning German, reading political economy, practising the violoncello – activities openly despised by his father. But there was no escape from banking, for by 1816, when he became a partner, his father was looking almost exclusively to pursue the country life, and Prescott was refusing to shift if he could help it from his comfortable home in Hendon. For the next seven years, until Prescott's son, William George, joined him, George Grote was the only working partner, though he took but a small share of the profits. During that time he fell in love with a bluestocking and, unable to secure his father's consent, married her secretly in 1820. The young couple lived at Fortis Green, beyond Highgate; but often they stayed at the banking house, he being required to open the safes in the morning and close them at night. On those occasions, Harriet Grote later recalled, 'when they took walking exercise, it was either on Southwark Bridge or in the Drapers' Hall Gardens, Throgmorton Street, amidst a grove of trees black with the soot of the City'. Grote seems to have been a conscientious banker, but that his real passions lay elsewhere are shown by diary entries for 1822:

Dec 3rd. Rose a little before 7. Read to the conclusion of Pausanias, being about 40 pages. After breakfast began to take down my rough notes upon these 40 pages; a task which I completed in the evening. Read some very interesting matter in the first volume of Goguet respecting the early arts, agriculture, baking, brewing, oil, drinks, and clothes. This is far the best part of Goguet which I have yet seen.

Dec 4th. Rose at 6. Read Goguet on the different Arts until breakfast; after breakfast read some articles in Voltaire's 'Dictionn. Philosop'. Had a headache this evening, which I whiled away conversing with W. Prescott.[28]

The following year Mrs Grote suggested to her husband that he write a history of Greece.

The square mile's share of intellectuals extended to its insurance arm. The story goes that one of Nathan Rothschild's many in-laws came up to him one day in the Royal Exchange and complained that he had failed to obtain the vacant actuaryship of a large insurance company (the Guardian) because he was a Jew. To which the great man exclaimed: 'Vat, not take you because of your religion! Mein Gott! Den I vil make a bigger office for you den any of dem.' True or not, the fact is that Rothschild was the prime mover in establishing in 1824 the Alliance Assurance, a joint-stock company capitalised at £5m; written into its deed of settlement was that Benjamin Gompertz should be appointed actuary. Gompertz was then in his mid-forties. His father and grandfather had been diamond merchants; he himself, in deference to his father's wishes, had spent most of his working life on the Stock Exchange, but from childhood it was mathematics that absorbed him. He made his reputation with tracts on imaginary quantities and porisms, being elected in 1819 a Fellow of the Royal Society, to whom the following year he presented a pioneering paper on Life Contingencies. He also proved a highly effective actuary at the Alliance and over the years was often consulted by government.[29]

The new company immediately launched a successful parliamentary campaign to strip Lloyd's, together with two chartered companies the Royal Exchange and London Assurance, of the marine insurance monopoly. The spokesmen for Lloyd's fought a stern rearguard battle, but Huskisson for one (in rare agreement with Rothschild) was adamant that the monopoly should go. One of the new competitors to Lloyd's was the Indemnity Marine Insurance Company, formed later in 1824. Assistant underwriter for its first three years, and chief manager for almost half a century thereafter, was William Ellis, himself the son of a Lloyd's underwriter. Ellis did much to establish the Indemnity, never took a holiday for thirty years, and yet found time to write books with portentous titles like *Education as a means of preventing Destitution, Where must we look for the further Prevention of Crime?* and *Thoughts on the Future of the Human Race.* He wrote a series of textbooks on teaching political economy to children and in time even lectured to the royal children at Buckingham Palace.[30] William Ellis and Benjamin Gompertz: two further reminders of the absurdity of seeing the City through a single cultural lens.

*

In 1824, after some temporary indigestion, the foreign loan boom revived with a vengeance. The emphasis was heavily on South America, and loans varied from the perfectly respectable, such as those arranged by Barings and Rothschilds for Buenos Aires and Brazil, to the frankly speculative, including further shots of Columbian and Peruvian scrip. A Mexican loan early in the year was particularly profitable, netting for its contractors B. A. Goldschmidt & Co at least $£\frac{1}{4}$m. By November the *Morning Herald* was reporting that 'the British Funds are now altogether considered matter of trivial importance, whether they advance or fall in value', whereas 'if the least report is circulated, or the least whisper abroad regarding any of the newly established States of South America, all persons are then in the greatest state of anxiety'. In the course of the winter there also began a phenomenal boom in joint-stock company promotion, with a whole host of generally baseless schemes coming forward to rapturous response. They ranged from mining and other companies in the new South American republics to more local ventures like Bognor New Town, Westminster Fish, and Economic Funeral. By January 1825, as the resident United States minister (Richard Rush) recorded in a letter home, the whole of London, not just the City, was in a state of heightened enthusiasm:

> Nothing was ever like it before, not even the days of the South Sea scheme . . . Shares in some of the companies have advanced to seventeen hundred per cent within a few months, and are bought with avidity at this price. I hear it said that noblemen of great estates, and directors of the Bank of England, participate; also that princes of the blood press forward to obtain shares.[31]

So the fever went on for a few months longer.

It was a mania that Barings and Rothschilds wisely eschewed. In the Commons that March, Alexander Baring openly compared noblemen gambling 'in the hells of St James's Street' to merchants doing the same in the Royal Exchange, adding bluntly that the mining companies in particular would 'turn out to be delusions'. Someone who disputed this prediction was the young Benjamin Disraeli, heavily embroiled in speculations and author of an anonymous, highly bullish pamphlet entitled *An Inquiry into the Plans, Progress and Policy of the American Mining Companies*, published that month. Disraeli's publisher, and partner in his syndicate in South American mining shares, was John Murray, to whom the sanguine author wrote on April Fool's Day that 'an immense and permanent rise is to be looked to'. And he added: 'I hope that this partnership is but the forerunner of mutual brilliancy of fortune'. So it was – eventually – but a few days later there was a hint of desperation when, after detailing to a creditor his share speculation, the debtor concluded: 'On the Mexican mines I rest my sheet anchor'.[32]

As Disraeli meditated his uncertain future, so Elia soon afterwards celebrated the end of his incarceration in the fortress of Leadenhall Street:

> Thou dreary pile, fit mansion for a Gresham or a Whittington of old, stately House of Merchants; with thy labyrinthine passages, and light-excluding, pent-up offices, where candles for one half the year supplied the place of the sun's light; unhealthy contributor to my weal, stern fosterer of my living, farewell!

'I have left the damned India House for Ever!', Charles Lamb announced to a friend on 29 March 1825, without a nod to literary artifice. Lamb had for the most part enjoyed the company of fellow-clerks but for him the City had been a place where he had felt his life slowly draining away. 'You don't know how wearisome it is to breathe the air of four pent walls without relief day after day, all the golden hours of the day between 10 and 4 without ease or interposition', he had written to Wordsworth a few years earlier. Retirement brought profound relief; and yet he could not forget the world he had left behind and those who had the misfortune to inhabit it:

> What is become of Fish-street Hill? Where is Fenchurch-street? Stones of old Mincing-lane, which I have worn with my daily pilgrimage for six and thirty years, to the footsteps of what toil-worn clerk are your everlasting flints now vocal?[33]

CHAPTER SIX

Curst be the Bubbles

'The abundance of money has led to a variety of speculations in England, and scarcely a week has passed but some new company was founded to direct a world projected adventure. What must be the cure of this mania time only can show.' Thus the private thoughts of Samuel Thornton on New Year's Day 1825. By March the person providing the answers was the Duke of Wellington, as recorded by his good friend Mrs Arbuthnot: 'He thinks the greatest national calamities will be the consequence of this speculating mania, that all the companies are bubbles invented for stockjobbing purposes & that there will be a *general crash . . .*' So it proved; during the second half of the year a combination of circumstances came together to produce arguably the most severe financial crisis of the century. The collapse of the absurdly overblown boom in foreign loans and company promotions, speculative overtrading in imported commodities, rashness on the part of the country banks, Bank of England policy that veered between complacency and an over-sharp contraction of credit – all these things, in hotly debated proportions, played a part. 'Sam Williams, the great American Merchant, stops payment & a universal pressure for Money prevails', recorded Churchill at the end of October, as the storm clouds gathered.[1]

There followed a difficult though not yet desperate month:

5 November. Business wants a good deal of pushing.

12 November. As to business, nothing done of any consequence, but Goods still arriving.

19 November. The Money Market very heavy which causes a universal Stagnation in all Trades. Our Sale of African Teak & wrecked Gothenburgh Cargo goes off tolerably well.

26 November. Money matters very alarming in the City. Stocks fall to 83 & rumours of different Schemes for alleviation.

The timber broker's weekly journal is complemented by correspondence to the Norwich Bank, a concern intimately bound up with the great Norfolk family of Gurney (from which Samuel Gurney came). J. J. Gurney on the 18th reported back from London in critical mood:

> There is a tremendous pressure upon this town, & I suppose almost *all* the Bankers are more or less distressed . . . The root of the difficulty is in the Bank of England, where they are extremely restricting their discounts with a view to producing a favourable effect on the exchanges, so as to prevent their being run upon for gold . . . It seems strange that the pecuniary facilities of the whole realm should thus depend on the management of a small despotic Committee.

By 1 December the head of the family, Hudson Gurney, was at the front line. Calling in at Barclays, London agents to the Norwich Bank and fellow Quakers, he found 'Jno Tritton's face very long, & Bevan running about the office and refusing Bill upon Bill offered for Discount'. Two days later Churchill himself was no less long-faced, though prematurely apocalyptic: 'Business increasing in Languor & the Stock in hand becomes enormous . . . Panic in the City now at a climax'.[2]

In fact, by the start of December, the Bank of England had reversed its policy and begun to discount largely. But, as one young private banker now discovered, the change came too late. Henry Sykes Thornton, 25-year-old son of Henry and nephew of Samuel, had been a partner for only a few months in the family bank (now called Pole, Thornton, Free, Down & Scott), but it was long enough for him to realise that Peter Free's management had left the bank in poor shape to cope with the run on it that began on Thursday the 1st. The following week Henry's sister and confidante Marianne Thornton wrote a vivid account to the aged Hannah More, like the Thorntons part of the evangelical Clapham Sect:

> On Saturday – that dreadful Saturday I shall never forget – the run increased to a frightful degree, everybody came in to take *out* their balance, no one brought any in; one old steady customer, who had usually £30,000 there, drew it out without, as is usual, giving any warning, and in order to pay it the House was left literally empty. Henry went out to endeavour to borrow but people made shuffling excuses – some said they would go and fetch some, and never returned – in short both he and Mr Free returned unsuccessful. Such a moment of peril completely turned Free's head; he insisted on proclaiming themselves Bankrupts at once, and raved and self-accused himself, and in short quite lost his powers of action.
> Old Scott cried like a child of five years old, but could suggest nothing, Pole and Down were both out of Town. Henry saw it all lay upon him . . .

They shut up always at five. At four, he ordered the balance for the day to be struck, and found that during the next hour they would have to pay thirty-three thousand, and they should receive only twelve thousand. This was certain destruction, and he walked out, resolved to try one last resource.

There had always been such a jealousy between their House and Smith's (the Carrington Smiths I mean) that Free had often observed that morning how pleased they would be to hear they had broken, but John Smith had been an early friend of the Sykes', and particularly kind to Henry, and to him he resolved to go – but not according to Banker's etiquette, as if he did not care whether he gave it to him or not – but he told him honestly he believed they must break, and he could hardly expect him to lend it, but yet if he could get them on till five, it would be an inexpressible relief. John Smith asked if he could give his word of honour that all was safe, that is, that the House was solvent, Henry said he could. Well! then he said they should have everything they could spare, which was not quite enough tho', for they had been hard-pressed themselves that day, but he went back with Henry to watch the event.

Two people had chanced to pay *in* some money whilst Henry had been absent, this, with what he had borrowed exactly met the demand upon them – but never, he says, shall he forget watching the clock to see when five would strike, and end their immediate terror – or whether any one would come in for any more payments. The clock did strike at last, and they were safe for the moment, but as Henry heard the door locked, and the shutters put up, he felt they would not open again at that dear House, which every association led him to love so dearly.

Yet that evening there emerged the possibility of further succour, for Smith arranged that those directors of the Bank of England who were in town should meet the following morning. Henry himself returned home to Battersea Rise well after midnight:

I ran to him, and found him perfectly white and bloodless with the anxiety and the exertion he had gone through, but so quiet and composed, I could scarcely believe it when he told me they must be proclaimed Bankrupts Monday morning, but not to mind it for no one would lose anything by it; but he was certain the House was solvent, and he had rather break at once than go through such another day. He said they were very kind to him in the City, but there *could* be no hope from the Bank; he was more sorry for the ruin it would occasion, as they reckoned that thirty-eight country Banks would fail in consequence. That it was owing partly to Free's folly in locking up the money partly to the pressure of the times, but help or hope he thought there was none. He next proceeded to do two or three things which almost broke my heart. He paid me and Nurse two or three pounds he owed us, for he said he shouldn't feel any was his own by Monday.

First thing on Sunday the Bank directors met, including the governor, Cornelius Buller, who was connected by marriage to Henry's elderly senior partner, Sir Peter Pole. After examining the books, and insisting that Free leave the business, they agreed to lend £400,000. It looked as though the house was saved, Henry's career was made, and in the words of a grateful Marianne, 'from the deepest sorrow, we are all at once the happiest of the happy'.[3]

It proved a false dawn. City tension was heightened by the rumour that Pole's, with its extensive country banks agency, had been bailed out; and on Thursday the 8th news came of the failure of Wentworth & Co, a leading Yorkshire bank. 'Our risk is in winding out on diminished values, & who may be able to stand on a general shrinkage nobody can well foresee', wrote Hudson Gurney that day, adding 'I have been run to death, apparently doing nothing, but am utterly bothered in mind & spirit'. 'The distress for Money among respectable Dealers & Merchants beyond anything ever experienced' declared Churchill on the Saturday. An almost tidal run on the country banks began the same day, which made up Henry Thornton's mind that there was no alternative but for Pole's to stop payment. 'If he had borrowed more money', Marianne explained, 'it would have only been to lend to Country Banks, who might all have stopped tomorrow. He felt sure that the House was solvent.'[4]

Henry took his decision (bringing down over three dozen country banks) calmly enough, but when the City found out on Monday morning its reaction was very different. 'The dense fog which prevailed throughout the day was scarcely more gloomy than the countenances of those who are affected by the present alarming state of the Money Market', reported the *Morning Chronicle*, adding that 'on no former occasion have we witnessed so decided a run on the different banking-houses, and especially on those connected with provincial establishments'. Tuesday was no better, as news came that Williams & Co of Birchin Lane was in trouble, and an impassable crowd gathered outside their door. ' "Never were such times", cried many of the oldest visitors of the 'Change, while others exclaimed, "If this state of things continues, we must ask not who is gone, but who stands? for unless something is done to relieve the pressure, and to restore confidence, few can resist so overwhelming a torrent of distrust".' Wednesday was a day of further stoppages and panic, during which 'the Royal Exchange was thronged long before the customary hour of assemblage, and Cornhill, Lombard-street, Nicholas-lane, and all the streets in which banking-houses are situated, were crowded to such a degree, as to impede the progress of passengers', so much so that police were called in. Gloom pervaded the Stock Exchange, where 'in the Foreign Stocks all were on the decline, and of Home Shares nothing was said except a hearty wish that they were all in a very warm place'. The only positive development of the day was a meeting that afternoon at Mansion House of about a hundred merchants and bankers, who passed a resolution expressing confidence in the Bank of England's attempts to stem the crisis.[5]

It was on the whole a justified confidence, for since the start of the week the Bank had been making every effort to bolster the market. Several years later Jeremiah Harman would recall with pride the assistance rendered:

> We lent it by every possible means, and in modes that we never had adopted before; we took in stock as security, purchased exchequer bills, we made advances on exchequer bills, we not only discounted outright, but we made advances on deposits of bills of exchange to an immense amount; in short by every possible means consistent with the safety of the Bank; and we were not upon some occasions over nice; seeing the dreadful state in which the public were, we rendered every assistance in our power.

With Buller more or less out of the frame because of his connection with Pole, the deputy governor, J. B. Richards, took charge. A key moment came on Thursday, when the cabinet gave its sanction to the Bank issuing £1 notes for the first time since the resumption of gold payments over four years earlier – on the condition that such issue was 'understood to be strictly temporary'.[6] By the next day these notes were in circulation.

Yet on Friday the 16th the situation was as grave as at any stage. That morning Mrs Arbuthnot and her husband (Joint Secretary of the Treasury) were put in the highly fractious picture by Herries, the member of government closest to the City:

> Mr Herries told us that such had been the extraordinary demand for gold to supply the country bankers & to meet the general run upon them that the Bank of England was completely drained of its specie & was reduced to 100,000 sovereigns . . . The Bank expects to be obliged to suspend cash payments tomorrow, and they want the Government to step forward to their assistance & order the suspension. Lord Liverpool is unwilling to do this & wishes the Bank to do it upon their own responsibility. By Mr Herries's account there seems to be considerable irritation between the Govt & the Governors of the Bank . . . Such is the

detestation in which Mr Huskisson is held in the City that Ld L & Mr Canning did not think it prudent to summon him to London till all the Cabinet were sent for &, in the discussions with the Bank, he is kept out of sight . . . Rothschild has made most gigantic efforts to assist the Bank & he told Mr Herries that, if he had been applied to sooner, he wd have prevented all the difficulty. As it is, if they can hold out till Monday or Tuesday, he will have enormous sums over in sovereigns from Paris, & the pressure will be entirely relieved . . . Mr Herries said that the City merchants appeared to have the utmost contempt for Mr Robinson [chancellor of the exchequer], who was wholly without plan or expedients & who did not appear to have the least idea what to do.[7]

Rothschild may not have been averse to the prospect of suspension, but clearly he was also mindful of larger responsibilities. The *Morning Chronicle*'s City correspondent reported that, in the course of the Friday morning, 'we were informed that 150,000 sovereigns had arrived from the Continent, which were immediately paid into the Bank of England by the house of Rothschild'; while according to Canning's private secretary half a century later, it was on the Friday night that 'the Rothschilds poured into the Bank £300,000 coin'. Whatever Rothschild's contribution, the Cabinet met that Friday evening and, in five acrimonious hours, hammered out a political compromise. The central figure was Wellington, who reluctantly accepted the insistent demand of Huskisson and Canning that the Bank must not be allowed to use the crisis as a device for once more going off gold, but convinced his colleagues that Huskisson's notion of depriving the Bank of its charter should it be forced to stop payment was preposterous. The Iron Duke held firm, as Mrs Arbuthnot admiringly recorded: 'He told Lord Liverpool that while there was life there was hope; that there was a chance of the Bank standing & while that chance remained, he wd not despair; that the Government were bound to support them to the very utmost of their power . . . for that their interests were those of the country'.[8]

'A gloomy foreboding seems to possess every mind' recorded Charles Churchill in his diary the next day. But the tide was about to turn. The Bank was not compelled to stop payment on the Saturday; over the weekend it ran out of £5 and £10 notes but then in the nick of time received a fresh supply from its printers; and by Tuesday, courtesy of Rothschild, major infusions of gold were arriving from France. A mild run on the Bank's gold reserves continued until Christmas Eve, but by then that precious intangible – confidence – had been restored. Churchill used the very term that day: 'This week a little quiet & confidence in the Bankers returning'. Quiet was sorely needed, as the leading bill broker John Overend wrote a few days later to a country correspondent. After describing 'the late bustle' as 'such a one as I never witnessed before in the 36 years I have been in Lombard Street', he went on:

> I hope never to see the like of it again, & if the Bank Directors had not seen the thing in its true light & given the prompt and immediate assistance they did, the game would have ben up . . . As to myself I may inform thee I get often very tired of the very great worry & close confinement of Lombard Street & for the last three months I have not been from the shop one half hour from nine in the morning until five at night, & often much later, but unless my health will not permit me I am determined to stick to my post until everything is in good order . . .⁹

Moving to a new post was Henry Thornton. Although it had stopped payment on the 13th, Williams & Co now managed to reconstitute itself as Williams, Deacon & Co, bringing in young Thornton and a former partner of Barings called John Deacon. At the last minute, just before the bank was about to reopen for business early in January and with gold still scarce in the City, the new partnership realised it needed a lot more sovereigns for the country banks. Marianne again takes up the narrative:

> Henry saw one resource, to get into a post chaise instantly, go during the night to Brighton where John Smith was, knock him up, persuade him to return to town with him, go with Alexander Baring to Rothshild, and those two Princes of the City might induce the Jew King of City, Rothschild, to give them the money, for he, probably, was the only man in England who *could* help them having it is suspected, been hoarding up sovereigns for exportation for some time.
> Henry did the deed, found Mr J. Smith quite willing to return with him, and by dint of a little persuasion and exhortation the Jew was induced to bring out his gold, first charging $2\frac{1}{2}$ commission, then saying he did it out of public spirit, and lastly begging they would never tell it or he would be besieged night and day. However, Henry and the sovereigns were in Williams's House before hardly any one knew he had been further than home during the night.¹⁰

It had, one way and another, been quite a learning curve for the prentice banker.

Who, in a larger sense, deserved credit for averting catastrophe? Historians have usually given the award jointly to the Bank and to Rothschild – the latter accolade no thanks to Alexander Baring. He sought to downgrade the contribution of French gold by putting about an inherently as well as circumstantially implausible story to the effect that what had really saved the day was the fluke of Bank officials happening to come across a box of unissued pound notes.[11] Yet perhaps accolades were hardly to the point. Thomas Love Peacock, the son of a London glass merchant, was not only a poet and novelist but also from 1819 an official of the East India Company; after the worst of the crisis was over, he reflected on the whole crazy phenomenon he had witnessed:

> Oh! where are the hopes we have met in a morning,
>   As we hustled and bustled around Capel court?
> When we laughed at the croakers that bade us take warning,
>   Who once were our scorn and now make us their sport.
>
> Oh! where are the regions where well-paid inspectors
>   Found metals omnigenous streaked and emboss'd?
> So kindly bought for us by honest directors,
>   Who charged us but three times as much as they cost.
>
> Oh! where are the riches that bubbled like fountains,
>   In places we neither could utter nor spell,
> A thousand miles inland 'mid untrodden mountains,
>   Where silver and gold grew like heath and blue-bell?
>
> Now curst be the projects, and curst the projectors,
>   And curst be the bubbles before us that rolled,
> Which, bursting, have left us like desolate spectres,
>   Bewailing our bodies of paper and gold.
>
> For what is a man but his coat and his breeches,
>   His plate and his linen, his land and his house?
> Oh! we had been men had we won our mock riches,
>   But now we are ghosts, each as poor as a mouse.[12]

CHAPTER SEVEN

Il est Mort

1826 was not the year of the silver lining. 'The manufacturers are almost entirely at a stand, credit is totally destroyed, the funds are today at 76, having this time last year been at 97, & every person in the City is in despair'. So recorded Mrs Arbuthnot on 10 February. Soon afterwards, on Wednesday the 15th, gloom was deepened by a crop of failures, including the prominent merchants and foreign loan contractors B. A. Goldschmidt & Co. It was not only distant Colombians, vainly hoping for their loan proceeds, who now paid the price:

> Mr L. A. Goldschmidt was the principal partner . . . From the time of the stoppage of the house until Saturday morning he was in a state of distraction. In the forenoon of Saturday he became more composed, and dressed himself to attend to the state of affairs to be laid before his creditors. The effort appears to have been too great for the acute feelings of Mr Goldschmidt – he threw himself on the sofa in despair, and remained for three hours in a state of inanimation . . . He passed from this life without a struggle or a groan. The immediate cause of his dissolution was the bursting of a blood vessel in his head, but there is not a question, that the ultimate cause of death was the suffering of his mind . . .

February was the worst month for failures and attendant dramas. Even in late April money remained scarce, and the mood was still very downbeat, as witnessed by a letter to Canton from Fairlie, Bonham & Co, one of the two leading East India houses:

> The stagnation experienced in general business is fully as great at the present moment as it has been at any time since the commencement five months ago of the extraordinary panic . . . Meantime our quotations for Produce, low as they are, may be considered almost nominal, it being impracticable to effect Sales to any extent, so that you may conceive in some degree the inconvenience that merchants and others must be exposed to.

As the summer wore on there was little restoration of confidence, and in particular a notoriety attached to the now thoroughly discredited sphere of foreign loans. In September one member of the Stock Exchange accused another of having exploited inside information about Chilean default; fisticuffs ensued, and after an exchange of cards it was very nearly pistols for two and coffee for one.[1]

Early next month Prince Hermann Pückler-Muskau, inveterate and impecunious traveller, spent the night anchored just below London Bridge, at the start of a tour of England in search of an heiress. In the morning he 'hastened as quickly as possible out of the dirty City, swarming like an ant-hill', and headed for the West End. But a few days later he was back, visiting first the Royal Exchange:

> The imposing statues of English sovereigns, combined with the antique and stately architecture, excite a poetical feeling, to which the thought of the boundless commerce of which London is the centre gives a still deeper significancy. The men, however, who animate the picture soon draw one back into the region of common-place, for selfishness and avarice gleam but too clearly from every eye. In this point of view, the place I am describing, and indeed the whole City, have a repulsive sinister aspect, which almost reminds one of the restless and comfortless throng of the spirits of the damned.

While at the Royal Exchange the prince took the opportunity to look in on 'the celebrated Lloyd's Coffee House, the dirtiest place of the kind in London, which exhibits few traces of the millions daily exchanged in it'. There followed brief glances at the Bank of England – 'the vast and beautiful building' where 'hundreds of clerks . . . mechanically conduct the gigantic business' – and the Lord Mayor in judicial action, before:

> Further still did we wander on in the tumultuous 'City', where you may be lost like a flitting atom, if you do not pass on to the right or left according to rule; where you seem to be in continual danger of being spitted on the shaft of a cabriolet driving too near the narrow 'trottoir', or crushed under the weight of an overloaded and tottering stage-coach edifice. At length we reached an extremely dark and mean-looking coffee-house, called Garraway's, where estates and houses of enormous value are daily put up to sale.

Finally, he could not resist making a call on Nathan Rothschild. 'I found him in a poor obscure-looking place, and making my way with some difficulty through the little court-yard, blocked up by a waggon laden with bars of silver, I was introduced into the presence of this Grand Ally of the Holy Alliance.' Speaking 'in a language quite peculiar to himself – half English, half German – the English part with a broad German accent but with the imposing confidence of a man who feels such trifles to be beneath his attention', the host 'did not stand much on ceremony' and 'broke out into bitter complaints that every poor devil who came to England had something or other to ask of him'. A courteous visitor could only pay the compliment that Europe was unable to manage without him, prompting the riposte from Rothschild: 'Oh no, you are only jesting – I am but a servant, whom people are pleased with because he manages their affairs well, and to whom they let some crumbs fall as an acknowledgement'. At which point exit Pückler-Muskau, discouraged from fortune-hunting in that particular direction.[2]

It was a pity he failed to penetrate the Stock Exchange, where he would have found plenty to amuse him. Many years later a veteran member recalled benignly the atmosphere of the 1820s:

> We were only a few hundred strong then, and everybody knew everybody else. We had some fine games. At 2, Capel Court, Mendoza had a boxing booth, where, instead of knocking prices about, a member could go and knock somebody about or get knocked about himself, if things did not suit him inside. An old woman had a stall *inside* the House, close to Capel Court door, where those who had not quite outlived their earliest tastes could feed on buns, cakes, etc. A gallery ran round the old House; seats and desks were fitted up for clerks and members. It was very convenient, because if a man wanted a book he simply called up to his clerk, who would throw it over. Some of the funny ones used to drop things over on unsuspecting members. Sometimes, in the afternoon, a jobber used to give us a tune on a cornet, and I reckon we had plenty of fun when things were dull. We used to buy our own chops and steaks in those days, and take them to a cook-shop or chop-house and have them cooked, paying a penny for the privilege. Almost over every bargain a glass of sherry used to be drunk. 'Who pays?' was a very common expression.[3]

All true no doubt, but perhaps the distance of time lent a certain enchantment. A couple of contemporary episodes suggest (Mendoza apart) a rougher, tougher environment. In the summer of 1826 there was the case of the partnership that went wrong – perennial of Stock Exchange life. William Knight and James Norman were both declared defaulters, and in the course of long drawn-out Committee investigations, prompted by complaining creditors, each made strong statements about the other. 'It has been my misfortune to be connected with a bad Partner – a Man capable of the basest deceit and falsehood and in many instances of most dishonourable conduct', declared Knight of Norman, not denying that 'these are hard assertions'. Norman for his part outlined how at the start of 1824 he had been persuaded to join Knight in partnership but then found him to be deeply in debt; emphasised that 'I was not brought up to the Stock Exchange, my introduction to Mr Knight took place before I knew anything of your House'; and added bitterly that 'Mr Knight appears to be as well off in the world since his Bankruptcy as before', whereas 'I was obliged to give up housekeeping and send my wife home to her friends', before going to the West Indies 'to renew my mercantile connexions'. It was not an exceptional case.

Still, it was better to be a mistrusted insider than a blameless outsider, as the hapless Mr Shevill discovered in April 1827. Following a press report that a gentleman had been ill-used in the Foreign Stock Market and robbed of four sovereigns, the Committee heard Shevill's account of what had happened:

> He stated that he is an auctioneer at Bethnal Green, and having occasion to go to the Excise Office on Business he saw there the card of a candidate for the London Orphan Asylum and on asking who had left that card he was told it was a Mr Copper who would be much obliged to any one who could procure some Votes.
>
> He recollected that Mr Inman of the Stock Exchange was a Subscriber to that institution and he therefore determined to call on him and solicit his Vote.
>
> Previously however to doing so, he went to the Bank to exchange some small notes for large ones and then proceeded up Capel Court to the Foreign Stock Exchange. He is quite confident that at the time he entered the House he had 4 Sovereigns in his breeches pocket and he had reserved them for the purpose of buying a pony harness in Fleet Street.
>
> As soon as he entered the House he was surrounded by a great many persons, some of whom asked him if he wished to buy Mexican or Colombian Bonds, and upon his answering that he was merely in search of his friend Mr Inman, he was pushed about very rudely, his hat was knocked off and he was otherwise very much insulted. At length one of the porters of the House came up to him and told him to walk out, as it was a private room and he had no business there.
>
> He accordingly went into the lobby and desired the waiter to call Mr Inman who answered that he had to go round to the door in New Court.
>
> As he was proceeding thither he had gone a very short distance down Capel Court when he missed his 4 Sovereigns. He returned immediately

and desired the Constable to go in and see if there were any improper persons there as he was sure his pocket had been picked.

The waiter sneered at him and refused to go, he then went to the Mansion House to lay his complaint before the Lord Mayor, who was not sitting at the time: and he was therefore obliged to postpone it.

He saw Mr Inman at the door in New Court to whom he stated what had happened, after which a search was made by the waiter in case the Sovereigns might have fallen on the floor, but nothing was found.

Other evidence was heard. Chapman, the waiter at the Capel Court door, after recollecting seeing Shevill 'apparently in a great passion and saying they were a pack of damned blackguards', admitted that 'he might have smiled on hearing such language'. Hadlow, a member, conceded that many people had 'flocked about and pushed him about, joked upon his name and knocked his hat off', but insisted that 'no violence was used nor was it possible that any money could have slipped out of his pocket'. He added that Shevill would 'not have been so much annoyed had he not persisted in remaining in the House after he was told to go out and had he not also been abusive on the occasion'. In the end the Committee admitted it could proceed no further in the case.[4]

Meanwhile the serious business of the City was going on. At about the same time that an intrusive auctioneer was being told to shevill off, the firm of Inglis, Forbes & Co was sending out its monthly letter on the East India trade. The familiar phrases recur. 'Continues very dull of Sale' (coffee), 'Good demand still exists for this Article' (sugar), 'Meets with a ready Sale' (rice), 'No disposition shewn by the Dealers to become purchasers except at very low rates' (cotton), and so on. Attached was a printed list of spices, drugs, dyes etc, 'shewing the Descriptions and Qualities which should be selected in preference for Shipment for the London Market', and it included:

Spices.	<u>Cassia Lignea</u>.......	as closely resembling Cinnamon as possible, high flavoured, not broken, and not false packed.
	Mace....................	reddish yellow, strongly aromatic, free from white pieces, flakes as perfect as possible.
	Nutmegs..............	large, heavy, and plump, and free from worms.
Drugs & Dyes.	*Castor Oil*..........	pale as water, without taste or smell.
	Dragons Blood....	clear, transparent and brittle, of a bright red color, in reeds.

Musk....................	sound flattish pods, dry, not opened.	
Sal Ammoniac.....	white and transparent, very sharp to the tongue.	
Soy......................	of a good consistence and taste not too salt.	
Elephants' Teeth	strait, sound, white teeth, the largest are the most valuable.	
Mother-O'-Pearl .... *Shells*	should be large, white, and of good lustre, free from cracks, grubs, or crust on the back.	
Tortoiseshell	large clear shells, heavy, not thin or light, without cracks or barnacles.[5]	

If the Victorian precept was to be that 'Servants talk about People, Gentlefolk discuss Things', it was clear on which side of the social divide the City of the 1820s was starting to line up.

Someone with no compunction about discussing things was Miles Stringer, partner of Stringer & Richardson, merchants and tea and spice dealers of 5 Monument Yard, Fish Street Hill. He maintained a sharp-tongued correspondence to many parts of the world, during 1828 particularly with Wilkinson & Petrie of Calcutta, the scene that year of much speculation in indigo. News between the two continents still travelled with frustrating slowness:

> *22 April.* Your lines of 28 Dec[r] have much surprised me, hearing you were in any difficulty to procure fine Indigo to complete my order & to use my Funds. I hope this will not turn out the fact, as I can trace others similarly situated who have either been more fortunate or decided.
>
> *28 April.* The absence of favorable winds has kept the Conach at Portsmouth & enabled me to follow up my lines of the 22nd inst: which I am desirous of doing under the impression excited by subsequent news from Calcutta 12 Jan via France which has reached me this day. I observe the high prices of the better kinds of Indigo & also the report of the difficulty of meeting with them, by which I cannot but infer you will not be able to complete my order in consequence of the advance & scarcity. I am quite disposed to give credit to your intentions & it may yet be explained by missing advices how it occurred, but reasoning only from present facts, I am bound to suppose you have committed a serious error in judgement by standing aloof as a buyer when you were fully justified by my instructions & having possessed yourself of the means of realizing upon me . . . I cannot but lament my expectations have been so sorely frustrated.
>
> *29 May.* I have caused the parcel of Indigo by Lady Macnaughton to be inspected by my Broker & am truly concerned to report his opinion has

disturbed me greatly. Far from finding the quality either such as I ordered or was induced to expect from your report, which should have been fine violet & blue, it is not better than middling violet & falls into that class of consuming & shipping qualities which are quite foreign to the purpose intended, & actually deprives me of making a sale in such markets in Italy & Germany as I might have addressed them to & saved that loss which is likely to hang over the article this Season. I feel this disappointment very keenly . . .

15 July. Since my letter of 29 May by Roxburgh I have been made uneasy by certain reflections forced upon me by comparing the business you have done for me this season in Indigo, & what you might have done had the concern been differently disposed, & I am free to confess it has rather been heightened by an accidental inspection of a parcel of 139 Chests marked I.P.S. & shipped by yourselves in the Lady Macnaughton, which has so far exceeded mine in quality that the comparison has been painful & prejudicial. I presume this Indigo must have been bought at the same time with mine & perhaps cost no more or even less. If it cost the same, you should have marked it for me, recollecting you had drawn largely on account, which I must again repeat you were not authorized in doing . . . But if it costs less, you were without excuse. I will suppose that fine qualities of Indigo were scarce, but having such an opportunity of compleating an order when under limits & money in hand I cannot understand why my interest was neglected, except to the advantage of a more favored customer . . .

The sequence of correspondence ended, 'I am sure you will not expect from me any further repetition of this confidence if I have not good reason to feel differently at the end of next season to what I have done this'.[6]

It is a relief to turn to the even temper of Charles Churchill's diary, very nearly cut horribly short:

8 December 1827. Providential Escape in Dowsons Timber Yard, – a Deal pitched from a high pile – after reaching the Ground – falling lengthways close to me.

22 December 1827. Another heavy Week in business but some Consolation perhaps in our Neighbours being as cold as ourselves.

10 May 1828. This Week got home my little Carriage wch is much approved of – hire a horse for the present . . .

3 August 1828. Saturday, run down to Worthing & after some little obstacles settle for No 2 Montpelier, for a Month certain.

31 October 1828. Business rather untoward at the early part of the Week – but we reap towards the end – Prices certainly advancing in Norway Deals, Timber pine deals & white plank.

12 September 1829. Business still in rather a larger way – with some disappointments – particularly with half of the Haubtly Cargo snatched away by Batten & White.

At the beginning and end of each year's journal Churchill usually made some more general entries, including this at the start of 1830:

> My Habits much as usual –
> In Business – pretty actively employed all the Morning – Dine at Bakers Coffee House – about 3 – to Change – & the Counting H^s & a Cup of Tea – with an Hour or two of Writing – winds up the business of the Day – then Home – the Children – & a light Supper concludes . . .

To which he added: 'I endeavour to get thro the World, without jostling, or being jostled, if I can help it'.[7]

An admirable aim, but the City was a pretty jostling place, where reputations rarely stood still and there was a ceaseless ebb and flow of firms rising and falling, individuals coming in and going out. There is no more telling, unsentimental source than the 'character books' which individual firms kept, in effect representing finely tuned credit ratings of other City houses. That kept by Barings in the late 1820s is a suggestive document:

> *C. A. Cordes.* Formerly a Clerk in the House of J. H. Schröder & Co and entered into Business (about 1824) with a Mr Schroder of Hambro [i.e. Hamburg] under the Firm of Schroder & Cordes. Mr Schroder died shortly afterwards & he has been alone about 12 months, is doing a fair Commission Business in the Export trade, principally in Sugar & Coffee to Germany. He has but little Capital, but is so cautious and prudent in what he does that the writer entertains the best opinion of him. In all his dealings he is scrupulously honest and there is not a Merchant in the City of London whose Character in every respect stands higher.
>
> *Lobeck, Strong & Co.* Mr L failed in 1819 under the Firm of L & Kraft, traded until March last as L & Co, and since then under the present Firm. He can have no money but Mr S with whom he has connected himself is Nephew of the late Mr Rundell of Ludgate Hill; and it is said has brought into the Concern £10,000, so that they may be considered safe for what they do; but the writer has no confidence of Mr L's ultimate success in Life, thinking him by far too sanguine a man. Their Business is executing Orders for the Shipment of Colonial Produce to the Continent, but their Connexions are not first rate.
>
> *George Meyer.* Is a Man of great experience having been 20 to 30 Years in the Foreign Trade. He was formerly the active Partner in the House of Simeon & Co, who were most extensive Foreign Merchants and realized a large Fortune during the War. He retired from this Concern in 1814 and took out of it £50 to 60,000. Afterwards he entered again into Business and in the Crisis of 1825 stopped payment. He is extremely clever and indefatigable and has most extensive Connexions on the Continent. It is

only of late that he has fully resumed his former Business, for which having been furnished with Funds by some powerful Friends, there is no doubt that he will obtain a fair share in the Exports of Indigo Cotton Coffee & Tobacco.

D. H. & J. A. Rucker & Co. A very old West India & Hambro' House. In almost every Crisis they have been looked upon in a most doubtful light, and yet have always stood their ground. They are certainly not thought the most highly of; there can be but little doubt however, that they must possess considerable capital. In the course of the Year their consignments from the West Indies are to a large extent. For many Years they have been large Receivers of Wool from Germany on consignment. The writer does not think them clever men and has observed that they have been generally unfortunate in making bad Debts. Mr D.H.R. used to live most splendidly at Melrose Hall, Wandsworth; but has recently gone to reside at Bath from whence he occasionally comes to Town. There are two other R^s in the House who conduct the Business.

Schmaeck & Co. The only Person known to be in the Firm is Mr S and a most unfortunate Adventurer he has been; Bankrupt in 1819 under the firm of S & Smith who failed again in the Crisis of 1825/26. The Man is well disposed, but has not sufficient Talent to compete with many of the other Houses in exporting Colonial Produce to the Continent.

Suse & Sibeth. Established here for some Years. Considered as great Rivals of all the other Houses and are not at all liked, being very sly and the most determined, pushing Characters than can be met with among the Foreign Merchants. To the Continent they are certainly the most extensive Export House there is. This Establishment has excited much attention of late; about 6 years ago the writer knew them to be very needy and it is generally understood that neither of them could be possessed of Property at the commencement of their Career: and as Indigo is a Money-Article, they must require large Funds to prosecute such a Business. It is conjectured & upon the Enquiries the writer has made he thinks it not improbable, that they have a sleeping Partner in the House – a Mr Westenholtz – who resides at Breslaw and is worth £20,000, the greater part of which is in the Concern, and this, added to their Savings & late years, for they are any thing but expensive Men, may give them a fair Capital. Mr Rothschild is the great Taker of their Paper and there is no doubt that most of the Houses they draw upon are substantial.

Walfords & Green. There is some difference of opinion as to whether there is much Capital in the Concern or not. In the Indigo Market, the Trade think them undoubted, but the Bill Brokers & Bankers on Lombard Street waver in this opinion and think them too much of Gentlemen to compete in the Market with the Industrious and that consequently their profits as Dealers must be limited. The writer has observed of late years that they have been most unfortunate Speculators and must have lost largely.

The book also records, in different handwriting and presumably some years later, the fates of these firms. That of Suse & Sibeth is illegible; Lobeck, Meyer and Rucker all 'failed'; Schmaeck was 'failed &c, poor'; Walfords & Green was 'done'; but the great survivor was Cordes who, fitting his character, left merchanting altogether and 'turned clergyman'.[8]

*

The City of the late 1820s was not a buoyant place. Churchill's year-end report in 1827 catches the prevailing mood: 'In Commerce, almost every one still smarting under the Losses wch the Climax of 1825 had left them – & fearing from the long Continuance of the Swell after the Storm – even now to venture far from Shore'. So it continued. One of the significant side-effects was even greater City scepticism about the benefits of free trade than had been the case in the first half of the 1820s: indeed, the 1825 crisis and its protracted aftermath seemed to many the direct result of the restructuring of the nation's economic system. Anxieties came to a head in the spring of 1829 when George Robinson – MP, merchant, banker, shipowner, future chairman of Lloyd's – spearheaded a campaign over the silk duties, invoking the City's residual dislike of Huskisson. Particularly susceptible to tariff changes, especially on sugar, were the West India merchants, who were in any case in long-term decline. Here there was no more poignant figure than William Manning, for so long that lobby's doughty advocate in the House of Commons and on the Court of the Bank of England. The famous cardinal recalled long afterwards his father's harrowing last years:

> After the peace of 1815, the great incomes of our merchants began to fall. The West Indian commerce suffered first and most. This shook his commercial house, and from 1820 to 1830 he had great cares . . . During those days he was in London most days in the week. When he came down to Combe Bank [an estate near Sevenoaks to where he had moved in 1815 from Totteridge], he was worn and weary. He was fond of fishing, and would stand for hours by the water at Combe Bank. He used to tell me that his chief delight was the perfect quiet after the strain and restlessness of London. We used to ride often together, but his time was too much broken, and his mind too full to allow of conversation on any subjects beyond the commonest . . .
>
> Just after I had taken my degree in the winter of 1830–31 the ruin came. I was with my father in 3 New Bank Buildings . . . I heard him say to one

of the correspondents of the house who came for business that 'the house had suspended payments'. After that all went into bankruptcy, and I went with my father to Guildhall, before a Commissioner in Bankruptcy, and saw him surrender his last possession in the world, his gold watch, chain, and seals, which he laid down on the table. It was returned to him as the custom is. After that I took him away, leaning on my arm. I remember some time before his saying to me with much feeling, 'I have belonged to men with whom bankruptcy was synonymous with death'. It was so to him.

Combe Bank was sold and Manning went into decline, dying in 1835 in Gower Street. He had made mistakes – including the rash purchase of estates in St Kitts without sufficient personal inspection – but overall he had been the victim of circumstances beyond his control.[9]

The 1825 crisis, and ensuing climate of uncertainty and recrimination, also focused attention on the banking system, not least on the Bank of England itself. For so long its directors had been the target of 'Country' abuse; by the 1820s it was the radicals who trained their rhetorical guns on Threadneedle Street. Yet, until very recently, the actual composition of the Bank's directorate has been shrouded in mystery. Walter Bagehot in the 1870s offered a helpful if faintly patronising sketch, in which he emphasised that since 'by old usage, the directors of the Bank of England cannot be themselves by trade bankers', therefore traditionally most of them were merchants, often with time on their hands, granted that 'the life of a man of business who employs only his own capital, and employs it nearly always in the same way, is by no means fully employed'. He did not deny their merits:

> The great respectability of the directors, and the steady attention many of them have always given the business of the Bank, have kept it entirely free from anything dishonourable and discreditable. Steady merchants collected in council are an admirable judge of bills and securities. They always know the questionable standing of dangerous persons; they are quick to note the smallest signs of corrupt transactions; and no sophistry will persuade the best of them out of their good instincts.

But what they had shown themselves to lack over the years, Bagehot believed, was that 'wise apprehensiveness' that was second nature to a trained banker, the tendency to take a pessimistic view of situations as a whole: 'Adventure is the life of commerce, but caution, I had almost said timidity, is the life of banking.'[10]

Bagehot might have developed his historical arguments further, for analysis shows that the directors of the Bank during the second quarter of the century were an undistinguished lot, though with some notable exceptions.[11] A few generalisations may be made: most were indeed merchants, with a particular bias towards the Russia and West India trades; there persisted a tight-knit recruitment pattern from within the traditionally influential City families; a university education was a rarity; and the strict rotation of the governorship was not an inducement to more able, dynamic merchants putting themselves forward for the Court. A particularly acerbic critic of his fellow-directors was George Warde Norman, the son of a timber merchant and a Bank director for many years after he himself took early retirement from business. In his memoirs he recalled Jeremiah Harman as 'ignorant, pompous, prejudiced and overbearing'; William Manning was 'amiable but feeble'; while George Dorrien, governor at the time of the resumption inquiry in 1819, was 'feeble but less amiable'. Norman himself, of undoubted intellectual calibre, had become a director in 1821 at the age of twenty-seven, given the nod by Manning on the recommendation of George Grote senior, even though he was not yet a partner in the family firm.

In the immediate aftermath of the 1825 crisis, with much blame being attached to inadequately capitalised country banks, legislation was passed permitting the establishment of joint-stock banks outside a radius of 65 miles of London, thus ending the Bank of England's monopoly of joint-stock banking. As for the conduct of the Bank itself, widely criticised for having allowed the crisis to reach the proportions it did, public attention now turned away from the question of cash payments and towards the less emotive area of how it could function more effectively, above all in terms of an effectively controlled note issue that in practice would operate as a national currency.[12] The Bank was fortunate at this stage to have someone capable of grasping the intellectual nettle, in the person of John Horsley Palmer, deputy governor from 1828 to 1830 and governor from 1830 to 1833. His origins were impeccably mercantile – he took over from his father the running of a prominent East India house – but unlike most merchants he had a keen interest in monetary questions, theoretical as well as practical. For six years from 1827 he was the key figure at the Bank: first he blocked Huskisson's plan to introduce a limited form of bimetallism, effectively arguing that the Bank already possessed adequate silver bullion; then he evolved his own currency principle, by which note circulation would fluctuate in relation to the Bank's holding of specie, a principle that in effect sought to further the Bank's independence of government; and in 1832 he cogently enunciated this doctrine to the Bank Charter Committee, so that it became known as the 'Palmer rule'. It was at that parliamentary committee, whose purpose was to consider the renewal of the Bank's Charter the following year, that the City's leading figures closed ranks around the Bank. 'It is exceedingly well managed', insisted Samuel Gurney, while Nathan Rothschild echoed the sentiments: 'I feel the management, and I know that it is good'. But perhaps the most striking testimony about the indispensable Bank came from George Grote junior:

> First, the commercial world has accustomed itself to the present routine of the Bank, and looks constantly to the Bank as the great centre of discount, especially in difficult times; next, the Bank is a perfectly well-known place, accessible to those who may not know how or where to find an individual discounter . . . A man can get to the Bank without that special, permanent, and exclusive connexion which he preserves with his own Banker, and which cuts him off from all other Bankers.[13]

The Bank's Charter was duly renewed – but at a price. Henceforth joint-stock banks would be allowed in London itself, though without the power to issue notes.

The new dispensation touched keenly on the City's private bankers, whose heyday was drawing to an end. Bagehot, with some classical phrases, would recall these fortunate creatures:

> He was supposed to represent, and often did represent, a certain union of pecuniary sagacity and educated refinement which was scarcely to be found in any other part of society. In a time when the trading classes were much ruder than they now are, many private bankers possessed a variety of knowledge and a delicacy of attainment which would even now be very rare.

And he explained:

> The calling is hereditary; the credit of the bank descends from father to son: this inherited wealth soon brings inherited refinement. Banking is a watchful, but not a laborious trade. A banker, even in large business, can feel pretty sure that all his transactions are sound, and yet have much spare mind. A certain part of his time, and a considerable part of his thoughts, he can readily devote to other pursuits. And a London banker can also have the most intellectual society in the world if he chooses it. There has probably very rarely ever been so happy a position as that of a London private banker; and never perhaps a happier.[14]

Certainly the calling produced some remarkable men, one of whom, as a shining self-made exception to the hereditary rule, was Lewis Loyd. Although trained originally as a Welsh Unitarian preacher, between the 1790s and the end of the war he transformed a small Manchester bank called John Jones & Co into the leading, City-based private bank known as Jones, Loyd & Co, whose annual profits by the 1820s were at times over £200,000. In 1835 the diarist Charles Greville referred to him as 'the richest Banker in the City, and perhaps the richest man in Europe'. The son of this particular preacher man was Samuel Jones Loyd, for whom the inevitable Anglican education at Eton and Trinity College, Cambridge preceded first a grand tour and then active partnership in the firm from 1821. The young Loyd did well in the shop, kept up a passionate interest in economic matters, and in 1832 was one of the private bankers who gave evidence to the Bank Charter Committee on the thorny question of the day:

> Do you think that any Joint Stock Company can conduct its business with the same degree of caution that a private Banker does? – I think that Joint Stock Banks are deficient in every thing requisite for the conduct of the banking business, except extended responsibility; the banking business requires peculiarly persons attentive to all its details, constantly, daily and hourly watchful of every transaction, much more than mercantile or trading business. It also requires immediate, prompt decisions upon circumstances when they arise, in many cases a decision that does not admit of delay for consultation; it also requires a discretion to be exercised with reference to the special circumstances of each case. Joint Stock Banks being of course obliged to act through agents and not by a principal, and therefore under the restraint of general rules, cannot be guided by so nice a reference to degrees of difference in the character or responsibility of parties . . .[15]

This was hardly consistent with the leisurely picture that Bagehot would later draw, but the implicit moral dimension was impressive enough: private bankers stood or fell by their own decisions; they knew their customers intimately; and to compare them with joint-stock functionaries was, in fine, absurd.

Yet be that as it might, the era was dawning of the City-based joint-stock bank, drawing its capital publicly, answerable to its shareholders, and not based on the traditional, quasi-hereditary system of a private partnership. After a share issue the previous year, the London and Westminster Bank opened in Throgmorton Street for deposit-taking business in March 1834: it had not only a paid-up capital of

£50,000, but a tough-minded, technically adept manager in J. W. Gilbart. It did not receive a cordial welcome. The Bank of England engaged in a protracted legal tussle to try to clip its powers, refused until 1842 to open a drawing account for it, and for a time would not discount bills payable at the London and Westminster. For their part the private banks declined to let the unwanted newcomer use the facilities of the London Clearing House. A typically hostile private banker was George Carr Glyn, an almost exact contemporary of S. J. Loyd. In 1832 he had also given evidence against joint-stock bankers as damning as he could make it – 'I should draw this distinction generally, that you cannot get a Director to do that for his proprietors, which a private banker would do for himself' – and he was soon relishing the difficulties the London and Westminster found itself in. 'Every day confirms the opinion of those who think that private banking is more suited to the peculiar wants of business of this City and consequently the new establishment makes no way', he wrote in February 1835 to a correspondent in Liverpool, adding that 'not one mercantile house of any eminence or large business has opened with it'. Glyn was a first-rate operator conducting a wide-ranging business, but in the end he was blinkered. A couple of years earlier, in the course of the same correspondence, he had referred complacently to 'the risk incurred by those who, not having been bred up to the arts of London business, engage in it under the idea of increased profit'.[16] Business history, alas, teaches the lesson that breeding alone is not enough.

It was not only the banking system that was being reshaped in the decade after the high drama of 1825.[17] The crisis had revealed all too palpably that the Bank of England's resources were not infinite, and the pragmatic response of the London banks was to cease relying on being able to discount bills there and instead to build up their own liquid cash reserves. The question then, faced in time by joint-stock banks as well as private, was how to make the most profitable use of those reserves; and the answer, from soon after 1825, was to put out such balances with the City's bill brokers, in effect as call loans secured on first-class bills. The implications of this were considerable, for the bill brokers in effect became bill dealers, holding their own portfolios of bills and dealing in them as principals. 'The business remained unchanged in character for some years after I became a partner', G. W. Alexander was to recall, 'but gradually it became a deposit business, money being left at call, the rate being $\frac{1}{2}$ per cent below that of the Bank of England. Any bills sold were guaranteed by the broker.'[18] From the point of view of the banks, confidence about these short-term loans took two main forms: that the bill dealer's reputation depended on using only unimpeachable bills as security; and that, should that not be the case, the Bank of England would be willing (on a selective basis from 1830) to discount the bills, in effect acting as lender of last resort to these embryo discount houses and thus ultimately the financial system as a whole. Put another way, the modern London money market was starting to emerge, discount houses now gained the City's acceptance in a way that had not been the case for bill brokers prior to 1825, and the Bank had taken up what would become its permanent position of sometimes recalcitrant long-stop.

The four leading firms to whom the Bank granted this discounting facility in the course of the 1830s were Overend, Gurney & Co (as that house was called from 1827, following the death of Thomas Richardson), Sanderson & Co, Alexanders (where Ann Alexander was gradually taking a back seat), and James Bruce. The dominant figure at Sandersons – a rising force partly on account of its extensive connection with the wholesalers of the Cheapside area – was William Morris. As a young man in 1820 he had come to the City from Worcester; after securing a berth via a distant family connection he became a partner in 1826; seven years later he moved from above the Lombard Street office to the village of Walthamstow, travelling daily to the City by stage coach; and in 1834 his wife gave birth to another William Morris, one who eventually would excoriate everything the City stood for.[19] But without a doubt the leading discount house post-1825 was Overend Gurney, from 1833 based at the corner of Lombard Street and Birchin Lane, or the 'Corner House' as it was invariably called. It was run as a very commercial, unsentimental operation, something that comes out in the response of John Overend in 1828 to the failure of Frys & Co, wholesale tea dealers of 5 St Mildred's Court, related to the Gurneys, and fellow-Quakers:

> They say we have just kept them on until we got out & they call me a great rogue & I tell them I care not what they call me if they do not call me a fool . . . What a fool I should have been after 40 years hard labour to have lost all my property & that of my Partners & have our house ruined to prop such a rotten concern, then I might have been called a fool indeed . . .

The firm profited greatly from the new banking strategy, and by November 1830 it was being reported that Overend Gurney 'owe £500,000 in Lombard Street at $2\frac{1}{2}$ per cent on good bills lodged'.

Moreover, it continued to build up its traditional business with the country banks, as reflected in an 1832 letter from the private bank Curries & Co to the Hull bank for which it acted as City correspondent:

> You will receive in this cover a letter from Messrs Overend Gurney & Co which will no doubt fully explain the terms upon which they will supply you with cash. I saw Mr Gurney on Saturday & he then proposed that you should send all your bills to him, which he engaged to discount at the market rate. I promised to give him the refusal of them. This I think perfectly fair & the best arrangement for you as you may depend at all times upon having your bills discounted at a fair rate & we are perfectly satisfied with the arrangement.

Judgement was all, and in 1842 one of the partners of Overend Gurney put down on paper the following summarising dictum: 'The one cardinal point for the employment of money to be repaid to the Public at call (especially in our scale of figures) is to have nothing fluctuating in value, nothing of a lock-up character, and if possible nothing insecure, and these have been our governing principles for many years past . . .'[20]

The author of those timeless criteria may well have been Samuel Gurney, for many years the leading bill broker. A financial journalist described him soon afterwards:

> Mr Gurney, who is a portly and robust man, must be 60 years old; but he possesses a hale and hearty constitution. He dresses strictly in the garb of the sect to which he belongs; and his dark brown, strait-collar cut coat, with a white broad-brim of beaver, make him almost a caricature of the Rev Sydney Smith's Pennsylvanian debtors . . . To the poor he is extremely munificent; and the cottagers in the neighbourhood of West Ham, where he resides, bear testimony to his worth and kindness.

He lived at Ham House in Upton, where he was an almost Dr Dolittle figure, one of his daughters recalling how before breakfast 'he used to take us about, the animals clustering round – the very tame kangaroos and peacocks, the dogs, as well as the horses and cows'. Then it was off to Lombard Street, where he tried his best to apply his Quaker principles. The story goes that on one occasion, after a large forgery upon the firm had been discovered, he said to the trembling culprit: 'By the law we must hang thee – but we will not do that; so, be off to the Continent, and beware of ever returning'. He was in the habit of referring every business event to the overruling providence of God, while he was as little depressed by loss as he was elated by gain. A rare surviving letter, to his brother in April 1825, conveys the inner man:

> I may fairly acknowledge I have been too much occupied in my worldly pursuits, and, what is worse, I do not at present see my way clear out of them. I mourn over this at times, but perhaps there is ground for hope that relief may come.
> A Lombard Street business, especially our own, is so very engrossing, and does in reality require such unremitting attention, that escape is not easy . . .

Perhaps the last word on Sam Gurney should go to the portrait painter George Richmond, who used to say that the face was a most extraordinary mixture of shrewdness and benevolence: each, in Gurney's case, demanded the other.[21]

*

Between the eminent bill broker and Nathan Rothschild there prevailed healthy mutual respect, and in 1824 Gurney was one of the backers of the Alliance Assurance. Sometimes, as Gurney's firm indicated three years later to the Norwich Bank, it was a respect born out of necessity:

> In reply to your note respecting the Rothschild's long bills remitted at $2\frac{1}{2}$ p Cent, we have to inform you that we took them of him exactly at that price. We have remonstrated against his sending bills of the description at such a price . . . There is such anxiety to get his bills which makes him so difficult to deal with that we are obliged to put up with much that is very unpleasant, or we should lose his connection . . .

Rothschild for another decade after 1825 remained the indispensable man, always on the lookout for appropriate new business: in the first half of the 1830s he acquired a monopoly of the Spanish quicksilver industry and arranged loans for (among others) Belgium, Greece and Portugal as well as the West India planters requiring compensation after the abolition of slavery in the colonies. 'The influence of Mr Rothschild is so great, that if much money should be wanted for any operations in which he is deeply engaged, there will be but little chance for other speculators to obtain the requisite accommodation', commented in 1835 the *Circular to Bankers*, the well-informed City organ

of the country bankers and no friend of Rothschild. That same year
Thomas Raikes, diarist brother of a recent governor of the Bank, paid
due tribute to Nathan and his brothers:

> The Rothschilds have become the metallic sovereigns of Europe. From
> their different establishments in Paris, London, Vienna, Frankfurt and
> Naples, they have obtained a control over the European exchanges which
> no party ever before could accomplish, and they now seem to hold the
> strings of the public purse. No sovereign without their assistance now
> could raise a loan.

Nathan himself to the Bank Charter Committee denied that either he
or the Bank could control the exchanges – 'all transactions, in India, in
China, in Germany, in Russia, and in the whole world, are all guided
here and settled through this country, so that it is not possible to guide
the Exchanges for so long as two or three months' – but contemporaries were fascinated by the great man in action on the Royal Exchange, as he dealt with other 'exchange-brokers' in all manner of
foreign bills, these bills being given in payment for goods shipped from
London.[22] The rates of exchange would fall when there were few takers
of bills to be found, rise when there were many.

One day, in November 1833, the smooth order of business was
rudely interrupted:

> A very curious scene occurred in the Royal Exchange this afternoon, at
> about four o'clock, which is considered the full-change hour. Mr Roths-
> child usually takes his station every Tuesday and Friday, with his back
> leaning against one of the pillars of the building at the south-east corner,
> in order to conduct his extensive transactions in the Foreign Exchanges,
> of which he is the great regulator. A person named Rose, perfectly
> unconnected with such business, thought proper to dispute Mr Roths-
> child's right to the particular spot. The latter gentleman remonstrated
> with Mr Rose, and explained to him courteously that it would be a great
> convenience to him not to be deprived of his customary post, whither the
> numerous brokers crowd in shoals to receive the offers of the great
> capitalist. Other persons interfered in order to induce the objectionable
> individual to retire. The Exchange porters also made their appearance,
> but all failed in their attempt, Mr Rose setting them at defiance, and fairly
> drove Mr Rothschild to the benches in the rear, where he sat down in a
> state of much excitement, and it was not until some time afterwards that
> he was able so far to compose himself as to conclude his negociations
> with the brokers.
> This affair created a very strong sensation for nearly half an hour, and
> the south east corner of the Exchange was greatly crowded during the

whole time. Annoyances of a similar description have repeatedly of late been offered to Mr Rothschild . . .

They seem to have stopped, for two years later an American traveller witnessed him in action at his familiar post: 'The persons crowding round him, were presenting bills of exchange. He would glance for a moment at a paper, return it, and with an affirmatory nod, turn to the next individual pressing forward for an audience'.[23]

Yet there remained, in society at large as well as in the City, a powerful undertow of prejudice against him, caught in Macaulay's description of a formal evening in 1831 at 'the Jew's': 'I did not see one Peer, or one star, except a foreign order or two, which I generally consider as an intimation to look to my pockets'. The attitude of politicians varied greatly: Huskisson was paranoid, Wellington was unashamedly dependent, and Althorp when he became Chancellor in 1830 'boasted of ordering his door to be shut against Rothschild'. Nathan himself could take or leave them, as Mrs Arbuthnot recorded in 1828: 'I asked him what was thought of the Duke in the City. He said they had unbounded confidence in him. I asked what they thought of Mr Peel, and he said they did not think about him at all.' Like most City people he probably assumed that politicians overrated their own importance, important though the course of politics could be to the City. Ultimately it was money, not legislation, that made the world go round. And in the context of a minor spat in 1830 between government and Rothschilds, it was a salutary lesson taught to Althorp by the Governor of the Bank, Horsley Palmer: 'Of this I am sure, that Mr Rothschild never drew a Bill without his receiving in one way or another ample remuneration, and the probability is, that what Government saved in Agency, they fully lost in the exchange'.[24]

And Barings? After its spell in the semi-doldrums, that still prestigious house was now fully restored by the distinctly unpatrician figure of Joshua Bates, who at Alexander Baring's instigation became a partner in 1828 and was for the next three and a half decades the dominant day-to-day presence at 8 Bishopsgate. Bates came from Boston and, entering his forties, already possessed wide mercantile experience in Europe and America. Above all he had the appropriate personal qualities for the job. A handful of contemporary estimates suggest something of the man. No one knew him better than the firm's American agent Thomas Ward, and after a visit by Bates he noted in his diary how he did not 'look very far ahead, nor understand general principles clearly', but had 'great nerve, and self possession and self confidence'.

On another occasion he wrote directly to Bates: 'You are the most uniformly laborious man I know'. Ward's son also got to know him, and in 1836 wrote to his father: 'I never saw a more busy, calm and dry man than Joshua Bates . . . His tone was dry, his words few.' Finally, there was the verdict of a compatriot who called on him in London: 'The man was illiterate and ignorant but possessed a strong mind and much business ability.'[25]

It is through his diary that one really begins to understand Joshua Bates. An entry at the end of 1832 evokes the dour underlying puritanism with which he sought to run Barings:

> Having been generally successful in business, we have become too free and open in our conduct and have incurred risks that it will not be wise to repeat. A system of secrecy should be encouraged in our office and none but clever persons admitted into the office. A rigid economy should also be enforced as much as in less prosperous times, avoid all pride & ostentation & unnecessary show.

Just occasionally, though, he could tire, as some two years later:

> I continue to suffer from headache & feel at times as tho I should drop to the earth. I hope my life may be spared for a while longer that I may retire from business and devote myself to the improvement of the moral condition of my fellow creatures.

But how to put these noble aspirations into practice? Even acts of charity could be a problem, as his entry on Christmas Day 1831 reflects:

> The operations of the past year have been generally successful and we have every reason to be thankful for the numerous blessings we enjoy, amongst them that of having it in our power to relieve those who are in distress. It is however one of the great inconveniences of London that you have no knowledge of those around you and feel an uncertainty whether you are giving to deserving persons or not.[26]

But Bates could not do without London, the stage for his operations, the place where he conducted his manifold business. With the ill-disguised pride of an adopted son he told a parliamentary committee in 1833: 'There is no place in Europe where such an assortment of goods can be collected together . . . Any person wishing to begin an operation to a distant country must, I think, begin it here.'[27]

Under the watchful direction of Bates, and serviced by some forty clerks who dealt with up to 200 letters a day, Barings by the mid-1830s was engaged in an extraordinarily wide range of transactions.[28] The staple acceptance business, in effect lending credit on commission, enabled a host of correspondents in Europe, America and the Far East to use bills on Barings and to facilitate the transport of raw materials and manufactured goods; while the firm itself not only bought and sold merchandise, securities, specie, bullion and bills of exchange for account of its many international trading clients, but also provided the credit for exchange accounts, received remittances and made collections and payments for those who required such services, and negotiated insurance and assembled passengers and freights on behalf of shipowners. The firm also acted on its own account – dealing in merchandise, specie, securities or whatever came to hand – and by 1834 had even become shipowners. For Barings, in contrast to Rothschilds, almost anything was fair game, provided there was sufficient certainty attached to it. That indeed was the crucial consideration, and comes out most clearly in the well-ordered approach that Bates, in tandem with the excellent Ward, adopted to the key question of the granting of credits. The golden rule, in Bates's words, was not to forget that 'by being too liberal we lose our money and not being sufficiently liberal we lose our business', and therefore 'the middle course is the one it should be our aim to follow'. What this meant in practice was trying to know as much as possible about the individual houses requiring credit, with credit ratings based as much as anything on personal assessments of prudence and honesty, and never granting credits that exceeded a firm's total capital. Bates was also adamant that if a correspondent required credit from Barings, then it was a condition of supplying it that the correspondent should not also seek credit from anywhere else. 'It should always be a condition of granting credits', he wrote in 1832, 'that the parties keep their account entirely with us.'

Control, above all quality control, also permeated the area of choosing and marketing securities, which were at this time usually American and with a bias towards states rather than corporate or municipal issues. 'It has been our invariable practice not to offer any stock which we did not ourselves deem good' was the guiding principle, enunciated to Ward some years later. The marketing of the $7m Louisiana loan of 1832 stands out, and prompted an interesting letter from Bates to Ward:

> We shall all make money, and pretty easily too. At one time . . . Rothschild gave out that he should take the loan. When he found out we had

got it he said he hoped we would give him a part of it. We told him we would gladly do so at the same price that we gave it to the public, which he declined.[29]

There was no doubting the profitability of the business as a whole: £98,000 in 1832 and £119,000 in 1833, with the volume of acceptances outstanding by the end of that latter year running at £2.3m. But had the firm expanded too far, too fast? John Macvicar, a London correspondent of Jardine Matheson, was a warm admirer of Barings, writing in November 1832 that 'nothing can be higher than the Credit they enjoy'; but by the following spring he was reporting a certain City scepticism:

> Baring Bros are extending themselves greatly as a commercial house – their Credit is beyond any question of doubt – but some people say, they don't like their extending their business to such a great length as they are doing – the amount of their engagements of one kind and another must be enormous. In the money market here their Bills are as current as Bank of Eng[d] paper . . .[30]

But the City did not yet properly know the Bostonian in its midst.

For all his innate caution, one episode revealed that Bates was as capable as the next merchant of taking a punt. 'I find myself on a speculation in Tallow . . . We think it as well to make sure of the control of the market by buying, and our Stock will now be including Mr Scheer's . . . We shall see what all this will come to', wrote a slightly apprehensive Bates in December 1830. The 'we' referred to Stieglitz & Co of St Petersburg as well as Barings. Tallow of course was a commodity with a rich speculative history, and with distemper raging among Russian cattle it seemed a fine stroke to attempt to corner the market in anticipation of rising prices. This, however, involved the purchase of such prodigious quantities of casks of the stuff that by early in 1831 Bates faced not only concerted attempts in the market to depress prices but also Radical attacks on his firm inside and outside Parliament. Nor was he made more comfortable by rumours of the imminent removal of the duty on candles. Late in March he received a strong letter from Frederick Scheer, the Russia merchant of 69 Old Broad Street with whom at the London end he had been conducting the tallow operation since the previous summer. After expressing his dissatisfaction should Bates's 'tallow speculation remain in its present stagnant state', Scheer went on:

> The Season has advanced too far, and we shall hardly be justified in leaving so important a business much longer to chance; and besides the

loss of money, which appears not impossible, a failure of this operation would more or less injure us all in the public estimation, and want of success in one instance leads but too often to defeat in future speculations . . .

Now, dear Sir, tho' you may differ from me in the opinion, which I have given more than once, yet the matter is of too much consequence to hesitate in stating again what I think my duty on this occasion to say. I feel perfectly certain, that if you attempt sales yourself that you will not succeed; that you will be betrayed intentionally as well as accidentally . . . Your many other occupations, the waiting of brokers, their watching each other, and many other circumstances constantly discover your transactions.

Bates seems to have taken the point, letting Scheer dispose gradually of the tallow holdings through the course of the year, almost certainly at a loss. And as he noted in his journal that Christmas, one clear moral had emerged from the whole sorry episode: 'It should be a warning never to embark in any operation of magnitude to attract universal attention'.[31]

*

It was not only tallow that gave Bates sleepless nights in 1831, for this was also the year of the Reform Bill and all the feverish excitement attached to it. 'It is impossible to describe, in adequate terms, the degree of interest felt by all classes in the City, as to the propositions which are to be brought forward by Ministers. On the Royal Exchange, scarcely any other topic meets with any attention.' Thus the *Morning Chronicle* in February. There ensued over the rest of the year a round of meetings, petitions and so on, generally in favour of reform, befitting the fact that since 1818 the City's parliamentary allegiance had been almost wholly Whig. Yet in the reform crisis itself, there is little evidence that *haute finance* – as opposed to the ranks of City shopkeepers who looked to the liverymen for political leadership – felt any enthusiasm for political democracy. Nathan Rothschild throughout maintained the closest relations with the obdurate Wellington; Alexander Baring (recently retired from business but still a significant City figure) actually moved over to the Tories, declaring that 'liberty for all' was his goal; and Joshua Bates confided to his diary in August that 'the reform bill will cause great uneasiness as to the value of property & if it pass there is no calculating its consequences'. Particularly revealing was the experience of George Grote, who now emerged as the City's

leading pro-reform spokesman. In October, after the Lords had rejected the bill, he organised a protest meeting of merchants, bankers
and traders at Mansion House, and for his pains was roundly criticised over his apparently timid handling of it by the radical tailor
Francis Place. The loyal Harriet would have none of it, replying
indignantly to Place:

> If those Bankers & traders were to be got together *at all*, you must
> adapt your style to their stomachs. To have spoken truth w^d have com-
> pletely severed Grote from them for ever & aye . . . Depend upon it if you
> heard all that I c^d tell you about that meeting & its preliminaries you'd
> say G was quite in the right to do as he did. Poor fellow it was a labour
> indeed to him to get them assembled & to utter what was put into their
> mouths.

She later recorded in her biography of Grote that 'he not unfrequently
avowed that the apathy, not to say aversion to Reform, on the part of
the City magnates, was unmistakeable'.[32]

To a degree the Whig government managed to tone down that
aversion when it presented a revised bill in December 1831. Bates
expressed the feelings of a propertied practical man:

> The reform bill will pass in some shape or other and thus the tranquill-
> ity of the nation will be secure which will be a great point. The new bill
> appears to me to be very different from the old one. The requiring of the
> £10 Electors to give proof of having paid assessed Taxes and poor rates
> appears to me equivalent to raising the qualification to £15, which will
> exclude all the worthless in the community.

There was one intense drama to come. These were the 'May days'
when King and Lords refused to back down, Grey resigned, and
Wellington attempted to form a ministry. The *Circular to Bankers*
accurately gauged opinion:

> On the first announcement of the Resignation of Ministers being ac-
> cepted, the feeling which we think prevailed most in the money-circles of
> the City, was one of exultation at the change . . . There was an obvious
> change in this feeling, however, on the succeeding day; and this change
> has made progress towards augmented doubt and apprehension.

Nothing augments doubt and apprehension more than a run on a
bank, especially if it is the Bank of England, and Place carried the day
with his famous placard (explicitly disavowed by Grote) 'To Stop the

Duke, Go for Gold'. As the City's leading bankers and others reluctantly yielded to the dictates of common sense over gut prejudice, Rothschild inevitably took the decisive initiative. He did his best to prop up
the Funds, but after a few days was compelled to report to Wellington,
through the person of Arbuthnot, 'that among the monied men there is
an alarm lest there should be such an opposition to all Reform as
would cause commotions . . .' With Rothschild's rider being that Wellington must grant some measure of reform, the Duke preferred to let
Grey do the work and so the Whig ministry was reinstated. Even then
some regret lingered. 'The power of the King & Lords appears to be
gone', Bates noted later in the month, 'and the only chance for good
gov' lies in the hope that people will find more profit in attending to
their business than to politics'. No one was more bitter at the apparent
supineness of the City than the King. In November 1832 Sir Peter
Laurie was about to become Lord Mayor and naturally hoped that
William IV would attend his banquet; but as he recorded in his diary,
'I was much mortified to find that the King had told Lord Melbourne
that he considered the opening of London Bridge a visit to the City and
would not come again'.[33] Sailor Billy had opened the rebuilt bridge in
August the previous year, but clearly that was enough for one reign.

The City's own pillar of the *ancien régime* was also about to crumble,
although, as Maria Edgeworth discovered in 1831, the arrogance of
Leadenhall Street remained undimmed: 'A superb mock majesty man
in scarlet cloak and cocked hat bedizened with gold motioned our
carriage away. "Coachman! drive on – no carriage can stand ever
before the India-house".' The writing had been on the wall for a long
time, even before 1813, but from the late 1820s the focus sharpened.
In 1828 Wellington's Cabinet discussed the East India Company, and
Lord Ellenborough, responsible for Indian affairs, paraphrased in his
diary the views he expressed: 'All, but the East India Company, were
opposed to the China monopoly, because all suffered by it. It was in
fact a mode of enabling the Company to govern India by a tax levied
on a necessary of life in England.' The necessary was of course tea, and
two years later the question returned to Ellenborough's attention:

> The Company have got into an awkward scrape. It seems that they have
> not made out their account of the prime cost of their tea as merchants do,
> that they have charged all losses whether from fixed rate of exchange or
> other causes, whereas merchants in general state prime cost on a calcula-
> tion of the price in the place where the article is purchased, the other
> calculations going in diminution of profit.

I begin to think that the maintenance of the monopoly will be impossible. I have long thought it very inexpedient. It would leave a sullen, settled feeling of discontent in the minds of the manufacturers and merchants of England.

The Duke himself read the evidence and declared that the monopoly could no longer be maintained. The Whigs eventually abolished it in 1833, in theory throwing open the Cantonese tea trade, and in October 1834 there took place the City's first sale of 'free trade teas'. Yet for several years the playing field of the London tea market remained distinctly unlevel, as the East India Company retained control of the Canton exchange until the end of the decade and the long-established tea brokers fought hard to prevent new entrants. By April 1835, Bates was complaining of the tea trade being in 'a very confused state', while soon afterwards James Matheson, on a visit to London, wrote back in some disenchantment to his partner in Hong Kong:

My deliberate opinion is, Jardine, that the Tea Market cannot mend . . . When I see the business still in the hands of only the few brokers who are wedded to the old Company system, and who are seeking to bolster up prices by perpetual recurrence to artificial arrangements, I cannot help having misgivings. Leave markets to take care of themselves is my motto.

The unsettled state of the market was also due to uncertainty about the government's intentions over a new rate of duty; Matheson had just been part of a fairly fruitless mercantile deputation to Lord Melbourne, with Horsley Palmer as spokesman. 'Going to the Prime Minister', he added to Jardine, 'is very much like going to the City Gate at Canton. We wait in the street, not his door, until he is disengaged.'[34]

Matheson should not have been surprised at the City's inherent conservatism, which was typified in the post-1815 years by the sluggish custom given to the splendid new London Commercial Sale Rooms in Mincing Lane; the overwhelming preference remained for continuing to hold sales either in coffee houses (above all Garraways's, often by candle light) or in the rooms of the brokers themselves. By the mid-1830s the pattern began to change and by the end of the decade some twenty sales by auction were being held daily at the LCSR. To look at the pages of the *Public Ledger* in 1834 and take a week at random, the first in September, is to catch a system on the cusp of change. Among the prospective sales advertised was one by James Vanhouse & Sons, brokers, at 37 Mincing Lane; the items on offer were 50 casks of plantation coffee, 20 casks of Cuba coffee, 35 bags of Grenada cocoa,

150 bags of pimento, 60 casks of Jamaica ginger, 50 boxes of West India arrowroot and 5 casks of Bermuda arrowroot. Tucker, Son & Co, brokers of 39 Lime Street, preferred to hold its sale at Garraway's in Cornhill: 9 chests of tortoiseshell, 1 ton of ivory, 'A Quantity of Horn Tips', 247 pieces of red wood, 61 casks of 'China M-o'-P Shells' and 40,000 bamboo canes were the attraction. If one wanted skins – whether 65,000 of raccoon or 52,000 of mink or a mere 10,200 of chinchilla – it was necessary to go to the LCSR on Monday, Tuesday or Thursday. Brokers for that sale were Wm. & Geo. Goad of 48 Mark Lane, a firm soon afterwards restyled W. T. Goad & Rigg and for many years content to fill one of the City's innumerable profitable niches.[35]

It was a niche that many on the Stock Exchange might have envied towards the end of May 1835, as in the context of war Spanish stock fell in one week from 72 to 50. The 'Spanish panic' seriously affected at least half the membership. It was memorialised by a contemporary account that transcends journalism and explores the collective psychology of a market under the severest pressure:

> The ruin was so comprehensive, both in its actual and probable results, that scarcely an individual could be found whom it did not reach, or fearfully threaten. There was, consequently, one common sense of danger, requiring united and simultaneous efforts to grapple with it; but which, from its very universality, paralysed and stupified all, none being sufficiently remote from the calamity, to be able to consult for the safety of those who were drifting into its vortex. It was as if a mine had been suddenly sprung beneath their feet; and the affrighted sufferers were running to and fro, calling for aid, but unable to render any . . .
>
> As the tide of devastation rolled on, there were daily and hourly increasing manifestations of its destructive progress. Haggard countenances and oppressed hearts began to show themselves, with the languor and morbid irritability produced by nights of sleepless anxiety. The dismay at what was approaching became stronger and more general; none could wholly resist the infection; distrust insinuated itself into every mind, and there prevailed a suspicious watching of each man's words for hidden meanings and intentions, lest unworthily bestowed confidence, or a too credulous reliance upon appearances, should aggravate circumstances already sufficiently afflicting . . .
>
> It was painful to witness the inroads which this state of suffering was making upon the habits and feelings of individuals. The usual hour for closing the business of the day was no longer a signal for returning home. Home had ceased to be the source of those serene delights, the expectations of which sustains a man through the toils he undergoes. Alas! what is home to him, who carries thither a vulture-secret gnawing at his heart, which it is mercy to keep from others while he can, but to do which, he

must deceive those whom he has never yet deceived. Is that a home, to which its master knows he is the messenger of sorrow, if his tongue speak the tidings that are upon it?[36]

The author of this feeling narrative was William Heseltine, one of the principal jobbers in Spanish stock. Like many members he defaulted at the end of May, but in July managed to secure his readmission to the Stock Exchange. Things would probably have been even worse but for an emergency whip-round in the City. Writing to the Bank of Liverpool on 28 May, George Carr Glyn noted that 'the exertions which have been made (in which we have felt it a duty to contribute to the utmost with prudence) will I trust prevent much further mischief'. Joshua Bates meanwhile could not resist drawing a moral on the Stock Exchange's behalf: 'I hope they will take a lesson from Experience and never carry their Speculations so far again. My House has nothing to do with it – we have never touched Spanish or any of the speculative stocks, and never intend to do so'. The inhabitants of Capel Court paid little or no attention to such austere moralisers. Soon afterwards, as if to prove the point, there appeared in *The Pickwick Papers* the debonair stockbroker Wilkins Flasher and his associate: 'Both gentlemen had very open waistcoats and very rolling collars, and very small boots and very big rings, and very little watches and very large guard chains, and symmetrical inexpressibles and scented pocket handkerchiefs'.[37]

Were Flasher and friend interested in events nearer to home than the Iberian Peninsular? Conventional wisdom would suggest not. Undoubtedly it is true that through most of the nineteenth century British industry had, in a direct sense, relatively little to do with the City; it preferred to rely on a mixture of self-finance and local finance in order to raise long-term capital. Instinctively, and not without reason, provincial industrialists tended to regard the City as a remote, rather baffling place where they would surrender control and probably be charged heavily for the privilege. The Stock Exchange for its part concentrated heavily on government stocks, whether home or foreign. An analysis of the stockbroking business of Marjoribanks, Capel & Co in 1830 reveals that hardly any transactions at all were done in British non-government issues. Inevitably this orientation led to charges of ignorance as well as indifference. Thus the *Circular to Bankers* in October 1829, shortly before the appearance of Captain Swing:

It is now greatly in fashion, amongst the frequenters of the Stock-Exchange, and those who participate in their feelings, to boast of a general improvement. There is no improvement yet, which affects the whole community; nor, essentially, any particular parts of it: while distress is increasing, rapidly, amongst persons engaged in agriculture.

It is perhaps typical that David Ricardo apparently never visited either the industrial Midlands or the North. Yet one should resist the temptation to caricature. Bates, for instance, made a fact-finding tour of Liverpool, Manchester, Birmingham, Leeds and Sheffield in 1833. A surviving price list of the stockbrokers Foster & Janson (forerunners of Foster & Braithwaite) for the same year shows that active securities included a wide range of British canals, docks, waterworks, and gas-light and coke companies, mostly the survivors of the 1824–5 boom. In general, not only was the City's textile quarter intimately involved with the rest of the country, but the London money market continued to act as effective conduit of short-term funds between the rural and manufacturing districts. Nor were all the Bank of England directors of the 1830s remote from industry: in particular, several had close links with metal and mining. To take a figure like William Thompson – MP for the City, director of the Bank and chairman of Lloyd's, but also leading ironmaster in South Wales – is to dispel simplistic notions of the City as an offshore island.[38]

Railways were a great case in point of City involvement that was crucial but not always beneficial. In the 1820s the pioneer Stockton and Darlington Railway borrowed heavily from Richardson, Overend & Co; in 1833 the first London meeting of the Great Western Railway took place at the fine old Jacobean house in Lime Street then occupied by the firm of Antony Gibbs, with the firm's head, George Henry Gibbs, becoming a director and a loyal supporter of Brunel; in the same year George Carr Glyn joined the London board of the projected London to Birmingham railway (eventually the London and North Western), becoming chairman four years later. Then in 1835 came the City's first railway boom, as the number of officially listed companies (twenty-one in July 1835) almost trebled in the next twelve months. 'The whole active interest of the Stock Exchange have lately directed their almost exclusive attention to Shares in Railways', noted the *Circular to Bankers* by February 1836, adding that 'the operations and purchases in them have been greatly accentuated by orders from the country, but especially from Lancashire'. What is significant, though, is the extent of misgivings felt by those most closely concerned with the new railways, or at least the respectable, non-speculative ones. 'I have done everything to stop the gambling in our shares not to the satisfaction of the Stock Exchange here or of the share brokers elsewhere',

Glyn himself wrote in October 1835. But even though the line was not yet built, he was unable to restrain extreme bullishness in the Birmingham shares, a phenomenon analysed the following February by George Gibbs, the cousin of George Henry, senior partner of the merchants Gibbs Son & Bright of Bristol and Liverpool, and himself until recently on the GWR board:

> The advance in these shares has been at least £55 in the last twelve months and yet for my life I cannot discover one fact bearing upon their value on which any rise can reasonably be built, that was not as well known before it commenced as it is now, with one single, and that to my mind alarming, exception – the patronage of the Stock Exchange.

Bates of course condemned the boom out of hand – 'there is at present great madness abroad in regard to rail roads . . . it is going too fast & will inevitably lead to disastrous results' – but for the Stock Exchange itself there was a greater good, even after the boom collapsed in 1837. This was the creation of a major and permanent market in non-government securities, sustained over the years by the high volume of shares issued by the railway companies, thereby ensuring ready marketability. 'Home Rails', in short, was set to become a feature of City life.[39]

In the mid-1830s, though, the main buzz came from across the Atlantic. Partly it was a case of London firms like Barings acting as intermediaries in the private placing of American securities; but essentially it was a question of American trade and its financing, with a particular emphasis on the cotton boom then being enjoyed by the southern states. No house exploited the opportunity more effectively than Barings, who seemed to hold all the aces: no shortage of capital; the capacious knowledge combined with fine judgement of Bates in tandem with Ward; and a Liverpool office, opened in 1832, that did most of the actual importing and exporting. It was an opportunity that for the most part Liverpool's own merchants failed to take, lacking the requisite financial and banking resources; the major exception, William & James Brown & Co, was the Liverpool branch of an American merchant house. It was in London that new rivals to Barings in the financing of American trade now emerged. There was no doubting the commercial possibilities, as one experienced merchant explained to a parliamentary committee in 1833:

> It is easy for a man without capital, but with good character and conduct, to embark largely in business in the American trade? – I think there never was a time when he could do it with more facility than now . . .

Is English or American capital employed in that trade generally? – London credit is employed to a very great extent; London credits are now used to a much greater extent in carrying on all commercial transactions than at any former period.

Then, in your opinion, the commercial transactions all over the world are to a greater degree settled in London upon credit than at any former period? – I think so. The foreign banking business of London appears to be much on the increase.

The testifying merchant, now turning himself into a 'foreign banker', was Timothy Wiggin, an American who earlier in his career had made a fortune in textiles in Manchester before coming out of retirement in 1825 to take over the London business of the failed American merchant Samuel Williams. By the mid-1830s, based at 7 Tokenhouse Yard, he was flourishing more than ever before. 'If I had to choose between Baring Bros and him', Macvicar even declared in 1833 to Jardine Matheson, 'I should under all circumstances give him the preference'. Timothy Wiggin & Co, however, was but one of the 'three Ws', a trio of Anglo-American houses now seeking to gain market share in the financing of transatlantic trade. The other two were Thomas Wilson & Co and George Wildes & Co, and of the latter firm Overend Gurney wrote in 1834 that 'we are always informed that their connections are very respectable which gives us great confidence in their acceptances'. By the beginning of 1836 there was one other major contender, Morrison Cryder & Co. Morrison was James Morrison, the immensely wealthy textile merchant, Cryder was John Cryder, an American merchant introduced to Morrison by Sam Gurney; and together their ambitions were such that from the start the City's jocular nickname for the new house was 'Over-Baring'.[40]

However, even Morrison, one of the shrewdest businessmen of the age, underestimated the dangers involved. Three were paramount: dependence on the continuing buoyancy of American trade; the problem in the pre-telegraph era of granting acceptance credits to traders beyond the realm of personal knowledge; and the increasing tendency of London houses to grant 'open credits', in other words accepting bills of exchange unsecured by invoices or bills of lading, a tendency that could not but produce undue speculation in the American trade itself.[41] All three were dangers that Joshua Bates zealously guarded against, and in February 1836 his diary contained a key entry:

Had long conversations with Thos Baring, Mildmay, John B in regard to the proper mode of conducting our business & we come to the

conclusion that the present system of credits is one of extreme hazard, &
that we should use great caution – not to keep goods on hand but to sell
as fast as consignments arrive, & to cultivate our rich correspondents
while we throw off the doubtful.

Five months later Glyn was reporting the Bank of England as getting
'very fidgetty' about 'the American houses'.[42]

One house anyway should have reassured the Old Lady. Bates indeed
felt moved to record on 25 July 1836:

> Commerce seems prosperous & the comfort of mankind more general
> than at any former period during the memory of man or than has been
> recorded in History. Emigration seems the natural cure for excessive
> population in old countries & if Peace continues there is no counting the
> increased wealth of this Country. Religion and Temperance seem to be on
> the increase also. Thank God for all these . . .

On that same day Lionel de Rothschild in Frankfurt wrote to his
brother in London: 'Yesterday evening he was in danger, but today is a
little better. He has this instant called me to tell you re Exchequer Bills,
&c'. The patient was Lionel's father, taken ill several weeks earlier
while in Frankfurt to attend Lionel's wedding. Three days later, on 28
July, Nathan Rothschild died at the age of fifty-nine. For a week
afterwards the City was bombarded by rumours and contradictory
reports – of his death, of his miraculous recovery – but at last (the story
goes) a pigeon was picked up on the south coast, bearing the words 'il
est mort.' And on 6 August there was published what became a famous
lithograph, 'The Shadow of a Great Man', showing a silhouette of
Nathan standing in front of his favourite pillar on the Royal Exchange.
Among the many tributes paid, one of the most telling was by the
Circular to Bankers:

> He had a clear and comprehensive view of weighty matters of business,
> a strong and unfettered will, a promptitude of decision, and a punctuality
> in execution unexampled, in their combination. To this were superadded
> a confidence in the success in any thing he undertook, a pride of temper
> resulting from his high new position which made him bear down at any
> personal risk all opposition, and a dexterity in working the unseen
> machinery requisite to his operations, that rendered his brief and brilliant
> career so remarkable.

On Monday the 8th a funeral procession of seventy-five carriages left
St Swithin's Lane, and such were the crowds that it took over a quarter

of an hour to pass through Cornhill, on its way to the Jews' burial ground in Whitechapel Road. Present at the interment was William Heseltine, who two days later published from the Stock Exchange his *Reflections at the Grave of N. M. Rothschild, Esq.* Most were to the effect that a shroud has no pockets, but one verse has a more satisfying roundness, last words from one City man to another:

> Upon thy struggling path of life
>   Strong lights and shades were cast,
> Which led through toil, suspense, and strife
>   To triumph at the last!
> In the continued conflict then,
> With selfish, artful, flattering men
>   Through which thy spirit pass'd
> What wonder though some stains of earth
> *Were* blended with thine inward worth![43]

CHAPTER EIGHT

No Luck About the House

The recently ennobled Lord Ashburton (the former Alexander Baring) was still by September 1836 offering words of instruction to his old partners: 'The variations of all stocks & their wild fluctuations seem to arise much from Nathan's death. In the end the emancipation of the money market will be a benefit, but the sudden cessation of a despotic rule is apt to exhibit such symptoms.' In fact, for reasons wholly unconnected with Rothschild's death and instead everything to do with the rapid and alarming downturn of the American economy, the City's latest round of monetary disturbances was only just beginning. The Bank's immediate response was to take ostentatious disciplinary action against all the leading firms engaged in American trade and finance, including even Barings. Bates was not amused: 'The Bank of England has been playing some shabby tricks. Refused to discount the Paper of seven Houses . . . This made it necessary for us to offer to discount our own acceptances.' The manoeuvre lasted only a few weeks, but in October the Governor, James Pattison, called in partners of each firm and formally told them that 'the extensive Credits hitherto given to the Bankers of the United States and others, either as open Credits or in anticipation of the Sale of States Securities in this Country, are objec-tionable so far as the Bank of England is concerned . . .' Undoubtedly the most over-extended of the houses were the 'three Ws', and that same month it required joint action by Overend Gurney and Jones Loyd to carry Wiggins over its difficulties. 'A very disastrous state of things is expected in New York & every one seems alarmed', Bates noted in mid-November, and he added without exaggeration: 'On the whole everything wears a gloomy aspect, with a prospect of failures'.[1]

As events unfolded in 1837, against the background of an unnerving-ly steady flow of bad news from across the Atlantic, the sharpest commentary was that provided by George Carr Glyn to the Bank of Liverpool. One of Glyn's main concerns was that too many of the Bank of England's directors were, in his own words, 'impregnated with political economy doctrines'; and during these anxious months he

placed great reliance on the 'practical knowledge' of Horsley Palmer
(who was still a director) to overcome these insufficiently pragmatic
tendencies. There was a particularly nasty moment early in March,
when the three Ws were under the cosh:

> I may tell you that had it not been for the firmness of Horsley Palmer
> & the Deputy Governor, the Governor and his party in the Court would
> have brought down every American house . . . I really think the Governor
> is mad upon this subject. He and I have been brought into disagreeable
> collision.[2]

Over the next few weeks, with the City straining on every rumour and
Bates working closely with Palmer on the detailed arrangements, the
Bank reluctantly agreed to a rescue package for the beleaguered Ws.
Was the *laissez-faire* Pattison – who in 1835 had somewhat reluctantly
joined Grote as one of the City's Liberal MPs – swayed by provincial
pressure? Two directors of the Bank of Liverpool came down to
London to see what they could do, stayed at St Paul's Coffee House,
and while there wrote to the governor in the strongest possible language of 'the great embarrassment which prevails in Lancashire both
in the Mercantile and Manufacturing interests, arising chiefly from the
want of confidence occasioned by the doubt and discredit thrown upon
American paper', adding that 'unless immediate steps are taken to
restore confidence and mercantile credit, we must soon inevitably witness the most awful crisis ever known in this or any other Country'.
After a detailed enumeration of those frightful consequences, the peti-
tioners concluded:

> We cannot doubt Sir that whilst on the one hand it must be distressing
> to your mind if the disasters which we apprehend should ensue, we are
> sure that it must be particularly gratifying to you at the close of your
> administration of the affairs of the most important institution in the
> World, to be instrumental in preserving the Country from the calamities
> with which it is now threatened.[3]

Pattison was indeed about to vacate the governor's chair, and Glyn was
hopeful that henceforth a larger view of the Bank's responsibilities
would more readily prevail.

By May remittances from the United States were still obstinately
invisible, many bills were arriving only to be dishonoured, and even
those bills accepted were difficult to discount. Bates on the 21st
confided in James Morrison: 'Has known the business in US all his life

& has been in London 16 years, never knew such a state of things before . . . If the Bank had not taken up the W's does not know the extent of the mischief which must have happened or where or when it would have stopp'd'. Bates believed that it now would not be so disastrous if the three Ws did stop, that the worst had been averted; but three days later Glyn more accurately reflected the City's mood when he wrote that 'we all entertain the strongest hopes of the Bank taking the decisive step and determining to carry these houses', adding the next day that 'every thing is progressing very satisfactorily with the Americans'. By Tuesday the 30th the crunch was imminent, as Wilson & Co and Wiggin & Co formally asked the Bank for further assistance, blaming 'the temporary and almost universal suspension of credit throughout the principal commercial Cities of the United States'. Morrison's diary was graphic enough: 'News from U.S. horrible. The Bank deliberating on the W's – and all consternation. Dismal forebodings – no sleep all night.' Wednesday brought no relief, as the Bank continued to delay its decision, 'and from what Mr Palmer tells me', wrote Glyn, 'I fear the result'. Glyn was confident of the governor, Timothy Curtis, and his deputy, Sir John Reid, but not of most of the rest of the Court.[4]

Thursday the 1st saw a stately but pointed minuet between merchants and politicians. The Court requested the governor and deputy-governor to lay before the prime minister and chancellor of the exchequer the Wiggin/Wilson application for further relief and to state to them 'the apprehension of many of the Directors, from the character of the accounts received from America, of the eventual solvency of the Houses in question'. They duly waited upon Melbourne and Spring-Rice, and later in the day returned to Threadneedle Street to present to their colleagues the following buck-passing minute:

> It appears that unless further assistance be given to certain houses in the American Trade their failure will ensue and very great and extensive commercial and manufacturing distress will inevitably follow. Lord Melbourne and the Chancellor of the Exchequer also collect from the statement made to them that less of eventual loss is apprehended by the Governors from taking this course than if further assistance were now to be refused.
>
> Lord Melbourne and the Chancellor of the Exchequer are deeply impressed with the public inconvenience which would result to the manufacturing and commercial interests from a suspension of the houses engaged in the American Trade, and are most anxious if it can be done with safety that these calamities should be mitigated if not averted.

But they do not possess either the data or the knowledge by which the solvency of commercial houses can be ascertained, and they feel that it is not within their province to direct or influence the decision of the Bank of England.

Was there an embarrassed pause before 'the Governor informed the Court that the opinions referred to in Lord Melbourne's Letter were stated as his own and the Deputy Governor's, and not of the Court, except as relates to the Solvency of the Houses'? Now at last the decision had to be made; and a furious Glyn reported soon afterwards that the proposal to extend relief was defeated by a single vote.[5] Curtis and Reid had fatefully overplayed their hand, the three Ws would never trade again.

Various small firms fell in their wake, but attention soon turned to Morrison Cryder and Browns of Liverpool, both of whom were also putting in for assistance. 'I believe that Morrison has taken his deeds & parchments to the Bank. It must have been a bitter step'. So Glyn recorded on the 8th, when in fact it became clear that the Bank was willing, on the security offered, to lend £325,000. Morrison's own feelings were mixed, and he wrote to his agent in the States the next day:

> The last ten days has been like a horrid dream! All the W's are gone and with them many others, indeed, as far as respects the American Houses, one looks about to see who is left standing, not who has fallen, the list is a brief one now! All who had not resources out of business like myself or opulent friends like Barings are gone . . .
> We shall of course lose & that I fear considerably, but we shall soon make it up. A few of us must have all the business hereafter.

A week later, to general City relief, the Bank also bailed out Browns, and the worst of the crisis was over. Only one major Anglo-American house had weathered it more or less unscathed. 'Probably in one way & another we may lose one year's commissions, which considering the nature of the crisis & the little warning to allow us to get out of it ought to convince people of our prudence & of our means.' Thus, with justified satisfaction, Joshua Bates later in the summer.[6] In a year of knock-outs and long counts, Barings had fought canny and won through conclusively on points.

*

On a Wednesday the following January, despite a temperature below zero and streets almost impassable with snow, Charles Churchill and family enjoyed a night out:

Mr Ernst Wolff & Mr Selby drop in to Dinner, wch leads to a Box at the Olympic, with young Todd, Mama, Charles, & the Girls. The Bengal Tyger & Puss in Boots.

The same night on coming out we learn the Conflagration of the Royal Exchange wch with all its attached Buildings becomes a heap of Ruins in a few Hours. Obliged to hold our Exchange at Guildhall.

It was horribly true – the Royal Exchange was no more, apart from its clock tower and some of its walls, left standing and covered in great icicles. The Gresham Committee, responsible for the building, held an immediate inquiry, and at least one of its witnesses lacked nothing in descriptive eloquence:

John Alley states that he left the Auction Mart Coffee House at $\frac{1}{4}$ before 11 returning home to Wood Street where he resides, perceived a strong light proceeding from the Northern Windows of the Captain's Room in the Royal Exchange, and smoke issuing through the Roof above – the windows below were perfectly dark – immediately assisted in breaking open the Iron Gates and padlock leading to the North Staircase and to Lloyds, and was first to ascend, he was followed by some of the fire Brigade – went immediately through the passage, turned to the right examined the Door of the Captain's Room found it in flames on the inside and also the Door of the Kitchen or Bar of the Captain's Room – had I knocked it, it must have fallen – returned to the Door of the Washing Room attached to Lloyds – the Skylight over was on fire – attempted to force the Door and while in the act was knocked down by one of the fire Brigade (into the burning embers which fell from the Skylight) who insisted that no doors should be forced. Notwithstanding the threat went to the apartments of the Secretary of Lloyds, forced open the Door and entered – the whole of the cornice of the inner room was on fire – saved many of the books which he gave to the Broad Street Watchman, Croker – returned for more books but found it impossible to enter the Secretary's Office without danger – turned his attention to the Subscriber's Room and assisted in removing the Drawers until it was considered unsafe longer to remain in the room . . .

The seventeenth-century Royal Exchange had long been a building waiting for its terminal conflagration, the weather badly hindered the brave if ill-organised attempt to save it, and the last tune rung out by the bells in the tower was 'There's Nae Luck aboot the Hoose'. London had known no worse fire since 1666 itself, but as Bates solemnly recorded, she was not alone:

During this month the superb Winter Palace at St Petersburg, The Royal Exchange in London & The Grand Opera House at Paris have been

destroyed by fire. It is said the description of the edifices destroyed
indicates the leading bias of the different Countries. Russia, despotic, has
lost a Palace; England, commercial, its Exchange; France, the arts &
theatrical representations, its Opera.

Glyn preferred to look to the future. 'It will give us the opportunity',
he wrote to Liverpool, 'of making a larger and more commodious
arrangement'.[7]

The regular frequenters of the Royal Exchange had no alternative but
to operate from elsewhere – the subscribers of Lloyd's, for instance, at
the South Sea House, the timber merchants and brokers at the Excise
Yard – as they waited an inordinate length of time for plans for a new
Royal Exchange to be settled. The delay gave Edward Moxhay his
opportunity.[8] He was an intelligent, self-made City man, who had made
a fortune out of baking biscuits and whose hobby was architecture, and
he now went ahead with a long-nurtured plan to erect in Threadneedle
Street a highly ambitious hall of commerce modelled on the large
general commercial rooms in Liverpool and Manchester. It opened in
1842 and contained a commercial newsroom and a reading room as
well as rooms for commission agents to show their samples, wool sales
to be held, railway shares to be auctioned, creditors to meet, and deeds to
be deposited. No expense was spared and Musgrave Watson the sculp-
tor designed an enormous frieze, consisting of a continuous line of
figures 'illustrative', in his own words, 'of Commerce and all its
influential consequences'. Moxhay's brainchild (some said brainstorm)
certainly put other establishments on their mettle, and by April 1843
the master of the Baltic Coffee House was appealing to subscribers not
to desert him for 'Mr Moxhay's Universal Hall of Commerce'. Stressing
his readiness to make improvements in terms of light and ventilation,
he went on: 'Some gentlemen have occasionally complained of unpleasant smells; these, by the removal of the kitchen and some additional
care as respects the water-closets, will, I believe, remove every complaint'.[9] Sadly for Moxhay, if not for the Baltic master, it proved a white
elephant. The initial annual subscription of five guineas per annum
was deemed too high, and the great majority of merchants and others
preferred to stick to their snug, familiar haunts (the North and South
American, the Jerusalem, the Jamaica, the Baltic and so on) and look
forward to the completion of the new Royal Exchange, the foundation
stone of which had already been laid by Prince Albert in January 1842.
Moreover, Moxhay's pioneer attempt to establish a new market in the
City for manufactured goods from the provinces misjudged the future,

more itinerant trend of industrial marketing. By the 1850s his building had been taken over by a bank and in 1975 Musgrave Watson's grandiose frieze was incorporated into the new Battishill Gardens in Islington.

All that lay ahead when, in November 1840, there was published an arresting piece of writing:

> Not long ago, about the closing in of an evening in autumn, I sat at the large bow window of the D— Coffee-House in London . . . I felt a calm but inquisitive interest in every thing. With a cigar in my mouth and a newspaper in my lap, I had been amusing myself for the greater part of the afternoon, now in poring over advertisements, now in observing the promiscuous company in the room, and now in peering through the smoky panes into the street.
>
> This latter is one of the principal thoroughfares of the city, and had been very much crowded during the whole day. But, as the darkness came on, the throng momently increased; and, by the time the lamps were well lighted, two dense and continuous tides of population were rushing past the door . . .
>
> By far the greater number of those who went by had a satisfied business-like demeanor, and seemed to be thinking only of making their way through the press. Their brows were knit, and their eyes rolled quickly; when pushed against by fellow-wayfarers they evinced no symptom of impatience, but adjusted their clothes and hurried on. Others, still a numerous class, were restless in their movements, had flushed faces, and talked and gesticulated to themselves, as if feeling in solitude on account of the very denseness of the company around. When impeded in their progress, these people suddenly ceased muttering, but redoubled their gesticulations, and awaited, with an absent and overdone smile upon the lips, the course of the persons impeding them. If jostled, they bowed profusely to the jostlers, and appeared overwhelmed with confusion. – There was nothing very distinctive about these two large classes beyond what I have noted. Their habiliments belonged to that order which is pointedly termed the decent. They were undoubtedly noblemen, merchants, attorneys, tradesmen, stock-jobbers – the Eupatrids and the commonplaces of society – men of leisure and men actively engaged in affairs of their own – conducting business upon their own responsibility. They did not greatly excite my attention.
>
> The tribe of clerks was an obvious one and here I discerned two remarkable divisions. There were the junior clerks of flash houses – young gentlemen with tight coats, bright boots, well-oiled hair, and supercilious lips. Setting aside a certain dapperness of carriage, which may be termed *deskism* for want of a better word, the manner of these persons seemed to me an exact fac-simile of what had been the perfection of *bon ton* about twelve or eighteen months before. They wore the

cast-off graces of the gentry; – and this, I believe, involves the best definition of the class.

The division of the upper clerks of staunch firms, or of the 'steady old fellows', it was not possible to mistake. These were known by their coats and pantaloons of black or brown, made to sit comfortably, with white cravats and waistcoats, broad solid-looking shoes, and thick hose or gaiters. – They had all slightly bald heads, from which the right ears, long used to pen-holding, had an odd habit of standing off on end. I observed that they always removed or settled their hats with both hands, and wore watches, with short gold chains of a substantial and ancient pattern. Theirs was the affectation of respectability; – if indeed there be an affectation so honorable.

The narrator observed many other types – pick-pockets, gamblers, Jew pedlars, street beggars, women of the town, drunkards, porters, coal-heavers, sweeps, organ-grinders, ragged artisans – before finally lighting on a decrepit old man and following him about London all night and all of the next day, only to discover that he was no more than 'The Man of the Crowd', the title of the story.[10] Edgar Allan Poe had not been in the City since his schooldays at Stoke Newington, but there would be few more compelling descriptions of the place and its inhabitants in the nineteenth century.

Charles Churchill, nearing the end of his career, would probably not have considered himself one of the Eupatrids. He knew his station and, though his diary starts to take on a valetudinarian quality, he continued to earn it:

31 January 1839. This day is the anniversary of my Entrance to the City & its Concerns in the Year 1801. I have therefore now completed 38 Years of constant undeviating attention to Business, until at last it has become a habit strong as nature.

25 January 1840. My Teeth giving way on all sides & obliged to resort to the expedient of an under as well as an upper front.

22 August 1840. Mr Sim absent on a little Tour & what with heat, fatigue & worry I knock up at the end of the Week.

29 August 1840. Hard worked all the Week. An interview with some of the Timber Merchants, not very agreeable – & without any result.

10 March 1841. Our Sale keeps us well employed, & we get rid of an amazing deal of Rubbish, at tolerable Prices.

28 August 1842. Business with us very hard, but the Buyers now more willing & the Sellers less so. Almost knocked up with daily visits to the Dock in this hot Weather. Mr Sim takes his Share ably.

7 September 1842. Again attacked with Boils. This Time I trust a short visitation but much interfering with out door business. At the Counting

House I find I can make myself useful, my head, hand & pen almost as good as ever.

    31 December 1842. This completes 30 Years partnership with Mr Sim & we both may acknowledge with Gratitude 30 Years prosperity altho certainly 30 Years of Care & Labor.

It was a source of comfort that his son, also called Charles, had entered the firm, at the age of seventeen; at the beginning of 1844 the father noted how 'his Horse, his Dog, his books, with a little amusement, a good deal of fag, & close attention to the Sabbath give me great cause for gratitude'.[11]

*

The late 1830s and early 1840s were not easy times in the City – though not as grim as they were in the British economy at large – and in the summer of 1839 the Bank of England found itself in what can only be described as a pretty pickle. For a variety of reasons, among them lax management and the drain on sterling caused by the need to pay for wheat imports, the Bank's bullion by the last week in July stood at barely £3.7m, just over a fifth of the circulation and palpably inadequate. The Bank's initial reaction seems to have been to look to the house of Rothschild, but Nathan's son Lionel, still finding his feet, received the most cautionary advice from his more experienced cousin Anselm on the Continent:

> Do not take any rash step in a large operation. Your mother tells me that Herries told your good father in her presence to mind and not trust the Bank without any guarantee . . . as the Bank being involved in difficulties may *stop* suddenly . . . Mind, you are not your good father and do not have his influence, and he was capable of acting in other ways than prudence would direct you.

So much for the Bank of England's rock-solid reputation. Instead, finding no joy at New Court, it turned elsewhere, as Bates recorded on 20 July:

> The Bank applied to my House yesterday to assist them in negotiating a Loan from the Bank of France which Tom Baring & I said there could be no hesitation about our entering on but Mildmay was violently opposed to. I went to the House of Lords to see Lord Ashburton & get his opinion, which was the same as that of Tom & myself.

Humphrey St John Mildmay was the over-cautious son-in-law of the former Alexander Baring; Tom Baring was the very able (if too often absent) grandson of Sir Francis Baring, and was mainly responsible for international loans. In tandem with Timothy Curtis from the Bank, Tom Baring went to Paris and, though encountering considerable hostility from the Rothschilds there, successfully organised a banking syndicate, under the Bank of France's auspices, to put up the loan. For Barings it was a great triumph, as well as an important marker in its relations with the Bank. Others focused on the plight of the Bank itself, and Churchill in his diary at the start of August 1839 caught the City mood: 'The Bank of England raise the rate of Disc to 5 p C^t & negotiate an arrangement with the Bank of France to draw 2 Millions, by way of a Check to the Exchanges!! The Bank of England & accommodation Bills!! What next.'[12]

The Bank and other City institutions had embroiled themselves in the affairs of the Bank of the United States, whose charismatic London agent, Samuel Jaudon, had been marketing whole rafts of American securities since 1838, on the back of an apparently recovering economy. 'I wish that I had a less stake in them', confided Samuel Jones Loyd to his friend George Warde Norman. Over the next few years his worst fears were realised: the Bank of the United States suspended specie payments in October 1839 and finally folded early in 1841, while in the course of 1841 and 1842 no less than eight American states defaulted. There developed in London an unbridled anti-American mood, and by June 1842 Bates was writing as much in anger as in sorrow that 'there never was a Country so disgraced in point of Credit as the United States of America, by the repudiation of some of the States & the inability of others to meet their engagements'.

This wretched story concealed two important trends for the future. One, in terms of the finance of Anglo-American trade as whole, was the speed with which the shock of 1837 was soon forgotten and the sway of Barings was again disputed. Although Morrison Cryder soon pulled out and was dissolved, Huths and Schröders each established branches in Liverpool (where Barings had had one since 1832), Rothschilds became more active in the field through the impatient urgings of its US agent August Belmont, and Brown, Shipley of Liverpool (as Browns there now became) vigorously pursued a policy of opening as many small credits as possible, involving an aggressiveness and willingness to take risks that Barings under Bates no longer countenanced. There was also the establishment in London of a permanent market for American securities, involving that remarkable figure George Peabody, merchant, financier and philanthropist.[13] He had been born in 1795 of fairly humble Massachusetts origins; by 1815 he had become a partner in a Baltimore-based firm which imported dry goods from Britain; by 1837 he had made five trips to Britain; and from 1838 he was a permanent resident, occupying offices at 31 Moorgate. Over the next seven years he moved decisively from merchanting to finance, above all marketing American securities and then trading heavily in them, soon becoming the City's acknowledged expert on the subject. Inevitably he found himself in an invidious situation as one after another state defaulted; quite apart from the strain it put on his own resources, he was even denied admission to the Reform Club on account of his nationality. Peabody, however, had a long-term faith in the United States: ultimately it would be rewarded.

The City's two dominant merchant banks – the reality existed even if the term had not yet been coined – remained Rothschilds and Barings. Lionel de Rothschild (formally Baron Rothschild from 1838, in belated recognition of the title granted to his uncles by the Austrian Emperor in 1822) lacked the genius of his father but was no fool. He had been educated at the University of Göttingen, spent apprentice years in London, Paris and Madrid, and essentially perceived his task as one of consolidation. Much more of a conformist than Nathan, he was disinclined to speculate on the stock market or indeed take major risks of any sort; in 1843 he closed his firm's account at the Bank of England, marking a break from Nathan's policy of large-scale borrowings there. Meanwhile other houses were on the rise, among them Huths, who by this stage was in active contact with almost all the leading commercial centres.[14] The key figure emerging was Daniel Meinertzhagen, who had married Frederick Huth's daughter in 1833 and who, in a rather touching letter back home to his mother in Bremen, was at pains to justify the unremitting character of his commercial duties:

> I beg of you not to think that because business occupies so much of my time, that it is the love of gaining money that keeps me tied to the desk. You must remember that in my mercantile relations I have serious duties to others. In such a world-wide business as ours there are many accidental circumstances which would bring about unforeseen losses and disasters unless each one of the chiefs faithfully and industriously sticks to his post. It is not the greater or smaller profits that matter, as much as the safety and regularity with which the concern is conducted.

But if Meinertzhagen was a German with a shining future in the City, the same did not apply to poor Frederick Scheer. In July 1838, seven years after the tortuous tallow speculation, the one-time merchant was again in plaintive correspondence with Bates:

> It has been my earnest endeavour, ever since my unfortunate [and unspecified] blunders of 1835, to right myself, without forcing myself on Public Notice, or troubling my private friends; I have however not been successful . . . I therefore make free to enquire of you, whether you could not use me as agent or otherwise, – or whether, if I were to establish myself as broker, you would encourage me in such an undertaking. This latter step, however painful it may be, seems in many cases to be the best resource, when necessity forces exertion upon us; but I have always felt an extreme repugnance to the business, and that is the chief reason, why I have ventured to trouble you, before I finally resolved what to do.

Scheer got little joy. Two days later he was writing again to Bates, 'I must try my fortune as broker', and asking for whatever favours circumstances would allow. Over the next few years he did conduct various tallow operations on behalf of Barings, but his high-flying mercantile days were over. In this harsh, uncertain world, did the Old Lady offer a comforting refuge? It all depended. The irascible Miles Stringer died suddenly at the Bank in December 1839, when about to transfer some stock for the Equitable; the octogenarian private banker Fuller went in much the same way in April 1842, in his case having caught cold when receiving the dividends. In 1841, however, following the highly embarrassing series of failures by individual directors over the previous decade, the Bank of England introduced the convention by which it would discount without limit the acceptances of a director's firm.[15] Failure was still possible for a Bank director, but there was no denying it had become a good club to belong to.

There was always a host of lesser fry who were afforded no such protection, and the sense of the City as a ceaseless, unresting whirlpool, full of fluctuating individual and family fortunes, is well conveyed by the circulars sent out by firms. From the collection kept by Brandts, here are four of 1840 and 1841, respectively from William Smith of Cross Lane, George Grenfell of New Broad Street Court, John Anichini of Bishopsgate Street Within and S. Cleasby of Brabant Court:

> I take leave respectfully to inform you that the state of my health which has suffered from the fatigue attendant upon two businesses has rendered it imperative on me, in accordance with the advice of my medical friends, to relinquish my connexion with Mr Brooks (as Hide & Skin Broker) and

to confine myself to my business of Warehouse Keeper at Cross Lane, to which my whole attention will be directed.

I beg to acquaint you that I have commenced Business as a Metal Broker, and flatter myself that my knowledge of the Market, and the ready access I have to the first information, will enable me to execute any orders which you may entrust to me, on the very best terms.

I regret to acquaint you that in consequence of a serious difference with my Father, on a subject unconnected with business, I have been compelled to leave his Establishment. For the future I shall have the pleasure of waiting on you with Mr Bailey.

Having had the severe misfortune some years ago to lose my Son and Partner, on whom it was intended the concern should entirely devolve, carried on under the Firm of Stephen Cleasby & Son; and feeling that my advancing years call for repose, I have determined, after having for some time past been gradually narrowing the extent of my commercial transactions, to retire altogether from Business, on the 29th instant, in informing you of which, I embrace the opportunity of thanking you for all past favors.

Pervading the circulars is the City's cosmopolitan character. At the start of 1841 Theodor Schlutow and Ferdinand Burmeister established themselves as Schlutow & Burmeister, ship and insurance agents; a year later Abraham Bauer & Co opened a London office, in King Street off Cheapside, 'for the general transaction of Mercantile Business, in conjunction with our houses at Manchester and Hamburg'. In the end, of course, so much depended upon whom one knew. Thus it was in October 1844 when, announcing that Daniel Fry was about to become a partner in his metal-broking business, Geo. W. Cotton of Riches Court, Lime Street made sure that he included the key piece of information: 'Mr D. H. Fry is a Nephew of my esteemed friend Samuel Gurney, Esq., (of the Firm of Messrs Overend, Gurney, & Co) who has encouraged the connexion, and is desirous to promote their success'.[16]

Meanwhile, the bitter joust continued between the City's old private banks and their new joint-stock rivals, of which by the end of the 1830s there were five. The long-term future lay with the upstarts – adequately capitalised, paying interest on current as well as deposit accounts, and not dependent on the caprices of a dynastic system producing satisfactory partners – but the short term was very different. 'Having come from an office where the accounts were on a large scale I was struck with the comparatively small amounts with which I had to deal': so recalled William McKewan, who as a young clerk moved in December 1839 from Morrison Cryder to the recently established London and County Bank. Three years later Daniel Hardcastle junior, in his cogent *Banks and Bankers*, conceded that 'the joint stock Banks are increasing in number and solidity, but as yet they are, as to means, credit and extent of operations, considerably removed from the elevated position occupied by their seniors and great competitors, the private Bankers'.[17] No one was more aware of this continuing inferiority than J. W. Gilbart, general manager of the London and Westminster from its inception. In January 1838 he explained to his directors why the bank's City office had advanced so less rapidly than its branches elsewhere:

> 1. The City Bankers have more influence over their customers than the Bankers in the Western parts of London. The City customers have occasion for discounts and loans which the Bankers most liberally grant. When they leave their Bankers to come to us they come to a Bank where they are less well known and where from that circumstance alone they might not be treated with the same degree of confidence. Hence we have drawn but few accounts from other Bankers and those few have been chiefly of an inferior class to whom their former Bankers have refused accommodation.
>
> 2. Our exclusion from the clearing-house. I need not say that this operated to our disadvantage in the City.
>
> 3. Our Influence is less powerful in the City. In the City of London the power of swaying the actions of other men and the opportunities of exercising this power are possessed chiefly by those who are extensively engaged in mercantile pursuits. Not many of our Directors and none of our large proprietors are thus engaged.

Though the joint-stock banks continued to be excluded from the clearing house, the London and Westminster had in Gilbart a remarkable man at its helm. A keen theoretician as well as astute practitioner, and in due course author of a standard treatise on banking, he was an austere, frugal bachelor who complained incessantly – that his directors underpaid him at £1,500 p.a., that being appointed to the office of bank manager failed to raise him to the same social position as a private banker, and that in the public estimation he was 'considered as holding an office analogous to that of chief clerk in a private bank'.[18] It all served to spur him on.

Despite the efforts of Smith, Payne & Smiths – which in its 1836 set of rules governing the admission of new London partners continued to state, as in the 1788 deed, that partners were forbidden to win or lose more than £50 in a day 'by play or betting at Cards, Dice or any other Game of Chance or by another species of Gaming whatsoever' – the writing was on the wall for the private banks. By 1841, only twenty-nine remained of the fifty-two which had been members of the clearing house in 1810.[19] It is tempting to argue that it was arrogance that proved their undoing. Barnett, Hoare & Co of Lombard Street were masters of the ostensibly courteous yet cool and haughty tone, as in a letter to the Bristol Bank in November 1840:

> Since you are so obliging as to consult our convenience, we are assured that it is your wish that we should freely express our sentiments. Any advance which you may require we are ready to make but at the same time we wish you to bear in mind that the present is a time of peculiar scarcity of money, from the continuance of the Bank having reduced their issues and that the liability of having forty or fifty thousand pounds taken out of our circulation cannot but be attended with inconvenience. Allow us to suggest that money may be borrowed upon Consols or reduced till the account at or under 5 p cent & that we presume Overend & Co or Sanderson & Co will gladly take your surplus money at the rate of $5\frac{1}{2}$. If therefore you should adopt our suggestion it will be attended with gain rather than loss.

Eight months later it was the Leith Bank that felt the patrician touch:

> We are favoured with your letter enclosing the Draft of a Bond for our approval, and proposing an Annual payment of £105 for our Conduct of your business. With reference to this sum we desire to call to your recollection your former proposal to keep £5,000 as a Cash balance in our hands, as our remuneration, which we did then and do now consider by no means excessive. The lowest sum therefore we can name for annual commission is £200 and we beg leave to add, without intending any disrespect, that even on those terms, we are not anxious to retain your account, subject to a call for £10,000, which we fear is likely often to be made upon us.[20]

One private banker happy to place himself above the fray was George Grote. In 1843, thirteen years after his father's unlamented death and two years after the end of his stint as one of the City's MPs (during which he had unsuccessfully attempted to introduce the principle of secret ballot), he retired from the banking house in order to devote himself to his *History of Greece*. The new senior partner was W. G. Prescott, his long-standing friend from those erstwhile evenings of headache.

The tea market continued to cause its own migraines, not least because of the devilish cunning ploys of the tea brokers, determined to wrest control of the market in the new area of free trade. By December 1837 Jardine Matheson, shippers of much of the 'free tea', was complaining to its London agents (now Magniac Smith & Co, including John Abel Smith of the Smith banking dynasty) about the bafflingly poor prices being paid. 'Really', the firm wrote, 'it seems quite a lottery what estimation the most carefully selected teas may meet with in the English Market'. It found that the same 'chop' of tea was given widely different valuations and soon it was sniffing a conspiracy: 'It appears to us that powerful and wealthy interests are combined in keeping up the mystery and uncertainty of the trade to which the Brokers seem to lend themselves with a too ready acquiescence'. The suspicion was justified, for the tea brokers were deliberately assigning bogus, inferior gradings of quality to the teas in order to force down the price to be paid to the shippers. Jardine Matheson in August 1838 accordingly instructed Abel Smith to do all that he could to prevent the firm's teas from being 'sacrificed by the over-fastidiousness and caprice of the Brokers who, when the market is overstocked, scruple not to attribute to inferiority of quality what is really the effect of flat and forced sales'.[21] Though he took effective action, making an arrangement with two firms of brokers, the tea market remained highly speculative – never more so than in 1840–41 during the Opium War with China, when in a rumour-ridden atmosphere it was believed for a time that supplies were in danger of ceasing altogether:

> Through the excitement following reports of total annihilation of the British forces, and of the poisoning process asserted to be adopted in the preparation of new teas, the quotation in the space of ten or twelve months, was run up from 11d to 3s 6d per lb; and in the meanwhile, on the arrival of every China mail, variations ranging from 3d to 6d, and even 9d per lb, ensued in the course of twenty-four hours. Mincing Lane was never before so crowded, even by 'outsiders'; not only were the brokers and the agents deeply engaged for themselves and their friends, but private capitalists, stock-exchange brokers, and a large number of the general public, were incited to take a few chests of Company's congou [the brand of the East India Company's import] . . .

So heavy indeed was the speculation that come the evening many of the dealers would adjourn to Garraway's, 'always the place of resort for the "late" men', and conclude their bargains amidst much consumption of 'champagne and anchovy toasts', presumably tea being considered inappropriate.[22]

The Opium War itself – fought by Britain largely for the sake of getting China to open up its economy to foreigners – was broadly supported by the City. 'Unjust but seemingly necessary' was the view of Bates, but Churchill was more enthusiastic and more representative, referring in January 1841 to 'cheering News from China, of the probable Success of the Expedition in bringing the Emperor to terms'. The news, however, was premature, and by March 1842, in fact with the Treaty of Nanking not that far off, there was a sour if macho tone in James Capel's regular City report to the Royal Bank of Scotland: 'The China business, it is feared, will be much longer about, and perhaps we may teach them to fight before it is settled'. The larger question remains as to whether Palmerston (foreign secretary at the start of the war and during most of its course) was the pawn of City-based mercantile interests. There is no doubt that he listened to what the City had to say, yet to judge by an insider's account of his meeting in August 1839 with some leading figures from the China trade, the *initiative* lay firmly with him. 'We were with him for an hour', reported one of those present, 'and he made very many enquiries which could not fail in impressing on our minds what he was looking to. We expect that vigorous measures will be resorted to, by sending out a naval force capable of acting in a way that will be felt by the Chinese.' The same implicitly applies to Palmerston's grateful letter to John Abel Smith in 1842, on hearing that the Treaty of Nanking was concluded: 'To the assistance and information which you . . . so handsomely afforded us it was mainly owing that we were able to give to our affairs naval, military and diplomatic, in China those detailed instructions which have led to these satisfactory results'. Palmerston and his predecessors had been notably unwilling to intervene on behalf of aggrieved bondholders in the affairs of defaulting countries, despite the often vehement wishes of City merchants and others. Yet in a broader sense it is undeniable that Palmerston was becoming very keenly aware of the close, conscious nexus between diplomacy and commerce, as is revealed in his letter to Lord Auckland (Governor-General of India) in January 1841:

> The rivalship of European manufactures is fast excluding our productions from the markets of Europe, and we must unremittingly endeavour to find in other parts of the world new vents for the produce of our industry. The world is large enough and the wants of the human race ample enough to afford a demand for all we can manufacture; but it is the business of the Government to open and to secure the roads for the market.[23]

It is unlikely that Bates would have demurred from these sentiments, necessity in the end counting for more than justice.

*

The political allegiance of the City remained predominantly Whig/Liberal. It was not, in terms of the City of London constituency itself, a passionate conviction: Grote in 1837 only scraped in above Horsley Palmer by a handful of votes; four years later, when Grote decided not to stand, Lord John Russell became his successor only because no leading City figure was prepared to come forward, and the support given to Russell by the Rothschilds and their satellites in that election owed less to larger political questions than the willingness of Russell to champion political privileges for Jews.[24] Similarly clouded, as in the 1820s, was the question of the City and free trade, firmly back on the agenda by the early 1840s. Once again debate was polarised along the lines of sectional interests, and in 1842 Charles Churchill (a supporter of the Conservative government) found himself uncomfortably near the centre of the storm:

> *12 March.* Our Sale on the 11th, rather heavy but very much interfered with by the news of the extraordinary alteration proposed by Sir R Peel in the Timber Duties, a reduction of 25/- on the Foreign & 10/- on the Colonial Duties. £100,000 Revenue absolutely thrown away.
> *19 March.* All business put to the Rout by the consideration of the Timber Duties. Meetings, Committees, Resolutions, petitions, letters & addresses, & one Contract in the course of the Week. My Calculations on the Duties [given to Gladstone at the Board of Trade the previous year] are charged with being the germ of the mischief.

In general terms, the City gave credit to Peel for financial and commercial competence – certainly in comparison with the preceding Whig ministries – but essentially felt, rather as towards Huskisson in the 1820s, that not necessarily wise policies of economic liberalisation were being thrust upon them. Bates for one was disgruntled, declaring in 1843 that 'all the doings of Sir Robert Peel in the Tariff etc by which he inclines towards the free trade system have been wrong, not only wrong in the abstract but wrong in reference to the condition of the country, its debt, poor laws etc'.[25]

The truly divisive question, of course, was the corn laws, the repeal of which would denote the final triumph of free trade. In the autumn of 1843 there took place a celebrated City by-election fought almost wholly on that issue. James Pattison, the prominent merchant and Bank of England director, was the candidate supported by the Anti-Corn Law League; while Tom Baring was the protectionist. From the start the League, and in particular its great orator John Bright, symbol of the radical industrial North, made all the rhetorical running:

> I know not what the electors of the City of London may do. I know not if they think that they at least have no interest in commercial prosperity, and that the world is wrong in supposing them to constitute the heart of our commercial enterprise; but I will tell them what their countrymen and the enlightened of all countries will say, if they should stultify themselves by voting for a monopolist, that as many of them revel in wealth, they are the spoiled children of commercial success, and that they crouch before a miserable aristocracy that must despise them in their hearts.

This was hardly the language to appeal to the money men of Lombard Street, though in S. J. Loyd the League found an influential City supporter. Polling day at the Guildhall was 21 October, a Saturday, and at the outset 'the only booth that was in any way crowded was that of the butchers', which 'arose from the members of that company having to attend Newgate market'. The eventual result was close but decisive – Pattison 6,532, Baring 6,367 – and the *Circular to Bankers* (supporters of Baring) acknowledged it to be 'a victory of money over land, of cosmopolitism over country, of democracy over aristocracy'. Nevertheless, the City electorate was hardly representative of the moneyed interest as such, the League had proved far more adept than the protectionists at mobilising the popular vote of the City, and according to Bates 'many Conservatives were out of Town', presumably because it was a Saturday. Yet for all that, there does seem to have been an emerging mood in the City by this time that, whether or not desirable, the movement towards free trade was becoming inevitable – and that therefore it was better to adjust to it than to fight it. The pragmatic Churchill put it best, in his diary at the start of 1843: 'The reduction of import Duties will open some new branches of Trade & the fears that have been entertained by others, which has produced a very general stagnation & distress, will give way to the experience of realities not being so bad as anticipated'.[26]

Was the City as a whole starting to be affected by a certain Peelite rigour? Those hoping to benefit from the Stock Exchange's quaintly named Fund for the Relief of Decayed Members would not have thought so, when in 1841 its treasurer Francis Wakefield, a prominent City figure who combined stockbroking with banking, absconded with almost £5,000 of the fund's reserves. Anthony de Rothschild would have been likewise sceptical, writing from Paris to his brothers in London the following year: 'I care nothing about J. Helbert, think he is a donkey & ought to be kicked all round the Stock Exchange by the members of that celebrated assembly'. Nevertheless, there is some evidence that the Stock Exchange itself, by this time comprising almost 800 members and still mostly trading in British government securities, was becoming more conscious of its public image. In 1843 it emerged that two broking firms had been doing business in the office of one of them, and this discovery earned the unstinting condemnation of the chairman of the day:

> Messrs Harrison & Cottle must well know that the Stock Exchange had been exposed to severe but most undeserved obloquy on the grounds of its being a close, instead of an open Market, tho' every possible pains was taken in the constitution and regulations of the House by giving the utmost publicity to its transactions, to protect the interests of the Public, towards which nothing contributed so effectually as the practice of making bargains in the open market, which was adopted by all the most respectable Brokers.[27]

The Stock Exchange was hardly 'an open market' in the eighteenth-century sense, but the broader point held, especially with the daily publication from that year of the Official List of prices – though whether the protection of 'the interests of the public' was really such a paramount concern remained another question altogether for a long time to come.

The following year saw the countervailing priorities of 'City' and 'public' fused intimately together in one of the cornerstones of nineteenth-century legislation: the Bank Charter Act of 1844. Its immediate antecedents lay in two pamphlets published early in 1837. The first, by Horsley Palmer, blamed the joint-stock banks and excessive speculation in foreign securities for the recent heavy pressure on the money market; the other, written in explicit repudiation by Samuel Jones Loyd, blamed the Bank of England itself and in particular, in a fine passage of proto-Victorian morality, called for a rigid separation of the Bank's issuing and banking functions:

> A Banker cannot contract his accommodation at a period when the whole trading and mercantile world are acting under one common impetus of expansion. If under these circumstances the Banker, in addition to what may be properly called his ordinary and legitimate resources, is

also entrusted with the power of issuing paper-money *ad libitum*; is it not inevitable that he should abuse that power? Can we expect that under such circumstances, whilst all his other resources are strained to the utmost for the accommodation of his customers, he will still keep a firm and unyielding restraint over the amount of his issues? Will he, under such temptations, in no respect confound or compromise his respective duties as a Banker of Issue and a banker of Deposit and Discount? or must we not rather conclude, whether we look to the principles of human conduct, or draw our conclusions from the lessons of experience, that he will certainly blend together his Deposits and Circulation on the one side, his Gold and his Securities on the other, and thus produce an account which shall throw a plausible appearance over the abusive use which he is making of his power as an Issuing Banker?[28]

Over the next few years two clear schools of thought crystallised: the pro-Palmer 'banking' school that wanted bankers to have discretionary powers over the volume of currency; and the pro-Loyd 'currency' school that explicitly refuted such powers. Unfortunately for the former, the Bank of England's track record remained such as to inspire little general confidence. Indeed, even at the time of the war of the pamphlets, James Capel was reporting to the Royal Bank of Scotland that 'there is a growing feeling in the commercial world (at least amongst those we are acquainted with) against the Bank . . . and many persons go so far as to aver that should their Charter be renewed, it will be on much less favourable terms than the present'. In particular, the 'Palmer rule' of 1832 was openly discredited, Daniel Hardcastle in 1842 bluntly declaring that 'it is effective against a Bank of issue, but not effective against a Bank of deposit also'.[29] By 1844 the Bank of England's charter was liable for renewal, the prime minister was Sir Robert Peel, and having become a convert to the 'currency' school he was determined to put through a fundamental overhaul of the Bank's working practices and its position within the national monetary system.

During the early months of the year he and Goulburn, his Chancellor, engaged in a round of negotiations with William Cotton the governor and Benjamin Heath the deputy-governor. They involved plenty of give and take but were harmonious enough, and both sides put forward fruitful suggestions. 'I must declare', Peel remarked to the Commons with apparent sincerity, 'that I never saw men influenced by more disinterested or more public-spirited motives than they have evinced throughout our communications with them'. Peel made an extremely lengthy speech on 6 May in which he outlined his measures, of which the main ones were separation of the Bank's note issue from its banking operations, restrictions on other banks of issue, a fixed ratio between notes and bullion, and a fixed fiduciary issue of £14m (i.e. the amount of notes that might be issued against securities). 'Sound & solid & generally approved of', noted Churchill on the 11th of the proposals; 'Peel has gained immense credit by his measure (and speech) about the Bank', recorded Greville the next day; while on the 13th the Bank's proprietors met and, encouraged by a typically capable speech from Loyd, gave their almost unanimous support to the bill. Opposition in Parliament was similarly muted, and it seemed that Peel and Cotton between them had created a very satisfactory consensus.[30]

Then came the revolt of Lombard Street, triggered by a belated realisation that an extension of issue on securities beyond £14m would only be permitted in order to replace the issues of country banks that were being withdrawn. On the last day of May, Horsley Palmer (still a Bank director) wrote to Peel asking him to increase the fiduciary limit to £16m, but to no effect, as Peel explained to Cotton on 4 June:

> My confidence is unshaken that we are taking all the precautions, which legislation can prudently take, against the recurrence of a monetary crisis. It *may* occur in spite of our precautions – and if it does, and *if it be necessary* to assume a grave responsibility for the purpose of meeting it, I dare say men will be found willing to assume such a responsibility.
>
> I would rather trust to this, than impair the efficacy and probable success of those measures by which one hopes to control evil tendencies in their beginning, and to diminish the Risk that extraordinary measures may be necessary.

Three days later, on Friday the 7th, the senior partners of the City's private banks held a meeting to consider the following memorial:

> We are apprehensive that the absolute limitation of the issue to £14,000,000, without any power of expansion being reserved, whether that amount be in itself a proper amount or not, will create a general feeling of uneasiness throughout the country, and, by preventing the satisfactory reception of the measure, will deprive the scheme of many of the advantages it possesses, and interfere with its success.
>
> We respectfully submit that the effect of such an absolute limitation will be to restrict the business of the country by leading to a general withdrawal of legitimate accommodation, unless some power be reserved by the bill for extending the issue . . .

Almost all the bankers signed, but then, as a clearly rattled Cotton explained to Goulburn the following Monday, there occurred a hiccup:

> If you have not yet received the resolutions from the Bankers I think I can explain the cause.
>
> Raikes Currie, Henry Thornton and some others did not approve of the proposed alteration of Sir Robt Peel's measures but their partners assented as did old Mr Loyd on part of Jones Loyd & Co. Prescott Grote & Co refused to sign just as the document was about to be forwarded to you. Mr Loyd came in great alarm and said the name of his house must be struck out as his son would not allow it to remain if he was to continue member of the Firm, that he was willing to retire and would do so unless the name of his House was withdrawn.
>
> I strongly suspect that Mr Palmer is very much at the bottom of this movement. He has been trying to influence members of the Court and I shall not be surprised if he brings forward some resolution which may probably place me in a Minority, but I will make the best fight I can and I shall be supported by the intelligence if not by the members of the Court.

A suggestive letter: Samuel Jones Loyd successfully terrorising his venerable father, Horsley Palmer trying to snatch victory at the last from his old theoretical rival, the governor outnumbered as he sided with Peel, and most of the great banking names of the City up in arms. In the event, Palmer did not seek to mobilise malcontent Bank directors; but on 11 May, West End and City private banks came together to sign and present to government the previous week's memorial. There were seven City refuseniks (including Jones Loyd and Prescotts), but twenty-one City banks signed, including Hanburys, Taylor and Lloyds, Barclay, Bevan, Tritton & Co, Smith, Payne & Smiths, Currie & Co, Glyn, Hallifax, Mills & Co, and Barnett, Hoare & Co. The reply from Peel, however, was couched in terms of the flattest refusal, and over the next few weeks the bill smoothly became law.[31] Precisely as with the resumption decision a quarter of a century earlier, the City had been powerless to prevent itself being imposed upon.

Yet, exactly as with the return to gold, the Bank Charter Act eventually became entrenched as one of the great Victorian orthodoxies. Almost thirty years on, Bagehot in *Lombard Street* was providing the classic exposition:

> By that Act the currency manages itself; the entire working is automatic. The Bank of England plainly does not manage – cannot even be said to manage – the currency any more. And naturally, but rashly, the only reason upon which a public responsibility used to be assigned to the Bank

having now clearly come to an end, it was inferred by many that the Bank had no responsibility.

Very rashly, for not only did the Act confer exclusive issuing rights upon the Bank, but in the very *narrowness* of its remit lay the possibility of a technical mastery over monetary affairs that henceforth few outside critics would be able to challenge. Peel's legislation may have been excessively inflexible and mechanistic, yet there are few things less susceptible to lay control than an esoteric machine. Moreover, it was a machine imbued with a powerfully moralistic character, capable of resisting merely technical arguments. To listen to the certain, unfaltering voice of Samuel Jones Loyd, the ultimate architect of the Act, as in July 1844 he published a pamphlet refuting the weak-kneed wish of his fellow-bankers to have a get-out clause in times of heavy monetary pressure, is to realise with a vengeance how the City too was being called upon to play its part in the emerging, thoroughly stern-minded Peelite-cum-Gladstonian dispensation:

> To accede to such a request would be virtually to destroy the efficacy of the measure. The commencement of a drain of bullion, and consequently of pressure on the money-market, is the period at which the provisions of the Bill become practically important; and unless they are then strictly adhered to, the whole measure becomes a nullity. A general conviction that they will not be suspended on such occasions is essential, for producing throughout the community that cautious forethought and that healthy tone of self-reliance, upon which the safety and utility of the measure must materially depend . . . [32]

CHAPTER NINE

Nuova Vita

A young man's diary, early in 1843:

> *16 January.* Extended carpet stock book, a very difficult task. Prayer meeting. Thought of many who were helped because they were hungering & thirsty after God.
>
> *30 January.* Bought goods at Caldicotts Ellis & Co & other Houses. Rather a trying day in business. How much do these things disorder the mind for meditation & prayer.
>
> *11 February.* Had a poor week in business, Gross & Cropper were discharged. Had a very dark & gloomy spiritual week, much to mourn over, scarcely had a moment's sweet communion.

George Williams was born in 1821 the son of a Somerset tenant farmer, was apprenticed to a Bridgwater draper, in 1837 was converted to evangelical Christianity, and four years later took up a position with Hitchcock & Rogers at 72 St Paul's Churchyard. There he found large, suitably elegant premises, geared to a wide range of fashionable retail business, but with haberdashery at its core. Less elegant were the lives of the shop's almost 150 assistants, most of whom lived in above the premises. Their hours were relentless (seven in the morning to eight or nine in the evening), the accommodation provided was bleak, and outside working hours there were few pleasures available apart from drinking, smoking and gambling at the Goose and Gridiron next door in the Churchyard.

It was this unredeemed existence, physically as well as spiritually unwholesome, that the intense young shop assistant now hoped to transform; and on 6 June 1844, the day before the disgruntled private bankers met, there took place in Williams's dormitory a very different sort of meeting. It was the gathering of thirteen young Christians 'for purpose of establishing a society which should have for its object the arousing of converted men in the different drapery Establishments in the Metropolis to a sense of their obligation and responsibility as Christians in diffusing religious knowledge to those around them either through the medium of prayer meetings or any other meetings they think proper'. Such were the origins of the YMCA: a child of the City. Williams himself was soon temporarily distracted:

> *16 July.* Mr May discharged & Mr H asks me or rather offered for my consideration the drapery department as buyer. And now Oh Lord another part of thy vineyard open to my view . . . Now Oh my God I ask thy directions. If it is thy will will thou cause Mr H so to appoint but if otherwise may his mind be set against it. I ask not honour nor wealth nor the luxuries of this life, but to glorify thy name.
>
> *17 July.* Mr Hitchcock very pleasant but not yet deciding as to my filling Mr May's situation . . . Went to Harts Coffee House with Valantine . . . nice evening only eat a little too much.
>
> *18 July.* Mr Hitchcock called me into his Counter house & appointed me Drapery buyer, & this day is a day of worldly exaltation. Oh Lord I now pray for wisdom. Give me wisdom, an understanding heart that in this great City I may by actions & words glorify thy name.
>
> *19 July.* For the first time went into the markets . . .

Over ensuing decades Williams flourished, the firm flourished, the YMCA flourished, and in 1894 its jubilee was marked by a knighthood for the strangely elfin draper from the West Country.[1]

The summer of 1844 gave birth not only to the Bank Charter Act and the YMCA. At the end of August, the Managers of the Stock Exchange 'met specially to enquire into a report seriously affecting the character of Maynard, a Waiter of this establishment, who occupies apartments over the Committee Room, viz – that he is the Father of a Child of which his own daughter has been delivered about three weeks since.' The meeting turned into quite a performance as the Managers sought to discover the truth of the charge. Evidence was heard first from three other waiters, one of whom said that 'he had been informed that a Mrs Eustace, whose husband keeps some offices in Bartholomew Lane, could throw some light upon the subject'. He was 'accordingly sent to request her attendance but returned saying Mrs Eustace declined coming before the Managers, but intimated her readiness to answer such questions as might be put by any individual Manager who would call on her'. Thereupon, two Managers were 'quitting from the Room for that purpose' when:

> The husband of Mrs Eustace presented himself, who said his wife had been informed some time since by a woman who sells Fruit in Angel Court, that Maynard had been in the custom of ill treating his wife, who exhibited Marks thereof on her Person; and that when they lived at

Haggerston while this House was building, Maynard was in the habit of sleeping with his Daughter, locking the door to prevent his Wife coming into the Room; also that, on the occasion of his absence some time ago, he took his Daughter *only* with him.

The two Managers then left and on their return reported that Mrs Eustace had confirmed her husband's statement, adding that 'her informant was a Woman who sells Fruit under the arch way in Angel Court, who said Mrs Maynard told her about Two Months ago that her Daughter was in the family way, adding that there was something in the case far worse than that circumstance *only*'. Mrs Maynard was then sent for and she proceeded to deny it all, except that her daughter had had a child. She also said that her daughter had been married at Shoreditch Church ten months ago to a man named Williams – 'this she knew Six Months since, but where he was to be found she could not tell, she believed somewhere at the West End of the Town'. Mrs Maynard was then sent upstairs to see her daughter, and returned to say that her daughter had neither marriage certificate nor knowledge of her husband's whereabouts. At last it was the turn of Maynard himself. He claimed to have seen the father of his daughter's child, when that man had worked as a porter in the City before going to the West End, and he flatly denied the reports of both ill treatment of his wife and paternity of his daughter's child. Apparently unconvinced, the Managers gave him a week to produce Williams.

On 5 September, Maynard had to admit that he had failed to track down the man in question. He also said that 'he could prove that his wife does not at all times know what she says, being occasionally not in her right mind'. His daughter, Sarah Ann, was sent for:

> She is not married, but Richard Williams, a Wine Porter, is the Father of her Child. They have been acquainted about two Years. He never told her where he lived. In fact she knows nothing whatever of him beyond their intimacy. He is about 30 Years of life, with rather florid complexion, and dark hair. Their intercourse had been confined to the apartments occupied by her Father overhead; this was carried on after her Parents were in Bed. She saw him last about 2 months before the Child was born.
>
> Her Father knew she spoke to some one, but never troubled himself, nor ever cautioned her about it. When in the Family way, she bought necessaries for the Child, the Money being furnished by Williams. Her Father never discovered her situation until about two months before her confinement.

It was resolved unanimously that Maynard and his family quit the premises within a week, and that he be suspended until 3 October but continue to be paid, 'in order to enable him to seek for, and produce before the Managers, the Father of his Daughter's Child'. On that date Maynard still could not produce his man, but the patient Managers gave him another three weeks. Finally, on 24 October, a letter was produced from the vestry clerk at Shoreditch Workhouse, where Sarah Ann and her child were staying. It stated his opinion 'that she has been made the dupe of a designing fellow named Williams, who is the Father of the Child, and who, after seducing her, has left her to chance, to shift for herself, and Infant'. The letter also included evidence from Maynard's doctor about Maynard's good character, as well as evidence that his wife often said things showing her not to be in her right mind. This conclusive letter read, the Managers reinstated Maynard – 'but at the same time cannot but express their regret at the very disorderly manner in which he has permitted his Wife and Daughter to conduct themselves, and for that reason they cannot allow him to reside on their Premises again'. Head no doubt suitably bowed, Maynard 'assured the Managers of his future circumspection'.[2]

Four days later, Monday the 28th, saw at last the official opening of the new Royal Exchange. Sadly Charles Churchill senior did not live to witness it ('make one or two efforts to get into business, but always punished for it' was almost his last entry), but by this time his son was also keeping a diary, and he noted that 'the merchants do not like being excluded by the corporation from the opening of the exchange'. It was certainly a splendid, classical edifice that William Tite (himself the son of a Russia merchant in the City) had built for the men of commerce. 'It is reported in the City that the Queen's mind is not in a right state', Greville had recorded back in January, but it was the grave Victoria who, cheered by great crowds and accompanied by Prince Albert, the Duke of Wellington and her ministers, opened what was still the City's most important building:

> As she slowly proceeded up the Lloyd's merchants' room, she frequently bowed in acknowledgement of the hearty greeting of her loyal subjects. On arriving at the top of the room, her Majesty paused for a moment to contemplate the effigies of her illustrious predecessors. At this period the *coup-d'oeil* was superb.

On Boxing Day the members of Lloyd's took possession of their 'commodious apartments', full of mahogany seats, benches and stands, and the merchants followed on New Year's Day. In the winter cold some of them regretted their decision that the courtyard should not be roofed – but tradition was tradition, and it remained open to the elements for almost forty years.[3]

PART THREE

1844–66

I have seen the West End, the parks, the fine squares, but I love the City far better. The City seems so much more in earnest: its business, its rush, its roar, are such serious things, sights and sounds. The City is getting its living – the West End but enjoying its pleasure. At the West End you may be amused, but in the City you are deeply excited.

CHARLOTTE BRONTË, *Villette* (1853)

CHAPTER TEN

City of Dis

'What true-bred City sportsman has not in his day put off the most urgent business', R. S. Surtees asked in 1838, 'that he might "brave the morn" with that renowned pack, the Surrey subscription fox-hounds?' A question that hardly needed answering, for:

> The members of the Surrey are the people that combine business with pleasure, and even in the severest run can find time for sweet discourse, and talk about the price of stocks or stockings. 'Yooi, wind him there, good dog, yooi, wind him.' – 'Cottons is fell.' – 'Hark to Cottager! Hark!' – 'Take your bill at three months, or give you three and a half discount for cash.' – 'Eu in there, eu in, Cheapside, good dog.' – 'Don't be in a hurry, sir, *pray*! He may be in the empty casks behind the cooper's. Yooi, try for him good bitch. Yooi, push him out' . . .
>
> It is this union of the elegant courtesies and business of life with the energetic sports of the field, that constitutes the charm of Surrey hunting; and who can wonder that smoked-dried cits, pent up all the week, should gladly fly from their shops to enjoy a day's sport on a Saturday?

There were few more enthusiastic followers to the hounds that John Jorrocks, 'a substantial grocer in St Botolph's-lane'; and the novelist pictured in gratifying detail his premises on a spring day at noon:

> Before Jorrocks & Co's warehouse, great bustle and symptoms of brisk trade were visible. With true City pride, the name on the door-post was in small dirty-white letters, sufficiently obscure to render it apparent that Mr Jorrocks considered his house required no sign; while, as a sort of contradiction, the covered errand-card before it, bore 'JORROCKS & CO'S WHOLESALE TEA WAREHOUSE', in great gilt letters on each side of the cover, so large that 'he who runs might read', even though the errand-cart were running too. Into this cart, which was drawn by the celebrated rat-tail hunter, they were pitching divers packages for town delivery . . . The warehouse itself gave evident proof of great antiquity. It was not one of your fine, light, lofty, mahogany-countered, banker-like establishments of modern times, where the stock in trade often consists of books and empty canisters, but a large, roomy, gloomy, dirty, dingy sort of cellar

above-ground, full of hogsheads, casks, flasks, sugar-loaves, jars, bags, bottles, and boxes.

The floor was half an inch thick, at least, with dirt, and was sprinkled with rice, currants, raisins, etc, as though they had been scattered for the purpose of growing. A small corner seemed to have been cut off, like the fold of a Leicestershire grazing ground, and made into an office, in the centre of which was a square or two of glass that commanded a view of the whole warehouse.

Presiding there was Jorrocks, a cockney 'frank, hearty, open, generous, and hospitable, and with the exception of riding up Fleet-street one Saturday afternoon, with a cock-pheasant's tail sticking out of his red coat pocket, no one ever saw him do a cock-tail action in his life'.[1]

'Banker-like establishments of modern times' may have been a caustic reference to the unpopular London and Westminster Bank. Its new head office in Lothbury was completed towards the end of 1838, its broad front marking a complete break with its Georgian surroundings and brashly towering above its next-door neighbour the private bank Jones Loyd. More than the banks, though, it was the insurance companies who changed the face of the early-Victorian City, erecting a series of grandiose headquarters, usually in the grand Italian manner. Between 1836 and 1843 the Atlas in Cheapside replete with pedimented cornices, the Globe, the Alliance, the Sun, were all testimony to a belief in the reassuring properties of uncompromising physical solidity. The Sun's old fire office had been in Bank Buildings, demolished in order to create a suitably impressive site for the new Royal Exchange, and its new head office replaced St Bartholomew's Church, likewise reduced to dust and rubble, on the corner of Bartholomew Lane and Threadneedle Street. The building of the new Exchange in 1844 altered the very hub of the City, creating more space, pulling down adjacent property, and prompting not only a widening of Threadneedle Street but also the construction of one of the City's first office blocks, the Royal Exchange Buildings directly opposite.[2]

1849 saw the construction of the Imperial Assurance Office, at the junction of Old Broad Street and Threadneedle Street, considered the equal to Tite's famous effort; that same year Bunning's New Coal Exchange was opened, in the presence of an eight-year-old Prince of Wales on his first appearance in the City, boasting a great domed interior one day to be fondly evoked by John Betjeman as 'impressive, vast and exquisitely detailed'; while in the early 1850s the creation of a western extension to Cannon Street cut mercilessly through the immemorial alleys of Great St Thomas Apostle, Basing Lane, Little

Friday Street and Great Distaff Lane, as to its south at the same time many crowded houses were being pulled down to make way for the erection of new warehouses. Even the august house of Barings could not resist the pace of change. 'It was determined about a month ago that we would enlarge our Counting House & make it comfortable', noted Bates in July 1853; and by November the new office, built on the site of the old counting house at 8 Bishopsgate and benefiting from gas lighting, was proving 'very convenient and looks imposing'.[3]

There were other aspects of change. As an upmarket shopping centre the City was now increasingly challenged by the West End, especially Nash's elegant Regent Street; while for residential appeal, the City was ever less the favoured spot for anyone of even a modicum of financial standing. The financial journalist David Morier Evans, in his pioneering, authoritative and eminently readable survey *The City; or, The Physiology of London Business* published in 1845, had no doubts on the score:

> The City is not now much chosen for a residence. The old houses, in the best thoroughfares, are either let as offices, or given up to the occupation of housekeepers who have the charge of the premises. At the banks, the rule is, for the junior partner to reside on the premises; and a certain number of clerks, also, live in the house.
>
> Merchants and others, who formerly located in the suburbs, have, in a great number of cases, chosen West-end domiciles. Regent's-park, and rows of villas that stud the neighbourhood of Kensington, Brompton, Hammersmith, and other places tending to those points, are thickly inhabited by City men. Clapton, Hackney, Islington, Peckham, and Clapham, were, at one time, considered very convenient distances by these people. Their taste has, however, even changed in this respect; and these spots have been denuded of a number of their former occupants. Clerks, instead of principals, now reside in these localities, all short walks or rides from the City being filled with the habitations of this class of persons.
>
> Thames-street, Queenhithe, and the thoroughfares to the warehouses at the water-side, some twenty or thirty years ago, were respectably inhabited by parties connected with mercantile life. They are all now left to humble tenants, and much of the grandeur formerly associated with City recollections, has passed away.

In short, concluded Evans about what marked the end of a venerable tradition, 'a dwelling in the City is a thing not now considered desirable, – all move either towards the west, or emigrate to the suburbs, – the one for fashion, the other for economy and fresh air'.[4]

There remained fundamental continuities between the Georgian and the early-Victorian City. For one thing its residential numbers held up (about 130,000) even though the social composition changed: by the time of the 1851 census, many of those living in the City were retailers and small-scale producers (such as watchmakers and tailors), who tended to use their homes partly as a place to live, partly as working premises for themselves and partly as an opportunity to sub-let to those needing office space for such burgeoning activities as stockbroking, shipping, insurance and merchanting in general – activities which for the most part were not yet housed in specialist office blocks. There remained in the City a plethora of small-scale family firms performing a bewildering variety of functions. Simply to walk down Cornhill in 1847, on the southern side towards Gracechurch Street, was to have a chance to inspect S. W. Silver & Co, shirt makers; Pretyman &Hobson, furnishing ironmongers; H. & J. Baldwin, woollen drapers and tailors; George Lowcock, watch maker and cutler; and Maclaren & Son, boot makers. The City was also an intensely *crowded* place, as Charlotte and Anne Brontë found when they set out from the Chapter Coffee House in Paternoster Row, by St Paul's Cathedral, in July 1848, heading for Cornhill, home of the publishers Smith, Elder & Co:

> When they had been discussing their project in the quiet of Haworth Parsonage the day before, and planning the mode of setting about the business on which they were going to London, they had resolved to take a cab, if they should find it desirable, from their inn to Cornhill; but that, amidst the bustle and 'queer state of inward excitement' in which they found themselves, as they sat and considered their position on the Saturday morning, they quite forgot even the possibility of hiring a conveyance; and when they set forth, they became so dismayed by the crowded streets, and the impeded crossings, that they stood still repeatedly, in complete despair of making progress, and were nearly an hour in walking the half-mile they had to go.[5]

Elizabeth Gaskell, Charlotte's biographer, did not even remark on the fact that it was a Saturday morning; Charlotte herself, surrounded by the rush and the roar, was clearly thrilled as well as alarmed.

Above all the City *felt* different. Flora Tristan (French socialist feminist and grandmother of the well-known Parisian stockbroker Paul Gauguin) wrote in her *London Journal* of 1840 of its 'great number of little narrow streets, crooked and poorly constructed' and went on:

The inhabitants of this part of town are considered by those of the West End to be of pure John Bull stock. They are, for the most part, worthy merchants who are shrewd where their business interests are concerned and who care for nothing but those same interests. The shops, where many of them have made fortunes, are so dark, so cold, so damp that the West End aristocracy would disdain to have them as stables for their horses.[6]

Private bankers always referred to the ground floor, where the business was done, as 'the shop', and Bertram Currie was to recall his family bank in Cornhill, which he entered in 1846, as 'narrow, low, and not over well lighted', though 'of considerable depth'. Even the main banking hall of Glyns, the largest of the private banks, was a dim, shabby and fairly ramshackle affair. The stubbornness emerges in a discussion in 1841 by the partners of Prescotts, faced by the regrettable need to make certain alterations:

> Attention was much taken up by listening to the statements and arguments, and inspecting the plans of Mr Moxhay of Threadneedle Street, who is extremely anxious that we should rebuild the front of our premises to accord in some degree with the Architectural Buildings which it is presumed will soon rise up around us; the eloquence of Mr Moxhay however failed to convince the Committee that they should be doing right to lay out money to render their premises pleasing to the eye of the Spectator; the expenditure requisite to make them comfortable to themselves and convenient to their Customers will be sufficiently heavy without the addition of Ornamental gratification.[7]

An aversion to show and ostentation lay deep within the City psyche: the gilt lettering on the Jorrocks errand-cart was strictly for the benefit of the West End.

'A most mysterious and unfathomable labyrinth of lanes and alleys, streets and courts, thronged with a bustling multitude' was how Evans in his opening sentences characterised this 'world within itself', and a brief tour may suggest something of its early-Victorian quiddity. Starting, in the company of Henry Mayhew, with the costers' barrows at Billingsgate Market very early on a Friday morning:

> As soon as you reach the Monument you see a line of them, with one or two tall fishmonger's carts breaking the uniformity, and the din of the cries and commotion of the distant market, begins to break on the ear like the buzzing of a hornet's nest. The whole neighbourhood is covered with the hand-barrows, some laden with baskets, others with sacks. Yet as you

walk along, a fresh line of costers' barrows are creeping in or being backed into almost impossible openings; until at every turning nothing but donkeys and rails are to be seen. The morning air is filled with a kind of seaweedy odour, reminding one of the sea-shore; and on entering the market, the smell of fish, of whelks, red herrings, sprats, and a hundred others, is almost overpowering.

The wooden barn-looking square where the fish is sold, is soon after six o'clock crowded with shiny cord jackets and greasy caps. Everybody comes to Billingsgate in his worst clothes, and no one knows the length of time a coat can be worn until they have been to a fish sale. Through the bright opening at the end are seen the tangled rigging of the oyster-boats and the red worsted caps of the sailors. Over the hum of voices is heard the shouts of the salesmen, who, with their white aprons, peering above the heads of the mob, stand on their tables, roaring out their prices . . .[8]

Elsewhere, later in the day, the produce brokers of Mincing Lane would be selling by auction in the Commercial Sale Rooms their 'foreign and colonial' produce of tea, sugar, coffee, spices and the rest, with up to 150 potential bidders 'all armed with catalogues and pens'; on 'Change the merchants gathered as of yore each afternoon between half-past three and half-past four, though Evans, a traditionalist at heart, quietly lamented that under the new dispensation 'there is now no fearfully sonorous bell' and 'separate places are set apart for the announcement of ships sailing, or quack advertisements, and the walls have ceased to display that immense amount of information which formerly could be gathered from them'; and across the road at the Bank of England, though no dealing in stocks had been allowed in the Rotunda since 1838 on the grounds of creating disorderly interference with the Bank's business, there was still the half-yearly ritual of dividend day to absorb the idle visitor:

We are in the middle of the year, and the interest on the three per cents is being paid. What crowding and sweeping to and fro. At least fifty clerks are sitting in a circle in a high vaulted saloon, well provided with a cupola and lanterns. They do nothing whatever but pay and weigh, and weigh and pay. On all sides, the rattling of gold, as they push it with little brass shovels across the tables. People elbowing and pushing in order to get a *locus standi* near the clerks; the doors are continually opening and shutting. What crowds of people there must be in this country who have their money in the three per cent Consols!

Strange figures may be seen in this place. An old man with a wooden-leg sits in a corner waiting, and Heaven knows how long he has been waiting already. Of course, a wooden leg is rather an encumbrance than otherwise in a crowd. The old man seems to be fully aware of the fact. He looks at his large silver watch – it is just twelve – puts his hand to the pocket of his coat, and pulls out a large parcel, something wrapped up in a stale copy of the *Herald*. What can the parcel contain? Sandwiches! He spreads them out, and begins to eat. He likes them too. He takes his ease, and makes himself perfectly at home. I dare say it is not the first time he has waited for his dividends.[9]

The scene was a tempting subject for any genre painter; it was not until 1870 that dividend warrants were despatched by post.

A chap needs a sandwich, and the City's coffee houses were still going strong, not least Garraway's with Messrs Funge and Bland as its proprietors. 'Large trays of ham, beef, and tongue sandwiches, cut in a most substantial manner, are ranged on the bar', Evans recorded of a typical lunchtime there, washed down by 'pale ale, stout, and sherry'; by the evening, 'coffee or punch' had become 'the favourite beverage', often 'accompanied by a choice Havannah'; and should there be any gaps to fill, the 'fruit-women' were allowed in, selling oranges and nuts. Over half a century later Edward Callow, who in 1845 had been a stockbroker's clerk, fondly recalled the Garraway's of his youth as 'furnished with cosy mahogany boxes and seats' and having a sanded floor and waiters who 'were such decorous and stately individuals as almost to deserve the name of attendants'. 'I do not suppose a woman ever entered the place during the present century' he added, presumably forgetting the fruit ladies.[10]

If it was something hot one wanted, Callow retrospectively recommended the Fleece and Sun in Threadneedle Street, 'a public-house of the old City type, with its dining-room fitted up with "boxes" '. There City people would repair for 'their mid-day steaks and chops, having previously visited Bannister's, the butcher's, and purchased their modicum of beef or mutton, which was handed to them in a piece of newspaper, with which they stepped in next door and gave it to the cook presiding over the grid-iron with full instructions as to its being well done or underdone'. As for the liquid aspect, 'the ale or porter – stout in those days was a term only used in reference to the brewings of Guinness of Dublin, or Lane of Cork – was served in its "native element", a bright, clean pewter pot'. And, 'in addition to the price of the liquid, beer or wine, a modest charge of threepence was made for what the waiters euphoniously termed "bread, cookin, and taters" '. Over the years vegetarianism would rarely be a growth stock in the square mile. 'The menu here consists principally of roast-beef, fish etc', wrote Joseph Hambro in 1843 back home to Copenhagen from his recently established office in Old Broad Street.[11]

Many and various types found their often perilous niche in the early-Victorian City, among them those desperate optimists called by Evans the 'little go' or 'alley men':

> They are a description of people including the lowest of the low among the outside speculators, who traffic in the letters and shares of railway, or any other joint stock company that may happen to fall into their hands. They frequent the purlieus of Capel-court, the Auction Mart, and the adjoining lanes and alleys, and principally consist of broken-down merchants' clerks, decayed tradesmen who have lost money by speculation, and others . . .
>
> The 'little-go' man, if he could realize a price for all the *securities* he holds, whether in the shape of letters of allotment for railway shares, old scrip of mining companies, or defunct steam and emigration projects, would soon realize his fortune; and therefore, to him, every scrap of paper of this description is part of his general store. He keeps them as mere lottery-tickets, with the chance of their turning up, some day or other, a prize.
>
> Visit Bartholomew-lane at any time in the year, and you will be sure to find several people of shabby exterior holding converse at the entrance of Capel-court, or on the steps of the Auction Mart. These are the 'alley men'. You will see one, perhaps, take from his pocket a goodly-sized parcel of dirty-backed letters, all arranged, and tied round with string or red tape, which he sorts with as much care and attention as if they were bank-notes. That parcel is his stock in trade; perhaps those letters may contain the allotment of shares, in various companies, to an amount, if the capital subscribed was paid, of many hundreds of thousands of pounds. They, doubtless, in his hands, are scarcely worth as many farthings; yet he makes a living on them, and is as busy as the most opulent stock broker in finding a buyer for his securities.[12]

A Dickensian scene, but for a Dickensian character the palm surely goes to 'Old Jack', the bearded, felt-hatted crossing-sweeper at the Royal Exchange who in 1850 told Mayhew his life story:

> I've had this crossing ever since '38. The Exchange was burnt down in that year. Why, sir, I was wandering about trying to get a crust, and it was very sloppy, so I took and got a broom; and while I kept a clean crossing, I used to get ha'pence and pence . . .
>
> I smoke, sir; I *will* have tobacco, if I can't get grub. My old woman takes care that I have tobacco.
>
> I have been a sailor . . . I was at the taking of Algiers, in 1816, in the Superb. I was up the Mediterranean three years, ten months, and twenty days, until the ship was paid off.

Then I went to work at the Dockyard. I had a misfortune soon after that. I fell out of a garret window, three stories high, and that kept me from going to the Docks again. I lost all my top teeth by that fall . . .

I was afeard of being taken up solicitin' charity, and I knew that sweeping was a safe game; they couldn't take me up for sweeping a crossing.

Sometimes I get insulted, only in words; sometimes I get chaffed by sober people. Drunken men I don't care for; I never listen to 'em, unless they handle me, and then, although I am 63 this very day, sir, I think I could show them something . . .

Those who think that sweepin' a crossing is idle work, make a great mistake. In wet weather, the traffic that makes it gets sloppy as soon as it's cleaned. Cabs, and 'busses, and carriages continually going over the crossing must scatter the mud on it, and you must look precious sharp to keep it clean; but when I once get in the road, I never jump out of it. I keeps my eye both ways, and if I gets in too close quarters, I slips round the wheels. I've had them almost touch me.

No, sir, I never got knocked down. In foggy weather, of course, it's no use sweeping at all . . .

I don't come to the same crossing on Sundays; I go to the corner of Finch-lane. As to regular customers, I've none – to say regular; some give me sixpence now and then. All those who used to give me regular are dead . . .

Old Bill, in Lombard Street! I knows him; he used to make a good thing of it, but I don't think he makes much now . . .

I gives threepence for my brooms. I wears out three in a week in the wet weather. I always lean very hard on my broom, 'specially when the mud is sticky – as it is after the roads is watered. I am very particular about my brooms; I gives 'em away to be burned when many another would use them.

Whereupon Old Jack parted from the social investigator and set off home to his lodgings, looking forward to 'a pound of bread, a quarter of an ounce of tea, and perhaps a red herring'.[13]

What about the men Mayhew ignored, the City's footsoldiers, the black-coated, white-collared army of clerks? The hours themselves were not staggeringly long (though of course included Saturdays), as Barings sought to make clear when it issued some formal regulations to its staff in 1845:

   I. The Junior Clerks are to attend at Half-past Nine o'clock; the Superior Clerks at Ten o'Clock every Morning.
  II. All under 60 years of age, are requested to sign the book.
 III. It is requested that there be no unnecessary conversation in the Office, one with another.

IV. Each Clerk is desired to attend to the duties assigned him, as soon as he enters the Office: by observing this Rule, the business of the day will be finished at an earlier hour.

V. One Hour is allowed for Lunch or Dinner.

VI. On ordinary days, when there are no Packets out, or Foreign Posts, the Clerks may leave the Office at Five o'Clock, if they have completed all that is required to be done in their several departments.

VII. On Packet Days and Post Days, all the Clerks are to stop until the duties of their departments are finished.

When it is considered that these Regulations, on ordinary days, only require attendance for the Superior Clerks about Six Hours per Day out of the Twenty-four, and the Junior Six and a-half Hours, and Two Hours additional on Post and Packet Days, it cannot be thought severe: it is therefore insisted on, that this short time be devoted earnestly to the duties of the Office.[14]

These encouraging words perhaps had their effect, for when the firm some years later gave a dinner at the London Tavern to its forty clerks, Bates noted 'they are certainly very excellent clerks'. Among them were the elite of clerkdom, the corresponding clerks, who at Barings and other merchant houses earned around £300 a year or more, and were often foreigners. In the words of Evans their all-important duty was 'to advise connexions abroad of whatever their principals have to communicate, through the medium of French, German, Italian, or Spanish, as the case may be'. Tuesdays and Fridays were especially onerous, being foreign post nights, when letters were posted for the Continent as late as eleven o'clock. That they and the other clerks in such firms thoroughly earned their screw is confirmed by Benjamin Davidson of Rothschilds, who visiting the Paris house in 1847 wrote to New Court that 'if you were to take the average quantity of work done by each clerk respectively, you would find, that one in London, would get through at least double what is performed by one in this House', adding disapprovingly of the Parisian clerks that 'it is astonishing how they contrive to come out such "swells" and to dress as well as they do'.[15]

In the City's private banks, appreciably more generous than the joint-stock variety, pay was reasonable rather than brilliant: Prescotts in 1843 paid twenty-four clerks total salaries of £2,870, Glyns in the same year paid 70 clerks and other employees £8,306 – in both cases an average of about £119 a year, which in conjunction with the discretionary hand-out of 'Christmas money' received from grateful customers placed the more senior clerks of a private bank at least up to the wage-earning level of a skilled manual worker (the so-called 'aristocrat of labour'). There were, however, the financially burden-some responsibilities to fulfil of being deemed a member of the mid-dling classes, as well as the fact that the banks rarely paid salaries upfront, as one inveterate debtor eloquently complained in an open letter to 'The Principals of the Banking Establishments in the Metro-polis' published in February 1845:

> I have been for eighteen years a bankers' clerk, during the whole of which time I have suffered more or less from a system, the hardship of which needs, I trust, but to be made apparent, to ensure its removal. I allude to the regulation by which the salaries of your clerks are paid only once in three months, after they are due, an arrangement presenting no advant-age whatever to the employer, but pressing with a degree of severity upon the necessitous clerk, of which the wealthy can have but very little conception. The manner in which I shall have to expend my quarter's salary just due, amounting to £40, will, perhaps, serve to make this intelligible.

Returned to my friend B, of whom I have been under the painful necessity of borrowing	£6	0	0
Butcher's, baker's, and grocer's bills	12	0	0
Rent, £6; bootmaker, £1 10s; tailor, £7 10s	15	0	0
Servant's wages	1	10	0

> You will perceive by this statement that I shall have £5 10s in hand, with which to commence the quarter, to meet those expenses for which I cannot possibly get credit; such as dining in the City, and other matters on which I need not enlarge. For these expenses the sum will be altogether inadequate; I must, therefore, again have recourse to my friend B, – again run up an account with the tradespeople, and, except your kindness interfere to prevent it, be thus embarrassed to the end of my days.[16]

There were, moreover, rarely any pension arrangements – clerks at private banks were usually expected to die in harness – and the work itself could be highly demanding. 'The counters are packed with clerks as close as they can stand together', one observer described Glyns at three o'clock of an afternoon, adding that 'two mighty streams of money are constantly ebbing and flowing across the counters, and half a million is said to be no uncommon sum for the firm to settle at the clearing house'. It was not easy work to perform in a poky, poorly lit banking hall, nor was it healthy work. In 1845 the newly established *Bankers' Magazine* launched a campaign to improve conditions; and that October 'A Bankers' Clerk' wrote to support it: 'No person, I am sure, can go into a Banking-house without discovering what a foul atmosphere the clerks are compelled to breathe, in consequence of so many persons being congregated together in a small ill ventilated space. It is to this circumstance that I attribute so many Bankers' clerks dying of consumption.'[17]

Six years later the publishers John Cassell brought out a guidebook, called *The London Conductor*, for the benefit of those trainloads of provincials coming up to town to visit the Great Exhibition. First stop was in front of the Bank of England:

> See, from where you stand, how each separate street, pours out its tide of young men into the City. From the east and the west, the north and the south, on it comes: clerks from Islington and Highgate, coming through Moorgate and Princes-streets; clerks from Mile End and Bow and Stratford and Hackney and Victoria Park, stepping briskly past the Exchange; clerks from Brixton, Clapham, Peckham, and other suburban places over the water, swarming up King William-street, and round by the Globe Insurance Office, that handsome building facing the main street, looking west; clerks from Pimlico and Bayswater and Brompton and Putney, coming east into the City; clerks of all ages, clerks of all sizes, clerks from all quarters, walking slowly, walking fast, trotting, running, hurrying into the Bank from the moment the clock strikes nine, till, at the latest, a quarter after – a very city of clerks.

All had walked to the City for want of an alternative: no clerk could conceivably afford his own carriage; it was a few years yet before the omnibus provided a real commuting alternative from the inner suburbs; and as for railways, the necessary lines were not yet built for romance to bring up the nine-fifteen. By the mid-1850s it was estimated that 200,000 people walked daily into the City along the principal roads. None, for those 'over the water', was more heavily used than the approach to London Bridge, and it was to that historic crossing that an American visitor drifted in 1849, having gone to Cheapside to see the Lord Mayor's Show:

> A most bloated pomp, to be sure. Went down to the bridges to see the people crowding there . . . Whilst on one of the Bridges, the thought struck me again that a fine thing might be written about a Blue Monday in November London – a city of Dis (Dante's) – clouds of smoke – the damned &c – coal barges – coaly waters, cast-iron Duke &c – its marks are left upon you, &c &c &c.

Herman Melville did indeed in time make a fine thing of it, and his novel *Israel Potter* (1855) summons up 'the greatest everyday crowd which grimy London presents to the curious stranger: that hereditary crowd – gulf-stream of humanity – which, for continuous centuries, has never ceased pouring, like an endless shoal of herring, over London Bridge'. There follows, from that vantage point, a passage akin to a John Martin painting, a reminder that death had undone so many long before another American came to the City and found it a wasteland:

> Whichever way the eye turned, no tree, no speck of any green thing was seen – no more than in smithies. All laborers, of whatsoever sort, were hued like the men in foundries. The black vistas of streets were as the galleries of coal mines; the flagging, as flat tomb-stones, minus the consecration of moss, and worn heavily down, by sorrowful tramping, as the vitreous rocks in the cursed Gallipagos, over which the convict tortoises crawl.
>
> As in eclipses, the sun was hidden; the air darkened; the whole dull, dismayed aspect of things, as if some neighbouring volcano, belching its premonitory smoke, were about to whelm the great town, as Hercula-neum and Pompeii, or the Cities of the Plain. And as they had been upturned in terror towards the mountain, all faces were more or less snowed or spotted with soot. Nor marble, nor flesh, nor the sad spirit of man, may in the cindery City of Dis abide white.[18]

CHAPTER ELEVEN

Horrid, Horrid Panic

The Bank Charter Act of 1844 was designed partly to curb speculation, but its framers could not be blamed for failing to take into account the lure of the iron monster. The railway mania, as it became known, was under way even before Peel's measure became law, and in 1845 it reached its height. The shocked partners of Prescotts convey something of its proportions:

> The gambling taking place at present in Railway Shares in every part of the Country, and amongst every class of Society, is quite alarming, and whilst it fills us with apprehension of an impending crisis, induces caution and circumspection leading apparently to loss of present advantages, but unquestionably preparing for us a comfortable Haven when the Storm shall come.

That was in June. Four months later, successive weekly meetings of the partners returned to the subject:

> The great feature of the present time is the speculation in Railroads, which has reached an awful magnitude ... Fresh projects make their appearance every day. Having kept ourselves free from the prevailing mania up to this time, it is not likely that we shall now yield to it ...
> It is estimated that the present *premiums* on the shares in quite new Companies amount to £28,000,000!! & that the *premiums* upon Companies of older date & in a more advanced stage, tho' still with their works incomplete, amount to £18,000,000!![1]

The grotesque bubble was about to burst. 'The Crisis in the Share Market' was the main headline by the end of October in the *Railway Monitor*, the newly-started weekly supplement of the *Economist*, and over the next few months premiums turned to discounts, members of the Stock Exchange were hammered, and new railway lines stopped being projected. 'Oh! the horrid, horrid panic! What a – what a dreadful bore!' lamented *Punch*, but in a Threadneedle Street parlour there was a certain grim satisfaction.[2]

151

The main speculative interest came not from the City but from the regions where the railways were actually being constructed, and though by October 1845 some 121 railway securities were being actively dealt in on the London Stock Exchange, this was a lower total than in either Liverpool or Manchester. Moreover, it was not only Prescotts Bank which kept its cautious distance but also powerful elements of *haute finance* in general. 'The mighty loanmongers, on whose fiat the fate of kings and empires sometimes depended, seemed like men who, witnessing some eccentricity of nature, watch it with mixed feelings of curiosity and alarm', wrote Disraeli in *Endymion* many years later. He was clearly referring to Rothschilds, probably discouraged by the experience of its Paris house in relation to new French railways, and Barings, where Bates in April 1845 argued that since 'the rage for railroads is great' and 'much swindling is going on in the Share market', it plainly followed that 'a crash is looked for sooner or later'.[3]

The running, however, was not just made by George Hudson ('The Railway King') and others from the provinces, for the City provided its share of railway bankers-cum-promoters. Glyns had already been to the fore in the 1830s, and that firm was now joined by Masterman, Peters & Mildred and Denison, Heywood & Kennard among others. John Masterman was a leading City figure, being not only a prominent private banker but also a Conservative MP for the City and one of the founders of the City Club, housed in Old Broad Street in second generation Palladian; Masterman had close links with the great railway contractors Thomas Brassey and Samuel Peto and was much involved, sometimes with the bankers and loan contractors C. Devaux & Co, in the building of foreign as well as domestic railways. The Stock Exchange itself during 1845 was in a state of almost permanent turmoil, with the arrival of many new members who were often of flimsy financial standing; dealings spilled over into the Auction Mart and the Hall of Commerce, and the clerks of stockbroking firms worked ferociously long hours to settle the business. It was a time for quick wits and shedding prejudices, and Evans in the autumn of 1845 recorded how 'the old and respectable members of the House have had the mortification to see persons who formerly had been of little reputation on the Exchange, and in many instances even their own clerks, carrying on an extensive and profitable business in shares'. It was now that there began the systematic practice of stagging – applying heavily for the shares in new companies with a view to selling them immediately at a premium – and *Punch* that year had plenty of fun satirising 'Stag-hunting in Capel Court'. Services were required in many and different ways as the mania raged and then messily expired, and it was no coincidence that new firms of solicitors now emerged, including one founded in Leadenhall Street by the Linklater brothers, sons of a provision merchant in Wapping High Street: there was no shortage of work for them and other legal gentlemen. After all, as the Stock Exchange's Edward Callow was to recall, 'a solicitor or two, a civil engineer, a Parliamentary agent, possibly a contractor, a map of England, a pair of compasses, a pencil, and a ruler, were all that were requisite to commence the formation of a railway company'.[4]

Undoubtedly there was a strong element of conscious fraud, especially when the mania was raging most fiercely. It was therefore no surprise when in 1846 the question arose of whether there should be formal controls over new railway issues, but Samuel Jones Loyd decisively expressed the City's view when he wrote from Lothbury to Lord John Russell that 'any measure of restriction which proceeds upon the principle of determining the amount of capital which the country can safely apply to any given purpose I think must be objectionable'. And he added, with an unconscious nod towards what would eventually become another contentious question: 'Can it be expedient to apply any restriction to the application of capital, either as regards time or amount, to public works in this country, whilst the power of exporting that capital for the promotion of similar works abroad necessarily remains unrestricted?' A masterful use of the adverb, but few in the City would have quarrelled with it. Still, in terms of the railway mania itself, it was not just the City that ultimately benefited with a vastly enlarged permanent market for domestic railway securities, among which the fixed-interest stocks of companies like the Great Western and London & North Western achieved an almost Consol-like status, but also the British economy as a whole. Over 2,000 miles of new line provided a more or less effective transport system for what was becoming the workshop of the world; the stimulus to the iron industry was both sharp and sustained; and for the first time, with the growth of the provincial stock exchanges, Britain had a national capital market.[5] An awful lot of money was spent, and much of it was wasted, but on this occasion it did not overly matter.

In the short term, the rollercoaster nature of the railway boom played its part in the major commercial and financial crisis of 1847, but it was not the main cause. Arguably as important was the Bank of England's unexpectedly aggressive discounting policy in the immediate wake of the Bank Charter Act, prompting the *Bankers' Magazine* to remark in April 1845 that the Bank's directors were 'now anxious to push their business, as bankers, to an extent hitherto quite unknown to their system of management'. This policy, perhaps at root a cussed response to the prevailing notion that the Bank was now no more than a mechanical instrument of parliamentary legislation, was one of the reasons why money was such a drug on the market in the mid-1840s and indeed why the railway mania flourished as excessively as it did. The crux, though, was the corn situation. Following the failure of the Irish potato crop in 1845, Peel the following summer pushed through the repeal of the Corn Laws, a measure that divided the City (and even individual City families such as the Barings) quite as much as it did the Conservative Party. Then not only did the Irish crop fail again but the European crop failed; the English harvest was poor; and that winter saw rising imports of ever more expensive wheat causing a massive drain of gold. By April 1847 the atmosphere was one of crisis and an anxious Chancellor of the Exchequer, Sir Charles Wood, looked in vain for guidance to the great mercantile names of the City, as he admitted to his banking confidant, Samuel Jones Loyd: 'I saw at Lord John's, Lionel Rothschild & Bates this morning & (low be it spoken), I am utterly confounded at the ignorance they displayed, of facts & circumstances which I should have thought every merchant in the City must have known. They really had little or nothing to say for themselves, & admitted that things were proceeding rapidly.'[6]

They were at least correct in that respect, especially as the 'company of merchants' had just performed a disconcertingly abrupt U-turn in its monetary policy, abandoning cheap money and, through temporarily restricting discounts, inducing a sense of panic about the lack of available credit. The pressure on discount houses like Overend Gurney became intense, even the bills of Coutts being refused in Lombard Street, and trade at large was more or less paralysed. By early May the news from Forbes, Forbes & Co in the City to Jamsetjee, Jejeebhoy, Sons & Co in Calcutta was dark-hued:

> Matters have been bad in London; but much worse we believe in Lancashire, particularly Liverpool . . . Deputation upon Deputation from the Country and one or two from the City have waited upon the Prime Minister and the Chancellor of the Exchequer with a view to including some measure of relief, principally aiming at a relaxation of our present Currency Law. No satisfactory reply has been given . . .

Nor would it if Loyd had his way. He was determined to keep the Whig government on the straight and narrow, and in a letter to Wood in June he with some justification put the blame on the Bank's failure to protect its banking reserve of notes during the enforced outflow of bullion: 'I could at any time convulse Manchester by gross mismanagement of my banking business – and the Bank of England, acting with infinitely larger powers, can and recently has convulsed the whole Country by mismanagement of its banking affairs'. Against which, 'the Bill never pretended to afford any protection'. But the City as a whole knew where to pin the blame, and in early July there was presented to government a 'Petition of the Merchants, Bankers, and Traders of London against the Bank Act', essentially a protest against credit rationing but with larger implications:[7] the Peelite cornerstone was starting to look shaky.

So it was against an uncertain background that Joshua Bates on 15 July left instructions at Bishopsgate before departing to Ems for a holiday and cure. He may not have impressed a Whig politician, but on his home patch we see a master businessman in action, looking into his murky crystal ball and, empirically and instinctively, knowing what courses to action to take:

Sugar. There will be a question about Sugar. My impression is that $\frac{30}{6}$ should not be refused . . . if not sold at that Antwerp is now as good a place of deposit as London (the ships going in Ballast to the Baltic for corn will take sugar in case it is desired to reship it as cheap as from London) and is much cheaper in point of charges . . .

Tea seems very low and is more likely to advance than recede. It will therefore be best to sell only the small parcels required to close sales . . .

Cotton we are agreed to realise gradually.

Tobacco. Altho' it is dreadful to keep Purton [where?] after the first of August I should prefer his remaining . . . His coming away might cause a fall in prices and it might be well to suggest his paying a double brokerage in order to disguise the purchases after he has left . . .

Wheat. Sales of Abbots should be *pushed*. The consignees should in my opinion be urged to get an offer subject to approval – and I would accept 50/- if no more can be obtained as I see no reason why such wheat should not be at 40/- before a month. The potatoes that I got from Sheen [where Bates lived when not in town] today are the best and the largest we have ever grown and were planted on the same ground where the crop failed last year.

Flour. There is no question in my mind as to the propriety of selling as fast as it arrives. I think there will be very little done in the corn markets until prices are 10/- @ 15/- lower per quarter. People have got high prices into their minds . . .

I cannot help thinking that the Free trade laws coupled with the immense expenditure for internal improvements and the high price and low stocks of Cotton will together keep the balance of trade against the Country until the laws are changed or the Railways finished, and that we shall be just on the verge of a panic for 18 months to come. At all events money will be valuable and we *must* be cautious about locking it up – and realise what we hold of *goods and stocks gradually* as the markets permit . . .

That evening he reached Dover and wrote to Tom Baring: 'Things always begin to rise the moment I leave Town. If good crops can make things better there is nothing to fear for never since I have known England did they look better. From London to this place I did not see a patch that was defective in the wheat fields.'[8]

In early August the question of the act continued to hover. 'I hear that George Glyn has become a convert to the necessity of repealing the act of 1844', Wood wrote to Loyd on the 9th, to which Loyd sharply replied the next day: 'I know nothing of G. Glyn's opinions or of his conversion. He is engaged in a very extended banking concern, and surrounded by all the influences of railroad vanity and speculation.' But what more immediately occupied men's minds was the deeply troubled state of the corn market, following the failure to adjust (as correctly noted by Bates) to the dramatically lower prices consequent upon the very heavy amount of wheat coming in from the Mediterranean and elsewhere since June. There were numerous failures in the trade, and on the 19th there fell to the partners of Prescotts a task of the utmost delicacy:

The Committee were occupied nearly the whole of this day, in closely inspecting the affairs of Messrs W. R. Robinson & Co, who through imprudent operations in Corn have found themselves in embarrassment . . . The great personal esteem they entertained for Mr W. R. Robinson, the head of the house, and the present Governor of the Bank of England, and the desire they felt of averting from the commercial body so severe a blow, as the failure of a house in their high position, would have led them to have incurred considerable inconvenience and even hazard, if they could have found themselves in any way justified after inspection of their accounts. It is therefore with the utmost regret that the Committee were compelled to inform Mr Robinson, that they could not assist him, as they took an unfavourable view of his affairs; it would seem that we have entertained a very erroneous impression of the amount of Mr Robinson's private property; we entertained the idea, from whence we derived we know not, that he was a Man worth upwards of £100,000, independent of his business; whereas it would appear his private property, including his Directorial qualification [i.e. his holdings of Bank stock] and a landed Estate in Gloucestershire, cannot be estimated at more than £25,000. His capital in the business is not more than £22,000; the stoppage of the House we fear is inevitable.[9]

The Governor of the Bank had failed. Loyd was unsympathetic, telling Wood that it was 'the result of extensive Corn Speculations, entered into and very foolishly conducted by his Son and partner and not properly controlled by himself', adding that the failure was 'merely a part of the general smash in the Corn Trade which sober minded persons have for some time past anticipated'. But most people in the City were profoundly shocked, and in the words of one correspondent on the 24th, 'it has created an extraordinary sensation, in consequence of the head of the firm occupying the prominent position of Governor of the Bank of England'.[10] The new Governor was James Morris, head of the merchants Morris, Prevost & Co.

The crisis deepened during September as a whole series of mercantile firms went down, among them several East India houses that had been badly affected by the recent alteration in the sugar duties. Gower, Nephews & Co, merchants over-committed in Mauritius sugar estates, failed on the 11th, and that meant another member of the Bank of England's Court, Abel Lewes Gower, having to leave it; as did the failure on the 18th of the East and West India merchants Reid, Irving & Co, whose senior partner Sir John Rae Reid had not long since been Governor of the Bank and who had vainly led commercial opposition to the Whig policy of equalising duties on foreign and colonial sugar. Between these two failures there occurred the stoppage with liabilities of over £2.6m of the discount house Sandersons, within days of the sudden death of its managing partner, William Morris senior. It was, as sports commentators like to say, all happening. The City's mood inevitably became ever more sombre. Charles Churchill junior noted on the 16th that 'business cannot be done on the usual scale, many of the large timber merchants holding off entirely'; John Abel Smith reflected on the 24th that he had never known such 'general alarm, discord, and distrust'; and at the start of October it was reported that 'on 'Change this afternoon business was as nearly as possible at a stand still'.[11]

The new month merely brought new turns of the screw, and on the 11th Magniac Jardine was reporting to Hong Kong that 'since the departure of the last mail the money difficulties have been progressively becoming worse, & the additional failures of important mercantile houses have been to an alarming extent'. The list included

Fry, Griffiths & Co, 'brokers, whose stoppage produced much sensation on the produce markets from the extensive business they had acquired through their means of giving facilities to holders of goods'. The letter went on:

> You may suppose how severely such disasters must cripple the means of other houses, while, though the resources of the Bank of England have been liberally afforded to the extent of its safety, the pressure has been so great as to compell the Directors occasionally to suspend assistance entirely, and other usual sources of accommodation are locked up. We confess we cannot see how the evil is to be arrested, unless by Government interference with the stringency of the currency act, of which there appears to be no present prospect. Want of confidence is extreme.

That was the ineluctable rub: an intense frustration by now existed that there was in the Bank's Issue Department a large reserve rendered inoperative by what *Punch* aptly termed 'The Obstruction in Threadneedle Street', in other words the Bank Charter Act.[12]

On Saturday, 16 October 1847, against a background of country banks starting to tumble, there assembled at the chancellor of the exchequer's the chancellor himself, the prime minister and the colonial secretary on the one hand; and on the other hand governor Morris, deputy-governor Henry James Prescott, his brother W. G. Prescott the private banker, the Bank directors G. W. Norman and William Cotton, and the inevitable Samuel Jones Loyd. Certainly the last four of these City representatives had, unlike most in the City, a strong emotional commitment to the full rigour of the 1844 act. There ensued what would become an almost ritualistic piece of by-play through the next twenty years:

> The Governor stated that it was quite within the means of the Bank of England, as far as that establishment itself was concerned, to carry out the provisions of Peel's Bill, but that they could not consistently with their own position as Bankers afford further extensive aid . . . They would afford what aid they could, but their present power of assistance was in fact limited to the amount of their daily receipts . . .
> Mr Loyd explained that the evil now to be apprehended and contended with was the destruction of confidence, which might result in the breaking up of the deposit system in Scotland and the North of England, by means of which capital is collected in small sums, and advanced in larger sums to the great industrial establishments, and that the suspension of this system would at once throw a large portion of the population out of employment. No aid which did not effect the restoration of confidence would be of any service.

The parties assembled then agreed that there was no remedy for this within the law ... After much discussion the conclusion was arrived at that the government might direct an unlimited issue of Bank Notes by the Bank of England on condition that no advance was made by them under a high rate of Interest: and it was hoped that when it was found practicable to obtain advances that confidence would be in a great part restored.[13]

The experts put 'the facts' of the case, the politicians take responsibility for the ultimate decision: such would become the convention, yet it seems that in this case even Loyd tacitly accepted that there was no alternative but to waive his cherished act.

For the moment, though, no action was taken, perhaps in the hope that the situation would improve of its own accord. If so it was a vain hope, as over the following week the money market 'suffered severely', nine and ten per cent being commonly charged on best short bills, and the Stock Exchange stayed 'a scene of continued alarm and excitement'. In the graphic words of one merchant to another on Tuesday the 19th, 'I would not advise you to take bills on Barings even'. Yet during that week there was an episode which is a reminder that times of falling markets and credit squeezed dry are by no means times of loss for everyone:

A manufacturer holding £100,000 – North-Western Railway Debentures (guaranteed 5 per cent for five years) – required bank notes to meet his liabilities. He went to Samuel Jones Loyd and desired to have his debentures discounted; Samuel Jones Loyd refused; the manufacturer replied, 'I must have money'. The banker rejoined, 'I can't do it. But stay; strike off 25 per cent and I will, but I give but five minutes to consider.' The wretched manufacturer had no choice but to submit to the extortion or to suspend payments. Samuel Jones Loyd gave £75,000 Bank of England notes and became possessed of £100,000 North-Western Railway Debentures.[14]

The teller of this unflattering tale was Lord George Bentinck, and something must be allowed for the prejudice of a Tory protectionist who tarred Loyd with the same brush as Peel.

Early on Saturday the 23rd ten leading City figures, including Samuel Gurney and George Carr Glyn, waited on the ministers and requested a suspension of the Act. Later in the morning, Morris and Norman also knocked on the door at Downing Street, and once again the ball was knocked over the net:

The Governor stated that in his opinion, the Bank was still in a position to maintain itself within the limits of the Act of 1844, but that he did not feel confident that this could be done without resorting to some active measures such as a Sale of Securities, or, the limiting accommodation in the way of Discounts.

Lord John Russell and the Chancellor of the Exchequer considered any restrictions in the way of Discount &c &c to be highly inexpedient and expressed a strong wish, that the Bank should act liberally today, with an emphatic assurance that happen what might, the letter authorising a possible deviation from the Law of 1844 should be sent to the Bank on Monday morning.[15]

News of the meeting leaked to the City, and the evening edition of the *Morning Chronicle* reported that 'Consols have improved today, and a better feeling is prevalent in the Stock Exchange'. George Grote the next day was privately scathing – 'the cry of "*must not let merchants fail*" is used just in the same way as that of "*must not let poor people starve*" in regard to Ireland' – but the City was still sufficiently merchant-dominated for the more ignoble cry to enjoy a certain compelling power.[16]

'The deed is done; and I hope it will succeed, but, I never did anything so unwillingly in my life. I am very curious to know the effect in the City. I am afraid that it will be too much approved.' Thus Wood, in all financial matters a strict Peelite, to Loyd on the Monday morning. Gurney later recalled that historic day as it affected him in the very nerve-centre of the City:

We had again a very heavy demand upon us; and we applied to the Governor, and said that, to supply Lombard-street with what was wanted, we should require £200,000 more . . . The Governor postponed a decision on our application till two o'clock. At one o'clock, however, the letter from the Government authorising relaxation was announced. The effect was immediate. Those who had sent notice for their money in the morning sent us word that they did not want it – that they only ordered payment by way of precaution. And after the notice we only required about £100,000 instead of £200,000. From that day we had a market of comparative ease.[17]

So easy that ultimately the Bank did not have to exceed the fiduciary issue of notes as laid down by the act: instead, it was the fact alone of the letter having been issued, potentially allowing such a relaxation, that turned the crisis. Disraeli, in the witty speech that he afterwards claimed made him party leader, compared the suspension of the act to the liquefaction of St Januarius's blood ('the remedy is equally efficient and equally a hoax') and he was not far off the mark. That, however, was what the City as a whole demanded, and the day after suspension Wood wrote to Cotton that 'the mode of doing it could hardly be wrong after the long & nervous consultations which we had with all you great authorities on the subject'.[18] The Chancellor was very sensibly determined not to be accused of imposing unwarranted government interference.

Out of the cumulative mercantile wreckage of 1847, Joshua Bates and his house once again came up smelling of roses: 'We do not hold on our own account £20,000 worth of goods, and our consignments, which are also moderate, will sell for enough to cover our advances', he smugly informed his American agent early in November. However, another major failure was about to shake the City. Two years earlier Evans in his survey had admiringly described Trueman & Cook as the leading colonial broking house in Mincing Lane:

> Such is the extent of their operations, that it is said, they dispose of produce of the worth of several millions of money in the course of the year. They are general brokers, and do not, like other firms, confine their attention to one special article; they sell largely of sugar, coffee, spices, indigo, &c, upon which they take the commission, which is their remuneration . . .
>
> Mr Cook is understood to be the 'great power' of the House 'out of doors', and Mr Trueman, the 'great power' of the House 'in-doors'. The one confines the whole of his attention to the arrangement of operations; the other, to the calculations, showing their probable success. Both partners pay much attention to the movements of trade; and the statistics, published in their 'Overland Circular', are generally regarded as accurate and instructive.[19]

On 15 November, Trueman & Cook failed; it was generally assumed that, like Fry, Griffiths a few weeks earlier, the firm had been undone by its practice of making advances on consignments to merchants who had foundered during the crisis.

But that was not the whole story, and early the next year Barings received from James Cook a lengthy narrative written for the sake of 'setting myself right before you'. Upset by accusations that he had 'suddenly and unexpectedly stopped the house after having by my exclusive management "ruined it" ', Cook explained in detail that the main unpaid debts to the firm were attributable to ill-advised accounts entered into several years before by Joseph Trueman senior against his wishes. And:

With regard to my having assumed the *sole* management of the house I can with earnest truth state, that it would have been the *greatest* possible relief to me if Mr Joseph Trueman Jnr had taken any portion of the burthen off my shoulders. By degrees however, from his great inefficiency and want of memory, I was compelled to withdraw all dependence upon him and of necessity to depend entirely upon myself. How gladly however I seized upon any arrangement for a division of labor, and how little anxious I was to keep the whole except from necessity, can be proved by my having gradually relinquished from 1845 a share of it to my present partner. I only required *active* help, and was happy enough to avail myself of it, for nothing but an iron constitution would have withstood all I had to encounter solitarily for many years, without any assistant council or help . . .

From the stoppage of the house until now I have been silent, it is my intention to be so still, for no spectacle to my mind is so degrading as the exhibition of private differences.

I would not trouble you with this but that, after the kindness I have always received from your firm, and the interest recently taken by Mr Bates, I do covet much to retain your good opinion.

I write this entirely for *your* perusal and with no view of putting the case before any other party.

There was a gratifying outcome to this trauma, for in the 1852 edition of his physiology Evans added a footnote that after the firm's failure 'the partners separated, and Mr Cook holds again a very prominent position in the produce-markets'.[20]

Within months of the 1847 crisis, France and much of the rest of Europe was convulsed by revolution. Early on there was talk of British intervention to restore the French monarchy, but James Capel fairly reflected City opinion when he told the Royal Bank of Scotland at the end of February 1848 that 'the time for Crusades in favour of Dynasties is over, and too much money has already been spent in favour of the ungrateful Bourbon Race'. Some London houses with intimate Continental connections (notably Rothschilds) were temporarily hit as a result of the turbulent European events of 1848–49, but in general the City benefited from the marked capital flight, totalling some £20m by the summer of 1849. 'Trade of course suffers, but the business of my House has been increased by the transmission of money from France & Spain for safety to this country', Bates noted as early as May 1848. Bates handled the crisis on a day-to-day basis with typical acumen, and there was a wealth of meaning in Tom Baring's remark to him that August that 'if I thought that one or two of your moves showed too rapid and short a tack for that character of steadiness which gives us a superiority over the Jews and makes people prefer doing business with us, it was because I was not on the spot and could not understand all the circumstances of the case'.[21]

London in 1848 had its own moment of threatened revolution. The Chartists gathered on Kennington Common on Monday, 10 April, and the City, as the *Morning Chronicle* explained, took no chances:

> The Bank of England was not only defended by an extra garrison, but its parapets were surmounted with a breast-work of sand bags, so placed as to defend and cover the besieged, but allowing apertures sufficiently large to permit him to take deadly aim upon his assailants. The Royal Exchange held within its area 200 pensioners; and the Mansion-house was also supplied with a strong guard. In fact, this was the case with the Mint, the Custom-house, the India-house, and many of the private banks and warehouses.[22]

The route of the main Chartist procession was from Fitzroy Square via Holborn, Farringdon Street and Blackfriars Bridge, thereby missing the City proper; but there were also eastern gatherings of Chartists, who met each other in Finsbury Square and, about 12,000 strong, marched down Bishopsgate Street and Gracechurch Street on their way to London Bridge.

Meanwhile, at 10.45 in the committee room of the Stock Exchange, there were anxious discussions, with William Hichens in the chair in the absence of the chairman and deputy-chairman, both on duty as special constables in the Royal Exchange:

> The Chairman said the Bankers in Lombard Street were sending over their Securities to the Bank of England, and recommended to confine all business today within the narrowest possible limits; and the present meeting was convened to consider the propriety of closing the House.
> Mr Mullens suggested that such a Step might occasion serious and unnecessary alarm, not only throughout the Country, but all over Europe, and most exaggerated conclusions would no doubt be drawn as to the State of the Metropolis, if the Stock Exchange was to be shut.

Outside the Bank of England a large crowd of spectators 'most vociferously cheered' whenever soldiers entered the building; but inside the Stock Exchange a nervous trading floor awaited developments south of the river:

> Between one and two o'clock, the deepest anxiety was evinced as to whether the Chartists would proceed with the procession in defiance of

the great force which the Government had brought to bear against its progress. About two o'clock, however, the news arrived that the procession had been abandoned, and that the Chartists at Kennington were fast dispersing. The intelligence was received with much gratification, and the national anthem was universally called for. The members instantly acted upon the suggestion, and being uncovered sang 'God save the Queen' in the most enthusiastic style. Consols immediately went up.

It was a turning point of British history, and the jubiliant tone to the *Morning Chronicle*'s 'Money Market and City News' written the next day caught the City's mood:

The triumph of the people over the mob, the victory of peace and order against violence and intimidation, which was so happily obtained yesterday by the loyal conduct of the citizens of London, is indeed a subject for great thankfulness, and should fill every honest heart with joy. The benefits arising from so happy a termination to those agitating disturbances will be speedily felt throughout the land ... Our energetic suppression of disorder will also tell to advantage in all parts of the world, and its effects will be speedily manifested in the confidence which foreign nations will have in directing their produce to this country, which is now almost the only one in which they can feel the security necessary to induce business: England has only to be quiet, and the trade of the world must centre in her.[23]

CHAPTER TWELVE

From Turds to Dibs

'It must', Loyd told Wood in August 1847 after the failure of Robinson, the Governor of the Bank, 'expedite the period for those general discussions and arrangements respecting the future management of the Bank, which could not under any circumstances have been long de-layed'. So it proved.[1] After a stalling meeting of proprietors the follow-ing month, at which one stockholder pointed out that six of the last nine governors had become insolvent and Governor Morris stiffly insisted that 'it was not customary for any discussion to be entered into' about the merits or otherwise of proposed new directors, significant reform was introduced in 1848. Though private bankers remained excluded from the Court (on the traditional grounds that they should not be privy to the secrets of a rival bank), a new emphasis was placed on mercantile weight and financial expertise, especially through a rule which meant that a busy City figure no longer had to leave the Court if he declined to become governor. Over the next twenty years the Court became a more substantial and better qualified body, and included a greater sprinkling of the emerging breed of merchant bankers, such as Tom Baring from 1848 to 1867. There was still, however, no immediate disposition to subscribe to notions of enlarged public responsibilities. 'I think the Bank of England should be conducted upon the same principle as any other bank is conducted', William Cotton informed the Commons Committee of 1848 into the previous year's crisis. Yet in actual if non-articulated practice that crisis did mark a certain water-shed: henceforth the Bank sought to refrain from being an active competitor in the discount market and instead tried to regulate the market by means of a variable Bank rate.[2] The process was not always conscious at this stage, but the implication was clear enough that considerations of profit were now becoming secondary to those of central banking.

The City changed in other ways as a result of the 1847 crisis.[3] The partners of Prescotts reflected at the end of the year that 'the ranks of the commercial world in London have been thinned so unsparingly it is a matter of gratification to see how well the Bankers of London have maintained themselves', while the Governor of the Bank of England calculated that in the course of the crisis some thirty-three significant commercial houses in the City had failed. Many of these were East and/or West India houses, dependent on the traditional colonial-cum-protectionist trading system that was now being overturned by the increasingly systematic adoption of free trade. The crisis effected a ruthless cutting down of the City's dead wood – and it left the protectionist cause there inadequately manned to resist the rising pressure to conform to the tenets of an international economy, as was eloquently shown by the City's inability in 1849 to mount an effective challenge to the repeal of the Navigation Acts, a repeal heartily celebrated by the Baltic Exchange. Some lingering doubts remained – 'the question still is what will be the effect of free trade on the balance of trade', Bates was asking himself in 1850 – but the potentially harsh truth was that the City was now playing in a different ball-game, one that internationally minded merchant banks would find easier to adjust to than old-style merchants whose interests tended to be bound up in a particular geographical area.[4]

Peelite free trade was about to become one of the City's cardinal orthodoxies, and so too, if more tentatively at this stage, was adherence to the Bank Charter Act. Why should this have been, granted that it was said in 1847 that only three people in the City supported it? One of those three (the figure was surely an exaggeration) was Loyd, and in the immediate wake of the crisis he did an extremely effective job in ensuring the Whig government followed his line of blaming the Bank of England for the turmoil rather than the act, a piece of legislation he continued to couch in terms of the higher morality. Wood was willing to be imbued and wrote to Loyd shortly before Christmas: 'Take Glyn for instance. Is not his judgement warped by the difficulties in which he was placed? Can you expect men who believe that an issue of paper would have saved them, to think so much of general good as of their own?' Yet it is arguable that the very *suspension* of the act in 1847 crucially blunted City opposition, for it was hard not to feel that it mattered much less now that it was apparent the government would relax its stringency in an emergency. And when in 1856 the directors of the Bank were asked to express their individual opinions on the subject, almost all affirmed that the act was fundamentally a fit and proper thing.[5] One way and another a holy trinity was being created – gold standard, free trade, Bank Charter Act – and it would take more than reason to shake it.

'The world', Joshua Bates reflected on his sixty-fifth birthday in October 1852 (though at the time he believed he was only sixty-three), 'seems very prosperous since the discovery of Gold in California & Australia, & the extension of railways & navigation by Steam are working great changes in the world'. He could not have been more right, for in the early 1850s the international economy was in the process of taking off spectacularly, so that by 1870 the volume of international trade would be five times what it had been back in 1840. Indeed, in retrospect the 1860s marked a unique decade: capital, goods and labour flowed almost unhindered round much of the known world in unprecedented quantities, the nearest we would ever come to a fully liberal, free-trading system. And at the heart of that system lay the City of London, providing not only unrivalled entrepôt facilities in terms of physical trade but also credit accommodation on a worldwide basis. In the words of a parliamentary committee in 1858, addressing a prominent City accountant who did not disagree: 'The trade of the world could hardly be carried on without the intervention of English credit. A man in Boston cannot buy a cargo of tea in Canton without getting a credit from Messrs Matheson or Messrs Baring.' Moreover, as a concomitant of this, the London money market found itself becoming increasingly sophisticated, increasingly international, with domestic bills of exchange gradually starting to give way in importance to foreign or external bills as London's great contribution to the provision of short-term commercial credit – bills guaranteed by the City's growing array of accepting houses. The pattern was similar in long-term finance. Although Paris until the end of the 1860s offered keen competition, London during the third quarter of the century consolidated and immeasurably strengthened its position as the world's leading international capital market, providing a string of foreign loans to capital-hungry states seeking to enjoy the fruits of scientific progress and industrialisation. British overseas investments, some £200m in the mid-1850s, increased about fivefold over the next twenty years and, in conjunction with the permanent effects of the railway boom, a fully-fledged *rentier* class was born.[6]

There was one other crucial component to all this global activity, and that was the profound transformation taking place in the world's communications. In 1851 a submarine cable was laid between Dover and Calais; and a year later Bates was noting that 'the Electric Telegraph is used more & more', adding that 'news is transmitted from Vienna in 12 hours, from Paris in half an hour'. Other European cities soon followed, and by 1860, in the context of negotiations over a

Russian loan, he was able to record with satisfaction: 'Rec^d a Telegram that the Contract for the Loan had been signed & despatched per mail, so that we shall have it in 5 days. The Telegraph is beginning to be much used and very usefull.' Six years later a cable was successfully laid under the Atlantic. One should not exaggerate the pace of change in practice – at Barings indeed, the twice-weekly foreign post day remained the fulcrum of business – but there was no denying the larger trend towards the City as hub of a global commercial wheel.[7] Mid-Victorian Britain is still remembered as the workshop of the world, Isambard Kingdom Brunel still holds imaginative sway, but it was in the under-publicised accounts department that the long-term future lay.

*

George Russell for one would not have doubted the future. He was a large Australian sheep farmer and in May 1851 was in London partly to visit the Great Exhibition. Walking the streets of the City 'the dark, smoky, sombre appearance of the buildings presents rather a striking and unfavourable contrast to many of the light cheerful-looking continental towns', he recorded in his journal, adding that 'the atmosphere also has usually a dull hazy appearance, even in fine weather'. But his main interest was less in air quality than in witnessing what happened at the London end to his adopted country's main export:

> On visiting the extensive docks crowded with shipping, the large roomy warehouses attached filled with merchandise from all parts of the world, with the great business activity and bustle which is here met with, it gives one an idea of the great commercial importance of England, quite surpassing anything of the kind I have hitherto seen.
>
> I saw more wool in the warehouses attached to the London Docks than I had ever seen before at one time, the operations of receiving it from vessels discharging, delivering that which had been sold, while numbers of buyers were examining the parcels that were to be offered for sale that evening. I was struck with the manner in which this examination is carried on . . . A large piece of the bagging is cut open at the end of each bale. The buyers walk along, pull out a handful of wool from each bale, examine it and note the value &c. The handful of wool is not generally returned, but thrown down on the floor . . . The bales appear generally much torn and out of shape in the warehouse, and the brokers cover them with numerous marks to identify the bales numbered in the catalogues &c.
>
> The sale-room in the evening was well-attended, each man with a catalogue before him, marking the prices of the lots as they are knocked

down, a remarkably speedy process. It is rather amusing to hear the rapidity and eagerness with which the biddings are made for favorite lots.

The Australian wool trade, a relative newcomer to the world's commercial panoply, was booming by this time; old-established City firms by no means succeeded in dominating the whole market, whether in terms of imports or re-exports; and among Australian wool merchants (though in his case originally a Canadian) who by the mid-1850s had set up their own City houses was Frederick Dalgety.[8]

Or take the Greeks. By 1852, six years after the repeal of the Corn Laws, over half the grain imported into Britain came from ports in the Mediterranean and Black Seas, and the following year A. Mongredien of 36 Mark Lane published in the *Mark Lane Express* a report on the phenomenon:

> This large and increasing trade is exclusively in the hands of a small body of merchants, all connected together by the ties of nationality, of religion, and in a great measure of kindred. They created this cargo trade, and they probably will keep it to themselves . . . In 1820, the trade with the Levant, then of small extent, was wholly in the hands of British merchants. In that year, two or three Greek houses were established in London, with moderate capitals and humble pretensions. Their operations, though at first limited, were highly successful, and received rapid development. Other Greek establishments were formed, and gradually the whole of the trade passed away from the British houses into the hands of the Greeks, who realized rapid, and in many instances colossal, fortunes . . .

It was not only corn, Mongredien emphasised, that these Greek merchants imported into England: there was also silk, opium, fruit and so on from Turkey and Greece as well as cotton from Egypt; and in return they largely sent back to these places cotton piece goods from Lancashire. The emphasis of these merchants (with such names as Rodocanachi, Spartali, Argenti) was firmly on cash and barter, on rapid turnover and low stocks of goods, and on 'on the spot' dealings with people personally known to them, indeed often related. Some were genuinely international houses, above all Ralli Brothers, which by the 1850s was extending its branches to India; and it was the London-based head of Ralli Brothers, Pandias Stephen Rallis, who was probably responsible for pioneering the Greek merchants' unique method of trading in cargoes of grain while they were still in passage from Odessa or wherever, a method that depended on the bill of lading and a sample of goods being sent by post to Britain as soon as the cargoes had been loaded. It was a method that depended on the tightest possible control. Pandias Rallis himself – married to Marietta Scaramanga, like himself the offspring of a Chios merchant – was Greek Consul in London and the most successful, best-known of all his countrymen in the City. He died in 1865; the dominance of the Greeks in the corn trade lasted only another generation.[9]

Wool and corn remain staples, but who now remembers guano? A pamphlet published in 1843 provides some exposition:

> Guano is the deposit of sea birds. Innumerable flocks of them frequent a great portion of the west coast of South America; and for ages immemorial these birds have left their deposits, either on the small islands lying contiguous to the mainland, or on the mainland itself. It is well known that in the regions where rains are frequent, the action of the same, conjoined with exposure to sun and air, eats out the virtues of the Guano; but where, as on the coast of Bolivia, and on a considerable portion of that of Peru, it never rains, the Guano retains and concentrates all the strength and fertilizing virtues of its original deposits.

A host of scientific and agricultural evidence was then adduced to prove guano's matchless fertilising properties. Publishers of this pamphlet were Antony Gibbs & Sons, who from 1842 to 1861 enjoyed a lucrative monopoly over the merchanting of Peruvian guano, a trade which peaked between 1850 and 1856, in which year Gibbs disposed of 214,707 tons of the stuff in Britain alone. Ironically, considering that it made the house's fortune (annual profits during the 1850s running at up to £100,000), the firm at the outset entered into the business with less than enthusiasm. William Gibbs, the senior partner, lamented in 1842 that his Lima branch had been induced 'to forsake the sound mercantile principles we have ever inculcated' and wrote melodramatically of 'dismay – distress – unfortunate Huano Speculation! . . . Let us now devise the best means of getting out of the scrape.' But Lima had already gone too far, while at the London end the overall control of the trade was soon in the much more confident hands of William's nephew, Henry Hucks Gibbs. Did he ever spare a thought for the Chincha Islands themselves? A journalist, giving new dignity to the term 'muck-raking', described life on 'three huge rocks, situated about 100 miles from Callao, the seaport of Lima':

> These islands, covered to a great depth with guano, are perfectly barren, from the excessive quantity becoming destructive of vegetation. Those

employed in transporting the manure to the loading places are Chinese, whilst negroes and the lowest of the mixed races of Callao and Lima are employed in stowing the cargoes. The Chinese, who, under specious promises, are inveighed to the island for a term of three years, seldom live to complete the term of their slavery, for the nauseous dust and the overpowering effluvia of ammonia in which they work are of themselves rapidly destructive of life.

The article then detailed the appalling treatment (including torture) of this peculiarly unenviable labour force. Eventually the Peruvian Government declined to renew the contract, local merchants taking it instead, but by then the financial foundations had been laid for what would soon become one of the City's most prestigious merchant banks. 'The House of Gibbs that made their dibs, By selling the turds of foreign birds': all things considered, the jingle was polite enough.[10]

High-minded and quite beyond satire, the textile quarter remained a flourishing, integral part of the commercial City. By mid-century Brettle's of Wood Street was no longer the market leader; George Brettle's eldest son, Edward, a partner from 1843, seems to have lacked entrepreneurial thrust and preferred the pursuits of a comfortable bachelor life based first in the Albany and then a substantial country house in Surrey. The Wood Street ascendancy passed to I. & R. Morley under the strong, paternalist control of Samuel Morley. He was effectively in charge from about 1840, rebuilt the warehouse in much enlarged form in 1850, and took over the Nottingham business in 1860. Morley himself, a strong Liberal and leading Nonconformist, moved in 1854 from Lower Clapton to a handsome house on Stamford Hill, complete with seventy acres of what his contemporary biographer called 'singularly well-timbered' grounds. That same year Cook's of St Paul's Churchyard moved into new premises there, given the full literary as well as visual treatment by the *Illustrated London News*:

> Unlike most of the large warehouses in the heart of London, it is not an assemblage of small buildings, incorporated from time to time to meet the exigencies of business, but a complete whole . . . On entering we are met by the presence of abundant light . . . In addition to the four-sided wells which pierce the several floors in various places, there is in the centre of the building a grand elliptic lantern, adorned with elegant friezes at the several stories, which admits a flood of light from the sky, illuminating every stage. The galleries are supported by slender Doric columns; and solid walls are supported by a lateral series of elegant arches, which, viewed from various points of elevation, present picturesque vistas

suggestive of indefinite space and distance. This structure in point both of design and execution leaves nothing to be desired. To most people, in fact, it would appear more like a Walhalla than a warehouse . . .

It was a very different world in Milk Street (just along Cheapside from Wood Street), where in 1852 the sixteen-year-old Joseph Chamberlain entered the family cordwaining business at his father's insistence. He found there a warehouse with no shop window and an enterprise struggling to remain afloat on profits of three figures.[11]

Another great Victorian statesman who also spent early years in the City's textile warehouses was Richard Cobden, the apostle of free trade and self-appointed conscience of the commercial middle classes. Early in 1850 he found himself confronted by the influence of the sixth great power. At Barings itself, Joshua Bates on Sunday, 13 January apparently did not suspect the storm ahead: 'Tomorrow we bring out a Russian Loan 4½ per Cent at 93, the amount £5,500,000. My belief is that the amount is too large, that the public will think so, & I should rather have brought it out at 92 but the Emperor has fixed the terms . . .' Two days later *The Times* City report allayed such anxieties, as well as unspoken ones:

> The new Russian Loan has been the chief topic of attention . . . That the terms are favourable is universally admitted, and the investment is still further recommended by the allegation that the money is wanted for the completion of a work of internal improvement. At the same time this allegation must be received with some allowance, since it is understood that the railway in question [from St Petersburg to Moscow] has long been nearly finished, that the iron and rolling stock are on the ground, and that little remains except to lay down the rails; so that it would appear probable the undertaking is in a great measure used as a pretext, in order to obtain in a popular way supplies for exigencies which have resulted from the recent war. A notice which has been given of the meeting in the City to reprobate the transaction has, it need hardly be said, produced no effect on the capitalists who may be expected to subscribe.

Unimpressed by the Bishopsgate subterfuge, so soon after the brutal Russian suppression of revolt in Hungary, Cobden was to address a protest meeting at the City of London Tavern (also in Bishopsgate) on Friday lunchtime. By then, unfortunately, the horse had bolted, for Bates on Thursday was noting that 'the Russian Loan goes wonderfully well'. The meeting itself was described by the *Economist*:

The body of the hall, the gallery, and even the staircase and landing leading to the large hall, were crowded long before the hour named for taking the chair. Mr Cobden made a speech, and declared that to lend money to the Emperor of Russia was to sanction the deeds of violence and blood committed by him in Hungary. The meeting appeared to meet with little sympathy from the monied classes. Mr Cobden's boldness was generally admitted, while his discretion was called in question.

During an interruption to Cobden's speech a chorus went up of 'three groans for Barings', but Bates the next day put such jeers in perspective: 'The subscriptions for the Loan amount to 13 millions . . . They talk of 2 to 4 premium in the Stock Exchange'. Or put another way, Barings earned a commission of £105,000, the Tsar got his money and, subterfuge or not, the line would be ready for Vronsky to catch his first glimpse one frosty morning of Anna Karenin.[12]

Railways were springing up everywhere, and much of the money came through the London capital market. There was increasing competition, both within the market and relative to Paris, and in April 1851 the Piedmontese finance minister, Cavour, gave detailed instructions to his representative in London:

It is necessary at all costs to get out of the unfortunate position in which we find ourselves vis-à-vis Rothschild. A loan contracted in England is the only means of regaining our independence . . . My intention is not to break with Rothschild at the moment, but only to prove to him that we can do without him . . . If we cannot obtain a loan in London very soon we will be reduced to submitting to the Rothschild yoke once more or suspending the work on our railways which is now being pressed forward with the greatest activity.

The Rothschild in question was Baron James, Nathan's brother, Paris-based and traditionally close to the Austrian Government. Cavour's man duly tried elsewhere, with an upshot recorded in another letter from Turin: 'Messrs Barings' refusal does not surprise me. I expected it. These gentlemen do not care to fight with Rothschild'. Cavour then suggested a secret approach to Hambros saying, 'if you allow it to be thought that you have given up serious negotiations for the moment, it would put Messrs Rothschild off the track'. The approach was a great opportunity for C. J. Hambro & Son, relative newcomers to the City, and in May a £4m loan was brought out at 85. James in Paris was crossness personified: he did all that he could to force down the price of Piedmontese securities, in both London and Paris, and so successful were his bear attacks that by August the loan was barely half subscribed. 'L'emprunt était ouvert', he remarked sardonically, 'mais pas couvert'. The turning-point came when Carl Joachim Hambro made an arrangement with a City speculator called Lewis Haslewood, who took £400,000 of the loan at just under 85; and when, later that autumn, Lord John Russell launched his popular cry 'Italy for the Italians' the success of the issue was assured. By early 1852 the price was up to 90, Hambro was able to sell at a profit the £400,000 tranche for which he had subscribed, and in terms of City rankings a new house was knocking at the door of the premier division of European loan contractors.[13]

By this time the City was also looking with renewed interest to the United States, thanks partly to the European revolutions of 1848–49, to the reviving state of the American economy, and also to the pertinacity of George Peabody. During the bleak mid-1840s he had operated in London virtually as a one-man market in American securities, calmly awaiting the restoration of public confidence in them; and now, in the early 1850s, he not only continued with that role, in close association with London's stockbrokers, but also operated to considerable effect on several other fronts, supplying iron for American railroads, short-term credits to American merchants and credit facilities to American travellers. 'We believe *we* pretty much regulate prices & are the principal controlers of the Market', Peabody remarked of his house in 1852 in relation to American securities in England. In June that year he played an important part in distributing to Britain and the Continent the pioneer issue of the Illinois Central, the first time the prospectus for an American railroad appeared in the London press. The next year Peabody himself brought out an issue (the Ohio & Mississippi Railroad), and soon it was clear that American railroads were to be a prominent feature of the London market, though it would be some time yet before their numbers proliferated there. Both Barings and Rothschilds declined to sponsor the Illinois issue, so that it was left to an assorted syndicate led by a decidedly lesser house, Devaux & Co, to bring it to the market. 'If we bring forward the good we shall be promoting the bad, and I have great doubts if we should touch them', Bates at the time wrote to his agent in the States; and that was very much the prevailing attitude in Bishopsgate towards the promotion of American railroads, though later that year both Barings and Rothschilds did agree to take a large block of Pennsylvania Railroad bonds.[14]

There was, however, one North American episode which stands out in these years, when native caution and sound judgement deserted

Barings. This was the over-ambitious issue which it handled with Glyns in the spring of 1853 for the Grand Trunk Railway Company of Canada, whose board of directors comprised the entire cabinet of the Province of Upper Canada as well as Thomas Baring and George Carr Glyn. It managed to raise over two-thirds of the projected £3.6m largely on the reputation of its backers, but within weeks the shares were at a discount and soon the railway was in severe financial difficulties; and though the contractors in 1859 triumphantly completed the line by building the Victoria Bridge in Montreal, it remained for many years thereafter an uphill, largely unrewarding financial struggle at the London end. 'The Grand Trunk business will go right, I think', Bates had reassured Baring in August 1853, but for once the Bostonian merchant got it wrong.[15]

On the Stock Exchange, arbiter of these matters, the emphasis in the 1850s was still heavily on domestic securities, whether government or railway: in 1853, of the total paid-up capital of quoted securities of £1215m, only £101m (less than 10 per cent) was foreign, predominantly representing the issues of foreign states. Nevertheless, whether in domestic or foreign securities, the tempo of business was perceptibly increasing. The advent of public telegraph lines from the late 1840s between London and other British cities led to the swift development of a far more responsive and integrated national securities market; while the submarine cable between Dover and Calais in 1851 meant for the first time prices in London and Paris were mutually available within business hours. With the number of members growing (up to 864 by 1850) and the volume of business expanding, the decision was taken in 1853 to pull down the old building and replace it with one over double the size. The new Stock Exchange, opened to business in March 1854, was architecturally rather undistinguished, but did have the compensating feature of a restaurant in the basement: this was Mabey's which, by the time it moved upstairs in 1872 to make way for a settling room, had acquired a reputation as the rendez-vous for many a daring deal.[16]

Along with the new building went the beginnings of a certain sense of professional status on the part of its inhabitants. A key text was *Practical Hints for Investing Money*, first published in 1855, often reprinted, and written by a member, Francis Playford. After giving the jobbers a clean bill of health ('they are in general men of considerable standing and reputed wealth') he stressed, with tortuous syntax, the unique expertise of his own fraternity:

It is not recommended that the public should entrust their stock-dealings to their banker's care; for they would far better consult their interests by employing their own broker. In fact, by adopting the latter course, they obtain the benefit of the broker's personal advice; whereas, by confiding stock transactions to the care of a banker who, having no discretionary power, merely gets the order executed without reference to its expediency or otherwise; for, in fact, it were idle to deny, that the public are thereby very often misled or induced to place their money in unsound securities, which would not be the case, if the business were entrusted to a broker; for, although the latter seldom possess the power of advising their principals in what particular stock they should invest, they frequently possess and exercise the negative influence of advising what securities to avoid; and this power is a far greater protection to the public than is generally believed.

Playford defended the broker's commission (traditionally $\frac{1}{8}$ per cent, but usually cut by half for speculative bargains) and called on the public to 'cheerfully pay to ensure for themselves the proper execution of the business', adding that 'few Brokers have ever been known to amass fortunes, though most of them, with a moderately good connexion, make fair incomes'. A fair, steady income was what Playford himself would have craved four years later, for in April 1859 he was declared as a bull; and on his readmission the following year, the chairman of the Committee issued an admonition, observing that at the time of the failure 'his means were very small and the account was of an alarming magnitude by which a most unjustifiable risk had been thrown on the Stock Exchange'.[17]

That was really the problem: a plethora of small-scale and in-adequately capitalised firms (the five partners and capital of £26,000 that the stockbrokers Laurence, Cazenove & Pearce had in 1846 was far above the norm); relatively easy entrance qualifications (recommendations from three members, each providing a surety of £300); and too many members, often of slender means, unable to resist the lure of speculation on their own account. A symptomatic if perhaps extreme example was William Le Grand. Following a large speculation in Consols he failed in May 1847 but was readmitted that August, when 'he promised most rigidly that he would not enter on any speculation for himself'. A year later he failed again, once more with a sizeable speculation in Consols on his own account, but by March 1849 an unabashed Le Grand was applying for readmission:

He stated that he is making exertions to liquidate the debts he owes in the House, he has two small estates, and he is also in expectation of recovering a portion of debts due to him from one or two of his old clients, and he intends if readmitted, of setting aside part of his forthcoming business for his creditors. With respect to having entered into a Speculation on his own account, he assured the Committee he was led into it in consequence of the defalcation of a principal, whom he knew to be of good property, and who had on all former occasions acted honorably by him, in many large share transactions.

Le Grand then explained how his client's defalcation had led him into the Consols speculation, and perhaps to his own surprise he was unanimously readmitted, lasting this time until May 1851. Only months later he was readmitted again, admonished, warned, and reminded of previous promises, such as to obtain sufficient cover to guard against possible loss; in replying Le Grand 'acknowledged gratefully the indulgence of the Committee, and would endeavour to act henceforward strictly in conformity with their wishes'. Finally, in September 1853, he failed again, and the following month:

> The conduct of Mr William Le Grand was brought under the notice of the Committee, and it having been shewn, that in two separate cases he had received sums of money for the purpose of investing in the English Funds, in the names of the respective parties, assuring them that the sums had been so invested, but the result proving that he had misapplied the money and made no such investments, it was resolved unanimously that William Le Grand having been guilty of dishonourable and disgraceful conduct, his name be ordered to be placed on the Black Board of the Stock Exchange.

The black board dated back to 1787, when many members had failed and not paid their creditors, and it remained the great moral pillory of the institution.[18]

Worse even than 'dishonourable and disgraceful conduct', there was nothing that vexed Stock Exchange creditors more than evidence of conspicuous consumption on the part of fellow-members who had failed owing them money. Henry Godwin, as the result of owning uninsured ships that went missing at sea, had failed in 1843 with debts of about £35,000. By June 1847 he had repaid only two shillings and ninepence in the pound to his creditors, appreciably less than the usual acceptable minimum to the Stock Exchange Committee of six shillings and eightpence, and his application for readmission was rejected, despite the assurance given that he was 'living now very economically in a house of £80 a year rent'. Two months later he tried again, and one of his recommenders stated that 'with respect to the charge of his living extravagantly, Godwin assured him he never spent up to his income, he never kept more than two horses, and always regretted the gift of a Carriage to him from his Father-in-law, which he felt bound to keep'. The vote still went against him, but in January 1849 another application at last succeeded, accompanied by the information that he was now in lodgings at a guinea a week.

Readmission alone did not always keep the creditors at bay. In April 1854 a complaint was lodged against a recently reinstated member called Thomas Trulock, who still owed £6,300. The Committee's attention was called to his squirearchical lifestyle: 'Mr Trulock has a house in The Regents Park and another at Crawley. He keeps six hunters, two carriage horses, a close carriage and several open ones, three grooms, coachman and footman and is constantly out with the hounds.' Trulock denied it all, stating that the hunting establishment belonged to a friend who stayed in his house at Crawley, that the house in Regents Park was rented out, that the marriage settlement stipulated that he should keep a close carriage for his wife, and that his annual expenditure was less than £500. While as to another of the complainant's charges: 'The Breakfast alluded to, did not deserve to be called a racing breakfast, being of a very simple nature and nothing beyond what any farmer would have given under similar circumstances'. The Committee was not convinced and Trulock was refused his annual re-election as a member.[19]

The lot of the solvent Capel Court population was to man the floor during the not very onerous trading hours of eleven to three. Sometimes there was frantic activity, but very often markets went quiet, even for days at a time. That was when elderly or frail members knew to beware. Towards the end of June 1851 the Managers of the Stock Exchange called upon the Committee to do something about 'the disgraceful scene which occurred in the Stock Exchange yesterday afternoon, a football having been introduced and between one and two hundred members engaged in the play for a considerable time'. One of these unmuddied oafs was identified as Henry Brown, and the Committee duly grilled him:

> The Chairman pointed out how derogatory it was to the character of the Stock Exchange that such disorderly conduct should be pursued, and expressed his surprise that the son of a member of the Committee so much respected as Mr Chas Brown should set so bad an example to the junior members of the House, and as the Committee were determined to suppress those disgraceful practices, he hoped Mr Henry Brown would aid them in so doing and would now give them an assurance that he

would not only refrain from them himself but discourage the practice whenever it was in his powers. Mr Henry Brown said he was afraid to give an absolute pledge, because on the impulse of the moment he might be led away to forget it, but he said he would endeavour to control any such impetuosity, and restrain himself as much as possible and avoid play for the future.

But if football was sidelined – though only temporarily, for in 1858 one of the Managers (James Capel) was 'grossly insulted' when he tried to blow for time – there was plenty of other work for idle hands. In January 1852 the Committee read a letter from William Hartridge complaining of the conduct of three members, who then appeared in person:

> Mr Mendes said that seeing Mr Hartridge going out of the House, with a blotting paper cap on, he could not help laughing but had no intention of giving offence.
> Mr Eykyn said he was going into the Stock Exchange, he met Mr Hartridge in New Court followed by several members, he turned round too, but had nothing to do with putting the cap on, and he denied that he made any noise, nor did he dance before him, as alleged by Mr Hartridge.
> Mr Pawle said that seeing Mr Hartridge leaving the House with a paper cap on, he followed to enjoy the fun.[20]

It was a place where, as in any school at any time, it was no fun being the odd person out.

*

There were few such japes in Lombard Street. In June 1851 a Swiss industrialist, yet another visitor to the Great Exhibition, went one morning to Smith, Payne & Smiths to cash a cheque for £30:

> I was shown to a seat facing a counter where five cashiers conducted their business. At five minutes to nine the official to whom I had to give my cheque took his place behind the counter. I had it in my hand and showed it to him. He did not say a word but emptied several little bags of gold coins into a drawer. Then he produced the well known little cash shovel that is used for coins in the banks. And then he just waited.
> At the stroke of nine he asked me if I wanted gold or bank-notes. I said I wanted gold. He did not count any of the sovereigns and half sovereigns but simply weighed them on his scales and then put them on the counter without taking any further notice of me. I counted the money and it was quite correct.

Complementing this genial atmosphere, a certain *gravitas* remained the leading characteristic of the best sort of private banker. It was a quality epitomised by Robert Bevan, the senior partner at Barclays for many years: a keen evangelical and prominent supporter of the YMCA, he was the severest of taskmasters towards any clerk who strayed in any detail. In general, it was still bottom that counted. 'He is not a brilliant man but perhaps not the worse banker on that account. I have a high opinion of his integrity and good sense.' Thus Loyd to his father in January 1850 about Henry Norman, a new recruit to the family bank, shortly before he himself was elevated to the peerage as Lord Overstone and left active business in Lothbury. Or as Raikes Currie was fairly criticised by his son Bertram: 'He had quickness, vivacity, and a considerable command of rhetoric, but these are not the qualities which make the ideal banker'.[21]

In the end, of course, it was an inherently unsustainable system. In 1853 the *Bankers' Magazine* analysed the twenty-five City-based private banks (twelve in Lombard Street) who were members of the clearing house and found that they had 104 partners between them, of whom sixty-seven had the same name as other partners. At Curries & Co all six partners were called Currie, at Smith, Payne & Smiths all but one of the six were called Smith. It was clearly neither an effective recruitment system nor a sufficiently certain way of ensuring adequate capital, even when in 1857 the legal maximum of partners was raised from six to ten. But there was also a sense in which the private bankers, as an endangered species, did not help themselves. Too many (such as the Lubbocks, the father renowned for astronomy, the son for entomology) did not put their best energies into the business; there was an almost doctrinaire refusal to pay interest even on deposit accounts, unlike the joint-stock banks; and there was a temperamental aversion to actively seeking business, an aversion so deep that even in the 1860s George Grenfell Glyn, himself one of the most vigorous private bankers, was remarking that 'it is apparently the fashion of the day boldly to ask for accounts, but I confess that is a course which I cannot bring myself to adopt unless in the case of personal friendship'. Joseph Dimsdale was senior partner during the 1850s of Dimsdale, Drewett, Fowler & Barnard. During the winter he and his family lived over the family bank at 50 Cornhill; and in the summer they moved to their country house in Essex, from where Dimsdale would ride to the City each day, stabling his horse at an inn close to the bank.[22] A happy life, but the age of steam now demanded something more than the traditional clip-clop.

The joint-stock banks – in the City, the London and Westminster, the London Joint Stock, the Union Bank of London, the London and County, and the Commercial of London – provided it with a vengeance. As early as 1845 Evans stressed the difference between the two animals:

> Instead of meeting in Joint Stock banks, as you do in private banks, cashiers and clerks peering through spectacles with a steady and staid appearance, whose only inquiries are respecting the weather and the prospects of business, you find yourself in the company of sprightly young gentlemen, who talk about new operas and the other amusements of the town with all the ease of connoisseurs in high life; and whose chief study is to give effect to chequered neckerchiefs, showy chains, and mogul pins . . .
>
> A Joint Stock Bank cannot be carried on without a fine building. Height of walls, extent of plate-glass windows, liveried porters at the entrance, and large chandeliers, seem to constitute the security of these concerns; and not sober, business-looking establishments, with anciently-fashioned railed counters, as in the case of the majority of our private banks.

Even this prejudiced observer, though, was compelled to concede that 'the Joint Stock banks enjoy a large proportion of public confidence, and the amount of business transacted is no doubt fast increasing'. In fact, pending their creditworthy survival of the 1847 crisis, the fast increase was yet to happen; and in the ten years after that panic the joint-stock banks of London not only broadened the range of their activities but increased their deposits from almost £9m to over £43m – a phenomenal expansion of banking and credit by any yardstick and in turn reflecting the thriving national economy. 'It is impossible to foresee the consequences of the failure of one of these large establishments', warned Thomas Weguelin, a Bank of England director, in 1856.[23]

Contempories were slow to realise, however, that the real danger of this rapid growth of deposits turned on the accompanying growth of the call loan system, by which the joint-stock banks employed an increasing portion of their reserves at call with the City's bill brokers (or dealers); and these bill brokers, headed by Overend Gurney, in turn used that money in order to finance bills and thus make a profit on it, keeping perilously low reserves in cash while they did so. But for the joint-stock banks themselves these were golden years, above all once the private banks in 1854 at last agreed, partly through the conciliatory counsels of W. G. Prescott, to admit them into the clearing house in

Abchurch Lane. Evans attributed this change of heart, after years of resistance, to 'a guerilla mode of warfare' on the part of the joint-stock banks, involving the private banks in 'sudden pressure upon tills, for note and cheque exchanges', and he may well have been right. Either way the joint-stock banks could now compete on equal terms for the country agency business and, quite apart from the symbolism of the climb-down, there was no doubt which way the contest was going.[24]

The dictates of economic logic had gone against the private bankers. Someone who may have doubted their continuing position as the City's elite was Nathaniel Hawthorne, well-known novelist now doubling as American Consul in Liverpool. In the autumn of 1855 he dined with Russell Sturgis in Portland Place and soon afterwards visited him on business:

> He is a partner with the Barings, and therefore a member of good society; though I have understood that the Barings are looked down upon by the body of London bankers, as being merely brokers. At any rate, Mr Sturgis's house is a very fine one, and he gave us a very quiet, elegant, and enjoyable dinner, in much better taste and with less fuss than Liverpool dinners . . .
>
> The house is at 8, Bishopsgate-street within; it has no sign of any kind, but stands back from the street, behind an iron-grated fence. The firm appears to occupy the whole edifice, which is spacious, and fit for princely merchants.

Herman Melville was equally impressed when, some years earlier, he dined at the East Sheen home of Joshua Bates:

> The dinner was superb – the table was circular – the service very rich. I ate of sundry mysterious French dishes. Everybody was free, easy & in good humor – all talkative & well-bred . . .
>
> The house is a large & noble one – the rooms immense – the decorations brilliant – statuary, vases & all sorts of costly ornaments. I saw a copy of *Typee* on a table. Mr Bates seemed to me quite a jolly old blade.

Young Henry Adams, son of the American minister to Britain, spent a few days in the 1860s as a member of a house party 'at Tom Baring's place in Hampshire, Norman Court':

> I suppose this place of Baring's is as near the true idea of aristocratic perfection as is permitted to imperfect mortality. Some people say that one's ear is offended by the rustle of bank-notes. It is a calumny, if said invidiously, for there could not be more luxury with less show.

Eye-witness reports from the Vale of Aylesbury would have perhaps laid greater emphasis on the show. By the early 1850s Mayer and Anthony de Rothschild acquired enormous estates there, Joseph Paxton built for Mayer the fantastic Mentmore Towers, and to be a Buckinghamshire stag was to experience life as nasty, brutish and short. The elder brother, Baron Lionel (this was still the Austrian barony), preferred for the time being to use Gunnersbury Park as his country house, and from the 1860s also inhabited an impressive new mansion at 148 Piccadilly, next door to Apsley House. Lionel had a serious, unflamboyant character and may well have been the model for Disraeli's Sidonia – 'a man without affections . . . void of all self-love, public approbation was worthless to him'. But even he had his rich man's whims, and so it was when Mathesons wrote to Jardine Matheson in January 1859: 'We venture to commend to your kind attention the accompanying letter from Baron Lionel de Rothschild who is anxious to procure some Pheasants from Japan, and whom we have assured that if at all possible, you will carry out his wishes'.[25]

Pride as much as avarice motivated the City's top merchant bankers by the 1850s. 'Half my pleasure is to work for a house which we intend to be perpetual,' asserted Tom Baring in 1849, matched a few years later by Bates: 'I do not any longer work for money but having arrived at that age when it would be impossible for me to arrive at any other distinction than that of a Merchant I feel that it *is* something to be at the head of the first commercial House in the World'. Beneath this comfortable sheen of self congratulation, there were considerable problems and tensions within the Barings partnership. They began in 1853 when Baring told Bates that he intended to devote less time to business. The reaction was typical: 'I told Mr Baring that I did not think it would answer for him to be much more absent than he is at present, that it would not look well for me as I should be supposed to be working for money which I should be sorry to have thought of me'. It was also decided at this time that young Edward ('Ned') Baring should enter the firm, in effect as the house's designated Baring of the future; and this likewise unsettled Bates, who while admitting that he was 'clever' also found the young man 'vain and desirous of playing the first fiddle'. There was also the disconcerting fact that most of the firm's capital came from himself and Tom Baring, and after totting up his personal fortune at just under £¾m, Bates decided in 1855 that despite advancing age there was no alternative but to stay in the partnership for at least another two years: 'If I go out the House must be dissolved and liquidated which would be a great folly. It would take 100 years to get up another House that would enjoy such unlimited confidence throughout the world.'[26]

The next focus for Bates's discontents was Russell Sturgis, an American merchant who had become a partner in 1849 and whose charm and good looks won over not only Nathaniel Hawthorne. Bates himself was an initial admirer, but the two were really chalk and cheese, and in August 1856 a day trip brought out all the puritan in him:

> Took a holiday it being Saturday and drove to Mount Felix at Walton on Thames to see the House Mr Sturgis thinks of buying. It was built by Barry, and is a palace beautifully situated on the Thames with 35 acres of Land . . . No one should live in such a house that has not a fixed income of £10,000 a year independent of business . . . It would be a delightful house for a large family, the Gentleman out of business, but too far from the City for a junior Partner in a commercial House. Mr S evidently wants to have it and would agree to pay £15,000 for it, if he gets the smallest encouragement from his Partners. That would take out all his capital. Who ever heard of a man laying out all his capital on a country House?

Sturgis (perhaps feeling that in his fifties he was old enough to know his own mind) would not be deterred and soon settled down to a daily regimen, recalled by his son, of rising at 6.30, bathing in the river, reading the family prayers at 7.45, breakfasting 'lightly on a leg of cold chicken and a cup of China tea', and then catching the 8.55 train to arrive at Bishopsgate by 10 a.m. As for the evenings, 'of business he never spoke'. Bates continued to grumble:

> I ought to retire, but who is there to succeed? The Junior partners have not £20,000 capital amongst them . . . Besides the present generation of young men appear to be educated very superficially. There is a great desire to get rich without the study of labor necessary to qualify them for business. They fancy they know all about it while they have no discovered that they know nothing.[27]

That was in January 1857, but it was another seven years – complaints about extravagance, wistful talk of leaving the firm one day – until at last Bates died in harness; and perhaps he would not have wished it otherwise.

What about the business itself? At a London dinner party during the 1850s there occurred the following exchange:

> Thackeray's daughter: 'And what is your profession?'
> The man from Barings: 'A merchant.'

> Miss Thackeray: 'A merchant! I picture you to myself sitting at your
> desk by an open window overlooking the broad estuary of the Thames.
> You glance from time to time at the distant reaches of the river. Presently
> you see a noble ship taking advantage of the incoming tide. She is yours
> and she is laden with precious tribute from foreign countries . . .'

The reply of Henry Bingham Mildmay (another partner not up to
scratch in the eyes of Bates) is not recorded. But though reality differed
from this romantic picture, there remained at Barings a significant
adherence to its general merchanting tradition, supplementing the
firm's financing of trade which was its bread-and-butter and in which
it was still the City's dominant house. In 1851 its volume of acceptances ran at over £2m, by 1855 they were over £4m. Rothschilds dominated the field of foreign loans. Placing most of a £4.4m Austrian
government loan in 1851, contracting for a Brazilian government loan
of almost £1.5m in 1852, organising the conversion of the Belgian
state debt in 1853 – all this was immensely profitable work carried out
at New Court.[28] There was at this time no underwriting in the state
loan business, and therefore a house needed substantial resources in
order to become a permanent player in that market, quite apart from
the range of quality contacts needed to secure the business in the first
place.

Nevertheless, as so often with the second generation, there was not
quite the same verve there once had been. John Francis (a permanent
official at the Bank of England who also wrote books) was a shrewd
commentator on City matters, and in 1849 he had this to say of
Nathan's sons:

> His children inherit his business; but they do not inherit his position in
> the stock-market. They are competitors for government loans; but though
> with the name remains a certain amount of its former power, they do not
> appear willing to entertain the extensive and complicated business in
> which their father delighted.

To a lesser but perceptible extent, the beginnings of a certain ossifica-
tion were starting to become apparent at Barings. In 1855 there was a
very suggestive sentence in a letter from the Liverpool partners of
Brown Shipley to their partners in New York: 'We aim, and with
perfect right, at a rank and position equal to the Barings, but it is
impossible that we can maintain it, if we are to be in the discount
market week by week . . . whereas they never discount and are known
to have always large sums lying at call'. Who could blame either Barings

or Rothschilds for obeisance to the god of liquidity? In both cases such an enviable business had been built up, such a high ranking secured, that to look for commercial adventure, or to make every financial asset sweat at the even faintest risk of being caught short, must have seemed worse than pointless. Bates may not have been quite convinced – 'as to hostility of us to Rothschilds we have none towards them but I am not sure they have none towards us' – but there were even signs that the old competitive animosity between the two houses was becoming blunted.[29]

Inevitably this left opportunities for other merchant banks. One increasingly powerful operator was R. Raphael & Sons, under the astute leadership of Henry Lewis Raphael from the mid-1850s. 'Mr Raphael called at 3.45 to request to have 40 odd Thousand Dollars delivered him out of the Bullion Office which was closed', the deputy-governor of the Bank of England recorded in May 1857. And three years later Rothschilds warned its New York agent 'not to accommod-ate houses we always find competing with us, for instance we did not like your taking a larger bill on Raphael'. Schröders was also making solid if somewhat anonymous progress mainly in international trade finance, though in 1853 it undertook its first foreign bond issue, for the Matanzas and Sabanilla Railroad Co of Cuba. John Henry Schröder continued to spend most of his time in Germany (where he was made a Prussian baron and eventually passed away in 1883 at the age of ninety-eight with the deathless words 'I die voluntarily'), but his son, also John Henry, became a partner at Leadenhall Street in 1849 and proved thoroughly able. The younger Schröder's personal as well as business orientation remained essentially non-British: in 1850 he mar-ried Eveline Schlüsser, the niece of his London partner and daughter of a German-Russian St Petersburg merchant; and, a devout Lutheran like his father, he attended a German church in London.[30]

From 1855, Alexander Kleinwort frequented the German Evangelical Church in Denmark Hill. He was a fellow-countryman who had served a lengthy mercantile apprenticeship in Havana and come to realise that the serious money was to be made not in the physical trade of sugar and other commodities but in the *financing* of that trade. Kleinwort & Cohen was in business by 1855, and within three years, now as Drake, Kleinwort & Cohen, it had a capital of £200,000 and was poised for future prosperity. But perhaps the most striking success story around this time was Hambros. Coming from a well-established Copenhagen mercantile family, Carl Joachim Hambro was permanently based in the City from 1839 and, despite a tendency to lengthy periods of depression, managed to expand the business steadily; other City houses were slow to pick up on Scandinavian accepting business. The Piedmontese episode of 1851 was the crucial breakthrough, and the rest followed: purchase of the extensive Milton Abbey estate in Dorset; his son Everard's education at Trinity College, Cambridge and marriage in 1866 to a daughter of Martin Tucker Smith, partner at Smith Payne & Smiths of 1 Lombard Street. The antisocial Carl Joachim never became a City insider, but his son would more than make up for it.[31]

Finally, of these rising merchant bankers, there is the American whom Morier Evans sought to evoke in a sketch in 1857:

> Through the dark portals of the Bank comes, emerging into the broad thoroughfare, the form of a stalwart gentleman, a little too burly, though tall, for grace in figure, but still erect, walking easily, in a manner which to a casual observer would indicate a person of position and means. He is well, but not extravagantly attired; a long blue frock coat, with velvet collar, black vest and black trousers being the style of his scrupulously neat and unexceptional apparel. There is not the slightest display in the shape of jewellery; no exhibition of chains or rings; everything is nicely ordered and well arranged.

George Peabody was a bachelor of miserly personal habits; he scrutinised newspapers with the greatest care but had no interest in literature; he once confessed that during all his time in London he had never visited either the Royal Academy or the National Gallery; in 1851 it was twelve years since he had been absent from his office for two consecutive business days; and not long afterwards he expressed his fear that 'we are all making money rather too fast, and not altogether by the "sweat of the brow" as stated in the Scriptures, as the lot of man'. Yet Peabody was also a great host, one of the acknowledged centres of American social life in London, and (in later life anyway) prone to considerable acts of philanthropy. During the summer of the Great Exhibition he held on the fourth of July a vast, much talked-about dinner and ball at Willis's Rooms, and among the guests was the aged Duke of Wellington. But not everyone in the City appreciated him, and in July 1853 Bates recorded some remarks recently made to him on 'Change by Daniel Meinertzhagen, by now the leading partner at Huths:

> 'Your countryman Peabody is a great boaster & does not do it cleverly. I was there the other day when he opened his book & said there my payments this month are £500,000'. This adds Mr M is out of proportion

with his means, for in 1851 he invited me to the opera [one of Peabody's favourite forms of entertaining] & after to take a glass of negus with him, when P said, how much do you think I am worth? Mr M said, I suppose you may have over £100,000. Yes replied Mr P, rather more. I had considerably more but lost some of it & which I have now newly recovered.

Towards the end of his life, Bates himself would reflect that Peabody was one of the few people with whom he had ever quarrelled, and referred to his 'want of sincerity' and 'fondness of show'.[32]

Huths as well as Barings were well established in the Anglo-American trade by the early 1850s, and there is no doubt that George Peabody & Co was emerging fast as competition, being an especial irritant to the other firms in the field through its practice of actively seeking accounts at a lower than usual commission rate. What really seems to have motivated Peabody was the desire, following the ignominious demise of the three W's in 1837 and the collapse of American credit soon afterwards, to establish a permanent American presence in the City. 'It has almost become a by-word among the English that no American House in London can long sustain their credit, that sooner or later all must fail', he reflected in 1852, adding that 'we not only, from self pride, but from feelings of Patriotism wish and intend with the smiles of Providence and the exercise of our best judgment and discretion, to refute hereafter such remarks'. But permanence demanded the exercise of foresight, and during the early 1850s he was much preoccupied by the search for a suitable American partner who could be trained to take the firm on beyond his own retirement or death. At last in 1854 he hit on Junius Spencer Morgan. He was forty-one years old and an established, highly thought of merchant in New England who had impressed Peabody by his demeanour at a dinner for the new American Minister in London. That same year the firm moved to more commodious premises at 22 Old Broad Street, its capital stood at almost £$\frac{1}{2}$m, and the all-American future seemed assured.[33]

The middling ranks of the City were also liable to rise or fall. Clearly on the way up in the merchant banking sphere was Henry Tiarks: his father, Johann Tiarks, had come to England in 1821 from Germany and was Pastor of the German Reformed Church in the East End of London; the fifteen-year-old Henry became a clerk in Schröders in 1847, following an introduction by one of his father's parishioners who was a partner in the firm; and by 1862 Tiarks was office manager and had married an adopted daughter of Alexander Schlüsser, whose partnership in the firm he would succeed to nine years later. Also on the way up in the 1850s, though in a quite different field and without the dynastic follow-through, was Manley Hopkins. He was by profession an average adjuster, whose task it was to assess, independently of both underwriter and owner, the pecuniary extent of shipping losses, in the cases of ships that had not actually sunk. It was an important and growing ancillary service within the City, and Hopkins flourished sufficiently to be able to move in 1852 from Stratford in the East End, which was being overrun by workmen's cottages, to a large, newly built house in Hampstead. Hopkins took his profession very seriously and over the years wrote several standard treatises, including in 1857 *A Handbook of Average*, in 1867 *A Manual of Marine Insurance*, and in 1873 *The Port of Refuge, or advice and instructions to the Master-Mariner in situations of doubt, difficulty, and danger*. Doubt and difficulty, if perhaps not danger, were his son Gerard's specialities; but Manley himself also wrote poetry, and in old age had privately printed by the Leadenhall Press at 50 Leadenhall Street 'A Gathering of Verses' called *Spicilegium Poeticum*, with titles like 'The Proëm', 'Eheu Fugaces', 'Love Sits Silent in her Silent Eyes', 'An Empty Quiver', and (almost Hardyesque) 'Far from the Madding Crowd'.[34]

Manley Hopkins may have failed to found a noble line of average adjusters, but that was nothing compared to the problems facing W. G. Lang, who was definitely on the way down in the 1850s. He was employed by Brandts and in August 1852 was sending to Edmund Brandt in Heidelberg very much the letter of the trusted confidential clerk, giving a résumé of business and concluding by 'sincerely hoping that you have found Mrs Brandt & your Family in good health'. But by June 1854 it was a different sort of missive that he was sending to Brandt from 4 Bath Place, Ramsgate:

> My health having much improved during the last week, I am most anxious to return to town, & purpose doing so next week, but unfortunately I am quite without means & am therefore, most reluctantly compelled to appeal to you. The very painful position in which I stand, I feel deprives me of all right to look for any consideration but still I venture to hope that my mental & bodily suffering will be taken into account, and that I may be allowed the opportunity to retrieve my past errors. The anguish of my mind has indeed been almost insupportable.

Lang asked for £12 and ended by again expressing the hope that 'you will for this time overlook what has occurred'. Brandt sent him £10, but the accompanying letter provoked more desperate appeals: 'The contents have overwhelmed me with grief. I hope & trust you may be induced to reconsider your resolve before consigning me to utter ruin.' And: 'I entreat you to grant me the opportunity of making up for the past'. And: 'Do, Sir, forgive what has occurred, & allow me to regain my position'.[35] What *had* occurred? The sources are silent, as they are about Lang's ultimate fate. He is left, like so many, to disappear into the long night.

In the spring of 1853 a group of young clerks with self-improvement in mind established the City of London Discussion Society, 'formed for the purpose of discussing any questions or propositions except those of a Theological character'. The first proposition to be debated, with eleven present, was 'Would it be beneficial to Society that the Crystal Palace should be open to the Public on Sundays?' and a decision was reached in the affirmative. Other, still weightier debates followed. 'Will Uncle Tom's Cabin go down to posterity?' (yes). 'Is there any standard of taste?' (no). 'Are early marriages desirable?' (yes). 'Is the character of the late Duke of Wellington entitled to our highest admiration?' (no). 'Is religion or commerce the best civilizer of mankind?' (religion). 'Should Brothels in this Country be licensed by Government?' ('decided in the Negative by the vote of the Chairman'). After the first year, however, the Society's secretary was complaining of dwindling interest and attendances ('We now have 14 Members only, and the continued adhesion of some of these is perhaps but very doubtful'); and in 1856 a merger took place with the City of London Elocution Society, thenceforth called the City of London Discussion and Literary Society and soon running a full programme of readings, lectures and debates. But by November 1860 there was once more gloom in the air about thin attendances, lack of quorums and so on:

> The Committee however reluctantly are compelled to arrive at the conclusion that the affairs of the Society have reached a serious crisis; illness, marriage and change of residence have thinned out ranks and reduced the robust man to a mere shadow ...
> It will only be by a long pull, a strong pull and a pull altogether that we can hope to restore the Society to its ancient prosperity; if the silver cord be once loosed, we shall look in vain for the formation of a similar Society, a bond of union so hallowed by old association, so cherished for its social gatherings, so memorable for its many intellectual conflicts.

The society pressed on during the early part of 1861 ('Feb 26. – Social Problems – 6. Woman'), but the minutes then fade out.[36]

Back in November 1853 these clerks had answered in the affirmative the question 'Should England go to War to support Turkey in her present quarrel with Russia?', thus reflecting mainstream City opinion as the public mood hardened that winter. The mood in Capel Court became especially feverish, inspiring a Stock Exchange special. One day the well-known member Sam Chard wandered into the consol market and inquired if there was anything doing. 'Well, there is nothing much doing; but I hear the Russians have taken umbrage –' 'The deuce they have', exploded Chard, and he at once rushed away and told everybody that the Russians had captured Umbrage, only to return a couple of hours later and ask his friend, 'I say, where the devil is Umbrage? I can't find it on the map.'[37]

During the Crimean War itself the City played a significant role: helping to maintain the servicing of existing Russian debts (despite government pressure to the contrary) but refusing to bring out any new Russian loans; mounting (through Barings) a full-scale corn operation on behalf of the French Government; and providing the mechanism for funding major quantities of new British Government debt, with Rothschilds again unrivalled as loan contractors. The market itself tended to groan when fresh money was needed, as markets do, and in February 1856 there occurred a charged episode involving the firm of Mullens, Marshall & Co, which for many years had acted as government broker and could not afford to be seen as other than whiter than white. On the afternoon of Friday the 15th the Committee met specially to consider a complaint from a member called Norman Wilkinson, to the effect that not only had the notice dated the 14th from the Treasury to the Bank of England announcing a new loan reached the Stock Exchange damagingly late (11.20 that morning), but also that William Mullens had taken advantage of inside knowledge of what was afoot to advise another member called Bostock to sell, to the detriment of jobbers in the market who were saddled with stock that was about to fall sharply once the news of the loan was made public. Some tense exchanges ensued:

> Mr Mullens reiterated that when Bostock asked him the opinion of stocks, he gave it in a general way as being against a rise from the state of money and the market being overloaded with securities, but never alluded in any way to a loan or funding.
>
> Mr Bostock was sent for, and asked by Mr Wilkinson, through the chairman, what were the exact words used by Mr Mullens, when he spoke to him this morning in the market.

Mr Bostock answered: 'He put me on my guard against buying stock, say perhaps "it is right to sell", but nothing about a loan or funding'. When pressed to give the exact words, he answered, 'He might have said, "sell a few for yourself" ' . . .

Mr Mullens complained that when he came into the Stock Exchange, he was assailed with hisses and hooting, by members who were standing on the benches and tables, and they appeared to be led on by Mr Norman Wilkinson.

Mr Wilkinson denied that he excited the members to hiss or hoot. The only thing he said was that 'It was a pity the Treasury Valentine came so late from the Bank, and that there ought to be another Bank broker'. He was under great excitement at the time, and was sorry if he had done anything to annoy Mr Mullens, but he could not avoid coming to the conclusion he had when he saw Mr Mullens whispering to Bostock both looking very pale, and the latter immediately selling stock in all directions $1/4$ per cent below the price.

The chairman and deputy-chairman then went over to the Bank of England to establish the facts of the case, and discovered firstly that the governor had not read the Treasury's letter until arriving at the Bank at ten past eleven that morning (having 'walked leisurely into the City'), and secondly that the chief cashier then put the letter in his pocket, walked at once to the Stock Exchange and there announced its contents, without speaking to anyone. All this digested, a unanimous vote duly vindicated Mullens and his partners.[38]

*

During much of the autumn of the following year, the governor was not even strolling into Threadneedle Street. In October 1857 the City was bracing itself for another full-blown financial and commercial crisis, largely the result of the collapse of banks and railroads in the United States. Sheffield Neave was laid up at home in Hampstead, reduced to sending a series of anxious messages to his deputy on the bridge, Bonamy Dobree. 'We clearly are going to have a heavy Squall & we must take in every reef we can', he wrote on the 9th, and on the 15th, 'I do nothing but fret that I cannot be with you'. From the start the main City focus was on the discount houses – 'My almost only fear is whether the great Bill Brokers are in such a position to bear a considerable drain on their resources', one Bank director wrote to Dobree on the 20th – and this time they were without the commanding leadership of Samuel Gurney, who had died the previous year. His successor, David Barclay Chapman of Overend Gurney, was particularly aggressive in putting pressure on the Bank, and on the 29th he even, according to Dobree's diary, 'called to know whether they could rely on the Bank for unlimited assistance if pressed'. Neave, back in action, studiously 'returned for answer that the Loans to the Brokers must depend upon Circumstances at the time'. Soon afterwards G. W. Norman (still a Bank director) was reporting to Overstone that the bill brokers 'now find themselves up to the ears in their Bills' and 'are I dare say a little frightened, and expect the old Lady to cash every thing'. That sounded calm enough, but by 5 November even Norman was admitting that 'things in the City are very sick, and more likely to be worse than better', so that 'we may again see Lombard St knocking at the door in Downing St'. A concerned observer of the deepening crisis was George Dallas, the US minister in London. 'A feverish anxiety pervades the mercantile classes', he had informed his secretary of state in October, and on 6 November he saw no relief: 'Every fresh steamer (the Vanderbilt last evening) brings gloomier accounts from the United States. All the merchants and manufacturers connected with American trade are startled and trembling.'[39]

On Monday the 9th, as Bank rate rose to 10 per cent, Dobree accompanied Neave on a summons to Sir George Cornewall Lewis: 'Chancellor stated that a Deputation from Glasgow was to have an interview with him Tomorrow. Asked in general Terms whether or no the Bank of England have any thing to suggest in regard to the Action of the Bill of 1844. The Gov'r replied that they had none'. The old dance was beginning again, but who would crack first? 'Men look as if they were beneath an impending avalanche, and scarcely dare to breathe', Dallas the next day with a certain flourish reported back to Washington, but Dobree in his diary was more terse: 'Gurney's ask for a dis: of 30 day Bills 400m [i.e. *mille*, the old-fashioned term for thousand]. Granted.' The climax of the crisis was now at hand, for the following morning, Wednesday the 11th, it emerged that the bill brokers Sandersons (reconstituted after its failure ten years earlier) had this time gone down beyond redemption, with liabilities of over £5m. Late that afternoon Dobree went with Neave and Weguelin to see Lewis again:

> The Chancellor desired to know if the time had arrived to adopt the Measure resorted to in 1847. He had had a visit in the Morning from Mr David Chapman who had represented to him such a state of affairs in Lombard Street, following upon the suspension of Sandersons Sandeman & Co coupled with other Circumstances (the request for the aid of

Troops in Glasgow) that in his opinion the simplest mode to meet the emergency was to issue a Letter to the Bank as in 1847.

But Neave and his colleagues would not play ball, telling the precipitate politician that 'the period had not arrived for such a Step' and that 'a strong opinion was entertained by the Court of Directors to maintain the Bill of 1844 at any sacrifice'. So matters rested for the moment, and as they left the room Neave told Dobree that his impression was that the government 'were prepared to issue 50 Letters and all they wished was that the Governors should make such a request'.[40]

Still, waking up on Thursday morning plenty of City men, and not just bill brokers, would have thought that Lewis had a point. Discounting had virtually ceased, the joint-stock banks were refusing to make advances, and the Bank's own banking reserve had fallen in barely a month from £4m to under £1m. The staid partners of Prescotts found the mood in Lombard Street both alarming and irrational, especially in the vaunted Corner House: 'We have called for £20,000 out of £120,000. OG & Co gave a cheque, but young Mr Gurney spoke unwisely about our demand, so much so indeed to make us doubt their power of answering the *call*. He talked of having 70/– in the £ which was never a question with us, as we know their means to be very ample.' Moreover, when Neave and Dobree went to see Lewis again at two o'clock that Thursday and give an update on the City latest, it transpired that Alexanders as well as Gurneys was by now under considerable pressure, as money held at call by them continued to be demanded in ever greater quantities. And, in the ensuing discussion, Neave conceded that some members of the Court were starting to waver in their opposition to a second potential infraction of the Act. Lewis pressed for names, but to no avail; in the end it was Lewis who produced the letter of his own accord (Neave did not give him the satisfaction of actually requesting it) and asked Neave to accompany him to Palmerston's, so that it could be signed by the Prime Minister and then taken back to the City. 'Do not on any account let Alexanders go down', Dobree was urged by James Wilson (who doubled as financial secretary to the Treasury and editor of the *Economist*) as they left the room, and it seems to have been the plight of this liked and respected house that carried the day. By the end of the afternoon the publication of the government's letter had again wrought its magic. 'Relief was immediately felt', the partners of Prescotts noted following the close of business, adding that Overend Gurney had 'paid off £800,000 of call money, and discounted £250,000 of Bills'. While two days later, Overend Gurney itself with marked equanimity informed a client in Yorkshire that 'there is a much better feeling prevailing & the Bank are giving every proper facility that can be desired'.[41]

Dobree, in the course of the final meeting with Lewis, had referred to how 'one Director, a consistent and heretofore staunch supporter of the Bill and well capable of judging the actual condition of affairs', had that crucial Thursday morning 'declared to his great regret that he saw no safety to the Bank or to the Mercantile Interest but in a relaxation of the restrictive Clause'. Who was the turncoat? Almost certainly Norman, who within hours was writing to Overstone from the Bank in notably unapologetic terms:

> We might of course have saved ourselves and the Bill, by refusing to advance for the money Dealers, but this might have brought down the whole credit system of the Country – a vicious system beyond doubt, but which ought to owe its gradual reform to the action of the country's good sense. Its extinction by a Catastrophe would have been awful.

Most leading figures in the City agreed with Norman that there had been no alternative – 'no doubt this measure was indispensable, for without it things would have come to a dead lock in 24 hours', reflected Bates – but among those still occupying the lonely high ground was W. G. Prescott, who wrote to Overstone on Friday the 13th: 'I paid Lothbury [i.e. the home of Jones Loyd & Co] a visit today to mourn over the event of yesterday. It is hateful to hear the exulting tone in which the overtraders speak of it.' Prescott made no bones about blaming the bill brokers for the crisis, and Overstone's mood was not improved when another correspondent told him that, in the immediate aftermath of the letter's publication, Chapman of Overend Gurney had 'avowed to his friends that he had threatened to compel the Bank to stop unless the Directors should obtain from Government a suspension of the Act'.[42]

It was as if Overstone acted as a one-man court of conscience, for on the 22nd Lewis sought to justify to him his action, asserting that before the suspension 'no pressure was applied to the government which they could not have resisted as easily as an application for a postponement of the hop duty' and that 'the pressure which was applied to them was the pressure of *facts*'. This was too much for the grand inquisitor, and two days later he exploded:

> The Bill brokers have been in the habit of holding probably from 15 to 20 Millions of Money *at call*!! The whole of this sum they invest in the

discount of Bills (to a large amount for the discounting J^t Stock Bk^s in the Country) and in advances upon Goods and Produce. – When general pressure arises, and calls for Money are made upon them by all their depositors – they have no source from which to met these calls, except that of rediscounting at the Bk of England. Hence the enormous demands upon the Bank – The Bill-brokers cease to discount – they send over-whelming masses of Bills to the Bank – and if this process sustains the slightest check – they at once exclaim, the world must stop payment, because there is an inadequate supply of money. In one, the last day before the Letter, Gurneys obtain 800 from the Bank!! and then they go to the Gov^t to urge the suspension of the Law, because the Bank is exhausted and can do nothing for trade. Either this system must be broken down, or it will in its turn break down any and every Monetary system which can be established. Each successive interference of the Gov^t encourages and stimulates this system. Gurneys, I am confident, will persist, with encreased confidence, in their present course, in consequence of what has now occurred . . .

Such is my conviction – and I believe it is the conviction of all the wisest and most thoughtful men in the City.[43]

The average City elder may ultimately have been as susceptible to pragmatic expediency as the next man, but a consensus began to emerge that something must be done as to the future – and there was no doubt who was target number one.

1857 was very much an American-induced crisis, and as much in the firing line as any of the bill brokers was George Peabody & Co, whose correspondents were either failing or finding it next to impossible to remit payments:

> I hope my house will weather the storm. I *think* it will do so even though so many in debt to me cannot pay. If I fail I will bear it like a man. In my conscience I know I never deceived or injured another human being . . . Nearly all the American houses in Europe have suspended operations and nothing but great strength can save them. It is the loss of *credit* of my house I fear.

Peabody's problems, as admitted in this letter to a favourite niece, were not helped by the attitude of Barings, which had extended him credit of £150,000 and during the crisis was relentless in pressing for repayment. The government's letter of 12 November was little use as far as he was concerned, and five days later he was compelled to go to the Bank of England to ask for assistance. Some hard bargaining ensued, and after several days during which Peabody trawled the City for appropriate lenders and guarantors it was eventually announced that the Bank of England would advance his firm £250,000 and other banks (headed by the Union Joint Stock, with the London and Westminster refusing) £550,000. In the event Peabody needed a total of only £300,000, and that was soon repaid, as American credit recovered surprisingly quickly from the crisis. Nevertheless, it had been a traumatic episode, and over the next few months he gradually eased out of business, so that by the spring of 1858 it was Junius Morgan who effectively headed the firm. That left him free to concentrate on philanthropy for the rest of his life, and in March 1862 Bates recorded without comment that 'Geo Peabody has given 150,000 pounds for the benefit of the poor of London'.[44] So were born the famous model dwellings, fortress-like monuments to one of the City's more admirable adopted sons, even if he did occasionally boast over a glass of negus.

Others also suffered during the autumn of 1857. Francis Bennoch was head of the firm of Bennoch, Twentyman & Rigg, who operated as wholesale silk dealers in London and manufacturers in Manchester. The previous year he had struck up a friendship with Nathaniel Hawthorne, who had found him 'a kindly, jolly, frank, off-hand, very good fellow', in his mid-forties and living prosperously at Blackheath. Hawthorne had lunched convivially with him at the premises in Wood Street ('a very narrow street, insomuch that one has to press close up against the wall, to escape being grazed when a cart is passing') and afterwards been given a tour of the extensive establishment, being shown 'innumerable packages of ribbons, and other silk manufactures, and all sorts of silks, from the raw thread to the finest fabrics'. Now, on 9 November 1857, Bennoch's firm failed for just over £¼m. 'Of all men on earth I had rather this misfortune should have happened to any other; but I hope and think Bennoch has sturdiness and buoyancy enough to rise up beneath it'.

A week later Hawthorne was asked to pay a visit to Wood Street. 'The interior of the warehouse looked confused and dismal; two or three clerks seemed to be taking an account of stock . . . Then appeared Mr Rigg, the Junior partner, looking haggard and anxious.' Rigg escorted Hawthorne upstairs to the dining room: 'Everywhere the packages of silk were piled up, and ranged on shelves, in paper-boxes and otherwise; a rich stock, but which had brought ruin with it'. Upstairs, Bennoch 'looked paler', while Twentyman, the middle partner, 'appeared as much or more depressed than his fellows in misfortune, and to bear it with a greater degree of English incommunicativeness and reserve'. The four of them, however, ate a hearty enough dinner: 'It was roast beef, and a boiled apple-pudding, and – which I was glad to see, my heart being heavy – a decanter of sherry and another of port'. Hawthorne then went on, as the inquiring consul gave way completely to the empathic novelist:

> I gathered from them a strong idea of what commercial failure is, to English merchants – utter ruin, present and prospective, and obliterating all the successful past; how little chance they have of ever getting up again; how they feel that they must plod heavily onward under a burthen of disgrace – poor men, and hopeless men, and men forever ashamed . . . It is not so in America, nor ought it to be so here; but they said themselves they would never again have put unreserved confidence in a man who had once been bankrupt, and they could not but apply the same severe rule to their own case. I was touched by nothing more than by their sorrowful patience, without any fierceness against Providence or against mankind, or disposition to find fault with any thing but their own imprudence; and there was a simple dignity, too, in their not assuming the aspect of stoicism. I could really have shed tears for them, to see how like men and Christians, they let the tears come into their own eyes . . . They talked of some little annoyances, half-laughingly. Bennoch has been dunned for his gas-bill at Blackheath (only a pound or two) and has paid it. Mr Twenty-man seems to have received an insulting message from some creditor. Mr Rigg spoke of wanting a little money to pay for some boots . . . It seems to me nobody else runs such risks as a man of business, because he risks everything. Every other man, into whatever depths of poverty he may sink, has still something left, be he author, scholar, handicraft man, or what not; the merchant has nothing.

There was to be a happy ending to this mercantile story. The firm did repay its creditors, it did get going again, and Bennoch himself flourished into old age. But for Hawthorne at the time, the episode caused a sharply diminished pleasure in London life. A fortnight later he found himself walking down Cheapside, a prey to the darkest thoughts:

> It is really an ungladdened life, to wander through these huge, thronged ways, over a pavement foul with mud, ground into it by a million of footsteps; jostling against people who do not seem to be individuals, but all one mass . . .[45]

Poe, Melville and Hawthorne: between them they located the imaginative truth of the nineteenth-century City.

CHAPTER THIRTEEN

The Fatal Day

Another American, Henry Adams, many years later recalled the world capital, almost in spite of itself, that he encountered in 1858: 'London was still London. A certain style dignified its grime; heavy, clumsy, arrogant, purse-proud, but not cheap; insular but large; barely tolerant of an outside world, and absolutely self-confident . . . Every one seemed insolent, and the most insolent structures in the world were the Royal Exchange and the Bank of England.' The Old Lady was indeed long renowned for a certain haughtiness, and after 1857 she was particularly frosty towards the discount houses, which were widely blamed for, if not causing the crisis, certainly exacerbating matters. These houses now included a joint-stock company, the National Discount formed in 1856, but the temperature truly dipped in relation to Overend Gurney. Not only was Samuel Gurney no more but his capable if unpopular deputy David Barclay Chapman (known in the City as 'Gurney's Liar') had also departed the scene, retiring at the end of 1857 with a handsome pay-off following a blistering attack upon him by *The Times* for his irresponsible conduct during the crisis.[1] Control passed to the younger generation, chiefly in the persons of the over-ambitious Henry Edmund Gurney and the extravagant David Ward Chapman, and the traditional Quaker virtues began to recede.

It was undoubtedly with Overend Gurney in mind that the Bank in March 1858 made it clear that it would no longer offer discount facilities to the City's bill brokers – a controversial policy from the start, being carried only by casting vote of the governor. It was intended to make the discount houses more self-reliant, but the *Economist* was not alone in expressing concern about its inflexible implications in times of monetary strain. Inevitably the Bank came under pressure to reverse it, as Dobree (by now Governor) noted on the last day of 1859:

> Mr Raymond Pelly visits me to announce his retirement from the House of Overend & Co on a/c of ill Health brought on from overanxiety greatly

encreased since the Bill Brokers have been excluded from the discount office. He believes that the Profits in Bill Broking will be so much reduced as to render the Business an unprofitable one. O.G. & Co will be obliged to retain a million of Reserve. He thinks that Messrs Gurneys are becoming impressed with the Notion that the Business does not now hold nett sufficient inducement to continue & that they will soon retire. Mr Pelly urges a reconsideration of the Exclusion of Bill Brokers by the Court of Directors.

A month later one of the Gurneys made a further personal appeal to Dobree, but received no encouragement at all. And by the beginning of April 1860, with Bank rate up to $4\frac{1}{2}$ and the onset of a certain tightness, the *Economist* (by this time under the high-charged editorship of Walter Bagehot) was calling for a truce. It did not deny that before the new rule the bill brokers had been 'perpetually competing with the Bank' and 'reducing its profits at the very time that they were relying on it for their safety', but it wanted a compromise, on the grounds that the credit of the bill brokers was being affected, potentially very damaging in the event of a crisis.[2] They were wise words, but the Corner House by now felt that words alone were not sufficient to concentrate minds.

The story of a momentous episode unfolds in Dobree's diary, beginning with a flat but meaningful entry on Thursday, 12 April: 'Barclays, Overends & Barnetts with Sheppard & Pelly & Co took away on the 9, 10, & 11th £1,600,000 in 1,000 Notes which Notes have not returned to the Bank'. In other words, Overend Gurney had mobilised its (largely Quaker) connections, including the stockbrokers Sheppard, Pelly & Allcard, to make major withdrawals from the Bank, all in £1,000 notes. By the end of the week Daniell of Mullens was telling Dobree 'that on the Stock Ex Messrs Gurney & Co avow that they took from the Bank a very large Amount of Bank Notes early in the Week with a view to reduce the Bank's Reserve to the lowest possible Amount'. The stakes of the game became clear on the Monday, when Dobree was informed through an intermediary that 'if the Rule excluding the dis Houses should be modified, the Notes withdrawn & still locked up in Lombard St shall be returned to the Bank "*tonight*" '. However, Dobree recorded, 'the Governors refuse to entertain any such proposal'.

The next morning there arrived on his desk a sinister anonymous message: 'Overends can pull out every note you have, from actual knowledge the writer can inform you that with their own family assistance they can nurse *seven* millions!!' But such threats were too late, for that same day Dobree heard that the game was over: 'Overend, Gurney & Co have told Mr Masterman that if it would be considered a conciliatory Step on their part, they will at once return to the Bank the Million, Five Hundred & Fifty Thousand Bank Notes locked up in Lombard St. They are sorry for what they have done.' The penitent bill brokers may have been affected by the imminence of a parliamentary question to be asked on the subject of the sudden sharp drop in the Bank's reserve, but in any case the notes were duly returned to Threadneedle Street on the Wednesday, 'identical but all cut into Halves'. The following day a relieved Court 'approved of the Course pursued by the Gov^rs in this disreputable Affair'. It had been quite a run-in, showing the Old Lady's mettle in a trial of nerves as much as strength, and auguring ill for a particular discount house should it ever come running to that elderly female for help.. 'I do hope you will remain obstinately firm against these tricksters', one of the Bank directors had written to Dobree during the episode, and no one on the Court would have disputed the epithet.[3]

How, as it endeavoured to reconcile the functions of commercial and central banking, was that Court chosen? Dobree in January 1858 received an instructive visit from someone who had himself been on the Bank direction for many years:

> Mr Palmer called to communicate, *confidentially*, to the Gov^ors the new Partnership of Dent, Palmer & Co. Mr Palmer & Mr McKillop retire & Mr Thomas Dent assumes the Head of the House with the intention of personally conducting the Business. Mr Edward H. Palmer [Horsley Palmer's son] has a Capital in the House of £60–65m [ie thousand] and at his Mother's Death will be encreased to 100m. The Capital in the House available for the conducting of the Business is a clear £500,000. In order to cement the connection of Mr Dent with the partners of DP & Co it would be very desirable he should be chosen as Director of the B^k of England & for which Mr D has declared himself a Candidate, and if his Age (60) should not be deemed a disqualification & he should be recommended by the Comm^e of Treasury, there should be a clear understanding that if he retired from the H° of Dent Palmer & Co he should at the same time relinquish his Seat in the Direction. Should Mr Dent not be accepted a Candidate (on a/c of his Age), then in such Case Mr Edw H. Palmer would be a Candidate.

Dent does indeed seem to have been considered too old, Bank directors traditionally being elected in their thirties or forties to allow them time to mature for a quarter of a century before assuming gubernatorial duties; but the ground had been judiciously prepared for a new Palmer to take the place of the old, his only obvious qualification being his firm's sound standing. Horsley Palmer himself died a month after his conversation with Dobree and was recalled by Bates as 'a respectable honest man of considerable ability', perhaps more fulsome praise than it would have been coming from other pens.[4]

If old-style personal recommendation still counted for everything, nevertheless, partly following the 1848 reforms, the system tended to produce a more able, usually university-educated Bank director than had once been the case. None was abler, at least on paper, than the director whom the City quickly tagged 'the fortunate youth'. Dobree recorded how, a week before Horsley Palmer's visit, 'Mr W. Goschen called to ask if there would be any objection to his son being considered a candidate for the Bank direction'. George Joachim Goschen, educated at Rugby and Oxford and a partner in the family firm of Frühling & Goschen, was twenty-seven when he became a director. Three years later he published *The Theory of the Foreign Exchanges*, an overnight City classic which went into its fourth edition in as many years. 'The object proposed is by no means to propound any dogmatic theories', Goschen reassured his readers in the introduction, 'but rather to call attention to many facts which are commonly believed to be peculiarly complicated and unintelligible, which, however, if carefully analyzed and illustrated, may be presented in a single form, and under such an aspect as to command general assent'.[5] His commercial and intellectual reputation made, he was returned unopposed as a Liberal MP for the City in 1863, having been put forward by two fellow-directors of the Bank; and two years later he became vice-president of the Board of Trade, which compelled him to retire from business and relinquish his directorship of the Bank and where he nobly refrained from grumbling that he had been set to govern packages. Goschen's relationship with the City would remain intimate if not always happy.

Few of the mid-Victorian directors of the Bank of England had more than tenuous links with the aristocracy, and the great majority were solid, socially unpretentious members of the London and Home Counties *haute bourgeoisie*.[6] Nor were they on the whole stunningly wealthy: of the twenty-three elected between 1833 and 1847, over half left fortunes of under £100,000. Nevertheless, these directors were significant figures in the national picture, for quite apart from their seats in the Bank direction and their individual mercantile bases a fair proportion of them were also MPs, no less than ten of them in 1863. Some no doubt sought parliamentary seats for reasons of social prestige, but others were highly conscious that, with monetary matters so often high on the political agenda, it was important for the Bank to be adequately represented in the Commons. These MPs were predominantly on the Liberal side, yet it is a striking fact of the period that easily the worst relations between Westminster and City were those between Gladstone and the Bank.

The man who embodied the financial conscience of the Victorians first became Chancellor at the end of 1852, and by 1854 he was displaying what Morley called 'a toughness, stiffness, and sustained anger that greatly astonished Threadneedle Street'. The bone of contention was recondite enough – involving certain well-enshrined conventions allowing the Bank to profit through the timing of payments to it of dividends on the national debt – but for Gladstone the abuse symbolised the continuing existence of 'old corruption' at the heart of the financial system. And though he won this particular battle, thereafter he never forgave the Bank for what he regarded as its obstructive attitude. By 1859 he was back at the Treasury, the object of considerable personal mistrust in the City. 'There never was a Chancellor of the Exchequer whose course it was less easy to predict', W. G. Prescott wrote to Overstone, while Overstone himself declared that 'surely Gladstone is a most dangerous finance Minister'. During the winter of 1860–61 he waged another fierce conflict with the Bank, this time over the price paid by government for the management of the public debt, and once again the Bank gave way amidst much thinly veiled animosity. At the same time Gladstone also succeeded, again against Bank opposition, in establishing the Post Office Savings Banks. In a late fragment he would recall his ulterior motive: 'I had an object of first-rate importance, which has been attained: to provide the minister of finance with a strong financial arm, and to secure his independence of the City by giving him a large and certain command of money'.[7] Ultimately, though, the irony of Gladstone's intervention was to be writ large. The Huskissonian return to gold became a City sacred cow; the Peelite Bank Charter Act in practice, if not by design, gave the Bank a permanent and unchallengeable pivotal role; and now the Gladstonian pursuit of balanced budgets, a pursuit aimed in part at freeing governments from dependence on the Bank, would become a hallowed orthodoxy that in time the City even believed was its own creation and certainly was prepared to defend at all costs. Gladstone may have regarded the Bank of England parlour as like a university common room – narrowing the point of view – but over the years successive governments could hope to escape from a certain subserviency to the City only if they were able to fight the good fight on the City's own ground, however 'narrow' and technical that might be.

*

Other, less illustrious Liverpudlians were also encountering the square mile, many of them through the tea trade. Harrisons & Crosfield, for instance, had started in Liverpool in 1844 to trade in tea and coffee, and within four years Joseph Crosfield was noting that 'there is scarcely any tea on its way from China to this port while ten ships have sailed to London', adding that 'this brings the London dealers into rather unpleasant competition with us'. In 1855 the firm opened a City branch at 3 Great Tower Street, almost opposite Mincing Lane, and by the mid-1860s this strongly Quaker house was London's third biggest tea dealers, behind Peek Bros and Moffat & Co. On a more modest scale, there was the experience of Frank Wilde, who early in 1859 opened a tiny office at 4 Mincing Lane Buildings, 14 Mincing Lane on behalf of the Liverpool tea brokers Bushby & Co. Wilde's letters back to Liverpool in the early weeks have all the poignancy of a newcomer seeking to establish himself in alien territory:

> *31 January.* I am writing comfortably in our own Office which is getting quite in Order.
> *1 February.* I called upon Mr Hardy [of S. Hardy & Sons] this morning, who received me very pleasantly asking me various questions about Liverpool people and also about the Dates we purchased for his house . . . I told him I was up here looking about me, and threw out a hint, that you might if you saw its practicality, at a later period, add General Business to our Tea branch here. He told me that he thought it would be no easy matter. It would take a considerable time to become acquainted with the different Buyers and their *standing* in a monetary sense; information was difficult to obtain and only Bankers could be questioned as a reliable source . . . He said he should see me perhaps in Mincing Lane occasionally no doubt.
> *4 February.* I am getting much more accustomed to the routine of sales here and shall no doubt gradually fall in but it must take time.
> *10 February.* Woodhouse [a City man who had shown friendliness to Wilde] as you know kindly put my name down for the Commercial Coffee Room for eight days. The time having expired I must either become a Subscriber or be refused admission. The subscription is two Guineas for 12 months and I shall be glad to know what you think. The room is frequented by people I ought to know & meet and I shall have access to important information.

16 February. I hope the 'Christy' soiree passed off with éclat. I should much have liked to have heard the minstrels.

18 February. Benares Sugar seems quite a drug at present and each sale as it is brought out has to be bought in. I have heard of 1000 bags to be put up for next Tuesday and it is not improbable that someone will one day knock the market down and establish lower prices. I should be inclined to move on.

19 February. I have made the acquaintance of a large Saltpetre operator which will I am sure be of use to me. I am feeling the ground firmer each day and shall work hard for success.

7 March. 'Not much doing in the Lane'.

8 March. The Sales today went steadily, I send Samples tonight.

9 March. I feel my position in London strengthening each day as of course from the fact of becoming familiarnest [sic] with people and customs, anticipation would lead one to expect: theory however is naturally predominant and is less remunerative than practice but necessary, though the latter goes a much longer way in indelibly fixing the methods of doing business in one's mind. I shall be glad to be doing something ere long and have little hesitation in saying that I can undertake business entrusted to our care. I am becoming better known in the 'room' and when I have business to transact no doubt a 'standing' will attract itself to me as your representative.

14 March. It seems quite natural to the London Brokers to talk Liverpool down and to increase prejudice against her but I must say that though terms $2\frac{1}{2}$% &c operate very much to her detriment, the way of doing business is vastly superior.

14 March (to his brother). It does seem so strange here, you may walk for hours and miles and you will not meet one soul that cares a scrap about you. I like Liverpool *very* much better than London as a residence . . . London from the distance looks glittering but becomes more tinselly when one looks into it. I hope my being here will turn out for my advantage otherwise I would have thought twice before leaving home . . . I am getting on very well with the 'Lane' and shall do well I think if my health keeps good. I fluctuate and suffer a good deal at times from old pains &c in my head . . .[8]

Frank Wilde may have been finding his feet in Mincing Lane, but it is hard not to feel there were some bleak moments in his lodgings at 42 St Pauls Road, Camden Town.

If he had it all to do, the same hardly applied to the young Richard Biddulph Martin, who in December 1859 graduated from Oxford, settled himself in at the family's London home in Eaton Square, and within days became the fifth generation of Martins to enter the family bank, where his uncle John Martin IV was senior partner: 'Walked with my father to a shop near Blackfriars Bridge – about a bookcase – saw

some good ones. Then to Lombard St where I was shewn the books &
received a first initiation into business. Went to the Bank & saw the
gold . . .' That was a Saturday, and a week later, on Christmas Eve, he
dipped his toes in the water again: 'Went to Lombard St and began to
learn Banking. Looked at the books, sorted cheques, &c. Dined with
the Partners. Fish, Mutton, 2 Boiled Chicken, Mince pies, Plum-pudding.'
Then, after Christmas, he went regularly. One day he 'ruled straight
lines & did a little with the books', on another 'the mistake in the books
was reduced to 5^d undiscoverable', on a third he 'saw a cheque of
Barings for £220,000 on the bank'.

Martin was a serious-minded young man who took to the business
quickly, and by February he was combining boyish enthusiasm with
worldly criticism in his response to the day's events: 'Baring paid in one
cheque of £249,300 14/7! on behalf of their share of the Canadian loan.
Bruce the Broker could not pay up £25,000 on demand & his bills have
been found to run as long as 6 mo which will never do.' In 1861 he
became a partner, and one day that year, with the money market tight,
he noted that Martins had been 'obliged to call in money (£50,000)
from Barings though inconvenient to them to repay it, which is a great
nuisance but cannot be helped', adding that 'it has not happened before
for years'. Two days later, at the end of work, he 'walked out of the
City with Mr Thos Baring', so presumably there were no hard feelings.
One Thursday morning in November 1862 occurred a typical City
story of informational asymmetry: 'A curious rumour got about that
the Bank had raised its rate. The clerk said "The rate will be the for-mer
rate". The Stock Exchange messenger bolted after "for" fancying it was
"4". The news went to Paris before it was stopped.' On the whole
young Martin's experiences were flat and prosaic – a typical entry, for
Christmas Eve 1862, reads 'hard work, usual work, calculating interests discounts &c' – and the diary serves as a reminder that even those
with the most copper-bottomed prospects had to put in the hours if they
were to be taken seriously.[9]

Traditionally the real test of the young City man was being left to
mind the shop, and in 1860 that was the challenge faced by Wentworth
Gray. Two years earlier he had gone into partnership with his older
brother Charles, an experienced West Indies and North America merchant, and together they operated from 31 Great St Helen's as Charles
William & Wentworth Gray. Charles was now away on an extensive
trip to see the firm's correspondents, and during a difficult year for
produce markets an anxious Wentworth tried simultaneously to keep
him in the picture and show that he was worthy of a partner's trust:

3 Feb. This will probably find you in Bermuda, I trust after a pleasant voyage. Things here are progressing pretty favorably, but very little *active* business to attend to.

10 Feb. We continue to be very slack here, no orders coming in and no sales to be made . . . I have not yet moved any of Halstead's provisions. The parcels already landed have all been examined and prove to be tainted throughout. Some casks of Pork which I saw this morning were *very* bad. Cocke [a broker] says that much of the stuff must be repacked but I shall endeavour if possible to sell it as it is.

15 Feb. I make no progress with Sales though I am constantly at the Brokers. Yesterday I refused 52/– for Halsteads bacon but would take it today as I find that, to judge from "Ledger" quotations, the price was a good one.

20 Feb. Halsteads bacon I sold @ 52/–, Cocke assuring me that this was really above its value . . . No offers whatever for Beef or Pork and some I think must be repacked . . . You will notice by Public Ledger that Tea is again on the decline, we shan't make our fortunes by our late speculation I fear.

Charles replied crisply from Hamilton on 7 March (having received Wentworth's slightly abject letter of the 15th) that '52/– seems to me a very good offer for Bacon & I should have been glad to hear of progress in that article'. And he added, as a helpful general maxim, that 'Bacon won't do to hold'.

But over the next few weeks, Wentworth's despatches continued to cause furrowed brows:

16 March. I have no sales of any consequence to report. Provision market quite stagnant and not a single Cask of Halstead's yet sold. We have now 2,700 packages of theirs on hand of the aggregate invoice value of $73,900. I am anxious to sell but Brokers say that if we forced any of it we should have to submit to very low prices, so I still hold on. Cocke expects every day to see some demand spring up. The quantities of provisions of all kinds now held here are enormous. At Brewers Quay they are quite full and could not receive a parcel I wanted to land there. The other Wharf also will shortly be overstocked.

30/31 March. I commence first by informing you of a little financial difficulty which I have lately experienced and relating how I have got out of it.

£3000 worth of Halsteads Dfts fell due between this and the 10th April and, being quite unable to move any of their Provision, I was at a loss to know where the money was to come from to meet the Bills.

The Balance at Glyns (today) stands at £1600 and in the 'box' I have a reserve of about £2000. This reserve however must go for various other acceptances falling due next week and for general payments which I have to meet. I therefore found it necessary to *borrow*.

This morning I went in to Glyn's and stated my case to Mr Williams and Mr Mills but they said they could 'do nothing for me', that it 'was quite against the rules of their house to advance money on *wharf* orders' &c. This afternoon however I called again by appointment and saw Mr Glyn who said that although it *was* against their rules to make such advances yet in the present instance they would consent to break through theirs and to make the advance of £3000 . . .

You need not I think give yourself any concern about my financial matters for the present. There will be about £8400 worth of Bills to meet during April but as I have obtained this advance from Glyns I hope to get on pretty well.

Both letters brought forth immediate replies from Charles, now in St Vincents. To the first he expressed his prescient concern that such an overstocked provision market 'may hamper you in finance' and added that 'you will of course give every care to keep *that* straight'. To the second he conceded that 'the transaction with Glyns, although not done by them in the most satisfactory style, is *so far* satisfactory that it opens the door with them, & I won't fain hope that having done the thing once they will not let you go to the wall for want of further help'. Charles even accepted a certain amount of blame: 'I believe indeed that our mistake heretofore has been the not making sufficient use of our Bankers – others *must* do it for we see houses of comparatively small position cultivating business which must require large advances'. So it continued into late summer, as the market obstinately refused to unblock itself and Wentworth faced daily humiliation at the hands of his brokers:

24 *July*. You may perhaps be surprised to learn that I have this day sold, to Phillips, a further lot of India Pork @ £6.10.0. I have tried to gain on this price without success and I learn that P was quite indifferent as to whether he had it or not. I debated the matter long before I decided on letting it go but the prospects for this article seem so very poor that I was induced to sell it . . . The Beef will be 'shewn' by Cocke today and I hope some business may result; we continue to have very large arrivals of this article and even Halstead & Co have lost their confidence in it. O'Ryan has sold nothing for us yet – he laughs at my prices saying that he has shewn the stuff repeatedly but that *his* buyers will not come *near* my limits. He insists that the price obtained for the I Pork is much above its value.

The business survived the strains of it all (the firm would last until about 1910), and three years later it was Wentworth who was in

Bermuda receiving letters from Charles in Great St Helen's. 'You should look about vigorously, try to pick up consignments however small. In these days there is no telling how soon small may grow into large & we cannot afford to lose even small.'[10]

As Wentworth Gray tried in 1860 to shift recalcitrant beef and pork, the senior clerks of the City's main banks met at the end of February to press for earlier closing than four o'clock on Saturdays. According to Legg of the London Joint Stock Bank, 'the great body of clerks, who now had to devote so much continuous labour in the performance of their duties, would have an opportunity, like other people, of enjoying the fresh air or improving their moral and social condition'. These sentiments were wholly endorsed by the Union Bank of London's chief cashier, who added with some pomp that 'he had been called upon in his official capacity frequently to make arrangements for extending the business of an establishment that he had seen grow from five clerks to one hundred and five, and could without difficulty make the arrangements necessary for closing at two o'clock'. The banks gave way, though at this stage only to the extent of closing at three o'clock on Saturdays.[11]

As for the chief cashier, a few weeks later on a crisp March late afternoon he was encountered by David Morier Evans as that hard-pressed financial journalist stood on a busy pavement near the Mansion House hoping to spot a friend or acquaintance who would be able to give him information on the day's monetary developments:

> For some time I wait patiently, but apparently without prospect of success, and the only reward for my perseverance is the kindly recognition from the insides of cabs, or the outsides of other conveyances, of friends who are in too desperate a hurry to fly the living maëlstrom to attend to me or my wants, though sore many may imagine my distress to be.
>
> At length I fancy I descry a style and appearance about which there can be scarcely any mistake, and which, if they shall represent in real reality the personage supposed, will relieve me from much of my difficulty, and at least satisfy my anxiety on points of importance, of little or no weight to him, but of vast interest to his willing recipient.
>
> I am right in my conjecture, it is one of my very best friends, one who can afford me the special knowledge I wish to secure, and who I feel will not hesitate or be stinting in his supply, if there be any to give. He approaches; his bearing is slightly imposing, being above the middle height, and exhibiting some regard to a substantial style of dress: he comes up, pressing through the crowd, who seem disposed to give him 'vantage ground. He is well enveloped in his fashionable brown coat; he

walks jauntily, but not with a supercilious or ostentatious air, and as our eyes meet he vigorously rubs his delicate, pulpy, well-formed hands.

'Ah! Ah!' he says, with a smile, and his bright eyes twinkle; 'this is glorious weather – they have been doing something over the way, to-day – taking it in by sackfuls – money I should think will be cheap after this'.

'Have they?' I respond. 'You are just the person I was in quest of. Detained late westward, I have not long reached the City. What has been doing?'

The speaker's playful allusion to the 'doing of something over the way' is in relation to enormous bullion operations at the Bank, whither large sums have been sent during the day. The sequence of his volunteered information is, that fine weather, with good bullion arrivals, will produce a favourable effect upon the money market.

I inquire the nature and extent of the transactions at the Bank. I am replied to in the same jocose vein, but find myself furnished with precise information. What the course and transactions at the Stock Exchange? No absence of intelligence of the principal movements and fluctuations, given in the same off-hand style, tinged with a spice of irony upon men and things in general. Has there been any fact of importance in the open money market – such as joint-stock bank stringency, or probability of increased abundance? He is not at a loss upon any of these questions; he answers glibly, but unerringly; and, finally, parting to catch his omnibus, asks with mock solemnity, if I can tell him the last price of Chinese Turnpike Bonds, since he purposes shortly making a considerable investment.

My end is accomplished, and he is soon lost in the human maëlstrom; but I have followed as long as vision enabled me his retreating figure. I am satisfied at having so amply gratified my thirst for knowledge of the day's proceedings, yet, at the same time, I cannot help reflecting that in following my cherished pursuit I make huge sacrifices that no emolument can ever repay.

How, on my way to my office, to shape and put into proper guise my required store of well-collected facts, the thought haunts me of his comfortable, easy, and steadily-attained position. How rebellious my heart rises, which at other periods is tractable and thankful, imagining the surfeit of pleasure he must enjoy in hastening home to spend his evenings with his wife – perhaps his little ones. And here am I working night after night into the silent hours for at most a precarious existence if head or hand should fail.

I, who at all times and in all seasons relish a sparkling or facetious colloquy, feel a peculiar description of *melancholia* follow this interview and conversation; but after chewing the cud of sober thought, I surmount my short but sharp hypochondriacal attack, and putting my back to my evening's labour, manfully go at it, and struggle through.

Morier Evans then fast forwards and gives the pay-off to his bitter-sweet *conte*:

A month subsequently, I am in the City rather earlier. I make my accustomed calls, and among other places at the joint-stock banks. An unparalleled fraud has been discovered – a fraud that appeared likely, when its magnitude transpired, to shake confidence to its centre; and when I inquire the perpetrator, I am told it is William George Pullinger – the individual who but a few weeks previously, inspired in my breast those transient feelings of envy, which certainly for the moment disturbed me more than I ever remember to have been before by any analogous circumstances.

It was indeed a scandal that rocked the City. Pullinger, chief cashier at the Union, was renowned for never taking a holiday, and it was only because of his unavoidable absence at a funeral on Thursday, 19 April (the day after Overend Gurney returned the bank notes) that a startling deficiency of over £260,000 came to light. On his return he acknowledged the crime and revealed that the defalcations had been going on for five years, since the time he became chief cashier and thus in sole charge of the bank's passbook. He also stated that, as a result of disastrous speculations on the Stock Exchange, the money was all lost.

Inevitably this led to a Stock Exchange inquiry, it being against the rules for a member to do speculative bargains on behalf of a clerk (however eminent a clerk), and the bank passed on to the Committee the names of a handful of brokers who had done business for Pullinger. They included Robert Johnston:

> He said he had known Pullinger intimately since 1842 [three years after Pullinger joined the Union Bank as a cashier].
> When Pullinger was taken up he had open for him £35,000 Consols, 300 Lombardos [i.e. Lombardo-Venetian Railway Company shares], 100 Great Luxemburg, £20,000 Mexican, £5,000 Berwick Stock.
> He used to go to the bank to Pullinger and has paid him in the bank, sometimes he met him where Pullinger went to dinner.
> Pullinger once said to him, 'if ever you are in a fix in carrying over Lombardo shares bring them to me as I have opportunities of getting money' ...

Another named broker was George E. Ball, whose firm Bell & Ball had failed in a Stock Exchange panic a year earlier, the cause almost certainly of the chief cashier's heaviest losses:

> He thought they began dealing for Pullinger in 1855.
> Mr Ball said he was a young man and Pullinger took him by the hand.

Pullinger always pretended that he was dealing for other people but he gave only one person's name, it was Mr Wessell who was a clerk in that bank and married a rich widow and then left the bank.

They had accounts with him every settling day in all the most speculative stocks such as Turkish, Mexican, Leeds and Midland.

When the failures occurred they had open for him near £200,000 Turks, about £500,000 Consols and from £120,000 to £200,000 Mexican.

He should suppose the clerks knew that Pullinger was speculating, there was no concealment on his part. He, Ball, went to the bank daily at eleven o'clock with the opening prices, he received orders across the counter, and should think the other clerks could hear.

Pullinger came to their office when he wanted anything, perhaps two or three times a week.

The Committee suspended Johnston and three other brokers (not including Ball, no longer a member). But its business was not done, for soon afterwards it was compelled to examine a Stock Exchange rumour that many bargains had been done for Pullinger by 'Messrs Scrimgeour the brothers of the Manager of the Union Bank'. John S. Scrimgeour pleaded that 'Pullinger was, at the time, a man looked up to by everybody and liked by everybody', and added with words he perhaps would not like to have had broadcast outside the Committee Room: 'His firm had maintained an unblemished reputation for 35 years. The other parties were on a very different footing'. The three Scrimgeours were, however, suspended until the following March, so that particular plea availed little.

By this time Pullinger had appeared at the Old Bailey and made his own plea, one of guilty. A press report described him as 'a stalwart, florid-complexioned man, perfectly self-possessed', and almost fifty years old. A week later, on 15 May, he addressed the court:

The moment the directors mentioned the suspicion that was entertained I at once confessed that I was culpable, and gave them every information as to the extent of the frauds, and gave all the assistance in my power to realise securities for the benefit of the bank. Myself and my wife have also assigned everything we possessed in the world with the same object, and in order that as much restitution as possible might be made. If it had not been for the bad faith of a broker who died last year I should have restored a much larger amount. From the first it has been my determination to plead guilty; and although my friends have endeavoured to persuade me from doing so, I persisted in that determination. It has gone forth to the world that I had made up a purse for my wife, but it is only due to her to say that from the first she has always urged me to make full restitution, and expressed her readiness to give up everything and retire to another land upon a small pittance allowed her by her own friends, and there hide her grief. (The prisoner was here a good deal affected.) If what I have just said should be considered by your lordship to afford any ground for mitigating the horrors of my imprisonment I shall be deeply grateful; but if your lordship, like the bank, should feel that you can show me no mercy, I shall still bow cheerfully to your decision. (There was a slight attempt at applause when the prisoner concluded.)

The judge was unmoved and gave him twenty years' servitude, whereupon 'the prisoner appeared quite overwhelmed at the sentence'. The following year he left Chatham by the ship *Lincelles* for Western Australia, to undergo his term of transportation. According to the official returns he died upon the passage, but it was generally assumed that Pullinger had committed suicide by jumping overboard.[12]

This gigantic fraud sent ripples through the wider banking community, and soon afterwards the Sheffield and Hallamshire Bank sent two of its directors to the City to make inquiries about the best means of protecting itself against a similar occurrence. They stayed at the Castle & Falcon in Aldersgate Street and began their inquiries on 12 June at Glyn Mills, who stressed to them 'that Consols are the very *best security* that a Bank can hold – and that they have seen three Panics, when for a time all other securities were absolutely unnegotiable, even Exchequer Bills – but they never knew a time when money could not be borrowed on Consols'. The next day, Wednesday, began with a visit to James Capel, which offered some trenchant opinions:

> Glyns, there cannot be a moment's doubt, are rich and indeed very rich – they are also men of business, and each of them daily attends at the Bank, and has a department to superintend.
> They think Overends very rich indeed, and the *only discount House* of *real wealth*. Alexanders very respectable . . .
> They thought that the London joint stock Banks were trading with *too little paid up Capital* – and trusting too much to their Deposits.

Then came a dilemma:

> Finding two Firms of Cunliffe in the Directory, & not knowing which was our correspondent, both being described as Bankers, we called first on Cunliffe Roger Son & Co in Bucklersbury, because nearest to us on the road.
> We handed in our cards with 'Sheffield & Hallamshire Bank written thereon' we said – we said to a Gentleman we were not sure, if theirs was the House we were in quest of, & asked if they had done business for our

Bank. The reply was that he could not very well recollect 'but he thought it must be sometime since'. We were then invited into an inner room where was an elderly Gentleman. He asked us to be seated, & went out with the younger Person. On returning the elderly Gentleman said 'he did not know the Sheffield & Hallamshire Bank' – & asked if 'Hallamshire was a little village near Sheffield'. He sent for what seemed a 'ledger'. He looked into the 'index' for our Bank's name, but said he could not find it.

We then said 'it was clear the other firm of Cunliffes was the House we wished to call upon' – & took our departure.

We give these particulars, because there was something about the bearing and manners of the old Gentleman, singularly mysterious & to us totally unexplicable.

They then made their way to Lombard Street, where Cunliffes & Co were not only the right firm of bill brokers but 'appeared to us respectable & orderly, & behaved with great courtesy'. The final visit that day was to Alexander & Co, who also made a favourable impression, 'thought our rules exceedingly good & proper', and agreed that 'Consols ought to be verified from time to time'.

On Thursday the main event was a visit to the Corner House:

Our interview was with Mr Gurney junior – the most intelligent & business like, & Gentlemanly Person, we had up to this time met with. We had a long conference, & although exceedingly busy (some six or eight persons waiting) he would not allow us to hasten our departure, until both we & himself had said all we wished to say.

He thought the alternation of duties among the Clerks, one of the most valuable checks that could be devised against fraud by collusion – they transferred Clerks from one duty to another – from one ledger to another, at a *moment's notice*.

We offered to attend again when they were not so busy, at any time of his own appointment, but he replied they were always the same & that they personally looked after their cash and Bills, as they found it necessary to make personal supervision of their Clerks.

He entered on the subject of their controversy with the Bank of England & said – that he thought this subject was not understood by the public – who thought that the question was solely between Bank of England and Overends, whereas it was between the Bank of *England* and the *Commercial public*. The latter would have to pay in *inconvenience* & the *price of money* for the restrictions now in force.

If the Bank of England did not relax, Peel's act would again have to be broken; but – not by *them*, but by the *Bank of England*, for its own salvation.

He further said –

We now do business on the principle known & acknowledged *of taking care of ourselves* – at all risks to our clients – we cannot do otherwise –

formerly we felt bound to discount in times of difficulty, for those who traded with us in good times – hereafter we cannot do this – all must take care of themselves in any future Panics.

It was Henry Edmund Gurney at his most magisterial, prompting his visitors to note that 'there is a large amount of business talent in this House'. Friday was the final day, and they called on the London and Westminster, where though disappointed not to see Gilbart ('having perused Mr Gilbart's books, we thought highly of his practical knowledge of Banking') they were politely received by knowledgeable deputies who supplied a fair amount of detail about the bank's system of checks and safeguards, happily in accordance with the new rules at the Sheffield and Hallamshire. The rest of the day was given over to writing up the interviews. 'We trust that our Colleagues will be of opinion that our journey to London has not been without good fruit', the report concluded, adding: 'We have worked hard & close this at $11\frac{1}{2}$ o'clock PM June 15, 1860.'[13]

*

A year and a week later the City was experiencing a conflagration even worse than the destruction of the Royal Exchange. This was the Tooley Street fire of 1861, just to the south of the river by London Bridge. Besides claiming the much-lamented life of James Braidwood, chief officer of the London Fire Engine Establishment, it completely destroyed five wharves and one warehouse, gutted eleven other warehouses, and reduced much of Tooley Street to rubble. It was a fire that not only provided human tragedy, material ruin and technicolour spectacle, but also in its immediate aftermath pointed up the City's distinctive combination of conservatism and innovation. The larger context was the moribund condition of the insurance business, one of the City's prime sectors: Lloyd's through a series of institutional reforms from the mid-1840s had semi-recovered from a period in the doldrums, partly caused by its rivals that appeared after 1824, but its unimaginative underwriters had signally failed to compete in the growing market of fire insurance; a long-established company like the Phoenix had got into the habit of making nondescript appointments to its board, and had allowed its management to ossify; and by the 1860s there was a host of strong provincial competitors to London's once near-monopoly in the field of non-marine insurance. In the summer of 1861 the City's fire offices reacted to the Tooley Street blaze by increasing their rates to such an extent that towards the end of July a large number of merchants and wharf property owners gathered at the Mansion House's Egyptian Hall to make their feelings known. The secretary of the Globe sought to defend the new rates, arguing that the fault lay at least in part with the indiscriminate storing of commodities in over-large warehouses, but his listeners gave him a cool reception. The upshot was *action directe*: merchants, shippers and others came together the following month to form the Commercial Union, at first concentrating on fire insurance but from 1863 embracing marine risks as well. Its chairman was the strong-minded Henry Peek, senior partner of Peek Bros & Co of Eastcheap, wholesale dealers in tea, coffee, cocoa and spice, and among those on a powerful board was Jeremiah Colman, whose mustard works in Norfolk had an important London distributive end in Cannon Street.[14] It was an impressive, speedy response to a specific contingency, reflecting the City (or one part of it) at its best.

What, however, the City has never been particularly good at, contrary to popular mythology, is the accurate anticipation of events in the wider world. Take this sanguine letter in November 1860 from Rothschilds to its American agent August Belmont, following the election of Abraham Lincoln:

> It is looked upon with satisfaction in this country from the check there will be upon slavery, and though there will be discontent in the Southern States, we expect things will go on peaceably, and that there will be no evil consequences such as a disruption of the Union or other division. You will see a good article upon the subject in *The Times* of today.

Two months later the message to Belmont remained adamant:

> We scarcely expected to receive such disheartening advices from you about Politics, as you look forward to an appeal to arms, and have gloomy foreboding about the future. The impression of American merchants here is much more hopeful. Bates, Peabody, Pickersgill and others are not wanting in confidence, as to a compromise or to means being effectually adopted for bringing the refractory States to order.

But the refractory states did not come to heel, and by May 1861 the same Bates was fearing 'a long and bloody war', one 'destructive of commerce' and likely to 'materially reduce the profits of B.B. & Co'. The American Civil War indeed affected both his firm and Peabody's, the latter for the first time looking seriously to Europe for business opportunities; but from the point of view of the City as a whole one significant by-product was the flow of 'hot money' from New York to London, harbinger of a coming era of increasingly volatile international capital movements. What was the City's attitude to the war itself? Henry Adams, as the son of Lincoln's man in London, was unimpressed when he wrote home in November 1861:

> How do you suppose we can make a stand here when our own friends fail to support us? Look at the Southerners here. Every man is inspired by the idea of independence and liberty, while we are in a false position . . . They have an object and they act together. *Their* merchants and friends in Liverpool have been warm and vigorous in their support from the beginning. *Ours* have been lukewarm, never uttering a hearty word on our side, and the best of them such as Peabody and the house of Barings invariably playing directly into the hands of our opponents. They have allowed the game to go by default. Their talk has been desponding, hesitating, an infernal weight round our necks.[15]

Adams, though, was referring specifically to houses with an American connection; and the probability is that the great majority of non-American houses in the City were not passionate either way, if perhaps with a certain innate bias (reflecting London society as a whole) towards the more 'gentlemanly' South. Markets, as Cobden would reluctantly have conceded, are rarely moved by abstract considerations, and the underlying tendency was to wait to see which side emerged the stronger.

In early 1863 the outcome was still uncertain, and that March there took place one of the more outrageous episodes in *haute finance*:

> The announcement has aroused an unusual amount of attention, and transactions have been already actively carried on throughout the day at prices ranging from 2 to 3 premium . . . The excitement connected with it is principally due to the fact that the affair is to be regarded almost exclusively as a cotton speculation . . . The loan will receive no official sanction – not even that of the Committee of the Stock Exchange . . .

Causing the excitement in Capel Court were the terms of a £3m bond issue on behalf of the Confederate States, bonds made peculiarly attractive by the option for holders to convert into cotton, then at a very high price. It was in effect a commodity speculation taking the form of a sovereign loan for a breakaway state in the middle of a civil war – an almost unparalleled tribute to nineteenth-century commercial freedom. Excitement continued to mount:

> In the foreign market the Confederate Loan has ranged between 3 and
> 5 premium, with very large and numerous transactions . . . As the affair
> will not be officially recognised the Stock Exchange dealers have adopted
> a general agreement to name a settling day of their own . . . Very little
> political feeling has been manifested in the business, and it seems evident,
> as far as London is concerned, that it is in viewing it as a cotton
> speculation, of which the advantages or disadvantages will be determined
> by the people of Manchester and Liverpool, that any attraction it pos-
> sesses is to be found. In other respects there can be no doubt that a
> majority of our merchants and capitalists would have wished that it had
> not been introduced.

That presumably was a reference to the official British attitude of
neutrality, but any such misgivings weighed little in the scales against
the prospect of a profitable spec. The loan as a whole was organised
by Erlangers in Paris, though the bulk of the bonds were brought out
in London where the issue was managed by Schröders. As with any
major issue there was an important distributive role for the better-
connected stockbrokers, one of whom was P. Cazenove & Co. It
assured one client, when the terms were announced, that Schröders
was 'a highly respectable firm', and then confessed to a certain indispensable secrecy:

> We have been obliged to prevent our names appearing on the pro-
> spectus in order to avoid the risk of the possible confiscation of a very
> large amount of Northern Railway property of which we are the regis-
> tered proprietors. We are still however acting unofficially having made
> friendly arrangements with Messrs Erlanger & Schröder.

In the event, it all went sour. The war shifted decisively against the
Confederacy, Erlangers and Schröders had to organise an expensive
support operation to keep up the price of the bonds, and despite their
best endeavours they were down by the end of the year to under 40 (the
loan having been brought out at 90), 'so that we may at length conclude', Henry Adams wrote with satisfaction, 'that the opinion among
capitalists is fairly become that the chances are against the independence
of the rebels'. So it proved: US railroads were already recovering much of
their prewar popularity as market counters, and by 1865, with peace
restored, a third of all the railway securities issued in London that year
were for American railroads. It was back to business as usual.[16]
Loan contracting was an inherently risky occupation, and a diary
entry by Joshua Bates in November 1858 accurately reflects the prim-

acy of judgement and the unsettling feeling sometimes attached to exercising it:

> Have had several interviews with Mr Ochagavia in regard to the Chilian loan. We had several weeks since offered him 92 for a 4½ per Cent Bond, payments spread over 6 ms. This he refused, but after trying in other quarters he probably found he could do no better and came back to us. Laurence [the stockbroker] thinks it would go well at 90, Capel that 92 would do. Fr[ancis] Baring thinks 90 enough, Thom⁵ Baring rather dislikes to give 92, Young seems to adhere to T.B., Sturgis is for 92 & the young partners go with the majority, so it is difficult for me to say take it without having the whole responsibility of the result.

Bates in the end opted for the more cautious 92, but his firm still managed to place only half the loan. Loan contracting, moreover, was becoming an increasingly competitive business, and a few weeks later Barings had the shock of discovering that a new Russian loan was to be undertaken not at 8 Bishopsgate but by Thomson, Bonar – reputable Russia merchants but an altogether lesser-known outfit on the international stage. Thomson Bonar, however, muffed its chance, and during the first half of the 1860s Barings and Rothschilds each did at least one Russian loan, both London houses maximising their European connections to ensure the widest possible subscriptions. Plenty of other houses were by now involved in the fray, including Dent Palmer (Turkey 1858), Frühling & Goschen (Egypt 1862, 1864), Hambros (Italy 1862), Raphaels (Denmark 1864, challenging the position there of Hambros), and of course Schröders (Sweden 1864). In April 1864 a rumour even got about the City, reported by Mark Collet of Brown Shipley, that 'Rothschilds have designedly caused the present tightness by locking up a large amount of notes in order to bother the Russian & Mexican Loans, from both of which they have been cut out', Collet adding that 'it is difficult to believe, this, but the story has gained currency'.[17]

As to whether a loan would go, much depended on the whims of the speculating public, and in the spring of 1862 the financial press was amazed by the enthusiastic reception given to a new Turkish loan, brought out by the Ottoman Bank, Charles Devaux & Co and Glyn Mills against a recent, all-too-familiar background of Turkish financial collapse. Soon afterwards Rothschilds brought out a new Russian loan, and the word from Cazenove's was that the stock was 'cheap & good at 92', but 'will not be a "sporting" thing like Turkish'. However, there were plenty of sporting things in the pipeline, as Morier Evans would confirm towards the end of 1863, in a survey of recent developments in the foreign loan market:

> Money, to the extent of many millions, has been subscribed to assist the necessities of Turkey, or to develop the resources of Egypt, and Morocco; and, whilst Portugal has not failed to come again into the market as a borrower, Peru has been allowed to consolidate her debt, though on a doubtful footing; Venezuela bringing up the rear, with two new financial arrangements.[18]

1863 was the year of a major bull market, in which almost 700 new companies were registered and the City was awash with speculative froth. It was also the year in which something approaching Continental-style joint-stock investment (as opposed to deposit) banking came to the square mile for the first time, throwing into sharp relief traditional English methods of financial intermediation. For over a decade the Crédit Mobilier, founded in Paris in 1852 by the Pereire brothers as an explicit rival to Rothschilds there, had been a talking point in the most eminent parlours. Barings was as keenly interested as anyone, appreciating its potential as a tool against Rothschild and even allowing Francis Baring to become a director, but in time it came to feel a gut hostility. Bates in 1855 asserted to Tom Baring that a joint-stock bank was essentially 'large capital, collected for purposes of speculation', while the next year he wrote to another partner: 'I should be disposed to cut loose from the Credit Mobilier. They will make a *smash* some day or other but probably not before they have done us all the harm they can by establishing a "Credit Mobilier" in London.' Nor was it only joint-stock investment banking that loomed as a threat to traditional City assumptions, for from the mid-1850s the advent of limited liability – against the vehement opposition of, among others, Overstone – meant that English company law was more liberal than anywhere else in Europe, challenging the conventional wisdom that the surest formula for prudence was for a businessman to have all his assets on risk. In the City itself, however, the tradition of unlimited liability partnerships remained sacrosanct for another half-century, and in 1863 the Russia merchant and Bank of England director J. G. Hubbard made no bones about attacking in Parliament French-style *commandite* (i.e. limited liability) partnerships, on the grounds that, though a lesser evil than incorporation as such, they still 'would powerfully tend to discourage measured and cautious trading, and would stimulate a system of reckless and irresponsible speculation'.[19]

Yet in the wider world the changes were irreversible, and from 1862 the codification of company law meant that there were few obstacles to starting a limited company. W. S. Gilbert was to famously encapsulate the process in *Utopia Limited*:

> Some seven men form an Association
> (If possible, all Peers and Baronets),
> They start off with a public declaration
> To what extent they mean to pay their debts.
> That's called their Capital . . .

By the spring of 1863 the financial boom was fully under way, and that April the formation took place or began to take place of three pioneering finance companies, consciously modelled on continental joint-stock lines and designed to be powerful vehicles of mobilising capital for governmental, industrial and other purposes. The first was the London Financial Association; the second was the General Credit and Finance Company of London, chaired by Samuel Laing, recently Finance Minister of India; and the third, and most important, was the International Financial Society, explicitly linked to the Crédit Mobilier.[20] It was time for the City to decide where it stood.

Henry Hucks Gibbs, in an explicit document, outlined to his uncle William on 1 May 1863 the crucial high-level preliminaries as the IFS took shape:

> It is proposed to establish in London an Association of the leading firms, to undertake between them any national financial operation which may offer – such as foreign Loans and the like – having the twofold object of doing a good business for themselves, and (as they would get rid of rivalry and competition of the various firms who now do such business) working better & more favourably than any individual firm can do.
>
> They would be formidable rivals to Rothschild, & would they think serve foreign Governments much better . . .
>
> The names are really first class.
>
> Peabody – Hodgson – Heath – Dobree . . . and other good firms whose names I don't at the moment remember. Meinertzhagen was much in favour; but old Huth said nay . . . Schröder is being asked. Frühling & Göschen the same . . .
>
> Baring, M. Mallet [the London envoy of the Crédit Mobilier] said, received the proposition better than he should have thought he would – said it was a necessity – that such a combination must come sooner or later – that he would think about it. Afterwards they saw all the partners in conclave when they declined for the present, Bates saying – You see

M. Mallet, we consider ourselves a sort of Credit Mobilier ourselves
alone. Still, T.B. said – we may have to join you sooner or later or else,
when you have taken away our business, Govern^ts may after all find that
the old ways are best and they may come back to us – think at present we
have too much to give away, having already a good connection in such
matters, and don't feel disposed to enter into combinations with others
who are not on equal terms with us.

This was the *gist* of what he said . . .

Gibbs added that there was to be a meeting the next day at Huths
and that 'they are much pressed for time – for fear I fancy Rothschild
should get the start of them'. As to his own attitude, he was 'not *much*
disposed to entertain the proposal, notwithstanding the respectable
character of the promoters', but said that he would consult Goschen
(probably George Joachim).

The following day he wrote again and explained his very English
reservations:

Goschen thinks better of the scheme than I do, and wished me to attend
the meeting with him; but as, the more I think of it, the less I should like
to compromise our House in it, I have declined . . . I don't like the idea of
companionship with the Credit Mobilier, nor indeed of associating ourselves on equal terms with some of the Houses named, or who might
hereafter join the Combination.

The French view of such matters is, I fancy, that a loan for instance
coming out at 20 pre^m is an affaire faite; whereas we should think *some
one* was being robbed, & should not like it. They would see with great
equanimity the same go down to 20 disc^t so that they had sold out. *We
shouldn't.* In short, I fear we might some day find ourselves dragged
through mud against our will and without our knowledge.

I should be willing enough to make an alliance – offensive & defensive
– a confederacy – with Baring, Hodgson, Goschen, Schröder and two or
three others, that we should undertake no business of this kind of any
magnitude without offering to participate with one another . . . but I
would not enter into any *Company* with such an object.

A week later Bagehot's *Economist* came out strongly on similar lines,
declaring that 'there is less call here than elsewhere for new developments of credit' and, taking on the City's behalf the moral high ground,
asserting that 'the notion of "rigging the market" is unpopular here,
but it might be considered as a "support" of friends or "industry" in
Paris'. In short, it concluded portentously, 'those concerned in the
matter must weight these considerations'.[21]

Such strictures did not prevent the International Financial Society from forming a reasonably powerful board. It included representatives from George Peabody & Co, Frühling & Goschen, Frederick Huth & Co, Samuel Dobree & Sons (Bonamy's firm), Heath & Co (another firm of merchants, edging into merchant banking, who provided a Governor of the Bank), Stern Brothers (a firm that had come from Frankfurt to London twenty years earlier, bringing out a Portuguese loan in 1863), and Robert Benson & Co (a Liverpool mercantile firm that had moved to the City a decade previously). The IFS's bankers were Glyns, a private bank conspicuous for its enthusiasm for furthering joint-stock enterprise. But quite apart from the fact that most of the directors were junior rather than senior partners in the individual firms, there were some notable gaps: Hambros, Schröders, Antony Gibbs, and above all Barings. For whatever reason – lack of clout, lack of commitment on the part of its members, an innate preference for doing things the traditional way – the IFS in practice proved something of an anti-climax, the turning-point indeed that failed to turn. It managed to establish itself as a long-term feature on the financial scene but was involved in relatively few major issues, and by April 1864 it may well have been with the IFS in mind that Tom Baring was observing complacently to a correspondent that it would soon be generally appreciated 'that business can be conducted with greater economy, activity and attention by private establishments where every partner has a direct interest, than by boards playing with the money of others'.[22] Put another, harsher way, it had been a triumph for the forces of conservatism, individualism and *amour propre*.

The new finance houses were not helped by the fact that during the year after their launch there took place, under the auspices of a sustained bull market, a wave of company promotions so relentlessly opportunistic as to darken the name of *any* new financial concern. 'Most unblushing have been the appropriations made for services in the establishment of banks', declared Morier Evans in his aptly named *Speculative Notes* (1864), asserting that 'the amount of transparent jobbery almost recognised in the light of day, has exceeded that known to have existed in the great bubble period of 1824–25, or the later railway mania of 1845'. A number of rip-off finance houses came to the fore during the winter of 1863–64, before the stock market at last ran out of steam. Such a one was the ambitiously named Crédit Foncier and Mobilier of England, promoted and run by Albert Grant.[23] His real name was Abraham Gottheimer and he had been born in Dublin in 1831, the son of a Jewish pedlar from Central Europe who then managed to become a partner in a foreign 'fancy' business in Newgate Street in London. Grant himself began as a wine merchant, in 1859 was actively involved in the promotion of the Mercantile Discount Co and became its general manager, and during the mid-1860s succeeded in systematically enriching himself. In 1865 he even became MP for Kidderminster: in sum, a tribute to social mobility but no sort of recommendation for financial Mobilier.

Integral to the operations of Grant was the activity known as making an artificial market. At the heart of this was the condoned existence of a 'grey' market, in which shares were traded prior to their allotment: these shares would be 'puffed' by the promoters and their friends to an extravagant premium; promoters and friends would be allotted a substantial quantity of shares; and the shares would then be sold to the general public at a handsome profit before they had time to tumble to a discount. Such in essence was the process rightly disparaged by the *Economist* as 'rigging the market', and it by no means only took place in perfidious Paris. Early in 1864 there occurred an episode of market-rigging in the flotation of the Australian & Eastern Navigation Company, a combination of three Liverpool shipping firms whose aim was to start a steamship line that would compete with the sailing ships that had hitherto dominated the Australian trade. What occurred was a classic corner, with the price rising to a steep premium, the directors and their circle managing to secure for themselves almost all the shares, and jobbers on the Stock Exchange facing acute difficulties in order to fulfil selling commitments. Eventually the Stock Exchange Committee not only refused the company's request for a settling day, on the grounds that the mode of allotment had been 'highly objectionable', but its chairman, F. L. Slous, persuaded the majority of his colleagues, against the opposition of S. H. de Zoete, to impose a total ban on dealings in the market prior to allotment.[24]

The Committee's long-serving secretary, Francis Levien, later recorded the aftermath:

> It soon became apparent that the view taken by Mr de Zoete was a correct one, for the attempted restriction proved worse than useless. Some of the dealers [i.e. jobbers] saw that by offering facilities for indulging in the proscribed dealings, they had an opportunity of creating business of so profitable a nature as to enable them to disregard the risk of losses through bad debts irrecoverable under the rules. The result proved that they were right. Large sums were made, and the object chiefly aimed at by the Committee – namely, an efficacious check to the tricks of the company promoters – was defeated.

Or in the feeling words of one member after some ten months of the ban, 'you might just as well attempt to stop the tide as to prevent dealing before allotment'. Inevitably those members who had obeyed the ban, and in so doing turned down business, lost patience, and in April 1865 the new rule was revoked.[25] For many years thereafter there would be no further attempt to clamp down on pre-allotment dealings, which, in accordance with the cardinal principle of the inviolability of the bargain, were held to be 'good' even though, by definition, a special settling day could not be granted until after allotment. This was not surprising: dealing before allotment was a valuable source of income to many members, *caveat emptor* remained the underlying philosophy of the markets, and no annually elected governing body was going to tamper a second time in that particular area, at least until the general climate of opinion in the House and elsewhere had much changed.

*

In the 1860s, at a time of intense financial activity in the world, the City became ever more indispensable. This applied with particular force in the field of international banking. Evans back in 1845 had noted the emergence of 'a number of Colonial Joint Stock banks' based in London, mainly connected with Australia; and there was also the Ionian Bank, established in Aldermanbury in 1839 to help further economic growth on those Greek islands still under British suzerainty until 1864. In the decade from the mid-1850s a series of important 'Anglo-International' banks were created, including the Bank of Egypt, the Ottoman Bank (from 1863 the Imperial Ottoman Bank), the London and Brazilian Bank and the Anglo-Austrian Bank. The City firm that specialised in acting as City midwife for these banks was Glyns; in 1863, when it was trying to secure support from Barings for the proposed Anglo-Austrian Bank, G. C. Glyn (a committed Liberal) wrote: 'Pray observe that I by no means surrender my political opinions . . . but I allow my commercial interests to take precedence in the present case'. Goschen two years later shrewdly defined what, in general, those commercial interests were: 'Joint-stock enterprise has been less anxious to invent fancy branches of commerce, or to find mysterious and recondite sources of wealth, than to get the highest rates for their capital by *lending* it to foreigners. To satisfy the foreign demand for capital in all its forms seems to be the leading idea . . .' The City, above all, was seen as the great source of funds. That was why at the end of 1862 Lewis and George Wallace set themselves up there – as

Wallace Brothers, East India merchants, of 8 Austin Friars – to provide finance, as well as charter shipping, for Wallace and Company of Bombay, trading there in a wide range of commodities. And that was why in 1866 the National Provincial Bank, with some 120 branches in the Midlands, was prepared to forfeit an annual note-issuing income of almost £½m as the price for acquiring a City base.[26] Money shading into contacts shading into influence: the lure was obvious and powerful.

So it was too, though given an extra twist by the fact of the American Civil War, in the case of the new transatlantic partnerships that now attained a presence in the City and sought to challenge the position of J. S. Morgan & Co (as Peabody's firm became in 1864) as the leading American house there. Three stood out: Speyer Bros (1861) originated from a rich Frankfurt family and, as Speyer & Co, had been in New York from 1837; Levi P. Morton was a New England merchant who opened banks in New York and London almost simultaneously (1863), the City firm from 1869 being known as Morton, Rose & Co; and J. & W. Seligman were two of eight brothers who in a short space of time opened offices in New York, New Orleans, San Francisco, Paris and Frankfurt as well as London (1864). The City's particular attraction for these ambitious newcomers was partly as a starting-off point for marketing American securities on the Continent but more importantly as a centre for conducting large-scale exchange operations. The buying and selling of bills on foreign countries was a growth industry, in the context of the mid-century global communications revolution, but according to Bagehot a few years later most English bankers would 'as soon think of turning silk merchants' as engaging in major remittance operations; and so it was foreign private bankers who cornered the business instead.[27]

These were all American houses, but there was also an important Anglo-American house that now came to the City. Brown Shipley of Liverpool had been contemplating the move since at least the mid-1850s, if not earlier, and in 1863 it at last set up in Founders' Court off Lothbury, though keeping open the Liverpool branch for another quarter of a century. The logic was compelling: the Civil War had fundamentally undermined Liverpool's cotton trade with America; while in terms of eventual peace the looming context of the transatlantic cable was likely to mean an end to the middleman role of the merchant in that trade, since it would put cotton brokers and manufacturers in direct communication with each other. Brown Shipley's future lay as City-based merchant bankers acting in close tandem (acceptance credits, foreign exchange business) with Brown Brothers in America. The firm was on a vigorous upswing, still prepared if necessary to cut its rates, and there was no doubt whom Mark Collet, in charge of the London house, saw as its principal rival. 'I do not wish to be envious', he wrote to his Liverpool partner in 1864, 'but it does seem hard that Barings should be getting everything the U.S. Government have to give when our New York people have at least some claim by their position & the sacrifices they have made'.[28] Brown Shipley would never become the seventh great power, but over much of the century, whether based in Liverpool or London, it did give 8 Bishopsgate cause for thought.

For all its preponderance of family firms, for all its increasingly hermetic institutional characteristics, the City overall was still a markedly 'open' society, capable of attracting talented outsiders and renewing itself. Take three men, each with their feet firmly under the table by the 1860s and each in their own way notable contributors. Montagu Samuel was born in 1832 the son of a Liverpool watchmaker and jeweller. When he left school at thirteen his parents changed his name round to Samuel Montagu, and as such he stayed. By the age of seventeen he was in the City working for his brother-in-law Adam Spielmann, a money changer; he then became manager of the Cornhill branch of a Paris firm; and in 1853, on the basis of £5,000 capital from his father, he established Samuel Montagu & Co, based at 142 Leadenhall Street and concentrating on bullion and foreign banking. Few in the City understood the workings of foreign exchange (which was perhaps why Goschen's book found such a ready market), but Montagu had a natural gift for dealing in different currencies, while his willingness to work on the tightest margins earned him the City tag that he had made his fortune (which he did comfortably while still in his twenties) on 'the quarter pfennig and the half centime'.[29]

Cast in the same hard-working, taskmastering mould was Julius Caesar Czarnikow, born in Germany in 1838 the son of a Polish-Jewish cloth merchant. He came to England in 1854, was soon working for Camphausen & Weber, produce brokers of Billiter Square, and in 1861 began on his own account as a colonial broker, first near and then in Mincing Lane. Not only did the business quickly take off on the back of rising British consumption of sugar, but from 1863 Czarnikow issued a *Weekly Price Current* full of market-related news about sugar, coffee and other commodities: it was popularly known in Mincing Lane as the 'Circular' and helped establish its publisher (and originally editor) as a dominant figure in that particular world.[30]

Another wordsmith, though of a more literary bent, was Edward
Clodd. His father was the captain of a trading brig and he was brought
up on the Suffolk coast. His parents prayed for him to become a Baptist
minister, but made the mistake of taking him to see the Great Exhibition, which 'made me secretly resolve, whatever might block the way,
to get to London when I left school'. In 1855 he became clerk to an
accountant in Cornhill – unpaid for the first six months – and then
had two other employees before in 1862 'I obtained a clerkship in the
London Joint Stock Bank'. The next ten years were a terrible struggle
(a large family to support, an inadequate salary, long and conscientious
hours in Princes Street, an aversion to borrowing, the frequent pawning
of his watch), but in 1872 he became Secretary to the bank, holding
that position until 1915. All the time, whenever he could, Clodd was
studying, and eventually he became a well-known rationalist, folklor-
ist, and populariser of scientific theories. He was, in short, one of the
classic Victorians, a deeply civilised man for whom the City was almost
certainly a place of drudgery rather than romance; yet his delightful
description of Cheltenham, as 'the city of three per cents', alone earns
him a place in any financial history of the period.[31]

One newcomer who gazed with seasoned eyes upon the City was
William Lidderdale. He had already had an interesting life: he was
born in St Petersburg in 1832, the son of a Scottish merchant there who
lost most of his money; as a young man he became cashier to Rathbone
Bros, leading Liverpool merchants; in 1857 he went to New York to
work in the firm's agency; and now in 1864, as a new partner, he was
sent to London to see to the firm's business with the City's tea brokers.
The balance of power since the opening-up of the tea trade was significantly shifting towards the importers, and Lidderdale's task was to
ensure that it stayed that way, as well as to find suitable brokers with
whom to cultivate new lines of business (the tea trade being seasonal),
and to look for investment opportunities. He despatched back to
Liverpool some illuminating accounts of his progress:

> The Wool Sales were a decided disappointment. I will put a minimum
> in future cases. Brokers here have no idea whatever of doing anything for
> one beyond the mere routine of their duties. Few of them seem to keep
> any statistics & altogether they do less work for the same money than in
> Liverpool . . .
> Mr Southey is chairman of the Board of Wool brokers. The sale I
> attended was conducted by him in person. He is a complete type of a slow
> going, prejudiced but rather shrewd John Bull – civil enough but quite
> indifferent – sturdy, red faced & short tempered. I should like to find

younger men, if their position were sufficiently good to attract attendance
to their sales. The difficulty with Southey is to obtain anything in the way
of information about the Market, that is beyond its current position . . .

I find my want of acquaintance with London money matters productive
of delay in making arrangements, but am getting into the matter. My
Liverpool notions of regularity don't appear to be appreciated. I particularly object to some of the customs in buying produce – it takes more than
a week to obtain delivery in many cases . . .

The peculiarity of business here is the amount of running about that it
involves . . .[32]

He and Frank Wilde would have found plenty to agree about concerning the inferiority of metropolitan ways.

For an individual family firm so much depended on skilful handling
of the partnership arrangement, more an art than a science. In 1858
Henry Hucks Gibbs wrote to his uncle William (thinking of retiring)
about the prospect of one or more of William's children joining the
firm as partners:

I doubt indeed if we shall ever have that pleasure . . . and I perhaps
doubt a little whether it would be altogether wise for a young man who
might well have of his majority some £8 or £9000 a year, to undertake
any such continuous application as that of a merchant: 'Le jeu ne vaudrait
pas la chandelle'. Occupation they should have, no doubt; but *continuous*
application is very far from desirable if it can be avoided, and tends to
shorten one's life.

It was soon clear that the young folk would not be coming to Bishopsgate (prompting Henry to remark to his brother that in terms of
recruitment 'the Brigadiers are the difficulty – the Subalterns and the
Rank and File are easy enough to find!'), and by 1862 the emerging
question was what to do about Augustus Sillem, whom three years
earlier had been head-hunted from his own firm to become manager at
the attractive annual salary of £2,000. Uncle William, still senior
partner but rarely in the City, seems to have regarded him as an
undesirable Continental merchant, but Henry was anxious to explain,
from more intimate knowledge, 'his faults and his virtues':

In the first place – He is hasty in temper – quickly moved and as quickly
calmed – does not always think first and speak afterwards – does not
always read & examine thoroughly before he gives an opinion: but as to
the latter part, I must say that he generally & *in matters of importance*
does read very carefully anything put before him. It is to a hasty question

that he sometimes gives a hasty reply. I think too that he might be disposed in his eagerness for business, to imitate the continental houses in cutting down commissions; and that partly from his aptitude for exchange operations, partly from his connection with Mieville [Sillem's father-in-law] which might suggest them to him, he *might* be inclined to go more into that kind of business than we should like. He is a man of strong prejudices – generally on the right side and with some foundation, but prejudices nevertheless, and carried too far . . .

Above all, Henry was adamant that the firm could not afford to lose such a capable man.

Two years later, in August 1864, matters came to a head, over the question of admitting into the partnership not only Sillem but also someone called Edward Stubbs. Henry (a person peculiarly obsessed by family relations and genealogy) conceded it went against the grain:

> Now it is a very pleasant thought that we should have only those of our own name in the house; a thought in which other people besides ourselves have indulged but which all, like ourselves, have had sooner or later to give up. Barings, for instance . . . It is pleasant I say; but I am not sure that it is always profitable. New blood is wholesome in Governments and in Houses of Business as well as in Families and in flocks and herds; and if the Head remains a Gibbs and as many of the members as the family will provide, we may well get other members from a different Stock, provided only that in the most important respects they are as well bred as ourselves. In the great requirements of Honour and Integrity I feel sure that both Stubbs & Sillem are as well bred, and therefore I think they would give strength to the House and help to maintain the strength it has.

Uncle William bit on the bullet, and both men became partners, the requisite capital being lent to them.[33] It was a classic exposition of the guiding principle of staying within the family if possible but being prepared to broaden out if necessary, and of the care taken when choosing new partners. The houses that survived tended to be the ones that took those infinite pains.

As the merchant banks, or at least some of them, now began to emerge as the City's elite, private banks were conclusively on the way out. They 'have struggled manfully and vigorously against the tide of competition which has set in so strongly against them', Morier Evans recorded perhaps too sympathetically, 'and though they have every now and then been able to place barriers temporarily in the way of their antagonists, they have never been able permanently to impede their operations'.[34] These antagonists were of course the joint-stock banks, and an increasingly common reaction among the private fraternity was to seek strength through union. Sir John William Lubbock, Forster & Co merged with Robarts, Curtis & Co in 1860; three years later Barclay, Bevan, Tritton & Co acquired the business of Spooner, Attwoods & Co; and in 1864 Glyn Mills took over Curries and Barnett, Hoare & Co fused with Hanburys & Lloyds, both steps occasioned by the lack of suitable partners coming through from the individual banking families concerned. All this made defensive logic, but undermined the prestige of the City's private banks as a whole.

But the real hammer-blow was the announcement in April 1864 that Jones, Loyd & Co was to be absorbed by its next-door neighbour and arch-rival, the London and Westminster. G. W. Alexander (whose own discount house had recently merged with Cunliffes, in the face of joint-stock competition) acted as marriage broker, and the news caused a sensation. Mark Collet of Brown Shipley sought to give his Liverpool partner the inside dope:

> It is difficult to say what truth, *if any*, there is in the thousand & one rumours that have been eagerly circulated the last few days about amalgamations concessions &c &c; but quite irrespective of any such real or supposed formation, *all* joint stock banks went up after the arrangement between Jones Loyd & Co & the L & Westminster became known and the mania (as well as prices) reached its height the day before yesterday . . . The scramble for Jones Loyd & Co accounts has been eager & in some cases (as that of the Imperial Bank) disreputable . . . I do not think from what I hear that the L & W^m B^k will lose many accounts they care about among Jones Loyd & Co's customers, except Frühling & Goschen, who, *I think*, will go to Smith Payne & Co . . .
>
> Jones Loyd & Co's case was peculiar; Lewis Loyd has no children, Wm Loyd only two quite young; they are both rich men, indisposed to work & yet Mr Norman's constant illness threw the onus on them; hence rather than go on or take new partners, they decided to sell out.

But whatever the immediate causes – according to John Biddulph Martin (Richard's younger brother and also a partner at Martins), 'the two Loyds were said to have been very unpopular with their customers and to have lost much business' – it was an event of major symbolic as well as material damage to the private banking system. 'The amalgamation of the still existing houses with great joint-stock banks has become a mere question of time', declared one commentator the next year, while soon afterwards George Carr Glyn was privately accepting that 'eventually private banking must give way'.[35] Bottom, in the end, was not enough.

Of all these nineteenth-century private bankers, one of the most sympathetic was surely W. G. Prescott, a man of intellect, high moral stature, unassuming tastes, and even a sense of humour. In September 1861 he wrote from Corfu to his friend Overstone:

> You will see by the date of this where I am – but you are not likely to picture to yourself the discreditable appearance I should make in Thread-needle Street or Lothbury were I suddenly transferred there – A wide brimmed planters Straw hat, an almost white dress, no waistcoat, white Canvas Boots, and a long white beard scarcely form a fitting dress for a Banker, unless he is, as I am, some way out of reach of his Creditors.

It is a pleasing glimpse of an eminent Victorian on holiday. However, on 29 April 1865, at his home in Roehampton, he cut his own throat. With phrases and assumptions redolent of the dying world of private banking, his appalled partners tried to explain why their senior had done it:

> Our Minds travel back to trace the first symptoms of declining powers in our poor departed Friend; the minutes of the 18th of August last record, that on the 30th of July he took leave of the Banking House for a while, and went with all his own family, his Son in Law, his Brother in Law, a retinue of Servants, and large consignment of Goods, to a very remote district of the Highlands of Scotland for Grouse Shooting, fishing, and other Sports, a course of life to which he was quite unaccustomed, and in which he was now too old to make a commencement; there he remained 'till early in October; indeed he did not return 'till the very day that he had to receive the Dividend Lists at the Bank of England; he came back an altered Man; care-worn, fatigued, and evidently out of health; the business appeared to oppress him; irrationally so; for altho' the times were gloomy, and some of our accounts were perplexing, there was nothing to create that great alarm which had taken possession of his mind as to great general monetary difficulty, and as to a straitened position on our part; he grappled fairly enough with the annoying and heavy account of Gillespie Churchill & Co, and with the positive fraud of that dishonest man, Thomas Kemp; but these he held as trifles in comparison with what he termed the very threatening aspect of Affairs (not participated in by others) and his excitement became very uncomfortable to those around him; C. Cave [Charles Cave, partner second in seniority to Prescott] was then taking his annual change of air at Bognor, but he made it a point to come up once, sometimes twice a week, specially to chat with and to soothe our poor Friend, and as he saw it would to a certain extent tranquillise his mind, he did not hesitate to transfer into his name all his private funded Property, and to alter from a fixed period, to call, deposits of money that he had with Overend & Co and Alexander & Co. But

nothing would do. The crowning feature of business that upset the brain of our poor Friend was the serious difficulties of the Bank of I. Barned & Co of Liverpool, and the very heavy loss with which at one time it appeared too clear we should on their account have to submit; but it was not business matters only that weighed him down; private affairs pressed heavily upon him; his only Son was a source of great and constant anxiety to him; much under par in intellect, and ungovernable in sensual appetites, his future seemed to promise the worst results; and this grief acted the more prejudicially upon him from the circumstance of his keeping, and brooding over it, almost entirely to himself; rarely naming it even to C. Cave to whom he generally talked freely on his private affairs. Then Mrs Prescott was constantly urging him, and with that pertinacity which Women so often display, and which gives no rest, to purchase some large landed Property at a long distance from London, a step which he knew he could not take without unduly and uncomfortably locking up his private resources; she was ever twitting him too on his continuing in business, but he felt the time had not yet arrived for his quitting it; so many young Partners in the concern, requiring if not the supervision, at all events for a certain period the countenance and the Capital of the Seniors; these two subjects were a source of great disquietude to him; for his Wife exercised very considerable influence over him, and there was a perpetual conflict in his mind between his desire to gratify her wishes, and his conscientious feeling of what was due to the Banking House, and those connected with him in it. Still with all this worrying about his Business and Private Affairs, never did we anticipate that his once Strong Mind would have quailed and broken down under it.

Prescott committed suicide on a Saturday, and on Monday there began a serious run on the bank that took two or three days to allay. Bertram Currie (now of Glyns) showed solidarity by calling at an early stage to place the resources of his own bank at the disposal of the remaining partners. Prescott's friends mourned the loss – 'it must be the result of some fearful physical disease', surmised Overstone, 'for a mind more calm, more steady, more firmly balanced has never come under my observation' – and a few weeks later his will revealed a personal estate of £205,000, with no legacy left to his son.[36]

There is no mention of this sad episode in the sparkling, witty, well-informed letters of Baroness Charlotte de Rothschild, Lionel's wife. Her main confidant was her son Leo, up at Cambridge in the mid-1860s, and a typical touch was how she and her husband had entertained the previous day the 'two Messrs Sassoon, who as you know are clever, good, liberal, charitable, generous, as precious as gold but as heavy as lead – and impossible to amuse'. In the course of the correspondence two very different stockbrokers feature. One was the middle-aged Lionel Helbert, senior partner of the Rothschilds' pet brokers Helbert Wagg. 'This morning both Uncles called', she wrote in February 1865 from 148 Piccadilly, 'escorted by the silent Prince of Stockbrokers, Mr Helbert, who, with his fine, grand manners, his conceit and his emptiness, without one grain of bonhommie, is perfectly insufferable to me'. Charlotte even referred to him as 'the horrid Helbert', and in another letter added further chapter and verse:

> At New Court Uncle Mayer rebuked Mr Helbert for having boasted in Mr Cazenove's presence of having secured for himself a pair of steppers, and having paid very nearly five hundred guineas for them. – Your Uncle was right, but what he said was wrong – he spoke of the caucasian broker's beggarly brother and beggarly sister – and their want of prosperity has nothing to do with Mr H's bragging propensities; it was cruel to drag their poverty to the light.

Perhaps, but it was cruel also of the prince of stockbrokers not to do more for his siblings. The end came suddenly at Bath in March 1866, as an epileptic fit seems to have followed attacks of gout, and Charlotte's tone was altogether gentler: 'Poor Lionel Helbert played whist with his friends on the eve of his death, and the last words he spoke before the terrible convulsions came on, were "I am perfectly happy" '.

Even more pleased with life was the other tame broker, the young Hon. Harry Bourke, a friend of Charlotte's children and a newcomer to the Stock Exchange. He had all the graces, and one evening in January 1865 entertained the Rothschilds at Gunnersbury with his songs – 'half a dozen of them, very gracefully and quaintly sung with humour, fun and wit, and the becoming modesty of a real gentleman'. Over the coming weeks he continued to earn glowing reports: 'Mr H. Bourke likes the City amazingly, and dines at the most charming West end parties every evening . . . Harry Bourke is much appreciated in the highest circles . . . He sings and recites wonderfully, and is really clever, though he never could pass an examination.' The highest circles indeed, for by the end of the year the news was that 'Mr Bourke has lost his head and heart to the Princess of Wales', and that going to a dance in the country 'he took a birthday bouquet down, and received in exchange a pin and a set of studs'. Was such intimacy with the royal family permissible from an inhabitant of Capel Court? The question arose explicitly the following autumn at a Gunnersbury dinner party, and Charlotte had no doubts on the score:

The guests talked with ill-natured astonishment of the selection made
by H.R.H. of H. Bourke – I really do not know why he should not be
considered – the son of Lord Mayo, the brother of Lord Maas – well
born, well connected and irreproachable in conduct and character,
antecedents and occupations, cannot be disqualified for society because
he earns his living in the City handsomely, but by great exertion, activity
and labour, instead of starving in the west end. I hate ill-nature in every
shape and I think the Prince has undoubtedly proved his good taste as
well as his kindliness of disposition by selecting for his travelling compan-
ion one of the cleverest, most amusing and most gentlemanlike among his
Cambridge friends.

Better a stockbroker than a lounge lizard, as Charlotte Brontë would
have agreed, but there was a pointedness too in the *Saturday Review*'s remark in May 1866 that 'the City is rapidly becoming another
branch of that system of relief for the aristocracy which Mr Bright
denounces'.[37]

*

May 1866 – a date forever associated with Overend Gurney. Back at
the start of the decade, not all country bankers had been as impressed
by the rock-like foundations of that house as the men from the Sheffield and Hallamshire. The Liverpool Union Bank was particularly
sceptical and pressed its London agents, Barnett, Hoare & Co, to
make enquiries. Lombard Street breathed reassurance:

> We have had constant and most confidential interviews with Messrs
> Overend & Co during the last few weeks.
> We believe they have exercised great prudence in their management,
> that they have very materially reduced their liabilities and are prepared
> for a much heavier pressure than it seems possible should come upon
> them.
> We know they are keeping a very large reserve (as much as a million and
> a half at least) so placed that it is at hand any hour.

That was on 15 February 1861. Soon afterwords, amidst false rumours
sweeping the City that Overend Gurney had stopped payment, Dobree
(in his last weeks as Governor) tried to give another anxious correspondent as precise a picture as possible:

> The house referred to has made, it is said, heavy losses during the last
> 18 months, – to the extent of £300m [i.e. thousand] @ £400m, – and is

considered to have as much more locked up in inconvertible securities: it does a rather reckless business and is continually incurring losses. It is however believed at the same time, that the *profits* are commensurate, and that the capital is ample enough to meet any contingency. The uncertain mode in which the business is conducted is the subject of general censure.[38]

Dobree, for one, had clearly not yet heard of the return to prudent management at the Corner House.

Over the next few years, the business there continued to be conducted by Henry Edmund Gurney and David Ward Chapman, and someone who encountered them both was Frank Wilde. Gurney he judged 'the most thorough man of business', but 'Chapman I don't think anything of at all and never did'. In August 1864 he found himself reporting to Liverpool a dispute with the firm, involving 'not the pleasantest' interviews with Chapman:

> They were evidently precipitate and I conveyed to them that it would only have been within the bounds of courtesy of commerce for *us* to offer to take up our bills . . .
>
> Chapman distinctly gave me to understand that they wanted the drafts taken up as they were a dead lock to them. There is no doubt that their course has been most unusual and I told them so. It was however no use to cut off one's nose to spite one's face and they volunteered that if we sent in acceptances of ours for £40,000 they would discount them.[39]

The sensible minnow knows when to cease protest, but it was all far removed from those standards of conduct once inculcated by old Sam Gurney.

The following July, encouraged by the recent example of the Morrison textile business successfully transforming itself into the Fore Street Warehouse Company, the firm of Overend Gurney went public. The new company was to pay £½m in goodwill, the capital was to be £5m, and Chapman was to retire from the business. The prospectus promised prospective shareholders that 'the Directors will give their zealous attention to the cultivation of business of a first-class character only'. Details of past profits, or of assets and liabilities to be transferred, were conspicuously absent. City reaction was mixed. The partners of Prescotts declared that they had 'no intention' of applying for any shares, but expressed satisfaction that 'the family of Chapman is to be expunged from the concern', not least since 'the present Gentleman of that name is considered to want steadiness of character'.

Another private banker, Robert Fowler, was just about sanguine: 'It is an extraordinary change. They have lost a good deal of money, but they must have a splendid business at bottom.' The *Economist* had its silent qualms, and laid implicit stress on the fact that accounts would at last be available; but to the uninitiated reader there was comfort in that eminent journal's assertion not only that 'Overend's must have much money left with them', but that 'as to the management, there ought to be, and must be, great traditional knowledge and skill in a concern which has been so very profitable so very long, and where such vast sums have gradually been made'. The *Bankers' Magazine*, the great proponent of joint-stock enterprise in all financial matters, was wholly enthusiastic: 'Without laying any claim to the gift of prophecy, we may confidently anticipate that the position of the new company will be relatively as high as the standing of the house to whose business it succeeds'. The terms of the issue were attractive, the name was a great one, and the shares went quickly to a premium. In August 1865 the customary question arose of settlement and quotation by the Stock Exchange Committee. Usually a formality, on this occasion the company's broker, Samuel Gurney Sheppard, was required to give evidence about some aspects of the flotation:

> The managing directors [two of them, including Henry Edmund Gurney] were to receive £5000 per annum between them, and also ⅓th of the residue of the nett profit after 7% was obtained. It could not be supposed that they would undertake the duties for £5000 a year alone ... Any one could have seen the articles of association before subscribing, in fact he – Mr Sheppard – had shown them to a great number of persons.

There ensued 'a very long discussion' before James Bury Capel (son of James Capel) moved that the application be granted, and this was carried by eight votes to one.[40] Caveat emptor, but had the buyer been adequately warned?

It was during the winter that Gurney proposed to borrow money from Glyns at a special rate on some securities which seemed to Bertram Currie of doubtful value. Currie dared to express misgivings, to which Gurney retorted indignantly: 'Do you presume to question the credit of Overend, Gurney, and Co?' By early in 1866 the City as a whole had the shakes, not just about Overend Gurney but about the whole mesh of finance companies created during the 1863 boom. Several had intimate connections with Overend Gurney, including one, the Contract Corporation, that went into liquidation at the end of March. War on the Continent also threatened, and by mid-April Mathesons was reporting serious 'want of confidence in monetary circles' and 'stocks of all descriptions being eagerly pressed for sale'. The moment of truth soon came. 'Things certainly look squally', admitted Lidderdale on Wednesday, 9 May and that evening the City report for *The Times* began starkly: 'The panic continues to increase in intensity, and this has been one of the worst days yet experienced'. Thursday the 10th paid for all. 'Very fine & hot' noted Richard Biddulph Martin, who found himself gratifyingly close to the centre of things:

> Usual work. Not much doing till about $\frac{1}{2}$ past 2. Birkbeck came in to say that Overend Gurney & Co had stopped. K. Hodgson came in & said it was for £10,000,000, with £3,500,000 unsecured. We had £50,000 with them . . . They could get no assistance from the Bank.

The first informant was presumably Robert Birkbeck, the other managing director of Overend Gurney; and the second Kirkman Hodgson, a former Governor of the Bank and senior partner of the merchants Finlay, Hodgson & Co. The formal announcement of the failure was made soon afterwards, probably waiting on the closure of the Stock Exchange, and another private banker, Currie, wrote in laconic style to his father: 'The fatal day, the long expected day has come & O.G. has put up his shutters. For some weeks I have ventured to predict this event . . . The panic is pretty smart & beats 47 or 57 . . . I think some of the new Banks will have a hard time & financial companies & contractors must go right & left.' It was indeed the third big crisis in twenty years, and all shared the immediate fear of Mathesons that 'the failures will not stop here, so many houses all over the Country depending upon that Company for their supplies'.[41]

Two retrospective questions at once arose. Why had the mighty Overend Gurney failed? Why had the Bank of England let it go down? The answer to the first did not publicly emerge for another three and a half years, when the directors of the company stood trial for having published a false prospectus – false in the sense that the firm had been bankrupt *before* it went public. Prosecuting counsel's opening speech contained a memorable and revealing passage:

> Whether stimulated by zeal or enthusiasm, or whether actuated by that insane cupidity which was too largely a characteristic of the present day, instead of adhering to the plain, honest, and rational system which had been adopted by the old members of the firm, they plunged into the most extravagant speculation . . . Not content with being mere money dealers

or bill discounters, they become partners in various undertakings. They covered the sea with their ships, ploughed up the land with their iron roads . . .

It was all true. Back in 1859 the new generation holding the reins at Overend Gurney had transformed the firm's business beyond recognition, becoming shipbuilders, shipowners, grain traders, ironmasters, railway financiers, and seemingly much else besides. These were lock-up investments, often poorly judged, and by 1861 the firm was in deep trouble. Undoubtedly large doses of vanity, ambition and greed played their part in this fateful diversification; but perhaps there was also some sense, as one of its partners had told Dobree at the end of 1859, in which the Bank of England's new, restrictive policy affected the firm's core business sufficiently to give such diversification added appeal. After 1861 the firm tried to recover, but its management was not up to the task, and problems were further compounded by an over-speculative approach to financing the new finance houses thrown up by the boom. Conversion in 1865 to a limited liability company, following the failure of merger talks with the National Discount Co, was a final desperate throw – a bold and in a way honest attempt by Gurney to shed extraneous commitments, return to the straight and narrow of discounting business, and end the whole Chapman era. It was implicitly recognised as such by the jurors in 1869, who acquitted Gurney and his fellow-directors, but the attempt itself came too late to save the Corner House in the troubled monetary conditions of 1866. Should the Bank have stepped in? Once it became clear that spring that Overend Gurney required assistance to survive, it appointed a committee of three (Hodgson and two private bankers) to scrutinise the books. The three wise men determined that the business was rotten beyond redemption, and no helping hand was held out.[42] Yet remembering the intensely strained relations between the Bank and Overend Gurney between 1857 and 1860, culminating in the infamous £1½m gun held at the Bank's head, it is hard to feel that the Bank in 1866 was making a strictly financial decision. Overend Gurney had once very much been members of the club – it is absurd to think of them by this stage as East Anglian upstarts – but it was a club that would never condone such bare-faced tactics directed against its ex officio chairman. *That* in the end was the new generation's most grievous misjudgement.

Their transgression of these unwritten rules was a mite academic as Black Friday dawned and City commuters read the confident prediction in *The Times* that the shock of Overend Gurney's failure 'will, before this evening closes, be felt in the remotest corners of the kingdom'. Among those travelling in from south of the river was Charles Churchill junior, and on arrival he somewhat breathlessly found 'City great excitement, Lombard S^t in uproar, talk of runs on nearly all the banks, the English Joint Stock stops . . .' Diarists and commentators vied with each other. 'Great confusion all day, the streets were crowded and almost impassable', recorded Martin, while according to the partners of Prescotts (who were falsely rumoured to have sold their business to a joint-stock bank), it was 'a day of most intense excitement and panic in the City, in fact such a day has never been experienced in the memory of any one'. The *Economist* thought Lombard Street 'looked more like a country fair than its usual self', *The Times* described 'throngs heaving and tumbling about' as by noon 'the tumult became a rout' and 'the doors of the most respectable Banking-Houses were besieged'. In the course of the day several stoppages were announced, rumours of many others gathered credence, and so seriously was the situation taken that 'even at Lady Downshire's ball', according to Charlotte de Rothschild, 'everybody spoke of the immense City failures'.[43]

Help, as was becoming the custom on these set-piece occasions, was already at hand. 'A complete collapse of credit in Lombard St and a greater amount of anxiety than I have ever seen', scribbled Bagehot that morning in a hasty note to Gladstone (nearing the end of a seven-year stint as Chancellor of the Exchequer), and Gladstone stilled his Peelite doubts and took the cue. His diary entry for the Friday characteristically records the process:

> From $2\frac{1}{4}$ till past midnight I was except 20m. occupied in receiving a stream of City magnates and deputations on the panic, in considering with Cardwell, Goschen, Ld Halifax [the former Sir Charles Wood], the Gov. & Dep. Gov., & Mr Hodgson, the proper course to take, & after obtaining all requisite information, arranging the letters & making the necessary announcements in the H. of Commons. Although the case was perplexing at the onset, & will be so in the *hereafter*, yet when we obtained the facts of the operations of the day our course became at once perfectly clear.

The paramount operational fact was that on a day of the severest credit panic, the Bank of England lent to banks, discount houses and merchants the phenomenal amount of £4m; but it is clear that the pressure on Gladstone to authorise suspension yet again of Peel's Act came not from the Governor, a linen manufacturer called Lancelot Holland, but from the successive deputations, which included country bankers as well as 'City magnates'. Again as usual, it was essentially psychological relief that was craved, and once more the trick worked. The next morning began in a mood of watchfulness rather than fear ('dear Papa, the Uncles and Natty are at New Court – a very unusual place for them to seek on the Saturday', Charlotte wrote to Leo in Cambridge), and by the end of the day Martin was able to record that 'the Government allowing the Bank to issue Notes at 10% gave relief & the panic subsided to a great extent'.[44] The worst of the Overend crisis was over.

'There is no longer any apprehension on the part of those who hold bona fide property that they will be denied reasonable facilities', reported Mathesons by the 17th, and over the next few months things gradually returned more or less to normal. But it was a long haul: Bank rate stayed at 10 per cent until August (partly in the context of war between Prussia and Austria, partly also against a background of agitation at home for further parliamentary reform); there was a handful of major banking stoppages; and a particular concern was the Agra & Masterman's Bank. This was another merged creation from 1864, when Mastermans was in effect taken over by the Agra and United Service, the great joint-stock Anglo-Indian bank that acted as repository for the savings of a whole imperial class. 'Of the Agra I hear in many quarters improving reports', noted Lidderdale on 25 May, adding that 'they are said to have paid out nearly all their deposits at short call & to be in no present danger'. One of his main informants was the leading stockbrokers Foster & Braithwaite, which on 7 June was still expressing confidence in the bank. That same day the Agra stopped, and apart from being a hard blow for thousands of people it was yet one more black mark for City competence in Lidderdale's view. 'I have lost all faith in their opinion unless on matters within very easy reach', he wrote soon afterwards of Foster & Braithwaite, though not denying that 'their facts are valuable very often'. Aiming to provide an altogether top-notch brand of service was Spencer, Hobbs & Co, which early in July announced to the world that it was opening for business as bill brokers at 11 George Yard off Lombard Street:

> Our determination is to deal solely with first class Commercial Bills of a strictly legitimate character, and we hope by diligent attention to the interests of our friends and principals to merit the confidence that may be reposed in us.
>
> Mr Spencer has been upwards of 18 years, and Mr Hobbs 10 years, in the Establishment of the late firm of Overend Gurney & Co, both

occupying positions of the greatest trust, and thus acquiring the experience so indispensable in a business of this nature.[45]

Several other new firms arose from the ashes of Overend Gurney, but all agreed that, for good or ill, there would never be another Corner House.

In September occurred a significant postscript to the crisis. Addressing the Bank's proprietors, Lancelot Holland looked back with pride:

> This house exerted itself to the utmost – and exerted itself most successfully – to meet the crisis. We did not flinch from our post. When the storm came upon us, on the morning on which it became known that the house of Overend and Co had failed, we were in as sound and healthy a position as any banking establishment could hold, and on that day and throughout the succeeding week we made advances which would hardly be credited . . .
>
> We would not flinch from the duty which we conceived was imposed upon us of supporting the banking community, and I am not aware that any legitimate application made for assistance to this house was refused.

In a leading article headed 'The Great Importance of the Late Meeting of the Proprietors of the Bank of England', Bagehot at the *Economist* pounced on this statement as a welcome acceptance of the doctrine that the Bank was lender of last resort and thus responsible for maintaining 'the sole banking reserve of the country'. It was not a reading of the Governor's remarks that found favour with Thomson Hankey, a West India merchant who had been on the Court since 1835, was Governor in the early 1850s, and besides being a member of the Political Economy Club was MP for Peterborough:

> The 'Economist' newspaper has put forth what in my opinion is the most mischievous doctrine ever broached in the monetary or banking world in this country; viz. that it is the proper function of the Bank of England to keep money available at all times to supply the demands of bankers who have rendered their own assets unavailable. Until such a doctrine is repudiated by the banking interest, the difficulty of pursuing any sound principle of banking in London will be always very great. But I do not believe that such a doctrine as that bankers are justified in relying on the Bank of England to assist them in time of need is generally held by the bankers in London.

Hankey was mistaken, for in the keen debate that ensued the balance of banking opinion came down on Bagehot's side.[46] There had been too many crises in too short a time for a 'purist' interpretation of the 1844 Act any longer to be tenable: the banking department of the Bank of England could not, in short, behave like any other bank. For a quarter of a century the moral rigour of the old currency school had been a perhaps noble attempt to evade inexorable banking realities, and now at last its insidious sway was unofficially declared over and out.

CHAPTER FOURTEEN

Change Alley

'Except for business purposes, the City may be said to be now unin-habited.' So declared the *Building News* in 1857, and if that was a slight exaggeration, it became ever less so over the next decade. By 1861 the City's residential population was down to 113,000 (having been 129,000 in 1851); by 1871 it had shrunk further to 75,000. Against a background of rapidly rising site and rental values, it was a remorseless process that brooked no alternative – and was hastened by the con-struction of not only new buildings and streets but also new railway lines, such as the laying down from 1863 of the North London line to terminate at Broad Street, involving the destruction of several hundred houses in the Sun Street and Long Alley area to the north of the new station. By mid-century the brokers, bankers and merchants had al-ready largely departed the residential scene; now it was the turn of the small traders, of whom there were few left living in the City by the time of the 1871 census. The nocturnal square mile they left behind, and in many cases the daytime one also, was inevitably a place of disappearing landmarks: between 1862 and 1865 alone, Crosby Hall in Great St Helen's, a notable specimen of fifteenth-century domestic architecture, was converted into a restaurant; the Spread Eagle Inn, one of London's oldest, standing at the Gracechurch Street entrance to Leadenhall Market, was pulled down; the old Flower Pot Tavern, immortalised by Lamb, made way for the National Provincial Bank in Bishopsgate; and Lamb's semi-beloved East India House also passed into the histori-cal ether.[1]

Still standing but of declining importance in a rapidly changing City was the Royal Exchange, increasingly superseded by specialist offices, specialist exchanges, and the revolution in international communica-tions. One of these new constructions was the Baltic Exchange, situated from 1858 on the floor of the old South Sea House (at the junction of Threadneedle Street and Bishopsgate Street) and populated by mer-chants and traders who had demanded larger, more convenient premises on the back of the prosperity created by the free trade in corn. The demise of the Baltic Coffee House was symbolic, for those wonderful monuments to the eighteenth century were now on the way out. None had more resonance than Garraway's; in 1866 major alterations in Change Alley necessitated its closure and subsequent destruction. Last drinks were served on Saturday, 11 August, and two days later the final sale took place, the lots comprising the furniture and effects of Garraway's itself. Just over a fortnight earlier, on 27 July, the cable under the Atlantic had at last been successfully completed, with conversations and messages being carried on throughout the day.[2] Two ages thus neatly overlapped.

There was no shortage of new buildings for West End visitors to judge whether the City's taste had improved. Of the insurance giants the Royal in Lombard Street now led the way, commissioning successive large headquarters from John Belcher in 1857 and 1863, the latter (demolished in 1910) full of panelling, plastered stories and allegorical sculpture. But the major thrust came from the joint-stock banks, almost all of whom between the mid-1850s and mid-1860s built or rebuilt on a lavish, even monumental scale. Typical was the imposing Italianate palazzo style favoured in 1856 by the new City Bank on a corner of Threadneedle Street, while ten years later John Gibson's magnificent classical banking hall in Bishopsgate for the National Provincial, resplendent with Corinthian columns and marble pillars, would have eased the doubts of even the most neurotic depositor. The new limited liability discount houses likewise put a premium on appearance. One result was the National Discount Co's palazzo-style building in Cornhill, completed in 1858 with distinctive cinquecento motifs and detailing; another was the General Credit and Finance Co's stunning effort at 7 Lothbury, completed by 1866 and admiringly described many years later by Pevsner as 'stone-faced Venetian Gothic, sumptuously handled, yet so crisp that it looks like a twentieth-century revival.' Even private firms joined the craze. Most of the best-known private banks did at the very least a respray job, earning from the *Bankers' Magazine* in 1863 the accusation that they were in their dotage succumbing to 'a love of show, leading eventually to excessive expenditure, and sometimes to embarrassment'. As for the merchant banks, Charlotte de Rothschild visited her husband at work in October 1865 and saw there for the first time the new portion of New Court, complete with spacious palazzo. It 'seems to me quite marvellous', she wrote, 'and intended for magnificent business'. Altogether, in the words of one expansive critic the following year, there appeared little doubt that 'the Roman Corso, the Neapolitan Toledo or even the glories of the Rue de Rivoli will be overtopped and out-vied by the continuous line of merchant palaces in Cornhill and Lombard Street and Bishopsgate Street and Cheapside'.[3]

City men also luxuriated in purpose-built office blocks, king-size warehouses and new, gleaming railway stations. Such office blocks were not new, but from the 1850s they started to mushroom almost everywhere, many in the immediate vicinity of the Stock Exchange in order to house stockbroking and jobbing firms. One, built in 1854, was at 5 Throgmorton Street. Owned by the two leading brokers James Capel and John Norbury, this housed not only their own firm but also several others. Another, constructed by the mid-1860s, was at Warnford Court just off Throgmorton Street, where one of the early tenants was the new firm of de Zoete & Gorton. If Capel and Norbury were only part-time property developers, by the 1860s there was at least a handful of full-time operators based in the City, including the City Offices Company and the City of London Real Property Company. It could be a chancy business, but with interest rates low and the formation of new financial companies all the rage, there was big money to be made as City rents soared until the shock of the Overend Gurney crisis. Significantly, it was a property speculator, George Myers, who in Great Tower Street in 1864 erected the suitably towering and memorably named Mazawattee Tea Warehouse, all eight floors of it and very ugly. That same year a major fire in Gresham Street led to the rebuilding of several of the main textile warehouses. As for the railway stations, their coming to the square mile signified that there no longer existed what one might call a City and suburban handicap, that the suburbs to the north and south of London were now readily accessible to the would-be City commuter. Broad Street opened in 1865 (serving leafy Hampstead, including no doubt Manley Hopkins), Cannon Street in 1866; while if one lived in Camberwell, for instance, it was possible from 1864 to entrain to Blackfriars, from 1866 to Farringdon Street. Cannon Street Station in particular was a superb creation, and from 1867 it had attached to it an equally splendid hotel, scene over the years of many company meetings.[4] Steadily the infrastructure of a modern, post-Dickensian financial centre was falling into place.

Yet such appearances in a sense deceived. The City remained a myriad of small firms, its street pattern defiantly not of the grid variety, and the streets themselves definitely not Haussmanised. In December 1860 members of the Baltic Exchange urged their committee to put pressure on the police to ban omnibus traffic in Threadneedle Street: 'Both the inconvenience and danger have recently been aggravated by the introduction of three-horse omnibuses, part of the iron fittings of which project considerably over the pathway, which is so narrow as not to admit of two persons passing when one of these large vehicles is in the way'.[5] Moreover, if such pedestrian danger was still an integral part of the City, so too was the relative absence of buildings seeking to scrape the sky. It is true that a prestigious new banking headquarters or an ambitious new office block often occupied the frontage space previously taken by several individual buildings; but in terms of height, few were significantly taller than their predecessors. Wren's skyline, in other words, remained intact, and it took a future generation to destroy it.

In the end, though, one wonders: how much did any of this matter to the wretches actually working in the place? For ultimately what abided – day after day, week after week, year after year – was not so much the larger environment as the actual, grinding routine: the voluminous ledgers, the salient account books, the endless, pernickety correspondence. *There* lies the true, inner, inscrutable history of the City, as draining of human vitality as the endless pleas of endless suitors recorded on the *peau de chagrin* in Balzac's famous story. From the thousands of firms, and many hundreds of thousands of sheets of inky paper, here, almost arbitrarily, is a surviving letter from P. W. Flower & Co, merchants of 62 Moorgate Street writing on 12 June 1866 to a firm in Glasgow:

> We are this Morning in receipt of your letter of yesterday handing in three signed Bills of Lading for 10 Casks Whisky shipped on board the 'Bruce' for Melbourne.
>
> We are sorry to find on the Bills of Lading that *seven* Casks out of ten are 'patched with Lead' – you ought not to have accepted the B/s Lading with such a clause, unless the Casks are as described, if they are, they ought not to have been shipped. We make it a rule never to accept Bills of Lading unless they are quite free from such clauses and we only receive those per 'Bruce' subject to your giving us a guarantee that you will make good any loss of Whisky caused through leakage. We shall feel obliged by your sending this guarantee by return.
>
> If you ship the 5 Barrels ordered yesterday you will be good enough to see that the Casks are *quite sound*, as we cannot in future accept B/s Lading with any clause whatever thereon . . .[6]

So it went, so it went.

Mr Rothchild

DrawnEtch Pub.d by R.t Dighton. Oct.r 1817

London Pub.d by Thos McLean, 26 Haymarket 1824

A View from the Royal Exchange.

1 *Nathan Rothschild in his prime*.

2 LEFT *Bartolozzi's engraving of the interior of the Royal Exchange, 1788.*

3 OPPOSITE *Richard Thornton's tallow corner, as recorded by Richard Dighton.*

A Scene on the Ball'r Walk. Royal Exchange, in November 1823

4 RIGHT *Joshua Bates,*
c *1840.*

5 BELOW *Muslin for caps,*
from Mr Hopps.

6 OPPOSITE *Cheapside in*
1823: poor Susan's plane tree
just out of sight, to the right
beyond the clock.

Mr Duthort

London, 11 May 1815

BOT. of **WILLIAM HOPPS,**
At his Cheap Linen Drapery, Hosiery, Mercery,
AND
FAMILY MOURNING WAREHOUSE,
The CANNON, No. 42, Corner of MARTIN's LANE, CANNON STREET.

ALL SORTS OF

£. s. d.

Irish Linens
Housewife Linens
Dowlas's
Russias
Diapers
Huckabacks
Table Linen
Cambricks
Lawns
Muslins
Dimities
Printed Cottons and Calicoes
Counterpanes
White Cottons and Calicoes
Lancashire and Russia Sheetings
Brown Hollands
Checks

Shawls
Handkerchiefs
Ready-made Shirts
Bombazeens
Bombarets
Stuffs
Thicksets
Velverets
Velveteens
Fancy Cords
Flannels
Blankets
Bed Ticken
Russia Drabs and Duck
Dyed Linens
And all sorts of Worsted, Thread
and Cotton Hose

Muslin for Caps   2

N.B. *Country Shopkeepers served on the most advantageous Terms.*

J. Plummer, Printer, 11, Little Eastcheap.

7 The Bank of England and the Royal Exchange *(1845)*: *line engraving by T.A. Prior, after A.L. Thomas.*

8 *Court Room of the Bank of England, from* London Interiors *(1841)*.

9 *Bankers' Clearing House in Lombard Street, 1847*.

Fair. | Change | Stormy

10 ABOVE *Rogers's Bank, on the corner of Lombard Street and Clements Lane, 1840s: the austere face of private banking.*

11 LEFT *Sir Richard Glyn, senior partner of Glyn Mills in the 1850s: an office sketch by H.B. Reynolds, a departmental head.*

12 View from the Monument, c 1857: still Wren's skyline, but the newly constructed Cannon Street West now cuts through to St Paul's.

13 LEFT *Corner of Bishops-gate and Threadneedle Street, 1862: just prior to demolition.*

14 BELOW *Same site, 1865: suddenly the City of Dickens has become altogether less human.*

15 Black Friday, 11 May 1866: the doors of Overend
Gurney are shut.

16 OPPOSITE London Bridge, c 1875.

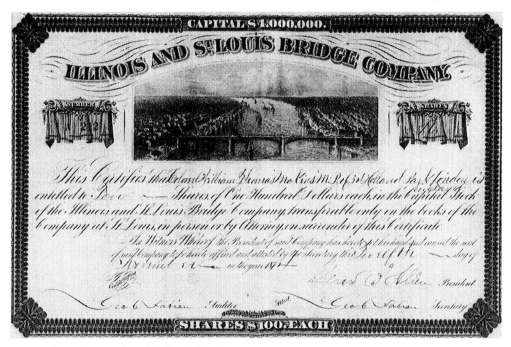

17 *Gentlemanly capitalism (i): the Colonel's investment.*

19 ABOVE LEFT *Lord Revelstoke: the man who caused the Baring crisis.*

20 ABOVE *William Lidderdale: the man who saved the day.*

18 *Gentlemanly capitalism (ii): Lord Rothschild's staghounds at Mentmore, 1889, with Natty himself (bearded, in profile) surveying the scene.*

21 *Bank Crossing,*
c 1885.

The sun from the west glares back,
And the sun from the watered track,
And the sun from the sheets of glass,
And the sun from each window-brass;
Sun-mirrorings, too, brighten
From show-cases beneath
The laughing eyes and teeth
Of ladies who rouge and whiten.
And the same warm god explores
Panels and chinks of doors;
Problems with chymists' bottles
Profound as Aristotle's
He solves, and with good cause,
Having been ere man was.

Also he dazzles the pupils of one who walks west,
A city-clerk, with eyesight not of the best,
Who sees no escape to the very verge of his days
From the rut of Oxford Street into open ways;
And he goes along with head and eyes flagging forlorn,
Empty of interest in things, and wondering why he was born.

Thomas Hardy, *Coming Up Oxford Street: Evening*
(As seen 4 July 1872)

CHAPTER FIFTEEN

Economical Power, Economical Delicacy

'The enquiries about Finlay Hodgson & Co have latterly become so numerous', wrote Brown Shipley in November 1866 to its partners in New York, 'and have come through such a variety of channels, that we can no longer close our eyes to, or leave you ignorant of the fact, that they do not for the moment occupy the same high & undoubted position for which they have so long been distinguished'. Finlay Hodgson was a long-established merchant house mainly trading with India; and the City was still trying to recover its nerve after the Overend Gurney smash. Brown Shipley preferred not to credit these rumours – 'the partners, with two of whom we are on intimate terms & in daily intercourse, do not give the slightest reason to suppose that they are less at their ease than ever' – yet seven months later it and the rest of the City were taken aback by news of an amalgamation between Finlay Hodgson and the mighty house of Barings. Most, like William Lidderdale, focused on the perceived weakness less of the former than the latter:

> The prevalent suspicion is that Barings begin to feel themselves short of brass & that both TB & Sturgis want more leisure – the latter indeed told Capel [probably the tea brokers Arthur Capel & Co] that the first result of the Amalgamation would be that he should get a month's holiday, which he had not had for years. Among the quiet folks it has created rather an unfavourable impression & several men think it will do Barings harm . . . Amalgamations have lately had so bad a signification that every one is studied. I should not be surprised to find that Barings did not object to an addition to their capital in view of the deaths among their partners in the last few years.

It was an accurate analysis of what was essentially a takeover by 8 Bishopsgate, for in the wake of Bates's death the firm's capital had dipped to £760,000, and it now rose to £1,390,000. But there was also the human factor, for quite apart from the possible desire for more time off, the ageing Thomas Baring had, like Bates before him, little confidence in either Sturgis or his younger partners and instead wanted to bring in the capable (indeed 'clever', according to Charlotte de Rothschild) Kirkman Hodgson, whom he knew well and who was a former Governor of the Bank of England.[1] It was a shrewd move, but in the event the longer-term destiny of the house still lay, for better or worse, in the hands of Ned Baring, whom the old grumbler had so mistrusted.

Things were different with the Rothschilds at New Court, where Baron Lionel continued to exercise complete sway and young Natty (Nathaniel) calmly awaited the succession. But life there could be humdrum enough, and Lionel's pen certainly did not seek to transmute base metals into gold. In July 1867 he wrote regularly to his wife while she was in Paris:

> *9 July.* There is nothing particularly new in the City, everything is very quiet.
> *16 July.* Here in the City on account of the rain everything was dull but the sun has just made its appearance and they close a shade better. We have been busy with a good many little things.
> *17 July.* Here in the City we have had a very quiet day; there is nothing particularly new. We have only seen Brokers who want orders.
> *18 July.* In the City no news today, everyone waiting [for] the weather, the harvest till now looks very promising, so we must hope for the best.

Yet in a sense these give a misleading impression, for it was precisely during the summer and autumn of 1867 that the foreign secretary, Lord Stanley, found himself virtually dependent on the information reaching him via Disraeli from the Rothschilds – even telling Queen Victoria that Lionel's 'information as to what is passing on the Continent is generally quite as early and quite as accurate as that which can be obtained through different channels'. Two years later, with the Liberals in power, their leader in the House of Lords had the boldness to suggest to Gladstone that he put forward Lionel for a British peerage. The Rothschilds represented, argued Lord Granville, 'a class whose influence is great by their wealth, their intelligence, their literary connexions, and their numerous seats in the House of Commons', adding with perhaps needless caution that 'it may be wise to attach them to the aristocracy rather than to drive them into the democratic camp'. Gladstone in turn twice tried out the idea on Victoria and twice encountered blanket refusal, the second time in language that encouraged no further discussion on the subject:

The Queen really cannot make up her mind to it. It is not only the feeling of which she cannot divest herself, against making a person of the Jewish religion, a Peer; but she cannot think that one who owes his great wealth to contracts with Foreign Govts for Loans, or to successful speculation on the Stock Exchange can fairly claim a British peerage.

However high Sir [sic] L. Rothschild may stand personally in Public Estimation, this seems to her not the less a species of gambling, because it is on a gigantic scale – and far removed from the legitimate trading which she *delights* to *honour*, in which men have raised themselves by patient industry and unswerving probity to positions of wealth and influence.[2]

Only the year before the Prince of Wales had paid a successful, very convivial visit to Mentmore, one of the Rothschild houses, but for the moment his mother, as society's acknowledged head, was not prepared to sell the pass.

They arranged things rather differently in the City, as Lidderdale found out. In November 1867 he reported to William Rathbone that he had just received an inquiry from the Deputy Governor of the Bank of England as to whether their firm would like him to be nominated as a director. 'I of course said yes', went on Lidderdale. Two days later a fuller letter to his senior partner in Liverpool manifested concern not to overplay their joint hand:

> I telegraphed you today if you had not written already to Mr Morris [a Bank director and former Governor] not to do so till you had heard from me.
>
> I am informed that the election of Directors is arranged by a very small Committee which is autocratic in the matter & which only in name takes the pleasure of the Board or Court. The Governor & Deputy are the strength of this Committee – to them I have been presented & have *subsequently* had the offer of nomination. I think therefore the thing is in as fair a way as RB & Co can expect or desire & it seems to me a case where any appearance of pressure or soliciting support had better be avoided. Perhaps some time you are in London, a few words with Mr Morris may hasten the matter – that is get me in ahead of someone of equal standing but at present after so definite an intimation, I think we had better sit still.

The following March the thing seemed in the bag as Lidderdale reported on a favourable summons from the Governor: 'He was very civil . . . I fancy RB & Co will be represented at the Bank by 1st May'. But then, early in April, came the cruellest blow about the vacant directorship: 'My chance was stopped by the heavy pressure brought to bear in favour of young Rothschild, who is only 24'. The fortunate youth was Alfred, Lionel's second son, and Lidderdale had to bide a while longer, which he did calmly enough. The news induced the most sardonic of responses from old Overstone in the course of his correspondence with G. W. Norman, himself still on the Court: 'I have before me a letter of Ricardo in which he expresses his astonishment that the Bank Directors with the opportunities before them had not accumulated much larger profits. I presume you do not mean any longer to expose yourselves to this censure.'[3] There had never before been a Jewish director at the Bank, and on the eve of Gladstone's momentous first ministry, that would end so much entrenched Anglican privilege, the City was already doing its bit.

As a general merchant, Lidderdale was only tangentially interested in the increasingly dominant and, in terms of the City's reputation, all-pervasive sphere of foreign loans; but in November 1868 he noted that 'Barings & Rothschilds are said to have coalesced to bring out the new great Spanish loan, for which they were competing'. His source was probably James Walker of Walker & Lumsden, at this time his stockbroking alternative to Foster & Braithwaite. Walker also told him that 'Barings are not in good odour with Investors on account of their apathy in protecting Central & South American bondholders – it is thought that they might have done more for men who bought stocks brought out under their protection . . .' It may not have been a fair charge, granted that Thomas Baring the year before had headed a deputation to the Foreign Secretary to press him, albeit unavailingly, 'to take active and energetic measures' against the Venezuelan Government for no longer paying interest on a loan Barings brought out in 1862. But it seems to have stuck, for Barings now let it be known that it blessed the creation of the Council of Foreign Bondholders, which held its inaugural meeting only a few days later and sought to unify all the different bondholders' committees, going back to the dog days of the late 1820s. Chairing that first meeting was George Goschen (who insisted that war on behalf of aggrieved bondholders was not a realistic option), but its founding spirit was Isidore Gerstenberg.[4] Born in 1821 in Breslau, where his father sold lottery tickets, he had come to London as a young man. He started as the City representative for Abraham Bauer's Manchester-based merchanting business, but by 1845 was a general merchant in Throgmorton Street operating on his own account, subsequently becoming both an exchange broker and a member of the Stock Exchange. He also in time became a naturalised Briton, married Bauer's daughter, and acquired Stockely House in Regent's Park.

Gerstenberg had fingers in many pies, including considerable interests in Latin America, and this initiative was to be the culmination of his career.

Few foreign loans were floated during the two years after the Overend Gurney crisis – and cautious authorities like the *Economist* insisted that, such were the intrinsic perils involved, 'clergymen, widows, old maids, pensioners, clerks, and small capitalists, have no business to put their money into any sort of foreign loans or speculations' – but by the end of 1868 the attractions of higher returns available abroad saw a pronounced revival of activity. The familiar names acted as issuing houses, while as ever the key role in British distribution was played by the City's leading stockbroking firms. 'Messrs J. H. Schröder & Co are to bring out the long talked of Russian Railway Loan on Saturday . . . Are you disposed to have a slice of it?' asked George Coulson of Cazenove's in November 1868 to John Fosters near Bradford. A year later he was on the selling trail again about an upcoming Turkish loan: 'The Loan has been taken by a powerful combination of French & Constantinople Bankers, & will be brought out by the Comptoir D'Escompte at Paris & its branches, & by Messrs Lionel Cohen & Sons here.' Coulson then gave details of the loan's terms, before going on: 'Some of our wealthy friends are participating & as we have been appointed Brokers to the Loan we shall be able to secure you any amount that you may require.' Lionel Cohen, a great grandson of Levi Barent Cohen and thus related to the Rothschilds, was a recognised expert on Turkish finance, a prominent dealer in the Stock Exchange's Foreign market who also engaged successfully in *haute finance*. This was one of his triumphs, for shortly before Christmas 1869 Coulson was reporting to Fosters, which had taken £25,000 of stock: 'The Turkish Loan operation has been a great success. We understand that the *whole* of the Stock taken *firm* has been placed.' Moreover, with the stock standing at a premium of $\frac{1}{4}$ to $\frac{1}{2}$ on the London market, 'you will have a profit to receive on the whole of your subscription, & then have the option for a similar amount'. Two months later there was a more apologetic note in the news travelling up to Yorkshire from 52 Threadneedle Street: 'We regret, with you, the small allotment of Russian that Rothschilds have sent you but your case is not a singular one. One of our friends, a well known and influential Banker who asked for £100,000, had only £5,000 allotted to him.'[5]

By the first half of 1870, enthusiasm for foreign loans was rising fast. There was even a pioneer loan for the Japanese Government, although it was brought out by Schröders with a less than flattering 9% coupon, a credit rating that caused considerable umbrage in Tokyo. As Coulson, with clarity rather than elegance, put it early in June, in the context of an imminent Peruvian issue: 'With the present fancy of the public for new Loans, the Loan is sure to be well received.' And six days later, no less sanguinely: 'The new Peruvian Loan has been a most perfect success. The Continental subscriptions have been exceedingly large. It closes $\frac{3}{4} - \frac{7}{8}$ pm here with good Market.'[6]

It was not a good market for much longer, for by the second week in July the City was rife with rumour and counter-rumour, occasional hard news and many straws in the wind, of impending warfare between France and Prussia. On the inside track, an inestimable privilege at a time of wildly oscillating markets, was Henry Raphael, who received a telegram from his Hamburg branch saying that war was inevitable. At once he sold his foreign stocks and ordered large quantities of bullion, news of which sent Cohen hastening round to New Court. 'Well', said Baron Lionel, 'if clever men, such as Henry Raphael is, do not some-times make mistakes, how are poor devils like us to live?' Within days Raphael had made a killing. In the Stock Exchange itself, the mood could hardly have been more febrile. At one point Arthur Wagg was accused by a client of having sold Turkish stock at an unduly low price; but in the words of the jobber who had bought the stock, words which helped convince the Committee of Wagg's innocence, 'Mr Wagg might have had the news of declaration of War in his pocket at the time he addressed him'. Coulson, meanwhile, was offering his client a notably frank commentary on the latest in Capel Court. On Monday the 11th pessimism reigned: 'All parties here think it is only a question of time. Jealousies like the present must be ventilated sooner or later.' Two days later markets were up: 'It was never reasonable that two such powers could fight on such a pretext.' Twenty-four hours later told a different story: 'We have had a day of continuous panic. Yesterday we were all in the stirrings for peace. Today we have every ugly rumour that fact or fancy can create.' And by Saturday the 16th, with war a reality: 'The darkest gloom we are told is before daybreak, so we have only to keep up good cheer & await the turn of the tide.'[7]

The first week of war brought no respite, as the partners of Prescotts grimly noted: 'The Foreign Stock Market has been in a constant state of ferment, the prices of many Stocks fluctuating 4 or 5 P C' in a day, even in an hour. Both parties are preparing for a severe struggle, and it remains to be seen whether the Prussian needle gun or the French Chassepot rifle is the most destructive weapon.' Inevitably there were many Stock Exchange failures (about forty during July) and it was soon clear that the City as a whole wanted a speedy end to the war, irrespective of who won. Thanks in part to the needle gun that wish was granted. 'It is now generally considered that the Continental War will not be of very long duration', reported Coulson on 8 August, adding that 'we have rumours at the close of business today that the Prussians have concentrated their forces & that severe fighting is going on before Metz'. Moreover, in the immediate as well as long term, there were significant benefits attached to neutrality. As Baron Alphonse in Paris wrote the next day to his Rothschild cousins in London: 'It is a general sauve qui peut. Everybody rushes upon the Bank to get cash and London is bought at any price . . .'[8] Three weeks later came Sedan, the capitulation of Napoleon III and the end of uncertainty, if not of bloodshed.

That autumn there was a piquant tailpiece to the war.[9] Gambetta's provisional government was still carrying on an increasingly desperate struggle against Prussia and sought to raise a £10m loan on the London market. Rothschilds and Barings were both approached and both refused, on the grounds of risk as well as not wishing to damage their relations with the Prussian Government. So the French turned to J. S. Morgan & Co, since 1864 an increasingly dynamic outfit under Junius Morgan. Before agreeing to take on the business, Morgan investigated (as he subsequently recalled to the American journalist George Smalley) the financial history of France since 1789, discovering that despite the several different types of government not one 'had ever repudiated or questioned the validity of any financial obligation contracted by the other' and that therefore 'the continuing financial solidarity of France was unbroken', that 'it was plainly a policy rooted in the minds of the people and of the governing forces of France'. And so: 'That was good enough for me. There was no gamble.' A furious Bismarck threatened that the loan would be repudiated by a victorious Prussia, but Morgan was undeterred and brought it out to a strong public response, especially from investors in France itself. The fall of Paris in January 1871 caused problems, almost halving the value of the bonds, but Morgan bought heavily and two years later was rewarded when the French Government duly redeemed them at full value, thereby netting him a clear profit of £1½m. This was a major infusion to the firm's capital; the prestige of Morgans had been immeasurably increased by its courageous handling of the loan; and, as Junius reminisced, Smalley rightly detected in his eyes 'a fire which showed he was not insensible to the triumph he had won'.

The episode was an important marker for the future, but in the immediate aftermath of the war it was back to business as usual, as Rothschilds in conjunction with Barings capably dealt with two enormous loans for France, issued in 1871 and 1872 and totalling some £239m in stock. As for the foreign loans market in general, there was only a fairly brief breathing space before, against the background of a booming world economy, the incipient mania that had been rudely interrupted by a thoughtless war was resumed, to flourish and intensify. Early in 1872 John Fosters found itself being almost bullied to participate by a shameless stockbroker called D. M. Katinakis of $8\frac{1}{2}$ Copthall Court:

> 2 *January.* The Hungarian Loan has been a very great success today. I have no doubt in my mind that it must have been asked at least 4 times over. I have marked some very large amounts to be *paid in full*, and if you have changed your mind, and you would like to have some, I feel almost sure that I will induce Messrs R Raphael and Sons to give it to *you.*
> Hungarian closes 2% prem [scrawled postscript].
> 24 *January.* Messrs C. J. Hambro & Son will bring out a 5% Russian Ry loan the day after tomorrow, for £1,500,000 at the price of $87\frac{1}{2}$% ... Although I cannot offer you any fixed amount, should you be inclined to take any and you would inform me the amount you would like, I feel sure Messrs H would give me the preference over nearly everyone else.
> 25 *January.* As the Loan will be largely written for, I would advise that you should apply for at least 5 times the amount you wish for.
> 27 *January.* I have no doubt that you will be thoroughly satisfied with the amount which will be allotted to you.
> 2 *February.* Messrs Hambro are extremely sorry that they could not allot you more than £5,000, on account of the numerous applications; as it is you are favoured; a great many applications being refused altogether and others only receiving 1%.[10]

So the merry game went on, but it has to be remembered that the more respectable houses were, to at least some degree, putting their reputations on the line each time they issued one of these sovereign loans. Certainly Lidderdale, by now safely ensconced on the Court and seeking to advise Rathbones in its investment policy, thought as much:

> I had today a long conversation with Rothschild (Alfred) about Foreign Securities & he told me his people thought very well of French, Italians & the new Hungarian Loan ... Of course the Rothschilds are interested – probably in all three Loans & that pretty largely, but they would not, I think, commit themselves as Agents or Godfathers with anything they did not think perfectly good ...

Moreover, it was incumbent on a top-notch issuing house to back a loan if it did not prosper at the outset, a fact which, in tandem with the growing size of many of these loans, resulted in the increasing practice of the London sponsors arranging a syndicate with other houses and interested parties before the issue came to the market. It was in effect a form of underwriting, in which, in the words of one commentator, 'each member of the syndicate agreed to take so much stock at a certain price, perhaps 5, or even 10 per cent below the price of issue in the prospectus', with a view of course to unloading it on the market sooner or later, hopefully sooner and at a profit. Some leading issuing houses tried to resist it as a novel practice (which it hardly was, bearing in mind the activities of syndicates during the French Wars) and as indicating weakness on their part. But the dictates of financial logic meant that a measure of risk-sharing gradually became the norm even in the better City parlours – though both New Court and 8 Bishopsgate remained aloof, at least when it involved their own issues.[11]

If foreign loans was one growth area, another was American business, following the laying of the transatlantic cable in 1866. By 1871 the volume of telegrams being sent between London and New York was running at some 42,000 a year, while trading on the floors of the two stock exchanges had become effectively integrated, with increasingly small price differentials for a substantial number of common securities. Not surprisingly a group of American houses flourished in the City, dealing on a large scale in American government bonds and American railroads as well as conducting extensive, highly competitive exchange business. 'We have seen no business of theirs except Exchange business – & this they did their best to spoil for everybody else last season', complained Brown Shipley in 1868 of Seligman Brothers. Rothschilds was still somewhat sceptical of the transatlantic drift. Its New York agent, Belmont, was ever-resentful of Baron Lionel's reluctance to pursue his suggestions – though from 1871 the firm did agree to take part at the English end in the complex international syndicates arranged to secure the series of massive post-bellum refunding loans on the part of the US Treasury. Barings was also a participant, though as it wrote early in 1871 to a friendly house: 'Of course these arrangements are not what would be most agreeable to us . . . but we do not think that it would be becoming to refuse to act.'[12]

Noblesse oblige certainly did not operate in the rough-and-tumble of American railroad financing, where there was often vigorous competition (including from stockbrokers) to act as London issuer, and where the lowest ethical standards tended to obtain on the other side of the pond. The classic case of stock manipulation was the Erie Railroad, a favourite speculative counter since 1861 and by now under the quick-silver auspices of Jay Gould, against whom powerful elements in the City made a dead set from 1869. Three years later he was ousted from control, marking the resolution of a long struggle between London and New York for command over the stock. A financial journalist some years later recalled the epic struggle:

> In ousting Gould, shares had to be bought by tens of thousands and shipped over to New York to be voted on. The Erie King was frequently seen on pay day half buried in bundles of stock. Spacious offices had not then come into fashion, and Mr Nickalls had sometimes so many Eries to receive that they had to be piled on tables or heaped on the floor. A carelessly dropped match might on one of those exciting pay days have annihilated a fourth part of the Erie capital.[13]

Tom Nickalls, one of the two leading jobbers in the American market, was crowned 'the Erie King' in 1872 and the tag would endure for the rest of his days.

Detached observers were conscious by the early 1870s that the City was entering a new phase. In January 1872 the *Quarterly Review* sought to pin down and explain what was happening. After referring to 'the great expansion of the trade of the country during the last fifteen, but particularly during the last ten, years, and the rapid way in which, for political and mercantile reasons, London is becoming the financial centre of the Old and New World', it went on:

> Political distrust and revolution in France, the absence of unity and coherence between North and South Germany, and the want of a great Teutonic financial metropolis, combine with the unquestioned stability and credit of English institutions, the benefit of firm and equal laws, and the facilities and inducements of the freest ports, the lowest tariff, and the cheapest manufactures in the world, to render London the place of ultimate settlement of the largest part of the business of both hemi-spheres. Hence the accumulation here of foreign capital and the growth of a powerful class of banks and financial houses . . .

This analysis rightly if only implicitly identified the Franco-Prussian War as a turning point. Its effects were manifold: the non-convertibility of the franc for eight years confirmed sterling as the unrivalled medium of settlement; the Bank of France's suspension of specie payments left London as the only world bullion market; the Paris Bourse's sharp loss of business; a flow of 'hot money' to London; and a human drain that included the ambitious, not always scrupulous international financier Baron Émile d'Erlanger, who took offices from the London and Westminster at 43 Lothbury and proceeded to lay the foundations of the firm Émile Erlanger & Co. Following the pattern of the 1860s, many other foreign houses were also establishing a foothold in the City, notably Crédit Lyonnais and Deutsche Bank.[14]

However, there were two other dimensions to the story. One was the importance of the continuing communications revolution, so that by 1872, for example, the City was in instant telegraphic contact with Tokyo and Melbourne as well as Europe and the States. Related to this was the increasing – and rapid – internationalisation of the money market, the waning of the inland bill (particularly from the 1880s) and the rise of the foreign bill on London, by which the City's discount and accepting houses financed ever-greater volumes of international trade.[15] More than ever, then, the City of London had become by the early 1870s indispensable. More thoughtful observers wondered what the implications of this seemingly gratifying development might be.

No one faced these implications more squarely than Walter Bagehot, the man whom G. M. Young would designate as *Victorianum maxime*, 'most Victorian of the Victorians', the man 'whose influence, passing from one fit mind to another, could transmit, and can still impart, the most precious element in Victorian civilization, its robust and masculine sanity'. In May 1873, six years after the appearance of *The English Constitution*, Bagehot published his classic treatise on *Lombard Street*, sub-titled 'A Description of the Money Market'. Its tone from the start was memorable and authoritative: 'The briefest and truest way of describing Lombard Street is to say that it is by far the greatest combination of economical power and economical delicacy that the world has ever seen.' Underlying all the detached analysis of that phenomenon was an almost passionate argument that the case of Overend Gurney and developments since then, above all the demise of Paris as a counterweight to London and the sheer volume of the City's liabilities as well as assets, meant that 'we must examine the system on which these great masses of money are manipulated, and assure ourselves that it is safe and right'. However:

> It is not easy to rouse men of business to the task. They let the tide of business float before them; they make money or strive to do so while it passes, and they are unwilling to think where it is going. Even the great collapse of Overends, though it caused a panic, is beginning to be forgotten. Most men of business think – 'Anyhow this system will probably last

my time. It has gone on a long time, and is likely to go on still'. But the exact point is, that it has *not* gone on a long time. The collection of these immense sums in one place and in few hands is perfectly new.

Or put another, even more ominous way: 'Money will not manage itself, and Lombard Street has a great deal of money to manage.' In a series of pithy, often wounding sentences Bagehot trained his particular guns on the Old Lady herself: 'No one in London ever dreams of questioning the credit of the Bank, and the Bank never dreams that its own credit is in danger. Somehow everybody feels the Bank is sure to come right.' Moreover: 'The Bank directors are not trained bankers; they were not bred to the trade, and do not in general give the main power of their minds to it. They are merchants, most of whose time and most of whose real mind are occupied in making money in their own business and for themselves.' And:

> We have placed the exclusive custody of our entire banking reserve in the hands of a single board of directors not particularly trained for the duty – who might be called 'amateurs', – who have no particular interest above other people in keeping it undiminished – who acknowledge no obligation to keep it undiminished – who have never been told by any great statesman or public authority that they are so to keep it or that they have anything to do with it – who are named by and are agents for a proprietary which would have a greater income if it *was* diminished, – who do not fear, and who need not fear, ruin, even if it were all gone and wasted.

What was to be done? In the core of his book, Bagehot suggested 'three remedies'. Firstly, that 'there should be a clear understanding between the Bank and the public that, since the Bank hold our ultimate banking reserve, they will recognise and act on the obligations which this implies'. Secondly, that in terms of improving the government of the Bank, 'we should diminish the "amateur" element; we should augment the trained banking element; and we should ensure more constancy in the administration'. Thirdly, that 'we should look at the rest of our banking system, and try to reduce the demands on the Bank as much as we can'.[16] Bagehot did not expect a warm reception for his arguments. 'In the *street* itself I fear I shall be sent into financial exile as neither the Directors of the Bank of England nor the Private Bankers nor the Joint Stock nor the Bill brokers will much like my remarks on them.' In fact the book was speedily reprinted, though it seems to have inspired little or any public discussion on the part of the City, nor even elicited a review in the *Bankers' Magazine*.

About the question of public acceptance of the Bank's public duties, it is extremely difficult to be precise about the effect of Bagehot's stirring words, though most historians of the British financial system have agreed that in some sense they did mark a turning point, that thereafter it was not possible even to pretend that the Bank was like other banks and could, when it came to it, evade its role as lender of last resort in time of crisis. Nevertheless, neither within nor without the Bank was this formally articulated at the time, and only future responses to specific contingencies would reveal how far the Bank was really moving along the road towards what would be called central banking. As for ending of the cult of the amateur in the Bank's direction, with an attendant wish for a permanent deputy-governor and a willingness to break the taboo of not allowing commercial bankers (as opposed to merchant bankers) on the Court, Bagehot seems to have met a brick wall. If the Bank of England considered his reform proposals, we do not know about it. Certainly there was no City agitation along these lines. What we do have, however, is the reaction to *Lombard Street* of one of the more independent-minded Bank directors, William Lidderdale. He wrote to Rathbones in Liverpool in October 1873, against a City background of alarm and despondency caused by bad news from both America and Europe:

> That our Banking and Monetary system in this Country is of an overcomplicated & interdependent nature which makes difficulties in any important quarter a serious matter for every one, is a fact upon which none of us are likely to differ. The system of taking enormous sums on deposit at call or short notice, on which interest has to be paid & which there is almost a necessity to employ if serious losses are to be avoided, is one which carries risk on its face. Mr Bagehot says things *are* so & that it is useless trying to change the system, & then throws upon the Bank of England the onus of providing a reserve adequate to the needs of all its competitors as well as regular customers.

According to Lidderdale, however, the system was perfectly capable of taking the strain; he asserted that 'so far as concerns the big Joint Stock Banks, they most undoubtedly have remembered their lesson & materially improved their practice in the last 6 years'. Crisis, what crisis? When the Bank raised its rate to 7% soon afterwards, prompting a certain raising of the moral eyebrows from his Liverpool correspondent, Lidderdale returned to the defence of the status quo with a robustness of language which suggested that it would be a while yet before meritocratic reform of Bank direction featured on the Threadneedle Street agenda:

You have a very curious notion about the action of the *Merchants* who occupy seats at the Bank Court – the effect of alterations of rate is generally much less felt in their business than in Banking arrangements, & people who do the latter on a large scale are much more constantly face to face with questions of self interest . . . Then many Directors, men like Morris, Latham, Hankey, Hubbard, Huth, Campbell, the present Governor Greene, & Gibbs are personally in a position so little touched by anything which goes on in the Bank that it cannot be a matter of material interest what the rate is. Certainly no body of men have a right to claim superiority to even unconscious promptings of self interest, but I am bound to say that I have never seen more honest endeavours to decide in the true interest of the Bank, even when I have differed with the majority.[17]

'In the true interest of the Bank': it remained a private institution with, as Bagehot deplored, only muffled, semi-acknowledged public responsibilities.

CHAPTER SIXTEEN

An Imaginative Faculty

As Lombard Street mulled or otherwise over *Lombard Street*, Anthony Trollope was writing what would be his greatest book. Published from February 1874 in monthly parts, *The Way We Live Now* is a panoramic novel of sustained moral disgust that deals with much else besides the City, but has at its centre the figure of the financial adventurer Augustus Melmotte – 'a large man, with bushy whiskers and rough thick hair, with heavy eyebrows, and a wonderful look of power about his mouth and chin'. His personal antecedents are shrouded in mystery (at one point Trollope refers to him as 'the boy out of the gutter'), at various times he has tried to make his fortune in New York, Hamburg, Frankfurt, Vienna and Paris, and finding the French capital too hot to hold him he has now moved to London, soon after the Franco-Prussian War. His offices are in Abchurch Lane ('the steps were narrow and crooked, and the rooms were small and irregular'), and the novel charts his rise and fall during the summer of 1873. Landmarks include the successful scam by which he launches at an irresistible premium an intrinsically worthless concern called the South Central Pacific and Mexican Railway; the desire of the English aristocracy to attach itself to his opulent coat-tails; the great dinner he hosts for the Emperor of China; his election as MP for Westminster; the discovery of fraud; and, amidst a dissolving financial empire, his suicide. He is a terrible man, being a shameless liar and quite prepared to use physical violence against his grown-up daughter when she thwarts his schemes. He is also without any of the graces, can hardly string two words together in public, and is willing to trust no one, with the partial exception of Croll, his long-serving confidential clerk. Yet as the novel progress it is hard not to feel a sneaking sympathy for him. He is the fox, and one knows that in the end the hounds are going to get him.[1]

Did the *Economist* conceivably have Melmotte in mind when in June 1875, as the serialisation of Trollope's novel drew to a close, it published one of its lofty editorials, on 'The Special Dangers of High Commercial Developments'? Much of it was a defence – in its way, a compelling and perennial defence – of the big operators of the day:

> Now, when a man has a great capacity for many wide combinations, it is not unnatural that his intellectual interests and calculations should far outrun the means at his disposal, and that he should, without any ignoble or unworthy unscrupulousness – though of course not without fault – be eager to avail himself of any advantage which the confidence of others may give him for extending his operations. We often talk as if the haste to be rich, the mere desire of wealth, were the only motive power in these great speculative transactions which, when they fail, cause so much misery and so much scandal. But no mistake can be greater . . . Our belief is that it is quite as much the natural heat of imaginative faculty, – for however odd the word 'imaginative' may sound in connection with the enterprises of the manufacturer or the merchant, it is an imaginative faculty of a particular kind, and nothing short of it, which fits a man for the conception and execution of those great commercial operations, – which leads men to embark in transactions larger then their resources will properly admit, as the haste to be rich, which, however, no doubt mingles with and vivifies that imaginative faculty . . . The sleepy-looking commercial man, who hardly knows what literature means, and never heard of either Mr Mill, or Mr Darwin, or the spectroscope, has often beneath that dull outside an intelligence as wakeful and restless as that of a French wit. And it is this eager intelligence of his, conscious of great power, or of the misleading symptoms of great power, which, quite as much as any mere thirst for wealth, leads him into operations extending beyond the scope of his legitimate means.

Bagehot then reached his moral burden:

> We are anxious that this should be fairly recognised, because we are quite sure that the world does injustice to the magnates of the City when it accuses the unfortunate among them of lightly playing of what is not their own to spend, in mere greediness and avarice. There is greediness and avarice enough, no doubt; but, probably, hardly more in the City than in the West-end.

Finally, Bagehot called on men of commerce to develop a larger hinterland, asserting that 'it is the men who have no other intellectual life except the life of commercial enterprise, who are the truly dangerous men'. And the article ends ringingly: 'Culture always diminishes intensity. And in the commercial world we could well afford to favour that result'.[2]

There is little doubt who was the real-life Melmotte. Albert Grant (né Gottheimer) had survived the Overend Gurney crisis but was not involved with his Crédit Foncier after 1868. Instead he set up as a company promoter on his own account, and that same year his services on behalf of the Milan Improvement Company, resulting in the creation of an elegant shopping arcade in the centre of that city, earned him an Italian barony from King Victor Emmanuel. Then came the feverish bull market of the early 1870s: Grant himself subsequently considered 1871 to be its apogee, when even the most highly respectable men and women were seduced by the lure of easy money:

> That was a year and an era when everyone was seeking what he could make on the Stock Exchange. There is a peculiar fascination to some people in making money on the Stock Exchange. I know hundreds who would rather make £50 on the Stock Exchange than £250 by the exercise of their profession; there is a nameless fascination, and in the year 1871 the favourite form of making money on the Stock Exchange was by applying for shares, selling them at whatever premium they were at, and that money was considered made – I say considered – honourably made . . .
>
> They seemed to think that premiums grew like mushrooms in the night, in a public way, and that in Capel Court, inside the Stock Exchange, they grew like cherries and had only to be plucked off the tree . . .

Grant in the early 1870s floated some nineteen new issues, a mixture of foreign and domestic, including four foreign mining companies. They covered a wide range and, whatever his dubious promotional methods, not all were complete rubbish. One that was, however, was the Emma Silver Mining Company of Utah, which paid him £200,000 for an English flotation and which in the autumn of 1871 he managed to puff to a handsome premium. Wealth flowed into his hands, he became a noted picture collector, and in 1873 he acquired slum land by Kensington Palace, cleared the area, and commissioned a veritable palace of his own, to be called Kensington House and set off by landscaped gardens and an ornamental lake. Early the next year he was not only returned again for Kidderminster (having lost the seat in 1868) but spent £30,000 on buying a rubbish dump in the centre of London known as Leicester Fields, with a view to transforming it into public gardens and presenting the finished article as a gift to the Metropolitan Board of Works.

Then came the fall. Markets in 1874 continued to feel the effects of the European and American financial crises of the previous autumn; Emma shares fell from a peak of over £30 to a nominal £2, being in fact barely marketable; a law suit initiated by a shareholder revealed

the murkiest details of stock market manipulation; charges of bribery
led to the MP for Kidderminister being unseated; and when a grateful
public gathered to witness the formal opening of Leicester Square,
what should have been Grant's finest hour was blighted by a hoard of
hired men with sandwich boards, which displayed a list of his bankrupt companies, details of the money that had been lost by the public,
and a verse that would become immortal in the City:

> Kings bestow titles,
> Honour they can't;
> Title without honour
> Is a Baron Grant.

The lines were pinned up on a wall at the Stock Exchange, where a wit
added a further couplet:

> Yes, but you're in an even worse dilemma
> If you cannot get a title to your Emma.

The rest followed with an inevitability: in 1876 an expensive law suit,
showing that another of Grant's 1871 promotions, Lisbon Steam
Tramways, had involved significant slush funds as well as systematic
share rigging; by 1877 the pictures on sale; two years later his failure;
and in 1883 the demolition of Kensington House, with the marble
grand staircase going to Madame Tussaud's and the beautiful entrance
gates to the East Sheen entrance of Richmond Park. Grant himself kept
an office in the City until 1888, but spent more and more of his time
living quietly at Bognor, last resort of barons as well as monarchs.[3]

In his heyday he had been masterly in his use of the press, which at
that time had poor coverage of financial matters. Before 1870 there was
no specialist financial daily, and even then the establishment of the
Financier left a gap, for it was little more than a journal of record,
desperately dull and with minimal editorial comment or genuine re-
portage to attract the interest of the average investor. Instead, the
unrivalled authority during the third quarter of the century was the
daily money article that appeared in *The Times* under the City editorship of Marmaduke Sampson, previously secretary to the Treasury
Committee of the Bank of England. 'Mr Sampson's first visit to me since
I was elected Governor. He comes to enquire if the Bank has received
any confirmation that the Bank of France has reduced its rate of
discount.' So recorded Bonamy Dobree, and over the years the man

from the Thunderer continued to enjoy the very best access to the highest places. 'He has exercised in a certain world an authority and power curiously superior to anything which his social position would suggest', the *Economist* was to recall at the end of his tenure, adding that 'there was "money in what he said", as the common phrase goes . . .'[4]

The implicit moral onus was considerable, and ultimately power corrupted him. *The Times* became known as the 'Jews' harp' on account of its systematic boosting of Russian and Brazilian stocks brought out by Rothschilds; and Sampson himself lived at Hampton Court House and enjoyed there a style of life (building a great floral hall, engaging Patti to entertain guests) way in excess of what would have been possible from his official remuneration as a journalist. An intrigued visitor there in 1870 was a representative of the unscrupulous American financier Jay Cooke, seeking to drum up support for Northern Pacific railroad bonds: 'Sampson, they say here, cannot be bought, and it would never do to offer him a pecuniary consideration, and I believe it, and there is no need of it, for a man who has saved £400,000 sterling as editor of the *Times*, and lived like a prince all the time, understands the art of getting along.' Whatever the implication, soon afterwards the infamous Emma flotation did see money changing hands, for it subsequently emerged in the law suit that in the course of just over twelve months Grant had donated some £7,500 to Sampson. At the end of the case in January 1875, *The Times* itself expressed its 'mingled astonishment and indignation', before going on:

> The explanation of these gifts, volunteered by Baron Grant, is that Mr Sampson had adventured in some speculations on his recommendation which had proved unsuccessful, and he had thought it fair to indemnify his friend against the losses he had sustained. The Baron's generosity is high-minded, yet it was not indiscriminate. Many persons must have lost money in speculations recommended by him – some who could worse afford to lose it than Mr Sampson – yet of all the unlucky men and women who had gone through this experience the one he selected to indemnify was the writer of the Money Articles in *The Times*, he himself being by profession a man who, month by month, and week by week, introduced new ventures to the Stock Exchange. We need say no more.

Sampson was compelled to resign his post and the reputation of financial journalism took a hammer blow. Perhaps fortunate not to witness his disgrace was his old assistant, David Morier Evans, who had died a year previously. In 1873 he had rashly sunk all his money into starting a paper called the *Hour*; by December he had been declared a bankrupt; his health broke down; and the end came on New Year's Day 1874 at a house in South Hackney.[5] Back in 1860 he had stilled his envy of Pullinger, but at the last he found that he did have no resources beyond hand and brain.

If Grant's nefarious activities were one of the main aspects of the boom of the early 1870s, then another was undoubtedly the craze for foreign loans, already under way in the late 1860s. It may not have been accidental that the publication in book form of *The Way We Live Now* in July 1875 coincided almost exactly with the appearance of the report of the Select Committee on Loans to Foreign States. The report did not inspirit *The Times*:

> The impression that it leaves on the mind is that no great intellectual power, no very rare ingenuity, no very elaborate artifices are necessary to victimize the public, but that the qualities chiefly required are boldness and assurance, a faculty for working in concert, and the discretion to keep a secret . . . It is evident that there is no credulity more absolute than that which is generated by the desire of a high dividend, and that no picture can be too glaringly coloured or too coarsely daubed to attract a certain portion of the public.

The *Economist* was also forcefully struck by the findings of the Committee, but seems to have considered that lenders and borrowers deserved each other:

> They have shown that little States, nearly without revenue, were able to borrow immense sums which they could never have paid, and which they never meant to pay – that they borrowed upon pretences which they scarcely even attempted to make good – that they forced these loans upon the English market by clever devices – and what is more extraordinary than all that, in several cases, they, the borrowing States, obtained scarcely any of the money, because it was intercepted by the persons who framed the devices. Those who cheated the English public cheated also – and that upon the largest scale – those in whose names they borrowed.[6]

Which were these sadly gullible states? The one that became a by-word for the whole inglorious process was Honduras, where it was hoped to construct an inter-oceanic railway and for which government loans came three times to the London market. By the third time, in 1872, the proposal was for a 'ship railway', by which ocean-going ships would be raised from the sea by hydraulic lifts, transported across the Isthmus on fifteen parallel tracks that would carry a giant cradle, and slid into the water on the other side – a fantastic scheme that was so comprehensively criticised that it was soon abandoned. Then there was the Republic of San Domingo, which raised a loan in 1869 but repudiated it the next year, to the indignation of many of Gerstenberg's foreign bondholders. In default all too soon was Costa Rica, for which loans were floated in 1871 and 1872, as they were also in the same years for Paraguay. The loans for all four states were characterised by the creation of artificial premiums and the unloading of stock on the public just before the price fell like a stone. Inevitably the main players in these operations varied from loan to loan, but two names stood out. The key figure in the Honduras loans was an international financier called Charles Lefevre, real name Joachim Lefevre, who had been imprisoned in Paris in the 1850s for breach of trust. Working closely with him was the firm of Bischoffsheim & Goldschmidt (depicted in Trollope's novel as Todd, Brehgert & Goldsheimer), with strong Continental connections and which had only recently based itself in London as an issuing house. Described by a member of the Gibbs family as 'keen enterprising people' ('as you will gather from their names', he could not resist adding), Bischoffsheims saw its chance for a killing and had few if any compunctions about taking it.[7]

The end of a boom always leads to recriminations and a search for scapegoats, and in March 1875 the Select Committee, which included Kirkman Hodgson, began taking evidence on the recent crop of disastrous loans to these Central and South American states. Quickly in the hot seat – one that neither Lefevre nor Henri Bischoffsheim was inclined to occupy – was Samuel Herman de Zoete, formerly senior partner of the stockbrokers de Zoete & Gorton and now chairman of the Stock Exchange Committee. A series of questions sought to elicit that body's general regulatory position:

> Do you make any inquiry whatever as to the probability of the State repaying that loan; does that come within the scope of your investigation? – No.
> Neither as to the reasonableness, nor as to the unreasonableness, of the amount? – No . . .
> Do you require any proofs as to the *bonâ fides* of the allotment? – I cannot say that we do; we take the assurance of the contractor that such and such an amount has been allotted; we do not ask for proof; we have no means of getting the proof, in fact . . .
> Am I right in assuming that if you were to make a more searching examination, you would be taking upon yourself too heavy a responsibility? – I am afraid we should never get through the business.

At the heart of the Committee's jurisdiction over new issues was its role in allowing settlement of bargains and authorising inclusion on the official list of prices – in both of which capacities, de Zoete stressed throughout his evidence a strictly minimalist interpretation of investor protection. Yet the facts being put to him were uncomfortable, and when towards the end of his evidence he was asked whether the Committee should have settled the Honduras loan of 1867, if it had known that Bischoffsheim & Goldschmidt had taken nineteen-twentieths of the allotment, his reply lacked a little in conviction: 'Probably not; I cannot say for certain; it is all a matter for the Committee.'

The investigators then tried to close in on the Stock Exchange operations, and made useful progress through Richard Evans, a financial agent who had worked for Lefevre in the first two Honduras loans:

> What dealings had you with respect to the 1870 Loan? – Before the loan was brought out Lefevre told me that he was going to have the management of that loan. He then said, 'Well now, the best thing to do when it is issued is this; if the bears attempt' (as there are always bears in every new loan, particularly if it is not a first-class loan) 'to knock this down, we must support it. I have full authority to do it.' Then he said, 'The wisest thing to do is to give, through a certain number of brokers, orders to buy or orders to sell, as the case may be . . .'
>
> When these instructions are given to the broker to communicate to the jobber, the jobber is the person to take action in the market? – Certainly.
>
> Does he run any risk at all? – Under those circumstances, certainly not.
>
> So that if any person comes into the market and offers to sell, a person in possession of a pocket order can always buy, and so speculate up to the extent of his pocket order? – Yes.

The next witness was a leading jobber in the Foreign market, Joseph Tucker, and the focus remained on Honduras 1870:

> Have you been in the room whilst Mr Evans has been examined? – Yes.
>
> Have you heard what he stated about authority being given, in order to keep the market straight, to jobbers to buy at a certain price? – Yes . . .
>
> Can you recollect what limit as to the amount of stock you were given? – They were limits left from time to time for half-an-hour to an hour, in a limited amount of stock at a limited price.
>
> Can you tell the Committee what sort of limits you would have: £50,000, £100,000, or what sort of amount? – I should think 50 thousands in Honduras.
>
> From whom did you receive that authority? – Chiefly from a Mr James Barclay.

It seemed a breakthrough, and the Committee summoned that retired broker to travel down from his home in Scotland, but failed to pin him down under questioning:

> The whole operation was artificial; it was the issuer of the loan who was buying in the market in order to make the public believe that it was a genuine affair, and that the public were anxious to take it? – Yes.
>
> That is commonly called rigging the market, is it not? – No, that is not rigging the market.
>
> But it has a very considerable family resemblance to rigging the market; what would you call rigging the market? – Making too large a premium and catching the bears, which they did not do; so they did not rig the market.
>
> They only rigged the public? – No, the public rigged the premium, I think.

So, no harvest from James Barclay; when asked to explain what a pocket order was, he replied that he did not know.

What about the big men? The second Costa Rica loan had been brought out by Émile Erlanger & Co in tandem with Knowles & Foster, the latter a highly respectable merchanting firm making its first tentative foray into the sphere of pure finance. Richard Foster explained to the parliamentarians how his firm had been led to the business by its brokers Hichens, Harrison & Co and how it had been introduced to Erlangers by Lionel Cohen. He also related how he had become very disenchanted on discovering a secret agreement between Erlangers and the Costa Rican representative, Señor Alvarado, giving Erlangers an extra 4 per cent commission. Next came Baron Erlanger himself, who admitted that, between the day of the issuing of the prospectus and that of the allotment, he had bought back most of the loan in order to ensure it went to a premium. There followed some fairly defensive remarks, before Erlanger came under stern questioning from Hodgson in an exchange that went somewhere near the heart of the matter:

> Therefore you think that the public is not allured by fictitious premiums which the bonds bear in consequence of the purchases made by those who have issued the loan? – I say that they are not allured, but I say at the same time that nobody would apply for a loan which is at a discount.
>
> All I want to know is whether you justify that buying which keeps a loan at a premium which is not the healthy result of applications from the public, but the result of artificial buying, for I must call it artificial buying? – Artificial buying, I do not understand.

> Such buying as yours I mean? – I beg your pardon, but I am not of your opinion.
>
> You think it is an advantageous thing to do? – I think it is a necessary thing to do.
>
> Necessary for what? – Necessary for this reason, that when a loan is brought out, as a rule nobody can tell beforehand what the reception of that loan will be; there may be circumstances quite apart from the quality of the loan, which may make it necessary for those who have an interest in the loan to buy, and in our own experience I can give you several instances of this . . .

Near the end of his evidence Erlanger stated that he preferred the Paris Bourse to the London Stock Exchange, because 'the Bourse in Paris is an open market', where 'everybody can watch the transactions, and can see what is going on': that was probably the last straw for the man from Barings.

Neither 8 Bishopsgate nor New Court was remotely implicated in any of this, and when the Select Committee towards the end of its labours came to examine Nathaniel (Natty) de Rothschild, himself already MP for Aylesbury, it perhaps expected an expression of intent to help cleanse the Augean stables:

> What is your opinion as to the disease? – It is rather difficult to say what the disease is; I should say the disease is the desire of people to get a high rate of interest for their money.
>
> Do you propose to remedy that? – No, not at all.
>
> You do not come here to suggest remedies, but to criticise the remedies which have been proposed? – Yes.

Natty then argued that if, for example, it became mandatory for a contractor to state the price at which he had taken a loan from the government concerned, then the foreign loans business would desert London for the Continent. And as for the notion that the Stock Exchange Committee should refuse a quotation unless told the terms of that agreement between contractor and state:

> Does the objection to that suggestion consist of its being unsound in theory, or in its being easily evaded in practice? – It relates to both. You have no more right to ask me at what price I have got a loan that you have to ask a man what price he gives for a horse.
>
> But supposing that the client of the broker cannot, without that information, be properly informed whether he should invest his money in that loan? – The majority of men do not write through brokers, they write for themselves.

The country clergymen and widows write through brokers, I presume?
– Those are not the majority of the people; the majority of the people
judge for themselves. The majority of the people, in my opinion, who
wrote for these loans wrote for them because they had made a good deal
of money by former foreign loans, and having done so they thought that
the new loan which had been introduced was equally as good as its
predecessors.

You think any provision of that kind would be easily evaded? – Very
easily evaded.[8]

Cool realism was Natty's forte, no less than his grandfather when
analysing the pioneer wave of foreign loans in the immediate aftermath
of the Napoleonic Wars.

Undeterred, the Select Committee towards the end of its report
(mostly given over to detailing the history of the various loans) did
turn to the question of possible remedies. It saw little good coming
voluntarily from Capel Court, noting that in the course of evidence
from Stock Exchange members it had not observed 'any very keen
appreciation of the evils of the present manner of manipulating loans,
or any fertility of resource in devising remedies'. There was, moreover,
an intrinsic problem:

> The Stock Exchange is a voluntary society. It has upwards of 2,000
> members. It exists for the purpose of buying and selling, to which all its
> other functions are subordinate. There is no reason to doubt that as
> between its own members it administers substantial justice. The power
> that it wields extends to expulsion, that is the taking away from the
> person expelled his occupation in life. Such a body can hardly be inter-
> fered with by Parliament without losing that freedom of self-government
> which is the very life and soul of the institution.
>
> The Committee which govern the Stock Exchange are annually elected,
> and any attempt to force upon the electors rules distasteful to the ma-
> jority would be resisted by the rejection of the Committee which framed
> them, and the substitution of a body more in harmony with the ma-
> jority . . .

Clearly, then, there would be no point advocating a return to a ban on
pre-allotment dealings, that experiment unsuccessfully tried (against
de Zoete's advice) a decade earlier. But the Select Committee did have
two specific suggestions to make: that the Stock Exchange's official list
should reveal not only the nominal amount of a loan but also the
actual amount held by the public; and that the Stock Exchange Committee should obtain statutory declarations from the contractor of a

loan. Still, such reforms could hardly be enough on their own, and the report concluded by expressing the conviction that 'the best security against the recurrence of such evils . . . will be found, not so much in legislative enactments as in the enlightenment of the public as to their real nature and origin'.⁹ It was not, in the end, so very different from the approach advocated by the member for Aylesbury.

*

Many contemporaries shared the evidently cool parliamentary opinion of Capel Court. 'Without taking a specially gloomy view of the world in general', declared *Blackwood's* in September 1876, 'we see that at least in its financial department and on the Stock Exchange, the powers of evil for the time are decidedly in the ascendant.' Many honest merchants in the City would not entirely have disagreed, perhaps among them Lidderdale, who back in 1868, following an invidious legal case involving Foster & Braithwaite, had come to the conclusion that 'the things practised daily for convenience on the Stock Exchange will rarely stand the light'. Lidderdale continued to do business through Foster & Braithwaite, but four years later was describing that firm as 'brokers whom it is necessary to keep in order, or you find yourself let in with the highest price in purchases & the lowest in sales'.

Fittingly, it was one of Foster & Braithwaite's most experienced partners, Charles Branch, who towards the end of 1876 took up the public cudgels in 'A Defence of the Stock Exchange' published in *Fraser's Magazine*. His attitude to the public was thoroughly robust: 'We, the Stock Exchange, never asked you to buy a bad security. If you thought fit to venture your money, and have lost it, so much the worse for you and your advisers.' Put another way: 'The Stock Exchange is a channel, not a filter. It argues no fault in the construction of an aqueduct that the water it conveys is often dirty.' And on this theme of what one might call a stringent passivity: 'We afford you every facility for buying what you want, and for getting what you have bought, and for selling it again if you are tired of it . . . But our duties, responsibilities, and powers end there.' There was a pleasing lack of cant about Branch's piece. He argued, as one might expect, that 'the trust confided to the members is but rarely abused', that 'principals seldom suffer loss by the failure of brokers'; but he also made the memorable assertion that 'a Stock Exchange restricted to investment business [i.e. as opposed to speculation] would be as useful and as popular as a

public-house licensed only for ginger-beer'. And he was not ashamed
of the quarter of a century he had spent in his occupation:

> The process of turning two shillings into half-a-crown, which is all that
> we profess to do, is not one calculated to arouse a moral, or even an
> intellectual, enthusiasm, like the work of a statesman, an artist, or an
> author. But it may nevertheless be necessary as to its purpose, honest as
> to its method, and satisfactory as to its results. We cannot all live by
> writing articles in *Fraser*. We cannot all join Ruskin's Company of St
> George. There must be readers as well as writers, workers as well as
> thinkers.[10]

Branch's defence proved in vain, for early in 1877 events moved
quickly against the Stock Exchange, starting with an internal squall
that aroused considerable unfavourable press attention. It began when
Baker & Sturdy, jobbers in the Foreign market, received a severe
censure from the Committee: their crime was that, 'having ascertained
the market price of Rumanian Bank shares to be $2\frac{3}{4}$ to $3\frac{1}{4}$ per share',
they 'were not justified in fixing $2\frac{1}{4}$ per share as the price to be
paid'. Lawrence Baker himself was a member of the Committee and,
not surprisingly, felt compelled to resign his place. This move, however, failed to appease the general feeling in the House that the guilty
parties had been let off too mildly, a feeling that culminated when
William Ingall, who had earlier resigned his position on the Committee
in protest at the tameness of the punishment, stood himself for the
vacancy he had created and defeated F. C. Charlesworth, the 'establishment' candidate, by a handsome 984 votes to 196. Thereupon the
rest of the Committee collectively resigned. The scene was set for a
bloody set-piece battle, over questions of market practice and appropriate disciplinary action; victory, to judge by the support manifested
for Ingall, would go to the hard-liners. In fact, most of the old Committee stood again during February for the places they had vacated and
with only two exceptions were returned. This was a mildly absurd
outcome:

> If the re-election of Mr Ingall meant anything, it was the approval of his
> conduct by the 'House' in refusing to be a party any longer to the
> proceedings of the late Committee. It was, in fact, as we have previously
> remarked, a manifest vote of censure, and plainly showed that the Stock
> Exchange was dissatisfied with the behaviour of its governing body. How,
> then, are we to explain the result of the ballot? . . . Evidently this proves,
> first, the desire of the electors not to exclude any particular member in the
> absence of actual evidence of his unfitness; secondly, the impossibility of

finding the requisite 30 competent men willing to serve; and thirdly, the relapse into their normal state of indifference of many of the electors.[11]

This convincing analysis came from the *World*, a particularly trenchant, well-informed critic of City men and matters.

Soon afterwards, on 20 March, J. R. Yorke proposed in the House of Commons that the affairs of the Stock Exchange be scrutinised by a royal commission. In the course of his speech he made much of how the Stock Exchange 'encouraged speculation by admitting a low class of members with small security'. Yorke was a Tory backwoodsman, as was the seconder of the motion, Sir Charles Russell, who reserved much of his disgust for the contractors of the recent disastrous foreign loans: 'A few years ago they would not have been allowed to put their foot within the pale of respectable society, but now-a-days respectable society not only tolerated, but toadied them, and enabled them to carry on their sinister practices . . .' The country gentlemen needed the support of a political heavyweight, and it came from Robert Lowe, a tough-minded former Chancellor of the Exchequer:

> The point was not that people gambled on the Stock Exchange; it was that the Stock Exchange, having rules, did not act upon them in many cases, and that in others they wilfully abstained from inquiry, where they well knew if they had inquired they would have found that a syndicate had been organised, and that the whole thing was a deception, and a fraud upon the public. It was not that people had lost their money foolishly, not that they had been deluded – for that would happen as long as human nature remained the same – but it was in order that we should not have a body receiving certificates and acting upon them, and who, knowing them to be false, and knowing that the loan had not been allotted, yet proceeded to give it all the vogue it could, just as if it had been allotted, that inquiry was needed.

George Goschen inevitably defended the status quo. 'Was it not the fact', he asked, 'that, although the French had legislated on the subject and laid down rules for their Stock Exchange, gambling had reached to an extent there to which it had never attained in this country?' But the tide was seemingly going the other way, and the Conservative government agreed to establish a Royal Commission – a decision, however, that immediately produced a hostile response from the two most eminent organs of the fourth estate. The *Economist* called it 'an attempt to give effect in a halting and hesitating manner to the vague feeling which prevails among the outside public that the Stock

Exchange is primarily responsible for most of the great frauds upon investors which have been perpetrated in recent years, and that such frauds may be prevented for the future by legislation of some kind'. While as for *The Times*, it argued root-and-Branch that the Stock Exchange machinery itself 'does not make the deceits and frauds, nor can their cure be found in a re-adjustment of the machinery', adding unequivocally that 'the remedy for fraudulent ventures is the punishment of those who concoct them'.[12]

Chairman of the Royal Commission was Lord Penzance, while those sitting on it included a significant cluster of high-level City insiders: Nathaniel de Rothschild; Henry Hucks Gibbs; Benjamin Buck Greene, a recent governor of the Bank; and Septimus Scott, chairman of the Stock Exchange Committee itself. Evidence was taken from June 1877 to April 1878, mostly on Saturday afternoons, and over fifty witnesses faced almost 9,000 questions. Francis Levien, secretary to the Stock Exchange Committee, was deputed to open the batting and most of the attack focused on the membership itself. Levien was pressed to concede that members ought to serve an apprenticeship before being admitted, but insisted that as qualifications 'credit and personal character are more desirable than anything else', adding that in practice 'the great majority of our members are those who have served as clerks'. It was then put to him that, notwithstanding recently hiked-up entrance fees and sureties, 'the very easy admission of a great many young men from the West end of the town has led to that very feeling of excitement out of which this Commission of Inquiry has grown, and that if you could prevent, by still greater restrictions, the easy admission of young gentlemen who go and play at lawn tennis, and tell their friends "I can put you on a good thing", that if you could restrict these sort of people from joining you, you would do a great deal to allay the excitement, and would do away with a great deal of the immorality into which this Commission is appointed to inquire'. This was a slow, twisting delivery, but Levien played the dead bat, denying 'that a money restriction would suffice' and reiterating that 'the best restriction is to take all the means in one's power to see that the applicant is a person of good character and credit'. He was, however, forced to concede not only that it had become increasingly common for people to go on the Stock Exchange without any previous connection with the business, but also that a recent survey of defaulters had shown that those who had served an apprenticeship as a clerk before becoming members were much less likely to fail. So character, yes, but it seemed that a little learning also helped.

Several Committee members gave evidence, including Percival Spurling and H. Rokeby Price, both brokers. Scott tossed Spurling an easy one:

> In your belief has the interest of members in any sense ever practically weighed in the decision of the Committee? – It has never affected the decision of the Committee. I am quite certain that since I have been there no settlement or quotation has been given by favour, nor has any loan or company been allowed to get through which has not complied with our published rules.

Yorke saw his chance:

> Do you recollect the case of the San Domingo Loan? – Yes, perfectly.
> Were the Stock Exchange rules complied with in that case? – I am now speaking from memory. We were not satisfied at the first coming up, and we required, before we would grant them a quotation, that they should bring up a letter showing what had been done with the remainder of the stock (I am speaking entirely from memory), and the result was that the broker employed came up upon another occasion and handed in a letter stating that the remainder of the loan had been placed; I think that those were the words which he used.
> 'Disposed of' I think were his words? – 'Disposed of'. There is no doubt that the Committee were deceived; but because they trusted merchants of London. I do not think that the Committee are to be so much blamed; it was a new thing, we had always been in the habit of trusting the merchants of London.

The evidence of Price focused in part on two of the more notorious cases of fraud and market manipulation this side of the Americas. One was the case of the Eupion Gas Company in 1874, a flotation infamous because of its volume of dummy applications, and he was asked whether the broker to that enterprise had believed the directors 'because of their names' or only after 'he made further inquiries'. 'I should not like to answer that question', replied Price. The other was Grant's Lisbon Tramways venture, an intrinsically hopeless project because the route from Lisbon to Cuitra was far too steep and narrow. In his speech to the Commons, Yorke had made much of how, even after Grant's evidence at the law suit had rendered the shares worthless, the company's broker, Harry Panmure Gordon of Scrimgeours, had 'come forward and said that in the interest of the Stock Exchange the scheme must be allowed to go on; that as a settling day had been appointed, the brokers and dealers must not lose their commission, and therefore the swindle must proceed'. Price insisted that this exaggerated what Panmure Gordon had done and added that, even if he had talked loftily of the interests of the Stock Exchange, this was without the sanction of the Committee. In general Price came across as a capable figure and provided detailed evidence of what the Committee *did* do in its ill-appreciated efforts to prevent malpractice.

Quite a few ordinary members gave evidence, though none as inform-atively or quotably as Charles Branch, who had recently retired from business:

> The great object of the promoters is to get the shares quoted at a premium so as to induce applicants? – Yes.
> They say, 'I will buy at a premium'? – Yes; and the dealers will sell some at say 1 premium, and the chances are that some other people who see this company announced, and who think that the shares will go down, or that they can get an allotment at par, will come in and sell some shares perhaps at $\frac{3}{4}$ premium, or presumably at something less than the jobber received from the broker who originally bought of him, and then a few transactions, or possibly many transactions, if it is a large company, take place. The object of those transactions is this, that the company's broker or some other person connected with it shall send to the newspapers in the afternoon a certified slip that the shares of the A.B.C. company are quoted at $\frac{3}{4}$ to $1\frac{1}{4}$ premium 'with an active demand'. The assurance they work upon is this; that a number of simple people amongst the public who would not be attracted sufficiently by the prospectus, and perhaps not at all, will often write for shares because they read and believe that the shares are in demand at 1 premium in the market . . .

For himself, Branch typically insisted that, 'whilst I should distinctly decline to take part in making an artificial market, I should not inquire into the object that a person had in buying shares if I thought he was good to pay'. But sometimes, as he recalled of the boom earlier in the decade, press items about premiums did not even reflect transactions at all:

> How came that to pass? – It came in this way, the premium was made with the view of working upon the public through the newspapers, and the people who worked the companies, and got into the habit of working them, saw at last that they might avoid the expense of the operation in the market, and get the benefit of a quotation without a bargain at all. So they would send a slip through the agent who had the advertisements for the company. It is a considerable business advertising a new company. I mean it is a matter involving a large payment of money; and that was generally done through an advertising agent.

To float a company in the first instance there is the bringing out of the prospectus, and then there is the employment of the advertising agent? – Yes, to advertise the prospectus in the newspapers.

Who would the advertising agent be? – Almost any news-agent in the City. Then if through the agent who sent the advertisements to the newspapers a slip was forwarded to the City department, saying, 'Such and such shares are in demand at $1\frac{3}{4}$ to 2 premium', that would in more than one newspaper appear in the City news the following day, notwithstanding the fact that there had been no transactions whatever in them.

Without any inquiry into the truth of it? – Without any inquiry into the truth of it.

The fact being that an expensive advertisement was put in on that same day? – Quite so.

The fact being that the newspaper having received an order for an expensive advertisement would be willing to receive and publish the fact in this little slip of paper without making any inquiries? – Yes.

The fact being utterly false? – Quite so.

The implication being, Branch did not need to say, that it was not the Stock Exchange that should have been the object of a royal commission. Still, he was probably as sceptical as the next man about the possibilities of wholesome change for the better. 'A good many people of the class of *rentiers* live for nothing else I think but to look at the quotations of their stocks', he remarked at one point, and when it came to it the job of Capel Court just as much as Grub Street was to service that curiosity.

It was not only members who gave evidence. Montague Newton was a seasoned half-commission man, in effect a denizen of the West End whose purpose in life was to bring business to a stockbroker and take for himself half the resultant commission; he was decidedly unimpressed by the men of the east:

> Men go in to the Stock Exchange now as a sort of refuge for the destitute. A man leaving the army who does not know what to do with himself, or how to get a living, says I will go into the Stock Exchange. A merchant breaks down, mercantile profits are so much reduced now in comparison with former years, owing to a variety of circumstances – possibly to the quickness of communication, telegraphs, and so on – and he does not see his way to making the profit that was formerly made. Then he goes into the Stock Exchange, and puts his sons into the Stock Exchange, men who have been brought up to utterly different pursuits. There is no inquiry made when a man applies for admission to the Stock Exchange as to his capacity for that work . . .
> Colonial brokers, tallow brokers, and many other signification of brokers, cotton brokers, and wool brokers, and all that class, only become

brokers after they have served an apprenticeship to their business. Further they deal in a limited number of articles. In the case of a colonial broker he possibly deals in a more extended variety of things than any other broker, but a cotton broker deals in cotton, a wool broker in wool. Among colonial brokers there are some of them that obtain a preeminence of speciality, some in coffee, others in sugar; it gets to be either their one article, or it is their leading article . . . But a stockbroker, unfortunately for him, with a limited education has to deal in or obtain a knowledge on a vast variety of securities. It would be difficult to count them, but there are several hundreds of different securities which he should properly speaking obtain some knowledge about . . .

The majority of stockbrokers are decidedly an ignorant class who know very little more beyond 8ths, 16ths, and 32nds . . .

Take a case which has frequently attracted the attention of the public. Some of you gentlemen may have heard of the Argentine securities. The Argentine securities used at one time to stand in the prices 95 to 100, and in those days the great majority of stockbrokers to whom you spoke would tell you that they were the finest securities open for investment; certainly the very best 6 per cent security that was ever introduced upon the market. And those same brokers, many of them who held arguments with me as to the sterling nature of these securities at about those prices of 95 to 100, when the prices went down to 30 to 40, told me that they ought to be sold, that they were thoroughly rotten, and that they ought never to have been introduced into the London market . . .

I have asked several of those gentlemen who took a particular interest in this stock, what they chanced to know about it and its intrinsic worth. 'Do you happen to know anything about the resources of the Argentine Confederation?' And their minds were an utter blank upon the subject. 'Do you know what their population is, and what their sources of revenue might be?' No answer could I get. 'Could you point out on the map to me within 2,000 or 3,000 miles where the territory lies?' And their minds were an utter blank; there was no answer. I state this as an absolute positive fact that has occurred within my own experience, and I should think amongst 20 or 30 different brokers . . .

Newton stressed that the advisory function had become increasingly indispensable to the occupation of stockbroking, gave other instances (including the Honduras loans) of woeful ignorance and complete inability to make an objective analysis, and offered for consideration his remedy 'that before a man is admissible to be a member of the Stock Exchange, he should have to undergo that which all men in any responsible position in life have to undergo, namely, an examination to show his capacity to act in a position where a great deal of responsibility is thrown upon him'.

Incompetence was one thing, dishonesty another. J. Smith Latham had been one of the big speculators of the early 1870s, with particularly massive dealings in French loans and Great Northern 'A' railway stock, and he proceeded to detail to the Commission how a conspiracy between his broker and other members had taken place to his severe detriment: 'When things were low, and it would have been right to buy they had advised me not to buy, but in the meantime they went and bought, and then sold to me at a higher price when they rose, so that between the lot I was very considerably done'. Latham was especially bitter that, having lost some £9,000 and brought this conspiracy to the attention of the Stock Exchange Committee in the summer of 1873, that body had failed to punish the offenders with adequate severity, in particular suspending his broker for three years rather than expelling him for life. He also took the opportunity, in a prepared statement, to offer a more general critique of the Stock Exchange: 'Secrecy permeates every branch, pervades all the acts, and shrouds the *arcana* of that mighty body – secrecy is the inherent and palpable cause of all its misdoings in the past, and the blot which, if not removed, must ever attend it, with its demon-like influence, in the future.' He went on to stress 'the unbounded facilities at present existing for collusion between the broker and jobber'; 'the total and entire absence of any check over the actions of stockbrokers who may be dealing for absent clients'; the fact that, amidst prevailing speculation and market-rigging, 'a would-be investor cannot possibly be in a position to know whether he is not about to plunge into a stock at its full "bull" height, until he finds, to his cost, that it soon commences to drop day by day and hour by hour'; and the iniquities of the Committee itself. Here Latham's invective reached full pitch:

> The Committee of the Stock Exchange is in one word corrupt. I am not using language one iota too strong when I say this . . . How can it be otherwise? The Committee is an irresponsible body. They frame their own laws to suit their own objects. Such of their laws as are framed with a view to protect the public, and these are few, they disregard when challenged to do so, by an outraged and plundered and indignant 'outsider', as I have proved to my cost . . . After they have heard his case they hold meetings in private conclave, and decide upon the best steps to take to insure, not the safety and well-being of the public, but the immunity of their own body from the effects of malpractices of portions of them. Protest after protest is read but with no influence whatever. Every advance is met with a corresponding frown from the vice-chairman, until one is forcibly reminded of the Inquisition. Even during the course of the

investigation the committee room is constantly being cleared, the accuser and the accused being thrust out, are brought face to face in an ante-room, whilst a private discussion is going on about procedure, and secrets of committee-men's practices, and how certain revelations will affect the whole body . . .

Septimus Scott, chairman of the benighted thirty, could not resist an intervention at the end of Latham's *tour de force*:

Do I understand you to object to speculative business as such? – Entirely.
I thought you said that you had been a large operator yourself? – Yes, I have been.
Then you really did what you think is wrong? – I certainly did, and earnestly desire to attest to the infamy and degradation which are its inseparable accompaniment.

The Stock Exchange never took kindly to exhibitions of piety, and no doubt Latham's friends advised him to stay well away in the future from Capel Court, or that 'plague spot' as he liked to call it.[13]

Predictably, the elephantine scale of evidence produced a mouse of a report. There were, when it came to it, only four significant recommendations put forward on a majority basis by the Royal Commission: that legislation was required in order to prevent pre-allotment dealings; that 'some public functionary' should determine certain questions relating to settlement and official quotation; that the Stock Exchange should be incorporated, as opposed to continuing as a voluntary, self-regulating institution; and that the public should be allowed to watch the members going about their business. 'Some minor proposals may be adopted', thought *The Times*, 'but they are certainly not of a kind to transform the Stock Exchange.' In particular, it saw the question of incorporation as more or less irrelevant, while as for a proposed ban on pre-allotment dealings, 'it is obvious that the prohibition would extend to honest transactions as well as to those that are dishonest, and in thus becoming offensive to the morality of the Stock Exchange would prove a dead letter'. To the even more *laissez-faire*, non-interventionist *Economist*, the whole thing showed once again that 'it is impossible to establish a tribunal whose verdict should effectively sift out the false from the true, and separate the doings of the honest man from those of the thief'.[14] In practice, the report elicited an almost entirely negative response from both government and the Stock Exchange itself. Pre-allotment dealings remained the norm; settlement and quotation remained wholly within the Committee's jurisdiction; the Stock Exchange remained a self-regulating, decidedly unincorporated body; and would-be public spectators remained excluded for another three-quarters of a century. The club, in short, preferred to stay just that, and the contrary trend of outside opinion was not yet strong enough to do anything about it.

It was a club, however, whose prestige in the larger world had hardly risen as a result of the events and successive inquiries of the 1870s. Such anyway was the judgement of T. H. S. Escott, leading journalist as well as author of an incisive survey published in 1879 on *England: Its People, Polity, and Pursuits*. His assessment of stockbroking is a reminder that there was a way yet to go before the stereotypical mid-twentieth-century image of the pinstriped paragon of boring respectability:

> Roughly it may be said professions in England are valued according to their stability, their remunerativeness, their influence, and their recognition by the State. These conditions may partially explain the difference which English society draws between the callings of the merchant and the stockbroker. Stockbrokers make immense fortunes; but there attaches to them a suspicion of precariousness infinitely in excess of that which, in some degree or other, necessarily attaches to all fortunes accumulated in commerce or trade . . .

Escott then discussed the noble heritage and the stability of being a merchant, before continuing in a delightfully malicious passage that may or may not have been pinned on the walls of Capel Court:

> It is different with the stockbroker, whose social position is so sudden that it cannot yet be looked upon as assured – whose wealth, though great, has the garish hue of luck, and the glories associated with which may dissolve themselves at any moment into thin air, like Aladdin's palace, and who himself is popularly supposed to be more or less on the tenterhooks of expectation and anxiety from morning to night. The merchant drives to his place of business in a family brougham or barouche; the stockbroker drives to the station, where he takes the morning express to the City, in a smart dog-cart, with a high-stepping horse between the shafts, and a very knowing-looking groom at his side.
>
> Such, at least, is the conception formed by the public of the two men of business, and it indicates not incorrectly the corresponding view of English society. The British merchant is very probably a member of Parliament; the instances in which stockbrokers are members of Parliament at the present day might be counted on something less than the fingers of one hand. The life of the ideal stockbroker is one of display; that of the ideal merchant, one of dignified grandeur or opulent comfort. Possessed of a certain amount of education, often acquired at a public school,

sometimes both at Eton and Oxford, the stockbroker of the period has decided social aspirations. He makes his money easily, and he spends it lightly in procuring all the luxuries of existence. He marries a handsome wife, sets up a showy establishment, lays in a stock of choice wines, hires a French cook; he has carriages and horses, a box at the opera, stalls at theatres and concerts innumerable. He belongs to one or two good though not always first-rate clubs. He has acquaintances in the highest circles, and congratulates himself on being in society. But the blissful experience is not one in which his wife shares. She has to be content with all the talk, stories, and scandal of society which she hears retailed at her husband's table by the young guardsmen and other patrician guests who readily accept the invitations to a house where cook and cellar are both excellent, where the hostess and such other ladies as may be present are pretty or attractive. As a consequence of this, there is a copious stream of male visitors at the residence of the fortunate speculator in scrip and shares, while the lord and master of the household is occupied in the City. Perhaps an uncharitable world begins to talk; at any rate, the glitter and show of the *ménage* acquire a certain flavour of Bohemianism, between which and the animating spirit of English society the only sympathy that exists is of a purely superficial kind . . .[15]

CHAPTER SEVENTEEN

The Ties that Bind

In January 1869 Arthur Munby, diarist of Victorian society and its underside, took a pleasingly melancholic stroll:

> In the afternoon, I rambled through some of the old backstreets of the City: the best possible substitute, on Sundays, for a quiet country walk. The course of the broad new street which is to run from Blackfriars northeastward, is marked by heaps of ruin; but these were quiet and lovely, and full of meaning and pathos. The old houses that encircled S. Ann's Blackfriars are gone, and the church stands high and bare above the open clearing. Just beyond it, are lines of tall costly buildings, facing at present nothing but ruined cellars and the débris of streets destroyed. Then came a mountainous hill, on the top of which a dozen withered trees, planted foursquare, stood out against the grey cold sky. They were almost all that remains of Doctors' Commons, except a few broken archways, & the foundations of what was the Probate Court. These, and the trees, and the hill itself, will all be carted away . . . Triumphant new things, and decaying old, are here brought into the sharpest saddest contrast. But, a little further on, in Great Trinity Lane, I found many quiet unmolested old houses, many silent unfrequented passages and little yards, with an old water tub at the far end, an old hooded doorway and mullioned kitchen window, an old whitecapped woman sitting peacefully before the fire within: places that are like rural England, that are hundreds of miles away from common London life. And so I came round over sombre Southwark Bridge, and back by the homely waterside streets to Blackfriars, where the river swirls through the half finished arches of the new bridge.[1]

The new street causing so much devastation, and now in the process of completion, was Queen Victoria Street, soon to include the Mappin and Webb turreted fantasy in Gothic at its top end. There could be no reversing the trend towards commercial palaces and away from old water tubs. By 1871 there were 75,000 residents in the City and 200,000 daytime workers, by 1881 the respective figures were 51,000 and 261,000. Many City churches were demolished: St Mary Somerset

(1867) on the west corner at Upper Thames Street; All Hallows Staining (1870) off Mincing Lane; St Mildred's (1872) in Poultry, where there had been a church on the site since the twelfth century; St Martin Outwich (1874) at the south corner of Bishopsgate and Threadneedle Street; St Antholin's (1875) on a corner of Budge Row, complete with one of Wren's very best spires, sold as scrap for a fiver; All Hallows the Less (1876) near Cannon Street railway station; and St Dionis Backchurch (1878) close to Fenchurch Street.

Meanwhile, some at least of the critics enthused. 'The City of London . . . is becoming more and more the *office* of the world. Stately buildings replace the ugly and cramped houses of the Georgian era, and these buildings are almost entirely parcelled out in offices. The City lives out of town,' crowed the *Builder* in 1868, echoed three years later by the *Architect*: 'There are few spaces in Europe of equal size which can compare for modern architectural interest with the mile radius round the Exchange . . . It may be that the exigencies of business-life, and the necessity which seems to grow stronger every day for putting on a good outside appearance, account for much of the elaborate and, one may say, lavish expenditure which has been made on buildings only intended for mere business purposes.'[2]

Mansion House Chambers, built in 1872 on the south side of Queen Victoria Street and containing some 500 rooms, epitomised the dawning age of the office block. But there was another approach, and the next year Norman Shaw, already renowned for his country houses, exhibited to general amazement at the Royal Academy a drawing of New Zealand Chambers that he was about to build in Leadenhall Street. Taking much of its inspiration from the nearby house of the Elizabethan merchant Sir Paul Pindar (itself soon to make way for an expanded Liverpool Street Station), its lovely oriels and overall lightness of touch pointed away from prevailing architectural tyrannies and towards the coming 'Queen Anne' revolution. Shaw himself was very much the coming man: in 1874 he was commissioned to rebuild Martins, partly on the old Garraway's site; and in 1880 Barings asked him to increase the available space in the Bishopsgate counting house and design a new frontage. This he did, using the finest, costliest materials, but in the most discreet, solidly unpretentious way: a further reminder, if reminder was needed, that architectural show in the City tended to emanate from those with something still to prove.[3]

People are usually more interesting than buildings, and early in 1868 a minor stir was caused when Lord Walter Campbell, nineteen years old, decided to try his luck in the City, starting at the bottom. The possibility emerged of a junior clerkship at the London branch of Rathbones, and Lidderdale, in sardonic vein, gave his reluctant approval:

> I presume it is hardly needful to explain to the Duke of Argyll that his Son will meet in our Office with no respect of persons but what is due to merit & faithful service – that he will have to begin at the lowest step, copy letters, go out with messages, prepare tea samples for tasting, run to the Post Office & fulfil every duty required of other junior clerks. This is not very agreeable especially to young men of Ld Walter's age, but unless he is prepared to take business ab initio he had better try another career.

For Lord Walter and almost everyone else in the vast clerical army, daily life in the City remained manual and laborious. It is true that in 1873 the first typewriter was spotted in the square mile, but it would be many years before it became a standard feature of office furniture – not least because of an innate reluctance to employ women typists, eventual superceders of the traditional male copying clerks. Barings recruited its first female member of staff in 1873, and by the mid-1880s there were ten of them, and Shaw thoughtfully provided a separate entrance. In general, though, they were still a somewhat *rara avis*. This conservatism was encouraged by the continuing small size of most staffs: less than thirty at Kleinworts by 1871, despite the firm's increasing prosperity, while five years later at Heseltine Powell, leading stockbrokers specialising in American issues, there were only seven on the books.[4] Put another way, these firms were small, self-contained worlds in which complete, indeed arbitrary power rested in the hands of the senior partner of the day, usually abetted in the fine detail by his office manager or (in the case of rather larger concerns) his departmental heads.

In 1874 the Civil Service Inquiry Commission quizzed William Newmarch, the robust and well-known secretary of Glyn Mills, about how he managed things:

> Do you think that any system of increase of salary by seniority merely would be likely to answer? – We could not carry on our business upon that plan at all. It would not answer. The state of efficiency at which the establishment has arrived (and its efficiency is generally admitted in the City) has arisen in the largest degree from every man knowing at the end of the year he will be dealt with according to his merits; that if he has turned out inefficient his salary will either not be increased, or will very likely be temporarily reduced, or that in an extreme case the man will be sent away altogether.

And they feel a sense of justice, and know that they will be promoted if they are worth it? – That sentiment is most entirely felt, and it operates in the strongest manner.

A few years later the following notice was sent round to staff by Barnetts, Hoares & Co:

> Complaints having frequently arisen owing to the bad writing of some of the clerks, the House wish it to be understood that in considering the increase of salaries, the question of writing will, for the future, form an important subject of consideration, and while a bad report on writing will materially affect the question of salary to the disadvantage of the bad writer, the House will be prepared to give special gratuities to those clerks who may render themselves conspicuous for the good book-keeping.

Yet it was rarely a thoroughgoing internal meritocracy, if only because of the strong element of paternalism that often obtained in practice. At Glyns itself, Lord Hillingdon, a solid, old-fashioned senior partner, would regularly invite the staff to cricket weeks at his country home near Sevenoaks; while at the Royal Exchange Assurance, the directors maintained generous pension arrangements, albeit at their own pleasure and entirely informal, and only in the most exceptional cases made someone redundant. In the more successful firms a benign paternalism came cheap at the price. In 1878, a not particularly profitable year, the thirty-five members of staff at Hambros were paid salaries totalling some £10,000 (less than £300 a head), while the three partners had to content themselves with £69,000, of which the lion's share (£52,000) went to Everard Hambro himself.[5]

Women were definitely not welcome in the coarser departments of the Bank of England. Allan Fea was to recall the very rowdy private drawing office that he entered as a clerk in 1881:

> The pandemonium was a little startling to a novice – jokes shouted from one end of the office to the other; the singing of a line from some popular song, winding up with 'Amen' in a solemn cadence of about a hundred voices. If you were not good at dodging you were liable at any time to have your hat knocked off your head by a flying Pass-book, for more hats were worn than not . . .

Typical nicknames given to clerks at the Bank included such cerebral concoctions as 'The Dead Horse', 'The Dook', 'The Ice-Cream Man', 'Job Lot', 'The Ghost', 'The Stiff Un', 'The Maiden Aunt' and (especially meaningful) 'The 'Orrid Old 'Og'. As for the heads of department, some were 'very rough diamonds', with the young Fea often wondering 'how such illiterate people could ever have got the job'. And he quotes the earful that a young 'masher' received having made the tactical mistake of turning up at the Old Lady wearing a monocle: 'What 'ave yer got that pane of glass in yer heye for? Best stick another in yer 'at, and make yerself into a bloomin' telescope.'[6]

It was marginally more decorous, if perhaps less enjoyable, at the Atlas Assurance in Cheapside, where Samuel Pipkin, a twenty-year-old hopeful from the Chilterns, secured a clerical berth in March 1868:

> All went merry as a marriage bell until the arrival of the first renewal period. After the commencement of those 15 strenuous days, with crowds clamouring for attention all day long, a cash book was thrown on to my desk – 'There you are, Mr Pipkin – there you are, take cash, enter what you receive in that book – you'll find receipts in numerical order, and if you are short you'll have to make it up. Ask everyone before issuing the receipt "Are any alterations required?" and, if so, send them over to the other side', where endorsements and new policies were attended to. Those were the elaborate instructions given by the Chief Cashier, who never wasted words in business, although he hummed operatic airs all day long. One had to pick up the right way of doing his work by doing it as seemed to him best and receiving corrections in unclassical and unquotable English. There was no *disposition* to teach in those days ... Juniors had then to ferret out the why and wherefore of office duties, or perform them by imitation or rule of thumb ... And so five years of humdrum work were spent, work which I could have done equally well at 14 years of age – lightened chiefly by the ever flowing tide of humans past my window, and now and then by the glimpse of a pretty face amongst them.
>
> But oh! it was awful! nearly all above me young – no sign of business development to create chances of promotion – a dismal vision of rounded shoulders, narrowed chest and atrophied muscles to be rewarded by a possible £200 a year at the age of 33 and ever after. The consolation was – the hours were short.
>> 10 to 4, 10 to 4, and then at 4
>> Brush your hat and flee the door.
> That was all most of us thought of – to get away from the mill – the dreary round, the common task. And most, or very many, never *do* get away.

Pipkin himself went to the Commercial Union in 1873, but returned to the Atlas in 1884 and, as general manager, transformed it into a modern institution. His eventual reward was to deliver to his peers a paper with the time-honoured title 'Fifty Years' Reminiscences in the City'.[7]

No such paper, alas, appears among the publications of Sidney Webb. The son of a small London shopkeeper, he went in 1875 at the age of sixteen into the office of a colonial broker. 'Disgusted with the petty cheating' (in Beatrice's subsequent words) that he encountered there, he started evening classes and in 1881 passed into the Inland Revenue, eventually taking his oblique revenge on the square mile by marrying an in-law of a leading partner of Huths. Similarly disinclined to last the mercantile course were the offspring of Julius Beerbohm, a Lithuanian who had arrived in the City in about 1830, prospered as a corn merchant, became a leading figure on the Baltic Exchange, and founded that invaluable bulletin, *The Evening Corn Trade List*. In the 1870s he employed all three of his sons as clerks, with a view to training them up for the succession. However, Ernest preferred to become a sheep farmer in the Cape; Julius an explorer in Patagonia; and Herbert a professional actor, taking the stage name of Tree. There was yet one more son, born in 1872, but the incomparable Max did not even try the joys of Bishopsgate Street.[8]

A good many men of foreign extraction continued to play a leading part in the City. In 1873, for instance, the Baltic Exchange's first printed list of members featured eleven bearing the name of Ralli, six of Mavrogordato, and six of Schilizzi. The dozen members of the Committee of Lloyd's in 1871 included George Joachim Goschen (chairman), Henry Caspar Heintz, Frederic Bernstein Natusch, James Bischoff and Solomon Israel Da Costa. An entry for May 1877 in the manager's information book at the Union Bank of London scrutinises M. R. Meyer of 16 Mark Lane:

> Meyer told me he is a native of Copenhagen where his business chiefly lies. Showed me his original memoranda in which is exhibited the gradual increase of his capital from a little below £5,000 in 1865 (when he commenced business) to somewhat beyond £50,000 at the end of 1876. His bad debts during the whole time have been less than £3,000 and from the list of his debtors, which he produced, his risks appear well spread, and his business is evidently well managed.

The 1870s, moreover, were characterised by a particularly able intake, including in 1872 Baron Joseph Rüffer, whose Rüffer & Sons quickly became a leading force in the financing of worldwide imports of goods into Europe. The Stock Exchange, with its relatively lax entrance qualifications, was especially open to foreign talent, perhaps epitomised by Ludwig Messel. His family had been bankers and financiers in Darmstadt for two generations; and soon after the Franco-Prussian

War he came to England, founding in his mid-twenties what before long ranked as one of the City's most successful stockbroking firms.[9]

Events in newly unified Germany further encouraged the drift, above all the creation in 1876 of a uniform currency, prompting a whole generation of Frankfurt-based operators in inter-German exchange business to migrate to London in pursuit of the rapidly expanding opportunities for dealing in securities between the different international markets. Arguably this was a sphere which the City's established merchant banks should have moved into – after all, they continued to control international money flows and had no shortage of international contacts – but in practice they preferred, for another hundred years, to leave the world of international securities dealing to members of the Stock Exchange, headed by opportunistic newcomers from abroad. Biedermann, Schwabacher, Lichtenstadt became among others familiar, not always welcome names in Capel Court. Often the hostility was but thinly veiled, a fact that perhaps explains Lionel Cohen's defiant outburst to the Royal Commission in 1877: 'It has been made a charge that there are adventurers, Jews, Greeks, and so on. I am a Jew myself, and possibly, therefore, not a fitting judge of the opprobrium intended to be conveyed by such a charge; and I do not see why it should be thrown (if it is a type of degradation) in the teeth of the Committee of the Stock Exchange that they impose no test of creed or nationality . . .'[10]

The City of the 1870s remained a competitive milieu. Abraham de Mattos Mocatta, of the leading bullion dealers Mocatta & Goldsmid, would not have denied the point, as he looked back at the end of 1872 on Ralli's having gone to a rival for its gold:

> We are exceedingly sorry as Pixley has never yet been in Ralli's door, and has now an excuse for going in, and may well sell Silver. Ralli's being very old friends of ours are not likely to give Pixley any order for Silver, but he is a pushing man & it is most vexatious. Also it is a step towards his getting a monopoly of small gold bars.

However, to view the City of this period – or, indeed, of any period – as a fully-fledged Darwinian meritocracy, where talent would always out and only the fittest survived, is to misconceive the essence of such a tight-knit, interconnected society, a society that has been aptly conceived as comprising (at its upper end anyway) a cluster of sometimes overlapping elites. Analysis of the composition of the court of directors of the Royal Exchange insurance company demonstrates continuous representation through the nineteenth century of members of the Grenfell and Lubbock families, leading mercantile and banking dynasties respectively. Blood mattered. The second son of George Warde Norman, for example, became a partner in Finlay Hodgson and in turn Barings, while the fourth son (the father of Montagu) became a partner in Martins in 1880, followed four years later by the seventh son. George Joachim Goschen may have abandoned active business in 1866, but one of his brothers became senior partner of the family firm and a director of the Bank of England, while another brother became a director of the London Joint Stock Bank. More recent newcomers also surrendered to the family way; the foreign bankers A. Keyser & Co was consciously maintained by Samuel Montagu & Co as an overflow firm for partners' relatives. And on the first floor of the Royal Exchange, overlooking the Iron Duke on his horse, blood truly ran thicker than water:

> There is, probably, no society or corporation in existence in which the hereditary element is so strong as in Lloyd's. Most of the names found in the old minute-books of Lloyd's a century ago still stand in the list of members, and of the more prominent names connected with the history of the ancient institution the only one missing is that of Angerstein, still represented, however, by his partner, Mr Francis Rivaz, admitted to the 'Coffee-house' in 1814 . . .

wrote a historian of Lloyd's in 1876. For further chapter and verse he might have cited the Secretan family, which in the third quarter of the century produced no less than five sons who made their careers there.[11]

There were in the City many other ties that counted. These ties could derive from school or university, they could be sporting or military, they could take any number of forms – but what signified was that they existed and were held by the great majority of practitioners to be indispensable. William Lidderdale, as usual, offered a wry slant on the phenomenon. He reported back to Liverpool in March 1867 on the opening of a permanent London branch (Rathbones sharing a new, purpose-built building in Fenchurch Street with those other sceptical outsiders, Kleinworts), and he was clearly amused by the behaviour of the inhabitants of Mincing Lane, behaviour that through force of habit had become something like second nature: 'Brokers are beginning to call at this office touting for business – professing a keen desire to make my personal acquaintance & "be of service" to the Firm. One or two gentlemen claimed to have fathers who "knew the name of your House 40 years ago" while another included it in his own juvenile recollections . . .'[12]

Nowhere did personal ties matter more than in the City's most rarefied circles, where the stakes were at their highest, the demands of trust at their most pervasive. Without a doubt one of the most prominent figures in those circles was Bertram Currie, by the 1870s the main man at Glyn Mills, which was still regarded as the leading City bank after the Bank of England itself. Not everyone fully appreciated his qualities: 'He was extremely clever, intellectual and agreeable . . . He was an avowed and mocking Atheist, extremely satirical and cynical, and I have never dined there without hearing him pass bitter and ironical remarks upon people.' This verdict was passed after his death by the wife of a former Governor of the Bank and she could have been dining at any one of three residences – in Whitehall, in Coombe near Kingston, or in Minley Manor on Bagshot Heath. Currie's intellectual authority was massive, he was regarded as a pillar of monetary orthodoxy, and in the words of Gladstone, in a rather differently couched tribute, 'he was so entirely first among the men of the City, that it is hard to measure the distance between him and the second place'. Currie himself, as one might guess from such warmth, was a committed Liberal in his politics, but declined to take the seat in the Commons that was his for the asking – it would, he said, 'have diverted my mind from money-getting'. In the City, his closest personal tie was with Ned Baring, in the 1870s the rising but not yet dominant force at 8 Bishopsgate, the man whom Joshua Bates twenty years earlier had found 'clever' but 'unattentive' and 'fond of society'. As young men they had often rented a summer house together on Wimbledon Common; by this time they were neighbours at Coombe; and it was only natural that Baring should have been godfather to Currie's eldest son.[13] It was an imperishable connection, the sort that ensured one friend's willingness always to go the extra mile on behalf of the other.

The woman who passed the harsh verdict on Currie was Constance Smith, married to Hugh Colin Smith. He was the third son of John Abel Smith; the eldest, Jervoise, was a partner in the family bank at 1 Lombard Street, but Hugh, after an early apprenticeship at Mathesons, made his career at Hay's Wharf, a large warehouse on the south side of the river. He was closely involved in its establishment in 1863 and remained a partner for almost half a century. As Constance reflected towards the end of his career: 'Gentlemen had not been Wharfingers before, and it was considered a rather infra-dig profession. That did not affect Hugh; he set to work and he thinks few people have had so successful and fortunate a life.' It was a mark of his prosperity as well as his name that he became a Bank of England director in 1876. *His* particular friend was undoubtedly Everard Hambro, who was not only married to a cousin of his but also lived next door to Hugh and Constance at 70 Princes Gate, just to the south (the right side) of Hyde Park. For three successive summers in the early 1870s the two families rented Mount Clare, a handsome property in Roehampton subsequently acquired by Hugh. Constance even began to harbour fears concerning Everard's ascendancy over her husband. It was certainly a physical ascendancy, for Everard towered over everyone at 6 feet 5 inches. He was also just starting to come into his own: senior partner at Hambros from 1877, a Bank director from 1879. There was little nonsense about him. 'Mr Hambro's ideas are always plain', the *Bankers' Magazine* noted some years later, adding that 'he has the City faculty of summing up a conclusion in three words.'[14]

Hambro was no intellectual, but several City eminents besides Currie manifestly were. None more so in the public mind than Sir John Lubbock, senior partner of Robarts, Lubbock & Co of Lombard Street. Honorary secretary and later chairman to the Committee of London Clearing Banks, a Liberal MP responsible for not only the Falsification of Accounts Act that benefited the few but also the Bank Holiday Act of 1871 that benefited the many, president at different times of innumerable scholarly societies or institutes (Statistical, Entomological, Ethnological, Anthropological, Linnean), a distinguished naturalist given to the study of the habits of insects, an equally distinguished archaeologist, and a prominent Darwinian whose *Origin of Civilization and the Primitive Condition of Man* was much translated – he was the very exemplar of the high-minded, broad-minded City banker. Lubbock was also the first president of the Institute of Bankers, founded in 1879, the first treasurer of which was Richard Biddulph Martin, himself closely linked with the Royal Geographic Society, the Anthropological Institute and the Royal Statistical Society, as well as being one of the early masters of photography. There was disagreement between the two men about the character of the Institute of Bankers: Lubbock wanted its syllabus to be broadly academic, Martin argued for an approach more rooted in current banking practice, and it was Martin who carried the day. Or in the words of his brother John some years later, 'if there is one term of reproach greater than another which can be levelled at a Lombard Street banker it is to say he is a theoretical man'.[15]

The question of the practical was a sensitive one. Henry Hucks Gibbs was a scribbler of the vigorous epistle (despite the loss of his right hand in a gun accident); architecture, books, pictures and genealogy all fell within his capacious interests; ecclesiastical politics fascinated him; he wrote authoritatively on card games (especially ombre) as well as questions of currency; and, a dedicated philologist, he contributed the better part of the letter 'C' to the *Oxford English Dictionary*. In its profile of him, however, the *Bankers' Magazine* was at pains to emphasise his proficiency in the counting house: 'His is a mind which is peculiarly open to the influence of facts. We should say he is really a man of business, and only by accident a man of theory – in other words, his theories insensibly fit his appreciation of facts. This, of course, is quite as it should be, and perhaps Mr Gibbs would not desire a better compliment.' Perhaps, but the fact was that the house of Antony Gibbs was moving into a period of relative decline, precisely because neither he nor his sons gave the business sufficient single-minded attention.[16] A gentle downwards progression similarly characterised the firms of Lubbock and Martin.

Gibbs was the first merchant banker to be a Governor of the Bank of England, but other capable governors in the 1870s included Benjamin Buck Greene, John William Birch and Edward Howley Palmer, all more or less traditional merchants, though Birch was a banker also. Greene's father had been a merchant trading with the West Indies, his own firm was Blyth & Greene of Philpot Lane, trading largely in Mauritian sugar; he lived at Kensington Palace Gardens and had a country estate at Midgham in Berkshire, where he built a church with a family vault in which he was eventually buried. He seems to have been a thoroughly reliable operator, a member of the Bank's inner councils for many years, and renowned for his private collection of statistics relating to its accounts. Nor was there anything mercurial about Birch. He was the son of a Suffolk clergyman, mastered Spanish as a young man, and eventually became senior partner of Mildred, Goyeneche & Co, the Hispano-English merchanting firm of his maternal uncle. At his offices a large card was displayed prominently on the mantelpiece in his private room: '*Business*. Call on a business man in business hours only on business; transact your business, and go about your business, in order to give him time to finish his business'. If small talk was low on his agenda, so was the free play of ideas. He was, one profile noted, 'impatient of the refinements of theorists', and had an almost Gradgrindian reverence for the facts. Horsley Palmer's son would probably have felt a temperamental affinity. Many years later his granddaughter recalled Edward Howley Palmer as an old man, not all that long after the end of his governorship and while he was still a director of the Bank:

He was a short man with a preternaturally long upper lip, a small grey eye in a large face and ginger hair. He was to me very alarming and had an early-Victorian habit of spitting into the fire ... Undoubtedly my grandfather was a lesser man than his father. I never remember hearing him make a remark of any length. He was surrounded by a complete and solid if austere comfort and he had the most perfect taste in old silver. His gilt Georgian sugar sifters and basin were heavily and I fancy fruitlessly protected in his will. This perfect taste failed him hopelessly when it came to buying pictures, and his walls were hung in later years with Sidney Cooper's cows for which he paid enormous prices ...

Etched vividly in my memory is a Sunday spent with my grandfather when I was eight and staying with him in London. I see myself in Sunday clothes walking in decorous silence through the Sunday stillness of Queen's Gate Gardens to 11 o'clock matins, hand-in-hand with my grandfather in a top hat and with an overcoat, his ebony stick tapping on the pavement. At St Stephen's, Gloucester Road, he had a comfortable pitch pine pew where he growled the responses and some suitable hymns. After Church I think I was exercised in the Park and then taken home to lunch. This I ate in solemn state in mingled pride and terror alone with him. The dining-room was rather dark and full of mahogany and silver. I felt the smallest and most worthless thing yet made. The large and deliciously tender English sirloin, the undercut uppermost, was perfectly carved by my grandfather on the table. I suppose I dimly realized that I was watching an artist at work and assisting at a solemn and in its way perfect ritual and the agony of humiliation that I felt when a gravy spot appeared beside my plate on the spotless and exquisite damask it still hurts me to recall. It was something terrible that had happened; something disordered and sordid in a perfect world of shining wood and silver and linen and well-cooked food of perfect choice; something that could never never be put right. The stern rebuke I got was wholly unneeded. We had a pudding for which my grandfather heated the sauce in a long silver saucepan on the table, and then he slept and I fled to a book, later to be re-dressed and taken forth again ... The day ends for my recollection in a solemn walk home in spring twilight, its atmosphere of soft greys and raw siennas unlighted by a single recollection of anything in the nature of a joke or words that would invite the confidence of a small person. Whether this entire aloofness was boredom or fear on the part of my grandfather I can never know. I think it was the latter. He remains a mystery from which only one solid fact emerges; his extreme generosity in money matters amounting to weakness to his wife and sons.[17]

Weakness indeed, for both sons proved something of financial ne'er-do-wells – the second, Cecil Horsley Palmer, trying his luck unsuccessfully on the Stock Exchange – and in general ended hopes of a Palmer dynasty in the City.

In this ever-changing world, personal touch and personal contacts both counted for much, but so too did staying power and, it has to be said, an adequate modicum of native ability. Take the faintly improbable figure of J. H. Puleston, as recalled in the memoirs of the late-Victorian company promoter H. Osborne O'Hagan. A poor medical student who emigrated to the States, he was by the late 1860s one of the managers of Wells, Fargo & Co, a job which 'brought him into touch with the greater part of the better-class visitors to that country, and as he had charming manners and was at all times ready to go out of his way to do things for people, he formed quite a considerable and valuable connexion amongst useful people'. The upshot was that when the leading New York house of Jay Cooke, McCulloch & Co decided to set up a branch in London and wanted a socially acceptable figure to be its nominal head, it 'came to the conclusion that the genial and popular J. H. Puleston was the man'. For a few years, on the back of the American boom, 'things went swimmingly with him', and 'he bought a beautiful estate – Marden Park, in Surrey – entertained on a large scale, and engaged in the fashionable hobby of horse trading', besides preparing to become Conservative MP for Devonport. Then in 1873 occurred the turning point, as Cooke came unstuck and the London branch was abruptly closed:

> It left J. H. Puleston at a loose end. No doubt very ample compensation was given to console him for the loss of his partnership and of his high position. But Puleston was ever the multi-millionaire, and could spend money like water, but he had not the training for the making of a successful financier, a role he now assumed.
>
> He . . . started a small and insignificant private bank in Princes Street, which he called Puleston, Brown & Co. In this, I think, he committed a mistake, for it called attention to the 'come down' from the great banking house, one of the largest in Lombard Street, to the unknown firm in two or three rooms in Princes Street, and his new firm was a bank in name only. His business of Puleston, Brown & Co was to some extent that of financiers, but he cut no great figure in the financial world once he ceased his connexion with the American bankers. His popularity still enabled him to hold his head high, both in political and social life, but the heyday of it was gone. He still thought in millions, even if he did not deal in millions. He always seemed to be hard up, and spent a good deal if he did not make a good deal. It was essential for his political and social aspirations that he should continue to make a good show, which he did, but only at cost to his peace of mind. I christened him 'The Impecunious Millionaire', a most appropriate name which attached itself to him . . . [18]

At about the time that Puleston was starting to fade out as a significant City presence, another name was being rescued from what would
have been an even more total City oblivion. In 1875 the merchanting
firm of Robert Benson & Co went bankrupt, at which point the
young Robert Benson was lucky enough to be taken into partnership
by John Walter Cross, an old family friend and someone with fully the
charm of Puleston and a lot more capacity. Cross was then in his
mid-thirties, his background was posh Liverpool followed by two
years at Rugby, and he had worked in both New York and London for
the family merchanting firm of Dennistoun, Cross & Co. Cross put the
capital into Cross, Benson & Co, which began business in September
1875 and soon flourished as, in effect, a rather select investment house.
He had made the acquaintance of George Eliot, and in the course of the
1870s he was handling her investments, giving her a guided tour of
the Bank of England, and introducing her to the novel pleasures of lawn
tennis. He was even deputed to arrange with the fishmonger at Waterloo Station to send her 'the fish of the day' on Wednesdays and
Saturdays. In May 1880 he became her second husband, despite an age
difference of over twenty years, but by the end of the year she was
dead, leaving him heartbroken. He pulled out of the business with
Benson, who by now hardly needed him, and in time he transformed
himself into a thoroughly amiable London clubman, occasionally sending off well-argued letters on financial subjects to *The Times*. He died
in 1924 a forgotten figure, perhaps the only City man to have read
Dante in intimacy with a great English novelist.[19]

Richard Foster would never have dreamt of abandoning the square
mile, even after the shabby treatment of him by Baron d'Erlanger over
the Costa Rica loan. The experience in fact reinforced his determination that Knowles & Foster should remain a purely foreign banking
and merchanting business, concentrating on its strong South American
connection, avoiding financial operations as such. Foster was representative of a City that was slowly passing.[20] He was born in 1822, a
nephew of the founders of the firm; in 1836 he began as an office boy;
and in 1853 he became a partner, remaining one until 1909, the year
before his death. Brought up in Stoke Newington, he lived from 1862
to 1879 at Upper Clapton (from where he would travel to the City each
morning by bus), eventually moving to Chislehurst. He was a philanthropist on a large scale and a church-builder; he was a great walker;
he occupied his holidays taking his family to the sea; he disliked society;
he was abstemious and used only one razor in his life, that of his father;
and he believed himself to be the last man to wear a stock and

swallow-tail coat on the Royal Exchange. His garb was appropriately anachronistic, for the Royal Exchange itself was in palpable decline by the last quarter of the century.

But if Foster was 'old' City, who was 'new'? None has quite the claim of Ernest Cassel, the most remarkable presence in the square mile since Nathan Rothschild and a financial genius who would no more have thought of standing on 'Change as trying to force his way through the doors of Capel Court. Biographical legends grew apace even in his lifetime, but this much seems more or less certain:[21] Ernest Cassel was born in 1852, the son of a small-time banker in Cologne, and after serving a brief banking apprenticeship in that city, he arrived in Liverpool at the age of sixteen with only a bag of clothes and his violin. For a year he worked for a firm of grain merchants there. In April 1870 he secured a clerkship with the Anglo-Egyptian Bank in Paris. Then came the Franco-Prussian War and a speedy evacuation to London, where Cassel managed to obtain a berth with Bischoffsheim & Goldschmidt, then at the height of its energetic, thoroughly cosmopolitan, not always scrupulous powers. Cassel quickly made a mark: he not only was instrumental in saving a Jewish firm in Constantinople in which Bischoffsheims was interested but he also managed to pull some crucial legal irons out of the fire in relation to the house's notorious Central American loans. By 1874 he was manager at an annual salary of £5,000; and soon he was poised to begin his career as an independent financier owing allegiance to no one but himself. In an age of instant communications across the world and ever more mobile capital, his rapid ascent would reveal piquantly how leaden-footed the traditional arrangement of a family-based network had become. Such an ascent relied utterly on personal qualities. Not many found Cassel a likeable man – for all his undoubted integrity, he had little grace and less humour – but only a fool doubted his judgement or his willingness to back that judgement.

*

Inevitably the Overend Gurney crisis caused a considerable shake-up in the discount market. Of the seven companies formed since 1856, four (including of course Overends itself) went down; and two suffered so badly that they had to be reconstituted, the Discount Corporation as the United Discount Corporation and the General Credit & Finance Co as the General Credit & Discount Co. Only one, the National Discount Co, the original joint-stock discount house, came through unharmed – and in fact much strengthened – as its rivals fell by the wayside. The National stayed as clear market leader for the next twenty years, until the United Discount Corporation and the General Credit & Discount Co came together in 1885 to form the Union Discount Co; while in terms of the three remaining discount companies as a whole, it was estimated by the *Economist* in 1877 that they were responsible for almost a third of total business. The private firms, therefore, still had a considerable role to play. In fact, in the 1870s there was a plethora of such firms; ten or more had been created in the immediate wake of Overend Gurney's demise, seeking to do its business with the country banks once done with such aplomb by the Corner House. Most of these new enterprises were pretty small-scale, such as Gillett Brothers & Co of 72 Lombard Street, founded in August 1867 by Alfred and George Gillett, the sons of a Quaker banker in Banbury. A third brother, William, was not a partner, but his help was crucial – for several years he had been a partner in the Finch Lane bill-discounting business of Brightwen & Co and now introduced former clients to his brothers. He insisted on being paid very handsomely for this help, and in time much fraternal acrimony ensued. But otherwise it was a placid enough firm, and each day in the office began with a prayer meeting which it was compulsory for all clerks to attend.[22]

Operating on a quite different scale with a bill portfolio of several million pounds, the daddy of the private firms was Alexanders, the great gainer along with the National from the 1866 crisis. No doubt delighted to have seen off Overend Gurney, its business sense remained well-developed. 'Do you desire to put out more money against bills?' Lidderdale asked head office in December 1870, and after mentioning a possible firm he went on: 'Alexanders we also know & have had dealings with – they are keener & more "screwy" but can often be managed.' A nasty moment came in 1877 when some key partners defected to the National, but the firm announced that it intended to continue on a private basis, a move that received a warm response, like this from Lewis Loyd:

> It is the natural consequence of the high honour and integrity that have characterised your now long business life, and is its appropriate award. Large as the development of the Joint Stock principles has been of late years, and many as have been the advantages that in some respects it has offered to the trading community, it has not succeeded in shaking the confidence which a long course of honourable dealing and high character inspires in men's minds towards old established private firms. Your case furnishes a gratifying proof that the personal attachment which attends a

long continued intercourse even in the hard matters of business is far from being extinguished among us . . .

Recipient of this letter was George William Alexander, the very same who, with his mother, had rescued the firm after his father's death in 1819. The following year he retired – with the firm's capital at a comfortable £400,000 – but occasionally the old Quaker gentleman would still visit the Lombard Street office, try to get through the heavy swing doors, and say a courteous 'I thank thee' to one of the clerks who came to help him.[23]

   Whether or not to go public was also a matter of keen debate in the City's textile quarter, where the leading merchanting firms had benefited greatly from the Franco-Prussian War. To quote the official biographer of Sir George Williams, grand old man of the YMCA and senior partner of Hitchcock, Williams & Co from 1863 until 1906, when these words were written:

> It was largely owing to the sudden cessation, at this juncture, of supplies from the two great Continental countries that Britain held her position for so long as the one great market place of the world. For years Continental competition in the Colonies and in America was crushed, while the British retail draper, who in some cases had begun to buy direct from the Continent, finding his orders unfulfilled, was forced to fall back on the home wholesale houses, holding as they did the only stocks available. The trade of the civilised globe passed, of necessity, through British hands, for the United States was then only feeling its way into outside markets. French and German ports were closed to commerce, and all British stocks of drapery goods, which are so largely of Continental manufacture, increased immensely in value, while orders poured in to London from all parts of the world. These were the golden years of English commerce.

Indeed, the City's great textile merchants were approaching their meridian in the 1870s: quite apart from the temporary boom caused by Continental warfare, the continuing disintegrated structure of the British textile industry, involving in turn a continuing crucial lack of working capital, meant that the commission merchants of the City remained firmly in charge of credit and marketing. Capital, however, was the crux, and by 1873 a series of firms (though not including the two biggest warehouses, Cooks and Morleys) had decided to incorporate, thus giving up traditional family control. Morrisons had become the Fore Street Warehouse Co, with a capital of £420,000 in 1864, followed by Bradbury Greatorex (generously admitting 'a few gentlemen of capital and experience as shareholders'), Foster Porter, and Pawsons of St Paul's Churchyard.[24]

At least one man's life was peculiarly affected by the dilemma of whether or not to incorporate. Leaf, Sons & Co, of Old Change, was a leading, long-established firm which specialised in a wide variety of fancy goods, including silk, ribbons, velvet, crêpe, dress goods, flowers and feathers. In the mid-Victorian period it had been run by three brothers, who lived close together in the Norwood area and would arrive each morning as a trio, driven by a smart pair of horses, punctually to open the post at nine o'clock. Disaster struck in the early 1870s: in 1871 one brother died; not long afterwards the decision was taken, through a mixture of sentiment and family pride, not to incorporate; and in 1874 a second brother died and the health of the third completely broke down. None were old men, and it was left to a wholly inexperienced next generation of Leafs to attempt to fill the gap and counter a serious shortage of capital. One of the three cousins stepping into the breach was Walter Leaf, aged twenty-two, educated at Harrow and Trinity, Cambridge, and already a fine classicist. He had originally been marked out for the Bar, but now there was no choice:

> On February 3 [1875] for the first time I took my seat on an office stool, and began my studies in book-keeping, theoretical and practical. I learnt to post a ledger, to draw a cheque, to take a parcel of bills to the bill-brokers for discount, to write a letter to a tardy debtor threatening him with legal proceedings if he did not pay up, and the thousand and one bits of routine which have to be mastered. I made no pretence of liking the drudgery, but it had to be faced; and from the very first day I determined that it should not make me forget the higher intellectual interests.

Nor did it. Three years later a friend working on an edition of Homer was drowned, and Leaf took it over, to such effect that he was eventually acknowledged as the foremost Homeric scholar of the day. He was also a more than capable linguist, economist, musician and mountaineer, as well as a student of psychical research. The satisfying life of a Renaissance man stopped, however, as soon as he passed through the doors of Old Change. He began to keep a journal, and some random entries for 1879 have survived:

> Not very much to do, except to brood over the miseries of business. Everything is wretchedness. C.J.L. is being rapidly worn out by it. I shall be soon. Only Homer keeps me going.

I have taken to work as some men would have taken to drink – to drive
away my thoughts.
Worked with a heart as heavy as the rain.
This strain will soon be too much for me, and then we shall be obliged
to give up business.
Things in O.C. look damnable.

Almost half a century later, near the end of his life, Virginia Woolf
called for tea. She found him 'bubbling & chubby', and went on in her
diary: 'Plunge deep into Walter's life & it is all sound & satisfactory.
His son kisses him & says "Bless you father". He sinks back chuckling
on his cushions. He chooses a maccaroon. He tells a story . . . Only I
am exiled from this profound natural happiness.'[25] As so often with the
writer looking in from the outside on the man of business, she could
not have known the price that he had paid.

In the transition from 'family capitalism' to a more modern, corporate form of enterprise so much depended on individual personality, and
the story of Dalgety & Co, by the mid-1860s the City's largest importers of colonial wool, makes an illuminating case study.[26] Frederick
Dalgety was a rugged character, possessed little sophistication of mind,
and by the early 1870s was being tugged in two directions. There was
his deep, instinctive desire to found a dynastic succession, acquire many
acres for his progeny, and stick come-what-might to the traditional
partnership system. (It was unfortunate that his first son had not been
born until 1866, when he was almost fifty.) There was also the uncomfortable fact that to be a successful wool-importing merchant in London required an ever-greater provision of credit and sometimes capital
– whether trade credit for the clip, long-term loans to the growers in
Australia, or for a variety of other purposes. Equally uncomfortable
was the fact that wool finance houses, providing long-term finance to
squatters, and the City branches of colonial banks like the Bank of New
South Wales, marketing the wool of growers to whom they had lent
long-term, were becoming an increasingly active, competitive presence.
These trends left Dalgety flummoxed and angry. He believed that the
integrity of the City's well-established wool merchants and brokers was
being unfairly challenged, and his particular *bête noire* was a London
director of the Bank of New South Wales whom he called a 'little
Sydney blaguard [sic]'.

Dalgety seems to have hoped the problems would go away, and in
1878, with the founding generation of partners starting to drop out and
his own appetite for work diminishing, he recruited into the partnership E. T. Doxat, an established wool broker with another firm and

with the reputation for being (in the words of a Kleinworts' character book) 'very clever but not scrupulous'. By the early 1880s this highly able operator realised that there was only one realistic solution: to convert the firm into a public company. Dalgety was aghast: 'From my experience of companies I have a horror of them – and know full well that they cannot be managed to compete with private firms where partners act in accord and common prudence and energy are expressed.' That was one of his milder, more constructive comments, but eventually, after the death of his wife in 1883 (during her thirteenth confinement), he gave in. Incorporation took place the next year and Dalgety's survived as main players in Australian wool, even as trading conditions changed even more drastically towards the end of the century. Anyway, the dynastic strategy, if one can call it that, would have been a futile one. None of Dalgety's four sons seemed to have a thought in his head apart from shooting, riding and fishing, and when one of them at least tried out the office in Lombard Street, directly after leaving Eton in 1889, his father was soon reporting that 'he has taken a hatred to the work and says the confinement will kill him – he has begged me to send him to one of my stations in New Zealand'. And the old man added, with a certain nobility: 'He is gentlemanly and has no vices – so I hope he will make a good colonist.'

The coming of the telegraph, together with the increasing use of steamships and the opening of the Suez Canal in 1869, inevitably put pressure on traditional merchanting. Lidderdale was typically alert to these trends:

> I do not appreciate fully your objections to contracting here for future Shipments, altho' I agree with you in preferring to import for ourselves. If you knew how jute was worked by the Greek Houses I don't think you would consider a contract made here at all illegitimate. Some of the best Greek Marks are offered here much more than in Calcutta – Rallis, Schilizzis &c all were selling here freely last autumn at £2 below the equivalent of Calcutta prices for Jute of equal quality . . .

That was in 1869, and three years later he returned to the charge, bluntly telling his partners in Liverpool that 'unfortunately trade is changing, whether we like it or not', and that there was no alternative but to operate in produce afloat, in effect pursuing an arrivals and futures business, as opposed to the time-honoured method of buying through correspondents. 'Commission business has many merits, but it is disappearing, nevertheless, except on terms which make it of very little value.' But if the trend was towards mercantile specialism, some still opted for general commission merchanting. Charles Oppenheimer, for instance, was originally from Frankfurt, came over to London as a young man in the late 1850s, and with his brothers and a brother-in-law built up a large import-export business, first in Watling Street and then Finsbury Square. His firm over the years continued to deal in a vast range of commodities, controlling at one time or another most of the French sardine trade abroad and the import and export of German porcelain dolls, Black Forest cuckoo clocks (a great favourite down under) and briar pipes made in France, as well as importing for the home market skins, silks, exotic timber, gums, rugs and carpets, oriental china and Japanese lacquer work.[27]

There remained in the daily round of mercantile life a strong sense of continuity, even of ritual. At Harrisons & Crosfield, for example, James Crosfield became a partner in 1871 and for the next forty years stood immovable at his high flap-top desk. Just round the corner in Mincing Lane itself, there was the popular William Pink, a coffee and cocoa broker recalled by his clerk as 'looking for all the world like Mr Pickwick, with his spectacles, his broad-brimmed silk hat and his rotund person'. Pink usually had 'a glass of port in the forenoon', with the produce sale always due to begin at one o'clock, and invariably he would ask his young clerk's opinion on 'the relative merits of the dozens on dozens of cups of coffee samples set out on the tasting trays'. Above all, there was that eternal verity, a due sense of caution, always to be observed:

> The Roquelle arrived on the 13th, bringing us your letter of the 29th March. It is painful to us that you draw upon us so largely . . . We must tell you very candidly that we do not see our way clearly to estimate the amount of produce from your side to cover the amounts we have sent to you for this season's trade, amounting now to £26,000. We cannot afford to have our capital locked up with you in debts and bad stock . . . The quantity of nuts you expect to get this season, 2500 tons, will not yield us an adequate return, of course we are ignorant of what Wax & Hides will come forward . . .[28]

Lintott, Spink & Co, Africa merchants of 5 New City chambers, Bishopsgate, was writing in April 1875 to James Topp, the firm's agent in Bathurst, Royal Gambia, but the sentiments could have come from any sound City merchant writing to anywhere in the world.

Something of the flavour comes through in Louis Bamberger's enticingly titled *Memories of Sixty Years in the Timber and Pianoforte Trades*. The son of a very small timber merchant, working mainly from home in Kentish Town, Bamberger came to the City as a young man in 1868, and gradually worked his way up. There he found three leading mahogany brokers: Thos Edwards & Son and Geo Shadbolt & Son, who both held their auctions at the Commercial Sale Rooms in Mincing Lane; and Churchill & Sim, whose catalogues for auctions in the Baltic Sale Rooms 'consisted of mahogany logs, black walnut, whitewood and other fancy wood logs', and whose Charles Churchill junior, approaching retirement, was a 'scrupulously fair' auctioneer and 'a great stickler for regularity' – both of which qualities his father would have approved of. Other leading auctioneer-brokers included Simson & Mason of St Peter's Alley, Cornhill and Henry Freeman & Co of Crooked Lane, near London Bridge. Then there was W. L. T. Foy who 'had the *bonhomie* and the pleasant manner in the rostrum that everybody liked, so that his sales were much sought after'. Indeed, 'he had a joke with practically everybody', and 'when my friend, Mr J. Archer Smith, used to bid, which he always did under the name of "Archer", Mr Foy would shout genially, "Archer up!", an allusion to the celebrated jockey, Fred Archer'. An important part of the timber trade as a whole was in Canadian wood, of which the leading importing firm was undoubtedly Browning & Castle, in turn drawing its supplies mainly from two pine shippers. One was R. R. Dobell & Co, whose principal 'would often arrive in London on Wednesday and take the next boat back to Quebec on the following Saturday'. The other was Price & Pierre, whose brands 'A', 'B' and 'C' were 'so excellent that they sold themselves – and the "C" mark in particular was quite a timber yard brand', there being 'so much good stuff amongst it that it could be profitably stored'. Overall, Bamberger reminisced fondly, it was in those days 'almost impossible to close a transaction without inviting one's customer into a "pub", and giving him the "run of his throat" '. And: 'As a personal example of the treating times, one of my customers, upon whom I used to call as early as 9 o'clock in the morning, invariably invited me to have a gin-and-water with him, or perhaps it was I who "stood".'[29]

The timber trade seems to have remained relatively impervious to larger trends, but elsewhere in the City the decline of the commission merchant helped to accentuate the century's underlying shift from 'merchanting' to 'merchant banking', though that latter term itself was hardly in use until the 1890s. It was this problem of semantics that prompted Francis Hamilton to write to the Marquis of Salisbury in 1871 in the context of Lubbock's impending Bank Holiday legislation: 'There are many Houses, such as Messrs Rothschilds, Baring Brothers & Co, and my own firm Brown, Shipley & Co, who are not legally

Bankers, but Merchants, tho' their transactions in Bills of Exchange, Home and Foreign Monetary operations are on a much larger scale than many Bankers.' Barings had by this time almost stopped trading in goods on its own account, though there remained for many years a house tradition that the firm was still willing to deal in anything provided that the operation was likely to yield a profit – despite the unsuccessful purchase in 1874, on behalf of the Chinese, of an ironclad frigate from the Danish Government, an exotic manoeuvre that should have stayed on the drawing board. Morgans was also more or less moving out of commodities, with the decision in 1873 to stop dealing in iron rails. At Antony Gibbs, following the loss of the guano contract and the rapid decline by the 1870s in the volume and profitability of the commission trading that had historically been the firm's life-blood, there was a conscious policy on the part of Henry Hucks Gibbs to give a higher priority to finance-based activities. However, it was by no means a simple or painless process, for not only did some of the firm's financial ventures come unstuck (including various speculations and uncovered loans), but also there was a reliance that would become increasingly unhealthy on nitrate trading as a substitute for guano.[30]

For most merchant banks there was, of course, the daily bread-and-butter business of accepting. A host of City firms, large and small, performed an accepting function, almost invariably relating to the particular part of the world with which they traded, and there was no particular mystique or splendour attached to the term 'an accepting house' until after the First World War. Between them these firms were responsible in the mid-1870s for guaranteeing trade bills amounting at any one time to some £55m, a volume of acceptances outstanding some £20m greater than the comparable figure forty years earlier. It was a volume that made London the trade capital of the world and reflected partly sterling's status as a world currency, partly the efficiency of the service provided, but above all the simple fact that the sheer international breadth and depth of people and firms gathered together in the City far exceeded those of any other financial centre. It was also a competitive market – increasingly so in the last quarter of the century – and at this stage the market leader was far and away Barings, with Schröders and Kleinworts very much as the houses on the way up. In 1871, for example, Kleinworts' acceptances stood at just under £3m (more than Hambros and Rothschilds combined), providing a commission income of £94,135. The countries responsible for the majority of that business were the United States, Britain, Cuba, Brazil and China, but ten other parts of the world each provided over £1,000 of commission. In all these countries many of the clients were of German origin and favoured a 'German' firm for trade credit. But how did Kleinworts itself decide to whom to give credit? The firm's founding father, Alexander Kleinwort, offered an incontrovertible axiom to his American agent not long before his death: 'It is most important to do a profitable safe business, to avoid reckless speculation and all parties who do not deserve and inspire full confidence.'[31] Joshua Bates could not have put it better, and in truth these qualities were always needed: local knowledge or access to local knowledge, sound judgement, and an infinite capacity to take pains. Some in the City had those qualities, most had not.

Accepting must have seemed an attractively profitable field to get into, and by the late 1860s those reputed iconoclasts of the square mile, the joint-stock banks, were tempted to dabble. Among them was the London and Westminster, whose chairman was in defensive mode at the annual meeting in January 1869:

> You can easily understand that a trader or manufacturer living in Dundee, and desiring to buy jute or hemp in Riga or St Petersburg, may be perfectly solvent and in good credit at Dundee, and yet not be known at those ports. Now in order to carry on his trade, he asks his country banks to get him a London credit, and we give him that credit, being ourselves covered by good commercial bills. These acceptances are usually accompanied by shipping documents. With the value of those documents we have nothing to do; we are not merchants . . .

The *Economist* was less than satisfied: 'The commercial public view with great and justifiable anxiety the growth of the new system under which London Bankers undertake, for a commission large or small, engagements which properly belong to a merchant.' A brief controversy died down but was resurrected in 1875, before a parliamentary committee in the context of Scottish joint-stock banks recently coming to London and going in for an aggressive accepting policy. The private banker Jervoise Smith, brother of Hugh and deputy-chairman of the committee of London bankers, expressed the viewpoint of the City establishment under some fairly friendly questioning from George Goschen:

> Is there in the City of London a recognised difference between banker's business and merchant's business? – We have always held that it is so.
> Is it considered that a bank which holds large deposits for other people is under certain obligations to refrain from risks which are considered

legitimate in mercantile transactions? – The leading establishments in London, I think, act under that rule.

Would it be considered contrary to the principle of banking to deal largely in goods? – Certainly.

A business in goods would, of course, be legitimate in a merchant? – Yes; but it would be perfectly foreign to the business of banking proper.

How far would it be considered legitimate in banks to involve themselves in transactions, the results of which were dependent upon the rise and fall of goods? – We hold it to be quite beyond the province of a London bank to engage in any business of that kind.

Even more telling was the testimony on the same day of William Crake, a director of the London and Westminster and a partner in the merchant house of Crawford, Colvin & Co:

Does the London and Westminster Bank accept largely? – The London and Westminster Bank, like all other banks doing business in London, can hardly escape accepting to a certain extent, but the London and Westminster Bank avoids it to the utmost of its ability. Many accounts of great value are refused, simply on the ground that they would involve foreign acceptances . . . We hold that the depositors have a right to look for the proceeds of their property entrusted to us being on the spot, and not used abroad.[32]

For another quarter of a century or so the City's leading joint-stock banks continued to hold back from mounting a significant challenge to the merchant banks. Undoubtedly the risk argument carried great weight; so too did a feeling that the established accepting firms, with their mercantile origins, international connections and linguistic skills, were inherently better suited to the business. Yet at some level this diffidence also reflected the culture of the City as a whole, a culture of specialist businesses fulfilling 'niche' roles – a culture that would have viewed with horror the late twentieth-century concept of so-called 'integrated' houses operating across the whole financial waterfront. In a City of alleys and courts that Dickens would still have broadly claimed his own, small remained beautiful.

That said, there was in the merchant-banking sphere little *glamour* attached to accepting, which remained for many years the poor cousin (in terms of status) by comparison with the variety of tasks that these firms undertook for foreign governments, above all the key role they played in floating loans on the London market. Not all of these loans were profitable – though some were immensely so – but provided the country concerned was more or less reputable, they had the great attractions of enhancing or entrenching a house's position within the City pecking order, and creating the strong possibility of future spin-off business from the foreign government concerned, ranging from payment of dividends and operation of sinking funds to the undertaking of exchange operations and provision of short-term credit. But how could firms break into the magic circle, above all in relation to high-profile European loans? As Morgans found in the 1870s, it was one thing to become a regular member of syndicates: this it was able to do partly through the ripening friendship of J. Pierpont Morgan (son of Junius) and Everard Hambro, the two men being neighbours in Roehampton each summer.[33] However it was quite another matter to be asked to take the lead in the most prestigious loans, and as yet Rothschilds, Barings and to a degree Hambros were the only London houses that consistently had that standing.

Conducting the London (and indeed European) end of the funding operations on behalf of the American Government was also a matter of keen jealousy and in 1874 Seligmans successfully muscled in on Rothschilds, to New Court's discontent. Five years later, not long after Baron Lionel's death, his son Natty was at the Bank of England making a transfer when he bumped into another merchant banker doing the same, Herman Hoskier of Brown Shipley. Hoskier asked him if Rothschilds was thinking of doing anything about the next funding operation, and in his letter to Brown Brothers in New York he quoted Natty's reply:

> Belmont wrote me lately on the subject, and after consulting our Paris friends, I wrote back by last Tuesday's Mail to say, that we were ready to go into the matter and would willingly take hold of it, but on one condition only, that we were not willing to join any American Syndicate and be at their mercy or command, and would only take it up if we were given the lead to work it our own way with a group of friends around us, as in my father's time.

Natty would ever be mindful of the weight of his inheritance, and Hoskier added of the new master of what was still the world's most famous wholly private financial institution, that he was 'a man of variable temper but an excellent man of Business'.[34]

The profits of Rothschilds remain a historical mystery, but we do have runs of figures for the 1870s for five other merchant banks. They show Barings making a very sizeable average net profit of £242,000 a year – sizeable for a firm of a handful of partners and a staff of well under a hundred, even though amounting to less than £10m in modern terms; Morgans averaging £154,000; Schröders just behind at £144,000; Gibbs some £85,000; and Kleinworts a little under £50,000. Anecdotal evidence suggests that another merchant bank, Huths, was making in this period a net profit of between £50,000 and £80,000 a year.[35] What about capital? Taking 1875, Rothschilds was way out in front, with the London house alone possessing a capital of over £6.5m, part of the total capital of the Rothschild banks of over £34m. Then (in terms of the figures and best guesses readily available) came Schröders on £1.68m, Barings on £1.62m, Morgans on £1.46m, Brown Shipley on £1.2m, Kleinworts on £0.84m, Hambros on £0.63m and Huths on £0.5m.[36] It is arguable[37] that historians have made too much of this question of capital – after all, the real trick is matching capital to business requirements, rather than building up capital for its own sake – but there is no doubt that City men themselves were much preoccupied by the subject, especially when the constituent elements of a partnership changed for any reason. That was the case with Morton, Rose & Co of Bartholomew Lane in October 1877, and the manager of the Union Bank of London recorded in his information book:

> Mr [Pascoe] Grenfell in handing me the circular announcing the dissolution of his firm so far as regards Sir John Rose & Mr Geo Milne, stated that the retirement of the two partners will make a difference in the capital of the concern of £40,000. As their credit has always depended upon that of the firm in the U.S. [i.e. Morton, Bliss & Co] which remains unchanged, he apprehends this will make no difference in their estimation here.

Grenfell estimated correctly, and over the next decade or so Morton Rose remained one of the most active houses in the City, above all in relation to American and Canadian railroad financing. If it had not got over-committed in the Argentine (perhaps because it had *too* much capital at its disposal?), it might still be a name on City lips.[38]

Two names were always at the centre. 'Such a bill would rank before a bill of Barings': so Bagehot in 1877 (shortly before his death) graphically described his new invention, the Treasury bill, which was to be 'the finest security in the world'. Barings was the most dependable of houses, always to be relied upon to do what it said it would do, and what was demanded in a partner at 8 Bishopsgate was character and competence rather than any more glittering qualities. One such partner in the 1870s was Henry Mildmay, son of the notoriously cautious Humphrey, and his own son, born in 1871, would later recall the family routine: breakfast together at nine o'clock, before Mildmay left for the

City; his return at six or soon after; and then 'the long and substantial dinner which my father liked', featuring 'always soup, fish, and at least two kinds of meat'. However, as one would also expect of a Barings partner: 'My father, for the times he lived in, was an abstemious man. For instance, he drank much less than most men. His ordinary drink at dinner was a pint of claret and perhaps a glass of sherry.'[39]

The other great City name was starting to move towards this Englishness in its domestic character, and in its case it was inevitably accompanied by a certain sluggishnes, an unwillingness to pursue entrepreneurial risk. One symptom was Belmont's chorus of complaints about missed American opportunities; another was the gradual physical withdrawal of first Baron Lionel and then Natty from regular attendance on the Royal Exchange, leaving the path clear for Samuel Montagu and others in the sphere of foreign-exchange dealing; and a third was broadly hinted at in Abraham Mocatta's retrospective on his business in 1871:

> In the course of the year we sold to Raphael from Rothschild several hundred thousand pounds of Silver which the latter wished to get rid of. It was a most mixed lot & some very coarse, some very rich in gold, some brittle &c. The fact was Sir Anthony did not wish the trouble of refining it ... The great difficulty was in settling the assays, the bars were so large, irregular & uneven. It must have paid Raphael well, for he continually asks for more.

A suggestive episode, yet equally suggestive is the remark of Sir Charles Dilke after meeting Natty and his wife at dinner in March 1879: 'Well knowing as I did two other members of the family, I could see how strangely like a Royal family the Rothschilds are in one respect – namely, that they all quarrel with one another, but are united as against the world.'[40] *Contra mundum*: whatever the fundamental long-term weaknesses of family capitalism, this abiding sense of family solidarity served as a powerfully effective, self-reinforcing reminder to successive generations of Rothschilds that vast wealth so quickly won can, as quickly, be lost again.

*

Escott's memorable depiction of the flash stockbroker, with his knowing groom and unfortunate young wife gravitating into the demimonde, may well have been an accurate reflection of how public opinion had come by the late 1870s to view members of the Stock

Exchange. The historical reality, however, was probably rather duller. For one thing, most inhabitants of Capel Court were not particularly wealthy. This is clear from average annual profit figures for three stockbroking firms operating in the 1870s: at Scrimgeours four or five partners shared just under £20,000; at Price & Pott two partners shared less than £5,000; and at Corthorn & Scott there was a little under £8,000 to go round each year. Enough to stock a decent cellar, but hardly the stuff of plutocracy. It is apparent from membership books that many members lived at perfectly respectable, wholly unassuming suburban addresses. In 1867, for example, Thomas Faulconer resided at 66 New Finchley Road, Hampstead; Walter Fearis at 7 Carlton Grove, Peckham; Charles Feiling at 1 Nightingale Terrace, Woolwich; Frederick Fenner at 12 Lime Villas, Putney; Samuel Field at 10 Rayner Street, Hackney; and John Fitzgerald at 19 St Aubyn's Road, Upper Norwood. Of course, there were great variations within the membership – in both directions. But for a representative figure one could do worse than the father of Molly Hughes, that supreme chronicler of London family life, who as a child in the 1870s lived in a big house in Canonbury:

> My father was on the Stock Exchange, and wavered between great affluence and extreme poverty. Neither he nor mother had a saving or economical disposition, but lived happily always, neither elated by wealth nor depressed by the lack of it . . .
> If things were going well, my father had no thought of enlarging his establishment or otherwise incurring bothers. His idea was that we should all enjoy ourselves a bit more along the old lines. When a shrinkage came we didn't notice much deprivation, or if we did it was put down to the weather.

Her father was a great cricket-lover, and 'when money was plentiful he would take the boys, and often mother and me as well, in a wagonette to a cricket match, and give us all a big lunch, and invite any cricketers home to supper'. Alternatively, on a Saturday afternoon, he would take the family to Kew on the North London line, and from there walk along the river to Richmond. He liked a rubber of whist and was also, like any self-respecting member of the Stock Exchange, fond of larks: 'One afternoon he came home early and suggested that it was just the sort of day for making toffee.' Family happiness ended abruptly in November 1879, a month of 'cold and dark with fogs', when this attractive man with a well-developed sense of life's priorities was 'run over and instantly killed' while he was in the City.[41]

There existed a gulf between the Capel Court fraternity (with probably only a few exceptions) and the leading houses which every day employed its services. It was a gulf epitomised by the almost dog-like relationship that the stockbrokers Helbert Wagg endured for the best part of a century with its main patrons, N. M. Rothschild & Sons. 'On the fortnightly settlement days', Alfred Wagg was to relate feelingly, 'my grandfather or father would go over to New Court with a statement of the position across which Baron Lionel would write £500 or £1,000, being an arbitrary fee which he fixed as our remuneration, varying in amount according to the humour he was in.' Running the fortnightly gauntlet by the 1870s was Arthur Wagg (Alfred's father), who in the spring of 1874 took a holiday in Nice, staying at the Grand Hotel. His regulation letter to Baron Lionel was not only canine in character, but also an almost textbook example of Stock Exchange middlebrowism:

> You were kind enough when I left to express a wish to have a few lines from me and as I have now been absent for some time, I will no longer delay in writing to you. We are enjoying our stay here very much and my wife has derived very great benefit from the change. I am afraid I shall make you envious if I tell you of the brilliant sunshine and of the floral beauties that prevail everywhere, but I must do myself the pleasure of sending some violets by 'grande vitesse' and these, if they arrive in good condition, as I hope they will, may give you some little idea of what we are surrounded with . . .
>
> The Times is looked for with great anxiety and fills up an hour or two very pleasantly. There are pleasant walks in the country, an al Fresco lunch at 'the London House', a trip to Monaco, or listening to the band, dinner and the opera or theatre and the day is soon passed . . .
>
> I am glad to hear from my brother that he is getting a liberal share of your business, from which I am in hopes that you are satisfied with his intelligence and zeal.

The brother was Edward Wagg, a year younger, and in 1879 it was he who was summoned by a very ill Baron Lionel to his bedside at 148 Piccadilly. 'I have been looking at my fortnightly account', the great man managed to say, 'and you have made a mistake in the addition.' Less than twenty-four hours later he was dead.[42] Within Capel Court itself, communications were changing even more rapidly than elsewhere in the City – in 1868 pneumatic tubes were introduced to link the market floor with the telegraph office, while four years later the conservative Managers reluctantly allowed the coming of the ticker-tape machine, by which Stock Exchange offices were kept in touch with the very latest market prices as collected on the floor by officials of the Exchange Telegraph Company – but the underlying club-like code of morality remained constant. It was communications that revealed the code in action at the end of 1874. The occasion was the railway smash at Shipton-on-Cherwell, near Oxford, just after midday on Christmas Eve, killing over thirty people. 'The overturned carriages, the heartrending shrieks of the injured, the dead bodies seen in all directions, and the scattered luggage combined to render the spectacle horrible in the extreme,' reported *The Times*, adding that 'the more slightly injured at once set to work with praiseworthy alacrity to help their distressed fellow-travellers'. But did they all? Within days, and possibly hours, a story passed into circulation that a stockbroker on the train had, on emerging unscathed from the debris, instead attended first to the speculative possibilities of the disaster. Apparently he had hied to the nearest telegraph office, wiring his authorised clerk to sell 5,000 of the railway (the Great Western) on which the accident had happened. A few days later he appeared in the House, to be greeted by the singing of the following verses:

> They tell a tale of an S.E. man:
>   One hardly can conceive it;
> But take the tale for what 'tis worth
>   And in charity disbelieve it.

> Saved by God's mercy in the crash
>   When better men were slain,
> His heart's no room for thankfulness,
>   'Tis filled with dreams of gain.

> Lusting for plunder, off he flies,
>   This wretched, greedy bug
> Wires his clerk to sell a bear,
>   And 'tises for his rug.

Over the years the story of this outrageous example of insider dealing became firmly embedded in Capel Court mythology. And it may be significant that on the Boxing Day there appeared in *The Times* a letter dated the 24th and sent from the Randolph Hotel, Oxford by K. ff. Bellairs, a member of the Stock Exchange. He stated that he had been accompanied from Paddington by three others and made much of the fact that 'we (or rather the two of us who were able to get about) went to work with brandy &c to help the wounded'.[43] Perhaps he was already covering his tracks, or perhaps the whole thing was merely one more example of the disinformation that invariably haunts markets.

Manning the London market, and setting the tone for the whole institution, were the jobbers, those little-known men whose activities have so largely effaced themselves from the historical record. Few in the outside world comprehended the art of jobbing and probably not many stockbrokers did either. It was an art that Bagehot, in one of his *Economic Studies*, made a valiant effort to evoke if not to explain:

> The trade in which Ricardo spent his life, and in which he was so successful, is of all trades the most abstract. Perhaps some people may smile when they hear that his money was made on the Stock Exchange, which they believe to be a scene of gambling. But there is no place where the calculations are so fine, or where they are employed on *data* so impalpable and so little 'immersed in matter'. There is a story that some dealer made very many thousand pounds by continued dealings in the shares of some railway, and then on a sudden asked where that railway was. The whole thing had been a series of algebraic quantities to him, which called up no picture, but which affected a profit and loss account. In most kinds of business there is an appeal of some sort to the senses; there are goods in ships or machines; even in banking there is much physical money to be counted. But the Stock Exchange deals in the 'debts', that is the 'promises', of nations, and in the 'shares' of undertakings whose value depends on certain future dividends – that is, on certain expectations – and what these expectations are to be, is a matter of nice calculation from the past. These imponderable elements of trade cannot be seen or handled, and the dealing with them trains the mind to a refinement analogous to that of the metaphysician.[44]

It is doubtful if 'the Erie King' ever thought of himself as a metaphysician. Tom Nickalls was born in 1828; at the age of five he was taken by his father to live in Chicago; he returned to England in 1845 and soon afterwards began jobbing; in 1860 he married into a well-known Stock Exchange family; and over the next three decades he was a dominant presence in the American market. A young clerk of the 1870s would recall his larger-than-life qualities: 'A great, burly man with the voice of the "Bull of Bashan", his habit was to come into the market and bellow, "I buy Eries", and the small fry of jobbers would gather around him and the price of the great American gambling counter of that time was pulled up and down as Tom Nickalls dictated.' The death in 1877 of the railroad tycoon Vanderbilt further enhanced his reputation, for he was almost the only leading jobber to stick to his buying guns, a policy that paid him handsomely. By 1891, when a brief depiction of him in action appeared in the financial press, both he and his market were somewhat on the wane, but the description was applicable to his prime and might almost have been penned in explicit repudiation of Bagehot: 'He had – and still has – any amount of pluck, taking a view and acting on it, sublimely disregarding the minute calculations on which smaller speculators pin their faith. It is no use talking to him about figures or dividends. "Who is buying?" or "Who is selling?" he asks, and then makes up his mind what to do.' Nor was his capacity for independent thought applied solely to railroad securities. 'Cricket, my boy, will take you round the world, and rowing, up and down the Thames', he would say to his children before they went to Eton.[45]

No one doubted there was a fundamental difference between brokers and jobbers, and the company promoter H. Osborne O'Hagan drew a sharp distinction between their respective qualities: 'Those who have much experience of the Stock Exchange will have found out that – there are, of course, exceptions – stockbrokers are generally honest but not particularly brilliant individuals, especially if they confine themselves to investment business; there is little scope for the development of the brain. On the other hand, stock jobbers and dealers who are actively working for themselves have a very different reputation.' Jobbers, in other words, were different animals, not necessarily possessing the social graces so desirable in a broker, and it was not until the 1890s that the first Etonian became a jobber, in the person of C. T. ('Pubbles') Barclay.[46] When the Royal Commission examined some jobbers, it was a pity that those they interviewed were all drawn from the more respectable end of what was always a very mixed trade. First up was James Renton, a large operator in the Home Rails market, and Lord Penzance himself led the questioning:

> I think that you are a member of the Stock Exchange? – I am.
> You are not a broker? – No.
> But you are what is called a dealer, and is sometimes called a jobber? – I believe that there are three classes of men in the Stock Exchange, namely, brokers, dealers, and jobbers. I think that there is a distinction between jobbers and dealers, because there are certain men who deal in the Stock Exchange who square their books, as it were, every day. They never go away uneven; they buy and sell and make their books square every day. Then again there is another class, of whom I consider myself one, who more properly speaking may be termed dealers or merchants, who have a considerable amount of stock on hand regularly. It is immaterial to us whether we sell the stock on the same day that we buy it or do not sell it for months or weeks afterwards . . .

Is there any difference, as regards the broker who deals, between the one class called the dealer and the other class called the jobber; is there any difference as to the broker in the mode in which he would deal with one class and with the other? – I should think not, except that as a rule the merchants, whom I call dealers, are generally of a more responsible character.

It is natural that with a large dealing you should like to know the responsibility of the man with whom you deal, but in other respects are you aware of any difference? – In other respects I am not aware of any difference.

Strictly speaking in Stock Exchange terminology a jobber was a jobber, whatever the somewhat murky historical connotations of that word and whether he maintained merchant-style a large open-ended book in particular stocks or whether he was always concerned to go home square at the end of each trading day. But even if 'dealer' sounded more acceptable, among the 1,800 or so jobbers there was enormous segmentation, and at least several hundred of them were not part of firms or partnerships as such, operating instead as one-man outfits on their own account with little more at their back than the proverbial book and pencil. Often they did not have offices, even though (for reasons of space) there were no longer desks available on the market floor for the purpose of settling accounts. 'Our firm bought some weeks ago £650,000 stock in a certain line', Renton at one point told the Commission, but such a transaction would have been in the realm of never-never land for many of his fellow-members.

Another jobber who gave evidence was the experienced, manifestly hard-headed Robert Marzetti. Penzance sought to nail him down on the vexed question of what constituted, in any given situation, 'the market price', especially in the context of the voluntary procedure (sometimes insisted upon by brokers on behalf of clients) of marking the price of bargains on a board:

If two people, acting *bonâ fide* in the open market, agree to a sale at 120, is not that necessarily the market price. What is it that constitutes the market price except a *bonâ fide* sale in the open market of a given thing? – When you make a price you do not always make it so that everybody can hear you.

By 'the open market' I mean in the market. I am a perfectly *bonâ fide* purchaser, and I go into the market and say, 'I want to buy Great Northern; what is the price?' The reply is '120'? – But that is what a broker does not do. He goes to you and says, 'I want to deal in 1,000 Midland; what price do you make for me?' You say '120 to $120\frac{1}{4}$', he says, 'I will buy £1,000 stock of you'.

Surely that is a *bonâ fide* bargain? – So it may be; but suppose that the jobber has been out for a minute or two, or that there has been some change in the market; when he last knew the market it was 120 to 120¼; there are sellers at 119½, now he has made a mistake.

At which point Septimus Scott, chairman of the Stock Exchange Committee, interjected: 'Does not he sometimes send to the broker and say, "I charged you too much for that stock, and must let you have it at so much less"?' And Marzetti replied: 'Yes; I have often done that myself.' A mildly incredulous Penzance then returned to the fray:

That happens? – Very often.
Then you alter the bargain on the board? – Yes, the mark will be taken out. The other day I gave a man about half per cent too little for some stock; he marked that price, and I found out that I had given him too little. The price came better from Amsterdam or Berlin. The market was better than I thought, I having made the price of the preceding day. I said, 'I hope that you have not marked it, as I will give you so and so for it'; I gave him the increased price, but in the meantime he had marked the bargain. I said, 'I am sorry that you have done that, because it will give rise to a bother with the Committee'. The custom is that every erasure on the board is reported to the Committee, and they wish to know the reason of it. There was nothing to be ashamed of in that transaction, but I thought that the Committee might send to me to know how it was to be explained, and I did not want my time taken up. The marking was expunged and the proper price was put in. These cases will occur . . .
Do persons ever voluntarily make a bargain at a price different from the market price, both of them knowing what the market price is? – That would be committing a robbery.
Never mind what it would be, I want to know whether it happens? – I do not know of it.

Would Marzetti have said so if he had known? Presumably not.

The classic defence of the jobbing system was that it provided ready marketability in the widest possible range of securities, but it was by no means clear to the Commission that this was necessarily the case. And when that reforming practitioner, William Ingall, of the Foreign market, referred to how 'the style of dealing has been changed very much indeed since I was first a jobber', Penzance pricked up his ears:

In what way? – It is rather difficult to explain how it is. In most cases when I began as a dealer in the Stock Exchange you could get a price made in all stocks. In nearly every stock they would make you some price.
By making a price you mean a price at which they could either buy or sell? – Yes, and they would deal; but for one or two reasons that has gone

321

very much out of use. It is very often the case now that a jobber will say, 'No, they call the price so-and-so, but I would rather not make a price', and he will not deal excepting by negotiation.

That is to say, he will know before he says anything as to what he will do, whether the individual who is about to deal with him wants to buy or sell, and then he will negotiate the price? – Yes, or else he will say himself what he wants to do. That gives him the advantage in negotiating either of seeing or listening to what the broker wishes to do.

It is not like making a price? – No. If you make a price you are considered bound to deal in a certain amount, not a very large amount, say a £1,000 stock.

You say that that is passing out of practice? – That to a certain extent is passing away, and there are various reasons for it.

With regard to stocks and securities in which there is a limited market, it has very much passed out of use? – Yes, very much passed away. Where there is a free market you do not find it so, but the fact is this: the number of securities in foreign shares and stocks have largely increased. Years ago, before these had increased, the price which a jobber would make was very much wider, and therefore it would pay him to take the risk and always make a price.

Ingall then explained that increased competition between jobbers had led to narrower price spreads (the difference between the buying price and the selling price), which in turn had led to this practice of 'negotiation' in many of the less popular securities, jobbers reckoning there was no longer sufficient incentive to take the risk of leaving themselves open to being burdened with stock they would find very hard to sell. 'When I started on the Stock Exchange as a dealer in foreign stock', Ingall added, 'I was one of the persons to introduce this practice of negotiating and I got very much scolded by my brother jobbers for doing so, but I felt it would be very unwise indeed to go and make a price in everything and anything.'

Unwise no doubt, but according to Branch, putting the broker's point of view, the resulting trend was a regrettable one. Although denying that 'the difference between the buying and the selling price . . . is too much to pay for the convenience of a continuous market', his key point was that too often that market was not continuous. Thus whereas Consols, Egyptian stock, and English railways were relatively marketable types of securities, problems arose with, for instance, 'National Provincial and Bank of England shares, East and West India Dock stock, the shares of water companies, gas companies, of insurance companies (almost all of them)'. Branch examined the Official List and estimated that some 285 of the securities on it were in practice marketable, representing about £610m in nominal value, and that some 1,082 securities were not marketable, representing about £563m. In consequence, the jobber was often a redundant figure, and 'many brokers spend very much time in trying to find a broker who has the business the other way, and they sometimes succeed and often fail'.

Branch, unconstrained because no longer a member himself, further elaborated on the plight of the brokers when they attempted to take independent action: 'We have in the Stock Exchange what is called a notice board, but it is in fact not a wall space at all, but it is on part, not even the whole, of a supporting pillar; a part of this pillar is supposed to contain the notices from brokers as to the stocks which they wish to buy or to sell, and the part of it which is devoted to that purpose is kept under lock and key, and is jealously supervised by jobbers, who exclude notices upon what have appeared to me to be the most idle pretences.' In short, said Branch, the whole thing was 'a farce'. Another veteran broker, Frederick Banbury senior, suggested that the Stock Exchange should introduce a register system for out-of-the-way stocks, in order to bring together prospective buyer and seller. This in fact became one of the Royal Commission's specific recommendations, but in the event the Stock Exchange failed to act upon it and never did institute a book in which brokers could enter securities they wished to buy or to sell. As the *Economist* wryly commented in 1885, with implicit reference to what was still almost certainly a jobber-dominated Committee: 'Although the House would undoubtedly gain by a measure which tended to make it a more comprehensive and effective dealing centre, yet when this involves, as in the present case, a prior collision with powerful interests inside the House, it is not surprising that but little is achieved.'

Still, there was one part of Capel Court where the question was more or less an irrelevance. There was no prouder witness before the Royal Commission than Richard Thorp, a leading jobber in British government securities for over twenty years:

We have been told that the London Stock Exchange is the best market, and the market affording the greatest facilities for dealing in securities in which there is a great demand, such as Consols, is that the case in your opinion? – I think it is the case. If you will allow me I will give you one or two instances, which perhaps may prove the point. An instance occurred with me less than a fortnight ago. One of our stockbrokers came in with an order from a banker to sell £150,000 stock, and wanted the money that very day. It was principally New and Reduced stock; there was about £80,000 or £90,000 of one, and about £60,000 or £70,000 of

the other. The broker having this order from the banker went to one of
the principal dealers in the market, and as it was rather a larger transaction than he chose to undertake by himself, he came to me. This was
about 20 minutes to 1 o'clock, certainly more than half-past 12, and by
1 o'clock this transaction was concluded and the money was paid.

Is that a thing which can be done on any other market, do you think? –
I do not know of any other market where such a thing could be done as
£150,000 of stock to change hands, and be dealt with in so short a time.

To what do you attribute that facility? – Simply because there are
dealers who are always ready for a certain nominal turn of the market, to
deal either way, in almost any reasonable amount of stock.

Such a transaction as you have spoken of implies your often having the
command of a sum of money as large as £150,000? – If we have not the
money of our own we know where to go for it. There are bankers in
London who are always ready to lend money upon such securities. If we
had not money at our own control (although some of the dealers have
very little capital employed in the business) we could not carry on the
business.

'A market where speculation, although sometimes active, wears a more
sedate appearance than anywhere else in the House' was how the
Economist some years later would describe the Consol market, as it
was generally called; and even as the price of British government stocks
moved into a period of long-term decline, its reputation for an unsur-
passed combination of respectability and marketability (including
daily settlement) remained intact.

What unfortunately the ten jobber witnesses before the Commission
failed to provide was significant insight into the psychology of their
very specialised craft. Near the end of the inquiry, George Medley, a
member for twenty-seven years and for the last dozen a jobber in the
American market, gave some clue. 'There is nothing a man dreads so
much as meeting another man the same way as himself. If two or three
meet together it amounts to a chicken panic, that is to say, we get
afraid of one another . . .' Not long after that vivid expression, discussion turned to the question of public access in order to counter charges
of the public being kept deliberately in the dark:

It has been suggested that it would be much better if the Stock Exchange
were open like any other market is? – They would not see the business
done, although they might fancy that they would, because important
business is done in a whisper. No dealer would allow what a broker does
with him to be known. It must be kept secret. That is the essence of the
business.

What do you think about the door being open? If the door were open, and people could go in, then their fancy would be satisfied, although they would not be much wiser; still, that source of suspicion would be removed from their minds? – That would be quite true. The only diffi- culty that I see in that is the physical one of want of room.

That matter might be got over if you had a sufficient building with large rooms like a large market? – I should have a great objection myself to have a crowd coming in. But perhaps after a little while the novelty of the thing would go off; if they were in a gallery, for instance, perhaps that would do.

It would lessen the confusion which exists on the Stock Exchange if the markets were separated so that the business might be done in different rooms? – But the confusion is not a hindrance, it is not inconvenient. We want to hear what is going on in other markets. Our markets move as it were by electricity; if we hear a shout in one market we want to know how things are going on there, one market affects another.

An alteration of $\frac{1}{8}$th in the Consol market makes a great difference? – Yes, just now [March 1878, with the Eastern Question at its most fraught] foreign stocks and Consols are what we look at. In fact, Russians and Consols, pending what we may call the tension between the two countries, are objects of great interest. I should not like to be dealing in stocks without knowing at the same time what is going on in other markets.

Would it not suffice for that purpose if it was in an adjoining room? – No, we could not hear.

How would a stranger who is supposed to be admitted hear it when it is done in a whisper? – I am speaking now of what may take place. There is a shout, and it is most important for us to hear it in other parts of the House. It is telegraphed all over the country immediately. If I was in another room I could not hear it. I certainly cannot see that anything would be gained by that . . .

Medley, however, was no blind defender of existing practices. He accepted that there had been much rampant speculation in recent years and blamed it on the fact that up to a quarter of the membership comprised 'young men who came in upon the top of the inflation of 1873'. He asserted that this gambling had been 'principally in the Railway markets and in the Foreign markets', thus implicitly exoner- ating his own market. And he argued that admission to the Stock Exchange should be made more restrictive: 'I should be most inclined to make a man pass an apprenticeship. I do not think that the mere possession of a certain sum of money qualifies a man for the practice of such a business.'[47]

The Royal Commission apparently failed to appreciate that there was an important vested interest involved concerning the whole question of admission.[48] Whereas Lloyd's was an institution which since the 1770s had been owned by its members, who therefore had a natural inclination to keep a lid on numbers in order to minimise competition, the situation was different at the Stock Exchange. There it was the shareholders who owned the building, and these proprietors had an equally natural wish to keep the Stock Exchange as open as possible to new members, in order to maximise their income through entrance fees and annual subscriptions. The proprietors elected the Managers, the members elected the Committee, only about a quarter of members were also proprietors, and inevitably there was a certain underlying tension between the two ruling bodies. Francis Levien on behalf of the Committee may have emphasised to the Royal Commission the continuing tradition of a stock market open to all the talents, but essentially it was a policy supported by the proprietors rather than the membership as a whole. That it *was* a relatively open market, in terms of admission and by comparison with either Lloyd's or the New York Stock Exchange, there is no doubt. It is true that the level of sureties was raised in both 1872 and 1874 – so that by the autumn of 1874 a prospective new member without a clerical apprenticeship on the Exchange was required to find three sureties for £750 each – but entrance fees remained low at a maximum of 100 guineas, as did annual subscriptions at no more than 20 guineas. In 1850 there had been well under a thousand members; by 1877 there were over two thousand; and the only future limitation seemed likely to be shortage of physical accommodation, as at the beginning of the 1880s the amount of space per person (members and their clerks) admitted to the House was down to appreciably less than three square feet.[49]

But if it was relatively easy to become a member of the Stock Exchange, it was another matter to flourish there. Family ties often remained of paramount importance – almost two-fifths of firms had at least two members of the same family amongst its partners – and indeed in 1867 Isaac Braithwaite drew up a new deed of partnership ensuring that for ever and a day his firm's full partners would come from three families only (Braithwaite, Barkworth, Savory), with any outside recruits to Foster & Braithwaite having to make do as salaried partners. Wealth and connection were also crucial ingredients of success, especially in relation to broking firms. Here the new, much-criticised West End intake particularly made its mark, and in July 1874 Charlotte de Rothschild was writing a little waspishly to her children in Trouville about what had been 'our chief topic of conversation at dinner yesterday' and would soon be causing an even bigger splash in the world beyond 148 Piccadilly:

The confidential clerk of Arthur Wagg is on the point of leaving him, and on account of the work which cannot be left undone on the Sabbath, the successor of the valuable employer must also be a Christian. Mr Bisch [presumably Henri Bischoffsheim?] knowing the complexity of the young jewish broker, has recommended to him, during one year as a confidential clerk, and afterwards as a partner, the scion of a noble house, no less a person than the Duke of Argyll's son, Lord Walter Campbell, who puts ten thousand pounds in the business, and is to receive ten per cent on the amount the first year and after that a proportion of the profits to be determined by Mr Bisch and your father. This is the proposal, very liberal on the part of Arthur Wagg, who is delighted, and who by his liberality gives great satisfaction to Lord Walter. Your father, however, has advised Lord Walter to go and speak to the Duke, as that proud nobleman might not like his son to enter into partnership with an Israelite. The Waggs will be overjoyed, if the partnership should really take place, to be connected in business with the brother-in-law of Her Royal Highness the Princess Louise.

Three days later Charlotte reported that 'one of the Bank directors, Mr L in the house of Rathbone, says that the red-haired young gentleman is very clever and has excellent business habits'. The journey to Inverary proved fruitful, and the following year, when the young aristocrat became a member, it was widely seen as a landmark in the Stock Exchange's history.[50]

However, not all of these 'orchids in a turnip field' (as the phrase went) were as satisfactory in character as Lord Walter. 'Com'é bello Cecilio, non altrimento lucido d'un paladino giovane crociato'. The beautiful Cecil, as resplendent as a young paladin on the crusades, was Cecil Boyle, the most admired boy of his generation at Clifton College and the special favourite of John Addington Symonds, who taught him there. 'His Soul is as beautiful as his body is wellgrown', affirmed Symonds; while others delighted in his aristocratic connections and his prowess as a cricketer. But there was little family money behind him, and after he left Clifton in 1872 he started to drift, sponging where he could. By 1874 the infatuation of Symonds was giving way to a certain disenchantment, as he found in Boyle 'a queer mixture of haughtiness, & resentful & quick temper, with a desire to have advisers & helpers'. Three years later Symonds was in London, writing to another old Cliftonian: 'I have just seen Cecil married. He looked rather green & yellow ... He makes £500 a year now, & hates the Stock Exchange. Yet I think from what he says about it that he is doing well there ... His health has been bad, but more I fancy from nervous depression than anything else – a sort of lack of vital energy.' Boyle had made a good

marriage (to the daughter of a former MP), his health improved, and
at the end of 1878 the not-so-young paladin was taken into partnership
by G. H. Pember, thus creating the stockbroking firm of Pember &
Boyle. Pember lost no time in writing to his bankers to commend his
new partner: 'Mr Cecil Boyle has I believe the two most important
qualifications: he is a thorough gentleman and a good man of business.
He comes to me through a first-rate introduction, and has himself a
nice business of a high class, and good means.' For his old, romantic
admirers, however, it was the final blow, as he settled down to become
a pillar of the Stock Exchange and the valedictory blessing he had
received from Symonds on leaving Clifton seven years before faded into
dim memory: 'Good Knight! to whom God has given strength, and with
it gentleness and anger. Use these rightly and be always the nobleman
you ought to be!'[51]

Another migrant from the West Country, though of a somewhat
lowlier native station, was Francis Carruthers Gould. He was born in
1844 the son of a Barnstaple architect and, after being educated
locally, became a member of the Stock Exchange for over twenty years.
There he found ample fodder for his gift for caricature, and collections
of his sketches of fellow-members were published for private circulation. Eventually he decided to leave Capel Court and during the second
half of his life he became a prominent political cartoonist, of Liberal
sympathies, as well as assistant editor of the *Westminster Gazette*. In
old age he looked back on the place with some fondness. 'A more
generous and kindly community of men it would be impossible to
find', he wrote, asserting also that nowhere in the City did there exist
'a higher standard of personal honour in all the relations of business'.
Nor did it worry him that the atmosphere had been 'like a big school
where all the boys knew each other's peculiarities or eccentricities,
applied nicknames with uncanny accuracy, and occasionally "ragged"
unmercifully'. Yet he had no regrets about having left the Stock Exchange. And in the only such retrospect ever written by a former
member, a passage going close to the heart of that institution's peculiarly unsettling and febrile collective psyche, he tried to explain why:

> I cannot say that it was ever a congenial occupation that suited my
> temperament. It was like living on a tropical volcanic island; when the
> sun shone and things went smoothly it was pleasant enough but there
> were too many sudden and unforeseen bolts from the blue. One might
> leave the City one evening with everything calm and serene, and the next
> morning there might be a wild storm with earthquakes and eruptions and

panics when the very foundations were shaken, and the crowd in the 'House', which had been merry and playful in the absence of care only a few hours before, were haggard with anxiety and dreading to hear the funereal knocking of the hammer which sounds the fate of those whom the disaster has wrecked. It was a life of alternations. Some men made fortunes swiftly, some plodded on cautiously, content merely to make a living, whilst others fell by the way. Some were fortunate or skilful enough to weather all the storms and even to profit by them, but there were others whose tragic fate it was to work all their lives only to fail at the end . . .[52]

CHAPTER EIGHTEEN

Playing the Game

'If England be the heart of international trade and cosmopolitan finance, and London be the heart of England, the City is the heart of London.' So affirmed Escott in 1879, and in an ambitious set-piece passage he convincingly depicted the Old Lady herself as lying at the *very* heart of the matter:

> Outside and beyond the specially national functions which the Bank is bound to discharge in being the banker of the Government, the issuer of notes that, under certain conditions, are legal tender and therefore national currency, in taking charge of Government securities and paying the dividends thereon to the holders, and in discharging the other various offices of a bank for the public, there are other multifarious functions which it is compelled by its position to fulfil. Bills from all parts of the world are drawn payable in London, as in other capitals, because it is convenient to have recognised places at which the international trading balances and the balance between the markets and traders of different countries may be settled; while, by mere force of geographical circumstances, London has, in a special degree, drifted into the position of international Clearing-House of the world, and the banking functions connected with it are largely, though not exclusively, discharged by the Bank of England, which is known as the bankers' bank at home. This is not all. In the final resort, when balances remain to be discharged as between one nation and another, after all the complicated mechanism of bills set off against each other has accomplished its utmost, they must be paid in gold. There is no other means of settling the final outcome of the mass of transactions in international commerce except through the precious metals – gold and silver; and while silver is mainly employed in the East, gold is chiefly used in the West. London consequently, as the convenient centre that may be drawn upon from all parts of the world, must possess a stock of gold sufficient to meet the demands that may be made on it. The Bank of England, as the banker of the nation, is the custodian of this treasure; and being thus constituted a bullion storehouse, to it flow all supplies of the precious metal that reach our shores. Circumstances have thus caused it to become a dealer in bullion as well as a banker. The Bank of England, in fact, discharges wider than national

banking functions. Along with the joint stock and private banks by which
it is surrounded, and with which its relations are close and intimate – for
as the central institution it keeps the reserves of the other banks as well
as its own – it represents the banking of the metropolis, and therefore, in
the final issue, of England. Owing to England's world-wide commercial
relations, this same banking system, and the subsidiary agencies by which
it is buttressed, acts as the general international Clearing House; and
bearing in mind the duties that further devolve on it from the fact that
London is the great bullion centre, we can form some faint idea of the
multiplicity and complexity of its operations, and the vastness of the
weight which presses on the central pivot around which the entire commercial and financial system revolves.[1]

A pressing and universal weight indeed, as not only did most of Europe
in the course of the 1870s move to a gold standard, but the sums of
money flowing through London became ever greater. The logic was
irresistible: sterling, backed by the Bank's undeviating adherence to the
gold standard, was *the* international currency; London was where the
world's trade was financed and settled; and there existed in the City a
short-term money market of unrivalled liquidity and security.[2] Could
the Bank of England, still predominantly run by merchants, cope with
its ever more demanding role as 'the central pivot'? Bagehot was not
alone in having his doubts.

The real problem was one of resources. The Bank's clout in the money
market was by the early 1870s becoming palpably weakened by the
rival impact of other banks, especially joint-stock ones, whose deposits
were continuing to rise at a far greater pace than the Bank's; this in turn
led to an ever-wider divergence between the actual, competitively
determined market rate and the official Bank rate. In December 1874
there appeared in the *Economist* a bold letter, probably written by
Newmarch of Glyns, asserting that 'it is felt on all sides that the old
system of paternal government is passing away' and that 'the Bank of
England, which once distanced every competitor, is now only *primus
inter pares*'. Newmarch even advocated that the London banks should
keep their own cash reserves (as opposed to the single-reserve system,
accepted by Bagehot as a fact of life) and settle the rate of discount
themselves, without reference to Bank rate. The proposal set all Lombard Street talking, but the next month the *Bankers' Magazine* came
down on the side of the sceptics. In part it argued that the plan 'does
not in any way connect the proposed reserve with the supply of bullion
or of gold coin, which should form the basis of every banking reserve'.
Its main thrust, however, was the key role that the Bank of England had

played, 'by pledging the resources of the nation', in the still vividly remembered crises of 1847, 1857 and 1866. And: 'If "Lombard Street" is prepared to face any storm that may arise without requiring this aid, then, and then only, it is strong enough to carry the proposed plan successfully through.' The journal was also doubtful if the government would come to the aid of the new joint-stock banks in the event of a crisis.[3] Over the next few months the debate fizzled out, but it had been a clear sign that the Bank could not, even after vanquishing Overend Gurney, take its authority in the City wholly for granted.

In fact, conscious in best Bagehot fashion of the importance of protecting its reserve, the Bank had already started to refashion its monetary policy. This was the so-called Greene-Gibbs policy – Benjamin Buck Greene was Governor from 1873 to 1875 and Henry Hucks Gibbs was Deputy Governor, before becoming Governor himself over the next two years – and what in effect it entailed was that when money was lent at home, Bank rate was simultaneously raised, so that gold came in from abroad and thus fortified the reserve. Or in the sanguine words of Gibbs himself, writing to a less than convinced Oxford economist in 1877: 'The Bank of England has but one weapon, the rate, wherewith they defend their own position, and make those who want to borrow money pay a little more for it, inducing, by the rise of interest, the foreigners to minister to the provisions of the Act of '44, and send more note-producing gold into our coffers.' The trouble was, however, the continuing difficulty of making Bank rate effective; unrealistic levels of Bank rate, geared to potential foreign drains of gold, had the invidious domestic effect of making the banks pay over the odds in their deposit rates; and in 1878 there was more, quite serious talk of an independent rate and an independent reserve. But it seems that once again Lombard Street failed to speak with one voice, and plans for what would have been little less than a unilateral declaration of independence were quietly shelved.[4] There, in a somewhat unsatisfactory state, matters remained for another decade, awaiting a strong, tough-minded man to come to the Bank's helm and try to assert in a more thoroughgoing way the dominance of Threadneedle Street.

That dominance would have to be asserted over a banking system that had been undergoing rapid change and was beginning to take something like its modern, mature shape. 1878 was an important year. The spring saw the failure of Willis, Percival & Co, and according to John Biddulph Martin (Richard's brother) in his year-end review, this 'caused a very bad feeling at the time, & was felt to be discreditable to private Banking'. Willis Percival was one of Lombard Street's oldest banks and, having failed with liabilities of over £½m, was absorbed into the Hampshire and North Wilts Banking Company. That joint-stock bank, which had recently tried to secure a seat on the London Clearing House but been rejected by the private bankers who still controlled it, now renamed itself as the Capital and Counties Bank and, after a further wait, at last got its prized seat. Meanwhile, in the autumn of 1878, there had taken place what Martin referred to as 'the scandalous failure of the City of Glasgow Bank'. There was no doubt that it was a scandal – involving over £8m of depositors' funds – and inevitably it shook the City profoundly. 'I have been busy all today about Discounts & have managed to do £45,000 out of £95,000. The other £50,000 I can't do at any price . . . The present state of affairs is a great deal worse than the panic of 1873 & 1866, bills could then be discounted under the Bank rate, but it is different today. No one wants bills even with the endorsement of foreign Banks.' That was the experience of David McLean, London manager of the Hongkong and Shanghai Bank, and many others shared it.[5]

The City's mood remained apprehensive for several months, and the story goes that shortly before Christmas one of the Rothschilds (presumably Alfred, being a Bank director) went to the Chancellor, Sir Stafford Northcote, and asked him if, before he went out of town, he would leave a signed letter suspending the act, the letter to be used on the moment should necessity arise. It is unclear whether this request was granted, but in the longer term the City of Glasgow crash proved, in two specific ways, a turning point in banking history. One was that it led to legislation providing for compulsory publication of balance sheets on the part of joint-stock banks; the other was that, to an extent still a matter of historical debate, it made banks increasingly preoccupied by the question of liquidity and as a direct result increasingly less likely to adopt a liberal approach in their lending policy.[6] The upshot was undoubtedly a more stable banking system – but arguably at the expense of overall British economic development.

By the early 1880s the City was increasingly the magnet to the provincial joint-stock banks, which by this stage had close, regular links not only with its discount houses but also the leading stockbroking firms. There could have been no clearer indication of how times were changing when in 1884 Lloyds of Birmingham, a bank hitherto confined to the Midlands, attained for itself a presence in London, and with it a seat on the London Clearing House, by the simple expedient of buying up Barnetts Hoares and Bosanquets, two of Lombard Street's more venerable private banks. Barnetts had come badly unstuck lending to the stockbrokers P. W. Thomas & Co, who had recently failed for £800,000; and both banks had acted as London agents to Lloyds. 'The result will be a very strong joint stock bank under the management of private bankers', one of the Barnett partners assured an intimate, adding that 'as far as we know, after privately communicating with many of our customers, the step we have taken meets with general approval'. But at least one customer decided to terminate the connection in consequence of the merger, and Barnetts wrote regretfully: 'We had hoped that as our business will still be conducted under the personal supervision of three of our old partners, our friends would not have disliked the reconstitution of the Bank in a form which appeared to us to be in accordance with the requirements of modern times.' The client was right, for the new bank – called, for the time being, Lloyds, Barnetts and Bosanquets – fundamentally represented a takeover, and it was symbolic that within a few years the dignified old premises of Bosanquets were being knocked down in order to allow the construction of a grand London office for the newcomer.[7]

Did the City's private banks have a future at all? One of their major problems, now acute in the wake of the recent legislation, was that they were mistrusted because of their continuing refusal to publish balance sheets. Yet quite apart from an instinctive reluctance to do so, they knew all too well the consequences of publicising the fact that, with very few exceptions, their capital and reserve were both negligible in comparison with most joint-stock banks. One of those exceptions was Glyn Mills, and in January 1885 it took the bull by the horns, issuing a circular that aroused much attention. 'The plan upon which they have hit', asserted the *Statist* (a relatively new, would-be rival to the *Economist*), 'does credit to their enterprise and forethought. They have decided to retain all the advantages which private banking offers, while giving to the public the information which is so highly prized in the case of joint-stock banks.' After noting the existing partnership's determination to retain private banking's traditional advantages of accumulated skills and unlimited liability, the *Statist* went on:

> Messrs Glyn, Mills, Currie, and Co have decided to register as a Joint-Stock Company; but the present partners remain the only partners in the business, and their liability continues to be unlimited. The management will remain without change; while a balance-sheet will be issued every half-year, as in the case of the joint-stock banks. The measure is a wise one, and opens out to private banking new and great possibilities. Indeed, under the new arrangement there seems no reason why private banking should not hold its own against joint-stock banking.

There was no denying that it was a clever arrangement, but this optimism was misplaced, for in the long run capital was always going to be king as far as deposit banking was concerned (even if the same did not apply in merchant banking), and that factor alone meant that private banking was ultimately doomed. Yet equally important was the human factor. Only a few weeks earlier, John Biddulph Martin had noted somewhat caustically in his review of 1884: 'Richard took his holiday principally in Scotland, but at the best was very little in Lombard Street . . .'[8] Richard Biddulph Martin, by now senior partner of the family bank, was an able banker and a far more attractive, 'rounded' figure than the average joint-stock banker; but no joint-stock banker remained on the payroll unless he put in the hours. That, in the end, made the difference.

*

Among those who regretted the Glyn Mills initiative of 1885 was Gladstone. 'Mr G says he is a Tory and old-fashioned enough not to wish to see the entire break up of the private bank system', recorded one of his private secretaries. But as he well knew, and sometimes acknowledged, the world was changing in all sorts of ways, not least in the conduct of British foreign policy – from the mid-1870s far more 'forward' than it had been for many years, and finding in the City an increasingly willing helpmate and ally. The decisive moment, of great symbolic as well as substantive importance, came in November 1875 when Disraeli's Conservative government was alerted to the possibility of buying a 44% share in the Suez Canal Company and responded to it with alacrity. Disraeli decided not to consult Parliament, bypassed the Old Lady, and turned instead to his long-time friends in New Court. 'They alone cd have accomplished what we wanted, & they had only 4 & 20 hours to make up their minds, whether they wd, or could, incur an immediate liability of 4 millions.' So the Prime Minister reported to the Prince of Wales almost immediately afterwards. In reality Baron Lionel had a little longer to make up his mind, but the gist was true: the British Government needed £4m virtually at once and Rothschilds agreed to advance it, making from the transaction a profit of almost £100,000. Sir Stafford Northcote, the Chancellor of the Exchequer, later admitted privately that 'we took their offer on their own terms without looking too closely into them'. Disraeli, however, was jubilant ('You have it, Madam'), the price of Egyptian stock rose sharply, and it was not until the following February that Parliament debated the purchase and its terms. A well-intentioned stockbroker suggested to Alfred de Rothschild that Disraeli should deflect criticism by publicly stating that Rothschilds had given its services gratis. Alfred passed the suggestion on to his father, who summoned the stockbroker and did not mince words: 'Arthur Wagg, you're a young man and will learn better. I've made £100,000 out of the deal, I wish it had been £200,000.' Baron Lionel, with all the insouciance of his own father, was unconcerned about any parliamentary censure and did not believe he had broken any unwritten City code. As Disraeli's secretary, Monty Corry, noted at the time:

> As to the question whether the Government should not have applied to the Bank of England, Baron Rothschild – giving no opinion as to the Bank's *power* – says that he understands the authorities to be about equally divided (even now) on the point of their *willingness* to have acted as the agents of the Government in this transaction. It is a point, moreover, which could only have been determined by the full Board, at the obvious sacrifice of despatch and secrecy. Mr Hubbard, for one, is clear that the Bank could not, and would not, have acted, while Mr Gibbs and Mr Thomson Hankey take the other view.

Corry added that Rothschild 'declares without hesitation that the Bank of England could not have found the required sum without grave disturbance of the money market'.

Altogether it was an episode destined for the history books, and it further cemented the close relationship between Disraeli and the Rothschilds, nominally Liberal though that family still was. 'The greatest man in England', Baron Lionel once called him, to which Natty is said to have added, 'In Europe, papa'. What of the larger consequences? 'We have now', *The Times* solemnly intoned on 27 November 1875, 'an abiding stake in the security and welfare of Egypt'. City opinion was divided, but the aged Overstone probably spoke for the majority when he sought to reassure G. W. Norman three days later: 'I admit the difficulties which you suggest as attaching to the Suez Land purchase. Nevertheless I believe it to be a wise step – indeed almost an inevitable step.' While as for the prospect of an increased British influence over Egyptian affairs, 'from this I think we cannot shrink'.[9]

There was no doubt that the City was becoming more bellicose, however little it welcomed the disruptive realities of war. Attitudes further hardened in the three years after the Suez purchase, as Britain on Turkey's behalf came close to going to war with Russia. In 1877 Natty Rothschild and Goschen were among those Liberals who sided against Gladstone on account of what was seen as his unacceptably soft approach towards Russian aggression; early in 1878 a copy of *The Times* was ceremoniously burnt in the centre of the Stock Exchange; and on the last day of January, as the *City Press* reported, patriotic passion ran unbridled:

> On Thursday afternoon the neighbourhood of Cannon-street Railway Station, the street, hotel, and railway-yard presented an extraordinary scene of tumult for nearly three hours. A meeting had been called for three o'clock by the City Neutrality Committee 'to protest against the vote of six millions for war purposes'; but at about two o'clock a large war-party, under the leadership of the agents of the Conservative organisations, marched into the hotel. Finding by the tablets on the stairs that there was a meeting of members of the City of London Liberal Club in one of the rooms, the mob burst into the room, and dispersed the occupants. Seeing that there was then no opposite party to combat, the war party occupied the corridors and the stairs, where they expressed in shouts their readiness to go to war, and engaged in horse-play. The police were sent for, and Inspector Forster, with a strong force of police, gradually cleared the hotel.

Various pro-government meetings were then held. In the hall of the hotel, Mocatta chaired one attended by 'numerous merchants of high standing'; outside, on the steps in front of the North Kent booking office, the private banker and chairman of the City Conservative Association, Robert Fowler, chaired another; and 'several small meetings were held about the station-yard', at one of which 'Mr Boyle took the lead', perhaps Cecil himself. The crowd then marched to the Guildhall, commandeering the Lord Mayor on the way, and held there another noisy, flag-waving meeting, addressed by the governor of the Bank, Edward Howley Palmer. Rounded off by a deputation to the House of Commons, the events of the day caused a considerable national stir, adding to the popular 'jingoism' (the word was just in the process of being coined) that moved public opinion decisively in the direction of the government. Was the City simply acting according to its own book? Certainly Palmer's own firm had considerable Turkish interests, but it is clear that the City's agitation was spread much wider, including as it did demonstrations at both Lloyd's and the Corn Exchange.[10] Gladstone may have inveighed against Turkish atrocities, but by this time most in the square mile were agreed that he was an atrocity far worse than any committed by the Turks.

Yet it was Gladstone who four years later, as Prime Minister, earned the ungracious thanks of the City through his reluctant decision to occupy Egypt.[11] The City's involvement with that country had been long and intimate: in trade from the late 1830s, mainly in cotton, so that by 1880 four-fifths of Egypt's exports went to Britain, which in turn supplied almost half her imports; and in finance from the 1860s, with loans issued by Frühling & Goschen under the most onerous terms to the debtor nation helping to cause almost permanent Egyptian financial crisis. In 1876 it was George Goschen who on behalf of the British bondholders designed the plan that effectively led to Anglo-French supervision of Egyptian finances; and two years later it was Rothschilds which issued an £8m Egyptian loan on the security of the khedive's domain lands. In 1879 the khedive (Ismail Pasha) was deposed, European informal supremacy was further reasserted, and in the early 1880s British investment poured into Egypt. This in turn led to a nationalist reaction, and eventually revolt, and so to the fateful occupation of 1882. What precisely were City attitudes, and what was the extent of City influence on this turning point in Gladstonian Liberalism as well as the evolution of British imperialism? No precise evaluation is possible, but there is some suggestive evidence.

By late March, Natty Rothschild, with an apparently threatening nationalist revolt well under way, was reported as being in a deeply anxious state, paying daily visits to the Foreign Office and, like St Paul, dying daily. It was also reported that half of the domain loan was still in the hands of Rothschilds, which perhaps explains the anxiety. It seems clear that, from late spring, Natty was helping to create a climate in which occupation appeared the only answer. By mid-June a British fleet was poised outside Alexandria and riots there had killed fifty Europeans. 'England has greater interests in Egypt than any other European Power, and those interests must be defended', declared the *Economist* on the 17th, no knee-jerk imperialist, and a week later it returned to the question:

> To the City and to business men, the matter presents itself under an aspect not uncoloured by the interests of trade. To them the question is rather of the prices of Egyptian securities, of rumours of possible embarrassments connected with the hurried closing of transactions in that country, of alarms about the unprotected condition of the canal.

The Times in its City report of 26 June anticipated difficulties at the impending Stock Exchange settlement: 'Egyptian securities have always been a favourite medium for speculation, and large accounts are known to have been open for the rise when the Egyptian imbroglio commenced.' Significantly, though, the same item referred to Gladstone's comforting statement 'a week ago' that 'the bondholders' interests would be protected'. By 5 July, Egyptian securities were going up on what transpired to be false rumours that Admiral Seymour's fleet 'had actually commenced a bombardment of the works that have been erected to command the harbour', while in the words of another market report soon afterwards, 'the prospect of an early intervention has certainly been well received in the City'. In short, 'the general feeling' at Capel Court was 'a wish for "some decisive action", the present suspense being regarded as intolerable'.[12]

That decisive action came on the 11th, as Alexandria was bombarded. The stock market itself waited on further events, but there is no doubt that the City as a whole was firmly behind Gladstone's action. The *Economist* would have been in danger of alienating its natural constituency if it had not toed the line and, with riots starting to spread inland, declared that 'whatever may have been the case a few days ago, it is no longer possible to speak of our action in Egypt as opposed to legitimate national aspirations'. And: 'Our interests in the Suez Canal, which it has all along been acknowledged we are bound at all hazards to maintain, are now distinctly threatened.' On 20 July the government decided upon a military expedition to Cairo, and Capel Court approved: 'There is nothing which the Stock Exchange apparently dreads so much as delay.' They were sentiments privately endorsed a week later by David McLean of the Hongkong and Shanghai Bank:

> I want to see England take Egypt and hold it. I am sure its the best thing for the Egyptians and I dont think the old Turk would object so long as we paid him the Tribute money. France would not like it but as she declines to fight now, she would not likely fight England & Egypt combined . . . I wish it was settled somehow and dont look for any revival in business until it is settled.

In August the *Bankers' Magazine* backed government policy, making much of the importance to British economic interests of the Suez Canal and arguing rather tortuously that while 'we do not say that because we have great commercial interests in Egypt we are therefore entitled to interfere by force of arms in the settlement of her internal affairs', nevertheless 'what we have a perfect right to maintain is, that as there exists a trade route over which we have a right of way, we cannot allow that right of way to be interfered with and our passage stopped'.[13] On

13 September at Tel-el-Kebir the British Army defeated the Egyptian insurgents; in the battle's immediate wake there began the de facto British occupation of the country, pending the return of full security to the canal and satisfactory stability to Egyptian finances; and few dissenting voices were raised in the City.

Historians have long debated the causes of the occupation of Egypt. Clearly the Suez Canal was thought to be at risk and thus the safety of India, that jewel in the imperial crown; clearly the internal disorder in Egypt was perceived as serious, even if it was somewhat overestimated; and clearly there were anxieties as to what the French might do if there was no British initiative.[14] Yet it is equally clear that the economic dimension was also very important, and that the well-vocalised interests of the Egyptian bondholders were no negligible concern. There existed a conjunction of interests, and their exact weighting will doubtless remain a matter of debate. Conjunction, not conspiracy. 'The bondholders are now in possession of Egypt', declared the Radical writer and thinker Frederic Harrison on 26 June to the Anti-Aggression League; and five days later, in an open letter to Gladstone published even as Seymour awaited his orders, he further activated a historical hare that would run and run:

> Turn it which way you will, it comes back always to this – that we are to go to war really for the money interests of certain rich men in London and Paris . . . Does it necessarily follow that, because certain Englishmen hold large sums in Unified bonds, and because they have invested much capital in Egyptian works, that Europeans are to be guaranteed as a dominant caste; and that, if the Egyptian people make any effort to displace one rivet of the dominion, there is instant appeal to war, ending in virtual conquest?

No, it did not *necessarily* follow – but it helped . . . And when Harrison made his final, vain, magnificent appeal – 'the permanent exploitation of Egypt by Western speculators and adventurers is an object which it is worthy of your career formally to repudiate as a national concern' – perhaps even Gladstone in the watches of the night would have conceded the point to that extent.[15]

*

It was in 1882 that, oblivious of impending foreign complications and amidst a wave of popular enthusiasm for anything to do with the pioneering world of electricity, electric lighting and the manufacture of electrical equipment, there took place the so-called 'Brush boom'. The Brush Company was the leader in the field, it had close links with a company formed by an ingenious electrical engineer called Hammond, and it proceeded to float various subsidiaries. Among them was Metropolitan Brush, licensed to work the patents of Brush arc lights in the London area and brought out in mid-May by H. Osborne O'Hagan:

> There was such a rush for the shares as had never been seen before in Lombard Street, the whole street being blocked by the crowd pressing to get to the bank to pay in their applications. Many gave up the attempt, contenting themselves with posting their applications in the nearest pillar-box. The capital was enormously oversubscribed, all the well-known City names being amongst the list of subscribers, and the shares, which on allotment were to be £3 paid, were on the day of the issue of the prospectus dealt in on the London Stock Exchange at £7 per share, or £4 premium. It was no wonder that Dick, Tom, and Harry put in applications in the hope of getting an allotment of a few shares . . .

So far so brilliant, from a company promoter's point of view anyway; but the awkward fact was that a handful of powerful bears on the Stock Exchange had decided that the Brush system was worthless and therefore were determined to force down the price. Their chosen instrument was the Jablochkoff Electric Light and Power Company, brought out in late May and reliant on what O'Hagan sincerely believed to be an inferior system of arc lighting. The Brush bears not only pushed up Jablochkoff shares to a big premium, but also went on a wrecking campaign.

> Rumours were actively circulated that there was nothing in the Brush system which would prevent a hundred rivals from entering the field and sharing the business with them. It was also put about that already the Brush system had been discarded in several places and one of its rivals substituted. The word went round, 'See what has happened in Paris'. No one knew what had happened in Paris, and no one inquired. It all helped to frighten speculators, and with a vigorous campaign against the Brush, Hammond, and Metropolitan shares, the bubble burst, the shares tumbled down many points in a week, and the Metropolitan Brush shares, which were a few days before selling at £4 per share premium, could not be sold at par. This was one of the worst slumps I have ever witnessed, for the speculating public were just as anxious to get out of their shares as a week or two before they had been anxious to acquire them, so that in a fortnight the shares of the Brush and Hammond Companies stood only at a small premium, although it was known that they had in their treasuries large sums for which they had sold their licences, and which would be distributed amongst the shareholders.

These abused companies, O'Hagan sagely concluded, 'were just a few years before their time'.[16]

O'Hagan's is the fallible account of an old man writing without notes many years afterwards, but there is no doubt that the 'Brush boom' was a remarkable episode in company promotion. Many enterprises were floated, a colossal £7m subscribed, few of the ventures survived, and a long-term legacy of mistrust was bequeathed to the whole British electrical industry:

> The existing state of things with regard to electric light companies is deplorable. Company after company is promoted and floated with a huge capital when it is absolutely certain that for years to come there will not be legitimate business enough to any per centage on a large part of the capital subscribed ... This speculative gambling is a curse to true enterprise. Rotten companies, not worth the paper their prospectuses are printed on, are always started when the public lose their heads, as they seem to have done now, to the loss of the ultimate holders of shares. Companies may be and are brought out legitimately, and are worked by honest men. Unfortunately the public will not discriminate ...

The bad drive out the good, and these words of the *Electrician* in May 1882 itself were echoed twelve years later by Alexander Siemens in his presidential address to the Institution of Electrical Engineers:

> However much other causes may have contributed to delay the development of electrical engineering, it is clear that the principal one must be looked for in the exaggerated expectations that were raised, either by ignorance or by design, when the general public first seriously thought of regarding electricity as a commodity for everyday use.
> At that time the promoters of electric companies preached to the public that electricity was in its infancy, that the laws of this science were totally unknown, and that wonders could be confidently expected from it. There was a short time of excitement to the public and of profit to the promoters; then the confidence of the public in electricity was almost destroyed, and could only be regained by years of patient work.[17]

Of course, as Siemens acknowledged, there were other causes: greed on the initial part of the companies themselves, including Brush; technical shortcomings; and legislation passed in 1882 that regulated prices as well as permitting local authorities to buy private electrical undertakings after twenty-one years, inevitably a discouragement to would-be long-term investors.[18] Yet the burden of Siemens' charge was justified, for above all it was the financial system itself that failed the fledgling industry. Ultimately it was a failure of quality control, a failure to distinguish between the bad and the good and then discourage the bad, keep faith with the good. No one can blame the public for succumbing to a mania – but the job of the professional intermediary, whether company promoter or stockbroker, is to apply objective analysis precisely at the times when it is not only reason that is at a premium.

It was a catastrophic start for the industry, as those public companies (including Brush, but not Hammond) that had survived the roller coaster of 1882 found themselves for most of the rest of the century hobbled for capital and having to pay out unrealistically high dividends in order to prevent a complete collapse of confidence on the part of an already deeply sceptical stock market.[19] This was disastrous, for by this stage in its economic development, starting to be caught up by Germany and the United States in terms of its mature industries, Britain should have been looking to the new industries – above all, electrical engineering, chemicals and in due course motor cars – in order to regain its unquestioned industrial ascendancy. All three of these new industries were high-tech and capital-intensive, so there could be no question of relying on traditional forms of self-finance and local finance. In other words, the role of the London capital market was pivotal.[20] The point, however, was not so much the *total* supply of funds that it did or did not channel into these new industries, but rather whether it was capable of effectively applying the element of long-term, disinterested discrimination. The experience of the 'Brush boom' suggested that, in terms of the crucial latter service, there was ample room for improvement.

Perhaps one could not have expected otherwise from the City in 1882. There were still very few industrial securities quoted on the Stock Exchange; an inevitable concomitant of this was poor marketability, not helped by the Committee's determination to preserve the monopoly rights of jobbers; and in the admonitory words of Erasmus Pinto's *Ye Outside Fools! Glimpses inside the Stock Exchange* (1877), 'Take no shares in industrial companies, unless fully acquainted with the concern'. A further discouragement until the turn of the century was the legal restriction on underwriting industrial shares, though O'Hagan among others was finding ways round the problem by the 1880s. Symptomatic of – and perpetuating – the Cinderella status of the Miscellaneous market (as the Stock Exchange's industrial department was called) was the reluctance of the leading merchant banks to sponsor domestic industrial issues, a reluctance attributable partly to their risky reputation and partly to the small and therefore unprofitable size of most of the issues. 'I never mean to have anything to do with industrial undertakings in the sense of lending our name', Everard Hambro asserted in 1882 itself, and with a few notable exceptions it was an attitude that would persist among the City elite for the best part of half a century. Nor were there many reputable stockbrokers willing to fill the gap and act as domestic issuing houses, or even act in harness with company promoters. As much as anything it was, as the *Statist* explained in 1886, a temperamental aversion:

> Company accoucheuring is not particularly popular in the House, and the best firms are chary of meddling with it. They prefer good steady everyday work which involves no special responsibility and only a reasonable amount of brain labour. To turn over familiar stocks like Trunks or Eries by the thousand day by day and week by week is the ideal existence of a prosperous broker. His morning letters and his afternoon cables are quite excitement enough for him. Surrounded by a circle of well-to-do clients, who can be trusted to take up their stocks or meet their differences without a murmur on pay-day, he is happy in his small world. From his office to the House, and from the House back to his office, is an ample round of existence for him. When he feels seedy or wants diversion he can have his Saturday to Monday at Brighton or the Isle of Wight. What could a well-endowed citizen wish for more? Such a man has no inherent love of novelty, and his predisposition is to suspect everything in the way of originality. Whatever might throw the big machine out of gear finds in him an avowedly prejudiced critic.[21]

So, the City's treatment of British industry was left for the most part to the tender mercies of an assorted band of company promoters. Some, like O'Hagan, were more or less honourable; most were not; and the results were well-nigh disastrous.

*

The world was the City's oyster, the future of British electrical engineering but a drop in the financial ocean. Take the Argentine where, in the context of monetary reform and apparent political stability under General Roca, there was much optimistic attention being focused. British investment in joint-stock enterprises in Argentina totalled some £25m in 1880, rising to £45m by 1885. There was then a minor crisis of confidence, but Dr Carlos Pellegrini, a Harrow-educated former finance minister, travelled to Europe and reached an agreement with some of the leading banks, including Barings and Morgans, that in effect imposed tight financial controls over the spendthrift Argentine Government, in return for a continuing flow of European investment.[22]

Control from London was also exercised in other ways during these years, by George Drabble and others. Born in Sheffield in 1823 into a family of cotton goods exporters, Drabble went to Buenos Aires as a young man and achieved considerable local prominence in ranch management and cotton trading. On his return to Britain in the late 1860s he was elected to the board of the Bank of London and the River Plate, soon became chairman, and for the rest of the century devoted his energies to ensuring that the bank was run much more professionally than it had been, with the initiatives of local merchants being firmly subordinated to the overall direction of the City-based board. The experience of the Mercantile Bank of the River Plate was similar. It was founded in 1872 by prosperous, locally based Anglo-Argentine merchants, the Wanklyn brothers, as an explicit rival to what was seen as Drabble's unduly conservative, City-dominated bank; it fared poorly against a background of political and economic troubles in the Argentine during much of the 1870s; and in 1881 it was absorbed into the River Plate Trust, a major investment vehicle controlled by Charles Morrison (son of James) and very much part of the City establishment. But, as they were to discover at 8 Bishopsgate, the balance of power between metropolis and periphery was not always what it seemed. In 1876 Barings sent a former member of staff, Nicholas Bouwer, to be its agent in Buenos Aires. He soon developed intimate relations with the local house of S. B. Hale & Co – an intimacy that extended to marrying the senior partner's daughter and becoming a partner in the firm himself, despite remaining Barings' agent. There were manifestly great opportunities in the Argentine (seemingly destined to be the United States of the southern hemisphere), Barings under the ambitious Ned Baring was determined to exploit them, and for the moment it did not matter that the affairs of the two houses were becoming increasingly entwined.[23]

Another Latin American bank run from London was the London and Brazilian, where John Beaton was a long-serving manager before becoming managing director in 1885 and eventually chairman. He was a mid-Victorian in outlook, retained a firm belief in the virtues of free trade, and in his old-fashioned way liked to call himself a 'cambist'. His concern for the integrity and good name of the bank was deeply felt, and a constant anxiety was how to prevent his local managers in Brazil from indulging in their penchant for exchange speculation. Much of the bank's business lay in financing the export of coffee from Brazil, often involving the issue of sterling drafts by the bank's branches to enable it to be sold in New York, and a perennial puzzle was trying to guess the likely course of the Brazilian exchanges. Beaton's correspondence from head office at 2 Old Broad Street was voluminous; fairly typical, in tone as well as substance, was part of this September 1879 missive to Rio:

> *Analysis of P/L.* This is to hand with thanks and the working of your Branch would have been highly satisfactory, but for the deduction on account of loss for Overdraft . . . We can only congratulate you on the result of your Exertions & we are assured you are as fully alive to the evil of another draft as we are.
>
> *Government.* We are well satisfied to learn that the Minister continues to give you a share of his patronage.
>
> *Telegram.* We note that you dare not express an opinion of Exchange, fearing its little value, it seems to us that it was for us to estimate the value! . . . Had the late Baron Rothschild been domiciled amongst you, you would all have realized, that he could form an opinion about the future course of Exchange![24]

Again, there is a contrast to be drawn between the firm hand on the tiller of a Beaton or a Drabble and the less than adequate hand of a well-established merchant bank. Here the case in point is Antony Gibbs, which in the 1880s found it hard to establish a satisfactory relationship with its Australasian house, Gibbs, Bright & Company. The London end fluctuated between on the one hand a pessimistic restrictiveness (and, in relation to exchange activities, even incomprehension) that significantly hampered the Australian business, on the other hand a failure to ensure that the Australian house was not over-committing the London partnership's capital. 'The several houses should be as far as possible all strands of the same cable, so that when *we* pull at home, they all feel the strain together.' So advocated Henry Hucks Gibbs to his son Vicary in 1884, referring to the five Australasian branches. By this time the total Antony Gibbs picture included a major involvement in Chilean nitrates, and the absence of full-time, wholly dedicated management in London was becoming palpably a problem.[25]

One area that Gibbs eschewed in the 1870s and 1880s was the financing of North American railroads, but plenty of other City houses had no such qualms. Clear market leaders by the 1880s were Barings, followed by Morgans, while other active railroad issuers included Speyers, Morton Rose, Brown Shipley, Seligmans, Robert Benson and even Thomson Bonar, hitherto best known for its Russian business. The 1880s was the decade in which 'Yankees' were at their consistently most popular in the London market, despite the occasional spectacular default or other scandal, and there was a certain bowing to the inevitable when Rothschilds, after Baron Lionel's death, engaged more actively in American matters than it had for many years. Nevertheless, an underlying ambivalence seems to have remained, even on the part of Barings, the dominant force in the field. From 1878 the firm was closely linked to Kidder Peabody, a thriving New York and Boston house that specialised in railroad business; and certainly Ned Baring was determined that Barings should stay the supreme financial and commercial Anglo-American institution. His right-hand man, T. C. Baring, expressed another view, however, when in 1883 he wrote with his congenital sourness to the firm's American agent that 'our experience in the business of railway loans in the US, though profitable in the main, has not always been of so satisfactory and smooth a character as to make us very passionately enamoured of it'; and the same year he and the other Bishopsgate partners resisted the suggestion that they should recruit into the partnership an expert on these unpredictable railroads. As for Morgans, there were clear signs in the 1880s that the London house was becoming rather cautious and risk-averse as Junius reached old age and that the main initiative in railroad financing was passing across the Atlantic to his decidedly less cautious son Pierpont, on his way to becoming a legend in his own lifetime. It represented a significant shift in the history of Morgans, and more importantly it reflected the way in which New York was, quite naturally, starting to grasp the lead in this sphere, though London would remain the focus for what was still the key component of a wide British and European distribution.[26]

It was also at this time that arbitrage business in the more popular railroad stocks – in other words, exploiting the difference in price at any one time on the two sides of the Atlantic – began to take off. The question of whether or not to enter this field was facing all the leading Anglo-American houses, and in October 1882 Brown Shipley addressed it with due circumspection:

> It will not suit us, with our Credit & Exchange business making such large calls as they do at present upon our time strength & resources, to embark in Arbitrage business to anything like the extent that such houses as for instance Raphaels do it . . . But there are firms who like Hambros do a certain limited amount of Arbitrage business & seem to find it profitable, & we have thought that to do something of the kind in a moderate way if it were only as an experiment might be well worth our while.

Brown Shipley, however, made it clear to Brown Brothers, who had recently acquired a seat on the New York Stock Exchange and were pressing to go into arbitrage, that it had serious reservations. After outlining the continuous application required if such arbitrage business between the two houses was to prosper, the letter went on:

> We may as well say at once, that no one of our existing partners in London can spare the requisite time nor are we any of us fitted by training, taste, or temperament to undertake it, besides it would be a new departure for us to discount & to borrow & might prove detrimental in other ways . . .[27]

In the event Brown Shipley failed to become significant arbitragists, while neither Barings nor Morgans made the attempt.

In fact it was a thoroughly trickly, 'nimble ninepence' kind of business that does not seem to have suited the stolid Anglo-Saxon temperament – an Achilles heel on the part of the City that perhaps also explained why, from the late 1870s, it was Vienna and Berlin, not London, that made the running in the evolution of futures markets for foreign exchange dealing. Or as a senior partner of Robert Benson & Co was subsequently to put it, 'Nobody understands arbitrage and foreign exchange unless born a Jew or an Armenian'. The partners of Raphaels and Samuel Montagu both fell into the former category, possessing a combination of aptitude, resources and capacity for sustained work that made their success in these demanding fields assured. In 1886 the *Statist* attempted to describe what happened at the London end as New York opened:

> Visitors to the City who are not familiar with its ways must observe a good many scenes which puzzle them. If they chance to be loitering about Bartholomew-lane or Throgmorton-street between three and four o'clock in the afternoon they may see telegraph boys racing along at a breakneck pace . . . They dash across streets, shoot round corners like greased lightning . . . dodge past hansoms, and rush up stairs into demure looking offices in the most unceremonious fashion. As soon as they reach the door they shout "cable!" . . . But these fleet footed youngsters may make as much noise as they please, and nobody objects . . .
>
> The afternoon cable race is one of the recent developments of Stock Exchange enterprise. It is carried on in the interest of the "arbitrageurs", who buy and sell on the small margins of difference there may happen to be between the London and New York markets. Arbitrage is also practised between London and the chief Continental Bourses, but on a smaller scale and with less scientific methods. On the Continent it is done largely

between one Bourse and another; in fact, it is of foreign origin, and foreigners take the lead in it even here. The market which offers the finest scope for it is American railways, the daily fluctuations in these stocks being active, and the deviations from parity between the New York and London prices being often considerable . . .

Translating dollar prices into sterling prices at the exchange of the day – a rate which is seldom two days alike – involves intricate calculation. Tables have been framed to facilitate the process, but an expert 'arbitrageur' carries in his head about all that he needs for his purpose . . .

From a quarter past 3 o'clock onwards the cables come pouring in. They have to be sent out from the cable offices to the offices of the arbitrage houses. There they have to be turned into sterling prices, and these compared with the London prices at the moment. Like a flash of lightning the 'arbitrageur' has to decide what he will buy and what he will sell. He rushes to the House and has his business done for him . . . Then he cables back to New York to 'cover' his transactions, that is, to buy against what he had sold or to sell against what he has bought. It may be also that his partner or agent in New York has entered into transactions which he must cover here if he can. The game is played simultaneously from both ends, and like duplex telegraphy there are generally two accounts of speculation crossing each other. Scores of buyings and sellings may be going on together, each of which carries a certain degree of risk, but the arbitrageur's hope is to come out right on the general balance. He makes his risks, so to speak, insure each other, and so long as the differences are comparatively small he stands a fair chance to come out well. The arbitrageurs themselves say that it is the small profits they make most by. A wide fluctuation in a stock, while a transaction in it is being covered, is pretty sure to end badly. If it is against the arbitrageurs, great judgement has to be exercised in deciding whether the loss should be cut at once, or the transaction kept open on the chance of its righting itself . . .

Having the first cable from Wall Street of an afternoon is better than having a 'moral certainty' for the Derby. The second cable is worth a good deal less, as the jobbers are quick enough to see how the wind blows from the west. If the arbitrageurs are buying they put up prices, and if they are selling they put them down. It is only the early bird that catches the arbitrage worm, and the late birds are more likely to be caught themselves. That is the moral of the headlong racing among the cable boys, of the lightning calculations, and the rushes of excited clerks into the House about half-past 3 o'clock. Capel Court and Wall Street are like two arms of a delicately poised balance. They are always deviating from the level, but the slightest touch brings them back to it. By forestalling that slight touch the arbitrageur makes his living.[28]

Was it a way in which a gentleman would choose to make a living? The silent implication was clear enough, and it did not flatter Armenians.

There were no such qualms about foreign government loans, even though they could involve some distinctly covert operations. Between 1877 and 1890 almost a quarter of the business (measured by value) still went to Rothschilds, while Barings and Hambros vied for second place, with the American houses of Morton Rose, Morgans and Seligmans in hot pursuit. For the really big loans, involving an international syndicate, it was significant that it was no longer a London house that invariably took 'the lead'; and when in 1880 the Russian Government authorised a £20m loan, not only was it floated in Paris, but only two of the fifteen banks who participated in the syndicate were British.[29] Nevertheless, London still maintained an overall edge over other capital markets, and the point was well illustrated in the early 1880s by the saga of the £29m Italian government loan, in many ways a replay of the Sardinian episode thirty years earlier.

The central City player was once again Hambros, this time with Everard in charge and making the most of his close personal as well as working ties with Ned Baring. The nub of a complex story[30] was that Italy in the intervening years had returned to being Paris Rothschilds country, but that Everard Hambro was now given the chance to show that his house could manage such a massive loan, based on the London market and without the assistance of Baron Alphonse de Rothschild. Accordingly he gathered together a powerful syndicate comprising his own firm, Barings, the Banque d'Escompte, the National Bank of Italy and the Crédit Mobilier of Italy. All went well in 1881, when the first tranche of almost £15m was successfully offered for sale, but then the problems began. Against a background of extremely nervous international markets because of the Egyptian situation, and Baron Alphonse conducting a superbly effective campaign to nobble the Banque d'Escompte, Hambro found himself by March 1882 coming under pressure from the non-British members of the syndicate to bring in the Paris Rothschilds before the second tranche was issued. This he refused, but the upshot in early May was disaster: subscriptions of barely £3m and the syndicate left with over £11m, with little or no sub-underwriting apparently arranged. The Italians again pressed for Rothschilds' help, but Hambro was adamant: 'The position of our two houses, that of Baring and mine – being what it is – would make it quite impossible for us to allow anyone to say that we had undertaken something which we could not carry to a good end.' An enormous amount of prestige was at stake, for the London market as well as Hambros and Barings; and in late September, after five weeks mulling things over on a Scottish grouse moor, Hambro deployed all his many contacts in order to mount a rearguard operation and most of the balance of the issue was sold to individual banks who would be firm holders of the stock until the market recovered. In effect he assembled a new, broad-based syndicate, which included Morgans and Brown Shipley; and early in 1883 when Hambro was able to relieve the syndicate of its responsibilities, placing almost £6½m of the loan with the market as a whole, he was justifiably congratulated by Brown Shipley on 'the very successful result obtained under all the peculiar circumstances of the case'. He could not have come out unscathed without the four-square support of Ned Baring, and the easy relationship between these two men at the very top of the City was illuminated in a brief note passed between them in 1885, presumably following another loan or operation. 'I should like my quarter if you are willing', scribbled Everard, 'but only if you are quite willing. You have had all the work so I feel I have no claim on the pickings. In haste as I am off to the Bank . . .'[31]

An increasingly competitive part of the world in terms of loan-issuing was the Far East. The first Chinese sterling loan on the London market was issued by Mathesons (the London house acting for Jardine Matheson) in 1875, while a decade later it was the Hongkong and Shanghai Bank making the running. McLean in London described the process to his chief:

> *15 October 1884.* The Chinese Ambassador wanted to know on what terms a Sterling Loan could be raised . . . I think we might get a Syndicate to take it @ 7% @ 95. But it is rather doubtful and at my request the Minister wired to Pekin recommending holding off for a time. If the French difficulty was settled, a Loan would go like smoke. The opponent against us is Rothschild, but we have the preference. Rothschild knows nothing of this proposed Loan and wont if I can help it. Marquis Tseng is most friendly to us & promised me that nothing will be done without first consulting us.
>
> *27 February 1885.* We have at last got the Syndicate to take up to £750,000 @ 94 net to us. The issue price is £98, but whether the public will take it remains to be seen . . . People are frightened to touch Loans just now owing to Political complications. The G.O.M. has made a nice mess all over the globe . . .
>
> *6 March 1885.* We have had large applications & judging by the amounts & the class of people applying I should say about £1,250,000 are bona fide Investors. The other 1 to 1½ Millions applied for by 'Stags', they simply apply to resell.

Soon afterwards, in June, two Chinese loans were prepared for the London market: one, for £1.5m, was to go to a central government department, called the 'Peking Field Force', and its purpose was 'the construction of an Arsenal, the extraction of Coal and Iron, and the experimental inauguration of a Railway in connection with these mining enterprises'; the other, for £757,000, was on behalf of the Viceroy of the Liang Kwang provinces. The first was to be issued by Barings (acting in tandem with Jardine Matheson), the second by the Hongkong Bank. Shortly before the day of issue there took place, as McLean noted with some irony, an attempt to pull City rank:

> Late this afternoon Mr Matheson sent for me to meet Mr Baring. They asked me to allow our Loan to be issued with theirs, without our name. *And they very kindly* said the business would be carried thro without Comm . . . I know what your answer will be, at least I hope so. Its a regular try on to shrink us in getting any more Loans from the Chinese . . .

Over the next few days, the Hongkong Bank pulled out all its stops to make sure that its loan was not issued after the Barings one, and exactly a week after the 'regular try on' McLean was writing triumphantly: 'Our Loan has been a great success. Barings, & Mathesons too, fancied that we were not ready . . .'[32] The Hongkong and Shanghai remained very much a player in the Chinese loans market, but it had been important that its London manager had kept his nerve at a critical moment.

Also requiring funding in the summer of 1885 was Egypt, the object of a £9m loan to be guaranteed by the French and German Governments as well as the British. The natural issuer of the loan was the Bank of England, which, since it usually issued for India and the Colonies, fully expected to issue for this new sphere of British influence; and indeed the Governor, James Currie, in liaison with Mark Collet, Everard Hambro and the government broker J. H. Daniell, drew up detailed proposals for Childers, Chancellor of the Exchequer in the dying days of Gladstone's second ministry. That was in April, but by July the situation had changed in two important ways: one was Bismarck's insistence that London allot a substantial proportion of the loan to Berlin as well as to Paris; the other was the advent of a Conservative government under Lord Salisbury. There occurred a discreet switching of horses, and on the 21st Sir Reginald Welby of the Treasury wrote to the new Chancellor, Hicks Beach:

> Lord Salisbury [Foreign Secretary as well as Prime Minister] sent over to me to come & meet Rothschild and Lord R [Natty had recently been ennobled] at once opened the question of Commission . . .

I told him of course that the reply must come from you and he said he would wait at the F.O. until the answer came . . .

I suggested to Lord R that he sh^d go back to the City & we would send to him, but he preferred waiting at the F.O.!

The deal was clinched, involving, at Rothschild's insistence, subscriptions to be invited at a fixed price; and on the 27th, Salisbury found himself writing an uncomfortable letter to the Bank of England. He explained that the peculiar circumstances of the loan – to be issued in three European capitals – had led to the government 'entrusting the issue of the English portion of the Loan to the agency of N. M. Rothschild, because that firm is one with the Houses of the same name in Paris and Frankfurt, and is in similar relations with the House of Bleichröder in Berlin'. Currie's reply was pained. 'We were prepared', he insisted, 'to carry out the issue in the centres of the Guaranteeing Powers, with, we believe, the greatest advantage to the Egyptian Government.'[33]

Would a Liberal government have acted otherwise? *Possibly* not, to judge by the shrewdest commentary on the whole episode, written on the 29th:

The Egyptian Loan has been brought out. It was entrusted to Rothschilds. Being the slave of Bismarck, the Gov were bound to allow part of it to be subscribed for in Berlin. Consequently, it was not convenient to employ the Bank of England, who have not been treated with too much courtesy; and, as the principle of tender is not understood or practised at Berlin or Paris, Egypt has had to lose the benefit of open competition. The price fixed was $95\frac{1}{2}$, which was subscribed for over & over again.[34]

Edward Hamilton had recently left Gladstone's service as one of his private secretaries and was now in the permanent employ of the Treasury. A bachelor, a gossip and a perceptive observer with a wide range of contacts, he left a diary that survives as a matchless document on the symbiotic relationship between high politics and high finance.

In terms of high finance, with fingers in pies all over the world, the visible embodiment was still Barings and Rothschilds, with Ned and Natty by the 1880s firmly at their respective helms. The more striking of the two was Ned Baring, a man self-evidently out of the ordinary ruck. 'Eyes of half-envious astonishment' used to follow him, a financial journalist would recall, 'as he daily drove a splendid pair of horses to his office, clad and hatted correctly, but with a short briar pipe between his teeth'. In every sense he was, in his prime, a full-blown character: somewhat overbearing, accustomed to his own authority, impatient of fools though not always able to recognise them, intelligent, cultured and hard-working, palpably ambitious for his firm and therefore himself (definitely in that order) – in short, very different from the grave, silent banker of City mythology. He had many attractive characteristics, including great generosity, but there remained the fundamental question mark of his judgement, which Bates had implicitly raised at the outset of his career. 'His qualities are those of a straightforward man of business, with little of the finesse possessed by his great rivals in financial business. He does not pretend to brilliant qualities, but makes his way by strict adherence to honest and straightforward methods.' There was some truth in this *Bankers' Magazine* description of 1888, but it hardly gave the whole picture. Indeed, arguably it applied rather better to Natty Rothschild, who had no great analytic intelligence, but made up for this with strength of character, sense of duty, and unwavering determination to hold what he had. 'Yes, by selling too soon': such was his typically blunt reply when asked if he had a secret for making money. As for imagination not being his long suit, implicit testimony came from his hero Disraeli, who once remarked that 'whenever I want to know an historical fact, I always ask Natty'. Natty, however, could also be very affectionate, even sentimental; he had little interest in the trappings of wealth; he abhorred unnecessary letter writing; and he possessed what a descendant would call 'enormous, almost ruthless vitality and drive'. He may not have been quite the man to advance the Rothschild position, but nor was he someone who would squander a unique legacy.[35]

We have glimpses of life in New Court under Natty and his two brothers. Carl Meyer had come to London in the 1870s, and by the 1880s this extremely able native of Hamburg was the rising man at Rothschilds, in effect acting as trusted confidential clerk. He would write to his wife when she was away, and his surviving letters reveal, among other things, that the preoccupations of *haute finance* were not always so high and mighty:

> The tape has just brought the result, at which I don't grumble. I suppose you know it by this time. The Lambkin, Sandway, Superba. I got 14 to 2 about Lambkin yesterday. I vainly tried all day yesterday to persuade Mr A. de R. to back the Lambkin but somehow he had a fancy for Queen Adelaide.

That was in September 1884, but the following August the nags were forgotten as the grind of the Egyptian loan – in particular, its complex

prompting the Managers to suggest that the market should change places with the Foreign market, which itself was adjacent to the inland telegraph lobby. An entirely commonsensical proposal, one might have thought, but it was soon causing ruptures. Proposed date for the new dispensation was 24 January, a Monday, when the Submarine Telegraph Company was to open its new office; but on the previous Wednesday, 98 railway jobbers petitioned the Committee to the effect that it objected to moving and that its rights were being infringed, while the Committee itself summoned one of the Managers and insisted that 'under no circumstances had the Managers any power to enforce orders against the subscribers'. On the 22nd, 114 dealers in the Foreign market sent in a memorial to the Committee supporting the proposed change. 'For several years past', it stated, 'business in the Foreign Market has been impeded, and great inconvenience and even risk have been caused, by the confusion and reckless rush across the House of members crowding to the telegraph office from the English Share Market [i.e. the Consol market] on the opposite side of the building.' And it predicted that if the change was not made, the situation would become even worse: 'The rush of members from west to east will be met by an opposite current from east to west.' The railway jobbers were unrepentant and the same day posted a notice claiming not only that 'the rushing to and fro is not caused by any particular market, but that the greatest offenders are the brokers, who deal between markets and their clerks'; and even asserting that 'many individual members consider that they have a sort of vested interest in the position they have occupied for years on the floor of the House'.

Monday morning proved predictably chaotic: the jobbers in the Foreign market sought to take up their putative new position in the Home Rails market, the jobbers there resisted them, and amidst scenes of considerable tumult it was only after the personal intervention of the deputy-chairman of the Committee (after Lionel Cohen of the Managers had failed to obtain a hearing) that order was restored and the invading jobbers persuaded to return pro tem to their usual position. Over the next fortnight the Managers conceded the wider point that the whole matter fell within the Committee's jurisdiction; while Septimus Scott, chairman of the Committee, for his part accepted that the actual proposal was a good one and stated that he would endeavour to have it carried out. That would have been the end of the story, whatever the wishes of the railway jobbers, if it had not been that on 3 February the jobbers in the Consol market mustered their own memorial against the proposed switch, on the grounds that the Foreign market moving to a smaller space would lead to an overflow foreign market that in turn would result in 'a very serious interference with our necessarily frequent passage to and from the Bank of England'. Accordingly, when Scott sought the Committee's adoption of the proposed change, he was defeated by eleven votes to five; the Managers, on being informed, expressed not unnatural 'regret and surprise'; the markets stayed where they were; and the renowned clout of the Consol market was once again made manifest.[37]

One railway jobber perhaps defended his pitch with particular vehemence. In March 1882 a notoriously strait-laced member, John Pyemont, complained of the 'systematic annoyance', both physical and verbal, to which he had for a long time been subjected from those standing in the Metropolitan market (a division of the Home Rails market), singling out Walter Tassell and Fraser E. Baddeley as his especial tormentors. In response, the Committee asked Tassell merely to apologise, but decided that Baddeley had been guilty of violating rule 16, involving 'disgraceful or dishonourable conduct' and liable to result in a substantive punishment. There followed a memorial from fellow-jobbers in the Metropolitan market, and in consequence Baddeley escaped with a censure and caution only. Eight months later, however, he was back in the Committee room:

> A letter was read from Mr H. Landau complaining that Mr F. E. Baddeley, to whom he had not spoken for many years, had, without provocation, grossly insulted him in the open market, by calling him 'a liar'.
>
> Mr Baddeley asked for an opportunity of explaining the circumstances. He said that it would be unnecessary for him to refer to the well-known custom amongst dealers, under which when a man challenged at a figure under the market price, he was understood to be a seller, and when he challenged at a figure over the market price, he was understood to be a buyer. Upon the occasion in question, Brighton 'A' stock was just 'sellers' at $\frac{3}{4}$, in fact a jobber who had bid that price had just been 'saddled', when Mr Landau suddenly challenged the market with 20,000 at $\frac{7}{8}$. He – Baddeley – called out 'I'll sell you five!' Mr Landau answered, 'No, I'm a seller'. He – Baddeley – was so disgusted at this that when a brother member said 'put them down to him', he replied, 'No, if that is the way he does business, the sooner he goes back to Poland the better!' He – Baddeley – did not know whether Mr Landau was a broker or a jobber; formerly he was a jobber in the very market in which this scene had occurred; then he turned broker; and now it was hard to say what he was, but as a fact he was constantly standing and dealing in his – Baddeley's – market; and it was not too much to assume that he must know the usages.

When therefore Mr Landau said, 'Well, I did wrong through ignorance of the customs', he told him that he had told a deliberate lie.

The explanation given, Baddeley was prevailed upon to withdraw the expression complained of; while Landau 'said he hoped that the Committee would express an opinion as to his conduct in the matter and was told that the case was closed'.[38]

There seems to have been something incorrigible about Fraser Baddeley, for a few years later he was the subject of a complaint that the support of some interior scaffolding had been cut away with a pocket knife, with the possibility of snapping and thereby causing an accident if a heavy weight was on the top. Yet again Baddeley was called in:

> He said that he did not know why he was picked out for complaint, as at least 40 people had done the same thing as he had done, which was simply to cut initials in the wood. There was one place where the wood was certainly cut to some extent, but there was no damage intended to the House. He considered it childish to suppose there had been any danger caused to anyone by what had been done, and there had assuredly been no idea of bringing the House down.

Childish maybe, but the Committee repaid the compliment when it informed him that it 'regretted to find that a member of his standing had allowed himself to be put in the position of being found fault with for an act which it might be thought could only be committed by a schoolboy, and they trusted he would never repeat such irrational conduct'.[39]

Meanwhile, the firms that would help mould the twentieth-century Stock Exchange continued to take shape. In 1882, the story goes, Henry Rudolph Laing and Fletcher Hayes Grant Cruickshank were on their way to a poker game when they decided to start their own stockbroking firm. Two years later, P. Cazenove & Co was in danger of falling apart on the retirement of its senior figures, but recruited two experienced brokers, John and Swainson Akroyd, to join the young Arthur Philip Cazenove, the firm becoming Cazenove & Akroyds. On the jobbing front, one young member, Fred Durlacher, after obtaining banking experience in Hamburg through a friend of his father's and spending a year as a broker, started on his own as a jobber in 1881 before teaming up with his brother Neville three years later, the new partnership dealing in breweries as well as railways; while in 1885, a well-established jobber called George Wedd set up in partnership with Harry Jefferson, the new firm soon becoming a significant presence in the Consol market.[40]

No prosperous future, however, awaited Rufus Isaacs in Capel Court. He had been born in 1860 at St Mary Axe into a family whose business was fruit importing; and after leaving school at thirteen, he spent some disagreeable years in the family firm (based in Mitre Street) before in 1880 going into the office of a stockbroker who had married his eldest sister. He soon became a member and then went into partnership with Gerald Phipps, a jobber in the Foreign market, before that was dissolved in 1883 and he tried jobbing on his own account. In these years Isaacs was a sharply dressed young man about town; he even won renown for standing on his head in a box at the Empire in Leicester Square and applauding vigorously with his feet. He also became particularly friendly with Jack Angle, the member of the Stock Exchange who doubled as one of the leading amateur heavyweights of the day. Isaacs himself took up boxing and together they spent many evenings in the East End cultivating the noble art among working men and boys, with Angle as referee and Rufus as timekeeper. Halcyon times, but they ended abruptly. 'The Stock Exchange settlement was concluded today', ran the City report of *The Times* on 14 August 1884. 'Only one very unimportant failure has been announced, and quotations were very strong all day in most departments.' The member so insignificantly hammered was Isaacs – in circumstances rather different to the subsequent family legend of his being caught unawares by a sudden slump – and soon he was reading for the Bar. 'I cannot say that I admire mankind, particularly City mankind', he wrote not long afterwards to a young lady friend.[41]

Although he once described himself as 'an ardent disciple of Schopenhauer', it is unlikely that Harry Panmure Gordon had any such qualms. The extrovert *par excellence* of an extrovert community, he had already by the 1880s had a very full and varied life. He was born in Perthshire in 1837, the only son of a well-known City figure who was a director of the Union Bank of London; he was educated at Harrow, Oxford and Bonn University; there followed four years in the 10th Hussars, before his spendthriftiness may well have played a part in his father's bankruptcy; he thereupon resigned his commission and went to China, joining a trading firm in Shanghai; and shortly after his arrival the Taiping rebellion broke out. This gave Panmure Gordon the chance to organise and command the Shanghai Mounted Volunteers, part of the 'Ever Victorious Army' that suppressed the Taipings. This military prowess won him a great reputation as well as a personal connection with Li Hung-chang and other Chinese notables. He returned to England in 1865 and, becoming a member of the Stock Exchange, joined the firm of J. & A. Scrimgeour. There followed his slightly embarrassing entanglement with Baron Grant and the world of Lisbon tramways, and in 1876 he established his own stockbroking firm.

Over the next quarter of a century Panmure Gordon flourished not only as an extremely successful practitioner, especially in the new issue sphere, but also as one of the most talked-about men in the City. The attention focused on a unique life-style. His homes (at Adelaide Crescent, Brighton and in time at Carlton House Terrace and near Rickmansworth) were lavish affairs in which he entertained freely; his penchant was to drive four-in-hand into the City; he was reckoned to have the best private collection of carriages in the world; his sartorial tastes were such that he possessed over a thousand neckties alone; and in *Who's Who* he listed his hobbies as salmon fishing, breeding collies, and running his estate. All this cost money. 'Well, I shall live a rich man and die a poor one', he once remarked, computing that his minimum expenditure was £2,000 a month. But, as he well knew, there was a pay-off, for his way of life, added to an attractive personality, enabled him to mix freely with the cream of society and gave him an entry into the best City parlours; altogether he was probably the most enviably connected of all late-Victorian stockbrokers. Nor was he remotely a fool in his conduct of business: his Chinese experience made him an invaluable helpmate of the Hongkong and Shanghai Bank; he had the good sense to recruit into his firm an extraordinarily able young Belgian, Willie Koch, who provided the financial brains; and he himself was always full of push and energy, one of his clerks later recalling how his 'restless temperament showed itself in staccato phrases, constantly repeated, accompanied by a gesture of the hands, like a player throwing out a card in bridge'. Panmure Gordon may have had a different pair of trousers for every day in the year, but there was more to his success than pants alone.[42]

The Capel Court climate in which 'PG' and others prospered in the 1880s was generally an invigorating one. In November 1884 the *Economist* offered its customarily magisterial perspective:

> The field for speculation afforded by the Stock Exchange is so various, the *rationale* of its methods has become so easy, and the initial credit or capital required is so small, that its popularity is easily explained. Its unreasonableness, however, is very clearly seen by those inside, who know that not only are the various factors which go to make up at any time the general condition extremely difficult to measure accurately, but also that the 'market' conditions are nearly always a matter of very wide conjecture. Take one set of stocks as an example. It would require the

closest study and the nicest calculation to arrive at any idea at all of the actual value of Grand Trunk stocks, while, as a rule, the 'market' movements, which are often the most important to speculators, are not known with the slightest certainty by the dealers themselves. The fact, however, remains, that a multitude of people are always ready to gamble in such issues, who would never dream of touching in a speculative way, iron, cotton, sugar, &c.

The article then described the inexorable increase 'in recent years' of the 'speculative element' in the House:

Firms with a large investment business, subsisting chiefly by that alone, are gradually diminishing. In fact, the number of first-rate houses of this description could almost be counted on one's fingers. The process by which they are dropping out – to be seen in all directions – is a perfectly natural one, and none can grow up to take their place; for it took in most cases fifty or a hundred years under the old order of things to build up a great investment house, with its connection of, perhaps nominally, three or four thousand clients. The most pretentious of the newer houses are very different, even the soundest of them. In their case, speculative business is the main thing, and apart from it many firms, with a very different reputation, could by no means exist.

Inevitably, the newer members of the Stock Exchange, which had increased greatly in numbers in recent years, tended to be speculative in their orientation. And, looking back over the past ten years or so:

Social reasons had begun to make the 'House' fashionable, owing to the apparent ease with which large fortunes were realised, and also the club-like nature of its life, when the Clearing House became firmly established [from 1880], and the necessity for a considerable degree of technical skill was largely swept away. As a consequence, a great influx took place, but the new element rather made up for want of business instincts by a greater liking and desire for business of a highly adventurous type.

In short, asserted the august journal, the Stock Exchange 'has undergone a greater permanent transformation than is generally recognised'.[43]

Nor was share speculation filtered solely through Stock Exchange firms, for in the 1880s there took place a mushrooming of brokers operating outside the Stock Exchange's jurisdiction. A few were powerful, reputable outfits, conducted by former members who had been frustrated by the Committee's refusal to allow its members to advertise; but the great majority were small-scale, opportunist affairs as described here by the *Statist*:

> The capital required to start an outside broker's office is the amount sufficient to pay the subscription to the Exchange Telegraph Company for their 'tape', to decently furnish the office, and provide a small balance at a bank. A modern development of an outside broker's office is the unlimited supply of cigarettes, and the favoured few do obtain an occasional glass of sherry . . .

The tape, it was clear, 'has become a faro-table for backing the rise or fall in prices', and more often than not what the business of these outside brokers comprised was clients betting on tape prices – for the rise or for the fall – rather than investing in the securities as such, even on a short-term basis. By 1886 as many as eighty outside brokers subscribed to the tape, and the more disreputable were commonly known as 'bucket shops'. Some controversy exists about the origin of the term, but the likeliest explanation is that it referred to the way in which the narrow coils of tape showing the latest Stock Exchange prices would eventually fall into a wooden bucket conveniently placed there for the purpose. Many Stock Exchange brokers resented the competition – in effect, an incursion into their monopoly – but for the time being were powerless to prevent the Exchange Telegraph Company from maximising its income.[44]

For brokers, punters and anyone else interested in the stock market, from January 1884 there was a daily paper that at last sought to provide a financial coverage that was trenchant and investigative as well as accurate and comprehensive. This was the *Financial News* (called for its first few months the *Financial and Mining News*), and the man behind it was the colourful, ambitious, none-too-scrupulous Harry Marks.[45] He was the fifth son of the head of the Reformed Congregation of British Jews and had served a youthful newspaper apprenticeship in the States, where he not only became editor of the world's first daily mining paper but also came to realise the gap that existed in the London market for a financial paper full of American-style verve and 'bounce'. He returned to England still in his twenties and, backed by an American engineer-cum-financier called Colonel McMurdo, began his life's work. Marks himself was editor as well as virtual proprietor, and his paper was soon making a considerable impact.

From the first the *FN* specialised in providing the most up-to-date, 'inside' information, with mines and American railroads as particular specialities. It also launched various campaigns, including one against dishonest bucket shops. As one of its best journalists, W. R. Lawson, was to recall: 'Our readers supplied us with the necessary information, and the bucketeer seldom showed fight. Either he returned the margin put up [i.e. by the client] or he compounded, or he made a bolt.' Indeed, the paper made a point of developing close relations with its readers, typified by its very popular 'Answers to correspondents' column. On 19 March 1885, for instance, a correspondent related that early the previous Monday morning he had wired his broker to buy 2,000 Metropolitan ordinary, but that the resulting purchase price of 102 was 'widely different from what I can find noted as the opening price in any paper'. The editor replied: 'Your broker certainly seems to have made a bad bargain, but the market for Metropolitans was somewhat excited and irregular on Monday morning.' In the same issue appeared a query from someone signing himself 'M. A. Cantab':

> Thoroughly sharing your opinion as to the value of Grand Trunks, I have lately sold the Second and Third Preference Stocks. At the last two accounts there has been, according to the *Financial News*, a small back-wardation of the Second, and a contango of 6d to 1s 6d on the Third Preference. At the account at the end of February I obtained a contango of 3d on the Thirds, and at the last account they were carried over at evens. On each occasion I paid a backwardation of $\frac{5}{16}$ on the Seconds, and they were all carried over at the very commencement of the account. My broker says he did the best he personally could for me. Can you kindly explain why I did not fare better?

This time the editor's reply was the soul of brevity: 'No'. In general, though, it was its *tone* that marked out the *FN*, a tone exemplified by its ironic critique of the large claims made by the East Florida Land & Produce Company in its prospectus: 'We are at a loss to understand why, in the estimates of profit, no account is taken of the luscious yellow pineapples that would grow under the tall yellow pine trees. Where are the profits from the fragrant and graceful banana; from the early strawberry and the toothsome green pea?'[46] Irreverent, caustic and often penetrating, the Marksian revolution in daily financial journalism was a much-needed one, despite the unfortunate side-effects that would soon reveal themselves.

In the Stock Exchange itself, the great problem by the early 1880s was one of *Lebensraum*. By 1883 the membership was over 2,500 (compared with less than 1,500 in 1870), while the following year the amount of space per person admitted to the House was down to an oppressive 2.08 square feet. Inevitably the poor clerks were blamed for the congestion – one year for crowding out the Foreign market on settlement days, another for loitering in general, yet another when the Hercules Passage entrance was deemed to be 'always obstructed by a crowd of clerks and foreigners'. Relief, however, was at hand. The Stock Exchange's architect, J. J. Cole, was commissioned to design a new building that would link with the existing one. The financial journalist Charles Duguid tried to describe it some years later, and he began with its dominant feature, the great dome:

> Its style is Italian, almost Roman, and the whole design is marked by a solidity and reality which forms a strong contrast to the plaster-work of the older building. The piers of the Dome are of solid Peterhead granite, many of the stones being more than three tons in weight. The Dome itself, covering the central octagonal area, is 70 ft in diameter and 100 ft high. The entrance lobbies and staircases are lined with marble, and the street fronts are constructed of Portland stone and granite. At the time of the addition the walls of the Old House were covered with Pavonazza marble to bring it into consonance with the New House, and the pillars were covered with Rosso and Giallo-Antico marble from the Roman quarries near Carthage. The peculiar veining of the new marble it was which immediately earned for the House the disrespectful title of Gorgonzola Hall!

In March 1885, soon after the new wing had been opened for business, the Prince of Wales paid a tour of inspection. Hearty cheers followed by enthusiastic renditions of the National Anthem and 'God Bless the Prince of Wales' were the inevitable accompaniments to the royal visit.[47] The Stock Exchange no doubt liked to think that it was becoming an accepted part of national life – those eighteenth-century outlaw days long gone – but the cheesy nickname was a gratifying reminder that its denizens could never take themselves quite seriously.

There were, in that hermetic, often hothouse world, plenty of other nicknames in everyday use.[48] Many referred to securities, and the schoolboy logic behind the tag was readily apparent. Thus 'Bags' were Buenos Ayres Great Southern Railway ordinary stock, 'Beetles' were Colorado United Mining Co shares, 'Berwicks' were North-Eastern Railway consolidated ordinary stock, 'Bulgarian Atrocities' were Varna & Rustchuk Railway 3 per cent obligations, 'Cream-jugs' were Charkow-Krementschug Railway bonds, 'Ducks' were Aylesbury Dairy Co shares, 'Haddocks' were Great North of Scotland ordinary stock, 'Matches' were Bryant & May shares, 'Pots' were North Staffordshire Railway ordinary stock, 'Sardines' were Royal Sardinian Railway shares, 'Sarah's Boots' were Sierra Buttes Gold Mine shares, 'Virgins' were Virginia new funded, and so on.

Similarly cerebral were some of the other terms frequently swopped between members. A 'turn' was well understood (even outside Capel Court) as the profit on a bargain, but few outsiders realised that a 'rasper' was a particularly big turn. 'Jam tart' meant exactly the market, in other words with buyers and sellers at the same price. A 'picker-up' was that unmentionable cad who not only tried to get a fellow-member to make a wrong price but then dealt with him. To 'bang' was to offer stock loudly with the intention of lowering the price, to 'puff' was to bid for stock loudly with the intention of raising the price. A 'squirt' was someone who hung about the market with a paltry order, not dealing fairly. To 'read' was to try to tell by a man's face or manner what he wanted to do, to 'shoot' was to make a man a close price in a stock without knowing if there would be a profit or loss on the bargain. A 'sweater' was a broker who undercut the competition by working for small commissions, a 'poacher' was a jobber who dealt out of his own market or continually changed markets. There were plenty of other slang expressions, but probably the classic of them all was the cry of 'Fourteen hundred!' – for some mysterious reason the shout that would go up whenever a stranger was spotted in the House, invariably prompting a vigorous, even bruising 'rat-hunt' to flush him out of the sacrosanct place.

In the mid-1880s a junior called Murray Griffith sought to penetrate this mysterious, compelling temple. He joined a firm of dealers in the Home Rails market, served a rather turbulent apprenticeship checking bargains, and then his big moment came:

> In quite an undue time, that is, quite early, I was admitted to the precincts of the Holy of Holies, the House, and then at once I realised that I had fallen amongst a lot of men who were always kind and helpful.
>
> The first day, passing along by the American market, I heard a big gentleman, with a big voice and a big beard, bid for a million Eries; that took me some time to digest and work out how much it came to in cash, and I wondered if he had all this money.
>
> When I was ordered to go before the Committee to be admitted as a clerk, I had been warned that I was never to loiter about in the markets, but in those days there was a fascination for me in hearing anyone bid for anything, and I spent all my spare moments in watching anyone bidding; I just worshipped them, but I had a kind of dislike to anyone who offered stocks. In those days we had giants in all the markets. Our market – the

Brighton market – dear old George Paine, who would help anyone who opened to him and played fair, but woe be to anyone who came the old soldier.

Roscoe, who was gentleness itself; in fact, when I became an authorised clerk all the big men acted more like fathers to me than competitors.

In the heavy rail market men like Robert Case, Walter Barron, and Hensley, no deal too big for them. The Foreign market, Lionel Cohen, Baker, and Sturdy, and many others, all dealing in huge amounts, but if I went to any of them with just a tiny little order, they were all just as kind and civil to me as to the biggest broker in the House.

All this struck me as true sportsmanship to help along a youngster. This kind of schoolboy comradeship in the hard battle for success, established in my mind the fact that the Stock Exchange was full of human beings. The only standard to live up to being that you 'play the game'. As time advanced I became an authorised clerk, which job is not the most pleasant, for though you may have the most broad-minded governor, it is so easy to job backwards. The most hardened dealers at some time or the other cannot help saying well it is all right, but I cannot understand why you bought so and so. Well, when you have made the wrong price, you, the clerk, know and feel what a fool you are, and you don't want it rubbed in. In my opinion the position of authorised clerk to a dealer is the most uncomfortable and worrying job anyone can take on; if you are on your own account and get landed on a falling market, you cut it, perhaps say a short bad word, pay up, and forget it, but when dealing for someone else you are full of anxiety; if you run the book it goes down, and if you cut it, it goes up. However, again comes into promise the good nature of the Stock Exchange man, rarely if ever do you hear of a governor rubbing in his mistakes to his clerk.

'Forty Years in the Best Club in London', Griffith called his fragment of memoirs. And as memoirs, they serve as a necessary antidote to the recollections (written at about the same time) of Carruthers Gould. Neither man denied the volatile, even seismic character of Stock Exchange life: but whereas the artist found it an existence unbearably ruthless in its practical working out, for Griffith it was an exciting, even exhilarating way of life fortified by the good fellowship of the club to which he was proud to belong. There is little doubt with whose view most members would have empathised. And, in a rather wonderful passage, the by now very successful jobber laid his faith on the line:

> I have always considered that the Stock Exchange is the real and true example of a socialistic institution, inasmuch that it gives everyone a chance of getting on, if he has the energy and brains so to do. Again, I say

they ask no questions; you do not require a banker's reference, etc, all you have to do is to 'play the game'; and even if a man is unfortunate and comes to an end financially, it is not a question of how he came to grief, 'but did he play the game?' . . .[49]

CHAPTER NINETEEN

Gentlemen of Property

'On June 15, 1886, about four of the afternoon, the observer who chanced to be present at the house of old Jolyon Forsyte in Stanhope Gate, might have seen the highest efflorescence of the Forsytes.' 'At home' to celebrate the engagement of his granddaughter, old Jolyon was a retired tea merchant in the City. His firm, Forsyte and Treffry, was by now a limited liability company and in decline, without the guiding influence of his celebrated palate and 'masterful power of selection' in the choice of agents. Directly or indirectly, the City played a significant part in the lives of all the Forsytes; and when the ultra-cautious Timothy, Jolyon's brother, put his savings into three per cent Consols, this made him an object of pity to the rest of his family, who 'had no dread in life like that of 3 per cent for their money'.[1] So this saga of the upper middle class would unfold, shadowed by a subtext of money invested in bricks and mortar, money invested in stocks and shares, and all underpinned, for good or ill, by a commercial society steadily pursuing its commercial goals. It was a masterly stroke of Galsworthy to begin his story in the summer of 1886 – for that was the moment when, with mid-Victorian reforming zeal finally exhausted, there emerged, in its hegemonic form, a social-cum-political compact devoted to the defence of property against the emerging threat of socialism. It was a compact of land and finance, of white-collar workers in proliferating suburbs, of 'Villa Toryism'. There were, of course, other elements to this late-Victorian compact, including the defence of Empire, but it was property that lay at the core. Galsworthy called his first volume *The Man of Property*, and again it was a felicitous touch. What specifically, though, was the importance of the City in all this? Not everything was resolved overnight in the mid-1880s, but in retrospect there are three critical areas: the City and politics; the City and imperialism; and the City and society. Taken together, with the question of bimetallism as an illuminating coda, they help to move the City of London, at last, into the mainstream of modern British history.

*

By the 1870s the decisive shift was under way of suburbia in general, and the City in particular, towards Conservatism. In 1874 the City returned three Conservatives and one Liberal, though the significance of this was masked by the fact of a Tory election victory. Soon, though, the writing was clearly on the wall. During the agitation over the Eastern Question, the City mood was as much anti-Gladstone and anti-Liberal as it was anti-Russian. And when George Goschen decided not to contest the City in the 1880 election and instead find a seat elsewhere, the City of London Liberal Association was unable to persuade Sir John Lubbock to ditch his Maidstone seat for the City. He consulted Liberal agents and others, who convinced him that the City could not be carried.[2] In 1880 itself, the Conservatives again took three seats and the Liberals (coming fourth) the other – and this despite it being a Liberal year overall. One City man still sitting on the Liberal benches was William McArthur, a successful wool merchant of Irish background who had been based in London from the mid-1850s.[3] He became MP for Lambeth in 1868, but by the early 1880s (having been Lord Mayor in 1880–81 and also been knighted) he was wholly out of sympathy with 'advanced' Liberalism. Sunday opening and temperance reform were what his Liberalism was about, not slum housing and unemployment; but as old-style Gladstonian Liberalism ran out of steam during the great man's second ministry, the Liberal agenda was moving irrevocably towards more materialist and there-fore, to its middle-class supporters, more threatening consider-ations. And when Gladstone sought to use Irish Home Rule as a way out, being an apparently ethical, non-economic issue of national self-determination, this merely compounded his problems, as much of what remained of his middle-class support, including in the City, struck camp en masse.

One episode during his second ministry had a particular significance. It began, from the City's point of view, in the Guildhall on a Saturday in September 1883:

> Something like half-an-hour elapsed before the aldermen returned to the hustings, and the impatient Livery [over 1500 strong] had for some time occupied themselves with shouting 'Time'. It was at once seen by the countenance of Mr Alderman Hadley that the choice of the aldermen had not fallen upon him, which gave rise to hooting and hissing and other signs of disapprobation, mingled with fierce crys of 'Hadley'. When the Lord Mayor came into the hall accompanied by Mr Alderman Fowler, they were received with hooting, interspersed with a few cheers.

> The Recorder, who was met with a storm of hissing, announced that the election had fallen upon Mr Alderman Fowler, MP, whereupon there were more hisses and groans, and cries of 'Shame' . . .
>
> The Lord Mayor-Elect, looking much distressed at the unusual reception given him by the gentlemen of the livery, tried for some time in vain to make himself heard above the noise and confusion . . .

No one, reported the *City Press*, could remember such turbulent scenes at the election of a Lord Mayor.[4] Their cause, almost certainly, was the need felt by the aldermen to mount an effective defence of the City's interests against the bill to reform London's local government that the Liberals were expected shortly to produce. So, instead of following hallowed convention by electing the senior alderman of the day, a Liberal called Hadley, they decided to entrust the defence of the City to Robert Fowler – the acknowledged leader of the City Conservatives, himself one of the City's MPs, and a forceful character.[5] He was also a well-known private banker, and his election as alderman for the ward of Cornhill in 1878 marked a clear break with the tradition of the City's leading bankers and financiers keeping their distance from the City Corporation.

Fowler duly became Lord Mayor, and in April 1884 Sir William Harcourt brought forward his London Government Bill. It sought to transform the City Corporation into a central governing body for the metropolis as a whole, in effect changing the Corporation beyond recognition and depriving the City of exclusive rights over its own estates. An 'able piece of constructive legislation' was the verdict of *The Times*, but immediately the City was up in arms, with Fowler leading an energetic and very expensive campaign. On 9 May the ratepayers of the City assembled at the Guildhall, and among those on the platform was the giant of the Foreign market, Lionel Cohen, who moved the first resolution. 'It was no exaggeration to say', he said, 'that in attacking the City of London they were attacking the very centre of commerce, and of the civilised world – (Cheers).' And: 'The Bill was a discredit to the Government, which had proved vacillating and weak in defence of our interests, not merely at home, but in all parts of the world – (Cheers).' At the end, the motion thanking Fowler for chairing the meeting was moved by the solicitor Edwin Freshfield and seconded by the stockbroker H. Rokeby Price. The City was thoroughly mobilised, and its opposition was a significant factor behind the government's decision in July to withdraw the bill. Four years later the Conservatives *did* reform London's local government, abolishing the Metropolitan

Board of Works and creating the London County Council, but they made very sure that the ancient privileges of the City of London were thoroughly ring-fenced.[6]

The relationship between the City and Gladstone had long been difficult, but in the mid-1880s it attained a new pitch of animosity. 'We want Gladstone turned out before any good can come to this country d—n his eyes.' That was the private view of the Hongkong Bank's David McLean in June 1884, and the events of the next two years compounded it, as the City became in every sense a Tory stronghold. In the 1885 election, fought mainly on Chamberlain's Radical programme but also offering a verdict on Gladstone's second ministry, both City seats (their number had been reduced by the recent Redistribution Act) fell comfortably to the Conservatives. Then, in a state of electoral deadlock, came Gladstone's suspiciously sudden conversion to Irish Home Rule. The City had always taken a very strong line against violation of property in Ireland, and on this most fundamental of issues it made its views clear at a mass meeting held at the Guildhall on 2 April 1886. 'It was a great success', noted Fowler in his diary. 'The hall was crowded and enthusiastic, though a few held up their hands against us. The great thing was getting the leading City Liberals to take the stand they took against Gladstone.' Among those Liberals who spoke against Home Rule were Lubbock, Richard Biddulph Martin, and the prominent copper merchant and former Governor of the Bank, H. R. Grenfell. Grenfell was unequivocal: 'If there was one thing the City of London would not stand it was the disintegration of the Empire – (loud cheers) – and the separation of this country from Ireland (renewed cheering).'[7]

Some City Liberals remained faithful to Gladstone, most notably Bertram Currie and Samuel Montagu, but most did not, including McArthur. The most prominent of all the defectors was Natty Rothschild: he had long been unhappy with Gladstone's foreign policy (his family had always been Palmerstonian in outlook), and now at last he made the formal break. The ordinary City man fully shared the views of his betters, as Edward Hamilton found a few weeks after the Guildhall meeting:

> In coming up on a crowded train from Sevenoaks this morning, I overheard characteristic remarks proceeding from (presumably) City men. 'That d—d fellow, Gladstone, is going to make another change of front. It is always with him, no matter what the means, so long as he secures his end – retention of office'. 'Perish the country; sooner than give up my official salary'.[8]

In June Gladstone's Home Rule bill was defeated in the Commons, in July he went down to a crushing electoral defeat – an election in which the Liberals did not even put up a candidate for the City. There was one final twist to 1886. Chancellor of the Exchequer in Salisbury's new ministry was Lord Randolph Churchill, a man renowned for his contempt for the new suburban brand of Conservatism, what he called the 'pineries and vineries'. Late in the year, in an ill-judged move, he resigned; but Salisbury called his bluff, accepted the resignation, and replaced him with George Goschen who, like so many City men, had broken with Gladstone over Ireland.

Perhaps inevitably, much nonsense has been written about the City's influence on politicians and the political process. Of course, it did exercise *an* influence – and one should hardly be surprised, for by the late nineteenth century, as Britain's visible trade deficit widened, the wellbeing of the economy was increasingly dependent upon the 'invisible' earnings provided by the City. Successive generations of politicians appreciated that it would be counterproductive deliberately to antagonise the City. Even Gladstone toed that particular line: when at the outset of his third ministry it was suggested to him that Joseph Chamberlain should go to the Treasury, he discounted the idea on the grounds that, in his secretary's words, 'the City would be terrified at his views'. Some of the City's leading figures, usually either merchant bankers or private bankers, also moved freely in the same social world as the leading politicians of the day, meeting as a matter of course and more or less as equals at clubs, dinner parties and country house parties. There are two examples of particularly close relationships. One was between Gladstone and Bertram Currie, the former invariably turning to the latter whenever he needed advice on financial subjects. The other was on the Tory side. 'Churchill and Natty Rothschild seem to conduct the business of the Empire in great measure *together*', Reginald Brett recorded in 1886 during Lord Randolph's brief chancellorship. And two years later, Hamilton was noting that 'R. Churchill turns to N. Rothschild for everything, according to N. R.'. There is no doubt that Natty loved being in the political know. Hamilton described him as 'an infallible retailer of political as of all other news', with 'a wonderful knowledge of what is going on'. Hamilton himself, as a significant presence at the Treasury and on good personal as well as business terms with Natty, was very conscious of the importance of ensuring that Whitehall was not seen to be unduly influenced by the City. And in April 1889, in the context of consulting the Rothschilds about an imminent issue of Exchequer bonds, he wrote the most telling of entries in his diary: 'Though I always think it well to keep clear of them in the East End I actually lunched in New Court.'[9]

All that said, there are some powerful negative points to be made. It is arguable that there existed an underlying conflict of interests, in that successive British Governments naturally pursued national interests, whereas the City by definition pursued international interests.[10] It was a conflict, though, that would surface more in the twentieth than nineteenth century. There is also the point that *if* a leading City figure did go into Parliament – and, increasingly, the leading City men did not – it was as likely to be for social as political reasons, and often he had little to say for himself once there.[11] Few bankers (if any) possessed any great global vision or unusual prescience about the future course of events. That did not prevent Natty Rothschild, as Hamilton recorded, from offering some disparaging judgements in the course of dinner at Gunnersbury one evening in August 1887. Of Rosebery (married to his cousin Hannah): 'His speeches were watery; his reputation as Foreign Secretary had been over-rated . . . Bismarck was greatly disappointed with him.' Of Chamberlain (who had also deserted Gladstone over Home Rule): 'He would never be a big man. He was the Radical wolf in Tory sheep's clothing. He was the typical democrat – a spendthrift & jingo.' And of Gladstone himself: 'He was hopeless – never knew his own mind two years or even two months running; & a continual danger to the State.' At the same dinner Natty predicted – wrongly – that 'Hartington will be Prime Minister very soon'. A year later Hamilton spent a Sunday in the New Forest, as one of a party that included Natty. 'According to N. Rothschild', he noted, 'the "Times" charges against the Parnellites, including *the* letters, will be proved up to the hilt.' While as to their political effects, Gladstone 'would be ousted from power for good' and, 'with Mr G gone, Home Rule would die a natural death'. Such was the hopelessly subjective view of perhaps the most eminent man in the City, a man renowned for his grasp of facts; and as Hamilton commented, 'this I believe to be the forecast of the representative man in the (London) street', adding that in his own opinion the question of Home Rule would 'still be the vexed question to solve' with or without Gladstone.[12]

There is evidence, moreover, that at least some politicians were determined to keep an arm's length relationship with the City. In 1882, for instance, Hamilton recorded Gladstone's determination to appoint Childers as Chancellor rather than the best-qualified candidate: 'Mr G won't hear of Goschen for the place. He seems to be prejudiced against Goschen for this place, believing, as he says, that no man connected with the City can make a good Chancellor of the Exchequer.' Four years later, Chamberlain was forthright in his condemnation of the City for planning to hold a big anti-Home Rule meeting: 'This is perfect madness. For the City to oppose a measure is as fatal as for the House of Lords to throw it out. It is enough to set up the back of the caucus from one end of England to the other.' Nor, later in 1886, was Churchill helped politically by his notoriously close relationship with New Court; after his self-induced fall, Hamilton reflected that he might have been in trouble anyway on account of 'the excessive intimacy of a man occupying the post of Chancellor of the Exchequer with a certain great financial house'. Even Churchill, as he committed political suicide, could feel a politician's pride. Brett recorded the immediate aftermath: 'I asked if I could tell Natty. He [Churchill] said no, because he is furious with Alfred Rothschild, who it appears is taking strongly against him. "He complains that I did not consult the Rothschilds. After all I am glad to have them as friends, but I . . . am not yet in their pay".'[13]

Yet if successive chancellors refrained from consulting the City as they framed their budgets – a budget being an essentially 'political' question – none could refrain from tapping the City's expertise when it came to more 'technical', seemingly apolitical matters. The classic case was Churchill himself. In October 1885, while at the India Office, he informed the Viceroy of his plans to place a future India loan 'in the hands of the Rothschilds, whose financial knowledge is as great as that of the Bank of England is small'. A year later he was Chancellor and, though staying close to New Court, found himself compelled to change his tune about the Old Lady. Hamilton described a memorable visit:

> Today the Chanc of the Exchequer came down with Welby & myself to the Bank. Tenders for Treasury Bills afforded a good opportunity of introducing him to the Governor & Deputy Governor with whom the Chanc of the Exchequer ought to be on good terms. He seemed quite nervous about presenting himself; but was I think rather interested with the proceedings . . .

Presumably this was the occasion when Lord Randolph was reduced, in his son's words, to 'hovering for half an hour outside in a panic of nervousness'. Once inside, he found that the 'proceedings' went, as usual, smoothly enough, to judge by Hamilton's set-piece account that same day:

> We sit round the Governor's table. The Cashier & two others bring in the Tenders, open & sort them. The Governor then proceeds to read them

out. The cashiers then give roughly the average price at which our requirements can be met by three months Bills & six months Bills ... Today we wanted about 2 millions, & as nearly a million falls due in 6 months Bills next December we took one million in three months Bills at about $2\frac{1}{4}$% per annum, & the other million in 6 months Bills at about $2\frac{3}{4}$% p.a. One of course defers to the judgement of the Governor & Deputy Governor; but it is generally a simple & straightforward business ... Randolph Churchill said he was interested in the ceremony. The Bank of England is certainly a grand institution. After we had done our business we had luncheon. The working of the Bank Act very appropriately formed a subject of discussion.

'One of course defers ... ' Perhaps there was no alternative, but it was an instructive phrase; and on another occasion, after being present at the same ceremony, indispensable to the short-term funding of the government, Hamilton noted that 'one must practically follow the advice of the Governor & Deputy Governor, but I am not satisfied with the bargain I made'. This reality obtained whichever political party was in power. Yet even grave merchants are human beings susceptible to prejudice, and by the late 1880s the collective political mood was very different to what it had been a generation or two earlier. Hamilton was again the witness, in January 1888 on one of his regular visits to Threadneedle Street:

I was at the Bank today, raising £2,000,000 in Treasury Bills. We got our money on wonderfully low terms ... At luncheon in the Bank parlour one generally hears grumbles, if not expletives, about Mr G. One Director said he intended to send Mr G a naive advertisement of an enterprising undertaker, who expressed surprise that people should go on living a life of trouble to themselves and others when they could be comfortably interred for £3 ... [14]

*

The 1880s was the decade of new imperial rivalries, of the 'Scramble for Africa', of new red splotches on the map of the world. Was finance the motor? Did the economic component behind the occupation of Egypt in 1882 represent a turning point? J. A. Hobson would claim, in his seminal work *Imperialism* (1902), that 'finance manipulates the patriotic forces which politicians, soldiers, philanthropists, and traders generate'. And: 'The financial interest has those qualities of concentration and clear-sighted calculation which are needed to set Imperialism to work.' Hobson's pioneering and actually quite subtle interpretation has often been parodied, but what is clear is that there are no easy generalisations about the role of the City in the late nineteenth-century expansion of the British Empire. Quite apart from anything else, there remained, even after the Egyptian episode, a strong political tradition that deplored interference by vested financial interests. Lord Cromer, Consul-General in Egypt, recalled that tradition in a letter in the 1900s to his nephew at Barings:

> In past days when Lord Palmerston ruled supreme in foreign affairs and subsequent years, the policy of the British government was not merely to abstain from direct encouragement to those who wished to invest their money in foreign states, but also to give them clearly to understand that, if they did so, they must take all the risks and that they could not expect any very effective support in the event of their foreign debtors failing to abide by any pledges they might have taken. It was held that this was the only course a nation which was the chief reservoir of capital for all the world could safely adopt and that the adoption of a policy of more active interference on behalf of British pecuniary interests abroad might and very probably would result in frequent and possibly serious political complications.[15]

To an extent, but only to an extent, it was an attitude that began to change in the 1880s, as it penetrated the 'official mind' that British economic supremacy was under threat, that the protectionist barriers being imposed elsewhere were hampering British trade which thus required new outlets, and that other countries were giving an increasingly sharp 'economic' edge to their diplomatic efforts. In particular, Turkey, Persia and especially West Africa were parts of the world where the British Government was starting to take initiatives. What categorically this did not mean, however, was the birth of any great wish to defend what were often perceived as narrow, even selfish City interests. Put another way, the relationship between diplomats and bankers remained a fundamentally awkward one, even if they increasingly could not do without each other.[16]

There were further ambiguities, beginning with the fact that it was by no means always the City which spoke most forcefully for a forward policy on the part of government. In the important case of West Africa, for example, provincial businessmen made the decisive running. Even setting aside political divisions, the City was not wholly united over imperial policy: merchants and shipowners, for instance, tended to speak with very different voices.[17] The City, in its conservative way, could also drag its feet. Such was the experience of the financier Vincent

Caillard in Constantinople in 1888, as he headed an Anglo-Italian group that unsuccessfully tried to prevent the Germans from winning the Anatolian railway concession. His London backers, he complained to the Foreign Office, 'failed to grasp the situation as I depicted it to them' and in general 'acted with that exasperating slowness which seems so often to seize City men'.[18] Indeed, detailed research shows that whereas the imperial component was appreciably higher in the portfolios of London investors as compared with those of non-metropolitan investors, this practical enthusiasm for empire did not apply to the City itself, where foreign non-imperial securities (especially those of the United States and South America) were much preferred.[19] A final point. For all the City's 'gut' imperialism during these late-Victorian years – ultimately reflecting a certain set of values, one that came out strongly over the Irish question – there was the uncomfortable fact that an aggressive expansionist policy was expensive and potentially dangerous, above all if it led to war, that state of affairs most inimical to City interests. Heart and head, in other words, were not always at one: but, in most City souls, the heart usually won.

Among these imperialists were those quondam Lord Mayors, Sir William McArthur and Sir Robert Fowler. McArthur was a Wesleyan evangelical, Fowler a Quaker who turned Anglican philanthropist, and neither saw any contradiction. McArthur in the 1870s had been much involved with the annexation of Fiji, something he viewed in essentially missionary terms, and in 1884 both were founder members of the Imperial Federation League.[20] In specific City terms, though, the key organisation was the London Chamber of Commerce, established in 1882. 'England is entering upon a new period of competition against the whole world', stated its *Journal* at the outset, 'and the whole world is as well-organised, if not better, than we are.' Significantly, the LCC was broad-based across the City as a whole, and the members of its first council included fifteen merchants, six brokers of various sorts, five warehousemen, three private bankers and two shipowners. Its first president was Charles Magniac of Mathesons, and he was succeeded four years later by J. Herbert Tritton of Barclays.[21]

Almost from the start its conscious goals were imperial federation, active colonial expansion, and a higher priority in foreign policy to be given to business considerations. Over the years the LCC fought many campaigns. In 1883, following the recent British occupation of Egypt, it vigorously attacked the question of French control of the Suez Canal and managed to get de Lesseps to give ground. Two years later there began a major City push, channelled through the LCC, for a stronger

British Navy, one that would more effectively guarantee protection to trade routes. By 1889 the point was tacitly conceded by Salisbury in his speech at the LCC's annual dinner: 'Our greatest duty is to provide the material for defending the splendid commerce which your enterprise has created'. The third campaign also took shape in 1885, and its goal was the annexation of Upper Burma, in order to ensure that British trade, not French, was dominant there. That autumn it was not only the LCC which was applying pressure on Churchill (at the India Office) to this effect but also Rothschilds, who had ambitions for Burmese ruby mines as well as railways. Hamilton, at the start of 1886, recorded the outcome:

> Burmah has been annexed – the inevitable result of the recent expedition. There is no end to the reputed richness of this latest appendage to the Crown; and, tho' probably the statements about its riches are exaggerated, its being annexed will probably redound to the credit of the Gov. The fact is (as I heard someone appositely remark in the railway carriage this afternoon) Jingoism is popular so long as it brings profit; and traders confidently expect to make a profit out of the new Burmah.

The Conservatives were still in office, and it was ironic that one of the merchants who stood to benefit most from this act of naked economic imperialism was Henry Gladstone, third son of the GOM and a Calcutta partner in the firm of Ogilvy, Gillanders & Co, the Liverpool merchanting house that had opened a City office in 1860.[22]

Even as Hamilton was noting the Burmese annexation, the press reported the imminent despatch of a German mission to Peking with a view to trying to secure there a mixture of industrial contracts and financial concessions. Within a week Panmure Gordon had, 'at the request of a large body of bondholders and others interested in Chinese commerce', written a letter to *The Times* that he took the precaution of first showing to Lord Salisbury. Describing himself as 'having been connected with all the China loans issued on the London market', Panmure Gordon began by holding out glittering prospects for the future of Chinese railway loans:

> It may not be out of place to state that from the geographical formation of the country, few countries can be more easily traversed by railways. The vast labour market of the country, so cheaply and abundantly stocked, added to the migratory habits of the people, all point to a speedier mode of transit being readily adopted. I was one of the first travellers by steamer up the Yantze to Hankow after that Treaty Port was

opened, and was greatly struck with the rapidity with which steam routes were adopted by the Chinese for the transit of produce and travellers in lieu of the old-fashioned junks, which had to wait for months for certain trade winds.

Sufficient credit is not given to the character of the Chinese, partly on account of ignorance, partly prejudice. The natives are very patient – perhaps a little slow to act, but deep thinking and given to master thoroughly all points of any proposed innovation. Present holders of Chinese securities need be under no alarm; the greatest caution will be exercised by the Chinese Government ere large monetary commitments are entered into.

That brought 'PG' to the question of international competition for new Chinese loans:

All countries will have a fair chance, as the Chinese Government will purchase in the best and cheapest market. Being well acquainted with the financial conditions of all the money markets of Europe, I consider that the London market is undoubtedly the chief and cheapest. This the Chinese Government are well aware of, and are not likely to pay additional commissions to foreign houses to float their loans on the London market.

However, then came the warning: 'It is an undeniable fact that the Ambassadors of all European nations, except our own, officially have instructions to support the financial and industrial schemes of their own countrymen.' Panmure Gordon called for a similar approach from the British Minister in Peking, and then wound up:

What a bright halo would encircle either the Conservative or Liberal party if this broad commonsense policy of supporting British commercial interests in the East were adopted? It would immediately strike the keynote of relief to the universal cry of depression of trade existing through our industrial centres, and if instead of 'Home Rule' any political party caused 'Home Interests' to be the popular cry, they would obtain a firmer grip in the saddle and endear themselves to the sympathies of all classes throughout the country.[23]

Salisbury took the cue, and later in January 1886 he wired to the Chargé d'Affaires at Peking the following instructions: 'In cases where foreign representatives interfere to the detriment of British commercial interests, you are at liberty to give the latter your support.' The Salisbury telegram marked a turning point in relations between business and state, even though diehard non-interventionism continued to linger at the Foreign Office. There was a sequel to this particular episode, and it occurred in the summer when the Chinese Minister in London, Marquis Tseng, returned to China via Germany, following the invitation of the German Government to meet Bismarck and tour German manufacturing centres. It was a development that caused hasty consultations between City and Whitehall, and early in August the latest information – and advice – was being passed on by Natty Rothschild at New Court to Sir Julian Pauncefote at the Foreign Office:

> I forgot to mention to you, when you did us the honour of calling here yesterday, that we had had advice from Berlin to the effect that the Marquis Tseng is now staying in the German Capital and that his presence there is being made the occasion for all manner of intrigues on the part of the German iron and steel manufacturers.
> I think it would be advisable for you to mention the matter to Lord Iddesleigh [formerly Northcote, now the foreign secretary] with a view to his taking such steps as will tend to secure for English manufacturers a fair proportion of any future contracts with the Chinese Government.

The tone was somewhat Richard Hannay – and almost certainly the City as a whole overreacted at this time to the German challenge to British interests in China – but the letter from this very Anglicised Rothschild was the clearest possible indication of the way in which the stakes were beginning to be raised in the intricate, worldwide game of finance and diplomacy.[24]

*

Natty Rothschild himself exemplifies the phenomenon that has been called 'gentlemanly capitalism', or alternatively 'integration'.[25] This is the phenomenon by which, in the late nineteenth century, the upper reaches of the City moved increasingly close to the traditional landed governing class, thereby achieving an intimate and privileged access to power denied to their industrial counterparts in the provinces. Such access, the argument runs, was in no sense conspiratorial, but rather the natural outcome of shared values and assumptions in turn deriving from, as much as anything, shared lifestyles. 'Manufacturers and merchants as a rule seem only to desire riches that they may be enabled to prostrate themselves at the feet of feudalism.' That dispirited verdict of Cobden as early as 1863 was echoed a quarter of a century later by Engels, who lamented 'the political decline and abdication of the bourgeoisie'.[26] Or put differently: W. G. Prescott's foray into the Scottish Highlands may have been ill-judged, and a cause of surprise to his thoroughly middle-class partners, but it pointed the way to a plutocratic, grouse-shooting future.

Why did the British aristocracy, a notoriously closed caste, let in the men of finance? Escott offered an explanation:

> All Englishmen, and a good many Englishwomen, if they have no vested interest in horses, bet, gamble, or speculate in some way. When it is not the Turf, it is the Stock Exchange, and perhaps this is the reason that the City plays so large a part in the arrangements of the West End. Duchesses and other ladies of rank, I may parenthetically observe, would scarcely be so demonstrative in their affection for the wirepullers of the London money market, to say nothing of a crowd of stock jobbers and stock-brokers, but for the speculative impulse within them.

That explanation, though, ignored a specific economic motive by the 1880s, which was that the rent rolls of the aristocracy were falling and thus many of its members needed to find not only a new investment strategy but also alternative sources of income. Both needs brought them into close and continuous contact with the City, which offered well-paid, light-duty jobs as well as investment portfolios to suit every taste and pocket. Sometimes these jobs took the form of partnerships within City firms, usually stockbroking; sometimes it might be a half-commission arrangement with a stockbroker, in effect touting for West End custom; and sometimes, if an impecunious aristocrat was very lucky, it might be what was called with delightful accuracy a 'guinea-pig' directorship. E. C. Grenville Murray, in his *Side-Lights on English Society* published in 1881, described how peers were 'at a premium for directing companies':

> If a Noble Lord's character can bear anything like the test of scrutiny – and so long as he is not on the turf it generally can – he may command good terms for letting his name be put on a prospectus. His patronage means success. What a peer offers for sale the public will buy; and if they are ruined it will console them greatly to hear that his lordship is a fellow-sufferer in pocket. Noble Lords always pretend to be heavy losers by joint-stock directing . . .

As company promotions boomed in the last two decades of the century, the opportunities were there for the taking; and by the mid-1890s about a quarter of the entire nobility were company directors. There was no doubt who was the most memorable guinea-pig:

> I sit by selection
> Upon the direction
> Of several companies bubble.
> As soon as they're floated
> I'm freely banknoted –
> I'm pretty well paid for my trouble.

So, in 1889 in *The Gondoliers*, sang the Duke of Plazo-Toro, that Spanish grandee 'unhappily in straitened circumstances' before his boat came home.[27]

On the other side of the compact, the City's great moment came in June 1885 when Natty Rothschild and Ned Baring were made peers, as Lord Rothschild and Lord Revelstoke respectively. 'It is thought desirable at this moment to give an addition of commercial strength to the House of Lords', explained Hamilton, little guessing that within a year both men would abandon Gladstone over the Irish question. There were, not least due to royal prejudice, few precedents for these new peers. Robert Smith who had the pencil taken from behind his ear; Loyd who became Overstone; and, in 1869, G. C Glyn who became Lord Wolverton. 'I did not know that you would be allowed to remain in business', wrote Glyn's partner, Sir Charles Mills, in his letter of congratulation, reflecting a traditional view of the nature of aristocracy. In 1885 itself, neither Rothschild nor Revelstoke had any intention of leaving the counting house, though for both men it was an honour gratefully received. Natty in particular was flourishing as never before, and a few of Hamilton's diary entries vividly convey the sense of him at the very centre of the social-cum-political elite:

> *15 April 1885*. Had an interesting dinner at the N. Rothschilds tonight. The Russian Ambassador was there in very good humour and was tackled in the evening by Sir W. Harcourt. There were also present the Bretts, Lady C. Beresford, Du Canes, Wolff, A. Balfour, Leighton, J. Morley, G. Russell &c.
> *27 May 1886*. Dined last night at the Rothschilds (Lord) – a big dinner – the German & Spanish ambassadors, both new, the Duke & Duchess of Wellington, Curzons, C. Beresford, W. Caringtons, Sir W. White, R. Spencer, Mrs Leo R & others. It was followed by an evening party, at which the house is always seen to great advantage.
> *26 July 1888*. I wound up my season last night with a dinner at the Rothschilds – a large party . . . After dinner there was an evening party – first, music . . . and then a recitation or two from Sarah Bernhardt . . .

Though perhaps lacking his rival's insatiable appetite for political gossip, Revelstoke was quite as much in the swim, and in April 1890

Hamilton accompanied him to Althorp for a house party at the home of Lord Spencer.[28]

For almost anyone who was anyone, the lure of a place in the country was more compelling than ever. Among merchant bankers (even setting aside the partners of Rothschilds, Barings and Hambros), Charles Goschen owned 'Ballards' near Croydon, built for him in 1873 by F. P. Cockerell in the innovative Queen Anne style; Henry Tiarks of Schröders moved four years later to 'Foxbury' in Chislehurst, a forty-room mansion set in 57 acres; and Henry Hucks Gibbs over the years made many additions to his fine country house at Aldenham in Hertfordshire. A particularly squirearchical figure was Brown Shipley's Mark Collet, as recalled by one of his American partners:

> While living in Liverpool, and later at his beautiful home at St Clere in Kent, he served as churchwarden of the parish churches, and in the latter place was accustomed to assist the clergyman by reading the Lessons. I can never forget the Sunday evening services at St Clere, when with guests and servants assembled in the upper hall, after the usual evening hymn and Scripture lesson, Sir Mark [as he became in 1888] gave a brief practical exposition of the passage he had read, never glossing over a difficulty, but drawing some practical lesson for the guidance of conduct.[29]

Other sectors of the City produced other landowning examples. Robert Fowler the private banker gradually acquired an extensive country property in Wiltshire, complete with ha-ha and obligatory stabling and kennels for hunting purposes. Charles Churchill junior the timber broker bought Weybridge Park in 1863 and spent happy summer hours sculling on the Thames. Henry Freshfield the solicitor bought Kidbrooke Park in 1874, becoming in time High Sheriff of Sussex. And William Peat, senior partner of the Mincing Lane commodity brokers Lewis & Peat, was by the 1870s living in a large house on Wimbledon Common, backdrop for his three sons to become such passionate, even brilliant polo players that they were nicknamed the 'Polo Peats'.[30] Or take some of the leading gentlemen of the Stock Exchange. Tom Nickalls celebrated his crowning as 'Erie King' in 1872 by moving his family to Patteson Court near Redhill, and then in 1887 bought a sporting estate in Sweden, whose 100,000 acres included a lake eight miles long and where he built a large house for big parties each August. Henry Cazenove, the leading figure at Cazenove's in the 1870s, acquired a country property near Aylesbury and threw himself into his new role with such enthusiasm that, in the words of the *Bucks*

Advertiser after his death, 'the poor of the parish, his servants, his tenants, the neighbouring farmers, the local tradesmen, with all these he was quite as much a favourite as with any of the county magistrates'. R. H. Harrison of the stockbrokers Hichens, Harrison & Co had built for him in 1889 Shiplake Court near Henley – 'a large well-behaved Tudor house of diapered red brick', according to one architectural historian, 'in a fine position above the Thames'. About the same time the self-made stockbroker and financier Alexander Henderson, who had made a fortune in Argentine railways, acquired the Buscot Park estate near Faringdon in Oxfordshire: 3,500 acres and a suitable setting for a medieval dreamland. Finally, there was Ludwig Messel, who acquired Nymans in West Sussex in 1890 and transformed a conventional garden into one of the glories of the land.[31] Capel Court was infamous for its noise and dust and acrid sweat, but sometimes its rewards could be beautiful.

What in base terms were the City's rewards? It is clear that, among those active in business in the late nineteenth century, few provincial industrialists left fortunes of the same magnitude as those accumulated by the City's leading operators.[32] There were, for instance, fewer cotton millionaires than merchant banker millionaires – millionaires who included Natty Rothschild, the three Raphael brothers, Herman de Stern and Baron Schröder. In the mid-1890s the *Statist* published some invaluable wealth statistics, compiled on the basis of deaths since 1887. They by no means claimed completeness, but they showed that 38 'foreign bankers and merchant bankers', presumably all based in the City, had left an average of £512,578 and that 93 'English bankers and money dealers', presumably many of whom were based in the City, had left an average of £211,450. By comparison, to take some occupations outside the financial sphere, 110 'coalowners and merchants, ironmasters, machinists, engineers and contractors', *some* of whom would have been City-based, left an average of £240,487; 193 'manufacturers, merchants, and warehousemen in the textile trade', which again would include City men, averaged £209,063; 119 brewers averaged £167,637; 101 judges, barristers and solicitors (again, a minority City component) averaged £84,933; and 67 physicians and surgeons could manage only £50,614. Significantly well down this league table were 84 members of the Stock Exchange, whose average was £95,685 – though it is worth bearing in mind that one has to multiply by over forty times to get a rough modern-day equivalent.[33] There was little doubt, then, where the serious money was to be made. Saving lives was all very well, even making things, but the world of issuing, accepting and exchange was what truly buttered the parsnips.

The successful City man had, therefore, something tangible to offer when he sought a marriage partner, and by the late nineteenth century it was no longer rare for that partner to be a daughter of an aristocratic family. There exists a heroic sample of leading bankers (including merchant bankers), 413 in all, who flourished in the City between 1890 and 1914, and by definition the great majority of these were also active in the 1880s. For the generation in the sample born between 1800 and 1820, only about five per cent married into an aristocratic family. But for the next generation, born between 1821 and 1840 and accordingly well-established City figures in the 1880s, the proportion rises sharply to at least twenty-four per cent – by any reasonable criterion, a proportion denoting significant upward mobility. That ratio of a quarter, moreover, applies to the next generation, those born between 1841 and 1860 and presumably the bankers who were actually getting married in the 1880s. If intermarriage was a crucial part of the 'integration' between land and finance, so too was education. The '413' again tell an interesting story, the sample showing an increasing tendency, culminating in the generation born between 1861 and 1880 but already well established by the 1821–40 cohort, for leading bankers to be educated at a public school followed by Oxbridge – precisely the education that was becoming a *sine qua non* in the political elite at large.[34] And in terms of the values inculcated by that education, few would deny that they were more 'gentlemanly' than 'capitalist'.

Attitudes matter. To return to that crusty old tea merchant, Jolyon Forsyte, when he and his brothers talked about their master-builder father, 'the only aristocratic trait they could find in his character was a habit of drinking Madeira'; and Jolyon heartily despised his club on account of its willingness to take someone 'in trade' like himself, reflecting that 'the members were a poor lot, many of them in the City – stockbrokers, solicitors, auctioneers, what not!' Or, from the more verifiable world of non-fiction, take Daniel Meinertzhagen VI, a leading partner of Huths by 1890. He was connected by marriage with Beatrice Webb (as she was about to become), and early that year she characterised in her diary various social types known to her. They included this 'great City financier, earning his tens of thousands each year, upright and honourable but cordially hating "the social question", describing frankly his ideal: English capitalists retired from business living on an income of foreign investment, the land given over to sport, the people emigrated or starved out, no inhabitants except a few dependants to serve in one way or another the fortunate capitalists.' Old Jolyon, who had little love of the common man, would no doubt have grunted his approval. It was a happy, albeit overpopulated world for those able to enjoy it at its best, and partaking of it on a Sunday in July 1888 was Edward Hamilton, that loyal friend of the City's cream:

> Went down in the afternoon yesterday to the house – the Old Palace – which the Bischoffsheims have taken for a time at Richmond. A suburban villa is certainly a charming possession. It is becoming more & more the vogue. It is far the pleasantest form of entertainment in summer. We had some Lawn Tennis, a very good dinner (which goes without saying) and pleasant company: the Duchess of Manchester & Lady Alice, Hartington, C. Beresfords, A. Sassoons, Clarendons . . .[35]

As a diary entry it has it all, and seemingly clinches the case for 'integration' game, set and match.

But of course, there are other perspectives on the whole phenomenon, beginning with the long-run assertion that there was nothing new about close links between the City of London and landed society. The copper merchant and Bank of England director Charles Pascoe Grenfell (1790–1867) married the daughter of the Earl of Sefton; while his son Charles William (1823–61), elder brother of Henry, married the grand-daughter of the second Earl of Harewood. One has only to examine the composition of the Phoenix Assurance board from 1840 to see there a strong cluster of City merchants and others whose *fathers* had actually had country seats. Nor, in terms of the accelerated integration that undoubtedly did take place in the late nineteenth century, should one be naive about the process. The country life may have had its inherent attractions, but for an astute operator like Ernest Cassel the motivation for learning to hunt was because the value of the contacts he thereby cultivated, along with assiduous attendance at the card table, the racecourse and the shoot, more than outweighed the pain and embarrassment of an unfortunate tendency to fall off. Not quite in the Cassel class, but impressive nonetheless, was Robert Benson, who in the last quarter of the century systematically utilised a socially deft marriage and a brother-in-law relationship with the 4th Earl Grey to build up for his house a select circle of well-heeled investors, who in effect employed him as a congenial financial consultant. It can even be argued that there was a specific business motive in the acquisition of land, despite the fact that rent rolls were falling: in the case of the Gibbs family, for instance, it is clear that there was a conscious strategy to acquire land partly as a way of preventing the firm from over-extending itself into riskier investments.[36]

Moreover, it seems extremely implausible that anti-City animus on the part of landed society could have died away overnight. Sir Gorgius Midas, that nouveau riche vulgarian in the pages of *Punch*, was an immortal creation of George du Maurier that rang many bells; while Hamilton in 1885 noted that 'some people are turning up their noses at the Rothschild Peerage'. Or consider what was in one sense the cardinal act of integration, the marriage in 1878 between the fifth Earl of Rosebery, a future Prime Minister, and Hannah Rothschild, a niece of Baron Lionel. Perfection, however, was marred by the attitude of the respective families: his mother strongly opposed the union, her male relatives stayed away in droves from the wedding. The barriers could go up, in other words, either side of the social divide.[37]

There is further evidence of Rothschild reluctance unconditionally to cross that divide. 'It is curious that all the Rothschilds (with one exception) should have preferred building their own houses & making their own places to buying old family seats with ready made parks which no amount of money can produce', remarked Hamilton in 1886, adding that 'it is moreover remarkable how clannish they are, & how they have all settled down in the same country' (referring to the Vale of Aylesbury). And two years later, Hamilton listened to Natty speaking 'with all his natural *class* prejudices' about the 'harm which a few of the aristocracy do to their class by frequently displaying a want of sense of honour in money affairs and by resorting to gambling in these days'. Such, even among Rothschilds, was the tenacity of City culture, which was essentially of a middle-class, non-aristocratic character. Or take the notable tribute paid to Tom Baring on his death in 1873. 'He was certainly a proof, if any were wanting', wrote Bertram Currie to his father, 'that a merchant may be as good a gentleman as an acred lord or squire and he was wisely content with and proud of his trade.'[38]

Currie himself, for all his properties, did not move in Society circles, eschewed the Season, and instead rented a house each summer in Littlehampton. Hamilton appreciated particularly his 'hard headedness & common sense', two of the qualities that made him such a City eminent. But in terms of non-integration, the classic case was surely Kleinworts, the merchant bank on probably the steepest ascent. The firm's founding father, Alexander Kleinwort, who continued living in Camberwell until his death in 1886, insisted that his two sons, Herman and Alexander, be educated on the Continent rather than going to an English public school. Thus equipped with fluent French and German, they then received a thorough commercial grounding, not an Oxbridge gown in sight, before finally becoming partners in the early 1880s.

These younger Kleinworts both married women whose first language was not English; they continued to work extraordinarily hard and had little or nothing to do with aristocrats or aristocratic pursuits; and when they eventually did buy country estates, they were on a fairly modest scale. Other successful Anglo-German houses, most notably Schröders, followed this pattern to at least an extent, as did the Anglo-Greek houses like Rallis. They all avoided wasting time being a director of the Bank of England; yet contrary to what one might expect, on account of the prestige of the institution, those who were Bank directors were, for the most part, distinctly non-integrating. Of the twenty-seven (still mostly merchants) elected as directors between 1848 and 1873, only ten of whom left fortunes of over £300,000, we have information about nineteen of their wives: they comprised the daughters of five clergymen, five City merchants, two MPs, two lawyers, two admirals, one ambassador, one landowner, and one banker – but no aristocrats. Charlotte de Rothschild in 1869 recorded with some bewilderment these tacit parameters: 'The Governor of the Bank called at New Court yesterday and told the Gentlemen he had been offered a Baronetcy, and had declined it; the reason of such a refusal I cannot comprehend; Mr Crawford thinks that a man in business ought not to be Sir Robert.'[39]

We know so little about the minds and habits of these mercantile men, but an exception, thanks partly to his correspondence, is William Lidderdale. His four sons all went to Winchester; he was serious minded, but enjoyed humorous quotations from *The Pickwick Papers* and Mark Twain; he was an assiduous reader of newspapers; his favourite authors were Scott, Burns, Thackeray and Dickens; he was fond of music, especially Scottish music and Mendelssohn; he subscribed to the Saturday 'Pops' concerts at St James's Hall; his favourite pastime was shooting in Scotland; and in 1887, on becoming Deputy Governor, he rented Yaldham Manor near Sevenoaks. If he integrated at all, it was almost certainly on his own terms.[40]

Underlining the problematic nature of this whole concept is the diversity of the City itself. For every Rothschild or Revelstoke there were many hundreds of smaller fry, few of whom inherited or made fortunes and almost none of whom had grandiose social or political ambitions. The world they inhabited was one of family capitalism, of low entry costs, and of high turn-over in firms and personnel – a world, in short, of work and all its attendant responsibilities and anxieties. Such a world included the notionally rip-roaring Stock Exchange, becoming arch-symbol of the late-Victorian age. Undoubtedly some members made the proverbial pile – enormous estates in Sweden do not come cheap – but the great majority did not. We know, for instance, how much the 74 members or former members left who died between mid-1894 and the end of 1896. Only one (the railway jobber James Renton) left over £½m, the average was £40,042, and as many as 39 failed to achieve five figures.[41] A representative figure of the era, although he features in none of the history books, was perhaps Stanley Scott. He was a member who for some years was also a leading batsman for Middlesex; his powerful build and large dark moustache made him instantly recognisable on the field of play; and, in true amateur style, he scored most of his runs in front of the wicket on the off-side. But his life was not all plain sailing. He had been educated at Streatham School and learnt his cricket on Streatham Common; he had little family money behind him; and eventually he had to give up the game in order to concentrate wholly on his Stock Exchange business. In old age he wrote his cricketing reminiscences, in the course of which he recalled playing in 1880 for a Stock Exchange eleven against Leopold Rothschild's eleven at the latter's home at Ascott, near Leighton Buzzard. There was a dream-like quality as two utterly different echelons of the City met on a once-in-a-lifetime occasion:

We went down from Euston in style by special train, and had numerous carriages to meet us on arrival. We drove to the ground, a beautiful park, capital wicket, plenty of room, big tents up – All A1. We won the toss. Felix Fielding and C. W. Burls went in first. Fielding got out very soon and I followed in. Burls and I had a 'beano'. We smote the bowling everywhere . . . We were not out at lunch time, the score being about 160. Then lunch! I must not forget the introduction to our host, Mr Leopold Rothschild. It was like being presented to Royalty. He was very gracious and pleasant. (We stood in a ring and were named and presented in turn.) He welcomed us heartily and then suggested lunch, and what a lunch! Everything you could wish for. Men servants to wait – they looked after us well, a bottle of champagne at each man's right hand and promptly repeated when the first got low – we did ourselves really well. Afterwards cheered up with excellent cigars, we were shown over the house and the stables. We saw a racehorse, a beautiful creature – 'Gunnersbury' I think it was, and then back to cricket. About the third ball I got pitched seemingly wide on the offside. I left it alone contemptuously, but to my astonishment and disgust it 'broke' back, scattered my stumps and I was out for 67. Burls, I think, made 90, and we were all out for rather more than 200. We bowled them out for less, but they gave us a good deal of trouble, and we had to work for our victory. It was a very fine day in every way, and I've never forgotten it, but I have never been there since.[42]

'I forget. Was I a bimetallist when I was at the India Office?'[43] Lord Randolph Churchill's sense of puzzlement in 1886 was shared by lesser mortals. Bimetallism was one of the more complex, arcane and now forgotten of nineteenth-century controversies; but during the debate's height, roughly the mid-1880s to mid-1890s, it was a rare time when the City had to address itself consciously to a major economic question, which it did in a most instructive way.[44] The crux of the bimetallist argument was that, against a post-1873 background of world economic depression and a falling general price level, including the price of silver, the only realistic solution was for the leading nations, above all Britain, to return to a bimetallic standard – in other words, abandoning the monometallism of the gold standard and thereby permitting the free coinage of silver in addition to gold.

The first meeting of what would become the Bimetallic League was held at the India Office in November 1881, with Henry Riversdale Grenfell, Governor of the Bank of England, among those present; and the second just before Christmas that year, at the Cannon Street Hotel, with Henry Hucks Gibbs in the chair. To many, brought up on the pure milk of the gold standard, this new movement seemed the most appalling heresy. 'The Yankees are going to try & force England & Germany into Bi-metallism' was the cynical reaction of David McLean, conscious of the United States as a silver-producing country, while just after the second meeting Hamilton recorded the response of the Prime Minister of the day:

> Old Thomson Hankey [still a Bank director] has written to 'draw' Mr. G. on bimetallism and has succeeded in eliciting an emphatic repudiation of any sympathy with the bimetallists. Mr. G. says he looks upon bimetallism 'as a departure from the very nature of a standard' and declares that, if he lived to the age of Methuselah, nothing would induce him to propose a measure which had any leanings in the bimetallic direction.[45]

In the course of the 1880s it became clear that, for once in his life, Gladstone was echoing the voice of majority City opinion. Nevertheless, Gibbs and Grenfell were weighty, articulate advocates of the bimetallist cause; among those in the City who supported them were Samuel Montagu (for once at odds with Gladstone), Edward Howley Palmer, and the increasingly prominent (especially socially) Eastern merchant Sir Albert Sassoon. Early support from the landed interest was joined from the mid-1880s by vocal bimetallism on the part of certain industrial and commercial interests in the provinces, especially Lancashire cotton merchants. In 1886, as trade depression deepened, the government agreed to appoint a Gold and Silver Commission to examine the whole question.

That October, as City figures prepared to give evidence, the Governor of the Bank, James Currie, asked his directors for their private views on the subject.[46] The individual replies included two from directors with strong industrial links, namely H. L. Holland, Governor during the Overend Gurney crisis and a partner in a firm of linen yarn manufacturers, and Henry Blake, a civil engineer who was London partner of the Birmingham-based James Watt & Co. Neither questioned the conventional wisdom:

> I believe it to be an impossibility to fix a permanent ratio at which gold and silver shall be interchangeable all over the world; and I shall expect that any attempt to do so would fail, in spite of national agreements, which cannot possibly become universal . . .
>
> The monometallic currency in Great Britain based upon a gold standard is admitted by general consent to be as perfect, if not more so, than that of any other country; and this, coupled with the universal trade which England possesses, and other reasons, makes London the chief centre of exchange for the settlement of commercial transactions . . .

Similar views came from three merchants, the still unknighted R. W. Crawford, Benjamin Buck Greene and William Lidderdale:

> My opinions have never inclined in the least to the side of, as it seems to me, an unpractical and dangerous economic fallacy . . .
>
> If there were any advantage to England in Bimetallism, which I deny, it would never do for her to rely upon any international agreement whatever . . .
>
> I prefer to make the best of existing circumstances rather than surrender our single standard with the advantages it possesses . . .

Finally, and equally characteristically, there were the judgements of a quartet of merchant bankers:

> It must be wiser to adhere to our present system of currency rather than 'take a leap in the dark', and enter upon an experiment the result of which no one can possibly foresee . . .
>
> To sum up the situation in a few words, London being the centre of the financial world, we have to be doubly careful to protect our stock of gold . . .

I am afraid I have not leisure at this moment, even if I had the inclination, to go into lengthened comments on the controversy . . . but I am glad to have the opportunity of stating that, as far as the general question goes, I have the pleasure to rank myself on the side of the firm monometallists . . .

I do not believe Bimetallism would be a cure for the so-called depression in trade . . .

The four were Charles Goschen, Alfred de Rothschild, Lord Revelstoke and Everard Hambro, the last two unwilling or unable to provide any supporting evidence or argument. But then, that was perhaps hardly the point, when it came to defending an article of faith.

Much of the evidence to the Royal Commission was given in 1887, producing impenetrable thickets of economics and statistics about gold and silver production, circulation and relative price levels. From the point of view of City orthodoxy, the key witness was undoubtedly Bertram Currie, whose answers were underpinned by an assumption that a healthy, internationally oriented square mile was synonymous with a healthy national economy:

Would you tell us why you say that the financial prosperity of this country is greatly due to the present standard? – I say it for this reason, that the fact that Great Britain is the only country where there is a real gold standard, the only place where, if a man has a bill for £100, he knows what he has got, and he knows that in all cases he can obtain for his bill for £100 a certain quantity of gold at a certain weight and fineness, attracts business to this country, and I think it can be asserted without fear of contradiction that the main reason why the great financial establishments of Europe have come to London and established themselves here is the fact that this is the only country in which there is a real gold standard.

Currie, given some inviting half-volleys by Sir T. Farrer (formerly of the Board of Trade), then elaborated his central theme:

I want to understand distinctly what is the position of London as regards the financial centre of the world. Is it that is it a sort of clearing house to which all debts are referred and through which they are paid? – Yes; I think its peculiar position is, that it is the only centre upon which bills from all parts of the world can be drawn. Wherever there is an exchange of any sort there is an exchange upon London. Bills upon London are always in the market; everybody has debts to pay in London, therefore everybody wants bills on London.

Just as it is the centre of the business of England it is the centre of the business of the world? – It is.

Bills from all parts can be sent to London and exchanged there? – Yes. A New York merchant wishing to buy goods in the East is obliged to supply himself with a credit upon England. That is distinctly to the benefit of London.

London becomes a sort of bank for the whole world? – Yes . . .

London is a sort of centre of banking which never existed before? – Yes.

The gold sovereign is the language in which it carries on its transactions? – Yes.

To disturb that language might very easily lead to the disturbance of that practice? – I have a very strong conviction that anything in the world which would shake the faith of mankind in the fact that what £100 means is a certain amount of gold of a certain weight and fineness, might disturb us very materially . . .

Should you think that the habits and desires of the community of London are in favour of gold? – I do most emphatically think so.

What about the horny-handed producers? Another convinced monometallist was H. L. Raphael, and he gave short shrift to bimetallist complaints from the provinces:

You are not aware of any manufactories or industries that are declining or decaying? – I daresay there are plenty of them; men who have not got the intelligence, or if they have the intelligence, have not got the opportunities. You may just as well ask me if every intelligent man in business succeeds? I say no. I have seen great fools succeed and intelligent men go to the wall, but I say in general the character of English trade at the present moment is that the profits are not anything like so great as they used to be, but there are profits and fair ones.

Elsewhere in his evidence, Raphael made plain his belief that the inevitable result of bimetallism would be inflation, which was why the various chambers of commerce were in favour of a double standard. And, in words that are hard not to read as at least mildly condescending, he explained that 'these bodies are composed of merchants, manufacturers, coal-owners, mill-owners, and people of that sort'.[47] It was an early sign, pointing to the century that lay ahead, that the City, manufacturing industry and the legendary goal of zero inflation would not always be easy bedfellows.

Asked by the Royal Commission in May 1887 if his bimetallist views represented 'the preponderating views amongst the directors' of the Bank of England, Gibbs conceded that he was 'in a small minority'. But the following April, chairing the Bimetallic Conference held at Manchester, the president of the Bimetallic League was in a more bullish mood about his pet cause: 'We began it – we Londoners – slowly and tentatively, and with no small array of opinion against us; but then came Lancashire into the field . . .' Gibbs overestimated the degree of Lancashire bimetallist unanimity, but was not deterred from fiercely attacking Currie's recent evidence to the Commission: 'I believe that the notion that England's prosperity is due to our having a single gold standard is merely a vain imagination. What a futile and miserable foundation on which to build the commercial greatness of England!' Grenfell was even more scathing, making much of Currie's unfortunate assertion that the problems caused to industry by the fall in prices represented the unavoidable 'fate of mankind' and acidly characterising his views as 'whatever you do, do not take away the banking supremacy of this country'. A copper merchant, with close links himself to Welsh mining, Grenfell likewise welcomed the northern drift:

> All the annuitants, the stock holders, and others of that class use London as a place where money is to be spent, and therefore they have no interest whatever in getting this matter put straight. But if London is the capital of the spending community, Manchester is the capital of the busy hive of bees who make the money . . .

It was a warmly received passage, but perhaps the most telling point in the entire proceedings was made by Professor H. S. Foxwell. He was a distinguished economist in sympathy with a move to silver, but he noted acutely the existence of a 'feeling' that 'there is something in bimetallism which is artificial, uncommercial, not precisely "cricket", if the expression may be allowed'.[48] Not to be cricket, he might have added, was to leave any cause without a prayer in the late nineteenth-century City.

The Royal Commission reported in November 1888, six members (including Sir John Lubbock) pronouncing against bimetallism and six (including Samuel Montagu) advocating its adoption. One specific recommendation, however, that it felt able to make was that of an issue of small-denomination notes (£1 and 10s) based on silver. The attitude of the Bank to this was hostile from the outset. Collet as Governor made strong representations to Goschen, Chancellor of the Exchequer, who in turn came down against the proposal in his budget speech the following spring. In 1889 it became clear that there was as yet no parliamentary majority for bimetallism; while Currie assured Hamilton that 'once let it be seriously projected, and you would have all the highest financial authorities with very few exceptions rise in revolt and blow the double-standard faddists into mid air'. Hamilton, as a good

Gladstone-inculcated Treasury man, bought this, reflecting later in the year that 'there is hardly a single City man of brains & standing who does not pooh-pooh the idea of a double standard'. And, of course, he was broadly right, despite the passionate beliefs of Gibbs, Grenfell and some others – beliefs that no doubt owed *something* to personal vested interests, City men with stakes in the silver-based nations of the Far East and South America being more likely to be bimetallist, but only something. The fault line was as much one of temperament, of willingness to countenance new solutions to new problems, of differing priorities between the national and international. One of the monometallist members of the Royal Commission, who was by now president of the Institute of Bankers and still a director of the Bank of England, was J. W. Birch. The *Bankers' Magazine*, in its profile of him in 1888, not only cited the reassuring 'business' card on his mantelpiece. It also caught the exact flavour of the archetypal City man, for whom there was no higher god than 'practicality', even if it was the practicality bequeathed to him by generations long dead:

> It is recorded of him that, if professors of refined political economy insist that there is much surplus gold in the country, he asks them to turn out their own pockets, and so at once get proof of the extreme economy of the gold currency in modern times. A detail of that kind stamps his character as a shrewd man of business, impatient of the refinements of theorists, careful of facts, and, therefore, as a necessary consequence, judicious in a crisis . . .[49]

CHAPTER TWENTY

Honest Guinness Stout

Members were at first reluctant to inhabit the new part of the Stock Exchange with its great dome, but then, in 1886, came the momentous discovery of gold on the Witwatersrand, and soon the New House was filled by the jobbers and raucous noises of what would become known as the 'Kaffir Circus'. By May 1887 the *Economist* was writing of 'A Mining Promotion "Boom" '; while two years later the *Statist* was detailing 'The South African Fever' and estimating that since 1886 the London capital market had channelled at least £50m into ventures like (to name some registered in January 1889) the Anglo Transvaal Prospecting Company, Madeline Witwatersrand Gold Mining Company, West Battery Reef Gold Mining Company, Doornplatz Gold Mining Syndicate, South Vogelstruis Gold Company and so on. In these free-for-all early years of the South African gold mining industry, the City acted as a conduit for information as well as capital. The Rothschild-backed Exploration Company was formed in 1886 to assess on behalf of its members (a select City elite) the potential investment value of the many mining propositions that sought London backing. In many parts of the City, however, even in New Court at times, there remained an underlying scepticism about gold mines that would prove hard to shift. In 1888 the *Economist* described mining shares as traditionally 'the happy hunting-grounds of organised gangs of promoters, who, together with their associates – low-class advertising agents, &c – care nothing about the value of a mine, provided only that it can be made a means of fleecing the public'. Or as an adage, beloved of the Stock Exchange, ran from about this time: 'A mine is a hole in the ground owned by a liar.'[1]

An important episode was the successful flotation in the spring of 1887 of Cecil Rhodes's Gold Fields of South Africa (later Consolidated Gold Fields). Rhodes himself was still an unknown force in the City; the person who secured the support for the flotation was his right-hand man, Charles Rudd, upper middle class, with a brother who was a director of the London Joint Stock Bank and now chairman of Gold

Fields. Between them the Rudds obtained influential backers, including the well-connected East India merchants Arbuthnot Latham and several leading operators on the Stock Exchange. Control at this stage stayed firmly in the hands of Rhodes in South Africa, but he would have conceded that it was the London flotation that gave his company the critical mass it needed.[2] Another key episode, which concerned diamonds not gold, came soon afterwards and also involved Rhodes. This was the convoluted establishment during 1887–88 of what became De Beers Consolidated, in effect the amalgamation of the Kimberley diamond mines. Rhodes came to London in July 1887, passed the informal test of an interview with Natty Rothschild, and was lent £$\frac{3}{4}$m by Rothschilds in order to effect one of the critical mergers in the process. Soon after De Beers was formed there arose the question of a debenture issue, and in August 1888 Rhodes wrote plaintively to Natty about the problem of getting adequate security for the loan:

> The whole case depends whether you have any confidence and trust in myself. Perhaps someone else can do it better, I really do not know; you know my objects and the whole case is a question of trust. I know with you behind me I can do all I have said. If, however, you think differently I have nothing to say.[3]

Much turned on that word 'objects', and over the years there would be a significant divergence between the empire-driven Rhodes and the commerce-driven City, whatever the latter's imperial sympathies. While as for 'trust', Natty's man on the De Beers board was Carl Meyer, in whom he invested somewhat more of that rare commodity than he ever would in Rhodes himself.

By 1890 the South African gold mining boom was temporarily over – awaiting a technological solution to the problem of non-remunerative pyritic ore below a certain level of the reef – but at its zenith in the late 1880s it was a major factor behind the mushrooming of the financial press. Most of these new publications were ephemeral and blatantly share-pushing, but one that was not was the *London Financial Guide*, which after a few weeks was renamed in February 1888 as the *Financial Times*. The new paper had a complicated early history,[4] including for a brief period finding itself under the chairmanship of Horatio Bottomley, who came from the East End and, still in his twenties, was trying to make an instant fortune out of printing and publishing; but by the end of 1888 he was trying his luck elsewhere and instead the dominant figure at the *FT* was Douglas MacRae, a shrewd, hard-working, rough Scotsman.

From the start the *FT*'s great rival was the *Financial News*, where Harry Marks was enjoying mixed fortunes. On the one hand, his paper was flourishing commercially; he was able to acquire a country seat near Broadstairs; and several of the *FN*'s vigorous campaigns earned wide attention, including ones against the Metropolitan Board of Works (before it was abolished), a bogus gold mining company called the Northern Transvaal, and even the bimetallist Bank of England director H. R. Grenfell – for his involvement in the promotion of the Harney Peak Tin Company, which had sought to obtain capital of £2m and been attacked so fiercely by the *FN* as to cause withdrawal of the prospectus. On the other hand, Marks's personal reputation, and also that of his paper, took some sharp blows in these years. First, in November 1888, a libel case brought by the promoter of the Ashley Bottle Company demonstrated that the *FN* had sought to obtain a large sum of money, up to £50,000, through ensuring the successful flotation of the company. And then, in two cases heard in 1890, an American company promoter revealed murky details about Marks's American past, and more importantly that Marks in 1886 had secretly promoted a worthless concern called the Rae (Transvaal) Gold Mining Company, advising readers over the next year to buy its shares while more or less simultaneously selling off his own shares through a variety of 'dummy' vendors. In general, the ethics of financial journalism were still at a rudimentary stage, and as the *Statist* sharply commented in 1887, presumably with itself as an exception, 'it is an understood thing that a big advertisement must be accompanied by a "good notice" '. Marks himself was remembered for years in the trade for how, when out canvassing for prospectuses of new issues, he would keep in his pocket three different draft critiques of the prospectus: a favourable one for the full prospectus, a less favourable one for the abridged, and a third that was outright hostile if he secured no advertisement at all.[5]

In the booming City of the late 1880s, there was one outsize personality over whom the two leading financial dailies locked horns. This was Colonel North, the self-proclaimed 'Nitrate King', who had earned himself the honorary military title on account of having founded and equipped a volunteer regiment in Tower Hamlets. The *Economist*, after his death in 1896, memorably described 'a millionaire stripped bare':

> He obtained, and knew that he obtained, his position in the City and in a certain kind of society solely through his money. He must have possessed inherent ability and power of governing, and he was a bold man,

and one who when unresisted was capable of kind acts, but for the rest he was from first to last just a workman who had made a great fortune, and who loved to proclaim it by extravagant expenditure, by ostentatious display, and by bearing everybody known. He never pretended to much education; his speeches when he was a candidate for Parliament made all England laugh, and if excited he could browbeat his associates as if he were still one of the roughest of workmen. He believed firmly and fully that his money gave him rights, and he asserted those rights to the full ... His great notion of hospitality was to drown his friends in champagne, and it may be doubted if he ever read anything in his life beyond a sporting newspaper.

John Thomas North was born near Leeds in 1842, the son of a well-to-do coal merchant, and from the 1870s he became involved in Chile's expanding nitrate industry. In the mid-1880s he established a producers' combination, and later in the decade, against a background of a raging bull market for nitrate shares that he himself did much to stimulate, he made a fortune out of promoting the Nitrates Railway Co and various nitrate companies. The Colonel at once bought a hugely expensive mansion near Eltham which he renovated to the nth degree; he played the country squire with great panache; he acquired a string of racehorses; and he was sufficiently accepted by the City establishment for not only Rothschilds to act as bankers at the end of 1888 to his newly launched Bank of Tarapacá and London, but for Natty the next year to send a gift to his daughter on her coming of age. North's rise was hugely galling to the house of Antony Gibbs, which had substantial interests in Chile, had pioneered the manufacture of nitrate of soda, and as London agents for the Chilean State Railway during its construction had even been responsible for sending the young North out to Chile in the first place. The Nitrate Railway, a bold venture conducted across difficult terrain, was an especially sore point, and in November 1888 Herbert Gibbs (a son of Henry Hucks) conceded as much to one of his managers in South America:

> Two years ago you and I discussed the question of the purchase of the railway shares, and our letters show that the desirability of doing so was a very open question, and no subsequent events can make it otherwise; at the same time North did seize what has turned out to have been a golden opportunity, and adding success to success he has made an enormous fortune under our very nose, in our own country, and at our own business, in which we have hardly participated at all. The result is that the gallant Colonel has completely eclipsed us in the Nitrate business and whatever he touches is dashed at by the public and driven to a premium immediately ...

North, however, had his public critics. The *Economist* was hostile to both him and the nitrate boom generally, while the *FN* in its best vein kept up a running attack. 'The Coming Crash in Nitrate Rails' was the headline of a typical editorial comment: 'Colonel North is a Pactolus among promoters. Whatever he touches turns, if not to gold, at least to premiums. In the end there is often a considerable difference between gold and premiums, but at the outset they may be easily mistaken for each other.' The *FT* by contrast offered the warmest support to the Colonel, especially in early 1889 when, amidst a fanfare of publicity and following a fancy dress ball at the Hotel Metropole at which a corpulent North dressed as Henry VIII greeted 800 guests including thirteen peers and two Rothschilds, he prepared to leave for a 'fact-finding' trip to Chile. His farewell banquet was at Liverpool's Adelphi Hotel, and the next morning the *FT* printed in full his extremely harsh remarks about the *FN*. For a time outright warfare between Marks and MacRae seemed likely, until a truce was called. North himself was now at his peak; the following year, partly in the context of political turmoil in Chile, nitrate shares tumbled, especially those of his own companies.[6] However, not unlike Cassel, his spectacular career had shown that in an expanding world economy knit together by instant communications, an adventurous City-based entrepreneur operating only for himself could move faster and more effectively than an old-established merchant dynasty.

*

Still, even 15 Bishopsgate could adapt, and had gradually done so since the end of the guano monopoly in the 1860s. Already in the spring of 1887 there had taken place the debut of Antony Gibbs as an issuing house. It floated on the London market the French-based Hotchkiss Ordnance Company, and Vicary Gibbs (another son) frankly described to his agent in Australia the morally, commercially nerve-racking and arduous business of embarking on a wholly new line of activity:

> I need not trouble you with all the pros and cons which were raised and the various doubts and anxieties which were expressed: suffice it to say that we finally consented to bring out the company for a very handsome commission though not so large as we should have asked had we known as much then as we do now.
>
> We had some trouble about the Board of Directors from their fidgettiness and other causes, but these were surmounted by Herbert who attended all the preliminary meetings and kept them straight.

The essential question as to whether the Hotchkiss business was good enough for us to invite the public exercised us very much, more especially as we knew that it had been frightfully sweated by intermediaries and groups of capitalists [including Morgans and Barings] before it reached our hands.

However we decided that when all was said & done it was still a very good speculative risk, in which we should be quite willing to take a substantial interest ourselves, after the profits of the last three years had been verified by Price Waterhouse the well known London accountants. As we looked to make a large portion of the profits of the business out of selling the shares which we might allot to ourselves at a premium and as extremely severe strictures had been passed upon our neighbours Barings for having made a very large allotment to themselves in the Guinness issue [of the previous October], we determined to fix beforehand with the vendors the maximum of shares which we were entitled to allot to ourselves, and disclose the fact on the prospectus. Such a step was entirely unknown beforehand, and some of the brokers doubted its wisdom, but the result has shown that it was at once proper wise and popular . . .

On the 2nd of March the evening before the prospectus was nominally issued, it became quite evident that the issue would be a success, and Rothschilds sent in an application for £600,000 . . .

There followed, when the prospectus was readily available, the penalties of success:

We began to see that there was a chance of some such rush as took place in Guinness & Allsopp [another recent brewery issue] so we made our preparations accordingly, we had the door of the cabin or little private room into the passage taken away and a barrier just like a ticket office erected with two clerks on the inside to distribute prospectuses. Then we ordered police to be in readiness to keep the crowd in order, and arranged for the semicircle in front of the general office to be cleared of its usual occupants . . . By eleven o'clock a dense queue of people had accumulated reaching from the semicircle to the street, and the semicircle itself became shortly so closely packed with people trying to make payments and hand in applications that it was impossible to get in or out of the office, while those further back who feared the lists might suddenly close fought & struggled and made matters worse. It became pretty clear that in spite of all our plans our organisation was breaking down. I addressed the crowd in a loud voice to keep them peaceable and promised that all applications should be received . . . For about 20 minutes great confusion lasted, and then the police got the people under control . . .

The principle on which we made the regrets was roughly as follows. We had ascertained that the proportion in which the capital was applied for was more or less ordinary shares forty times, preference twenty times and debentures ten times: we therefore sent regrets with great freedom to everyone of whom we knew nothing who had applied for a large line of ordinary shares alone as we thought they were in all probability mere premium hunters. We further asked the brokers with whom we were well acquainted to furnish us with lists of their clients among the applicants for whom they desired special consideration, and all who did not appear on such lists we condemned: we were also very severe on stock jobbers not dealing in that particular market, viz the miscellaneous, and on all unimportant mercantile houses and stock brokers. On the other hand the destroying angel did not enter the houses of single women, military men, important issuing houses, and those who did not apply for ordinaries, and those who applied for very small amounts, as all these for one cause or another appeared to us suitable shareholders . . .

The infinite pains were not yet over, for late on the night of making up allotments a mistake was discovered, as a result of which all the envelopes had to be re-opened and an alteration made. The partners and clerks (a workforce of about forty-five in all) did not finish their task until almost three o'clock in the morning, when the last sack of allotment letters was carried off to the post:

> Most of the clerks went off to the Cannon St Hotel, and we three [Vicary, Herbert and a third brother, Alban] walked home highly delighted not only at the way everything had been managed, but at the extremely loyal and active way in which all the clerks had strained every nerve to do what we wished and make the thing a success. We on our part had done our best to make it pleasant for them, allowing smoking all over the office and private rooms, and free dinners, and generally being as genial as our natures would permit . . .

Finally, Vicary announced that he was off to Paris for Easter and, as a conscientious merchant banker, would take the opportunity of inspecting the Hotchkiss factory.[7]

Three years later, relatively seasoned hands at the issuing game, the brothers found themselves playing in the big league. The occasion was a Mexican state loan, jointly issued with Bleichröders of Berlin. August was an unseasonable time of year to be doing such business, and on the 18th Vicary in Bishopsgate wrote to Herbert, presumably out of town: 'I am glad your place is a success, & I wish you much enjoyment. Akroyd [of Cazenove & Akroyds, the stockbrokers closest to Gibbs] had heard your bag the first day through a Miss Curtis before I did!' The following week Vicary was in ebullient mood as he wrote to Alban, also away: 'The tendency seems so good for Mexican things and the idea of our new subvention loan seems to be so well received that I would recommend our running half of our share and getting the other half underwritten at $2\frac{1}{2} + \frac{1}{2}$ brokerage.' Vicary added that the price would not be under 94 and that 'with luck we ought to clear £50,000'. On 1 September, with the loan about to be launched and questions of pricing and allotment still to be decided, Vicary's temper had swung sharply: 'J. Akroyd is away partridge shooting. I am met at every turn by these sacré holidays.' And: 'I am hampered by not knowing what Bleichröder and Cassell [sic] are doing.' The latter was apparently representing Bleichröder's interests, and in the event these allies of Gibbs insisted on $93\frac{1}{2}$ as the price. A final piece of correspondence – from Harry Gibbs, yet another brother, to Alban on the 16th – revealed even more clearly where the whip hand lay:

A.G. & S keep for themselves £100,000 and Cassel retains like amount for himself, both these sums are included in the £1,700,000 allotted to English. We originally intended to allot £200,000 less than we finally did in London, £300,000 less in Berlin; we meant not to allot this £500,000 in all, but on the morning of the day we did the allotment Cassel came, & was most urgent we should allot the whole amount, saying it would not matter for the 'Stags' to get more than they ought to, & that the more we allotted the more widely the stock would be diffused, also that it would not do for the Stock Exchange to find out we had said that the whole amount had been subscribed for by the Public & that we were keeping back £500,000. Vicary (who was here for an hour or two just before he went to bed with the gout) did not agree with Cassel's views, but was overruled in the matter.

Cassel was entering his prime by the late 1880s – acting with Rothschilds to carry through the important armaments amalgamation of Maxim Gun and Nordenfelt Ammunition, working with Hirsch to finance railway construction in Turkey and Eastern Europe, helping to arrange loans for Egypt as well as several South American states – and Gibbs gives us a rare glimpse of the master in typically decisive action.[8]

Cassel left few papers and probably never even considered writing his memoirs. There was no such reticence about H. Osborne O'Hagan, in a sense the City's home-grown equivalent to Cassel, if operating at a less exalted level. In retirement on the French Riviera in the late 1920s he wrote *Leaves from my Life*: boisterous, vainglorious, often extremely detailed, a guaranteed tonic to tired spirits and a compelling story. O'Hagan was born in Blackburn in 1853, his father was a civil engineer from Ulster, and he went to Rochester Grammar School. But his schooling was abruptly terminated by his father's entanglement in the

Overend Gurney crash, not long before he died while working on the madcap Honduras Railway scheme. The fifteen-year-old O'Hagan became a junior clerk in the City, spending his spare time on an intensive course of self-education. He abandoned novel reading and began a lifetime's habit of devoting at least two hours daily to *The Times*, at first on loan for a halfpenny the third day after its issue: 'I was not after the news, but the wealth of knowledge it diffused.' By the mid-1870s he had managed to set himself up as an independent company promoter, with early specialties including tramways and collieries.

It was in the 1880s that, through his newly founded City of London Contract Corporation, O'Hagan really came into his own, going far beyond anything attempted by Baron Grant in previous decades, as well as being altogether more honest. The key lay in his invention and popularisation of underwriting for industrial issues, which meant that, as the vendor would not suffer if the public failed to respond to the issue of shares, he was thereby encouraged to go public; and this farming out by O'Hagan of underwriting on a commission basis was particularly important before 1900, when the Companies Acts still precluded a company from issuing its shares at a discount or itself paying a commission to anyone for taking up its shares. Successful underwriting required a good City connection, and by the late 1880s, when he was at his height, O'Hagan was working particularly closely with Harry Panmure Gordon, who always called him 'the Chief'. During these hectic years he engaged in promotion of a mass of English breweries, various American breweries, the Cardiff timber merchants John Bland & Co, the Chicago Junction Railways and Stockyards, the Chicago Packing & Provision Co, the entertainment complex Ronacher's of Vienna, and the Havana cigar business of Henry Clay & Bock Ltd. Amidst all this activity he tried hard to maintain quality control, genuinely seeking to convert only worthwhile concerns into public companies and endeavouring to ensure a distribution of the capital sufficiently equitable not to wreck the company's future prospects.

Underpinning O'Hagan's career was a combination, very rare in the City then, of judgement and industry. Of the first:

> There is no profession or occupation or whatever it may be called which requires such patient and careful attention as that of the financier, whose task it is to sort out the good from the large number of businesses which come before him. If he allows himself to be influenced only by whether

the public would take up a venture, he will not be long before he finds that ugly chickens come home to roost. He must investigate with great patience and sometimes with considerable expense each undertaking which impresses him, assuming that all is not gold that glitters, and when he has incurred a considerable outlay and perhaps embarked some of his own capital, he must have resolution to drop the concern and lose his money if he finds a nigger in the fence, in other words, danger in the enterprise.

And of the second:

Success rarely comes to those who take to their offices their sports, their theatricals, or other amusements. To really succeed, a man must make his work his first love. It has been said to me, If you are thinking of your business day and night, how can you get any pleasure out of life? To which I replied that I loved pleasure as much as anyone, and the busy man, no matter how hard he may at times be put to it, will find time to taste of the pleasures; but when I was hard put to it, then I found my business my greatest pleasure, for it was like playing a lot of games of chess at the same time . . .

When at work I could do so much because I would work from twelve to eighteen hours a day. I could do with so little sleep, having convinced myself that the amount of sleep required is just a question of habit. I am now seventy-five years of age, but I claim that I have lived eighty-five years. I have cheated the demon Sleep out of a good ten years.

O'Hagan also had considerable personal charm. 'I looked upon him as a strange man whose confidence I could not gain in the course of two or three interviews . . . I have rarely conducted any negotiation without a smiling face and one or two anecdotes.' The resourceful promoter had systematically collected and stored in his memory over 10,000 such 'amusing stories', yet another card up his capacious sleeve.[9]

O'Hagan claimed, with some plausibility, that his system of underwriting made the promotion of industrial companies both attractive and respectable to the City as a whole. But there were other reasons why, between 1886 and 1890, there took place an upsurge of home industrial issues, and these included the advent of smaller share denominations, a diminution of uncalled liabilities, a need for external capital on the part of more technologically driven industries, and (not least important) a natural wish by families owning businesses to reap the considerable material fruits of converting to a public company. One such family was Guinness of Dublin, which offered its inimitable business to Barings in 1886, having had it turned down a few years earlier by Rothschilds. The total size of the issue was £6m, and Edward Hamilton that October recorded the outcome: 'There has been nothing within the recollection of the City like the rush for shares in the Guinness Co . . . It seems pretty clear that the Barings put the rate of interest on the preference & debenture shares 1% too high.' Whatever the truth of that charge, there were some sensational scenes at 8 Bishopsgate, as the merchant bank was besieged, desperate applicants hurled through windows their forms wrapped around stones, and (in the words of the *Daily News*) 'special policemen kept back the pushing crowd of clerks, agents, messengers and City men'.

But that was not the only thing that the City (and the partners of Antony Gibbs) would remember about this flotation: for it eventually emerged, partly as the result of assiduous digging by the *FN*, that despite, or perhaps because of, the phenomenal over-application for above all the £4.5m ordinary and preference shares, Barings had kept back almost £1m of them for itself, set aside handsome portions for favoured City houses, and made available barely a quarter of the shares for the public at large. The experience was summed up in some verses in the *St James's Gazette*, modestly entitled 'A Disappointment':

What means this crowd, so dense and denser yet,
That Baring's solemn portal has beset?
  What do they hold so dear?
Has some great western nation once more sought
For English loans, perchance too dearly bought?'
  They answered me: ''Tis beer!
Not the light sparkling foam of Bass's ale,
Not even Allsopp – his "East India pale";
  'Tis honest Guinness stout,
Which for three weary livelong nights and days,
With eager greed and venturesome amaze
  Has turned the world about.
Be it the firm debenture, (money lent),
Be it the winsome preference (6 per cent!)
  Be it the hopeful share –
Be it whate'er it may, our simple task
Is the allotment due to us to ask –
  If aught there be to spare'.

'Give me a form! a cheque!' I cried; 'th' amount
My bankers hold I scarcely need to count.

I sell whate'er I get!'
My cheque was cashed. All seemed to promise well.
I sold; and then came all I had to sell, –
   A letter of regret!

Miss Otis should have been a merchant banker, but, amidst some fierce press criticism, other disappointed applicants reacted in a vein more bitter than sweet. 'One of the most disgraceful Frauds on the Public that in my experience has ever been concocted': that was the view of Robert Cecil, addressing Barings from his writing desk at the Carlton Club. The firm itself took it all stoically on the chin, finding solace in a profit of over £½m; but it had been an illuminating experience, with the pros finely balanced against the cons.[10]

For the two great rivals, there was an immediate sequel to the episode. On the same day that he noted the rush of applicants for Guinness shares, Hamilton added intriguingly: 'Apropos of the success of this undertaking and the failure of the Manchester Ship Canal which was in the hands of the Rothschilds, an invidious comparison is drawn between "Rothschild's water" and "Barings' beer".' The following year, July 1887, the two houses came together to offer jointly to the public a £4m issue to try again to enable the canal to be built. It proved a miserable flop, with the public applying for less than a fifth, little interest being shown outside Lancashire, and the City remaining indifferent. It was an awkward baby to hold, with Barings and Rothschilds each being left with over 40,000 shares, and it may well have been the moment when New Court anyway decided that British industrial promotions were not for it. Revelstoke perhaps had his moment of revelation the following year, in the course of negotiations for the conversion of a Liverpool brewery, Messrs Walkers, into a joint-stock company. 'During the discussion', the *Bankers' Magazine* related soon afterwards, 'some strong words were used in Lord Revelstoke's presence. He pointed to the door, and the firm lost the quarter-million or so which might have accrued from the business'. But for whatever cultural and commercial reasons, Guinness and the Manchester Ship Canal would for many years stand out like sore thumbs in the issuing history of Barings and Rothschilds, where the foreign remained firmly their home patch. For the Ship Canal itself, however, there was a surprisingly happy outcome to its relations with the City. An issue in 1889 proved appreciably more successful, while much of the financial initiative passed to Glyns and Alexander Henderson, who between them helped to ensure that the Canal could be opened by Queen Victoria in 1894.

'But for your timely assistance and valuable counsel', its deputy chairman informed Bertram Currie in a notable tribute, 'it is very doubtful if the Manchester Ship Canal would have been begun.'[11]

Other industrialists would have been more muted in their praise for the services of the square mile, notwithstanding the example set by O'Hagan. Among the many brewery conversions of the late 1880s, several were sold to the public for absurdly inflated values; and in January 1888, when the Bass issue was puffed up and then much oversubscribed, Hamilton noted of the trend to turn private businesses into joint-stock concerns that 'Guinness started the fashion, & since then the Brokers [and presumably also the company promoters] whose appetite for spoils was so whetted over that transaction are putting great pressure on the proprietors of all big undertakings to follow the Guinness suit'.[12] The issuing house in this case was Glyns, which as in the old railway days somehow combined propriety with an eye for the main chance.

But if the City was overly enthusiastic about breweries in the late 1880s, it was quite the reverse about things electrical, following the sour end to the 'Brush boom' of 1882. A revealing source is the correspondence of Colonel R. E. B. Crompton, a distinguished electrical engineering entrepreneur who in the summer of 1888 became highly disenchanted as he sought to increase his firm's capital: 'We have contemplated putting the affair before the public, but are staggered by the huge fees asked by the London brokers.' And: 'I have had a harrassing time, chiefly due to the rapacity of all the various people who think they have a gold mine in the transformation of a private concern into a public company. For instance, the valuers charged me £700, the solicitors wanted to do the same, and Eddy Bourke's firm [the stockbrokers Brunton, Bourke & Co] actually had the cheek to ask £1,000 – no, a *thousand guineas*!! – for the use of their name on the prospectus.' Crompton eventually used a different broking firm, but thereafter showed a reluctance to come to the market, despite palpable shortages of working capital. A similar hostility to the City marked the gifted Sebastian de Ferranti, who in 1890 refused to go public despite the certain knowledge that this would create acute liquidity difficulties for his private company.[13]

In other industries, flotations did go ahead, but at a significant price. In 1888 the newly formed chemical cartel, the Salt Union, was brought to the market by Morton, Rose & Co – whose qualifications for the task were less than obvious – with such watered-down capital that its future profitability was severely affected. The following year, gross overcapitalisation characterised the flotation of Walkers, Parker, the first lead manufacturers of any size to be converted. And in 1890, the advisers of the Paisley sewing thread combine, J. & P. Coats, misjudged the likely success of the flotation and left that company with less working capital than it should have had. All these episodes mattered greatly to the industries concerned, but far less to the City as a whole. 'Still a happy hunting-ground for young jobbers seeking to make a business' was how the *Economist* in 1889 described the Stock Exchange's Miscellaneous market – it would be a long time before senior jobbing firms gravitated to it and dealt in home industrials.[14] British industry was coming by fits and starts to need the City, but as yet the City in return was hardly giving British industry its best shot.

*

Perhaps there was an excuse in the overheated late 1880s, when there was so much going on. One of the most striking developments was the rapid growth of investment trusts.[15] These trusts were quoted on the London Stock Exchange and spread their assets across a wide range of investments, being designed, in the words of the prospectus in 1868 of the pioneer Foreign and Colonial trust, 'to give the investor of moderate means the same advantages as the large Capitalists'. That at least was the theory, though in practice they were found most attractive in the late 1880s by existing investors who felt they were no longer obtaining an adequate return on British government securities. Scotland played an important part in the origins of investment trusts, and by this time the emerging giant in the movement was Dundee's Robert Fleming, whose Investment Trust Corporation was launched in London in 1888, though he himself did not open a London office until the turn of the century. Another key individual was Robert Benson, whose Merchants Trust also began in the late 1880s. He and Fleming were very respectable, but many of their contemporaries were not, and by April 1889 the *Statist* was writing distinctly scathingly about 'The Trust Craze'. Noting that about eighty investment trusts had either registered or offered additional capital since the start of 1888, it asserted that 'promoting syndicates and limited liability ventures, which have failed to successfully float various companies and scratch issues, find a "Trust" a valuable receptacle for all sorts of indigestible rubbish.' The *Economist* was also sceptical: 'We cannot help thinking that the existence of a good many recent trust companies is due partly to the desire for easy directorates.' Perhaps that stricture applied to the young John

Wynford Phillips. His father was the Prebendary of Salisbury Cathedral and he himself had trained as a barrister after coming down from Oxford in 1882. But then, six years later, he married Leonora Gerstenberg, daughter of the bondholders' friend, and this gave him sufficient means to jettison the law for the joys of finance. He quickly became involved in two investment trusts and so started a remarkable City career.[16]

Phillips was 'new' City, and at this stage 'old' City had relatively little to do with investment trusts, if only because they were new. Few in the City – on the financial side at least – were now 'older' than Natty Rothschild, and very soon after the Guinness affair he was asked by the journalist Frank Harris if he was jealous of the large profit made by Barings:

> 'I don't look at it quite in that way', retorted Lord Rothschild. 'I go to the House every morning and when I say "No" to every scheme and enterprise submitted to me, I return home at night carefree and contented. But when I agree to any proposal, I am immediately filled with anxiety. To say "Yes" is like putting your finger in a machine: the whirring wheels may drag your whole body in after the finger.'

Was his firm already entering upon a slow but inexorable decline? One might think so, to judge by a remark in January 1887 from Morgans in London to Drexel Morgan in the States: 'Since failure in Manch Ship Canal issue & small success in one or 2 other enterprises their name does not carry with it that persuasion to the public w^h it used to do.' It is also perhaps significant that the revolution in Brazil in November 1889 took Rothschilds completely by surprise, despite that country being very much Rothschilds' turf.[17] Of course one can exaggerate, for not only did the house continue to bring out a steady stream of foreign government issues but earlier in 1889 it was responsible for the phenomenally successful Burma Ruby Mines issue, when the crowd in St Swithin's Lane became so great that Natty reputedly had to climb up a ladder to get into the bank. Yet even that venture was double-edged, for it caused plenty of trouble as well as profit and may have played a part in persuading Natty that all company promotions, foreign as well as domestic, were simpler eschewed.

An increasingly pivotal figure inside New Court was Carl Meyer – 'the ever industrious C.M.', Cassel called him – and in January 1890 he wrote a formal letter to Alfred de Rothschild requesting to be relieved of his duties unless he be transformed from a salaried clerk into a financial adviser. Meyer's terms included 'that my name should be removed from the list of clerks under the control of the worthy Allard'; that he should receive a minimum yearly income of £6,000 to replace his salary; 'that, if possible, some structural alteration should be made in the office enabling me to have a small room to myself instead of sitting right in the middle of the general office which is particularly inconvenient for talking to strangers whom I have often to see on business of the house'; and 'that, if at any future time you should determine upon conferring the procuration of the house (as is done at Vienna and Frankfurt) upon any of the members of the staff, I should be one of those entrusted with that mark of confidence'. Meyer added that 'you may have an opportunity of explaining my views to Lord Rothschild'. Though some changes were made to Meyer's position, he never became a partner. Instead, over the years, he became increasingly close to Cassel, while Rothschilds remained an autocracy. In February 1890 two great autocrats came together, as Revelstoke was a guest at a house party held by Natty at his country home near Tring. The inevitable Hamilton (an almost Jamesian figure) watched closely: 'It is rather amusing to see the heads of the two great rival financial Houses together. They take stock of each other with jealous eyes, the jealousy being somewhat ill-disguised.'[18] The two men, temperamentally so different, knew each other well, and both may have wondered whether the ultimate spoils would go to the hare or the tortoise.

Hamilton's diary also makes it patently clear how, by the late nineteenth century, no Chancellor of the Exchequer could get very far in a financial operation without, in his words, 'taking the financial "bigwigs" into confidence', none of whom was bigger than Revelstoke and Rothschild. There was no bigger operation than Goschen's enormous conversion in 1888, when he sought to convert £500m of British government three per cent stock to two and a half per cent. On paper everything was in his favour, helped by the cheapness of money, the dearness of securities and his own high reputation in the City, not least after his recent political switch; but for any Chancellor a major conversion was a severe test of nerve, and that it could never be regarded as a cast-iron certainty to carry the market had been shown by the unexpected failure of poor Childers's debt conversion scheme four years earlier. 'I am more & more convinced that the right way to set about a conversion is by persuasion rather than by force', wrote Currie to Goschen on 11 January, as preliminary discussions began, and a week later Hamilton was reflecting along the same lines: 'The Chanc of the Exchequer must nerve himself into giving the stock-brokers some consideration, if he is to succeed with any conversion on a large scale. I am glad to say he has taken into his confidence men like Lord Revelstoke, Rothschild & B. Currie. Without their cooperation he will embark in a hopeless task.'[19]

Over the next few weeks Hamilton's well-placed social and professional life enabled him to offer an informed commentary on the scheme's progress. He was frustrated by Goschen's 'inability to make up his mind & come to decisions', but generally it went well enough:

> 5 *February* [a Sunday, staying with Leopold de Rothschild at Ascott]. N. Rothschild rode over from Tring. He seemed pleased at having been consulted by the Chanc of the Exchequer about possible Debt Conversion. According to him the practicability of carrying through a large measure – it was no use nibbling – depended mainly upon the European situation.
>
> 21 *February* [Goschen having paid a visit to the Bank of England to discuss the operation]. City people are apparently making up their minds more & more to face a reduction in interest.
>
> 1 *March.* I see that the great difficulty we shall have is to induce him [Goschen] to accept the principle of a small brokerage which I believe in these days to be absolutely essential to assure success to that part of his scheme which is optional.
>
> 4 *March.* The Chanc of the Exchequer is fortunate in having a very sensible Governor of the Bank (Collet) and a shrewd hard headed Deputy Governor (Lidderdale) with whom to consult. He is going the right way to work moreover in taking into his confidence some of the leading financial people, like Lord Revelstoke, Rothschild, and one or two representatives of the Joint Stock Banks. He still shies at the idea of brokerage . . .
>
> 8 *March.* Yesterday Goschen declared he would not face the idea of brokerage. However he has today yielded to further pressure and has accepted a compromise . . . All the City authorities believe some *douceur* to be a *sine qua non*. Dining at Lord Bath's last night, I found Lord Revelstoke, whose judgment is very good, most strong on this point.

Three days later Goschen formally put forward his scheme in Parliament. Hamilton was cheered by the early response:

> 14 *March.* Everything promises well for the Conversion scheme. Its success ought to be assured. The City are going to work at it with a will. Being all Tories, they are ready enough to carry through a project emanating from a Conservative Government; though the actual terms are not nearly as good as the terms offered by Childers 4 years ago . . . The Rothschilds have taken up the Conversion scheme quite warmly & are advising foreign holders of Consols to come in.

17 March. The Conversion scheme continues to promise well. There have been grumbles on the part of some of the big Joint Stock Banks, who would like to squeeze better terms out of the Chanc of the Exchequer – a larger bonus & a higher commission; but I doubt if there is much heart in the opposition.

Nor was there, and the same day the *Economist* declared that 'Mr Goschen has every reason to be gratified with the reception his Debt Conversion scheme has met with', that 'probably, indeed, he was just a little astonished at the enthusiasm with which it was first greeted on the Stock Exchange'. Goschen's conversion was the great triumph of his chancellorship, though Gladstone, whose own attempted conversion of 1853 had not come off, growled afterwards that the whole thing was no more than a 'magnificent swindle'.[20] But if so, it was a swindle which the City, properly remunerated, was prepared to countenance.

Early in 1889, however, as Goschen and the Treasury prepared the rather technical endgame of the conversion operation, all was not such sweetness and light. Hamilton again:

> *16 January.* The most formidable financial job ahead is the redemption of the balance of old Consols & Reduced threes ... I am convinced it ought to be done *en bloc*, & if we go the right way to work I don't believe it will be as formidable a business as many people think. The way to do it is to get certain big houses like Barings & Rothschilds to form a syndicate which would take at a given price such amount of new stock as will be required to replace the old stock ...
>
> *31 January.* In consequence of a talk I had with Lord Revelstoke in the autumn, he has made an informal proposal through me. It is that he would take 20 or 25 millions of stock at par ...
>
> I have impressed upon him [Goschen] the importance of taking the Rothschilds likewise into confidence; and he will give them a hint that he has had a 'nibble'. We must have the cooperation of both houses, between which there is a considerable amount of jealousy.
>
> *7 February.* Revelstoke & Rothschild are in communication with one another, & the Revelstoke proposal seems to have elements of success in it; but the terms originally proposed will have to be materially modified. Rothschild won't look at them: the possible margin of profit being considered wholly out of proportion to the risk run.
>
> *13 February.* Agreement with financial houses has broken down; they opened their mouths a deal too wide. They would not take the new Stock (20 or 25 millions), running all risks, higher than $97\frac{1}{2}$, as against present price of $98\frac{3}{4}$ to 99 and Revelstoke's original offer of £99.13.6.

Perhaps the two houses were simply too greedy, perhaps Natty was once again displaying his excessive caution, or perhaps Goschen at his end of the negotiations was unduly anxious about criticism from Gladstone if he made his terms too generous. In any event, the government was left with no alternative but to turn to its faithful retainer, the Bank of England, to help it redeem the old stock.[21]

Conversion, let alone redemption, would not have been possible without the blessing of the Stock Exchange, where *la vie spirituelle* continued. In 1889 there was the scandal of members defying the Committee by openly smoking all day long, as a way of protesting against the House's inadequate sanitation in the context of prevalent enteric fever. Early in 1890 the Committee considered a complaint from the Managers about 'a sudden rush made by a crowd of persons at the main entrance on the 23rd of December whereby a pugilist named Slavin was carried, or forced, into the House', but decided it would not be politic to interfere. That spring the *Rialto* noted the practicalities of maintaining sartorial standards: 'There is a hat shop on the Royal Exchange where the members of the House deposit their bowlers on arriving in the City, and receive silk hats from dust-proof boxes in exchange. When going home, they return the silk hats and get back the bowlers. They pay rent for the boxes, and the hat shop makes a very good thing out of them.' A few months later the same paper reported a lively episode when presumably the topper was laid aside: 'The Stock Exchange was much excited by a bet made by one of its members – that he would go from the House to the top of the Monument and back inside 15 minutes. As a matter of fact he did it in a little over 8 minutes, and a good deal of money changed hands over the event.' But sometimes there was business too, and from the mid-1880s the American market was particularly industrious, maintaining an after-hours market in Shorter's Court (just outside the Stock Exchange) in order to continue dealing while Wall Street was open. Elsewhere, there were inevitable comparisons being drawn towards the end of the decade between the chaotic, extremely busy Kaffir Circus – 'mainly composed of foreign elements, especially, perhaps, the Jewish' – and the Consol market – 'where speculation, although sometimes active, wears a more sedate appearance than anywhere else in the "House" '.[22]

For the Stock Exchange as a whole these were marvellous years. Membership was up to 2,640 by 1887; as many as ten firms had five or more partners; James Capel & Co was probably typical in enjoying annual profits over the next two years of well over £50,000; and in 1890 the *Bankers' Magazine* asserted that 'the stockbroker who kept a modest man-of-all-work in the year 1885, perhaps now has two gardeners, a coachman or "tiger", and even a footman or two, in place of the factotum'. Probably not employing a nursemaid was a member called Hugh Stutfield, who some years later, in an article memorably entitled 'Celibacy and the Struggle to get on', recalled the heady late 1880s:

> About five years ago [*circa* 1889] there was quite a rush of gilded youth within the portals of Capel Court. Nearly every firm of standing could boast of one or more sprigs of nobility on its staff of clerks, and smart cavalry officers were glad to act as 'runners' [half-commission men] if they could not become partners. The talk in the smoking-rooms of fashionable West-End clubs was of the comparative merits of American and Nitrate Rails, of the coming rise in frozen meat and land companies' shares . . . These were the palmy days of 'booms' and general inflation. The loan-monger and the company-promoter were on the war-path, and the public tumbled over each other in the wild rush after premiums on new issues. Financial houses and firms of old standing vied one with the other in foisting unmarketable rubbish on the guileless investor, who, through the medium of trust and other companies, fell a victim to various ingenious devices to part him and his money . . .

One member no longer in Capel Court to greet the noble sprigs was Spencer Herapath junior. He was the son of a successful stockbroker and, by early 1888, was in partnership with Algernon Delmar. 'Spencer called morning, jumpy & jerky, disappointed with horse he bought at Tattersall's', his sister Marion recorded in her diary that spring, but far worse was to follow:

> *14 June.* Bad news. Spencer failed on Stock Exchange.
> *15 June.* Spencer declared on Stock Exchange – disgrace . . .
> *22 June.* Cling to hope it's all Delmar's fault.
> *9 July.* Letter from Spencer, can't think he realises awful nature of failure.
> *November.* Spencer's failure in Times – no idea such failure, over £135,000.

Spencer was a feckless ne'er-do-well rather than a crook and, since his partner had done a runner, he was left to bear the brunt. Old Herapath's firm was ruined, and Marion's husband, the well-known artist and cartoonist Linley Sambourne, must have been tempted to depict a heart-rending scene.[23]

Almost as tragic a sight was a cornered stag. O'Hagan, for whom stags were a veritable *bête noir*, explained how they went about their usually, but not invariably, risk-free business:

The *modus operandi* pursued is that the moment a prospectus appears, someone on the Stock Exchange begins offering to sell shares of the company at a premium. If those interested in the success of the issue come forward to protect the issue and buy these shares for the special settlement (which means that the shares so bought are not to be taken up and paid for until the Stock Exchange appoints a day for the settlement of all bargains made in the shares), then the game goes on merrily, for people will come forward and sell what is called a bear of these shares so long as they can force the promoters to buy them at a premium. Then they send in applications for the amount they have sold, and if they secure allotments they just wait for the special settlement to deliver the shares they have sold, and take their profits. If they hear that the shares have been badly subscribed for, they hastily withdraw the applications they have made; while if they learn that the shares have been overapplied for, they increase their applications thrice or four times the amount they have sold, hoping that a part of their applications will be allotted to them.

These men are called 'bears' or 'stags'. Sometimes when a company's capital has been largely oversubscribed, these stags are 'caught', for the promoters scrutinize the list of applications, and put on one side any which look as though they came from stags. There have been instances when the 'stags' have been badly caught and made to suffer very severely, but such instances are rare, as if there are many stags who are out of the shares, they do all in their power to depress the price of the shares and frighten shareholders to sell their holdings at a sacrifice. It is so easy to spread unfounded rumours, which are eagerly taken up by Stock Exchange speculators and inserted in a certain class of paper, and frequently people are frightened into parting with their shares at a loss, and the 'stag' gets out of his troubles.

I am not speaking of isolated cases, but it is what went on from day to day when I was in the City. Brokers and jobbers got fat on it. I have in mind one very prominent member of the Stock Exchange who boasted to me that he sold before allotment one or two hundred shares of every company which offered its shares for subscription, and on average did very well indeed; but goodness, how he squealed when he was badly caught, and came to me to help him in his trouble!

Most stags were jobbers rather than brokers, with a sprinkling of hardened outside professionals. The majority of ordinary speculators were understandably nervous of being stags, granted that to be a seller in pre-allotment dealings carried with it an unlimited liability, in the sense that a cornered stag would have to pay literally whatever price was asked in order to procure the stock he had promised to sell. So the practice was left mainly to the inhabitants of Capel Court. O'Hagan, who suffered often from these tactics, remarked elsewhere in his memoirs that 'the mentality of members of the Stock Exchange is strange', in that 'men who hold their heads high, who would be horrified if it were suggested that they were not the soul of honour, would boast of the profit they made out of stagging a new venture'.[24]

Successful corners were indeed relatively rare, and the stag usually bounded away free, but in the winter of 1889–90 an episode occurred that passed indelibly into the Stock Exchange collective consciousness. The London flotation of the American company H. H. Warner and Co took place in November 1889, involving the issue of £550,000 in preference shares and 35,000 ordinary shares of £10 each. After itemising Warner's various proprietary medicinal products, including Warner's 'Safe' Remedies, Warner's 'Log Cabin' Remedies and Warner's 'Safe' Yeast, the prospectus went on: 'These preparations are sold in almost every part of the civilised world. In the United States, where they have been longest before the public, the total number of voluntary testimonials received is almost beyond belief. The large profits derived from proprietary medicines are well known.' Predictably, the issue, brought out by the stockbrokers Coates, Son & Co, was heavily stagged. Less predictably, Hulbert Harrington Warner – who, unbeknown to anyone in the City, was a member of the New York Stock Exchange and well versed in market practice – secretly instructed over a dozen brokers to buy up large quantities of the shares. He also ensured, when it came to allotment, that no shares went to stags, and as a result his carefully planned corner was perfectly in place. O'Hagan had been asked by Warner to bring out the business but had declined, though finding in 'Warner the Safe Man', as he was known in the States, 'a commanding presence and an impressive manner, the more so perhaps that he disclaimed any knowledge of things or affairs outside the scope of his own business'; and he relates what happened next, as the supply of shares completely dried up:

> The 'stags' began to feel that their tails had been twisted and made strong efforts to close their commitments, but their frantic efforts to buy sent the shares quickly to £25. Then they knew that they were caught out of the shares they had sold and they were at the mercy of the manipulators who were pulling the strings in this knife-cut-knife gamble. Away went the shares up to £40–£50, and there was nothing to put a brake upon their advance . . .

Possibly following an intervention by O'Hagan – who was friendly with some of the hardest-hit stags, little though he liked the breed in general – the druggist at last showed mercy, as the *FT* reported on a Monday in April 1890:

Business in the Miscellaneous market has been paralysed by the claims of Warners to attention. Talking of the rig in these shares occupied dealers' time almost exclusively today as it did on Saturday, and the wildest possible stories were afloat. 'The big bears, "Wicked Willie" included, had been given up to two o'clock to close at 50'. If this magnanimous offer were not accepted promptly, '100 would be the next price'. Certainly there was a good deal of bear closing at 50 to 54, and the broker to the company was generally on the spot and open to let bears out at 50, in spite of the fact that his presence in the market led to his being mobbed and hooted at. In the afternoon it was confidently asserted that all big bears had agreed to cut their loss at 50, and the rig may be looked upon as practically over . . .

The *FT* at the time reckoned that 'the clique' had made a profit of nearly a quarter of a million, O'Hagan years later that 'Warner must have returned to the States the richer by several million pounds'. The case of Warner's Safe Cure rig went to the courts in 1891, but they found, to general disbelief, that the charge of conspiracy was not sustained, declining therefore to relieve jobbers of their bargains. Among those jobbers would have been 'Wicked Willie', whose real name was William Morris (no relation); but he had already died – of, so it was said, a broken heart.[25]

The Warner squeeze took place over several months, but sometimes a few minutes could make or break a man's career on the Stock Exchange. In September 1890 a non-member called W. R. Brand, of Elm Grange, Finchley, accused a broker, Percival Preeston, elected in 1882, of having forestalled his market. Brand's precise charge was that he had given Preeston an order to sell 100,000 Mexican Rails (a notoriously volatile, speculative security) and that Preeston had then sold 15,000 at $61\frac{1}{4}$ for himself before selling 10,000 on Brand's behalf at $60\frac{3}{4}$. The protagonists attended the Committee, and Preeston read out his account of the events of the morning of Monday the 22nd:

I entered the Stock Exchange at Capel Court at twenty to 11 and passed through, as my invariable custom is, my office being in Old Broad Street.

I passed through the Mexican Rails Market and noticed a move and excitement. I had not been in the City on the Saturday previous, and had gone away a bull of £5,000 Mexican Ordinary.

These were on my mind, and seeing an excited crowd I took Mr Jackman [a Mexican Railway jobber] aside and asked him what was up. He said there was a serious fall in silver, he believed. I then said, 'Make me a price in £15,000'. He said, the market had not developed, and then

418

made a wide price $61\frac{1}{4} - \frac{3}{4}$. I sold him them at $61\frac{1}{4}$ and went round to one or two others to ascertain if there was really any news in . . .

I then went to my office at 61 Old Broad Street and saw Mr Brand waiting outside for me. He said, 'How late you are, I have been waiting half an hour'. I replied, 'I am a little, but it is not yet eleven'. I said, 'What is it?' He said, 'I want a deal in £100,000 Mexican Rails'. I said, '£100,000? This is rather a big order, is it not?' as I was not anxious to undertake it, and I said, 'No turn to me, remember I do not do your regular business, and it is no turn to deal in such a market in £100,000'. He said, 'You said I might come and deal'. I said, 'Yes, but not in £100,000'. He said, 'Run in, there's a good fellow, and sell £10,000'. I went into the Stock Exchange immediately. I entered the side entrance to avoid the Mining Market and sold £10,000 at $60\frac{3}{4}$ to Messrs Kennedy & Robertson . . .

In answer to questions, Preeston 'distinctly denied that he had Brand's order in hand when he sold the 15,000 at $61\frac{1}{4}$'. Clearly, as the next set of reported statements showed, much turned on the precise time of that sale; and though 10.40 was no longer tenable, it was in Preeston's interests to make it, and thus his alleged arrival in the market before going to his office, as early as possible:

Brand: His train was due at Broad Street at 10.33, but was normally [being the North London line] five minutes late. It took him 10 minutes to walk to the Bank Stores, where he generally met a friend and had a glass. On this day he did so and, receiving a cable, he walked to Mr Preeston's office, arriving about 11. There he saw the clerk, who said that Mr Preeston had not come up to town yet. He – Brand – said, 'What a nuisance!' He stood outside the office waiting until he saw him coming along. It was about 11.15. He – Brand – admitted he was not in the best of tempers. Mr Preeston had his gloves on, and his umbrella in his hand.

Jackman (also present): His book showed that he had bought 15,000 Mex Rails off Mr Preeston at $61\frac{1}{4}$. He could not say what the time was. He denied that he dealt with Mr Preeston before 11. He believed it was about 11.15. He did not observe whether Mr Preeston had his gloves on, or carried an umbrella. Mr Preeston asked him the reasons for the fall before he dealt. He – Jackman – thought he told him there was a rumour of an accident on the line.

Preeston: On the morning in question, he left Brighton by the 9.25 train, which was due at London Bridge about 10.38. He took a hansom, and there being a crowd of carriages, and obstruction at the Mansion House, he got out of the cab and walked direct to the House.

Brand: Mr Preeston might have come up by the 9.48 train.

Preeston: Having regard to the loss of time occasioned by the stoppage of the vehicular traffic opposite the Mansion House, he thought it might have been about five minutes before 11 o'clock before he actually sold the 15,000 at $61\frac{1}{4}$.

The Committee deferred consideration, and at a further meeting Prees-ton, faced by the evidence of tape prices for that morning running against his version of events, made a final chronological bid: 'As he had luggage to see after, he could not have sold the 15,000 at $61\frac{1}{4}$ before three minutes to 11.' But he insisted that he 'had sold at $61\frac{1}{4}$ before he saw Brand'. Finally, on 16 October, the Committee voted 21–0, with 22 present, that Preeston had been guilty of the proverbial 'dis-graceful and dishonourable conduct'; and a fortnight later a unani-mous vote expelled him. The *Economist* applauded the severity of the punishment, welcoming it as a break from the Committee's unfortu-nate tradition of dealing with erring members 'not so much according to their deserts, but more from an inside standpoint, which is based to some extent upon a club-like feeling of good fellowship'.

Preeston himself gave vent to his feelings in a strong letter to the *Statist*, in which he returned obsessively to what exactly had happened immediately after getting off his train from Brighton due at London Bridge at 10.38:

> This train, however, as shown by the railway company's books, was some minutes late. I wish to draw special attention to the following details, as the whole matter rests on a question of time . . . I found my luggage in the van, engaged a four-wheeler (at London Bridge Station) to take my luggage to my chambers, the cabman requiring a written address; having no change, I had previously borrowed on the train 3s from a member of the Stock Exchange to pay my cab on arrival at London Bridge, thus fixing the train by which I travelled and arrived. I then took a 'Hansom', but, getting in a block near the Mansion House, jumped out, and proceeded on foot to the Stock Exchange, where, as nearly as I can judge from the foregoing facts, I should arrive somewhere about 11 o'clock . . .

Near the end of his letter, he reiterated: 'I cannot fix my own time within a few minutes, owing to the circumstances already mentioned; also that the transactions from beginning to finish only occupied five to seven minutes, and that there is no official record kept as regards time in dealing.' And, most solemnly: 'I must leave others to judge the possibility of accurately determining the grave issues involved with re-gard to myself.'[26] However, his protest availed him little, and the rest of the City seems to have shown a massive indifference as to the fate of Percival Preeston. Perhaps he was also unfortunate in the timing of his letter, for it was published on 8 November 1890, and that particular Saturday the City was starting to have other, even graver things on its mind.

CHAPTER TWENTY-ONE

A Friend in Need

In October 1889, not long after the London Dock Strike, William Lidderdale pondered the age he lived in and attempted to apply the dictates of commercial common sense:

> Personally I have a strong feeling that the Social & Political Revolution in progress will try the stability of values very much in the next five or six years. The transfer of power to the least educated class promises to be accompanied by a competition on the part of politicians to attract the attention & favour of the new voters, & the latter will hear what is likely to please rather than the truth. There will be Labour troubles & questionable legislation, & I much doubt the effect for some time on property being favourable.

The Governor of the Bank of England then turned specifically to 'the present tendency of finance':

> It is distinctly in the direction of danger – too much capital is being forced into industrial developments, financiers are taking larger & larger risks in securities which require prosperity & easy money to carry without becoming a burden, & an increased number of investments have been driven up in price by the combined effects of a long period of cheap money & depression in trade, & of the transfer from Gov' securities of heavy amounts before employed by Consols. Trade is now profitable & needs more capital, new enterprises promising speculative results compete with trade for money. People are now attracted only by the promise of profits beyond interest. On the basis of 20 years ago we have most of the elements of a Crisis, with the additional danger that our collective liabilities are enormously increased with but a small increase in the central cash reserve of the country.

So, was a crisis inevitable? The Governor thought not, placing his faith in the current mode of 'financial operations':

> No great loans are taken without the issuing firms taking in numerous associates who share the risk for a consideration. London & Paris,

London & N York, London N York & Berlin or Hamburg, combine to carry out the operation thus greatly lessening the dangers of unsuccessful issue by a division & spreading of the liability. It is impossible to say which is at present the more important consideration – the tendency to excessive finance or the enlarged power to meet bad times – the position would take long study. My impression is that a *great deal* more reason for distrust would have to exist than formerly in order to produce serious discredit.

Lidderdale was offering advice to Rathbone about the latter's holdings, and from his privileged vantage point he was sufficiently sanguine to assert that 'so great has become the solidarity of Finance that it seems to me it would need something like a sudden outbreak of war, under present circumstances, to produce a crisis'.[1]

Over almost three decades Lidderdale had made himself into a City insider, but someone wholly on the outside was a young American called J. Walter Wood who, after graduating from Harvard, started working for Barings in the autumn of 1888 in the 'Bills Payable' department. Many years later, an established Wall Street figure, he recalled what was clearly a mellow experience at 8 Bishopsgate:

> The general office was a large room with no windows, the ventilation being in the high ceiling, where skylights admitted a portion of such light as there happened to be outside – which, on foggy days, was none at all. The only artificial light was from candles in fixed candlesticks on all the desks. There were no 'cages', telephones, 'tickers', or even typewriters (all letters were handwritten by each department) ... The silence was impressive, and the great banking room, with its mellowed fixtures seen through the soft light, was very dignified.
>
> No one seemed in a hurry. The bank messengers were called 'walkers', not 'runners', as in New York. Business did not really begin till about 11 o'clock, and was usually over by 4 o'clock. For those clerks who remained at work till 5 o'clock, tea with thin slices of buttered bread was served by the liveried 'walkers'. The partners' room adjoined the general office, and was more like a gentleman's library with a cheerful open fire in a marble mantelpiece at the end of the room, and a soft red and blue rug. The mahogany desks were massive, and the chairs deeply upholstered in dark leather. In the center of the room was a large table with a limited number of necessary reference books, and from the walls deceased partners of the House looked down from their mellowed-gilt frames.[2]

Perhaps by 1888 they no longer liked what they saw. At the start of December the *Statist* published a well-informed, highly critical article on 'Messrs Baring Brothers' Issues'. It itemised the firm's thirty-one principal issues since 1882 (of which all but two, Guinness and the Manchester Ship Canal, had been foreign) and stressed recent developments:

> Since 1884 Messrs Baring have been growing bolder and bolder in their invitations to the public. In that year they offered altogether little more than $6\frac{1}{2}$ millions sterling; in 1886 they offered over $18\frac{1}{4}$ millions sterling; in the present year, up to date, they have offered somewhat more than 28 millions sterling, irrespective of the Buenos Ayres Drainage, &c, Loan, which we are glad they did not succeed in placing with the public.

The *Statist* then proceeded to accuse Barings of not fulfilling its moral duties as an issuing house:

> Their prospectuses too frequently are not merely meagre, but quite insufficient to enable anyone to judge of the character of the security. The Messrs Baring, moreover, never state what compensation they receive for bringing out either a loan or a company, though surely this is a material circumstance.

The paper went on to assert that Barings had failed to 'exercise a restraining influence upon borrowers, especially upon Argentine borrowers, when it became evident that they were piling up debt too fast'. And it concluded on a frankly ominous note: 'It is much better, in the long run, that bad business should not be embarked in than that insecure loans should be foisted on the public by one of the greatest of our houses. In the long run the latter policy does not pay.' The *Bankers' Magazine* had only recently, and justly, cited this household name as the prime case of a firm that had 'never known, during the present century, anything but first-class credit, into which enters the elements of dignity – moral, personal and commercial alike'. Solid, deeply respectable and rather unimaginative, there was on the face of it no more English house in the City.[3]

What was going on?[4] The answer lies primarily with one man and one country. The man, inevitably, was Revelstoke, who may well have had his head turned by the phenomenal success and profitability of the Guinness issue, even to the extent where he came to believe that simply to have the name of Barings attached to an issue was sufficient to guarantee its favourable reception. And the country to which from the mid-1880s he devoted ever more of his firm's resources was the Argentine, into which British capital was pouring at an astounding rate, totalling up to £150m (over £7bn in present-day terms) by the end of the decade. That seductive land of rich pampas had long held a fatal attraction for the City, and amidst considerable competition from other houses Barings was responsible for about a quarter of the funds now flowing to it. The main conduit, of course, was the Buenos Aires firm of S. B. Hale & Co, examined and given a clean bill of health by Brown Shipley:

> That they are the first House in the Argentine Republic there can be no doubt, & that they have Barings confidence we have had good proof. As the field they occupy is a promising one for profit, all deductions made, the country rich in resources & rapidly increasing in population, & the government improving, we think that, with people of such old & high standing there, & of such responsibility, we ought to be able to do some business . . .[5]

That was in November 1887. Less than a year later Revelstoke was paid a visit by the firm's leading director, C. H. Sanford, who had recently obtained from the Argentine Government the much-sought concession to develop the sewerage and water system of Buenos Aires. Was Sanford a man to trust? According to the invaluable O'Hagan, he was 'an American medical man' who had become established in Buenos Aires, and achieved a friendship with the president of the republic, having originally been 'travelling in the Argentine on behalf of an American firm, manufacturers of "Florida Water", made, I believe, from the flower of the elder tree'.[6] Barings had had at least one unfavourable report on him, yet Revelstoke not only agreed to bring out the Buenos Aires Water Supply and Drainage Company but also, with his propensity for double-or-quits, decided against the increasingly common custom (as he no doubt saw it, but which so reassured Lidderdale) of having the issue fully underwritten. The flotation took place in November 1888 and, as the *Statist* noted with grim satisfaction, flopped. The implications for Barings, left with a vast number of unmarketable shares, were dire: it had agreed to operate on joint account with Hale & Co and it was committed to finding further capital for a massively expensive project as well as stumping up the rest of the purchase money to the Argentine Government. Judgement was all, and Revelstoke's had deserted him.

All might have been well if from late 1889, mirroring the world economy, there had not occurred a sharp crisis of confidence in all things Argentine. That October, Revelstoke wrote to Sanford in perhaps milder terms than he felt:

> The accounts we get from B. Ayres are not very satisfactory. It seems to
> us that a crisis is almost inevitable and the consequences may be very
> serious. Our money market is getting tighter daily . . . Argentine se-
> curities of all kinds are depressed and practically unsaleable in any
> quantity and are likely to remain so for the present.

Matters got worse in 1890, fuelled by a lethal Argentinian combination of financial maladministration and political turmoil. Edward
Hamilton provided a shrewd commentary towards the end of July:

> The news of the day is that a revolution has broken out in the Argentine
> Republic, which has borrowed too much – speculated & peculated. Many
> people will be hit by this unsettled state of things, especially some of the
> big City houses. The Barings are said to be up to the neck in Argentine
> securities . . . Not so the Rothschilds, who are much more cautious.

Up to the neck and rising: Barings had managed to find takers for less
than a tenth of the £2m of ordinary shares of the company it had so
foolishly backed. The work of the Buenos Aires Water Supply and
Drainage Company had virtually ground to a halt. With large holdings
in other South American securities likewise locking up the firm's
capital, Revelstoke and his partners had placed themselves in a position of appalling exposure, where the company was owed in November a further substantial payment but Barings simply did not have the
funds to meet it. The mood in the City's best partners' rooms was
hardly upbeat during the summer of 1890 – 'It is impossible to sell any
stocks except in the most retail way, I do not expect to do more than
hold our own in London this year, and indeed I shall be thankful if the
result of our trading all round in 90 is to pay counting house exs and
leave us where we were', reported Vicary Gibbs in August to the retired
Sillem – but as yet it was only at 8 Bishopsgate that merchant bankers
sank in despair into their deeply upholstered chairs.[7]

During September the situation remained on hold, though Barings
achieved some temporary alleviation through borrowing some £½m
from its good friends at Martins. On 7 October, Hamilton dined with
(among others) Natty Rothschild, who 'confessed to being very uneasy
about the present state of things in the City'. And Hamilton glossed:
'Nobody knows exactly why an uneasy feeling should prevail: beyond
that there is a sort of general apprehension that certain big houses are
not in a very comfortable or easy position, mainly due to the Argentine
crisis & the general fall in securities which causes their lock-up to be
so enormous.' Within a few days Goschen, still Chancellor, was record-

ing a similar mood in his diary: 'Went to the Bank, things queer! Some of the first houses talked about. Argentine, etc, have created immense complications. Uncomfortable feeling generally.' Then, on the 13th, Bertram Currie of Glyns received the first intimation that his old friend and neighbour was in serious trouble. The intermediary was Sidney Brunton, a partner with the stockbrokers Brunton, Bourke & Co and a leading figure in the money market:

> He came with a message from Lord Revelstoke to say that the firm required a large sum of money, and that it was difficult for them to appear in the market as borrowers. Before replying to this proposal, I told Mr Brunton to ask Lord Revelstoke for a statement of the bills payable and receivable. He returned with the answer that the acceptances of the firm amounted to ten millions sterling, and the bills in portfolio to nine millions sterling.[8]

The upshot was that Glyns advanced £$\frac{1}{2}$m, and later in the month another £$\frac{1}{4}$m.

All was intensely secretive, no one could yet name names, and the City's perturbed frame of mind was accurately reflected in an out-letter of the Imperial Ottoman Bank written on the 24th:

> We are going through peculiar times in London just now. Money is not so scarce, otherwise we would have a panic, but it is almost impossible to sell stock of any class from Consols downwards. 'The Market' won't buy excepting to close a/cs, and none of the 'big houses' here are free to buy, their commitments being already as much as they can carry.

The impossibility of selling securities compounded the problems of Barings, as did the policy of the Russian Government of steadily withdrawing its large-scale deposits from the house, with another major withdrawal ($1\frac{1}{2}$m) due on 11 November. The probability is that, by the end of October, Revelstoke had sufficiently swallowed his pride to take into his confidence perhaps a handful of leading figures, who in turn realised that something must be done. At this time a twelve-year-old boy had been sent home from boarding school for three weeks, having dislocated his shoulder at football. He was Richard Meinertzhagen, son of Daniel Meinertzhagen of Huths, and on 2 November, a Sunday, this was his diary entry:

> C'lou [Daniel's brother] is staying here [Mottisfont Abbey in Hampshire], also Charles Goschen owing to an upset in the City . . . Apparently

a firm called Barings is going to smash, so today they all drove over to Norman Court [where 'old Lady Baring' lived and Tom Baring had lived] and they took me with them. I never saw such a lot of long-faced bankers all looking as though it was the end of the world. Father says it is a most serious matter and may involve the whole City but I don't pretend to understand it . . . As soon as we arrived at Norman Court all those old gentlemen shut themselves up in the smoking-room whilst I was sent out into the garden . . . After the conference everyone seemed pleased and smiling and I was introduced to a Mr Robert Benson and a Mr Nathan [sic] Rothschild.[9]

Smiles all round, but there seem to have been no instant solutions, and in fact the Baring crisis was only just beginning.

The next sighting in a largely invisible process occurred at 8 a.m. on Saturday the 8th, when Everard Hambro – second only to Currie as a close friend of Revelstoke – caused some raised eyebrows by calling at such an unusual time of the week on Natty Rothschild in New Court. Their discussions were inconclusive, but Hambro pressed on and saw Revelstoke himself, who said bleakly that he would be able to say on Monday whether Barings could go on or would have to stop. The two men were both directors of the Bank, and Hambro told Revelstoke that the only man who could help him now was the Governor; he arranged that Lidderdale should come to Hambros in the afternoon so that he could discreetly see Revelstoke. At that meeting – before which Lidderdale scribbled a note to Goschen asking him to come to the Bank first thing on Monday – Revelstoke and a fellow-partner laid before Lidderdale and Hambro 'a preliminary statement of their affairs', in Lidderdale's words soon afterwards, 'which rendered it uncertain whether the Firm would have any surplus after payment of their liabilities'. Inevitably the atmosphere was strained. Lidderdale, who had probably learnt only that day that Barings was in such trouble, contented himself with saying that he needed more precise information and would wait until Monday to see whether Barings could go on. Hambro had already passed on to Lidderdale his earlier conversation with Revelstoke, and all the evidence is that the head of Barings was in an emotional state this second Saturday in November 1890.[10]

Lidderdale whiled away the next day by taking his small son to London Zoo. Perhaps even at this stage he saw the crisis as an opportunity as well as a challenge, for already that summer he had acted decisively to achieve for the Bank a greater degree of control over the money market than any Governor had managed for a long time. As a good merchant, he was inherently hostile to bankers as a breed – 'a less public-spirited class . . . I do not know', he declared – and in particular resented their tendency to remove at a drop of the hat their already inadequate balances from the Bank. His words to Welby at the Treasury, a few weeks before the crisis, were heartfelt:

> I don't think any one who has not sat for 2 years in the Governor's chair during the last decade can realise fully – the dependence of the English Banking system upon the Bank – the difficulty that this dependence creates in our management. Banking liabilities have enormously increased, not so Bankers' reserves, and this makes our burden much heavier than before and leads to fluctuations in rates quite out of proportion to actual movement of currency.

His special ire was reserved for the joint-stock bankers, but on this Sunday he also felt considerable contempt for Revelstoke's gross mismanagement. He later told Hamilton that Revelstoke 'did not seem the least to know how he stood' and that 'it was haphazard management, certain to bring any firm to grief'. It is also possible that Revelstoke was no special favourite at the Old Lady, for in 1887 he had had a slight run-in with the Governor of the day, James Currie. 'I am sorry that you express a feeling that the Junior Members of the Court [i.e. including Revelstoke] have practically nothing whatever to do with the management of the affairs of the Bank', Currie had written to him.[11] Still, personal feelings aside, there was no getting away from the almost unthinkable consequences should Barings go down: not only would the failure of the City's leading accepting house inevitably bring down a host of other firms, including all the discount houses, but the very status of the bill on London would be threatened and thus the pre-eminence of the City as an international financial centre.

Yet what could the Bank do? The post-1873 intellectual legacy of Bagehot's *Lombard Street* meant that indisputably it would have to do *something*, but the equally indisputable fact was that a private institution, responsible to its shareholders and with reserves roughly half the size of Barings' estimated liabilities, could not hope to act as sole lender of last resort. It was all very difficult, and at this particular juncture in its affairs the square mile was extremely fortunate to have at its helm someone described by Welby as 'a model of a calm shrewd bold Scotch man of business'. Or as Hamilton, ear ever to the ground, had noted not long before the crisis broke: 'It is said that Lidderdale is considered in the City to be the best Governor the Bank has ever had (not excepting Collet). He always knows his mind, & his judgement is very good.'[12]

He had come a long way from those early dealings with the tea market, and now that judgement was to meet its supreme test.

Goschen kept his Monday morning appointment in Threadneedle Street, and years later Lidderdale recalled that his first words were 'You gave me an unhappy Sunday, Mr Governor'. Goschen himself recorded the course of the interview in his diary:

> To the Governor of the Bank. Found him in a dreadful state of anxiety. Barings in such danger that unless aid is given, they must stop. — came in while I was there; almost hysterical. Governor and he both insisted that the situation could only be saved if Government helped . . . Picture drawn of the amount of acceptances held by various banks, which would have to stop. All houses would tumble one after the other. All credit gone. I entirely understood their reasoning, but remembering action taken in France when [in 1889] Comptoir d'Escompte was in difficulties, I said the great houses and banks in London must come together and give the necessary guarantee. This was declared impossible if the Government didn't help.

The Chancellor then went to see two other (unnamed) bankers, both of whom insisted that government help was necessary. And he noted tartly: 'Both quite demoralised. Lidderdale much more of a man and keeping his head, though certainly he pressed me hard.' Goschen returned to the Treasury in mid-afternoon and informed Hamilton of the plight of Barings. 'Every effort will have to be made to keep them on their legs', Hamilton wrote later in the day, though adding that Goschen 'does not at present see his way to doing more than giving every support to the Bank'. And: 'I gathered from Goschen that poor Revelstoke seems to have well nigh lost his head, which is not to be wondered at. Though the City is very uneasy, depressed, & excited, they have not yet got word of the immensity of the storm that is brewing . . .'[13]

That evening, as it happened, was the Lord Mayor's banquet, and just before it began Goschen told Salisbury about Barings. 'Is it as bad as that?' asked Salisbury, and in his speech he calmly concentrated on foreign affairs. Following the turtle soup, there was little sleep for Goschen as he wrestled with himself as to what his policy should be. 'If I do nothing and the crash comes I shall never be forgiven: if I act, and disaster never occurs, Parliament would never forgive my having pledged the National credit to a private Firm.' Eventually, his 'night thoughts' convinced him that it was impossible as well as undesirable to carry direct aid in Parliament: 'How defend a supplemental estimate for a loss of half a million! And would not immediate application put the whole fat in the fire?'[14] Goschen, like all Chancellors of the era, was a finance minister formed in the Gladstonian mould; and at the heart of Gladstonian Liberalism was an immutable belief in *laissez-faire*. The City, it seemed, would have to stand or fall on its own.

Between Tuesday and Thursday, as rumours flew with ever greater velocity, there were four main developments. The first was that Goschen continued to insist to Lidderdale that the government could offer no tangible help, while Lidderdale for his part was adamant that the Bank could act only within a larger umbrella provided by the government. Secondly, the Bank managed to persuade the Russian Government not to make its £1.5m withdrawal from Barings. Thirdly, Natty Rothschild emerged as a constructive figure, not only persuading the Bank of France to lend £3m in gold to bolster the Bank of England's badly stretched reserves, but applying discreet pressure on his good friend Salisbury to adopt a more interventionist attitude to the crisis. Significantly, 'he said that if the catastrophe came', Salisbury recorded after their conversation, 'he thought it would put an end to the commercial habit of transacting all the business of the world by bills on London'. Rothschild seems to have been sceptical about the chances of Barings' long-term survival as a significant business, even if it did not sink immediately, but as Hamilton noted with pleasure after a dinner party on Wednesday, 'N. Rothschild spoke very nicely & unboastfully about the situation'. The fourth development was probably the most important – Lidderdale's decision to appoint Bertram Currie and the octogenarian Benjamin Buck Greene to determine between them whether Barings was solvent in the long run, in other words whether it was worthy of rescue. It was an appointment that on the Wednesday brought forth the most pitiful letter from Revelstoke to Currie: 'I don't like to come & see you & hardly think I ought to write, but I cannot help sending one line in my wretched agony to implore you to do what you can. I know you will & I am sure you feel for us all in our nightmare.'[15] Pitiful, yes, but aimed at an old friend's heart with deadly effect.

Friday the 14th paid for all. In the course of a trying morning it became clear that, in the eyes of Currie and Greene, the assets of Barings did show a substantial surplus over its liabilities, despite the firm's pressing need for an enormous cash advance of up to £9m, mainly in order to meet acceptances falling due over the coming weeks. Some ten years later Greene wrote to Lidderdale about his memories of that morning: 'I must frankly say that as the amount required was so large . . . I considered the shutters must go up soon after I reached The City, instead of which on delivery of the report to my surprise you instantly said "They must be carried on . . ." ' Meanwhile, it was also becoming clear that, after almost a week of astute news management, including a degree of self-denial on the part of the press, the City at large was starting to succumb to outright panic. At about noon John Daniell, senior partner of Mullens the government brokers, burst into the Bank, crying to Lidderdale with his arms aloft: 'Can't you do something, or say something, to relieve people's minds? They have made up their minds that something awful is up, and they are talking of the very highest names – the very highest!'[16] During the next hour, Barings' bills started to pour into the Bank at an alarmingly rapid rate. With the entire credit of the City at peril, the moment was nigh for Lidderdale to earn the greatness that was being thrust upon him. At about two o'clock he slipped quietly out of the Princes Street door.

He took a roundabout route until he secured a hansom, which drove him to Downing Street. There he did not meet Goschen, who was committed to a speaking engagement in Dundee that evening and felt that he had to fulfil his programme to avoid panic. Instead his place was taken by W. H. Smith, first lord of the Treasury and widely known as 'Old Morality', and he was soon joined by Salisbury. For at least an hour neither side would back down from the positions taken at the start of the week. At one point Salisbury offered authority to break the 1844 Bank Charter Act, but this Lidderdale (he was to recall) 'emphatically refused', telling the Prime Minister that 'reliance on such letters was the cause of a great deal of bad banking in England'. And, 'after a short pause', Salisbury replied, 'I believe you are right'. Eventually, with stalemate looming, Lidderdale played his highest card:

> I told Lord Salisbury I could not possibly go on with the matter at the Bank's sole risk; that the Bank had been taking in Baring's Bills all the week, pending the investigation; that they were probably coming in fast now that alarm had set in, and that unless Government would relieve us of some of the possible loss, I should return at once and throw out all further acceptances of the Firm.[17]

This threat prevailed. The two politicians in effect gave Lidderdale just under twenty-four hours to save Barings, promising that the government would bear half the loss resulting from taking in Barings' bills up to early afternoon on Saturday. By five o'clock, mercifully unhindered by the notorious traffic jams of late-Victorian London, the Governor was back in the City.

Currie was among those waiting for him, as Lidderdale called an immediate meeting in his room at the Bank and announced his intention of starting a guarantee fund for Barings, with the Bank itself putting up the first million pounds. Currie at once declared that Glyn Mills would contribute half a million on the condition that Rothschilds did the same. Moments later Natty Rothschild arrived at the meeting. Would he agree? To quote Currie's subsequent, carefully measured account: 'He hesitated and desired to consult his brothers, but was finally and after some pressure persuaded to put down the name of his firm for £500,000.' What pressure? According to Hamilton the next day, it needed Lidderdale to say bluntly to Rothschild: 'We can get on without you.'[18] What would have happened if Rothschild had called Lidderdale's bluff is another question. But he did not, and the success of the guarantee fund was assured: over the next half hour the City's inner circle rushed to contribute. Subscribers to the first list included Raphaels (£250,000), Antony Gibbs and Brown Shipley (£200,000 each), and Smith Payne & Smiths, Barclays, Morgans and Hambros (£100,000 each). In the evening, Lidderdale met representatives of the five leading joint-stock banks, who put themselves down for an impressive total of £3.25m. Effectively the fund guaranteed the Bank against any losses arising out of advances made to Barings to enable it to discharge its liabilities; and the happy consequence was that, in some form still to be determined, Barings was saved. 'We will do our best not to be unworthy of what has been done', wrote Revelstoke to Lidderdale on Saturday morning.[19]

The existence of the fund remained secret most of that day, as it steadily grew to almost £10m by mid-afternoon, eventually reaching some £17m by the following week. And, until news of it did leak out towards the end of Saturday, the mood of the City as a whole was encapsulated by the *FT*'s graphic leading article that morning on what it could only call 'The Agony':

> The City is becoming enveloped deeper and deeper in a baleful, mysterious crisis. Day by day thick clouds gather over the Stock Markets, and where they come from, and who is responsible for them, no one has a definite opinion. All who have financial interests at stake feel as if they were standing on the brink of a volcano which at any moment may open up and swallow them. This slow-killing agony has been going on now for about two months without coming to a head. The worst kind of fever would reach its climax in less time.

Meanwhile, from those in the know, there were a couple of instant verdicts on the dramatic solution of the previous day. 'It appeared to us that it was to the interest of our joint account to come forward, not only to diminish our loss on Barings' bills but to avoid the danger of losing by other firms stopping', wrote Raphaels to its New York agents. Baron Alphonse de Rothschild in Paris, given the news of the guarantee fund by his London cousins, concurred: 'Evidence indeed that the English houses perfectly understand their responsibility and by preventing the catastrophe threatening the house of Baring they are shielding their self interest in as much as the house of Baring just now is the keystone of English commercial credit'. By Sunday the outlines of what had taken place were generally known, and Hamilton reported the very revealing reaction of the West End:

> Nobody talks of anything else but of the Barings . . . There is a strong feeling of sympathy for them. This is not unnatural for more reasons than one: everyone is relieved that the catastrophe has been averted, there is no suspicion of fraudulent intent, the House has always been popular & greatly respected, poor Revelstoke himself is known to have been the most generous & large-hearted man, there is the feeling ingrained in John Bull for the fallen, and moreover not a few are sorry to think that the downfall of Barings means the undisputed supremacy of the Jews in the commercial world.

Still, they were not universally shared sentiments. 'What a time you must have had in the City', wrote Lord Randolph Churchill to Alfred de Rothschild the next day from Monte Carlo. And he went on as only he could have: 'Fancy those Barings being brought so low . . . Lord Revelstoke will not be able to ride the high horse so much as he used to.'[20]

'Saved' was the *FT*'s bald headline on Monday the 17th. The paper declared that, if Barings had gone under, 'what might have happened on the Stock Exchange is a prospect too fearful to contemplate', and that 'not a. living man in the House has witnessed anything approaching the catastrophe which would have been inevitable'. The following evening, at Reginald Brett's, Natty Rothschild was emphasising that (in words reported by his host) 'had Barings been allowed to collapse, most of the great London houses would have fallen with them', adding that 'about 6 millions' worth of Bills are drawn daily upon London, and an enormous proportion of this business passed through their hands'. In fact, the atmosphere of crisis did not pass quite so abruptly as these affirmations of relief might suggest. On Wednesday the 19th, Harry Gibbs wrote to Vicary in Athens and mentioned that, over the past few days, all important firms, 'except possibly Huths', had been 'talked about'. His explanation showed a good understanding of City psychology: 'Of course the fact is that Barings having collapsed so fearfully, people are saying "Who then is safe?" & the Stock Exchange having received a tremendous shock & having no "business" to occupy their minds with, are simply talking wildly about the great houses, no matter how strong they may be.' Indeed, for a few hours that same day it seemed in Capel Court as if the guarantee fund had never been. John Biddulph Martin, in his retrospective account of the Baring crisis, related a sharp encounter:

> A rumour, more or less well founded, that the joint stock banks had announced that they would call in all loans from the Stock Exchange, caused almost a panic in the morning; it was certain that the Governor of the Bank of England called the managers in and told them that if they would not give their customers reasonable accommodation, they must not themselves look to the Bank in case of need. Thereupon they let it be known that they would make advances as usual, and a general improvement all round took place immediately. This seemed to be the turning point, and the crisis was at an end.[21]

Quite why the joint-stock banks lost their nerve at this thirteenth hour is unclear, but undeniably there was a touch of the triumphant central banker as Governor Lidderdale sent them on their way.

And Barings itself? 'A great Nemesis overtook Croesus', one partner at the time famously described the humiliation, adding that 'the line has never been out of my head since the Guinness success'. By Saturday the 22nd arrangements were well in hand for the old partnership to be wound up and replaced by a new company, called Baring Brothers & Co Ltd, with capital of £1m subscribed by many of the leading City houses as well as members of the family. 8 Bishopsgate remained in a state of shock, and one visitor that day was John Biddulph Martin: 'Went to Barings about prospects of keeping the a/c. Painful interview with Ld Revelstoke, he almost broken down.' There was plenty of pain to come, for over the next few years the winding up of the old partnership involved the selling of all assets; and these included the private property of the partners, whose liability was (in the best City tradition) unlimited. None suffered materially and emotionally more than Revelstoke himself, who before his death in 1897 lost not only his country estate and his wonderful collection of French furniture and pictures, but also his position in the City and much of his self-esteem. In the depressed financial climate of the early 1890s, liquidation proved a protracted business, but eventually, in 1895, the Bank of England's loan was paid off and the long-suffering guarantors were no longer on risk. The Chancellor of the day, Harcourt, took the opportunity to write to Lidderdale, by now an ex-Governor: 'The Baring Guarantee was a bold and probably a necessary stroke. It has ended well. May it never be repeated. Such turns of luck do not often occur in the nature of things.' The warning note of admonition was there, reminiscent of the celebrated *Punch* cartoon in November 1890 itself, showing a stern-looking Old Lady scolding a group of schoolboys with heads bowed and playing cards hidden at their back: 'You've got yourselves into a nice mess with your precious "speculation"! Well – I'll help you out of it, – for this once!!' And, with an implicit throwback to the earlier financial crises of the century, the cartoon was entitled 'Same Old Game!'[22]

'Goschen has at last found a happy land as protector of City princes', Beatrice Webb noted rather sourly in her review of 1890, but otherwise there was near unanimity that the crisis had been resolved as satisfactorily as could possibly have been hoped. The greatest plaudits went to Lidderdale, who at the end of the year received a deputation and address of gratitude from the Stock Exchange Committee. His reply was wholly in character: 'I shall always remember with pride and satisfaction that, in the opinion of such a body as yours, in a moment of danger I was able to do my duty.' He had done so in an intense, peculiarly British crisis, played out almost entirely behind closed doors. It was a crisis that, through the device of the guarantee fund, had fully reaffirmed the Bank's authority within the City. As never before, the leading houses of the City had come together in conscious, collective action to rescue one of their own – a club to which the main joint-stock banks now clearly belonged, though arguably as second-class members being charged double for the privilege. Certainly there was some resentment on their part that they had not been taken into the inner councils of the Bank and had not featured on the initial subscription list.[23] But pehaps above all the crisis showed the importance of the personal touch. Almost a quarter of a century earlier, it would have been perfectly possible to save Overend Gurney, which in time did pay its creditors; but the firm had made the fatal mistake over the previous decade of antagonising the rest of the City elite. Whatever the dislike in some quarters of Revelstoke's rather arrogant personality, the same did not apply to Barings in 1890. 'The House has always been popular & greatly respected': Hamilton's words hit the nail squarely on the head. Barings, supremely, was the establishment's – political, social, financial – *inside* house; and in Bertram Currie and Everard Hambro it had two exceedingly well-placed, powerful allies. This is not to deny that there was a more generalised fear for the future of other firms and the future of the City should Barings go down. But in the end, the lesson of the crisis, a lesson applicable not only in 1890, was that it will always pay to be fortunate in one's friends.

Notes

ABBREVIATIONS

B of E	Bank of England Archives
BB	Baring Brothers & Co Archives
BBJB	Journal of Joshua Bates, Baring Brothers & Co Archives (DEP 74)
BS	Records of Brown, Shipley & Co (Guildhall Library)
Barclays	Barclays Group Archives: Bank of Liverpool records, Langton Papers
Brandt	Records of Wm Brandt, Sons & Co (Nottingham University Library)
Churchill	Diaries of Charles Churchill senior and Charles Churchill junior (Guildhall Library)
DBB	David J. Jeremy (ed), *Dictionary of Business Biography* (1984–6)
Gibbs	Records of Antony Gibbs & Sons (Guildhall Library)
Hambros	Records of C. J. Hambro & Sons (Guildhall Library)
Hamilton	Diaries of Sir Edward Hamilton (British Library)
JF	Records of John Foster & Sons (Brotherton Library, Leeds)
JM	Records of Jardine Matheson & Co (Cambridge University Library)
Lloyds	Lloyds Bank Archives
McLean	Letter books of David McLean, 1875–89, at the School of Oriental and African Studies Library, London (SOAS Ms 380401/13)
Martin	Diaries of Sir Richard Biddulph Martin and John Biddulph Martin (the Holland-Martin family archives)
NW	National Westminster Bank Archives
Overstone	D. P. O'Brien (ed), *The Correspondence of Lord Overstone* (Cambridge, 1971)
RAL	N. M. Rothschild & Sons Archives (London)
RBS	The Royal Bank of Scotland Archive (London)
Rathbone	Records of Rathbone Bros & Co (Liverpool University Library)
SE	Records of the London Stock Exchange (Guildhall Library)

CHAPTER ONE

1. Kenneth Garlick and Angus Macintyre (eds), *The Diary of Joseph Farington* (1979), vol VI, pp 2253–4; *Public Characters of 1803–1804* (1804), p 387; *John Julius Angerstein and the Woodlands* (Woodlands art gallery, Greenwich, 1974); *Select Committee on Marine Insurance* (P. P. 1810, IV), p 67.

2. J. Leighton-Boyce, *Smiths the Bankers, 1658–1958* (1958), pp 130–5.

3. *Annual Register* (1810), pp 403–5, *Gentleman's Magazine* (October 1810), S. R. Cope, 'The Goldsmids and the Development of the London Market during the Napoleonic Wars' in *Economica* (1942), L. Alexander, *Memoirs of the Life of Benjamin Goldsmid* (1808), p 95; *Cobbett's Weekly Political Register*, 3 Oct 1810.

4. Charles Buxton (ed), *Memoirs of Sir Thomas Fowell Buxton* (1849), pp 288–9; Stanley Chapman, *N. M. Rothschild, 1777–1836* (1977), Lord Rothschild, *The Shadow*

of a Great Man (1982), Richard Davis, *The English Rothschilds* (1983); RAL, XI/82/10; RAL, T29/364; RAL, T31/1/5.

5. Van Akin Burd (ed), *The Ruskin Family Letters* (1973), vol I, pp 54–6, 64, Tim Hilton, *John Ruskin: The Early Years* (1985), pp 1–12, Wolfgang Kemp, *The Desire of My Eyes: The Life and Work of John Ruskin* (1991), pp 3–11.

CHAPTER TWO

1. J. M. Price, 'What did Merchants do? Reflections on British Overseas Trade, 1660–1790' in *Journal of Economic History* (1989).

2. S. D. Chapman, 'The International Houses: The Continental Contribution to British Commerce, 1800–1860' in *Journal of European Economic History* (1977), pp 9–10.

3. Stanley Chapman, *The Rise of Merchant Banking* (1984), p 9; *The Picture of London, for 1815* (sixteenth edn, 1815), p 101.

4. Hugh Barty-King, *The Baltic Exchange* (1977), pp 28–9; Bryant Lillywhite, *London Coffee Houses* (1963), pp 20–1.

5. S. W. Dowling, *The Exchanges of London* (1929), pp 4–5.

6. S. E. Fairlie, 'The Anglo-Russian Grain Trade, 1815–1861' (London D Phil, 1959), pp 262–3.

7. T. S. Ashton, *An Economic History of England: The 18th Century* (1955), p 140; David Kynaston, *Cazenove & Co: A History* (1991), pp 11–12; Stanley Chapman, *N. M. Rothschild, 1777–1836* (1977), p 4.

8. W. R. W. Stephens (ed), *A Memoir of the Right Hon William Page Wood, Baron Hatherley* (1883), vol I, pp 1–4; Philip Ziegler, *The Sixth Great Power: Barings, 1762–1929* (1988), pp 17–19; Kenneth Garlick and Angus Macintyre (eds), *The Diary of Joseph Farington* (1979), vol VI, p 2060; Ziegler, p 51.

9. K. F. Dixon, 'The Development of the London Money Market, 1780–1830' (London D Phil, 1962), p 80; S. R. Cope, 'Bird, Savage & Bird of London: Merchants and Bankers, 1782–1803' in *Guildhall Studies in London History* (1981); S. D. Chapman, 'British Marketing Enterprise: the Changing Roles of Merchants, Manufacturers and Financiers, 1700–1860' in *Business History Review* (1979), pp 217–25; Lucy Sutherland, *A London Merchant, 1695–1774* (Oxford, 1933).

10. D. E. W. Gibb, *Lloyd's of London: A Study in Individualism* (1957); S. D. Chapman, 'Hogg Robinson: the rise of a Lloyd's broker' in Oliver M. Westall (ed), *The historian and the business of insurance* (Manchester, 1984); *Select Committee on Marine Insurance* (P. P. 1810, IV), pp 64, 76, 42.

11. Sir John Clapham, *The Bank of England: A History* (Cambridge, 1944), vol I; Michael C. Lovell, 'The Role of the Bank of England as Lender of Last Resort in the Crises of the Eighteenth Century' in *Explorations in Entrepreneurial History* (1957–8); Stanley Chapman, *Merchant Enterprise in Britain: From the Industrial Revolution to World War I* (Cambridge, 1992), p 56.

12. D. M. Joslin, 'London Private Bankers, 1720–1785' in *Economic History Review* (1954–5); P. W. Matthews and A. W. Tuke, *History of Barclays Bank Limited* (1926), p 35; Roger Fulford, *Glyn's, 1753–1953* (1953), pp 2–6; Joslin, p 181; L. S. Pressnell, *Country Banking in the Industrial Revolution* (Oxford, 1956), Dixon, 'Money Market'.

13. RBS, WD/3/4, 10 June 1814; Clapham, vol I, p 166; Matthews and Tuke, pp 41–2; George Chandler, *Four Centuries of Banking*, vol I (1964), pp 210–14.

14. Perry Anderson, 'The Figures of Descent' in *New Left Review* (Jan/Feb 1987), p 31; E. Victor Morgan and W. A. Thomas, *The Stock Exchange: Its History and Functions* (1962), W. J. Reader, *A House in the City: A Study of the City and of the Stock Exchange based on the Records of Foster and Braithwaite, 1825–1975* (1979),

S. R. Cope, 'The Stock Exchange Revisited: a new look at the market in securities in London in the eighteenth century' in *Economica* (1978); Larry Neal, *The Rise of Financial Capitalism: International capital markets in the age of reason* (Cambridge, 1990); S. R. Cope, 'The Stock-Brokers find a home: how the Stock Exchange came to be established in Sweetings Alley in 1773' in *Guildhall Studies in London History* (1977); Anon (J. Lancaster?), *The Bank – The Stock Exchange – The Bankers – The Bankers' Clearing House – The Minister, and the Public* (1821), p 7.

15. P. G. M. Dickson, *The Financial Revolution in England: A Study in the Development of Public Credit, 1688–1756* (1967), p 493; Lucy Sutherland, 'Samson Gideon: Eighteenth-Century Jewish Financier' in Lucy Sutherland, *Politics and Finance in the Eighteenth Century* (1984).

16. Philanthropos (Thomas Mortimer), *Every Man His Own Broker* (1761), pp 79–81.

17. A. Heertje, 'On David Ricardo' in *Transactions of the Jewish Historical Society* (1970–73); Piero Sraffa (ed), *The Works and Correspondence of David Ricardo* (Cambridge, 1952), vol VI, pp 150–1.

18. Lancaster, p 9; NW, 2456, Smith Payne & Smiths correspondence, 30 April 1802; *Rules and Regulations Adopted By The Committee for General Purposes of the Stock-Exchange* (1812), p 46.

19. Dixon, p 24; S. R. Cope, 'The Goldsmids and the Development of the London Market during the Napoleonic Wars' in *Economica* (1942), p 182; S. R. Cope, *Walter Boyd: A Merchant Banker in the Age of Napoleon* (1983), p 2; Elizabeth Gaskell, *Cranford* (Oxford, 1972 edn), pp 12, 187; George and Pamela Cleaver, *The Union Discount: A Centenary Album* (1985), pp 33–4; Martin Daunton, 'London and the World' in Celina Fox (ed), *London – World City, 1800–1840* (1992), pp 21–33.

20. Dr William Fleetwood, *A Complete Collection of the Sermons* (1737), p 732; Daniel Defoe, *The Anatomy of Exchange-Alley* (1719); Dickson, p 28; George Birkbeck Hill and L. F. Powell (eds), *Boswell's Life of Johnson* (Oxford, 1934), vol III, p 353.

21. M. Dorothy George, *Hogarth to Cruikshank: Social Change in Graphic Satire* (1967), p 77; Diana Donald, ' "Mr Deputy Dumpling and family": satirical images of the city merchant in eighteenth-century England' in *Burlington Magazine* (Nov 1989); Peter Pindar, *The Fat Knight and the Petition; or, Cits in the Dumps!* (1815), p 29, Clive Trebilcock, *Phoenix Assurance and the Development of British Insurance*, vol 1 (Cambridge, 1985), pp 50–1; Ziegler, p 36.

22. P. J. Cain and A. G. Hopkins, 'The Political Economy of British Expansion Overseas, 1750–1914' in *Economic History Review* (1980), p 469; P. J. Cain and A. G. Hopkins, 'Gentlemanly Capitalism and British Expansion Overseas: I. The Old Colonial System, 1688–1850' in *Economic History Review* (1986), p 513, Nicholas Rogers, 'Money, land and lineage: the big bourgeoisie of Hanoverian London' in *Social History* (1979); *Boswell's Life of Johnson*, vol II, p 126; Cain and Hopkins, 'Gentlemanly Capitalism', p 514.

23. H. V. Bowen, 'Investment and empire in the later eighteenth century: East India stockholding, 1756–1791' in *Economic History Review* (1990); Sutherland, 'Samson Gideon'; Leighton-Boyce, p 129; Ziegler, p 51; Jane Austen, *Sense and Sensibility* (Oxford, 1980 pb edn), p 145; Rogers, 'Money, land and lineage', Lucy Sutherland, 'The City of London in Eighteenth-Century Politics' in Sutherland, *Politics and Finance; Diary of Joseph Farington*, vol VI, p 2059.

24. Barry Supple, *The Royal Exchange Assurance* (Cambridge, 1970), pp 76–8; Chapman, *Merchant Enterprise*, pp 55–6.

25. James C. Riley, *International Government Finance and the Amsterdam Capital Market, 1740–1815* (Cambridge, 1980), pp 195–204; Cope, 'Bird, Savage & Bird'.

26. F. M. L. Thompson, *English Landed Society in the Nineteenth Century* (1963), p 63; Walter Bagehot, *Lombard Street: A Description of the Money Market* (1873), p 161.

27. Gibb, pp 71–2; John M. Sherwig, *Guineas and Gunpowder: British Foreign Aid in the Wars with France, 1793–1815* (Cambridge, Mass, 1969), pp 263–4, S. D. Chapman, 'The establishment of the Rothschilds as bankers' in *Jewish Historical Studies* (1985–6), pp 179–81; Cope, 'Goldsmids', p 191, Cope, *Walter Boyd*; Ziegler, p 58; Ralph W. Hidy, *The House of Baring in American Trade and Finance: English Merchant Bankers at Work, 1763–1861* (New York, 1949), p 53; Cope, 'Goldsmids', pp 204–6, Norman J. Silberling, 'Financial and Monetary Policy of Great Britain during the Napoleonic Wars, II' in *Quarterly Journal of Economics* (1924).

28. Chapman, *Merchant Enterprise*, pp 167–74; N. B. Harte, 'The Growth and Decay of a Hosiery Firm in the Nineteenth Century' in *Textile History* (1977).

29. Dixon, 'Money Market', pp 21–137, 220–9.

30. Anon, *Letters from an Irish Student in England to his Father in Ireland* (1809), vol I, p 131; Chapman, 'British Marketing Enterprise', p 218; Ian P. H. Duffy, *Bankruptcy and Insolvency in London during the Industrial Revolution* (New York, 1985), pp 182–94.

31. Chapman, *Merchant Enterprise*, chs 2 and 5; Chapman, *Merchant Enterprise*, p 56.

32. Anthony Webster, 'The political economy of trade liberalization: the East India Company Charter Act of 1813' in *Economic History Review* (1990).

CHAPTER THREE

1. *The Post-Office Annual Directory for 1815*, p 241.

2. Richard Rush, *Memoranda of a Residence at the Court of London* (Philadelphia, 1833), pp 77–8.

3. Defauconpret, *A Fortnight in London* (1817), p 49; Jon Lawrence, 'From Counting-House to Office: The Evolution of London's Central Financial District, 1693–1871' (forthcoming); Edmund Sheridan Purcell, *Life of Cardinal Manning* (1895), vol I, p 3; *The Times*, 17 Jan 1815, 4 May 1815; Philip Ziegler, *The Sixth Great Power: Barings, 1762–1929* (1988), p 48; Lawrence, 'Counting-House'; Dorothea Mozley (ed), *Newman Family Letters* (1962), p xiii.

4. J. H. Dunning and E. V. Morgan, *An Economic Study of the City of London* (1971), p 34; Roger Fulford, *Glyn's, 1753–1953* (1953), p 101; John Arthur Gibbs, *The History of Antony and Dorothea Gibbs* (1922), p 202; W. Marston Acres, *The Bank of England From Within* (1931), vol II, p 351; *National Provincial Bank Review* (Nov 1967), p 14; Fulford, p 104; *The Autobiography of William Jerdan* (1852), vol I, p 28.

5. Algernon West, *Recollections* (1899), vol I, p 314; Richard Gatty, *Portrait of a Merchant Prince: James Morrison, 1789–1857* (Northallerton, 1977?), p 11; NPBR; RBS, S: 16, Aug 1814; *Jerdan*, vol I, p 29.

6. Charles Duguid, *The Story of the Stock Exchange* (1901), p 93; B'side 14.53 (Guildhall Library); *The Picture of London, for 1815* (sixteenth edn, 1815), p 204.

7. *Picture of London*, pp 183, 192; Anon, *Letters from an Irish Student in England to his Father in Ireland* (1809), vol I, pp 130–1; *Leigh's New Picture of London* (1818), p 294; John Summerson, *Georgian London* (1962 Pelican edn), pp 157–8.

8. Robert Hawker, *The Royal Exchange* (c 1808), pp 3–6.

CHAPTER FOUR

1. This chapter is heavily reliant on the pioneering work of Boyd Hilton, *Corn, Cash, Commerce: The Economic Policies of the Tory Governments, 1815–1830* (Oxford, 1977).

2. Huskisson papers (British Library), Add Ms 38,741, fos 201–8.

3. Liverpool papers (British Library), Add Ms 38,271, fo 317.

4. Huskisson papers, Add Ms 38,741, fos 251–2.

5. *Secret Committee on the Expediency of The Bank resuming Cash Payments* (P. P. 1819, III), pp 26, 157, 51–2.

6. *The Times*, 19 May 1819; Hansard, 21 May 1819, cols 598–604, 612–13, 24 May 1819, cols 683, 741, 747.

7. Charles Duke Yonge, *The Life and Administration of Robert Banks, Second Earl of Liverpool* (1868), p 384.

8. Yonge, pp 416–7.

9. William Smart, *Economic Annals of the Nineteenth Century, 1801–1820* (1910), p 744; Thomas Tooke and William Newmarch, *A History of Prices* (1857), vol VI, pp 337–9.

10. *The Times*, 17 May 1820; Piero Sraffa (ed), *The Works and Correspondence of David Ricardo* (Cambridge, 1952), vol VIII, p 197.

11. Tooke and Newmarch, vol VI, p 342; Barry Gordon, *Economic Doctrine and Tory Liberalism, 1824–1830* (1979), pp 19–21; Francis Bamford and the Duke of Wellington (eds), *The Journal of Mrs Arbuthnot* (1950), vol I, pp 390–1; Hansard, 24 Feb 1826, col 812.

CHAPTER FIVE

1. John Arthur Gibbs, *The History of Antony and Dorothea Gibbs* (1922), p 296.

2. Dorothea Mozley (ed), *Newman Family Letters* (1962), p xvi; Vivien Noakes, *Edward Lear: The Life of a Wanderer* (1968), pp 13–17; K. F. Dixon, 'The Development of the London Money Market, 1780–1830' (London D Phil, 1962), pp 159, 172; Churchill, Mss 5,762, vols 1–2, Augustus Muir, *Churchill and Sim* (1963).

3. Philip Ziegler, *The Sixth Great Power: Barings, 1762–1929* (1988), pp 80–5.

4. Stanley Chapman, *The Rise of Merchant Banking* (1984), p 83.

5. D. C. M. Platt, *Foreign Finance in Continental Europe and the United States, 1815–1870* (1984), pp 8–10; Chapman, *Merchant Banking*, pp 83–4.

6. *Commercial Chronicle*, 16 Jan 1817; *Select Committee on the Expediency of The Bank resuming Cash Payments* (P. P. 1819, III), pp 53, 158.

7. Gibbs, Mss 19,879, fos 10–12, 19,866, vol 1, 9 June 1821.

8. Churchill, Ms 5,762, vol 3.

9. SE, Ms 14,600, vol 9, 26 Nov 1821–24 Dec 1821.

10. On all these episodes, see Frank Griffith Dawson, *The First Latin American Debt Crisis: The City of London and the 1822–25 Loan Bubble* (1990).

11. *New Times*, 14 Oct 1822, Dawson, pp 37–8.

12. Dawson, pp 39–40; *Morning Chronicle*, 12 Oct 1822, 18 Oct 1822, 25 Oct 1822.

13. W. G. Hoskins, 'Richard Thornton: A Victorian Millionaire' in *History Today* (1962).

14. *Morning Chronicle*, 23 Oct 1822, 9 Nov 1822, 16 Nov 1822.

15. Hugh Barty-King, *The Baltic Exchange* (1977), pp 62–6.

16. RAL, T42/4; Richard Davis, *The English Rothschilds* (1983), p 33; RAL, T3/230; Liverpool papers (British Library), Add Ms 38,271, fos 173, 248; Chapman, *Merchant Banking*, pp 18, 48.

17. Lord Rothschild, *The Shadow of a Great Man* (1982), p 14, quoting *The Times*, 3 Aug 1836; *Cash Payments*, p 161; RAL, T27/219; Chapman, *Merchant Banking*, p 40.

18. Nina L. Kay Shuttleworth, *A Life of Sir Woodbine Parish* (1910), p 201.

19. RAL, T5/164; B of E, G8/21, 18 June 1823; Davis, p 37.

20. *Cash Payments*, p 114; Ziegler, pp 94, 76.

21. BB, character book, late 1820s (not catalogued).

22. Richard Roberts, *Schroders: Merchants & Bankers* (1992), pp 32–40; C. Amburger, 'Wm Brandt and the Story of his enterprises' (typescript, *c* 1937, University of Nottingham Library); Georgina Meinertzhagen, *A Bremen Family* (1912), pp 251–2.

23. Anon, *Cook's of St Paul's* (1957), pp 4–5; Anon, *A Short History of Bradbury Greatorex and Co Ltd* (197–?); N. B. Harte, 'The Growth and Decay of a Hosiery Firm in the Nineteenth Century' in *Textile History* (1977), pp 22, 28–9; Stanley Chapman, *Merchant Enterprise in Britain: From the Industrial Revolution to World War I* (Cambridge, 1992), pp 175–8; Richard Gatty, *Portrait of a Merchant Prince: James Morrison, 1789–1857* (Northallerton, 1977?), p 23.

24. William Cobbett, *Rural Rides* (1948 edn), p 104; SE, Ms 17,957, vol 22; M. C. Reed, *A History of James Capel and Co* (1975), pp 1–4, 19–21; Roberts, pp 356–8; David Kynaston, *Cazenove & Co: A History* (1991), pp 15–16; Stanley D. Chapman, *Raphael Bicentenary, 1787–1987* (1987), pp 5–13.

25. Dawson, p 40; *Morning Herald*, 5 Nov 1824.

26. *Cash Payments*, p 178; Dixon, pp 200–04; L. S. Pressnell, *Country Banking in the Industrial Revolution* (Oxford, 1956), p 103.

27. Dixon, pp 220–34.

28. Mrs Grote, *The Personal Life of George Grote* (1873), pp 47–8.

29. G. Clayton, *British insurance* (1971), p 100; Sir William Schooling, *Alliance Assurance, 1824–1924* (1924), pp 2–14; *Dictionary of National Biography*.

30. Sarah Palmer, 'The Indemnity in the London marine insurance market, 1824–50' in Oliver M. Westall (ed), *The historian and the business of insurance* (Manchester, 1984); *Dictionary of National Biography*.

31. *Morning Herald*, 3 Nov 1824; Dawson, p 106.

32. *Hansard*, 16 March 1825, col 1063; Benjamin Disraeli, *Letters: 1815–1834* (Toronto, 1982), pp 25–9.

33. A. C. Ward (ed), *Everybody's Lamb* (1933), pp 167, 156; E. V. Lucas (ed), *The Letters of Charles Lamb* (1935), vol II, p 319; *Everybody's Lamb*, pp 167–8.

CHAPTER SIX

1. Samuel Thornton, *Yearly Recollections* (1891), p 196; Francis Bamford and the Duke of Wellington (eds), *The Journal of Mrs Arbuthnot* (1950), vol I, p 382; Frank Whitson Fetter, *Development of British Monetary Orthodoxy, 1797–1875* (Cambridge, Mass, 1965), pp 111–13; Churchill, Ms 5,762, vol 7.

2. Churchill, Ms 5,762, vol 7; K. F. Dixon, 'The Development of the London Money Market, 1780–1830' (London D Phil, 1962), pp 178–9, 181; Churchill, Ms 5,762, vol 7.

3. E. M. Forster, *Marianne Thornton, 1797–1887: A Domestic Biography* (1956), pp 106–14.

4. Dixon, p 181; Churchill, Ms 5,762, vol 7; Forster, p 115.

5. *Morning Chronicle*, 13–15 Dec 1825.

6. Walter Bagehot, *Lombard Street: A Description of the Money Market* (1873), pp 51–2; Liverpool papers (British Library), Add Ms 38,371, fo 77.

7. *Mrs Arbuthnot*, vol I, pp 426–7.

8. *Morning Chronicle*, 17 Dec 1825; *Macmillan's Magazine* (Dec 1874), p 157; *Mrs Arbuthnot*, vol I, p 428.

9. Churchill, Ms 5,762, vol 7; Dixon, pp 183–4.

10. Forster, pp 117–23.

11. Philip Ziegler, *The Sixth Great Power: Barings, 1762–1929* (1988), p 98.

12. Thomas Love Peacock, *Paper Money Lyrics, and other poems* (1837), pp 26–8.

CHAPTER SEVEN

1. Francis Bamford and the Duke of Wellington (eds), *The Journal of Mrs Arbuthnot* (1950), vol II, pp 10–11; *Morning Chronicle*, 21 Feb 1826; JM, II.A.1.10, reel 287, no 96; Frank Griffith Dawson, *The First Latin American Debt Crisis: The City of London and the 1822–25 Loan Bubble* (1990), pp 128–9.

2. A German Prince, *Tour in Germany, Holland and England* (1832), vol III, pp 43, 59–63.

3. G. Duckworth Atkin (ed), *House Scraps* (1887), p 150.

4. SE, Ms 14,600, vol 10, 7 Sept 1826 – vol 11, 20 Dec 1827, vol 11, 24 April 1827.

5. JM, III, box 24, 16 April 1827.

6. Records of Stringer & Richardson (Guildhall Library), Ms 21,755.

7. Churchill, Mss 5,762, vols 9–12.

8. BB, character book, late 1820s (not catalogued).

9. Churchill, Ms 5,762, vol 9; Barry Gordon, *Economic Doctrine and Tory Liberalism, 1824–1830* (1979), p 109; Edmund Sheridan Purcell, *Life of Cardinal Manning* (1895), vol I, pp 8, 71; Richard Pares, *A West-India Fortune* (1950), p 311.

10. Walter Bagehot, *Lombard Street: A Description of the Money Market* (1873), pp 212, 214, 219, 222–3.

11. This paragraph derives entirely from A.C. Howe, 'From "Old Corruption" to "New Probity": the Bank of England and its Directors in the Age of Reform' in *Financial History Review* (1994).

12. This paragraph is largely drawn from Frank Whitson Fetter, *Development of British Monetary Orthodoxy, 1797–1875* (Cambridge, Mass, 1965), pp 120–64 and Boyd Hilton, *Corn, Cash, Commerce: The Economic Policies of the Tory Governments, 1815–1830* (Oxford, 1977), pp 232–68.

13. *Committee of Secrecy on the Bank of England Charter* (P.P. 1831–2, VI), qq 3689, 4946, 4772–3.

14. Bagehot, pp 268–9.

15. DBB, Ranald C. Michie, 'Samuel Jones Loyd, Lord Overstone of Overstone and Fotheringhay', vol 3, pp 868–72; Lytton Strachey and Roger Fulford (eds), *The Greville Memoirs, 1814–60* (1938), vol III, p 136; *Bank of England Charter*, q 3306.

16. Edward Nevin and E. W. Davis, *The London Clearing Banks* (1970), p 61; *Bank of England Charter*, q 3113; Barclays, 25/265 (94, 43).

17. W. T. C. King, *History of the London Discount Market* (1936), pp 35–101, K. F. Dixon, 'The Development of the London Money Market, 1780–1830' (London D Phil, 1962), pp 186–204, W. M. Scammell, *The London Discount Market* (1968), pp 133–49.

18. K. F. Dixon, *Alexanders Discount Company Limited, 1810–1960* (1960), p 4.

19. Charles Harvey and Jon Press, 'The City and Mining Enterprise: The Making of the Morris Family Fortune' in *Journal of the William Morris Society* (1990).

20. Dixon, 'Money Market', pp 193, 194; RBS, CU/98, outgoing letters, 19 Nov 1832; Dixon, 'Money Market', p 195.

21. Anon (David Morier Evans), *The City; or, The Physiology of London Business; with Sketches on 'Change, and at the Coffee Houses* (1845), p 20; Augustus Hare, *The Gurneys of Earlham* (1895), vol II, pp 238–9; Hannah Geldart, *Memorials of S. Gurney* (1857), p 44; Hare, vol I, p 241.

22. Dixon, 'Money Market', p 191; *Circular to Bankers*, 9 Oct 1835; *A Portion of the Journal kept by Thomas Raikes, Esq from 1831 to 1847* (1856), vol II, pp 221–2; *Bank of England Charter*, q 4799.

23. *Morning Chronicle*, 27 Nov 1833; J. Rumney, 'Eighteenth Century English Jewry through Foreign Eyes, 1730–1830' in *Transactions of the Jewish Historical Society* (1932–5), p 339.

24. George Otto Trevelyan, *The Life and Letters of Lord Macaulay* (1881 edn), p 160; A. Aspinall (ed), *The Correspondence of Charles Arbuthnot* (1941), p 136; *Mrs Arbuthnot*, vol II, p 200; B of E, G23/53, 4 Dec 1830.

25. Ralph W. Hidy, *The House of Baring in American Trade and Finance: English Merchant Bankers at Work, 1763–1861* (New York, 1949), p 84; Philip Ziegler, *The Sixth Great Power: Barings, 1762–1929* (1988), p 123; Hidy, p 83; Ziegler, p 123.

26. BBJB, 31 Dec 1832, 9 Nov 1834, 25 Dec 1831.

27. *Select Committee on Manufactures, Commerce, and Shipping* (P.P. 1833, VI), q 1020.

28. This paragraph is wholly drawn from Hidy, pp 124–50.

29. Hidy, p 150; Ziegler, p 150.

30. Ziegler, pp 136, 134; JM, II.A.1.10, reel 291, no 795, reel 292, no 889.

31. BBJB, 6 Dec 1830; Ziegler, pp 131–2; BB, HC3.8.1; BBJB, 25 Dec 1831.

32. *Morning Chronicle*, 4 Feb 1831; Ziegler, p 114; BBJB, 21 Aug 1831; Place Papers (British Library), Add Ms 35, 149, fo 107; Mrs Grote, *The Personal Life of George Grote* (1873), p 77.

33. BBJB, 25 Dec 1831; *Circular to Bankers*, 11 May 1832; *Despatches, Correspondence, and Memoranda of Field Marshal Arthur Duke of Wellington* (1880), vol VIII, p 308; BBJB, 24 May 1832; *The Journal of Sir Peter Laurie* (The Saddlers' Company, 1985), p 59.

34. Maria Edgeworth, *Letters from England, 1813–1844* (Oxford, 1971), p 538; Lord Ellenborough, *A Political Diary, 1828–30* (1881), vol I, p 85, vol II, pp 218–9; *Morning News and Public Ledger*, 9 Oct 1834; BBJB, 25 April 1835; JM, II.A.5, private letters I.10 from London, reel 463, no P.14.

35. Anon, *The history of Goad, Rigg & company* (1952).

36. W. Heseltine, *A Family Scene during the Panic at the Stock Exchange, in May 1835* (second edn, Canterbury, 1848), pp 22–3, 27–9.

37. Barclays, 25/265 (104); BBJB, 31 May 1835; Charles Dickens, *The Pickwick Papers* (Oxford, 1986 Clarendon Press edn), p 854.

38. P. L. Cottrell, *Industrial Finance, 1830–1914: The Finance and Organization of English Manufacturing Industry* (1983 pbk edn) is the fullest guide to the overall theme; M. C. Reed, *A History of James Capel and Co* (1975), pp 28–32; *Circular to Bankers*, 23 Oct 1829; R. S. Sayers, 'Ricardo's Views on Monetary Questions' in T. S. Ashton and R. S. Sayers (eds), *Papers in English Monetary History* (Oxford, 1953), p 94; W. J. Reader, *A House in the City: A Study of the City and of the Stock Exchange based on the Records of Foster and Braithwaite, 1825–1975* (1979), pp 36–7; M. J. Daunton, '"Gentlemanly Capitalism" and British Industry, 1820–1914' in *Past and Present* (Feb 1989), p 138.

39. *Circular to Bankers*, 26 Feb 1836; Barclays, 25/265 (120); Jack Simmons (ed), *The Birth of the Great Western Railway: Extracts from the Diary and Correspondence of George Henry Gibbs* (Bath, 1971), p 78; BBJB, 5 May 1836; T. R. Gourvish, *Railways and the British Economy, 1830–1914* (1980), pp 16–17.

40. Stanley Chapman, *The Rise of Merchant Banking* (1984), pp 39–42; *Manufactures*, qq 2009, 2014–5; JM, II.A.1.10, reel 292, no 1,021; Barclays, 25/265 (68); Richard Gatty, *Portrait of a Merchant Prince: James Morrison, 1789–1857* (Northallerton, 1977?), pp 156–8.

41. Chapman, *Merchant Banking*, pp 109–11, Michael Greenberg, *British Trade and the Opening of China, 1800–42* (Cambridge, 1951), pp 168–9.

42. BBJB, 14 Feb 1836; Barclays, 25/265 (185).

43. BBJB, 25 July 1836; RAL, T23/148; *Circular to Bankers*, 5 Aug 1836; *Morning Chronicle*, 9 Aug 1836; Heseltine, pp 53–6.

CHAPTER EIGHT

1. BB, HC1.20.1.2C; BBJB, 17 Sept 1836; B of E, G8/29, 26 Oct 1836; BBJB, 13 Nov 1836.

2. Barclays, 25/265 (286, 278, 286).

3. B of E, G4/59, 21 March 1837.

4. Muriel Emmie Hidy, *George Peabody: Merchant and Financier, 1829–1854* (New York, 1978), p 84; Morrison Cryder records (Guildhall Library), Ms 11,720, folder one, 21 May 1837; Barclays, 25/265 (289, 290); B of E, G4/60, 30 May 1837; Richard Gatty,

Portrait of a Merchant Prince: James Morrison, 1789–1857 (Northallerton, 1977?), p 164; Barclays, 25/265 (292).

5. B of E, G4/60, 1 June 1837; Barclays, 25/265 (293).

6. Barclays, 25/265 (297); Morrison Cryder, Ms 11,720, folder one, 9 June 1837; BBJB, 20 Aug 1837.

7. Churchill, Ms 5,762, vol 16, week ending 13 Jan 1838; Gresham Committee Repertories, Report of the Special Committee of Enquiry into the destruction of the Exchange by fire, 18 Jan 1838; BBJB, 20 Jan 1838; Barclays, 25/265 (342).

8. Jon Lawrence, 'From Counting-House to Office: The Evolution of London's Central Financial District, 1693–1871' (forthcoming), NW, 229, Bank of London records, Anon (David Morier Evans), *The City; or, The Physiology of London Business; with Sketches on 'Change, and at the Coffee Houses* (1845), pp 156–61.

9. Brandt, correspondence (49).

10. Edgar Allan Poe, *Poetry and Tales* (New York, 1984), pp 388–90.

11. Churchill, Mss 5,762, vols 17–20, 22.

12. Sir John Clapham, *The Bank of England: A History* (Cambridge, 1944), vol II, pp 167–8; Stanley Chapman, *The Rise of Merchant Banking* (1984), p 165; BBJB, 20 July 1839; Churchill, Ms 5,762, vol 17.

13. Overstone, vol I, p 245; BBJB, 4 June 1842; Chapman, *Merchant Banking*, p 42, S. D. Chapman, 'The International Houses: The Continental Contribution to British Commerce, 1800–1860' in *Journal of European Economic History*, p 29; Hidy, *George Peabody* is the best book on Peabody.

14. Richard Davis, *The English Rothschilds* (1983), pp 58, 80, 129–30, Chapman, *Merchant Banking*, p 165; J. R. Freedman, 'A London Merchant Banker in Anglo-American trade and finance, 1835–50' (London D Phil, 1969).

15. Georgina Meinertzhagen, *A Bremen Family* (1912), pp 253–4; BB, HC3.8.1; Lloyds, A13/3d/3, Stevenson, Salt & Co, scrapbook, 22 April 1842; R. S. Sayers, *The Bank of England, 1891–1944* (Cambridge, 1986 pbk edn), p 268.

16. Brandt, commercial circulars, 1829–45.

17. NW, 337, London and County Bank records, reminiscences of William McKewan; Daniel Hardcastle, jnr, *Banks and Bankers* (1842), pp 21–2.

18. T. E. Gregory, *The Westminster Bank Through A Century* (1936), vol I, p 255, vol II, pp 205–7.

19. J. Leighton-Boyce, *Smiths the Bankers, 1658–1958* (1958), p 271; George Chandler, *Four Centuries of Banking*, vol I (1964), p 301.

20. Lloyds, A12/1b/7, Barnett, Hoares & Co, private letter book, 1840–71.

21. Michael Greenberg, *British Trade and the Opening of China, 1800–42* (Cambridge, 1951), pp 188–9.

22. D. Morier Evans, *Speculative Notes* (1864), p 117; Evans, *The City*, p 167.

23. BBJB, 15 April 1840; Churchill, Ms 5,762, vol 19; M. C. Reed, *A History of James Capel and Co* (1975), p 52; JM, II.A.5, private letters I.10 from London, reel 463, no P.35; Greenberg, p 214; Jasper Ridley, *Lord Palmerston* (1972 Panther edn), pp 354–5.

24. Mrs Grote, *The Personal Life of George Grote* (1873), p 141; Davis, p 70, Charles Stuart Parker (ed), *Sir Robert Peel from his Private Papers* (1899), vol II, pp 570–1.

25. Churchill, Ms 5,762, vol 20; BB, HC1.20.8.

26. *Economist*, 30 Sept 1843, 28 Oct 1843; *Circular to Bankers*, 27 Oct 1843; A. C. Howe, 'Free Trade and the City of London, *c.* 1820–1870' in *History* (1992), pp 397–8; BBJB, 22 Dec 1843; Churchill, Ms 5,762, vol 21.

27. SE, Ms 14,600, vol 17, 26 Nov 1841, *The Times*, 8–9 April 1841; RAL, T23/446; SE, Ms 14,600, vol 18, 8 Feb 1843.

28. J. Horsley Palmer, *The Causes and Consequences of the Pressures upon the Money-Market* (1837); S. J. Loyd, *Reflections Suggested by a Perusal of Mr J. Horsley Palmer's Pamphlet* (1837), pp 45–6.

29. Reed, p 47; Hardcastle, p 164.

30. *Hansard*, 6 May 1844, col 750; Churchill, Ms 5,762, vol 22; Lytton Strachey and Roger Fulford (eds), *The Greville Memoirs, 1814–60* (1938), vol V, p 173; *Economist*, 18 May 1844, *The Times*, 14 May 1844, Evans, *The City*, p 9.

31. *Sir Robert Peel*, vol III, p 140; *Circular to Bankers*, 14 June 1844, *Economist*, 15 June 1844; B of E, M5/206 (item 65); *Circular to Bankers*, 14 June 1844, *Economist*, 15 June 1844.

32. Walter Bagehot, *Lombard Street: A Description of the Money Market* (1873), pp 161–2; S. J. Loyd, *Thoughts on the Separation of the Departments of the Bank of England* (July 1844 edn), p 55.

CHAPTER NINE

1. Diary of George Williams (YMCA); Clyde Binfield, *George Williams and the Y.M.C.A.* (1973); DBB, Clyde Binfield, 'Sir George Williams', vol 5, pp 825–33.

2. SE, Ms 19,297, vol 3, 30 Aug 1844–28 Oct 1844.

3. Churchill, Mss 5,762, vols 22, 26; Lytton Strachey and Roger Fulford (eds), *The Greville Memoirs, 1814–60* (1938), vol V, p 152; *Economist*, 2 Nov 1844, 28 Dec 1844, 4 Jan 1845.

CHAPTER TEN

1. R. S. Surtees, *Jorrocks's Jaunts and Jollities* (1924 edn), pp 1–3, 14, 32, 62–3.

2. Jon Lawrence, 'From Counting-House to Office: The Evolution of London's Central Financial District, 1693–1871' (forthcoming); Harold P. Clunn, *The Face of London: The Record of a Century's Changes and Development* (1932), pp 66, 24–5, P. G. M. Dickson, *The Sun Insurance Office, 1710–1960* (1960), pp 113–5.

3. Clunn, pp 29–30; Pennie Denton (ed), *Betjeman's London* (1988), p 53; Richard Trench, *London before the Blitz* (1989), p 154; BBJB, 13 July 1853, 5 Nov 1853.

4. Anon (David Morier Evans), *The City; or, The Physiology of London Business; with Sketches on 'Change, and at the Coffee Houses* (1845), pp 189–90.

5. Lawrence; Peter Jackson (ed), *John Tallis's London Street Views, 1838–40, Together with the revised and enlarged views of 1847* (1969), pp 260–1; Elizabeth Gaskell, *The Life of Charlotte Brontë* (1975 Penguin edn), pp 345–6.

6. Flora Tristan, *London Journal* (1980), p 4.

7. Bertram Wodehouse Currie, *Recollections, Letters and Journals* (Roehampton, 1901), vol I, p 18; Roger Fulford, *Glyn's, 1753–1953* (1953), pp 166–7; NW, 11,520, Prescotts committee minutes, 3 June 1841.

8. Evans, p v; Henry Mayhew, *London Labour and the London Poor* (New York, 1968), vol I, p 64.

9. Evans, pp 178, 99–100; Max Schlesinger, *Saunterings in and about London* (1853), p 219.

10. Evans, pp 163–7; Edward Callow, *Old London Taverns* (1899), pp 5–8.

11. Callow, pp v-ix; Hambros, Ms 19,047, 29 Aug 1843.

12. Evans, pp 62–4.

13. Mayhew, vol II, pp 471–2.

14. BB, Partners File, 323, 1845–1923, vol I.

15. BBJB, 1 Jan 1854; Evans, p 173; RAL, T6/233.

16. *National Provincial Bank Review* (Nov 1967), p 14; Fulford, p 167; *Bankers' Magazine* (Feb 1845), p 257.

17. Daniel Hardcastle, jnr, *Banks and Bankers* (1842), pp 37–8; *Bankers' Magazine* (Oct 1845), p 40.

18. *The London Conductor: Being A Guide For Visitors to the Great Industrial Exhibition* (1851), p 1; H. J. Dyos, *Victorian Suburb: A Study of the Growth of*

Camberwell (Leicester, 1977), pp 66–70; Herman Melville, *Journal of a Visit to London and the Continent* (1949), p 22; Herman Melville, *Israel Potter* (1925 edn), pp 255, 257–8.

CHAPTER ELEVEN

1. NW, 11,521, Prescotts committee minutes, 19 June 1845, 9 Oct 1845, 16 Oct 1845.

2. *Economist*, 25 Oct 1845; *Punch*, 22 Nov 1845.

3. *Economist*, 4 Oct 1845 (estimated from market reports); *Endymion* (1881), p 356; BBJB, 25 April 1845.

4. W. J. Reader, *A House in the City: A Study of the City and of the Stock Exchange based on the Records of Foster and Braithwaite, 1825–1975* (1979), pp 39–40; Anon (David Morier Evans), *The City; or, The Physiology of London Business; with Sketches on 'Change, and at the Coffee Houses* (1845), pp 56–7; G. Duckworth Atkin (ed), *House Scraps* (1887), p 109; Judy Slinn, *Linklaters & Paines: The First One Hundred and Fifty Years* (1987), pp 10, 16; Charles Duguid, *The Story of the Stock Exchange* (1901), pp 148–9.

5. Overstone, vol I, p 373; Reader, pp 42–3; E. J. Hobsbawm, *Industry and Empire* (1969 Pelican edn), pp 114–5, T. R. Gourvish, *Railways and the British Economy, 1830–1914* (1980), p 17.

6. *Bankers' Magazine* (April 1845), p 53; Overstone, vol I, p 378.

7. Churchill, Ms 5,762, vol 29, 29 April 1847; JM, II.A.1.10, reel 300, no 3,096; Overstone, vol I, p 383; Frank Whitson Fetter, *Development of British Monetary Orthodoxy, 1797–1875* (Cambridge, Mass, 1965), pp 206–8.

8. BB, HC1.20.8, part I.

9. Overstone, vol I, pp 387–8; NW, 11,521, Prescotts committee minutes, 19 Aug 1847.

10. Overstone, vol I, p 391; JM, II.A.1.10, reel 300, no 3,128.

11. Sir John Clapham, *The Bank of England: A History* (Cambridge, 1944), vol II, pp 198–204; W. T. C. King, *History of the London Discount Market* (1936), p 142; Churchill, Ms 5,762, vol 29; JM, II.A.5, private letters from London, 1812–82, reel 463, no P.115; *Economist*, 2 Oct 1847.

12. JM, II.A.1.10, reel 300, no 3,141; Fetter, pp 209–10.

13. NW, 11,521, Prescotts committee minutes, 21 Oct 1847.

14. *Economist*, 23 Oct 1847; Clapham, p 207; Louis J. Jennings (ed), *The Croker Papers* (1884), vol III, p 152.

15. B of E, M5/517.

16. *Morning Chronicle*, 23 Oct 1847; Mrs Grote, *The Personal Life of George Grote* (1873), p 179.

17. Overstone, vol I, p 397; *Secret Committee on Commercial Distress* (P.P. 1847–8, VIII.I), q 1600.

18. David Kynaston, *The Chancellor of the Exchequer* (Lavenham, 1980), p 134; B of E, M5/206.

19. Philip Ziegler, *The Sixth Great Power: Barings, 1762–1929* (1988), p 137; Evans, *The City*, pp 183–4.

20. BB, HC.3.6; Evans, *The City* (1852 edn), p 161.

21. M. C. Reed, *A History of James Capel and Co* (1975), p 52; D. C. M. Platt, *Foreign Finance in Continental Europe and the United States, 1815–1870* (1984), p 13; BBJB, 28 May 1848; Ziegler, pp 137–8.

22. *Morning Chronicle*, 11 April 1848 (two separate reports).

23. SE, Ms 14,600, vol 20, 10 April 1848; *Morning Chronicle*, 11–12 April 1848.

CHAPTER TWELVE

1. Overstone, vol I, p 391; much of this paragraph derives from A. C. Howe, 'From "Old Corruption" to "New Probity": the Bank of England and its Directors in the Age of Reform' in *Financial History Review* (1994).

2. *Economist*, 18 Sept 1847, Frank Whitson Fetter, *Development of British Monetary Orthodoxy, 1797–1875* (Cambridge, Mass, 1965), p 272; Fetter, p 261; W. T. C. King, *History of the London Discount Market* (1936), pp 161–8.

3. The argument of this paragraph is taken from A. C. Howe, 'Free Trade and the City of London, *c.* 1820–1870' in *History* (1992), pp 401–7.

4. NW, 11,521, Prescotts committee minutes, 31 Dec 1847; D. Morier Evans, *The Commercial Crisis, 1847–1848* (1848), p 108; Hugh Barty-King, *The Baltic Exchange* (1977), p 94; BBJB, 27 July 1850.

5. Overstone, vol I, p 403; B of E, M5/209.

6. BBJB, 10 Oct 1852; E. J. Hobsbawm, *Industry and Empire* (1969 Pelican edn), pp 139–40; *Select Committee on the Bank Acts* (P.P. 1857–8, V.I), qq 1700–02; G. A. Fletcher, *The Discount Houses in London: Principles, Operations and Change* (1976), p 17; E. Victor Morgan and W. A. Thomas, *The Stock Exchange: Its History and Functions* (1962), p 88; Hobsbawm, p 119.

7. BBJB, 10 Oct 1852, 9 June 1860; Stanley Chapman, *The Rise of Merchant Banking* (1984), p 108.

8. P. L. Brown (ed), *The Narrative of George Russel of Golf Hill* (1935), pp 293–4; M. J. Daunton, 'Firm and Family in the City of London in the Nineteenth Century: the case of F. G. Dalgety' in *Historical Research* (1989), pp 157–9.

9. *Mark Lane Express*, 31 Jan 1853; Chapman, *Merchant Banking*, p 127, S. E. Fairlie, 'The Anglo-Russian Grain Trade, 1815–1861' (London D Phil, 1959), pp 273, 341; Timotheos Catsiyannis, *Pandias Stephen Rallis* (1986).

10. The whole saga is covered in W. M. Mathew, *The House of Gibbs and the Peruvian Guano Monopoly* (1981); Antony Gibbs & Sons, *Guano: Its Analysis and Effects* (1843), p 4; Chapman, *Merchant Banking*, p 130; Gibbs, Ms 11,047, 1 Aug 1842; *Nautical Magazine and Naval Chronicle* (April 1856); Mathew, p 226.

11. Stanley Chapman, *Merchant Enterprise in Britain: From the Industrial Revolution to World War I* (Cambridge, 1992), ch 6; Negley B. Harte, *A History of George Brettle & Co Ltd, 1801–1964* (1975?), pp 65–6; Edwin Hodder, *The Life of Samuel Morley* (1887), p 118, DBB, Stanley D. Chapman, 'Samuel Morley', vol 4, pp 319–23; Anon, *Cook's of St Paul's* (1957), pp 6–7; J. L. Garvin, *The Life of Joseph Chamberlain*, vol I (1932), p 38.

12. BBJB, 13 Jan 1850; *The Times*, 16 Jan 1850; *Economist*, 19 Jan 1850, 26 Jan 1850 (a fusion of two separate reports); *The Times*, 19 Jan 1850; BBJB, 19 Jan 1850; Philip Ziegler, *The Sixth Great Power: Barings, 1762–1929* (1988), p 171.

13. Bo Bramsen and Kathleen Wain, *The Hambros* (1979), pp 263–72, deal with the episode; Hambros, Ms 19,051, 25 April 1851, 9 May 1851, 24 May 1851; David S. Landes, *Bankers and Pashas: International finance and economic imperialism in Egypt* (1958), p 46.

14. Muriel Emmie Hidy, *George Peabody: Merchant and Financier, 1829–1854* (New York, 1978), pp 342–51; Ziegler, p 210.

15. D. C. M. Platt and Jeremy Adelman, 'London Merchant Bankers in the First Phase of Heavy Borrowing: The Grand Trunk Railway of Canada' in *Journal of Imperial and Commonwealth History* (1990); Ziegler, p 225.

16. R. C. Michie, *The London and New York Stock Exchanges, 1850–1914* (1987), pp 37, 8–10, Jeffrey Kieve, *The Electric Telegraph* (Newton Abbot, 1973), p 51; Charles Duguid, *The Story of the Stock Exchange* (1901), p 181.

17. Francis Playford, *Practical Hints for Investing Money* (1855), pp 17, 62–3, 23–5; SE, Ms 14,600, vol 25, 27 Feb 1860.

18. David Kynaston, *Cazenove & Co: A History* (1991), p 30; SE, Mss 14,600, vol 20, 31 May 1847 – vol 22, 7 Oct 1853; John Francis, *Characters and Chronicles of the Stock Exchange* (1855 edn), pp 168–9.

19. SE, Mss 14,600, vol 20, 28 June 1847–1 Jan 1849, vol 23, 3 April 1854.

20. SE, Mss 14,600, vol 21, 30 June 1851, vol 24, 12 April 1858, vol 22, 5 Jan 1852.

21. W. O. Henderson, *J. C. Fischer and his Diary of Industrial England, 1814–51* (1966), pp 162–3; P. W. Matthews and A. W. Tuke, *History of Barclays Bank Limited* (1926), p 45; Overstone, vol II, p 475; Bertram Wodehouse Currie, *Recollections, Letters and Journals* (Roehampton, 1901), vol I, p 19.

22. *Bankers' Magazine* (May 1853), pp 352–61; Horace G. Hutchinson, *Life of Sir John Lubbock, Lord Avebury* (1914), vol I, pp 3, 25; Roger Fulford, *Glyn's, 1753–1953* (1953), p 162; Dornford Yates, *As Berry and I were Saying* (1952), p 110.

23. Anon (David Morier Evans), *The City; or, The Physiology of London Business; with Sketches on 'Change, and at the Coffee Houses* (1845), pp 14–16; Edward Nevin and E. W. Davis, *The London Clearing Banks* (1970), p 68, Sir Albert Feavearyear, *The Pound Sterling: A History of English Money* (Oxford, 1963 edn), p 288; B of E, M5/209.

24. King, pp 182–5; NW, 11,523, Prescotts committee minutes, 16 June 1853; D. Morier Evans, *Speculative Notes* (1864), p 32; W. F. Crick and J. E. Wadsworth, *A Hundred Years of Joint Stock Banking* (1936), p 30.

25. Nathaniel Hawthorne, *The English Notebooks* (1941), pp 225, 256; Herman Melville, *Journal of a Visit to London and the Continent* (1949), p 43; J. C. Levenson and others (eds), *The Letters of Henry Adams*, vol I (1982), p 465; Richard Davis, *The English Rothschilds* (1983), pp 92–102; Benjamin Disraeli, *Coningsby* (1927 Bodley Head edn), p 299; JM, II.A.1.10, reel 304, no 4,430.

26. Ziegler, p 162; BBJB, 12 June 1853, 5 Nov 1853, 9 Dec 1855.

27. BBJB, 30 Aug 1856; Julian Sturgis, *From Books and Papers of Russell Sturgis* (Oxford, c 1893), pp 257–8; BBJB, 3 Jan 1857.

28. BB, DEP 135, Alfred Mildmay, 'Notes and Recollections'; Ziegler, p 180; Davis, p 139.

29. Francis, p 308; Edwin J. Perkins, 'Managing a Dollar-Sterling Exchange Account: Brown, Shipley and Co in the 1850s' in *Business History* (1974), p 48; BB, HC1.20.4, part 3; Ziegler, p 169.

30. Stanley D. Chapman, *Raphael Bicentenary, 1787–1987* (1987), p 15; B of E, M5/454; RAL, II/10/28, 21 Dec 1860; Richard Roberts, *Schroders: Merchants & Bankers* (1992), pp 43–61, 79, 85–6.

31. S. J. Diaper, 'The History of Kleinwort, Sons & Co in Merchant Banking, 1855–1961' (Nottingham D Phil, 1983), pp 1–49; Bramsen and Wain, pp 250–1, 262, 298–300.

32. Evans, *Speculative Notes*, p 39; Franklin Parker, *George Peabody: A Biography* (Nashville, 1971), pp 39, 51–3, Hidy, pp 305, 341; BBJB, 31 July 1853, 25 Oct 1862.

33. Hidy, pp 300, 340; Kathleen Burk, *Morgan Grenfell, 1838–1988: The Biography of a Merchant Bank* (Oxford, 1989), pp 16–18.

34. Roberts, p 84; D. J. Wilson, *100 Years of the Association of Average Adjusters* (1969), p 84, Robert Bernard Martin, *Gerard Manley Hopkins: A Very Private Life* (1991), pp 1–6; Manley Hopkins, *Spicilegium Poeticum: A Gathering of Verses* (1892).

35. Brandt, correspondence (47).

36. City of London Discussion Society records (Guildhall Library), Ms 988, vol 2.

37. G. Duckworth Atkin (ed), *House Scraps* (1887), p 7.

38. Olive Anderson, 'The Russian Loan of 1855: An Example of Economic Liberalism?' in *Economica* (1960); SE, Ms 14,600, vol 23, 15 Feb 1856.

39. B of E, M6/65, M5/454; Overstone, vol II, pp 758, 764; George Mifflin Dallas, *Letters from London* (1870), vol I, pp 324, 334.

40. B of E, M5/454; Dallas, vol I, p 338; B of E, M5/454, M6/65.

41. Overstone, vol II, p 784, Walter Bagehot, *Lombard Street: A Description of the Money Market* (1873), p 179; NW, 11,524, Prescotts committee minutes, 12 Nov 1857, B of E, M6/65; JF, 190, 14 Nov 1857.

42. B of E, M6/65; Overstone, vol II, p 786; BBJB, 14 Nov 1857; Overstone, vol II, pp 794, 810–11.

43. Overstone, vol II, pp 819, 822–3.

44. Burk, pp 20–23, gives the fullest account of this episode; Parker, p 94; BBJB, 21 Nov 1857, 26 March 1862.

45. Hawthorne, pp 282, 287, 591, 604–7.

CHAPTER THIRTEEN

1. *The Education of Henry Adams: An Autobiography* (1918 edn), p 73; NW, 11,525, Prescotts committee minutes, 13 July 1865; *The Times*, 17 Nov 1857.

2. B of E, M5/455; W. T. C. King, *History of the London Discount Market* (1936), pp 201–3; B of E, M5/456, M5/457; *Economist*, 7 April 1860.

3. B of E, M5/457, M6/65.

4. B of E, M5/455; BBJB, 7 Feb 1858.

5. B of E, M5/455; Thomas J. Spinner, Jr, *George Joachim Goschen: The Transformation of a Victorian Liberal* (Cambridge, 1973) is the best book on Goschen; George J. Goschen, *The Theory of the Foreign Exchanges* (1879 edn of the third edn), p xii.

6. This paragraph is culled from A. C. Howe, 'From "Old Corruption" to "New Probity": the Bank of England and its Directors in the Age of Reform' in *Financial History Review* (1994), as are some of the earlier points in this chapter.

7. John Morley, *The Life of William Ewart Gladstone* (1905 two-vol edn), vol I, p 518; Howe, 'Bank of England'; Richard Shannon, *Gladstone, 1809–1865* (1984 pbk edn), p 319; Overstone, vol II, pp 912, 936; Morley, vol I, p 686.

8. Peter Pugh and others, *Great Enterprise: A History of Harrisons & Crosfield* (1990), pp 9, 11; NW, 11,431, Alliance Bank, letter book of Frank Wilde.

9. Martin (R), 17 Dec 1859–31 Dec 1859, 2 Feb 1860, 11 Feb 1861, 13 Feb 1861, 20 Nov 1862, 24 Dec 1862.

10. Charles William & Wentworth Gray records (Guildhall Library), Mss 21,411, 21,412, bundle 1.

11. *Bankers' Magazine* (April 1860), pp 217–19.

12. D. Morier Evans, *Speculative Notes* (1864), pp 1–6; *Economist*, 28 April 1860; SE, Mss 14,600, vol 25, 2 May 1860 – vol 26, 1 June 1860; Peter G. Laurie, *Sir Peter Laurie: A Family Memoir* (Brentwood, 1901), p 275; *Bankers' Magazine* (June 1860), pp 398–9; Laurie, p 275.

13. Midland Bank archives, AM 25/9.

14. Harold E. Raynes, *A History of British Insurance* (1948), pp 338–41, Edward Liveing, *A Century of Insurance: The Commercial Union Group of Insurance Companies, 1861–1961* (1961), pp 3–14; D. E. W. Gibb, *Lloyd's of London: A Study in Individualism* (1957), pp 88–9; Clive Trebilcock, *Phoenix Assurance and the Development of British Insurance*, vol 1 (Cambridge, 1985), pp 667–704; Ranald C. Michie, *The City of London: Continuity and Change, 1850–1990* (1992), p 155.

15. RAL, II/10/28, 20 Nov 1860, 11 Jan 1861; BBJB, 28 May 1861; Kathleen Burk, *Morgan Grenfell, 1838–1988: The Biography of a Merchant Bank* (Oxford, 1989), p 26; Edward Nevin and E. W. Davis, *The London Clearing Banks* (1970), p 105; J. C. Levenson and others (eds), *The Letters of Henry Adams*, vol I (1982), p 260.

16. Richard Roberts, *Schroders: Merchants and Bankers* (1992), pp 63–9; *The Times*, 19–20 March 1863; JF, 268, 17–18 March 1863; *Letters of Henry Adams*, p 413; Mira Wilkins, *The History of Foreign Investment in the United States to 1914* (1989), p 105.

17. BBJB, 10 Nov 1858; Philip Ziegler, *The Sixth Great Power: Barings, 1762–1929* (1988), p 175; Leland Hamilton Jenks, *The Migration of British Capital to 1875* (1938 edn), pp 421–2; Collet papers (Kent Record Office), C 79/3, 21 April 1864.

18. P. L. Cottrell, 'The Coalescence of a Cluster of Corporate International Banks, 1855–75' in *Business History* (1991), p 39; JF, 189, 30 April 1862; Evans, *Speculative Notes*, p 77.

19. Ziegler, p 182; BB, HC1.20.8, part 3; M. J. Daunton, 'Inheritance and Succession in the City of London in the Nineteenth Century' in *Business History* (1988), p 272.

20. Sir W. S. Gilbert, *The Savoy Operas* (1935), pp 600–1; P. L. Cottrell, *Investment Banking in England, 1856–1882: A Case Study of the International Financial Society* (1985), vol 1, pp 97–9.

21. Gibbs, Ms 11,036, vol 3; *Economist*, 9 May 1863.

22. Cottrell, *Investment Banking*, vol 1, pp 133 ff, eg p 318; Ziegler, p 182.

23. Evans, *Speculative Notes*, pp 78–9; DBB, P. L. Cottrell, 'Albert (Abraham) Zachariah Grant (Gottheimer)', vol 2, pp 623–9.

24. SE, Ms 14,600, vol 28, 3 March 1864–21 March 1864.

25. D. T. A. Kynaston, 'The London Stock Exchange, 1870–1914: An Institutional History' (London D Phil, 1983), p 142; SE, Ms 14,600, 2 Feb 1865, 19 April 1865.

26. Anon (David Morier Evans), *The City; or, The Physiology of London Business; with Sketches on 'Change, and at the Coffee Houses* (1845), p 16; Anon (Paul Bareau), *Ionian Bank Limited: A History* (1953); Cottrell, 'Coalescence'; Roger Fulford, *Glyn's, 1753–1953* (1953), p 160; David Joslin, *A Century of Banking in Latin America* (1963), p 17; A. C. Pointon, *Wallace Brothers* (Oxford, 1974), pp 19–22; Nevin and Davis, p 81.

27. Stanley Chapman, *The Rise of Merchant Banking* (1984), pp 45–6, Dolores Greenberg, 'Yankee Financiers and the Establishment of Trans-Atlantic Partnerships: A Re-examination' in *Business History* (1974); Walter Bagehot, *Lombard Street: A Description of the Money Market* (1873), p 213.

28. Aytoun Ellis, *Heir of Adventure: The story of Brown, Shipley & Co, merchant bankers, 1810–1960* (1960), pp 93–5; Collet papers, C 79/3, 13 April 1864.

29. Lilian H. Montagu, *Montagu, Baron Swaythling: A Character Sketch* (1913), DBB, Edwin Green, 'Samuel Montagu, 1st Lord Swaythling', vol 4, pp 298–301.

30. Hurford Janes and H. J. Sayers, *The story of Czarnikow* (1963).

31. *In Memoriam: Edward Clodd* (1930), Joseph McCabe, *Edward Clodd, a Memoir* (1932).

32. DBB, Sheila Marriner, 'William Lidderdale', vol 3, pp 786–90; Sheila Marriner, *Rathbones of Liverpool, 1845–73* (Liverpool, 1961); Rathbone, files of general correspondence 1851–73, XXIV.1.14–15, 24 March 1864, 21 May 1864, 23 May 1864.

33. The account of this episode owes much to Daunton, 'Inheritance and Succession'; Gibbs, Mss 11,021, vol 19, 24 Sept 1858, 4 Feb 1859, 11,036, vol 3, 29 March 1862, 8 Aug 1864.

34. Evans, *Speculative Notes*, p 31.

35. Collet papers, C 79/3, 6 April 1864; George Chandler, *Four Centuries of Banking*, vol I (1964), p 307; Frederick Martin, *Banks and Bankers* (1865), pp 186–7; Fulford, p 195.

36. Overstone, vol II, pp 963–4; NW, 11,525, Prescotts committee minutes, 1 (4?) May 1865; Overstone, vol III, p 1073; *Bankers' Magazine* (June 1865), p 787.

37. RAL, RFamC/21, 6 March 1865, 3 Feb 1865, 22 July 1864, 8 Feb 1865, 17 March 1866, 7 Jan 1865, 20 Feb 1865, 10 March 1865, 5 Dec 1865, 3 Nov 1866; W. D. Rubinstein, 'Wealth, Elites and the Class Structure of Modern Britain' in *Past and Present* (1977), pp 114–5.

38. Lloyds, file 4553 (Sayers notes); B of E, M6/65.

39. NW, 11,432, Alliance Bank, letter book of Frank Wilde, 8–10 Aug 1864.

40. *The Times*, 15 July 1865; King, pp 239–40; NW, 11,525, Prescotts committee minutes, 13 July 1865; John Stephen Flynn, *Sir Robert N. Fowler* (1893), p 150; *Economist*, 15 July 1865; *Bankers' Magazine* (August 1865), pp 905–9; SE, Ms 14,600, vol 29, 18 Aug 1865.

41. Bertram Wodehouse Currie, *Recollections, Letters and Journals* (Roehampton, 1901), vol I, p 61; JM, II.A.1.10, reel 320, no 8,429; Rathbone, files of general correspondence 1851–73, XXIV.1.16–17, 9 May 1866; *The Times*, 10 May 1866; Martin (R), 10 May 1866; RBS, GM/600/3; JM, II.A.1.10, reel 320, no 8,448.

42. *Bankers' Magazine* (Jan 1870 supplement), p 3; King, p 247; Ziegler, p 182.

43. *The Times*, 11 May 1866; Churchill, Ms 5,762, vol 42; Martin (R), 11 May 1866; NW, 11,525, Prescotts committee minutes, 11 May 1866; *Economist*, 19 May 1866; *The Times*, 12 May 1866; RAL, RFamC/21, 12 May 1866.

44. Norman St John Stevas (ed), *The Collected Works of Walter Bagehot*, vol XIII (1986), p 608; H. C. G. Mathew (ed), *The Gladstone Diaries*, vol VI (Oxford, 1978), p 436; Sir John Clapham, *The Bank of England: A History* (Cambridge, 1944), vol II, p 264; RAL, RFamC/21, 12 May 1866; Martin (R), 12 May 1866.

45. JM, II.A.1.10, reel 320, no 8,456; Rathbone, files of general correspondence 1851–73, XXIV.1.16–17, 25 May 1866, 1 Aug 1866; Brandt, commercial circulars, 1862–66.

46. *Economist*, 22 Sept 1866; Bagehot, *Lombard Street*, pp 169–70; Sir Albert Feavearyear, *The Pound Sterling: A History of English Money* (Oxford, 1963 edn), p 305, Frank Whitson Fetter, *Development of British Monetary Orthodoxy, 1797–1875* (Cambridge, Mass, 1965), pp 272–5.

CHAPTER FOURTEEN

1. Donald J. Olsen, *The Growth of Victorian London* (1979 Peregrine edn), p 121; John Summerson, 'The Victorian Rebuilding of the City of London' in *London Journal* (1977), p 164; Jon Lawrence, 'From Counting-House to Office: The Evolution of London's Central Financial District, 1693–1871' (forthcoming); Harold P. Clunn, *The Face of London: The Record of a Century's Changes and Development* (1932), pp 38, 29, 33.

2. Hugh Barty-King, *The Baltic Exchange* (1977), pp 109–28; *City Press*, 18 Aug 1866; *The Times*, 28 July 1866.

3. Summerson, 'Victorian Rebuilding', Corporation of London, *Continuity and Change: Building in the City of London, 1834–1984* (1984), pp 15–27; Nikolaus Pevsner, *London: I. The Cities of London and Westminster* (1973 Penguin edn), p 265; David S. Landes, *Bankers and Pashas: International finance and economic imperialism in Egypt* (1958), p 37; RAL, RFamC/21, 16 Oct 1865; Donald J. Olsen, *The City as a Work of Art* (1986), p 27.

4. M. C. Reed, *A History of James Capel and Co* (1975), p 61; Hurford Janes, *de Zoete and Gorton: A History* (1963?), p 29; Lawrence, 'From Counting-House'; Richard Trench, *London before the Blitz* (1989), p 154; H. J. Dyos, *Victorian Suburb: A Study of the Growth of Camberwell* (Leicester, 1977), p 71.

5. Barty-King, p 141.

6. P. W. Flower & Sons records (Guildhall Library), Ms 19,343, vol 1.

CHAPTER FIFTEEN

1. BS, Ms 20,111, vol 1, 10 Nov 1866; Rathbone, files of general correspondence 1851–73, XXIV.1.18, 27 June 1867; Philip Ziegler, *The Sixth Great Power: Barings, 1762–1929* (1988), p 183; BB, DEP 135, Alfred Mildmay, 'Notes and Recollections'; RAL, RFamC/21, 7 Aug 1867.

2. RAL, RFam/C/4; Richard Davis, *The English Rothschilds* (1983), pp 146, 101; Albert M. Hyamson, 'The First Jewish Peer' in *Transactions of the Jewish Historical Society* (1951–52), p 290.

3. Rathbone, files of general correspondence 1851–73, XXIV.1.18, 4 Nov 1867, 6 Nov 1867, XXIV.1.19, 11 March 1868, 6 April 1868; Overstone, vol III, pp 1148–9.

4. Rathbone, files of general correspondence 1851–73, XXIV.1.19, 6 Nov 1868; Leland Hamilton Jenks, *The Migration of British Capital to 1875* (1938 edn), p 287; Jenks, pp 290–1, *Economist*, 14 Nov 1868; Alexander Behr, 'Isidore Gerstenberg: Founder of the Council of Foreign Bondholders' in *Transactions of the Jewish Historical Society* (1951–52).

5. D. C. M. Platt, *Foreign Finance in Continental Europe and the United States, 1815–1870* (1984), p 168; JF, 106, 26 Nov 1868, 12 Nov 1869; Chaim Bermant, *The Cousinhood: The Anglo-Jewish Gentry* (1971), pp 175–8; JF, 106, 20 Dec 1869, 10 Feb 1870.

6. Richard Roberts, *Schroders: Merchants & Bankers* (1992), pp 70–2; JF, 106, 3 June 1870, 9 June 1870.

7. Stanley D. Chapman, *Raphael Bicentenary, 1787–1987* (1987), p 20; SE, Ms 14,600, vol 34, 11 July 1870; JF, 106, 11–16 July 1870.

8. NW, 11,526, Prescotts committee minutes, 21 July 1870; JF, 106, 8 Aug 1870; RAL, T10/209.

9. Kathleen Burk, *Morgan Grenfell, 1838–1988: The Biography of a Merchant Bank* (Oxford, 1989), pp 34–5, Ron Chernow, *The House of Morgan: An American Banking Dynasty and the Rise of Modern Finance* (1990), pp 26–7.

10. Ziegler, p 198; JF, 107.

11. Rathbone, files of general correspondence 1851–73, XXIV.1.24 (1–50), 29 Dec 1873; *Bankers' Magazine* (July 1876), p 518; Stanley Chapman, *The Rise of Merchant Banking* (1984), pp 155–60.

12. R. C. Michie, *The London and New York Stock Exchanges, 1850–1914* (1987), pp 46, 48, 70; Edwin J. Perkins, *Financing Anglo-American Trade: The House of Brown, 1800–1880* (Cambridge, Mass, 1975), p 208; Chapman, p 156, Vincent P. Carosso, *The Morgans* (1987), p 179, John J. Madden, *British Investment in the United States, 1860–1880* (New York, 1985), p 117; Ziegler, p 216.

13. Dorothy R. Adler, *British Investment in American Railways, 1834–98* (Charlottesville, 1970), pp 99–100; Charles Duguid, *The Story of the Stock Exchange* (1901), pp 249–50.

14. *Quarterly Review* (Jan 1872), p 120; Baron E. B. d'Erlanger, *My English Souvenirs* (1978), pp 103–4; Youssef Cassis, *La City de Londres, 1870–1914* (Paris, 1987), p 40.

15. Ranald C. Michie, *The City of London: Continuity and Change, 1850–1990* (1992), pp 72–3.

16. G. M. Young, *Victorian Essays* (1962), p 126; Walter Bagehot, *Lombard Street: A Description of the Money Market* (1873), pp 4, 19–20, 40–2, 71–4.

17. Norman St John Stevas (ed), *The Collected Works of Walter Bagehot*, vol XIII (1986), p 642; R. S. Sayers, *Central Banking after Bagehot* (Oxford, 1957), p 9; Rathbone, files of general correspondence 1851–73, XXIV.1.24 (51–113), 17 Oct 1873, 21 Oct 1873.

CHAPTER SIXTEEN

1. Anthony Trollope, *The Way We Live Now* (Oxford, 1951 World's Classics edn), pp 31 (ch IV), 106–7 (ch XI), 81 (ch IX), and *passim*.

2. *Economist*, 19 June 1875.

3. DBB, P. L. Cottrell, 'Albert (Abraham) Zachariah Grant (Gottheimer)', vol 2, pp 623–9; A. Grant, *Twycross v Grant and Others: Speech of Albert Grant* (1876),

p 126; H. Osborne O'Hagan, *Leaves from my Life* (1929), vol I, pp 32–5; Francis W. Hirst, *The Stock Exchange: A Short Study of Investment and Speculation* (1911), p 170.

4. B of E, M5/454; *Economist*, 23 Jan 1875.

5. Leland Hamilton Jenks, *The Migration of British Capital to 1875* (1938 edn), p 399; O'Hagan, vol I, p 37; Ellis Paxson Oberholtzer, *Jay Cooke: Financier in the Civil War* (Philadelphia, 1907), vol II, p 193; *The Times*, 19 Jan 1875; *Dictionary of National Biography* (Evans).

6. *The Times*, 31 July 1875; *Economist*, 14 Aug 1875.

7. *Select Committee on Loans to Foreign States* (P.P. 1875, XI), pp lxi–xcvi; Gibbs, Ms 11,037, vol 4, 25 Oct 1871.

8. *Loans to Foreign States*, qq 96–7, 109, 234, 510 (de Zoete), 2257–62 (Evans), 2415–20 (Tucker), 2861–4 (Barclay), 3496–3603 (Foster), 3719–4006 (Erlanger), 5765–5866 (Rothschild).

9. *Loans to Foreign States*, pp xlvii, 1.

10. *Blackwood's Edinburgh Magazine* (Sept 1876), p 310; Rathbone, files of general correspondence 1851–73, XXIV.1.19, 18 March 1868, XXIV.1.23 (43–90), 22 Oct 1872; *Fraser's Magazine* (Oct 1876), pp 493–503.

11. SE, Ms 14,600, vol 41, 8 Jan 1877–6 Feb 1877; *World*, 21 Feb 1877.

12. *Hansard*, 20 March 1877, cols 209, 216, 237, 239; *Economist*, 24 March 1877; *The Times*, 21 March 1877.

13. *Commission appointed to inquire into the Origin, Objects, Present Constitution, &c, of the London Stock Exchange* (P.P. 1878, XIX), qq 242–311 (Levien), 1120–25 (Spurling), 1968–2132 (Price), 3955–4117 (Branch), 4265–89 (Newton), 7265–7453 (Latham).

14. *London Stock Exchange*, pp 19–27; *The Times*, 17 Aug 1878; *Economist*, 7 Sept 1878.

15. T. H. S. Escott, *England: Its People, Polity, and Pursuits* (1879), vol II, pp 39–42.

CHAPTER SEVENTEEN

1. Derek Hudson (ed), *Munby: Man of Two Worlds* (1974 Abacus edn), pp 264–5.

2. Richard Trench, *London before the Blitz* (1989), p 136; Ranald C. Michie, *The City of London: Continuity and Change, 1850–1990* (1992), p 14; Harold P. Clunn, *The Face of London: The Record of a Century's Changes and Development* (1932), pp 49, 83, Trench, pp 165, 159; Edgar Jones, *Accountancy and the British Economy, 1840–1980* (1981), p 66; Donald J. Olsen, *The Growth of Victorian London* (1979 Peregrine edn), p 122.

3. Clunn, p 53; Andrew Saint, *Richard Norman Shaw* (1976), pp 136–7, 238, 244, John Summerson, 'The Victorian Rebuilding of the City of London' in *London Journal* (1977), pp 181–2.

4. Rathbone, files of general correspondence 1851–73, XXIV.1.19, 3 Jan 1868; Mary Cathcart Borer, *The City of London: A History* (1977), p 288; Philip Ziegler, *The Sixth Great Power: Barings, 1762–1929* (1988), p 204; S. J. Diaper, 'The History of Kleinwort, Sons & Co in Merchant Banking, 1855–1961' (Nottingham D Phil, 1983), p 348; D. T. A. Kynaston, 'The London Stock Exchange, 1870–1914: An Institutional History' (London D Phil, 1983), p 116.

5. *Civil Service Inquiry Commission* (P.P. 1875, XXIII), qq 8779–80; Lloyds, file 4553 (Sayers notes), 22 May 1878; Roger Fulford, *Glyn's, 1753–1953* (1953), p 219; Bo Bramsen and Kathleen Wain, *The Hambros* (1979), p 304.

6. Allan Fea, *Recollections of Sixty Years* (1927), pp 142–6.

7. *Post Magazine and Insurance Monitor*, 23 Dec 1916; Barry Supple, *The Royal Exchange Assurance* (Cambridge, 1970), p 378.

8. Norman and Jeanne Mackenzie (eds), *The Diary of Beatrice Webb*, vol 1 (1982), p 329; Hesketh Pearson, *Beerbohm Tree: His Life and Laughter* (1956), pp 6–8, DBB, Michael Sanderson, 'Sir Herbert Draper Beerbohm Tree', vol 5, pp 543–6.

9. Hugh Barty-King, *The Baltic Exchange* (1977), p 163; Frederick Martin, *The History of Lloyd's and of Marine Insurance in Great Britain* (1876), p 359; NW, 4,337, vol 1, Union Bank of London, 23 May 1877; Stanley Chapman, *The Rise of Merchant Banking* (1984), p 51; Shirley Nicholson, *A Victorian Household* (1988), pp 137–8.

10. R. C. Michie, *The London and New York Stock Exchanges, 1850–1914* (1987), pp 65–7; *Commission appointed to inquire into the Origin, Objects, Present Constitution, &c, of the London Stock Exchange* (P.P. 1878, XIX), q 3425.

11. Mocatta & Goldsmid records (Guildhall Library), Ms 18,644; M.J. Daunton, 'Financial elites and British society, 1880–1950' in Youssef Cassis (ed), *Finance and Financiers in European History, 1880–1960* (Cambridge, 1992), pp 130–9; Supple, pp 352–3; Martin, *Lloyd's*, pp 365–6; Michael D. K. Turner, *Contract Unbroken: Secretar's 200 Years at Lloyd's, 1789–1989* (1989), p 17.

12. Rathbone, files of general correspondence 1851–73, XXIV.1.18, 5 March 1867.

13. Youssef Cassis, *Les banquiers de la City à l'époque Edouardienne* (Geneva, 1984), p 35; Bertram Wodehouse Currie, *Recollections, Letters and Journals* (Roehampton, 1901), vol I, p xi; Fulford, pp 199–203; John Orbell, *Baring Brothers & Co., Limited: A History to 1939* (1985), between pp 42–3; Currie, vol I, p 44, vol II, p 8.

14. Cassis, *Banquiers*, p 285; Bramsen and Wain, p 300; Cassis, *Banquiers*, p 301; *Bankers' Magazine* (Jan 1889), p 40.

15. Clive Trebilcock, *Phoenix Assurance and the Development of British Insurance*, vol 1 (Cambridge, 1985), pp 680–2, *Bankers' Magazine* (April 1886), pp 323–6; DBB, P. E. Smart, 'Sir Richard Biddulph Martin', vol 4, pp 169–71; Edwin Green, *Debtors To Their Profession: A History of the Institute of Bankers, 1879–1979* (1979), pp 39–48; *Journal of the Institute of Bankers* (Feb 1887), p 75.

16. Anon (Wilfred Maude), *Antony Gibbs and Sons Limited: Merchants and Bankers, 1808–1958* (1958), p 27, Rachel Gibbs, *Pedigree of the Family of Gibbs* (1981 edn), p xix, DBB, William M. Mathew, 'Henry Hucks Gibbs, 1st Lord Aldenham', vol 2, pp 548–54; *Bankers' Magazine* (March 1888), p 268; Chapman, *Merchant Banking*, pp 130–1, 166–7.

17. Augustus Muir, *Blyth, Greene, Jourdain & Company Limited, 1810–1960* (1961), pp 20, 24, B of E, ADM 30/6; *Bankers' Magazine* (Feb 1888), pp 147–50; family memoir by Guendolen Morris (in possession of the family).

18. H. Osborne O'Hagan, *Leaves from my Life* (1929), vol II, pp 219–24.

19. Chapman, *Merchant Banking*, pp 129, 153, Gordon S. Haight (ed), *The George Eliot Letters* (1954), vol I, pp lxii–iv, Gordon S. Haight, *George Eliot: A Biography* (Oxford, 1968), p 504, *The Times*, 4 Nov 1924.

20. Anon, *The History of Knowles & Foster, 1828–1948* (1948), W. F. Foster, *Richard Foster* (1914).

21. Kurt Grunwald, ' "Windsor-Cassel" – The Last Court Jew' in *Leo Baeck Institute, Year Book* (1969), DBB, P. Thane, 'Sir Ernest Joseph Cassel', vol 1, pp 604–14; Anthony Allfrey, *Edward VII and his Jewish Court* (1991), p 137.

22. W. T. C. King, *History of the London Discount Market* (1936), pp 256–61; R. S. Sayers, *Gilletts in the London Money Market, 1867–1967* (Oxford, 1968), pp 5–29, 33.

23. Rathbone, files of general correspondence 1851–73, XXIV.1.20–21, 1 Dec 1870; K.F. Dixon, *Alexanders Discount Company Limited, 1810–1960* (1960), p 6; NW, 4,337, vol 1, Union Bank of London, manager's information book, 20 March 1878; Dixon, *Alexanders*, p 6.

24. J. E. Hodder Williams, *The Life of Sir George Williams* (1906), p 257; Stanley Chapman, *Merchant Enterprise in Britain: From the Industrial Revolution to World War I* (Cambridge, 1992), pp 181–5, 179.

25. Chapman, *Merchant Enterprise*, p 180; Walter Leaf, *Some Chapters of Autobiography, With A Memoir by Charlotte M. Leaf* (1932), pp 121–2, 144; Anne Olivier Bell (ed), *The Diary of Virginia Woolf*, vol III (1982 Penguin edn), p 73.

26. This and the next paragraph derive wholesale from M. J. Daunton, 'Firm and Family in the City of London in the Nineteenth Century: the case of F. G. Dalgety' in *Historical Research* (1989).

27. Rathbone, files of general correspondence 1851–73, XXIV.1.20–21, 31 March 1869, XXIV.1.23 (43–90), 11 April 1872, 17 June 1872, 8 July 1872; Sir Francis Oppenheimer, *Stranger Within* (1960), p 22.

28. Peter Pugh and others, *Great Enterprise: A History of Harrisons & Crosfield* (1990), p 16; John De Villiers, *My Memories* (1931), pp 40–1; Lintott, Spink & Co records (Guildhall Library), Ms 10,624, 14 April 1875.

29. Louis Bamberger, *Memories of Sixty Years in the Timber and Pianoforte Trades* (1930), pp 4–36.

30. Richard Roberts, 'What's in a Name? Merchants, Merchant Bankers, Accepting Houses, Issuing Houses, Industrial Bankers and Investment Bankers' in *Business History* (1993); Aytoun Ellis, *Heir of Adventure: The story of Brown, Shipley & Co, merchant bankers, 1810–1960* (1960), pp 102–3; Ziegler, pp 202–4; Kathleen Burk, *Morgan Grenfell, 1838–1988: The Biography of a Merchant Bank* (Oxford, 1989), p 38; Mathew, 'Henry Hucks Gibbs', Chapman, *Merchant Banking*, p 130.

31. Chapman, *Merchant Banking*, pp 106, 124–5; Diaper, pp 155, 180, 72.

32. *Economist*, 30 Jan 1869; *Select Committee on Banks of Issue* (P.P. 1875, IX), qq 7026–30, 7318–20.

33. Burk, pp 32–3, 43–6.

34. Chapman, *Merchant Banking*, p 46; BS, Ms 20,111, vol 2, 29 Dec 1879.

35. Ziegler, p 376; Burk, p 264; Richard Roberts, *Schroders: Merchants & Bankers* (1992), pp 75, 107; Gibbs, Ms 19,880; Youssef Cassis, *La City de Londres, 1870–1914* (Paris, 1987), p 141; Richard Meinertzhagen, *Diary of a Black Sheep* (1964), p 29.

36. Chapman, *Merchant Banking*, p 44, Roberts, *Schroders*, p 528, Ziegler, p 376, Burk, p 264.

37. Roberts, *Schroders*, pp 110–11.

38. NW, 4,337, vol 1, Union Bank of London; Chapman, *Merchant Banking*, p 53, Dolores Greenberg, *Financiers and Railroads, 1869–1889: A Study of Morton, Bliss & Company* (Newark, 1980).

39. Ziegler, p 196; BB, DEP 135, Alfred Mildmay, 'Notes and Recollections'.

40. Chapman, *Merchant Banking*, p 47; Mocatta & Goldsmid records (Guildhall Library), Ms 18,644; Stephen Gwynn and Gertrude M. Tuckwell, *The Life of the Rt. Hon. Sir Charles W. Dilke* (1917), vol I, p 285.

41. Kynaston, 'London Stock Exchange', p 119; *Members and Firms of the Stock Exchange* (1867); M. Vivian Hughes, *A London Family, 1870–1900* (1946), pp 13–19, 140–1.

42. Roberts, *Schroders*, p 358; RAL, T11/67; Alfred Wagg, 'Autobiography' (unpublished typescript, *c* 1958, held by Schroders), p 15.

43. Michie, *Stock Exchanges*, pp 9, 19; *The Times*, 25 Dec 1874; *Financial News*, 14 Nov 1902; *The Times*, 26 Dec 1874.

44. Walter Bagehot, *Economic Studies* (1905 edn), pp 197–8.

45. DBB, David T. A. Kynaston, 'Thomas Nickalls', vol 4, pp 439–41; J. Hall Richardson, *From the City to Fleet Street* (1927), p 51; *Rialto*, 25 July 1891; Guy Nickalls, *Life's A Pudding* (1939), p 38.

46. O'Hagan, vol II, p 335; Elizabeth Hennessy, *Stockbrokers for 150 Years: A History of Sheppards and Chase, 1827–1977* (1978), p 27.

47. *London Stock Exchange*, qq 1185–90, 1219 (Renton), 2662–70 (Marzetti), 4998–5006 (Ingall), 3435, 3438, 3447–59 plus App VI, 3492–3 (Branch), 4580–6 (Banbury); *Economist*, 30 May 1885; *London Stock Exchange*, qq 5358–62 (Thorp); *Economist*, 19 Jan 1889; *London Stock Exchange*, qq 8419, 8495–6, 8500–04, 8486, 8491, 8493 (Medley).

48. The argument in this paragraph owes much to Daunton, 'Financial elites', pp 136–8.
49. SE, Ms 14,609, vol 2, 11 May 1904.
50. Kynaston, 'London Stock Exchange', p 99; W. J. Reader, *A House in the City: A Study of the City and of the Stock Exchange based on the Records of Foster and Braithwaite, 1825–1975* (1979), pp 61–2; RAL, RFamC/21, 28 July 1874, 31 July 1874; Reader, p 82. Jehanne Wake, *Princess Louise: Queen Victoria's Unconventional Daughter* (1988), pp 274, 288, gives the poignant story of what happened subsequently to Lord Walter's City career.
51. Mark Girouard, *The Return to Camelot* (1981), p 173; Herbert M. Schweller and Robert L. Peters (eds), *The Letters of John Addington Symonds*, vol II (Detroit, 1968), pp 186, 209, 337, 449; Kynaston, 'London Stock Exchange', p 100; Girouard, p 173.
52. F. C. Carruthers Gould, 'Draft Autobiography' (House of Commons Library manuscript collection), pp 73–7.

CHAPTER EIGHTEEN

1. T. H. S. Escott, *England: Its People, Polity, and Pursuits* (1879), vol I, pp 190, 192–4.
2. R. C. Michie, *The London and New York Stock Exchanges, 1850–1914* (1987), pp 145–7.
3. G. A. Fletcher, *The Discount Houses in London: Principles, Operations and Change* (1976), p 30; *Economist*, 5 Dec 1874; *Bankers' Magazine* (Jan 1875), pp 5–7.
4. L. S. Pressnell, 'Gold Reserves, Banking Reserves, and the Baring Crisis of 1890' in C. R. Whittlesey and J. S. G. Wilson (eds), *Essays in Money and Banking* (Oxford, 1968), pp 186–9, Fletcher, pp 32–3; B of E, M6/28, p 5; W. T. C. King, *History of the London Discount Market* (1936), pp 295–6.
5. Martin(J), review of 1878; R. S. Sayers, *Lloyds Bank in the History of English Banking* (Oxford, 1957), p 246; Martin(J), review of 1878; McLean, 18 Oct 1878.
6. Pressnell, p 189; Michael Collins, *Banks and Industrial Finance in Britain, 1800–1939* (1991), p 42.
7. A. R. Holmes and Edwin Green, *Midland: 150 years of banking business* (1986), pp 50, 64, 81; Sayers, *Lloyds*, pp 247–8; Lloyds, file 3944 (Sayers notes), 4 March 1884, file 4553 (Sayers notes), 9 June 1884; R. S. Sayers, *Gilletts in the London Money Market, 1867–1967* (Oxford, 1968), p 192.
8. *Statist*, 17 Jan 1885; Martin (J), review of 1884.
9. Dudley W. R. Bahlman (ed), *The Diary of Sir Edward Walter Hamilton, 1880–1885* (Oxford, 1972), vol II, p 774; Robert Blake, *Disraeli* (1969 pbk edn), pp 581–7; Lord Rothschild, *'You Have It, Madam': The purchase, in 1875, of Suez Canal shares by Disraeli and Baron Lionel de Rothschild* (1980), p 22; Iddesleigh papers (British Library), Add Ms 50,017, 19 Feb 1876; Alfred Wagg, 'Autobiography' (unpublished typescript, c 1958, held by Schroders), p 11; George Earl Buckle, *The Life of Benjamin Disraeli, Earl of Beaconsfield*, vol V (1920), p 448; Stephen Gwynn and Gertrude M. Tuckwell, *The Life of the Rt. Hon. Sir Charles W. Dilke* (1917), vol I, p 285; *The Times*, 27 Nov 1875; Overstone, vol III, p 1285.
10. Hugh Cunningham, 'Jingoism in 1877–78' in *Victorian Studies* (1971); *City Press*, 2 Feb 1878.
11. This account is indebted to B. R. Johns, 'Business, investment, and Imperialism: the relationship between economic interests and the growth of British intervention in Egypt' (Exeter D Phil, 1982), A. G. Hopkins, 'The Victorians and Africa: A Reconsideration of the Occupation of Egypt, 1882' in *Journal of African History* (1986).
12. Wilfred Scawen Blunt, *Secret History of the English Occupation of Egypt* (1907), p 240; *Economist*, 17 June 1882, 24 June 1882; *The Times*, 27 June 1882; *The Times*, 6 July 1882, *Economist* 8 July 1882.
13. *Economist*, 15 July 1882, 22 July 1882; McLean, 27 July 1882; *Bankers' Magazine* (Aug 1882), p 606.

14. Andrew Porter, ' "Gentlemanly Capitalism" and Empire: The British Experience since 1850' in *Journal of Imperial and Commonwealth History* (1990), pp 282–5.

15. Frederic Harrison, *National and Social Problems* (1908), pp 199, 218–9, 224.

16. H. Osborne O'Hagan, *Leaves from my Life* (1929), vol I, pp 118–24.

17. P. L. Cottrell, *Industrial Finance, 1830–1914: The Finance and Organization of English Manufacturing Industry* (1983 pbk edn), p 189; *Electrician*, 20 May 1882; *Journal of the Institution of Electrical Engineers* (1894), pp 12–13.

18. I. C. R. Byatt, *The British Electrical Industry, 1875–1914* (Oxford, 1979), pp 15–21, J. F. Wilson, *Ferranti and the British electrical industry, 1864–1930* (Manchester, 1988), pp 12–18, Ranald Michie, 'The Finance of Innovation in Late Victorian and Edwardian Britain: Possibilities and Constraints' in *Journal of European Economic History* (1988), pp 510–16.

19. William P. Kennedy, 'Capital markets and industrial structure in the Victorian economy' in J. J. van Helten and Y. Cassis (eds), *Capitalism in a Mature Economy: Financial Institutions, Capital Exports and British Industry, 1870–1939* (Aldershot, 1990), p 31.

20. This is the case forcibly argued by William P. Kennedy, *Industrial structure, capital markets and the origins of British economic decline* (Cambridge, 1987), especially pp 134–47.

21. Erasmus Pinto, *Ye Outside Fools! Glimpses inside the Stock Exchange* (1877), p 34; Hambros, Ms 19,063, vol 22, 15 April 1882; *Statist*, 25 Dec 1886.

22. H. S. Ferns, *Britain and Argentina in the Nineteenth Century* (Oxford, 1960), pp 397–403.

23. Ferns, pp 333–4, Charles A. Jones, *International Business in the Nineteenth Century: The Rise and Fall of a Cosmopolitan Bourgeoisie* (Brighton, 1987), pp 170–1; Jones, pp 129–33, 171–3; John Orbell, *Baring Brothers & Co., Limited: A History to 1939* (1985), p 57.

24. David Joslin, *A Century of Banking in Latin America* (1963), pp 161–2; London and Brazilian Bank records (University College, London), G2/7, 3 Sept 1879.

25. G. J. Whitwell, 'Charles and Reginald Bright' in R. T. Appleyard and C. B. Schedvin (eds), *Australian Financiers: Biographical Essays* (Melbourne, 1988), pp 137–59.

26. Stanley Chapman, *The Rise of Merchant Banking* (1984), pp 95–7, *Statist*, 15 Dec 1888; Philip Ziegler, *The Sixth Great Power: Barings, 1762–1929* (1988), pp 216–7; Kathleen Burk, *Morgan Grenfell, 1838–1988: The Biography of a Merchant Bank* (Oxford, 1989), pp 49–50.

27. BS, Ms 20,111, vol 2, 28 Oct 1882.

28. Edwin J. Perkins, *Financing Anglo-American Trade: The House of Brown, 1800–1880* (Cambridge, Mass, 1975), pp 222–3; Stanley D. Chapman, *Raphael Bicentenary, 1787–1987* (1987), p 23; *Statist*, 14 Aug 1886.

29. Chapman, *Merchant Banking*, pp 88, 158.

30. Bo Bramsen and Kathleen Wain, *The Hambros* (1979), pp 309–19.

31. Bramsen and Wain, p 315; Hambros, Ms 19,111, part 1; BB, HC3.10.

32. McLean; BB, Particulars of Loans issued by Baring Brothers & Co (not catalogued); Frank H. H. King, *The History of the Hongkong and Shanghai Banking Corporation*, vol I (Cambridge, 1987), pp 554–6; McLean, 12 June 1885, 19 June 1885.

33. Sir John Clapham, *The Bank of England: A History* (Cambridge, 1944), vol II, p 316; PRO, T 250/13.

34. Hamilton, Add Ms 48,641, 29 July 1885.

35. Hartley Withers, 'The New Face of the City' in The Times, *Fifty Years: Memories and Contrasts* (1932), p 149; Ziegler, pp 186–7; *Bankers' Magazine* (June 1888), pp 607–9; Virginia Cowles, *The Rothschilds: A Family of Fortune* (1973), pp 167, 164; Miriam Rothschild, *Dear Lord Rothschild: Birds, Butterflies and History* (1983), pp 10–12; DBB, S. D. Chapman, 'Nathan Meyer Rothschild, 1st Lord Rothschild of Tring, Hertfordshire', vol 4, pp 946–53.

36. Letters of Sir Carl Meyer (unpublished), 10 Sept 1884, 3–6 Aug 1885, 11 March 1886; DBB, P. Thane, 'Sir Ernest Joseph Cassel', vol 1, pp 604–14, Pat Thane, 'Financiers and the British State: The Case of Sir Ernest Cassel' in *Business History* (1986); Meyer, 10 Aug 1886.

37. SE, Mss 14,600, vol 46, 12 Jan 1881–7 Feb 1881, 19,279, vol 9, 4 Feb 1881, 19,515, app 54.

38. SE, Mss 14,600, vol 48, 3–6 March 1882, vol 49, 20 Nov 1882.

39. SE, Ms 14,600, vol 52, 28 Oct 1885.

40. *Independent*, 15 Dec 1990; David Kynaston, *Cazenove & Co: A History* (1991), pp 76–7; Wedd Durlacher brochure (c 1984).

41. The Marquess of Reading, *Rufus Isaacs, First Marquess of Reading*, vol I (1942), pp 1–35; *The Times*, 15 Aug 1884; Reading, p 38.

42. H. Panmure Gordon, *The Land of the Almighty Dollar* (1892), p 4; DBB, David Kynaston, 'Harry Panmure Gordon', vol 2, pp 611–13; King, *Hongkong and Shanghai*, vol I, p 545; Vivian Nickalls, *Oars, Wars and Horses* (1932), p 81; *Evening News*, 23 April 1934.

43. *Economist*, 22 Nov 1884.

44. *Statist*, 9 Jan 1886, 19 Dec 1885; Henry Warren, *The Modern Bucket-Shop* (1906); SE, Ms 14,608, vol 1.

45. DBB, Dilwyn Porter, 'Harry Hananel Marks', vol 4, pp 133–5, Dilwyn Porter, ' "A Trusted Guide of the Investing Public": Harry Marks and the Financial News, 1884–1916' in *Business History* (1986).

46. *Financial News*, 3 Oct 1921, 19 March 1885; David Kynaston, *The Financial Times: A Centenary History* (1988), pp 8–9.

47. SE, Ms 14,609, vol 2, 11 May 1904; Charles Duguid, *The Story of the Stock Exchange* (1901), p 303; *City Press*, 4 March 1885.

48. This and the next paragraph are almost entirely taken from G. Duckworth Atkin (ed), *House Scraps* (1887), pp 12–17.

49. W. A. Morgan (ed), *The Stock Exchange Christmas Annual*, 1925–6 (1925), pp 64–7.

CHAPTER NINETEEN

1. John Galsworthy, *The Forsyte Saga* (1922), pp 4, 29, 20.

2. Horace G. Hutchinson, *Life of Sir John Lubbock, Lord Avebury* (1914), vol I, p 164.

3. H. L. Malchow, *Gentlemen Capitalists: The Social and Political World of the Victorian Businessman* (1991), pp 78–159.

4. *City Press*, 3 Oct 1883.

5. Malchow, pp 160–257.

6. John Davis, *Reforming London: The London Government Problem, 1855–1900* (Oxford, 1988), pp 77–80; *The Times*, 11 April 1884; *City Press*, 10 May 1884; Davis, *Reforming London*, pp 106–8.

7. McLean, 27 June 1884; John Stephen Flynn, *Sir Robert N. Fowler* (1893), pp 315–6; *City Press*, 3 April 1886.

8. Hamilton, Add Ms 48, 643, 10 May 1886.

9. Y. Cassis, 'Bankers in English Society in the Late Nineteenth Century' in *Economic History Review* (1985), p 211; David Kynaston, *The Chancellor of the Exchequer* (Lavenham, 1980), p 130; R. F. Foster, *Lord Randolph Churchill* (1981), p 277; Hamilton, Add Mss 48,649, 21 Aug 1888, 48,642, 4 Dec 1885, 48,647, 31 Aug 1887, 48,650, 18 April 1889.

10. Andrew Porter, 'Which City? What Empire? Shipping, Government, and the Limits of Co-operation, 1870–1914' in R. V. Turrell and J. J. Van-Helten (eds), *The City*

and the Empire (Collected Seminar Papers no 35, Institute of Commonwealth Studies, University of London, 1985), p 61.

11. Cassis, 'Bankers', p 227.

12. Hamilton, Add Mss 48,647, 31 Aug 1887, 48,649, 19 Aug 1888.

13. Dudley W. R. Bahlman (ed), *The Diary of Sir Edward Walter Hamilton, 1880–1885* (Oxford, 1972), vol I, p 280; Blanche E. C. Dugdale, *Arthur James Balfour* (1936), vol I, p 97; Foster, p 331; Richard Davis, *The English Rothschilds* (1983), p 205.

14. Foster, p 194; Hamilton, Add Ms 48,644, 3 Sept 1886; Kynaston, *Chancellor*, p 124; Hamilton, Add Mss 48,644, 3 Sept 1886, 48,641, 3 Sept 1885, 48,647, 31 Jan 1888.

15. J. A. Hobson, *Imperialism: A Study* (1938 edn), p 59; Pat Thane, 'Financiers and the British State: The Case of Sir Ernest Cassel' in *Business History* (1986), p 91.

16. D. McLean, 'Commerce, Finance, and British Diplomatic Support in China, 1885–86' in *Economic History Review* (1973), p 465; D. C. M. Platt, *Finance, Trade, and Politics in British Foreign Policy, 1815–1914* (Oxford, 1968), Andrew Porter, ' "Gentlemanly Capitalism" and Empire: The British Experience since 1850' in *Journal of Imperial and Commonwealth History* (1990). The typescript for this volume was completed before the publication of the path-breaking survey by P. J. Cain and A. G. Hopkins, *British Imperialism: Innovation and Expansion, 1688–1914* (1993).

17. S. R. B. Smith, 'British Nationalism, Imperialism and the City of London, 1880–1900' (London D Phil, 1985), p 78.

18. R. P. T. Davenport-Hines, 'The Ottoman Empire in Decline: The Business Imperialism of Sir Vincent Caillard, 1883–98' in *City and Empire* (35), p 124.

19. Lance E. Davis and Robert A. Huttenback, *Mammon and the pursuit of Empire: The political economy of British imperialism, 1860–1912* (Cambridge, 1986), pp 198–217.

20. Malchow, pp 110–18, 141, 194–5.

21. Smith, pp 30–9.

22. Smith, pp 81–6, 176–7, 374, 137–41, 144–6; Hamilton, Add Ms 48,642, 2 Jan 1886; Stanley Chapman, *The Rise of Merchant Banking* (1984), p 143.

23. McLean, 'Commerce'; *The Times*, 9 Jan 1886.

24. McLean, 'Commerce'; PRO, FO 17/1038.

25. Significant contributions to the debate include: W. D. Rubinstein, 'Wealth, Elites and the Class Structure of Modern Britain' in *Past and Present* (1977); Geoffrey Ingham, *Capitalism Divided? The City and industry in British social development* (Basingstoke, 1984); José Harris and Pat Thane, 'British and European bankers, 1880–1914: an "aristocratic bourgeoisie"?' in Pat Thane, Geoffrey Crossick and Roderick Floud (eds), *The Power of the Past* (Cambridge, 1984); M. Lisle-Williams, 'Beyond the Market: the Survival of Family Capitalism in the English Merchant Banks' in *British Journal of Sociology* (1984); Cassis, 'Bankers'; S. D. Chapman, 'Aristocracy and meritocracy in merchant banking' in *British Journal of Sociology* (1986); P. J. Cain and A. G. Hopkins, 'Gentlemanly Capitalism and British Expansion Overseas: I. The Old Colonial System, 1688–1850' in *Economic History Review* (1986); P. J. Cain and A. G. Hopkins, 'Gentlemanly Capitalism and British Expansion Overseas: II. New Imperialism, 1850–1945' in *Economic History Review* (1987); Perry Anderson, 'The Figures of Descent' in *New Left Review* (Jan/Feb 1987); Y. Cassis, 'Merchant bankers and City aristocracy' in *British Journal of Sociology* (1988); S. D. Chapman, 'Reply to Youssef Cassis' in *British Journal of Sociology* (1988); M. J. Daunton, ' "Gentlemanly Capitalism" and British Industry, 1820–1914' in *Past and Present* (1989); Porter, ' "Gentlemanly Capitalism" and Empire'; Malchow, *Gentlemen Capitalists*; W. D. Rubinstein, *Capitalism, Culture, and Decline in Britain, 1750–1990* (1993); P. J. Cain and A. G. Hopkins, *British Imperialism* (2 vols, 1993).

26. Daunton, ' "Gentlemanly Capitalism" ', p 119.

27. *Society in London, By a Foreign Resident* (seventh edn, 1885), p 118; E. C. Grenville Murray, *Side-Lights on English Society* (1881), vol II, pp 163–4; David Cannadine, *The Decline and Fall of the British Aristocracy* (1990), pp 406–20.

28. *Hamilton*, vol II, p 880; Roger Fulford, *Glyn's, 1753–1953* (1953), p 198; *Hamilton*, vol II, p 839, Hamilton, Add Mss 48,644, 27 May 1886, 48,649, 26 July 1888, 48,652, 30 April 1890.

29. Mark Girouard, *The Victorian Country House* (1971), p 175; Richard Roberts, *Schroders: Merchants & Bankers* (1992), p 85; DBB, William M. Mathew, 'Henry Hucks Gibbs, 1st Lord Aldenham', vol 2, pp 548–54; John Crosby Brown, *A Hundred Years of Merchant Banking* (New York, 1909), p 340.

30. Malchow, p 174; Augustus Muir, *Churchill and Sim* (1963), p 57; Judy Slinn, *A History of Freshfields* (1984), p 118; Anon, *Two Centuries of Lewis & Peat, 1775–1975* (1975), p 18.

31. Vivian Nickalls, *Oars, Wars and Horses* (1932), pp 17–22, 62, Guy Nickalls, *Life's A Pudding* (1939), pp 19–49, DBB, David T. A. Kynaston, 'Thomas Nickalls', vol 4, pp 439–41; David Kynaston, *Cazenove & Co: A History* (1991), pp 67–8; Girouard, p 187; David Wainwright, *Henderson: A History of the life of Alexander Henderson, first Lord Faringdon, and of Henderson Administration* (1985), pp 48–50; Shirley Nicholson, *A Victorian Household* (1988), pp 137–8.

32. W. D. Rubinstein, 'The Victorian Middle Classes: Wealth, Occupation and Geography' in *Economic History Review* (1977).

33. *Statist*, 31 March 1894–21 July 1894, 21 Nov 1896.

34. Youssef Cassis, *Les Banquiers de la City à l'époque Edouardienne* (Geneva, 1984), pp 242–5, 121–9.

35. Galsworthy, pp 19, 31; Norman and Jeanne Mackenzie (eds), *The Diary of Beatrice Webb*, vol 1 (1982), pp 321–2; Hamilton, Add Ms 48,649, 2 July 1888.

36. Cassis, *Banquiers*, pp 265–8; Clive Trebilcock, *Phoenix Assurance and the Development of British Insurance*, vol 1 (Cambridge, 1985), p 702; DBB, P. Thane, 'Sir Ernest Joseph Cassel', vol 1, pp 604–14; Chapman, *Merchant Banking*, p 153; M. J. Daunton, 'Inheritance and Succession in the City of London in the Nineteenth Century' in *Business History* (1988), p 279.

37. R. G. G. Price, *A History of Punch* (1957), pp 91–2; *Hamilton*, vol II, p 899; Harris and Thane, 'British and European bankers', p 226.

38. Hamilton, Add Mss 48,645, 12 Dec 1886, 48,649, 21 Aug 1888; Fulford, p 208.

39. Hamilton, Add Ms 48,651, 17 Oct 1889; S. J. Diaper, 'The History of Kleinwort, Sons & Co in Merchant Banking, 1855–1961' (Nottingham D Phil, 1983), pp 66–70; Roberts, p 113, Chapman, 'Aristocracy and meritocracy'; A. C. Howe, 'From "Old Corruption" to "New Probity": the Bank of England and its Directors in the Age of Reform' in *Financial History Review* (1994); RAL, RFamC/21, 17 Sept 1869.

40. DBB, Sheila Marriner, 'William Lidderdale', vol 3, pp 786–90.

41. D. T. A. Kynaston, 'The London Stock Exchange, 1870–1914: An Institutional History' (London D Phil, 1983), p 122.

42. Benny Green (ed), *The Wisden Book of Obituaries* (1986), p 794; *Cricketer*, 3 May 1930.

43. Kynaston, *Chancellor*, p 124.

44. The controversy is resurrected in: E. H. H. Green, 'Rentiers versus Producers? The Political Economy of the Bimetallic Controversy, c 1880–1898' in *English Historical Review* (July 1988); A. C. Howe, 'Bimetallism, c 1880–1898, a controversy re-opened?' in *English Historical Review* (April 1990); E. H. H. Green, 'The Bimetallic Controversy: empiricism belimed or the case for the issues' in *English Historical Review* (July 1990).

45. A. Cotterell Tupp, *The Early Proceedings of the Bimetallic League, with some account of its origin* (1895), p 9; McLean, 15 Dec 1881; *Hamilton*, vol I, p 203.

46. B of E, G15/145.

47. *Royal Commission appointed to inquire into the recent Changes in the relative Values of the Precious Metals* (Second Report, P. P. 1888, XLV), qq 6670, 6797–6810 (Currie), 7036, 6918 (Raphael).

48. *Precious Metals* (First Report, P. P. 1887, XXII), q 5880; Bimetallic League, *The Proceedings of the Bimetallic Conference held at Manchester, 4th and 5th April, 1888* (Manchester, 1888), pp 27, 22, 46, 42, 67.

49. B of E, G15/146; Hamilton, Add Mss 48,650, 4 Jan 1889, 48,651, 4 June 1889; *Bankers' Magazine* (Feb 1888), pp 149–50.

CHAPTER TWENTY

1. *Economist*, 21 May 1887; *Statist*, 2 March 1889; the role of the City is examined in S. D. Chapman, 'Rhodes and the City of London: Another View of Imperialism' in *Historical Journal* (1985), Robert Vicat Turrell with Jean-Jacques van Helten, 'The Rothschilds, The Exploration Company and Mining Finance' in *Business History* (1986), Charles Harvey and Jon Press, 'The City and International Mining, 1870–1914' in *Business History* (1990); *Economist*, 4 Feb 1888; Max Karo, *City Milestones and Memories* (1962), p 3.

2. Robert V. Kubicek, *Economic Imperialism in Theory and Practice: The Case of South African Gold Mining Finance, 1886–1914* (Durham, N. C., 1979), pp 87–90.

3. Colin Newbury, 'The Origins and Function of the London Diamond Syndicate, 1889–1914' in *Business History* (1987); Robert Vicat Turrell, ' "Finance . . . The Governor of the Imperial Engine": Hobson and the Case of Rothschild and Rhodes' in Rob Turrell (ed), *The City and the Empire* (Collected Seminar Papers no 36, Institute of Commonwealth Studies, University of London, 1986), p 88.

4. David Kynaston, *The Financial Times: A Centenary History* (1988), pp 14–22.

5. Dilwyn Porter, ' "A Trusted Guide of the Investing Public": Harry Marks and the Financial News, 1884–1916' in *Business History* (1986); Kynaston, *Financial Times*, pp 11–12, 22–3, 29–30; *Statist*, 9 April 1887; Kynaston, *Financial Times*, p 80.

6. The fullest account of North's career is in Harold Blakemore, *British Nitrates and Chilean Politics, 1886–1896: Balmaceda and North* (1974); *Economist*, 9 May 1896; Anon (Wilfred Maude), *Antony Gibbs and Sons Limited: Merchants and Bankers, 1808–1958* (1958), p 30; Gibbs, Ms 11,042, vol 2, 28 Nov 1888; Kynaston, *Financial Times*, pp 23–5.

7. Gibbs, Ms 11,042, vol 2, 1 April 1887.

8. Gibbs, Ms 11,040, vol 1, 18 Aug 1890, 26 Aug 1890, 1 Sept 1890, 16 Sept 1890; Pat Thane, 'Financiers and the British State: The Case of Sir Ernest Cassel' in *Business History* (Jan 1986), p 83.

9. H. Osborne O'Hagan, *Leaves from my Life* (1929), including vol I, pp 35–6, 262–3.

10. Philip Ziegler, *The Sixth Great Power: Barings, 1762–1929* (1988), pp 199–201, gives a full account of the Guinness episode; Hamilton, Add Ms 48,645, 23 Oct 1886, 27 Oct 1886; G. Duckworth Atkin (ed), *House Scraps* (1887), p 123.

11. Hamilton, Add Ms 48,645, 23 Oct 1886; Ziegler, pp 201–2; *Bankers' Magazine* (June 1888), p 609; Roger Fulford, *Glyn's, 1753–1953* (1953), p 207.

12. Hamilton, Add Ms 48,647, 25 Jan 1888.

13. Crompton records (Science Museum Library), B 113, 6 July 1888, 9 July 1888; J. F. Wilson, *Ferranti and the British electrical industry, 1864–1930* (Manchester, 1988), pp 56–8.

14. P. L. Cottrell, *Industrial Finance, 1830–1914: The Finance and Organization of English Manufacturing Industry* (1983 pbk edn), pp 171–2; D. J. Rowe, *Lead Manufacturing in Britain: a history* (1983), pp 243–8; Graham Turner, *Business in Britain* (1971 Pelican edn), p 18; *Economist*, 19 Jan 1889.

15. Youssef Cassis, 'The emergence of a new financial institution: investment trusts in Britain, 1870–1939' in J. J. van Helten and Y. Cassis (eds), *Capitalism in a Mature Economy: Financial Institutions, Capital Exports and British Industry, 1870–1939* (Aldershot, 1990), pp 140–2.

16. Fulford, p 163; A. R. Hall, *The London capital market and Australia, 1870–1914* (Canberra, 1963), p 55; Stanley D. Chapman, 'Venture Capital and Financial Organisation: London and South Africa in the Nineteenth Century' in Stuart Jones (ed), *Banking and Business in South Africa* (1988), p 36; *Statist*, 13 April 1889; *Economist*, 6 April 1889; P. N. Davies, 'Business History and the Role of Chance: The Extraordinary Phillips Brothers' in *Business History* (1981).

17. Frank Harris, *My Life and Loves* (1966 Corgi edn), p 518; Morgan Grenfell records (Guildhall Library), Ms 21,799, fo 79; Hamilton, Add Ms 48,651, 20 Nov 1889.

18. Letters of Sir Carl Meyer (unpublished), 25 Jan 1890; Hamilton, Add Ms 48,652, 16 Feb 1890.

19. Hamilton, Add Ms 48,647, 7 Jan 1888; RBS, GM/7, 11 Jan 1888; Hamilton, Add Ms 48,647, 18 Jan 1888.

20. Hamilton, Add Ms 48,648, 5 Feb 1888–17 March 1888; *Economist*, 17 March 1888; Hamilton, Add Ms 48,649, 18 Oct 1888.

21. Hamilton, Add Ms 48,650, 16 Jan 1889–13 Feb 1889; S. R. B. Smith, 'British Nationalism, Imperialism and the City of London, 1880–1900' (London D Phil, 1985), p 247.

22. Charles Duguid, *The Story of the Stock Exchange* (1901), p 315; SE, Ms 14,600, vol 57, 13 Jan 1890; *Rialto*, 3 May 1890, 4 Oct 1890; *Economist*, 19 Jan 1889.

23. M. C. Reed, *A History of James Capel and Co* (1975), p 68; *Bankers' Magazine* (Oct 1890), p 1638; *Blackwood's Edinburgh Magazine* (Dec 1894), p 786; Shirley Nicholson, *A Victorian Household* (1988), pp 96–7.

24. O'Hagan, vol I, pp 272–3; Hubert A. Meredith, *The Drama of Money Making: Tragedy and Comedy of the London Stock Exchange* (1931?), p 146; O'Hagan, vol II, p 28.

25. O'Hagan, vol II, pp 32–8; *Financial Times*, 23 Nov 1889, 22 April 1890; Duguid, p 319; W. J. Reader, *A House in the City: A Study of the City and of the Stock Exchange based on the Records of Foster and Braithwaite, 1825–1975* (1979), p 99.

26. SE, Ms 14,600, vol 58, 2 Oct 1890–3 Nov 1890; *Economist*, 1 Nov 1890; *Statist*, 8 Nov 1890.

CHAPTER TWENTY-ONE

1. Rathbone, IX.8.12, 15 Oct 1889.

2. BB, DEP 115.1, J. Walter Wood, 'Business Activities of Some Members of the Wood Family'.

3. *Statist*, 1 Dec 1888; *Bankers' Magazine* (June 1888), p 609.

4. Helpful accounts of the Baring crisis include: Sir John Clapham, *The Bank of England: A History* (Cambridge, 1944), vol II, pp 326–39; L. S. Pressnell, 'Gold Reserves, Banking Reserves, and the Baring Crisis of 1890' in C. R. Whittlesey and J. S. G. Wilson (eds), *Essays in Money and Banking* (Oxford, 1968), pp 192–207; Philip Ziegler, *The Sixth Great Power: Barings, 1762–1929* (1988), pp 235–66; John Orbell, 'When Croesus stumbled and the City shook' in *Independent on Sunday*, 4 Nov 1990.

5. BS, Ms 20,111, vol 2, 12 Nov 1887.

6. H. Osborne O'Hagan, *Leaves from my Life* (1929), vol I, p 377.

7. Ziegler, p 240; Hamilton, Add Ms 48,653, 27 July 1890; Gibbs, Ms 11,040, vol I, 12 Aug 1890.

8. Hamilton, Add Ms 48,654, 8 Oct 1890; Arthur D. Elliot, *The Life of George Joachim Goschen, First Viscount Goschen* (1911), vol II, p 169; Bertram Wodehouse Currie, *Recollections, Letters and Journals* (Roehampton, 1901), vol I, p 90.

9. Imperial Ottoman Bank records (Guildhall Library), Ms 23,993, vol 2, 24 Oct 1890; Richard Meinertzhagen, *Diary of a Black Sheep* (1964), p 267.

10. B of E, G15/192, f.176, G15/189, f.15A.

11. Pressnell, p 191; Hamilton, Add Ms 48,654, 8 Jan 1891; BB, HC3.52.8.

12. Pressnell, p 169; Hamilton, Add Ms 48,653, 9 Aug 1890.

13. B of E, G15/192, f.176; Elliot, vol II, pp 170–1; Hamilton, Add Ms 48,654, 10 Nov 1890.

14. Elliot, vol II, pp 171–2.

15. Ziegler, pp 247–8; Hamilton, Add Ms 48,654, 12 Nov 1890; B of E, G15/192, f.183.

16. B of E, G15/192, f.177; Clapham, vol II, pp 330–1.

17. B of E, G15/192, f.179, G15/189, f.15A.

18. Currie, vol I, pp 92–3; Hamilton, Add Ms 48,654, 15 Nov 1890.

19. B of E, G15/189.

20. *Financial Times*, 15 Nov 1890; Stanley D. Chapman, *Raphael Bicentenary, 1787–1987* (1987), p 31; RAL, T15/44; Hamilton, Add Ms 48,654, 16 Nov 1890; RAL, XI/109/127.

21. *Financial Times*, 17 Nov 1890; Maurice Brett (ed), *Journals and Letters of Reginald Viscount Esher* (1934), vol I, p 145; Gibbs, Ms 11,040, vol 1, 19 Nov 1890; George Chandler, *Four Centuries of Banking*, vol I (1964), pp 333–4.

22. Ziegler, pp 251–2; Martin (J), 22 Nov 1890; Ziegler, p 265; *Punch*, 8 Nov 1890.

23. Norman and Jeanne Mackenzie (eds), *The Diary of Beatrice Webb*, vol 1 (1982), p 349; B of E, G15/189, f.29A; R. S. Sayers, *Lloyds Bank in the History of English Banking* (Oxford, 1957), pp 213–14.

Acknowledgements

I am grateful to the following for allowing me to consult and reproduce material in their possession: The Bank of England; Barclays Bank; Baring Brothers; The Joint Grand Gresham Committee; Hambros; The Holland-Martin Family Archives; The House of Commons Library; University of Liverpool; Lloyds Bank; Matheson & Co; Sir Anthony Meyer; Midland Bank; Morgan Grenfell; National Westminster Bank; School of Oriental and African Studies, and Mr David McLean; Elizabeth Robbins; N. M. Rothschild & Sons; The Royal Bank of Scotland; Schroders; University College, London; National Council of Y.M.C.As.

The following kindly supplied illustrations and, where appropriate, permission to reproduce: The Baltic Exchange (3); The Governor and Company of the Bank of England (jacket, 7, 8, 20); Baring Brothers (4, 19); British Museum (6); British Newspaper Library (9,15); Cazenove & Co (18); Guildhall Library, Corporation of London (1, 2, 5, 12, 13, 16, 21); Lloyds Bank (10); National Westminster Bank (14); The Royal Bank of Scotland (11).

Many archivists have helped me, and I would like especially to mention John Booker, Christopher Cove-Smith, Henry Gillett, Edwin Green, Katy Hooper, Serena Kelly, Fiona Maccoll, Simone Mace, Elizabeth Ogborn, John Orbell, Alison Turton and Philip Winterbottom. Much of the research for this book was done at the Guildhall Library, and I am grateful for all the help I have received there.

A grant from the Authors' Foundation was timely and appreciated.

A book like this owes much to those working in the same field, and historians to whom I feel a personal as well as professional debt include Kathleen Burk, Martin Daunton, Richard Davenport-Hines, Anthony Howe, Derek Keene, William Kennedy, Jon Lawrence, Ranald Michie, Dilwyn Porter, Judy Slinn and Jehanne Wake. No one has done more important pioneering work on the history of the City than Stanley Chapman, and I hope to have built a little on his foundations. Finally, to two other historians, Youssef Cassis and Richard Roberts, I owe a

Acknowledgements

particular debt: not only for the example of their work, but also for many conversations about this maddening village which we can only pretend to understand.

My greatest debt of all is to Lucy, great great granddaughter of a 'capable Governor'.

London, summer 1993

INDEX

Note: in the case of a firm that changed its name, the name given is the one by which it was most usually known during the period.